*World History by the
World's Historians*

World History by the World's Historians

Paul Spickard
Brigham Young University–Hawaii

James V. Spickard
University of Redlands

Kevin M. Cragg
Bethel College

Boston   Burr Ridge, IL   Dubuque, IA   Madison, WI   New York
San Francisco   St. Louis   Bangkok   Bogotá
Caracas   Lisbon   London   Madrid   Mexico City   Milan
New Delhi   Seoul   Singapore   Sydney   Taipei   Toronto

McGraw-Hill

*A Division of The **McGraw·Hill** Companies*

WORLD HISTORY BY THE WORLD'S HISTORIANS

This book is printed on recycled, acid-free paper containing 10% postconsumer waste.

1 2 3 4 5 6 7 8 9 0 DOC/DOC 9 0 9 8 7

ISBN 0-07-059835-5

Editorial director: *Jane E. Vaicunas*
Sponsoring editor: *Leslye Jackson*
Editorial coordinator: *Amy Mack*
Marketing manager: *Annie Mitchell*
Project manager: *Cathy Ford Smith*
Production supervisor: *Deborah Donner*
Photo research coordinator: *John L. Leland*
Cover designer: *Elise Lansdon Design*
Compositor: *Carlisle Communications Ltd.*
Typeface: *Palatino*
Printer: *R. R. Donnelly, Crawfordsville*

Credits section begins on page 639 and
is considered an extension of the copyright page.

Library of Congress Cataloging-in-Publication Data

World history by the world's historians / [compiled by] Paul Spickard,
    James V. Spickard, Kevin M. Cragg.
       p. cm.
    Issued also in two volumes.
    Includes bibliographical references.
    ISBN 0-07-059835-5
    1. World history.   I. Spickard, Paul R., 1950–   . II. Spickard,
James V. III. Cragg, Kevin M.
    D20.W887 1998   97-34362
    909—dc21   CIP

www.mhhe.com

Contents

Part 3
EVOLVING TRADITIONS

Part 4
GROWTH OF THE WEST

Part 5
SCIENCE AND CRITIQUE

Part 6
PASSICONS OF THE PRESENT

Dedicated to the
memory of

Frank Wong
1935–1995

Of Canons and Questions: Some Prefatory Remarks

World History by the World's Historians presents some of the finest historical writing ever produced by writers from all parts of the globe. There are historians here who wrote as much as three thousand years ago, and others who are writing today. They come from all around the world: from East and South Asia, the Americas, Africa, Europe, the Middle East, and the Pacific. These selections provide the reader the opportunity to contemplate the nature and purposes of history as it has been practiced by people from many different traditions and in many time periods.

Great historical writing is, in the first instance, a pleasure to read. We offer this collection of fine historical writing to any student or casual reader who likes a good story, who is curious about the past, who is stimulated by ideas, and who likes to think about what we know and how we know it. There is good writing here to suit many tastes: the vivid storytelling of Anna Comnena, the broad social analysis of Marc Bloch and Ibn Khaldûn, the abstract philosophy of Fukuzawa Yukichi, the interdisciplinary breadth of Euclides da Cunha, the faith of Luke and al-Tabari, the passionate political commitment of Gertrude Himmelfarb and Charles Beard. For the general reader, it may be enough to read and reflect, to enjoy these historians simply for the pleasure of their company.

This book is also intended for use as a college text in courses on historical method. The book introduces the reader to the study of history as a discipline by exposing her to a variety of excellent historical writers. We contend that the writers whose work appears here are great historians. The book proceeds from the rather old-fashioned premise that there are certain historians every history major ought to read before she leaves college. Such an approach embodies the idea that there is a canon, a consensus list of the best historical writing. We offer the historians in this anthology as our nominees for inclusion in such a canon—but it is a different canon than those we have seen before.

Our choices of historians speak to two issues: excellence and representativeness. Not all historical writing is equally good. Among the Romans, Suetonius is wonderful and was widely read for many centuries, but few informed modern readers would argue that he is the equal of Tacitus. Among early Chinese, Dong Junshu is a fine historian, but Sima Qian is the giant of his age. Inevitably, our choice of something over fifty outstanding historians involves judgments of quality, even as we recognize that our notions of quality are to some extent conditioned by the intellectual values of our own era.

Although we would argue it is possible—in fact, important—to make judgments of quality within the contexts of particular times and traditions, we are less comfortable comparing historians from different eras and places on the axis of quality. We may compare Tacitus and Suetonius, both Romans, and make a judgment. But on what basis can we compare the excellence of Tacitus and that of Braudel? They are both extraordinary historians, but their eras and places and purposes are so different that it seems ludicrous to attempt to judge one better than the other. It would be like trying to decide who is the greater athlete, Michael Jordan or Tiger Woods. It is a question that cannot be answered.

But just as we may decide that Jordan is an outstanding example of basketball excellence and Woods is a model golfer, so too we may choose Tacitus to stand for the highest development of Roman historical writing and Braudel to exemplify the modern French. It is on these two bases, then, that the historians included in this anthology are chosen: each is excellent in his or her way, and together they represent the best of many traditions.

We have purposely included a larger variety of traditions than some European-oriented traditionalists might expect. Indeed, the other book most similar to this one, Peter Gay's *Historians at Work*, is unsuitable for classroom use, not only because it is four volumes long but also because it includes only European and North American historians, and only males. When we began this book, we had in mind creating a shorter, more manageable imitation of Gay's work. But as we proceeded we kept finding historians who were obviously important who were outside the male, Euroamerican canon Gay chooses. It is just not true that only men and only Europeans and North Americans have written history and written it distinctively and well. No one can read al-Tabari, Arai Hakuseki, and Sima Guang and fail to be struck by the breadth of their vision, the depth of their insight, the richness of their interpretation—and the importance of their work to the development of historical writing, even if they did not write history of a modern Western type.

Type of history is an issue. The ways people wrote history—indeed, their conceptions of what history was and what its uses were—differed in different times and cultures. Most modern Europeans and North Americans have thought of history as the stories of the past retold with lessons for the present and guides for the future. A premium has been put on getting the story straight, on basing one's account on an accurate record and care for context. History has not been viewed that way in all times and places. Ibn Khaldûn was not much concerned with the stories, the details of the past, but was very concerned with broad generalizations that could be drawn from the past. Early Indian historians, by contrast, cared a great deal for the story and not much for accuracy, though Kalhana, whom we include here, did his best to get the facts right. Machiavelli and Guicciardini saw history not as a subject in itself but as a branch of political philosophy that used examples drawn from the past. Most of the historians in this volume (particularly the nineteenth-century British, Germans, and their intellectual descendants) regarded written documents as superior to oral accounts, and so relied mainly on the former. Kenneth Dike, however, regarded oral traditions as superior for understanding the fundaments of African history, and regarded documents as mere supplements; in this he was rather like Herodotus. So there are many kinds of history represented here. Not all will fit equally well with the preconceptions or interests of a particular reader, but all of them will edify the reader if he or she is open to learn. Every reader wears spectacles fashioned by his or her time and culture, but to read the varieties of history only through the lenses of the present and of one's own culture is to blind oneself to the breadth of that which one might learn.

Just as an unbiased reading compels one to include historians from many traditions—Arai Hakuseki along with Gregory of Tours, Romesh Dutt along with William Bradford—so, too, it is worthwhile reading women historians as well as men. One can hardly read Macaulay and Martineau and judge the former a superior example of Victorian British historical writing, even though most traditional Euroamerican historiography courses eschew the woman, Martineau, and include the man, Macaulay. So, too, there are subjects that women historians have illuminated more fruitfully than have men. Anna Comnena and Ban Zhao are two examples of court historians whose accounts are much more vivid than their male colleagues' because of the personal connections and the woman-oriented sensitivities they brought to their work. Gulbadan Begam shows aspects of Mughal life that Abu'l Fazl, her better-known male contemporary, misses. Thus, there are women historians included here along with the men, and Asians, Africans, Latin Americans, Pacific Islanders, and Middle Easterners along with Europeans and North Americans.

Even so, the reader will quickly observe a bias toward writers whose work has appeared in English. The work of many great writers in other languages has been translated into English and therefore will be available to our readers. That is more true, however, of Europeans than of Asians or Africans. We offer no new translations, so our collection inclines toward writers who are accessible to an English-speaking audience and slights those writers and traditions whose work has not yet been translated.

This English-speaking bias is perhaps most apparent in the final section, "Passions of the Present." That section differs from the others in that it is intended to introduce the reader, not to the past development of many historical traditions, but to the current concerns of the American historical profession. We assume that most of our readers will be working in the United States (this text is intended primarily for U.S. colleges), and therefore their major interaction will be with the questions that animate U.S. historians. At this time, despite considerable convergence, there is not one single set of questions that occupies historians all over the world. Still, the concerns of American historians are also concerns in more than a few other places, and we describe them in Part 6.

The reader will also note a bias toward history that is written as opposed to that which is recorded by film, video, or other means. For the purposes of this book, historians are writers of history and, in nonliterate cultures, tellers of history. Historians who have used other media, such as film, painting, and the plastic arts, are worth contemplating, but, by the nature of their media, their tasks are so different that they properly constitute a separate study.

World History by the World's Historians, then, proposes a more inclusive canon, and one designed to support a worldwide understanding of the historical discipline. Nonetheless, it leaves out many fine historians; our editors insist we limit our collection to a certain number of printed pages. That is within the design of our project. We have gathered the work of 56 great historians into six roughly chronological categories: "In the Beginnings," "Early Historians," "Evolving Traditions," "Growth of the West," "Science and Critique," and "Passions of the Present." "In the Beginnings" contains four selections typical of the histories found in primarily oral societies. It also presents three early works of written historical literature. All show how history writing probably began. The former show the pressures shaping oral histories; the latter show history mixed with literature, religion, and philosophy. It is out of such materials that the later traditions of history writing grew. "Early Historians" shows the founding of formal historiographical traditions in many parts of the world. "Evolving Traditions" carries the development of historiographical traditions further, up to about 1500 C.E. Part 4, "Growth of the West," contains selections that reflect the rapid and powerful expansion of Europe onto the world scene and the responses of historians in many parts of the world to that expansion. "Science and Critique" shows nineteenth- and early twentieth-century historians around the world grappling with the idea of history as a science and with objectivist aspirations. The final section, "Passions of the Present," gives examples of the kinds of historical questions, topics, and perspectives that frame the work of the current generation of American historians.

Each part of the book begins with a discussion of the common features in that era of the development of historical thinking and writing around the world. Then we present selections from the work of several historians. Each selection is preceded by an introduction that addresses certain common questions and is followed by questions for students to consider and suggestions for reading. Each introduction describes the life and work of the writer, lays a context for that person's writing, and highlights distinctive features. It seeks to help the reader understand not only what the author wrote, but why she wrote what she did, what were her favorite topics and themes of interpretation, and where she stood in the development of the art of history. We keep these analyses brief because, frankly, we believe it is better to read great historians than to read about them. It is like the study of literature: it is a good thing to read criticism of Conrad's themes and style, but it is a better thing to read *Nostromo* and *Lord Jim* and discover their wonders for oneself.

We encourage students to ask questions like these as they read: Who was this historian? Where did he fit in the structure of his society? Why did this person choose to write history? Why did he write as he did? What kinds of problems or topics did this historian choose to investigate? What kinds of sources did she use? What are the strengths and weaknesses of those sources? What other sources might she have used? What are the methods the historian used to frame questions and to collect and analyze information? On what assumptions and toward what ends did he fashion an interpretation of his subject? What were the responses of others to her writing? How can the work of this historian inform the student's own emerging sense of how he or she wants to write history? How does that student's own cultural context shape the kind of history that he or she finds most compelling?

Because history has been so variously conceived and written, *World History by the World's Historians* does not present a formal philosophy of history. Instead, it employs a broad, inclusive definition of history as the study, record, and interpretation of the human past. In our time in Europe and North America there is a major dispute over the philosophical question "What is history?" On one side are empiricists, who think of history as what happened or what people thought happened, and who spend their time trying to find out what happened. On the other side are constructivists, who contend that history is whatever historians study, and who are more interested in how people construct their historical visions of the world. This debate is compelling to historians today. Other philosophical debates have been compelling to historians in other times. We shall not take sides in this debate or any other—to do so would be to recast the past in present dress—but we shall point out some of the issues from time to time. Insofar as there is a philosophical theme to this volume, it is that history and philosophy of history are diverse. *World History by the World's Historians* presents the work of historians who operated on the bases of a variety of different philosophies.

Some professors will use *World History by the World's Historians* as the only text for a course in historiography or historical methods. But most will want to use it as the foundation for their course, supplementing it with the writing of their personal favorites. Each professor will choose different other books—probably half a dozen—for students to read. Some who value the Victorian era will want their students to read Acton, Macaulay, and Martineau in their entirety in addition to the excerpts from many historians here. Philosophers of history may prefer Collingwood, Carr, and Kelley. Postmodernists may choose Foucault, Davis, and Darnton. Asianists may insist on Sima Qian, K. M. Panikkar, and Naito Konan. The choice is theirs. The pleasure and the learning, we hope, will be the reader's.

FOR FURTHER READING

Aron, Raymond. *Introduction to the Philosophy of History.* Boston: Beacon, 1961.

Barker, John. *The Superhistorians.* New York: Scribner's, 1982.

Barzun, Jacques, and Henry F. Graff. *The Modern Researcher.* 5th ed. New York: Harcourt Brace, 1992.

Benjamin, Jules R. *A Student's Guide to History.* 6th ed. New York: St. Martin's, 1994.

Boia, Lucien, et al., eds. *Great Historians from Antiquity to 1800: An International Dictionary.* New York: Greenwood, 1991.

––––––. *Great Historians of the Modern Age: An International Dictionary.* New York: Greenwood, 1989.

Breisach, Ernst. *Historiography.* Chicago: University of Chicago Press, 1983.

Carr, Edward Hallett. *What Is History?* New York: Knopf, 1962.

Clive, John. *Not by Fact Alone.* New York: Knopf, 1989.

Collingwood, R. G. *Essays in the Philosophy of History.* New York: Oxford, 1956.

Dray, William H. *Philosophy of History.* 2nd ed. Englewood Cliffs, NJ: Prentice Hall, 1993.

Fischer, David Hackett. *Historian's Fallacies.* New York: Harper and Row, 1970.

Fitzsimons, M. A. *The Past Recaptured.* Notre Dame, IN: University of Notre Dame Press, 1983.

Gay, Peter, et al., eds. *Historians at Work.* 4 vols. New York: Harper and Row, 1972–75.

Gilderhus, Mark T. *History and Historians.* Englewood Cliffs, NJ: Prentice Hall, 1987.

Kammen, Michael, ed. *The Past Before Us: Contemporary Historical Writing in the United States.* Ithaca, NY: Cornell University Press, 1980.

Kelley, Donald R., ed. *Versions of History from Antiquity to the Enlightenment.* New Haven, CT: Yale University Press, 1991.

Levine, Lawrence W. "Clio, Canons, and Culture." *Journal of American History* 80 (1993): 849–67.

Lowenthal, David. *The Past Is a Foreign Country.* Cambridge, MA: Cambridge University Press, 1985.

Mazlish, Bruce. *The Riddle of History.* New York: Harper and Row, 1966.

Mink, Louis O. *Historical Understanding.* Ithaca, NY: Cornell University Press, 1987.

Stern, Fritz, ed. *The Varieties of History.* New York: Vintage, 1972.

Editors' Comments and Acknowledgments

The creation of an anthology as broad as this one required both an initial editorial division of labor and the assistance of several people. The very fact that ours is the first attempt to collect selections from the world's historians in one book meant that we had no models and no clear canon from which to draw. We therefore had to specialize and to consult other scholars with expertise different from our own. Were it not for their kind assistance, plus the help of our universities' librarians, students, and staff, this volume would not have been possible.

The editors' labors were arranged as follows: Kevin Cragg is the most classically trained of us, so he took primary responsibility for the Greeks, Romans, and early Christians, plus medieval and early modern Europe. Jim Spickard is the most familiar with anthropology and with social science, so he took responsibility for Native and Latin America, the Middle East, Africa, and India, plus the social scientifically oriented historians we have included. Paul Spickard, with expertise in Asian as well as American history, took responsibility for China, Japan, and many of the modern historians. We each chose passages and wrote drafts of introductions, which we modified based on the others' suggestions. After we had a full manuscript, we each read and revised the entire work. Paul Spickard collated and adjudicated among these revisions, making changes as clarity and style demanded. We have therefore listed him as first editor, though our efforts have been as equally divided as we can imagine on a project of this type. We are fully joint editors who take collective responsibility for our work.

Several other scholars contributed to our efforts. Noriko Usuda, a former student of Paul Spickard at Brigham Young University–Hawaii and now an independent scholar working in Tokyo, provided an analysis of Japanese historiography that undergirds both the authors and the books chosen to represent that tradition. In addition, she undertook translations of some works of Yanagita Kunio that are not otherwise available in English; although those translations are not part of this anthology, they helped us understand Yanagita and we are grateful. Four other students provided valuable analyses of other authors and advice on the passages selected: Kerri Ritchie, Karina Kahananui Green, Gerald D'Sena, and Richard Schuchart. In addition, we have tried out most of these passages in our courses at Brigham Young University–Hawaii, the University of Redlands, and Bethel College. Our thanks go to all the students who helped make this a better text.

Several of our professional colleagues made timely suggestions that helped determine the book's shape and contents: Jeff Belnap, Robert Eng, David Grandy, Greg Gubler, Carl Hanson, Bill Huntley, John Martin, Alida Metcalf, Richard Reed, Ronald Toby, and William Kauaiwiulaokalani Wallace. In addition, several readers offered suggestions that helped us fine-tune our manuscript for publication: Wayne Hamilton Wiley, Central Virginia Community College; Juanita Smart, Washington State University; Steven W. Guerrier, James Madison University; Gerald Herman, Northeastern University; and Marian Nelson, University of Nebraska–Omaha. While we are grateful for their advice, we are also mindful that they should not be held responsible for our editorial decisions.

Charlene Keliiliki was a paragon of energy, dedication, efficiency, and grace as she typed much of the manuscript. We also thank Bernadette White, Chuck Freidel, Amy Deeds, Sarah Weingartner, and Tricia Rafanan for help with typing. We are grateful to the librarians at Brigham Young University–Hawaii, the University of Redlands, the University of Hawaii, UCLA, Trinity University, and Bethel College for sharing with us the books they prize and for many kindnesses as we tried to track down odd pieces in strange places.

The University of Redlands granted Jim Spickard a timely sabbatical, and the Institute for Latin American Studies at the University of Texas provided him a visiting scholarship. Paul Spickard received a sabbatical from Brigham Young University–Hawaii and a visiting fellowship from the East-West Center. Bethel College granted a sabbatical leave to Kevin Cragg. For all of these, we are grateful.

Finally, our families know what they have had to endure while this book was being made; thanks go to them as well.

Note regarding the spelling of non-English words

All the selections in this anthology are presented with words spelled as they were in their published forms, whether those be books written in English or English translations of works written originally in other languages. We have not reworked the translators' transliterations of names or terms from other languages. This leads, inevitably, to certain inconsistencies, but not, we hope, to confusion.

The inconsistencies exist for each of the non-English traditions, but they are most apparent in the Chinese selections (Chapters 7, 10, 11, 22, and 37). The Chinese writings we present were translated between 1922 and 1975, all using one form or another of the Wade-Giles romanization system. The same system was used by the publishers of most of the books in the Chinese chapters' bibliographies. We have left those writings as they were first published in English. In our own introductions to the Chinese selections, however, we have employed the Pinyin romanization system that is currently used in the People's Republic of China. So, for instance, the authors of our selections write of the Hsia Dynasty and the Chou dynasty; we write of the Xia Dynasty and the Zhou Dynasty. They identify the authors of Chapter 11 as Pan Ku and Pan Chao; we write their names Ban Gu and Ban Zhao.

The selections from Arab, Persian, and Indian traditions are presented here with a minimum of diacritical marks, usually just apostrophes.

We believe that the careful reader will not be confused by all this. We must write in our era, as others have written in theirs.

Note regarding footnotes

Most modern Western historians used footnotes to indicate the sources from which they drew their material and to make parenthetical comments on their narratives. Most other historians did not use footnotes, and either told their reader the nature of their sources in the body of the text or else left the reader to guess. The modern Western quest for scientific objectivity and verifiability has led to a vast increase in the use of footnotes, especially in the twentieth-century West.

This presents the editors with a problem: we wish to communicate to our readers how these historians did their work, but we do not wish to spend too many pages on footnotes—we would rather those pages display the authors' writing. We have ended with a compromise. In certain cases we have kept the footnotes intact, because we believe they will substantially help the reader understand how that historian went about his or her work, or because they comprise such an integral part of the text—a kind of two-level exposition—that they cannot justly be left out. Those authors include Gibbon (Chapter 31), Ranke (38), Dike (44), Braudel (48), Blassingame (50), Thompson (51), Bynum (52), Davis (53), and Himmelfarb (55). In other instances we have omitted the footnotes: Dutt (34), Weber (40), Turner (41), da Cunha (42), Panikkar (43), the Beards (45), and Bloch (46).

Historians in
Complete Volume

VOLUME II

Authors' Note: About the Photographs in This Text

McGraw-Hill has kindly provided a photograph to accompany each chapter. Specialists searched diligently for an image of each historian. When such an image could not be found, the publisher's researchers substituted an image that highlighted the writer's milieu or some aspect of his or her work. We appreciate their diligence.

This means, regrettably, that we have proportionately more pictures of male historians than female, and many more photos of European writers than historians of color. Is that not a sad commentary on the way archives have been kept in a European-male-dominated world?

Our publisher tells us that what appears here is absolutely the best we can do at this time for images of Third World and women authors. We continue to hope for improvement and invite our readers to suggest sources of more appropriate photos for any subsequent editions that might appear.

Author's Notes About the Photographs in This Text

PART ONE

In the Beginnings

M ost historians today work with texts. Libraries, musty archives, old manuscripts and records—these are the sources from which they fashion their insights into the past. True, historians of recent events often talk with those who took part in them, but this is not possible for times long ago. The written word, occasionally augmented by clues from archaeology, is their usual guide.

Just as modern historians mostly read words, so also do they write words. Despite the recent advent of electronic and visual media, most historians report their findings in books and journal articles. These fill our libraries and subsequent historians' lives. Through these words, historians try to capture the past "as it really was." That is, they strive for objectivity: they write fact, not fiction, and clearly distinguish the two in their minds.

Yet history was not always so practiced. Some societies lacked writing, and so could neither consult records nor produce them. Other societies' tales of the past sat somewhere on the border between history and literature. In both cases, the past was recounted to entertain or edify as much as to inform; indeed, early historians did not think these aims separate.

Whence came the various historical traditions that are the subject of this book? Clearly, they grew out of early oral and written literatures. Each of the world's civilizations began without writing, and each of their historical traditions began with something that modern scholars would call "not quite history." If we are to understand the various ways of writing history collected in this volume, we must get a sense of the "not quite history" that came before.

We have labeled this first section of our anthology "In the Beginnings." By this, we wish to highlight both the emergence of historical writing from the oral traditions of nonliterate societies and the precursors of some of the major schools of written history that we shall be tracing. Our selections seek breadth, not depth. We have chosen four passages that are typical of various oral traditions, and three early texts from three of the world's great civilizations. We wish we could include more of each. Both types of passages, however, bring several interesting historiographic issues to the fore.

1

First, how did the historians of nonliterate societies ply their trade? For all societies have had historians. Hunting bands, tribes, and kingdoms, from the stone age to our own time—all have found ways to recount their past. And like modern people, all have used their stories of the past to orient themselves to the present: to explain, to justify, and to sanction what they do.

By and large, nonliterate historians told about "the way things used to be." They collected tales, sayings, and bits of folk wisdom, which they sifted and ordered into stories that made sense of past events. And they presented these accounts in a social context: as tales to specific audiences, in specific milieus, and for specific purposes. This, indeed, is much like literate historians, none of whom merely presents facts without regard to audience or meaning. Such lists of facts, as Lewis Carroll had his Dodo say, are "the driest things I know of." All historians, lettered and unlettered, must try to tell a tale.

Are these oral accounts "histories"? That is, are they believed by their tellers to be true records of the past? Or are they fictions, designed merely to entertain and inspire? The accounts in this section are clearly the former. Each does amuse and charm its audience, but each is also seen as a true tale by its tellers. As such, these sagas are no different from the well-written histories of our own day. Entertainment is an aid to knowledge, not an end in itself.

Here a second question intrudes: are such oral "histories" accurate? Modern scholars disagree about this. The most well-developed debate has been between Africanist historians

and Africanist anthropologists. Many of the former, led by Jan Vansina, regard oral traditions as largely accurate, though subject to much the same skepticism as one would aim at written records. Many of the latter, led by T. O. Beidelman and Luc de Heusch, argue that oral traditions are so deformed by present social needs as to be historically useless. They can teach us about today, but not about the past.

This dispute has had some interesting twists. A linguist in the 1930s discovered an Albanian bard who could accurately recite 13 hours at a stretch—about the same amount of material as in a 200-page book. By observation, the linguist learned that the oral reciter used techniques that cued his memory about what should come next. The fact that he was working with poetry helped; humans can best memorize to music or rhythm. Virtually all oral traditions are poetic in one form or another, increasing their consistency. For years, this case was used to support Vansina's position. Yet when the bard recorded his tale again in the 1950s, it was different from the tale he had told two decades before. Comparing the tapes showed that it had changed in subtle ways. Still, the bard claimed that he had made no changes and that he had told the tale exactly as he had 20 years before. Clearly, what it means to tell "the same" story in an oral society is not the same as in a literate culture. This supports the anthropologists' position.

Still, internal evidence in some tales argues for a degree of historical accuracy. The *Iliad*, for example, which was passed on in oral form long before it was written, records the names and locations of many cities in Greece whose existence was unknown at the time the poem was compiled in the eighth century BCE. Not until after nineteenth-century excavations could scholars show that the list is accurate for the Trojan War period. On the other hand, the traditions from which the *Iliad* was built included references to the use of chariots in battle—something that had dropped out of eighth-century warfare. The composer creatively portrayed the chariots providing a kind of taxi service to bring the heroes to the battleground where they alighted and battled with spears and swords in proper eighth-century style. That is, the composer reworked some of the material so it made current sense but left some of it alone. In many oral traditions, events, names, and descriptions seem to be relatively stable; chronology and sequencing get lost or confused.

Most historians assume that oral traditions are uneven at best, though they contain many kernels of truth. The tellers try to be faithful to a tradition and to match their audience's expectation that a story will correspond to what they have heard before. Yet that story must also touch the audience's present concerns. These contradictory requirements shape histories that are oral, as they shape written ones; the exact dynamics—and thus accuracy—vary from case to case.

We shall see both change and continuity at work in the passages we have collected in this section. As noted later, the griots of West Africa have preserved the deeds of their great king Son-Jara for over seven centuries. Much fantasy has accrued to this tale in the intervening time, and Son-Jara's epic has become a political charter for Mande-speaking peoples. The Mande emphasize his greatness, and so claim it as their own. Yet, despite their aggrandizing, a factual core remains. At the other extreme, Hopi origin tales surely have some factual basis in the treks of various clans and tribelets across the American Southwest. Yet inter-clan rivalry has buried the past beneath a present in which the tales are used as weapons, pitting one group against another. Oral traditions are indeed histories, but they must be weighed with care.

This section shall not worry too much about accuracy, however. If the historians of nonliterate societies did not get all the details right, they were still true to their traditions and believed themselves to be telling true tales. As such, they were historians. They thought that the past was important. They used some sources and discarded others. And they tried to tell about the past in a clear and accurate way. Readers who wish to explore the historical accuracy of the ensuing selections should scan the books and articles following this introduction or those following each passage. Accurate or not, however, tales such as these are the first histories.

A third issue arises when oral traditions are written down—as were all those that appear here. The Hopi text we have chosen is traditional, yet its teller is no primitive. He is clearly influenced by modern writing and by the modern world. Indeed, he comments on anthropologists' ideas about his people and puts forward a distinctly more pan-Indian world view than would have been likely two centuries ago. He also shapes his story for a non-Hopi audience, going into detail about things that Hopis would automatically understand. The text is thus neither "aboriginal" nor purely "oral"; ironically, this lets it illustrate many facets of the oral tradition extremely well.

Similarly, the passage from the Sundiata epic appears not as it would be told to Malian villagers, but as a piece of literature modeled on European epic stories, by one of West Africa's best-known Francophone writers. It is, in short, a translation of a traditional *griot*'s tale into a modern idiom, whose narrator ironically goes to some pains to emphasize the superiority of the spoken word over the written. Again, such ironies show us something about the complexity of history in an oral setting. We have included this version of Sundiata because of this, and also because it is accessible to the modern reader. Our selection from the Hawaiian *Kumulipo* is less accessible, because it was designed for the native Hawaiian aristocracy, not for us. These three passages, plus the Kaguru tale—retold by an anthropologist enmeshed in the aforementioned controversy—give the reader a good sampling of history in an oral context. They are not exactly history as it was told around campfires before writing, but they are as close as we are apt to get in the modern day.

As mentioned earlier, the last three passages in this section are somewhat different. The first two were once oral, yet have long been written and are among the foundation epics of Western civilizations. The third was probably never oral, but is also something of a foundation story. All three sit on the border between history and literature. They raise some new issues that readers may wish to note.

The first issue concerns authorship. The histories in the rest of this anthology have single, identifiable authors. These three probably do not. The *Iliad* and *Genesis* were oral long before they were written; they were thus shaped over considerable time by a large number of people. Their final composition consisted of weaving together shorter tales, poetry, and songs into a cohesive whole. Some scholars think such a task would be too great for any single bard and so postulate a committee or bardic school as a joint author. Others think the consistency of character and style in the two works just cited means that the final compilation was the work of one mind. No one knows which happened, though textual analysis provides clues, as Richard Friedman's work on the Bible has shown. It is only when these tales were committed to writing that we got the fixed text that we now read. The Chinese *Book of History* is similarly a compilation of prior oral traditions and court records. They have clearly been modified to fit the concerns of their compilers—a practice common to all of the passages in this section.

The second issue concerns genre. Though the Greeks thought the *Iliad* was history, we moderns usually treat it as literature. We analyze its plot and characters, trace its narrative structure, and use literary techniques to explain its emotional appeal. Similarly, most modern readers encounter *Genesis* either as narrative religious philosophy or as myth. Even if we regard it as true, we see its truth as different from the truth about what we ate for yesterday's breakfast or how we voted in the last election. Though it is about the past, it is not ordinary history in our minds. The *Book of History* more overtly recounts the past, yet it similarly slides into ethical advice and homilies. As we could call the *Iliad* literature and *Genesis* religion, so we could call the *Book of History* philosophy. Such works do not easily fit the modern definition of history; yet they are important histories all the same. The distinctions between genres we make in the twentieth century did not exist at the beginning of the historical enterprise.

FOR FURTHER READING

Beidelman, Thomas O. "Myth, Legend and Oral History: A Kaguru Traditional Text." *Anthropos* 65 (1970): 74–97.

Friedman, Richard E. *Who Wrote the Bible?* New York: Summit Books, 1987.

Goody, Jack. *The Interface between the Written and the Oral.* Cambridge: Cambridge University Press, 1987.

Henige, David P. "The Problem of Feedback in Oral Tradition: Four Examples from the Fante Coastlands." *Journal of African History* 14 (1973): 223–35.

Heusch, Luc de. *The Drunken King: or The Origins of the State.* Bloomington, IN: Indiana University Press, 1982.

Hill, Jonathan D., ed. *Rethinking History and Myth: Indigenous South American Perspectives on the Past.* Urbana, IL: University of Illinois Press, 1988.

Lord, Albert Bates. *The Singer of Tales.* Cambridge, MA: Harvard University Press, 1960.

Schoffeleers, Matthew. "Oral History and the Retrieval of the Distant Past: On the Use of Legendary Chronicles as Sources of Historical Information." In *Theoretical Explorations in African Religion,* edited by Wim van Binsbergen and Matthew Schoffeleers, 164–88. London: KPI, 1985.

Vansina, Jan. *Oral Tradition.* London, 1965.

———. "Once Upon a Time: Oral Tradition as History in Africa." *Daedalus* 100 (1971): 442–68.

CHAPTER 1

Hopi

Migration Stories

Albert Yava
NAU . . . PH . . 658.320, Leo Crane Collection, Cline Library,
Northern Arizona University.

The Hopi Indians have dwelt on the edge of Black Mesa, in northern Arizona, for several hundred years. Like other Western Pueblo groups, they live in villages perched on cliffs and farm the flat land below. Indian corn, squash, beans, and cotton grow well there despite the dry climate; springs on the valley floor bring water south from the snowy Colorado plateau. Before the modern era, the Hopi depended on such crops and on hunting to survive.

Hopi families and clans are matrilineal: a person belongs to the same group as his or her mother. These groups traditionally had economic, political, and ritual duties. Goods were produced and shared within the family, not between families (though there was some ritual trading). Clans governed the villages, often with much infighting. Hopi religious life still centers on the clans and on *kiva* societies, which carry out some of the most complex and closely guarded of all Native American rites.

The Hopi first met Europeans when Don Pedro de Tovar explored the area for Coronado in 1539–1540. Two centuries before, the region had many more settlements, more intensively farmed and tied to each other by trade. Whole villages sometimes moved to seek better water and land, especially during dry spells; this accounts for the many ruins found in the area. One such dry spell, and perhaps Spanish-borne smallpox, shrank the Hopi towns near the time of de Tovar's arrival so that the society he saw then was in decline. Hopi villages were smaller in the 1500s than they had been before and than they would be in later years.

Unlike the more accessible parts of their empire, the Spanish could not control this region. Few expeditions visited the Hopi in the years after contact, and the Pueblo revolt of the 1680s kept the tribe free for nearly two centuries. That revolt brought many eastern refugees to Black Mesa; some of them joined Hopi groups. A few villages split as their population grew; others waned and were abandoned. Their relative independence has let the Hopi keep more of their traditions than is the case with many other Native American groups. Yet despite their seeming stability, Hopi villages have seen much change.

The Hopi record some of these changes in their clan legends. Framed as origin myths, these tales both recount former roving and justify today's clan pecking order. As the following passage shows, the Hopi believe that this is the fourth world, into which people came to escape evil. After climbing up through a bamboo or reed, they scattered over the earth. Groups who were to become the Hopi clans wandered across the Southwest, coming to Black Mesa at various times to settle the several hamlets. The author, Nuvayoiyava (Albert Yava), attributes some of these treks to the search for land, and others to interclan fighting. If events of the last hundred years are any guide, both reasons are likely. But the constant alerts against evil and conflict may be less historical than cautionary. The Hopi are as much averse to infighting as they are prone to it; it makes sense that they would use their legends to warn themselves of its consequences. Note the criteria Yava uses to separate "true" from "false" stories; this is the oral historian at work.

Note that this passage was collected in the middle of the twentieth century. Nuvayoiyava is not only both a Hopi and a Tewa, as he indicates (a

Tewa village was absorbed by the Hopis after the Pueblo revolt, and he is related to both groups); he is also an American. He has learned many Hopi and Tewa oral histories but has also read what anthropologists say about his people and about their ancestors and has taken pains to disagree with them. He is thus no untutored "primitive," as his version of the Hopi origin story shows. This history is both traditional and shaped by modern concerns. For example, versions collected a century ago do not say that Hopi villages took in Apaches, Shoshones, and Indians of groups other than the Tewa. Nor did they link the Bahanas (White people) to the emergence myth. This version of the story, however, uses the myth to explain Whites' evil—plainly a comment on the way Europeans appear from a modern Hopi view. Such modern concerns cannot be separated from "tradition," as if the former were some pollutant from which the latter could be extracted. Historians in oral societies inevitably shape received material in the crucible of the present. What appears now as "traditional" may well just be yesterday's issues. This passage is typical of oral histories in such mixture. It is more explicit than most in its recognition of other variants and in its attention to the reach of history into the present day.

Migration Stories[1]

As to where all these Hopi clans came from, every clan is the custodian of its own story. But adding it all up you can say that they came from just about every direction. Some of those who came from the north, from the neighborhood of Tokonave (which the white people renamed Navajo Mountain)—they include the Snake and Horn clans—originally were from farther west, probably in California. Other clans came from a place far to the south called Palatkwa. No one knows for sure where Palatkwa was. A number of clans traveled up and down the Colorado River and the Little Colorado for a good many years, maybe centuries, before they arrived here. Some, like the Coyote Clan (not the same as the Water Coyote Clan) came from Eastern Pueblo country.

Looking at all these facts, it's clear that the modern Hopis are descendants of numerous different groups, including Plains Indians, that merged after gravitating to this place. Those people who say we are all descendants of those Basketmakers who lived up in the San Juan Valley make it sound too simple. We Hopis (you have to remember that I am a full-fledged Hopi as well as being a Tewa) can't be explained so easily. Those migrating groups that came here spoke several different languages. For example, the Water Coyote group that came here from the north spoke Paiute or Chemehuevi or some other Shoshonean dialect. We had clans, even whole villages, coming here from the Eastern Pueblos, where various languages are spoken. We had Pumas coming in from the south. And there's an Apache strain too. Those clans that came here from Palatkwa, such as the Water Clan, the Sand Clan and the Tobacco Clan, brought Pimas and Apaches with them. My father's group, the Water Clan, claims to be Uche—that is, Apache—in origin. It could be that the first people to settle these mesas were Shoshonean-speakers from the San Juan Valley, but other people joined them and it was this mixture that came to make up what we now call Hopitu, the Hopi People.

Anthropologists believe that the earliest Hopi villages were established around the twelfth or thirteenth century when a big drought came to the San Juan Valley and drove the people south. Shongopovi is supposed to have been our first village—the old Shongopovi, that is, built down below the mesa at the place called Masipa. It was settled by the Bear Clan. But from the evidence, you'd have to say that those Bear Clan people weren't actually the first to settle in this region. For one thing, according to their own tradition, the first morning after they arrived they saw smoke rising from Antelope Mesa. They investigated and found that a village was already established up there. That village was Awatovi.

All through this country around here are hundreds and hundreds of old ruins. Anthropologists haven't paid much attention to them, only to the larger, more spectacular ruins. Some of those people living in the smaller villages of only a few houses may have been here long before the Bear Clan, the Snake Clan and other clans built the main Hopi settlements. In fact, some other clans claim to have arrived here before the Bear Clan. There could have been settlements scattered all through this mesa country long before Betatakin and Mesa Verde were abandoned.

One thing we can be sure of is that people weren't just moving down from the north. They were traveling in all directions. It isn't clear to us as to what they were looking for. Maybe it was water and good fields. Maybe they were told in their old prophecies to behave in such and such a way, or to find such and such a place. According to the main Hopi creation story—there are a number of different creation stories, but this is the one most Hopis accept—the beginning of our earthly experience was when the people emerged from the underworld. Where they emerged from, that was already their Third World, and up here it was the Fourth World. At that time they were advised to look for a place called Sichdukwi, Flower Mound. The clans separated and went in different directions, but eventually they converged here in the belief that Sichdukwi was at First Mesa. At least, that is the traditions that some clans have. The ones that gravitated to the other mesas had another thing that they were looking for. Some clans say they went in that direction looking for Masauwu, the Death Spirit who owned all the land around here.

But there's another reason for all the migrations and the abandonment of one village and another. Time after time, contention within a village, or between villages, or between clans caused the people to leave, and in the journeys that followed, they were looking for a place of harmony where they could follow good teachings and a good way of life. That didn't mean having bounteous crops, but living together as people who were civilized and worthy of being in the Fourth World. Time after time, in our traditional stories, the people had to leave a certain place because they'd fallen into evil ways. Sometimes their villages were destroyed because of the corruption that had come into their lives. Sometimes one village had to pack up and leave because of dissension with another village. Palatkwa, that southern village of the Water Clan, was destroyed and the people had to leave because they'd forgotten about spiritual values.

The people of Sikyatki had to go away because of evil things that had occurred, and because of enmity with Keuchaptevela, the old Walpi. The chief of Awatovi asked that his village be destroyed by the other villages because his people had lost respect for their spiritual traditions and had become undisciplined and ungovernable. The Snake Clan had to leave Tokonave because of friction with other people in the village. The chief of Pivanhonkapi had his village destroyed because, as in the case of Awatovi, the people had turned away from decent living. The Payupkis abandoned their village because of quarrels with nearby Tsikuvi. Oraibi was broken in two by dissension, so the Fire Clan and the Water Coyotes had to go away and build new villages.

Sometimes, traditions say, sorcerers were responsible for these events. That is a way of saying that evil forces came into play. Always, time after time, there is that theme of flight from evil and the search for virtue and balance. The theme goes back to the first recollection of all, the emergence of the people from the underworld. That's where it begins. The story is usually told to boys after they have been initiated into the Kachina Society. It's quite long, with elaborate details, but I will make it brief, telling enough, though, to explain about that long flight from sorcerers, dissension and evil.

Way back in the distant past, the ancestors of humans were living down below in a world under the earth. There weren't humans yet, merely creatures of some kind. They lived in darkness, behaving like bugs. Now, there was a Great Spirit watching over everything, and some people say he was Tawa, the sun. He saw how things were down under the earth. He didn't care for the way the creatures were living. He sent his messenger, you might say his representative, Gogyeng Sowuhti—that is, Spider Old Woman—to talk to them. She said, "You creatures, the Sun Spirit who is above doesn't want you living like this. He is going to transform you into something better, and I will lead you to another world."

So Tawa made them into a better form of creatures, and Gogyeng Sowuhti led them to another world above the place where they were living. This was the Second World, still below the ground. The creatures lived here for some time, but they were still animals in form, not humans. There were some with tails, some without. The ones that were eventually to become human did not have tails.

But life in the Second World wasn't good. The creatures didn't behave well. They didn't get along. They ate one another. There was chaos and dissension. So the Great Spirit sent Gogyeng Sowuhti down again after he transformed those beings without tails into a human like form. But they weren't yet true humans, because they were undisciplined—wild and uncivilized. Gogyeng Sowuhti led them to another world up above, the Third World. Things were better at first, but after a while there was more chaos and dissension. Evil individuals caused all kinds of difficulties. There were sorcerers who made people fall sick or quarrel with one another. The evil ones made life hard for everyone.

When at last things became too difficult to bear, the ones who wanted to live orderly and good lives said, "This must come to an end. When the Great Spirit brought us up here he wanted us to be better than we were before. How can we get away and leave the evil ones behind?" Gogyeng Sowuhti told them, "Above us is a Fourth World. Up there life will be better for you. But to get there we have to go through the sky of the Third World. And there are other problems. The Fourth World is owned by Masauwu, the Spirit of Death. You will have to have his permission to go there."

* * *

The people who wanted to escape from the Third World decided to send a scout up to see what it was like up there and make contact with Masauwu. They chose a swift bird, the swallow. The swallow was swift, all right, but he tired before he reached the sky and had to come back. After that they sent a dove, then a hawk. The hawk found a small opening and went through, but he came back without seeing Masauwu. Finally they sent a catbird. He was the one that found Masauwu.

Masauwu asked him, "Why are you here?"

The catbird said, "The world down below is infested with evil. The people want to come up here to live. They want to build their houses here, and plant their corn."

Masauwu said, "Well, you see how it is in this world. There isn't any light, just greyness. I have to use fire to warm my crops and make them grow. However, I have relatives down in the Third World. I gave them the secret of fire. Let them lead the people up here, and I will give them land and a place to settle. Let them come."

After the catbird returned to the Third World and reported that Masauwu would receive them, the people asked, "Now, how will we ever get up there?" So Spider Old Woman called on the chipmunk to plant a sunflower seed. It began to grow. It went up and almost reached the sky, but the weight of the blossom made the stem bend over. Spider Old Woman then asked the chipmunk to plant a spruce tree, but when the spruce finished growing it wasn't tall enough. The chipmunk planted a pine, but the pine also was too short. The fourth thing the chipmunk planted was a bamboo. It grew up and up. It pierced the sky. Spider Old Woman said, "My children, now we have a road to the upper world. When we reach there your lives will be different. Up there you will be able to distinguish evil from good. Anything that is bad must be left behind down here. All evil medicine must be thrown away before you go up. Sorcerers cannot come with us, or they will contaminate the Fourth World. So be careful. If you see an evil person going up, turn him back."

The people began climbing up inside the bamboo stalk. How they got through the bamboo joints I don't know, because the story doesn't explain about that. The mockingbird guarded them on the way up. He was like a scout. He went ahead, calling, "Pashumayani! Pashumayani! Pash! Pash! Pash!—Be careful! Be careful!" The people came up in groups, until everyone reached the top. The opening in the place where they came out was called the sipapuni. The people camped near where they emerged. The light was grey and they didn't know where they would be going. Spider Old Woman—that is, Gogyeng Sowuhti—said, "Well, we are all here. Did you leave the evil ones down below?"

They said, "Yes, we didn't see any evil ones coming up."

Spider Old Woman said, "Good. Now plug the bamboo up with this cotton."

All this time, the mockingbird was telling the people how to arrange themselves, some over here, some over there, group by group, and he gave each group the name of a tribe. So there were Utes, Hopis, Navajos and so on, and one of the groups was called Bahanas, or white people.

After the bamboo was plugged with cotton, it turned out that an evil one had come up without being detected. When they discovered him he laughed.

They said, "We don't want you here. It was because of people like you that we left the Third World."

He said, "You couldn't get along without an evil one. I have a part to play in this world." So according to this version of the story, the evil one taught them how to make the sun, moon and stars and to loft them into the sky to make the world light.

There are other explanations of who put the Sun, moon, and stars in the sky. Some say that Spider Old Woman told the people how to do it. There is also a story that Coyote scattered the stars in the sky. Over in Oraibi some of the traditions say that the spirit Huruing Wuhti, Hard Substances Old Woman, put the sun up there. But the way it was told to me, it was the evil one who came through the sipapuni with the people who showed them how to get the sky work done. Sometimes you hear that the evil one was a powaka, a witch or sorcerer. Because he came into the upper world instead of staying below, sorcery and evil have plagued the people ever since. In my version of the story, sorcery and knowledge were sort of linked together. A sorcerer was supposed to know how to do things that ordinary people couldn't do. I suppose that in the old days they would have said that he was a man with powerful medicine. That's how the evil one knew what to do about making the sun and moon.

When the Hopis left the sipapuni to begin their migrations, they told the sorcerer that he couldn't come with them, because the whole purpose of the emergence was to get away from evil. So he went with the Bahanas, or white people, instead, and the Hopi leaders said that everyone must be wary of Bahanas if they met them anywhere, because their possession of the sorcerer would give them more knowledge than the Hopis could cope with. But time and again in later days other sorcerers found the Hopis and caused dissension and corruption in the villages.

You can see that the theme of dissension and evil, and of the search for a place of harmony, starts with the emergence story. I've told only a little of that story, because it's very long. Different villages and clans have their own special details, and different explanations. A clan in Shongopovi or Oraibi has different explanations than the same clan in Walpi has. The reason is that clan groups kept branching off during the migrations. The Bear Clan was going in a certain direction, then part of the clan left the group and went another way. They all expected to meet again somewhere, maybe at the place foretold in their prophecy. When the Water Clan was coming north from Palatkwa, it was the same thing with them. So you had different branches of clans scattered all across the country, and then they started coming together again at the Hopi mesas. By that time the fragments of the clan had accumulated different experiences. Up to the point when they'd separated, they all had the same traditions, but after that each branch acquired experiences of its own. When they came together again they couldn't tell the same story any more.

*   *   *

The way they tell it, the Bear Clan stopped in various places and made villages when they had to grow their corn, then they went on. One of the places they stopped at was Wupatki, where those ruins are, north of the San Francisco Peaks. The Hopis call those mountains Nuvatikyao, Snow Peaks. After a while the wise old men told the Bear Clan people, "This is not the place we are supposed to go to. The land is too rich here. We will become obsessed with easy living. We are supposed to settle at a place where life will be austere. Let us move on. Our guiding spirit will take care of us." So they moved from there and eventually arrived at Hopi country. Masauwu, the Death Spirit, was living over on Third Mesa near where Oraibi is today, according to the Oraibi Bear Clan story, and he saw them coming. (The Walpi people say Masauwu was living over here.) He went out to meet them, and asked who they were.

They said, "We are the Bear Clan."

He said, "I have been expecting my children, the ones called the Fire Clan. They are the ones I was going to give this land to."

They answered, "Well, the Fire Clan was the first to come through the sipapuni, we acknowledge that. But then they pulled back and refused to take the responsibility of leading the people. So we accepted the responsibility. This is the place we were told about, so we came here. We are the first of the clans to arrive."

Masauwu said, "Yes, since you are the first to come, I will give you a place to build your village."

The place he gave them was where the ruins of Old Shongopovi are, down below the mesa on the east side, and he assigned land for them to cultivate. They called that place Masipa. I think I already mentioned that the morning after their arrival they saw smoke rising from Antelope Mesa in the east, and when they investigated they found that another village was already there. (That would be Awatovi, of course.) But that fact never interfered with their claim that they were the first to arrive in Hopi country. After a while some of their affiliated clans and other clans arrived and joined them.

* * *

Well, after a while the Fire Clan arrived. They found Masauwu and announced that they had come to receive the land he had promised them. He told them, "You Fire Clan people, you were the ones I selected to favor. But the Bear Clan came first. You were my chosen people, so why didn't you take the lead?"

The Fire Clan chief said, "Because we wanted to be respected. When we arrived up here in this world we didn't know any more about it than the others did. Everything was strange to us. We didn't want to be accused of leading the people in the wrong direction. If something bad happened, we didn't want the others to say we were guilty of bringing them into a hard life." Masauwu answered, "Well, you let the Bear Clan get here first, and now they are the paramount clan. Still, you are my clan. You are the Fire Clan, the Masauwu Clan, and I will watch over you. But I don't want to stay where all these people are living. I'm going to disappear from this place. You won't see me any more, but I'll work with you in spirit. I'll guide you. I'll show you the right way by giving signs such as sparks or flares in the night." After that, Masauwu went away from there and didn't show himself to the people any more. He became invisible unless he wanted to show himself as an apparition.

The Fire Clan stayed on in Oraibi until 1906, when they were forced to leave. They founded a new village, Hotevilla. Still today, the Fire Clan has credentials going back, so they say, to the emergence from the Third World. They own a piece of a broken stone tablet that, according to their tradition, they have possessed ever since leaving the sipapuni. They say that the other portion of the tablet was given to good Bahanas right after the emergence. The reason for that was that there was already a prophecy saying that one day far in the future a good Bahana was going to come from the East bringing harmony and good fortune to the Hopis. But the Hopis had already been warned that there were bad Bahanas as well as good ones. So when the right Bahana came he was supposed to carry the portion of the broken tablet. If the two pieces fit together properly, then the Hopis would know that it was the good Bahana that arrived, not some impostor.

The broken tablet of the Fire Clan really exists, at least their part of it. They have it over in Hotevilla. A number of us have seen it. Yukioma, the last Fire Clan chief in Oraibi, went to Washington with a BIA Official in 1911 or 1912, and he took that broken tablet with him just in case he might run into the white man who was supposed to have the other part. When he returned, some of the people asked him, "Did you find the real White Father who has the other part?" He said, "No, they took me to the Commissioner. That's as far as I got. I didn't get to see the Big White Father."

QUESTIONS TO CONSIDER

1. How does the narrator use these stories to tell us who the Hopi are?
2. Why does he disagree with other versions of the stories, especially those recorded and interpreted by anthropologists many years ago?
3. How does writing down these oral histories change them?

FOR FURTHER READING

Courlander, Harold. *The Fourth World of the Hopis.* Albuquerque, NM: University of New Mexico Press, 1971.

Dozier, Edward P. *The Hopi-Tewa of Arizona.* Berkeley: University of California Press, 1954.

Eggan, Fred. *Social Organization of the Western Pueblos.* Chicago: University of Chicago Press, 1950.

Hopi Voices: Recollections, Traditions, and Narratives of the Hopi Indians. Recorded, transcribed and annotated by Harold Courlander. Albuquerque, NM: University of New Mexico Press, 1982.

Rushforth, Scott, and Steadman Upham. *A Hopi Social History.* Austin, TX: University of Texas Press, 1992.

NOTES

1. Albert Yava, *Big Falling Snow: A Tewa-Hopi Indian's Life and Times and the History and Traditions of His People,* ed. Harold Courlander (New York: Crown, 1978), 36–53.

CHAPTER 2

The Kaguru

An East African Migration Tale

Tanzania, home of the Kaguru
© Gary Olsen

The Kaguru are a Bantu-speaking people living in east-central Tanzania, in East Africa. They occupy the central part of that country, in and around the Itumba mountains, where they grow crops and hunt wild game. Like many of their neighbors, they are organized into matrilineal clans that trace their descent from key female ancestors. Those clans, however, are ruled by men—the brothers and uncles of the women who bear the clan name.

The following tale describes the movement of the Mukema clan to its present locale from the northwest, whence they were driven by enemies. Led by their ancestor, Lugode, a group of women and young boys stayed at various places in Kaguru-land before settling in the vacant Talagwe region. Lugode built a fire to claim the land, then made her home in a west-facing cave. Within a few years she was joined by a youth from Musongwe, who had lost his way hunting. His own people later found him and initiated him into manhood (Kaguru boys are initiated by circumcision at puberty). He then returned to marry Lugode. All the Mukema clan leaders descend from this union.

The story presents a plausible history of the Mukema, up to and including contact with the Europeans. Yet as Thomas Beidelman, the anthropologist who collected this tale, points out, much of it reflects Kaguru beliefs and justifies current Kaguru social relations. For example, the Kaguru believe that the spirits of babies live in the west before birth, and that the north is unlucky. How appropriate, then, for the Mukema to have fled from the northwest, the land both of origin and of ill luck. And how right that Lugode's womb-cave faced west, ready to receive the spirit-babies of the clan leaders. Similarly, Lugode's fire justifies the Mukema claim to clan primacy in the Talagwe region, as does the grant of headship by the German "Kasimoto" (which is Swahili for "fierce work"). The various stopping points on the clan trek explain the presence of clan members at other sites. And the prominence of women in the tale until Lugode's marriage marks the fact that Kaguru women bear the clan's name, even though they do not rule it. Lugode, after all, disappears from the story as soon as she bears sons.

Beidelman also notes that before this marriage, the traveling Mukema lacked one major feature of any social group: adult men. They had all the things that the Kaguru consider necessary for civilization, except men to hunt and to rule. As a result, they were unproductive; Lugode, their ancestor, is even called "Old Woman"—by implication she is past menopause. After the boy's circumcision and their marriage, she becomes fertile, the true mother of her people. These two institutions, one that makes boys into men and the other that makes women their wives, make social life possible, in the Kaguru view.

Despite this, the Mukema believe this story to be true, just as other Kaguru clans believe their own clan legends. Most of these share similar elements, some of which are likely based on real events. Though Beidelman unfortunately does not tell us the name of his informant, the Kaguru who pass on these tales are, in short, the group's historians. This tale is their idea of how history should be told.

18   Part 1   In the Beginnings

History of the Mukema of Talagwe[1]

The Mukema clan is among the clans which came from far away into the land
of Ukaguru. The Mukema came from Irangi. They had stayed there for many
years along with other clans. Later that land of Irangi was entered by two
other groups and those groups were fierce, the Masai and the Little-People.

Because of their fierceness those people made people afraid to stay in that
land, so they deserted group by group and went down from out of the north.
They marched slowly and then they reached a certain land in Ugogo called
Ifunda. There at Ifunda they stayed for a long time and then they went on
down [south] slowly until they reached the Ruaha River and here many
groups of people failed to cross the river while others succeeded so then that
group started to return back where it had come from. During that journey the
group of people was led by three female elders for even though there were
males, those were youths.

The first of those people was Old Woman Lugode and she was the eldest
and she was with her younger sister who was called Nechala but the name of
their third comrade is not known. They marched like that back again to Ifunda.
When they left Ifunda they reached Chimagai Swamp and then they reached
Igombo. There at Igombo they settled for some time. Then they climbed up into
the Itumba Mountains and then passed through Munyela Pass.

When they left Munyela they reached Munhindili in Uponela. There they
didn't spend much time but continued on with their journey to find a good
land in which to settle. Then they entered Itungo in the land of Maundike.
From Itungo they went to Malmdike but they didn't like that land, so they
soon left and went to Ikonde in the land of Mamboya. There they stayed for
five years and some of their comrades remained there but all of that
[Mukema] group left and passed along the way to Chimhinda at Mugugu and
so they reached the land of Talagwe.

At that time the land of Talagwe had no clans which had reached there
and so Old Woman Lugode and her comrades climbed Talagwe Mountain and
then they made a fire in order to show that they themselves were the first to
arrive. Consequently the clans that appeared later had to go ahead to find
lands on which to settle.

Old Woman Lugode had reached a cave in the rock on the west side of the
mountain near the trail at the pass to Iwale and Ngutoto. There that younger
one named Nechala and the others said goodbye to Lugode so that they might
go on ahead to find more land at Mukundi and that land pleased her very
much so she made a fire on top of the hill to show that she herself was the first
and therefore the owner of the land.

The others who appeared later passed through to go ahead to find lands
on which to settle. Consequently even today the land of Mukundi is the land
of the Mukema. Old Woman Lugode and others had settled there and she was
the leader of all the lands which stretched around Talagwe Mountain.

Long ago when a person or group of people were the first to enter a land
they made a fire so that their fellows that came later would [know] that they
would be their subjects [in case] they [also] wanted to settle in that land.

Now when Old Woman Lugode stayed in that land she was followed later by Gweno people. Those just passed on ahead for they wanted a land in which to settle. But they failed, so they returned later to Talagwe and told Lugode that they wanted gardens to cultivate, so she gave them some and later many other clans arrived in that land and they also failed to get lands for [their own] settlement, so they became residents of Talagwe.

Lugode stayed there in the cave for years and then one year six people came from the land of Itumba and they were hunters. They hunted animals in the land of Talagwe and then one of their comrades was lost on the mountain and he was an uncircumcised person (viz., minor). Those five comrades of his returned to Itumba and announced that their comrade was lost. Then his kin despaired and ate the mourning-feast because they thought he was dead.

That youth who was lost on the mountain had seen a place near a rock cave from which smoke was coming, so he went there and then he saw the old woman and she was alone there outside the cave. That one had a garden of fresh edible maize and he greeted her, and that woman replied and she took him there to the cave and gave him food which he ate. So he stayed there for many days.

That youth told her that his home was at Musongwe in Itumba and that his clan was Njowe. Many days passed and then one day Old Woman Lugode saw some travellers on the path to Iwale, the main path being used there long ago and those were coming from Ungulu. Then she called to them and then she asked them where they were going and they told her that they were going to Itumba. Then she instructed them that when they reached Musongwe in Itumba that they should tell them there, "There is a child who may be seen at Talagwe Mountain."

Those people kept on with their journey and then they reached the land of Musongwe in Itumba and they told them as they had been instructed. When his kin heard that, a group of men and women set out and went to Talagwe. When they got there they saw Old Woman Lugode and that boy there. They were welcomed nicely, though they had come weeping. They stayed there for many days and then they circumcised that boy there at the cave. When he had recovered they returned home to Musongwe in Itumba so that he could be anointed with oil.

Then later those people returned that boy to Old Woman Lugode and he became the husband who married her. When he married her he stayed there and then she bore her first child, Segala; the second, Sembaya; the third, Mulunguwafula. And then there were two girls and those were Malagala and Muhaima. This Malagala bore Maluta and others and Muhaima bore Mfundo.

At that time the first white people arrived in that land and they found Sembaya in his land of Talagwe and those people were Arabs who were trading for elephant tusks and also catching people to make them into slaves. Up to that time no other clan or other clans were known there but the Mukema with their land of Talagwe, Iyogwe, Makuyu, Chinyolisi, Chikunde, Masimba, Makutwi, Luseka, Ngutoto, Diola and others around the mountain. Sembaya and Mulunguwafula were known even before the English, Germans and Arabs arrived in this land, but they were known first [by others] then.

The capital for Sembaya and Mulunguwafula was Talagwe and all the inhabitants obeyed the summons of the elder of Talagwe at the capital of his eldership or chiefship.

Now one should know how the Mukema got the headmanship of this land. Sembaya himself was not a headman but rather just an elder or chief, the first who stayed and cultivated his land [there]. But he was therefore like a headman. When Sembaya died, another elder of Talagwe appeared and he stayed there. We all know that when many white people arrived that those were the Germans and that that was a difficult time because of battles with the Masai. They entered the land to seize Kaguru property and [the Kaguru] fought them so that they would not enter their land, but the Kaguru failed. Many cows and goats were seized and very many people were killed, men and even women and children.

Some were killed at the rivers while drawing water. Others slept in their houses and the houses were burned and those people died. Therefore this was a time of great trouble so that many people fled to the Itumba Mountains. Now Talagwe escaped from the battles with the Masai. The Masai were unable to climb the mountains and so all the Kaguru fled to the mountains and if the Masai tried to climb the mountains, very many were killed by the Kaguru.

Consequently, there were no people in the lands below the mountains. Later the Kaguru again tried to fight with the Masai of the previous time and this time they defeated the Masai and so they drove them off and chased them from the land of Ukaguru. Mulunguwafula was one of the leaders of the land of Ukaguru known since long ago because of his heroism in fighting with the Masai in Ukaguru.

*   *   *

This European [named Kasimoto] travelled around the land in order to stop the battles that the Kaguru and Masai and Ngulu were fighting at that time. When that German left Mpwapwa that year he arrived at Rubeho and then he met an elder of that land and he was named Pembamoto and he led him to the land of Kibedya. There at Kibedya he met an elder Masingisa and he made him the leader of his journey along with Pembamoto.

When they left Kibedya, they arrived in the land of Talagwe and he met the elder of that land, Mulunguwafula at his village. Because of his strength in fighting with the Masai he was also taken up as the third leader along with his comrades to lead him [the European] on his way to Ungulu where there were still battles with the Masai and Ngulu. Now from Talagwe they passed through the lands of Nhunguli [and] Lwande to Masige, to Majanda until Toga to Mondanya [in Ungulu].

When they reached that land they found fierce battles were still being fought with the Masai and Ngulu so that European and his guides killed many Masai and even captured cattle [which the Masai] had and returned them to the Ngulu and to the other people who were travelling with him and guiding him.

That German had returned the majority of Masai back to the bush of
Kijungu and then he himself started to return with his people. At the time of
their return from the bush at Kijungu, they passed through Bokwa [and]
Pagwi and then they passed the bush on the borders of Mpwapwa and
Ukaguru and then they arrived at Sagara and then Mpwapwa and at the time
those who were with that German were also with Mulunguwafula and his
comrades. Those two and the other people came from out of Ungulu and
brought herds of cattle and goats which were captured from the Masai.

Now when they finished their journey the elder went to return to
Mpwapwa and then that European Kasimoto spoke saying, "Those people
who came first to their land long ago before other people and clans should be
the ones to get office of power for their lands which they controlled." They
wore caps as badges [of office], so the elder of Talagwe, Mulunguwafula, wore
a cap and turban of headmanship.

When the Germans had ruled for a few years, Talagwe had already got its
headmanship and all its lands were under Mulunguwafula. Truly then
Mulunguwafula had become the first headman, on account of the support of
the Germans and he was called "headman." When he had worn his cap and
turban it was a sign showing his elderhood over all his land and he was given
a herd of thirty-five goats because he had troubled himself to fight the Masai
and therefore Kasimoto liked him much. Then he came with that herd of goats
into his land of Talagwe.

I go on to tell of the land of Talagwe and its sides which were its
boundaries when the Arabs had yet to enter the land and meet Sembaya, and
the Germans [had yet] to meet Mulunguwafula. Its boundaries were as
follows: from Lion Stone Rock it passed Ngulugo, a hill at Rudewa, then
through the bush of Muheneke until Changulu Hill, Masimba. From there the
boundary continued to the valley of Mangala and from there the boundary
passed Nhyanga Hill and then passed through the mountains to Luseko and
then to Makutwi Rock. From there the boundary passed Magela at a large
rock, Ifuma, and then through Chilume Hill and then to a baobab tree on the
path leading to Mugugu. From there the boundary passed Mugego Hill and
then to Walambe Hill and from Walambe to Ibong'o Hill and from Ibong'o it
rejoined Lion Stone Rock where it had first started.

This is how Sembaya ruled according to those boundaries from the time of
the Arabs up to when his brother Mulunguwafula ruled his land according to
that boundary.

Talagwe is the base for the chiefship of all the land of Talagwe and its
parts where Sembaya and Mulunguwafula and all who followed later stayed.
At the time of this first headman, Mulunguwafula, his village was known as
that of the chiefship by the Europeans who were travelling about the land
below Talagwe Mountain.

Headmen who have ruled since the cap was first taken are: Mulunguwafula, a Mukema, into whose hands was given the cap of headmanship;
Chadibwa Musulwa, a Mukema; Sanghole, who was a child of the Mukema;

he was given the headship of the land by his fathers so that he might lead people. Mwana Mbusi also held the chiefship through his fathers. Tepe-tepe was a child of the Mukema. Mahungo Mfundo was a child of the Mukema. Mfundo Chalasa was himself a Mukema. Chilimo Munyengu was a Mukema; Mfundo Asumani was a Mukema.

At the arrival of the clans of all black people in the land they reached Talagwe and the majority settled in all parts of the land of Talagwe and for many years all those clans accepted the command of the leader of the owning clan of the land and were always judged by them, and the owners of the land were rulers. If an elder died, another was selected from the same clan which were owners of the country.

QUESTIONS TO CONSIDER

1. How does this story help the Mukema clan claim the land they occupy?
2. How does this story justify the social power of adult men?
3. Why does the story include Europeans?

FOR FURTHER READING

Beidelman, Thomas O. *The Kaguru, a Matrilineal People of East Africa*. New York: Holt, Rinehart and Winston, 1971.
_____ . "A History of Ukaguru, Kilosa District: 1857–1916." *Tanganyika Notes and Records* 58/59 (1962): 11–39.
Douglas, Mary, and Phyllis Kaberry, eds. *Man in Africa*. London: Tavistock, 1969.
Forde, Daryll, ed. *African Worlds: Studies in the Cosmological Ideas and Social Values of African Peoples*. London: Oxford University Press, 1976.
Onwuejeogwu, M. Angulu. *The Social Anthropology of Africa*. London: Heinemann, 1975.
Turner, Victor W. *The Forest of Symbols: Aspects of Ndembu Ritual*. Ithaca, NY: Cornell University Press, 1967.
Wilson, Monica H. *Good Company: A Study of Nyakyusa Age-Villages*. Boston: Beacon Press, 1963.

NOTES

1. Thomas O. Beidelman, "Myth, Legend, and Oral History: A Kaguru Traditional Text," *Anthropos* 65 (1970): 78–87.

The Kumulipo

Hawaiian Mythic Genealogy

King David Kalakaua
© 1995 North Wind Pictures

L ike the Hopi emergence myth, the Kumulipo is an origin story; "beginning in deep darkness" and tracing the descent of Hawaiian kings from the birth of the world to the early eighteenth century. A poetic chant rather than a narrative, tradition says it was composed to hail the son of Keawe, a chief on the island of Hawai'i. Hawaiian nobility used such chants to prove their status, and this one promoted Keawe's lineage over that of Kuali'i, an Oahu island rival.

The Kumulipo was recited at least twice publicly during the next century. Kalani-opu'u, Keawe's grandson, had it told to Captain Cook in 1779, believing Cook to be the god Lono mentioned in the myth and seeking to bind their relationship. It was chanted again in 1804 at the death of Ke'eaumoku, an uncle of Kamehameha, the king who had united the islands some years before. Kamehameha, himself a lineal heir of Keawe, sought to sanction his rule as well.

King David Kalakaua wrote down the Kumulipo in Hawaiian in 1889 to bolster his claim to the throne. He had been chosen king in a stormy election after Kamehameha's line died out in 1874. His sister-successor, Queen Liliuokalani, wrote an English version while under house arrest during the U.S. takeover of the islands. Descended from Keawe, though not from Kamehameha; the chant tied them to the old Hawaiian kings and to the beginnings of time.

Yet the Kumulipo is more than just a political tract. As Martha Beckwith, translator of the following version, asserts, the text is as much literature as history. Constant pairing of male and female (see Chant One, lines 13 and 14) marks the centrality of sex in the Hawaiian world view. The onomotopoesy, vivid in the original though largely lost in translation, mimics the crabs, rats, and gossipy neighbors appearing in the story. And the image of life emerging from a primeval slime reflects a Polynesian sense of the cosmos that is at odds with the Christian emphasis on creation.

Early folklorists called this a "creation myth," but this is inappropriate on two counts. First, there is no creation per se, but an evolutionary continuity from the earliest beings to the gods to godlike kings and to mortal humans. The Kumulipo grounds the present in the past as one long, unbroken generative chain. The gods are part of that chain, not beyond it. Second, to its authors, it was not myth but history. Keawe's kin called it a true record of the past. Dorothy Barrère finds it the oldest and most authentic of the Hawaiian tales—though it clearly does not record history in the way we do. Marshall Sahlins, on the other hand, warns that all Polynesian histories are rife with ritual elements; we cannot take even the seemingly more objective parts of the Kumulipo at face value, because it recasts events to fit native ideas of the proper ties between gods and people. One example: Hawaiian kings often claimed to poison their predecessors, not because they actually did, but because kingly *mana* made a normal succession impossible. Hawaiian histories thus report more usurpations than truly befell.

But these caveats are no more serious for Hawaiian oral history than for any other. The Kumulipo was a record of the past to its hearers, doing for them what our histories do for us.

The Kumulipo[1]

Chant One

1   At the time when the earth became hot
    At the time when the heavens turned about
    At the time when the sun was darkened
    To cause the moon to shine
5   The time of the rise of the Pleiades
    The slime, this was the source of the earth
    The source of the darkness that made darkness
    The source of the night that made night
    The intense darkness, the deep darkness
10 Darkness of the sun, darkness of the night
    Nothing but night.
    The night gave birth
    Born was Kumulipo in the night, a male
    Born was Po'ele in the night, a female
15 Born was the coral polyp, born was the coral, came forth
    Born was the grub that digs and heaps up the earth, came forth,
    Born was his [child] an earthworm, came forth
    Born was the starfish, his child the small starfish came forth
    Born was the sea cucumber, his child the small sea cucumber came forth

                              *   *   *

35 Born was the Ekaha moss living in the sea
    Guarded by the Ekahakaha fern living on land
    Darkness slips into light
    Earth and water are the food of the plant
    The god enters, man can not enter
40 Man for the narrow stream, woman for the broad stream
    Born was the tough landgrass living on land

Refrain

46 Man for the narrow stream, woman for the broad stream
    Born was the 'A'ala moss living in the sea
    Guarded by the 'Ala'ala mint living on land

Refrain

52 Man for the narrow stream, woman for the broad stream
    Born was the Manauea moss living in the sea
    Guarded by the Manauea taro plant living on land

                              *   *   *

106 Man for the narrow stream, woman for the broad stream
    Born was the hairy seaweed living in the sea
    Guarded by the hairy pandeanus vine living on land

Darkness slips into light
Earth and water are the food of the plant
The god enters, man can not enter
The man with the water gourd, he is god   112
Water that causes the withered vine to flourish
Causes the plant top to develop freely
Multiplying in the passing time   115
The long night slips along
Fruitful, very fruitful
Spreading here, spreading there
Spreading this way, spreading that way
Propping up earth, holding up the sky   120
The time passes, this night of Kumulipo
    Still it is night

*   *   *

Chant Three

A male this, the female that
A male born in the time of black darkness
The female born in the time of groping in the darkness   275
Overshadowed was the sea, overshadowed the land
Overshadowed the streams, overshadowed the mountains
Overshadowed the dimly brightening night
The rootstalk grew with dark leaves
The sprout that shot forth leaves of high chiefs   280
Born as Po'ele'ele the male
Lived with Pohaha a female
The rootstalk sprouted
    The taro stalk grew
Born was the Wood borer, a parent   285
Out came its child a flying thing, and flew
Born was the Caterpillar, the parent
Out came its child a Moth, and flew
Born was the Ant, the parent
Out came its child a Dragonfly, and flew   290
Born was the Grub, the parent
Out came its child the Grasshopper, and flew
Born was the Pinworm, the parent
Out came its child a Fly, and flew
Born was the egg [?], the parent   295
Out came its child a bird, and flew
Born was the Snipe, the parent
Out came its child a Plover, and flew
Born was the A'o bird, the parent
Out came its child an A'u bird, and flew   300

*   *   *

Chant Six

Many new lines of chiefs spring up
540 Cultivation arises, full of taboos
[They go about scratching at the wet lands
It sprouts, the first blades appear, the food is ready] [?]
Food grown by the water courses
Food grown by the sea
545 Plentiful and heaped up
The parent rats dwell in holes
The little rats huddle together
Those who mark the seasons
Little tolls from the land
550 Little tolls from the water courses
Trace of the nibblings of these brown-coated ones
With whiskers upstanding
They hide here and there
A rat in the upland, a rat by the sea
555 A rat running beside the wabe
Born to the two, child of the Night-falling-away
Born to the two, child of the Night-creeping-away
The little child creeps as it moves
The little child moves with a spring
560 Pilfering at the rind
Rind of the 'ohi'a fruit, not a fruit of the upland
A tiny child born as the darkness falls away
A springing child born as the darkness creeps away
Child of the dark and child in the night now here
565   Still it is night

                          *   *   *

Chant Eight

595 Well-formed is the child, well-formed now
Child in the time when men multiplied
Child in the time when men came from afar
Born were men by the hundreds
Born was man for the narrow stream
600 Born was woman for the broad stream
Born the night of gods
Men stood together
Men slept together
They two slept together in the time long ago
605 Wave after wave of men moving in company
Ruddy the forehead of the god
Dark that of man
White-[bearded] the chin

Tranquil was the time when men multiplied
Calm like the time when men came from afar 610
It was called Calmness [La'ila'i] then
Born was the La'ila'i a woman
Born was Ki'i a man
Born was Kane a god

Lo'a ke kane [the husband]	Nakelea ka wahine [the wife]	718
Le	Kanu	719
Kalawe	Kamau	720
Kulou	Haliau	
Na'u	Ka-le	
'A'a	Hehe	
Pulepule	Ma'i	
Nahu	Luke	725
Pono	Pono'i	
Kalau	Ma-ina	
Kulewa	Kune	
Po'u	Kala'i	
Po'ulua	Kukulukulu	730
Pae	Ha'a'a	
Paeheunui	Ki'eki'e	
Hewa	Kulu	
Maku	Niau	

* * *

Chant Thirteen

Taboo was the house platform, the place for sitting
Taboo the house where Wakea lived
Taboo was intercourse with the divine parent
Taboo the taro plant, the acrid one 1805
Taboo the poisonous 'akia plant
Taboo the narcotic auhuhu plant
Taboo the medicinal uhaloa
Taboo the bitter part of the taro leaf
Taboo the taro stalk that stood by the woman's taboo house 1810

* * *

Chant Sixteen

Kahekili [the first] was the man, Hauanuihoni'ala was the wife
Born was Kawauka'ohele and [his sister] Kelea-nui-noho-ana-'api'api 2090
    ["Kelea-swimming-like-a-fish"]
She [Kelea] lived as a wife to Kalamakua
Born was La'ie-lohelohe, [she] live with Pi'ilani, Pi'ikea was born
Pi'ikea lived with 'Umi, Kumalae-nui-a-'Umi [was born]
His was the slave-destroying cliff

2095 Kumulae-nui-a-'Umi was the man, Kumu-nui-puawale the wife
Makua was the man, standing first of *wohi* rank on the island
Kapo-hele-mai was the wife, a taboo *wohi* chiefess, the sacred one
'I, to 'I is the chiefship, the right to offer human sacrifice
The ruler over the land section of Pakini
2100 With the right to cut down *'ohi'a* wood for images, the protector of
    the island of Hawaii
To Ahu, Ahu son of 'I, to Lono
To Lono-i-ka-makahiki

QUESTIONS TO CONSIDER

1. What is the line of descent, from primal slime to human beings? What
   significance might this have for Hawaiians?
2. What is the role of taboos in Chant 13?
3. How is this genealogy like the Hopi (Chapter 1) and Kaguru (2) legends?
   How is it different?

FOR FURTHER READING

Barrère, Dorothy B. *The Kumuhonua Legends.* Honolulu, HI: Bishop Museum Press,
    1969.
Beckwith, Martha W. *Hawaiian Mythology.* New Haven, CT: Yale University Press,
    1940.
Kame'eleihiwa, Lilikala. *Native Land and Foreign Desires.* Honolulu, HI: Bishop
    Museum, 1992.
Ne, Harriet. *Tales of Molokai.* Ed. Gloria Cronin. La'ie, HI: Institute for Polynesian
    Studies, 1992.
Sahlins, Marshall. *Historical Metaphors and Mythical Realities: Structure in the Early
    History of the Sandwich Islands Kingdom.* Ann Arbor, MI: University of Michigan
    Press, 1981.

NOTES

1. *The Kumulipo: A Hawaiian Creation Chant,* trans. and ed. Martha Warren
   Beckwith (Honolulu, HI: University of Hawaii Press, 1972; orig. 1951),
   58–60, 71–72, 87–88, 97, 124–25, 138–39, 206.

CHAPTER 4

The Sundiata Epic

The Founding of a Mande Empire

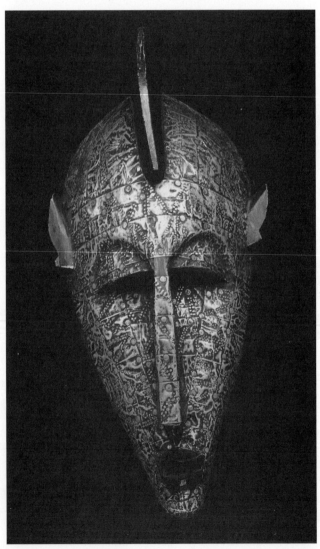

Tribal mask of the Mali
© Dean Fox/SuperStock

W est Africa's oral traditions are among the world's most well developed. Native bards or *griots* recite long stories about past events, especially tales of old kings and warriors. Despite the cautions to which all such oral records are subject, these tales contain our best accounts of much West African history.

The *Epic of Sundiata* is a case in point. Sundiata (or Sunjata, Son-Jara, etc.) was a Mande prince and warrior, the founder of the Mali kingdom in the early thirteenth century. Arab records mention him as a great *mansa,* or emperor, who freed his country from the Soso and went on to build a great realm. He and his successors extended their rule from the Gambia and Senegal rivers in the west to the southward bend on the Niger river past Timbuktu in the east, and from the upper reaches of that latter river north to the edge of the Sahara desert. Archaeological evidence shows the center of this region to have been much more densely populated then than it is now—as is likely under the peace that such a realm brings. Arab travelers wrote of its great wealth, but only the griots give any details about Sundiata's conquests or his rule. Outside this oral tradition, we know next to nothing.

Though the core of the Sundiata epic is historic, it has become much mixed with folklore. The prophecies at the hero's birth, for example, are clearly narrative devices. Having him master childhood paralysis shows his strong will and his ability to win against odds. His skill at tracking wild game ties him to Mande hunters, who were believed to have great magic. His persecution and exile may have been real but could as easily have been introduced to give an outside victor the right pedigree to rule. And the culmination of his battle with Soumaoro, in which the latter is overthrown when Sundiata finds the secret of his magic, is plainly fabulous. Similarly, the wider set of tales of which this epic is a part compress 400 years of Malian rule into just four generations. Events from later wars appear among Sundiata's battles; some of his generals may have been rulers in their own right. Yet it is just such devices that make this tale real for its audience. By tying Malian history into an intelligible whole, the epic gives its audience a proud tradition. This, it says, is who our ancestors were— and also, by extension, it tells who we are.

There are many extant versions of the Sundiata epic, nearly as many as there are griots to tell it, though their customs demand as exact a performance as they are able. Mande bards are born to their jobs through membership in an endogamous caste. Like the other Mande occupational castes, bards train extensively for their work. They have many tales to tell and must master them all. A full performance of the Sundiata tale may take four to five hours, during which time the griot is expected to present and interpret the story for his listeners as well as keep their attention through good delivery.

The variation below, compiled by D. T. Niane, is the most accessible one for an American audience. Johnson, Innes, and others have recorded more exact versions, which read much like extended free verse and include ritual audience responses at key points. They are free of some of Niane's Europeanizations, but they are much harder for an outsider to follow. Niane's version gives us a good picture of West African oral history, while still being within our reach.

The Sundiata Epic[1]

The Words of the Griot Mamadou Kouyaté:

I am a griot. It is I, Djeli Mamoudou Kouyaté, son of Bintou Kouyaté and Djeli Kedian Kouyaté, master in the art of eloquence. Since time immemorial the Kouyatés have been in the service of the Keita princes of Mali; we are vessels of speech, we are the repositories which harbour secrets many centuries old. The art of eloquence has no secrets for us; without us the names of kings would vanish into oblivion, we are the memory of mankind; by the spoken word we bring to life the deeds and exploits of kings for younger generations.

I derive my knowledge from my father Djeli Kedian, who also got it from his father; history holds no mystery for us; we teach to the vulgar just as much as we want to teach them, for it is we who keep the keys to the twelve doors of Mali.

I know the list of all the sovereigns who succeeded to the throne of Mali. I know how the black people divided into tribes, for my father bequeathed to me all his learning; I know why such and such is called Kamara, another Keita, and yet another Sibibé or Traoré; every name has a meaning, a secret import.

I teach kings the history of their ancestors so that the lives of the ancients might serve them as an example, for the world is old, but the future springs from the past.

My word is pure and free of all untruth; it is the word of my father; it is the word of my father's father. I will give you my father's words just as I received them; royal griots do not know what lying is. When a quarrel breaks out between tribes it is we who settle the difference, for we are the depositories of oaths which the ancestors swore.

Listen to my word, you who want to know; by my mouth you will learn the history of Mali.

By my mouth you will get to know the story of the ancestor of great Mali, the story of him who, by his exploits, surpassed even Alexander the Great; he who, from the East, shed his rays upon all the countries of the West.

Listen to the story of the son of the Buffalo, the son of the Lion. I am going to tell you of Maghan Sundiata, of Mari-Djata, of Sogolon Djata, of Naré Maghan Djata; the man of many names against whom sorcery could avail nothing.

* * *

The Lion's Awakening

[Sundiata, here called Mari Djata, is the son of King Naré Maghan and Sogolon, his favorite wife. When Naré Maghan dies, his wish to pass on the throne to Sundiata is thwarted by Sassouma Bérété, one of his other wives. Sassouma Bérété claims the throne for her son, Dankaran Touman, and the council agrees.]

As men have short memories, Sogolon's son was spoken of with nothing but irony and scorn. People had seen one-eyed kings, one-armed kings, and lame kings, but a stiff-legged king had never been heard tell of. No matter how great the destiny promised for Mari Djata might be, the throne could not be given to someone who had no power in his legs; if the jinn loved him, let them begin by giving him the use of his legs. Such were the remarks that Sogolon heard every day. The queen mother, Sassouma Bérété, was the source of all this gossip.

* * *

Sogolon Kedjou and her children lived on the queen mother's left-overs, but she kept a little garden in the open ground behind the village. It was there that she passed her brightest moments looking after her onions and gnougous. One day she happened to be short of condiments and went to the queen mother to beg a little baobab leaf.

'Look you,' said the malicious Sassouma, 'I have a calabash full. Help yourself, you poor woman. As for me, my son knew how to walk at seven and it was he who went and picked these baobab leaves. Take them then, since your son is unequal to mine.' Then she laughed derisively with that fierce laughter which cuts through your flesh and penetrates right to the bone.

Sogolon Kedjou was dumbfounded. She had never imagined that hate could be so strong in a human being. With a lump in her throat she left Sassouma's. Outside her hut Mari Djata, sitting on his useless legs, was blandly eating out of a calabash. Unable to contain herself any longer, Sogolon burst into sobs and seizing a piece of wood, hit her son.

'Oh son of misfortune, will you never walk? Through your fault I have just suffered the greatest affront of my life! What have I done, God, for you to punish me in this way?'

Mari Djata seized the piece of wood and, looking at his mother, said, 'Mother, what's the matter?'

'Shut up, nothing can ever wash me clean of this insult.'

'But what then?'

'Sassouma has just humiliated me over a matter of a baobab leaf. At your age her own son could walk and used to bring his mother baobab leaves.'

'Cheer up, Mother, cheer up.'

'No. It's too much. I can't.'

'Very well then, I am going to walk today,' said Mari Djata. 'Go and tell my father's smiths to make me the heaviest possible iron rod. Mother, do you want just the leaves of the baobab or would you rather I brought you the whole tree?'

'Ah, my son, to wipe out this insult I want the tree and its roots at my feet outside my hut.'

Balla Fasséké, who was present, ran to the master smith, Farakourou, to order an iron rod.

* * *

The royal forges were situated outside the walls and over a hundred smiths worked there. The bows, spears, arrows and shields of Niani's warriors came from there. When Balla Fasséké came to order the iron rod, Farakourou said to him, 'The great day has arrived then?'

'Yes. Today is a day like any other, but it will see what no other day has seen.'

The master of the forges, Farakourou, was the son of the old Nounfairi, and he was a soothsayer like his father. In his workshops there was an enormous iron bar wrought by his father Nounfairi. Everybody wondered what this bar was destined to be used for. Farakourou called six of his apprentices and told them to carry the iron bar to Sogolon's house.

When the smiths put the gigantic iron bar down in front of the hut the noise was so frightening that Sogolon, who was lying down, jumped up with a start. Then Balla Fasséké, son of Gnankouman Doua, spoke.

'Here is the great day, Mari Djata. I am speaking to you, Maghan, son of Sogolon. The waters of the Niger can efface the stain from the body, but they cannot wipe out an insult. Arise, young lion, roar, and may the bush know that from henceforth it has a master.'

The apprentice smiths were still there, Sogolon had come out and everyone was watching Mari Djata. He crept on all-fours and came to the iron bar. Supporting himself on his knees and one hand, with the other hand he picked up the iron bar without any effort and stood it up vertically. Now he was resting on nothing but his knees and held the bar with both his hands. A deathly silence had gripped all those present. Sogolon Djata closed his eyes, held tight, the muscles in his arms tensed. With a violent jerk he threw his weight on to it and his knees left the ground. Sogolon Kedjou was all eyes and watched her son's legs which were trembling as though from an electric shock. Djata was sweating and the sweat ran from his brow. In a great effort he straightened up and was on his feet at one go—but the great bar of iron was twisted and had taken the form of a bow!

Then Balla Fasséké sang out the 'Hymn to the Bow,' striking up with his powerful voice:

> Take your bow, Simbon,
> Take your bow and let us go.
> Take your bow, Sogolon Djata.'

When Sogolon saw her son standing she stood dumb for a moment, then suddenly she sang these words of thanks to God who had given her son the use of his legs:

> 'Oh day, what a beautiful day,
> Oh day, day of joy;
> Allah Almighty, you never created a finer day.
> So my son is going to walk!'

Standing in the position of a soldier at ease, Sogolon Djata, supported by his enormous rod, was sweating great beads of sweat. Balla Fasséké's song had alerted the whole palace and people came running from all over to see what had happened, and each stood bewildered before Sogolon's son. The queen mother had rushed there and when she saw Mari Djata standing up she trembled from head to foot. After recovering his breath Sogolon's son dropped the bar and the crowd stood to one side. His first steps were those of a giant. Balla Fasséké fell into step and pointing his finger at Djata, he cried:

'Room, room, make room!
The lion has walked;
Hide antelopes,
Get out of his way.'

Behind Niani there was a young baobab tree and it was there that the children of the town came to pick leaves for their mothers. With all his might the son of Sogolon tore up the tree and put it on his shoulders and went back to his mother. He threw the tree in front of the hut and said, 'Mother, here are some baobab leaves for you. From henceforth it will be outside your hut that the women of Niani will come to stock up.'

*   *   *

[Sogolon and Sundiata go into exile. After many adventures, they take service at the court of Moussa Tounkara, in Mema, a neighboring kingdom.]

It was at the court of Mema that Sundiata and Manding Bory went on their first campaign. Moussa Tounkara was a great warrior and therefore he admired strength. When Sundiata was fifteen the king took him with him on campaign. Sundiata astonished the whole army with his strength and with his dash in the charge. In the course of a skirmish against the mountaineers he hurled himself on the enemy with such vehemence that the king feared for his life, but Mansa Tounkara admired bravery too much to stop the son of Sogolon. He followed him closely to protect him and he saw with rapture how the youth sowed panic among the enemy. He had remarkable presence of mind, struck right and left and opened up for himself a glorious path. When the enemy had fled the old 'sofas' said, 'There's one that'll make a good king.' Moussa Tounkara took the son of Sologon in his arms and said, 'It is destiny that has sent you to Mema. I will make a great warrior out of you.'

From that day Sundiata did not leave the king any more. He eclipsed all the young princes and was the friend of the whole army. They spoke about nothing but him in the camp. Men were even more surprised by the lucidity of his mind. In the camp he had an answer to everything and the most puzzling situations resolved themselves in his presence.

Soon it was in Mema itself that people began to talk about Sundiata. Was it not Providence which had sent this boy at a time when Mema had no heir? People already averred that Sundiata would extend his dominion from Mema to Mali. He went on all the campaigns. The enemy's incursions became rarer and rarer and the reputation of Sogolon's son spread beyond the river.

*   *   *

The Return

Every man to his own land! If it is foretold that your destiny should be fulfilled in such and such a land, men can do nothing against it. Mansa Tounkara could not keep Sundiata back because the destiny of Sogolon's son was bound up with that of Mali. Neither the jealousy of a cruel stepmother, nor her wickedness, could alter for a moment the course of great destiny.

The snake, man's enemy, is not long-lived, yet the serpent that lives hidden will surely die old. Djata was strong enough now to face his enemies. At the age of eighteen he had the stateliness of the lion and the strength of the buffalo. His voice carried authority, his eyes were live coals, his arm was iron, he was the husband of power.

Moussa Tounkara, king of Mema, gave Sundiata half of his army. The most valiant came forward of their own free will to follow Sundiata in the great adventure. The cavalry of Mema, which he had fashioned himself, formed his iron squadron. Sundiata, dressed in the Muslim fashion of Mema, left the town at the head of his small but redoubtable army. The whole population sent their best wishes with him. He was surrounded by five messengers from Mali and Manding Bory rode proudly at the side of his brother. The horsemen of Mema formed behind Djata a bristling iron squadron. The troop took the direction of Wagadou, for Djata did not have enough troops to confront Soumaoro directly, and so the king of Mema advised him to go to Wagadou and take half of the men of the king, Soumaba Cisse. A swift messenger had been sent there and so the king of Wagadou came out in person to meet Sundiata and his troops. He gave Sundiata half of his cavalry and blessed the weapons. Then Manding Bory said to his brother, 'Djata, do you think yourself able to face Soumaoro now?'

'No matter how small a forest may be, you can always find there sufficient fibres to tie up a man. Numbers mean nothing; it is worth that counts. With my cavalry I shall clear myself a path to Mali.'

QUESTIONS TO CONSIDER

1. How is the story of Sundiata's childhood like American legends of the young George Washington?
2. How might the fabulous elements of this tale have enabled it to survive for several hundred years?
3. Granting that much of this epic is folklore rather than history, how can these folkloric elements help us understand the Mande past?

FOR FURTHER READING

Conrad, David C. "Searching for History in the Sunjata Epic: The Case of Fakoli." *History in Africa* 19 (1992): 147–200.

Innes, Gordon. *Sunjata: Three Mandinka Versions.* London School of Oriental and African Studies, University of London: 1974.

Johnson, John William, and Fa-Digi Sisòkò. *The Epic of San-Jara: A West African Tradition.* Bloomington, IN: Indiana University Press, 1992.
Levtzion, Nehemia. *Ancient Ghana and Mali.* London: Methuen, 1973.

NOTES

1. Djibril Tamsir Niane, *Sundiata: An Epic of Old Mali,* trans. G. D. Pickett (Essex: Longman, 1965), 1–3, 36–38, 43.

CHAPTER 5

The Hebrew Bible

Genesis

The Hebrew Bible - Book of Genesis
The Granger Collection, New York

From the creation of the world to the Babylonian exile, the Hebrew Bible presents itself as a history of God's chosen people. Its various books recite their wanderings, their kingdoms, and those kingdoms' eventual fall. Tradition assigns the authorship of the Torah—the first five books of the Bible—to Moses, in the late second millenium BCE. Scholars generally now place their actual writing much later. Before they became texts, though, they were transmitted orally. All the Hebrew tribes told stories of their beginnings, and later systematizers formed those stories into the books we now read. Together, they are the mythic history of a nation, key to both its identity and its religion.

The term "mythic history" is apt. The Hebrews saw their tales as a true record of the past, and the stories do lack the extravagant supernaturalism of the myths of other peoples. Yet we cannot take them simply at face value. Like the legends of the Hopi and the Kaguru, the Torah also had political uses. David, Solomon, and their kingly heirs used it to justify Hebrew rule over their predecessors in Canaan. As well, priests used it to criticize kings. Scholars have traced these battles through the text, showing how the various oral traditions may have been shaped into the books we now read.

Most scholars identify what are probably four main collections of stories in the "Five Books of Moses." The "Yahwist" collection was most likely written in Jerusalem during Solomon's reign, about 950 BCE, building on previous oral traditions (some historians date it much later, a few earlier). It refers to God as "Yahweh" and emphasizes the role of kings and leaders in Hebrew history. The "Elohist" collection may have been written a hundred years later in the northern kingdom of Israel. Its name for God is "Elohim," and it emphasizes the tie between God and the whole Hebrew people. About 620 BCE, according to most scholars, a "Deuteronomic" collection was added, which emphasized laws and God's special designs for the Judean kingdom. For years, scholars dated a fourth "Priestly" collection to the time of the exile, when defeated Judeans were forcibly moved to Babylon. More recent historians have argued that this collection predates the Deuteronomic additions. The exact dates and outlines of each collection are still in dispute. The majority of scholars does not doubt their existence, however.

The passages below come from Genesis, the book that recounts the beginnings of Hebrew history. The first selection, which we have labelled *In the Beginning,* is from Genesis 1–2. It is an account of the beginning of the world and the origins of humankind, similar in some ways to the origins account in the *Kumulipo.* Philosophical and possibly symbolic in nature, it is difficult to pin down in place and time. One must look with the eyes of faith to believe in its accuracy. Most likely part of the Priestly collection, it grounds the ritual seventh day of rest in God's example.

The second passage, *Abram's Story,* taken from Genesis 11–12, is probably also part of the Priestly tradition. It traces the Hebrews' ancestors back to the Flood, much as the Kumulipo traces the genealogy of Hawaiian kings. It is still mythic, yet different from the first passage. Some of the Hebrews' ancestors may well have come from Mesopotamia, traveling with their family and flocks to Haran, and thence to Canaan. Though the detailed descriptions of people and places and events are surely enhanced by literary elaboration, they conform to the pattern of a remembered past. Archeological and other sources confirm that something happened in these spots, though they cannot give us the details historians need. Although the Bible is preeminently a religious book, it is also the most detailed very old written document that historians possess. These chapters are the point at which Genesis becomes a document that historians can use and evaluate, albeit with great caution about any factual claims.

The third passage, *Jacob and Esau,* from Genesis 27, is generally regarded as Yahwist in origin. Here the issue is who possesses legitimate rights to the Promised Land. According to the story, God had given Canaan to Abraham and to all his descendants. Isaac inherited that promise from him and should have passed it on to his first-born son Esau, whose descendants were the Edomites, a neighboring non-Hebrew people. Yet second-born Jacob (later called Israel) is the Hebrew ancestor. The tale shows how Jacob stole Esau's birthright, then fled to his mother's brother Laban, from whom he gained two wives and many sons. Their sons were the mythic ancestors of the tribes of Israel, as Esau's sons were the ancestors of their nearest neighbors.

Genesis[1]
In the Beginning

In the beginning God created the heavens and the earth. Now the earth was formless and empty, darkness was over the surface of the deep, and the Spirit of God was hovering over the waters.

And God said, "Let there be light," and there was light. God saw that the light was good, and he separated the light from the darkness. God called the light "day," and the darkness he called "night." And there was evening, and there was morning—the first day.

And God said, "Let there be an expanse between the waters to separate water from water." So God made the expanse and separated the water under the expanse from the water above it. And it was so. God called the expanse "sky." And there was evening, and there was morning—the second day.

And God said, "Let the water under the sky be gathered to one place, and let dry ground appear." And it was so. God called the dry ground "land," and the gathered waters he called "seas." And God saw that it was good.

Then God said, "Let the land produce vegetation: Seed-bearing plants and trees on the land that bear fruit with seed in it, according to their various kinds." And it was so. The land produced vegetation: plants bearing seed according to their kinds and trees bearing fruit with seed in it according to their kinds. And God saw that it was good. And there was evening, and there was morning—the third day.

And God said, "Let there be lights in the expanse of the sky to separate the day from the night, and let them serve as signs to mark seasons and days and years, and let them be lights in the expanse of the sky to give light on the earth." And it was so. God made two great lights—the greater light to govern the day and the lesser light to govern the night. He also made the stars. God set them in the expanse of the sky to give light to the earth, to govern the day and the night, and to separate light from darkness. And God saw that it was good. And there was evening, and there was morning—the fourth day.

And God said, "Let the water teem with living creatures, and let birds fly above the earth across the expanse of the sky." So God created the great creatures of the sea and every living and moving thing with which the water teems, according to their kinds, and every winged bird according to its kind. And God saw that it was good. God blessed them and said, "Be fruitful and increase in number and fill the water in the seas, and let the birds increase on the earth." And there was evening, and there was morning—the fifth day.

And God said, "Let the land produce living creatures according to their kinds: livestock, creatures that move along the ground, and wild animals, each according to its kind." And it was so. God made the wild animals according to their kinds, the livestock according to their kinds, and all the creatures that move along the ground according to their kinds. And God saw that it was good.

Then God said, "Let us make man in our image, in our likeness, and let them rule over the fish of the sea and the birds of the air, over the livestock, over all the earth, and over all the creatures that move along the ground."

So God created man in his own image, in the image of God he created him; male and female he created them.

God blessed them and said to them, "Be fruitful and increase in number; fill the earth and subdue it. Rule over the fish of the sea and the birds of the air and over every living creature that moves on the ground."

Then God said, "I give you every seed-bearing plant on the face of the whole earth and every tree that has fruit with seed in it. They will be yours for food. And to all the beasts of the earth and all the birds of the air and all the creatures that move on the ground—everything that has the breath of life in it—I give every green plant for food." And it was so.

God saw all that he had made, and it was very good. And there was evening, and there was morning—the sixth day.

Thus the heavens and the earth were completed in all their vast array. By the seventh day God had finished the work he had been doing; so on the seventh day he rested from all his work. And God blessed the seventh day and made it holy, because on it he rested from all the work of creating that he had done.

This is the account of the heavens and the earth when they were created.

* * *

Abram's Story

Two years after the flood, when Shem was 100 years old, he became the father of Arphaxad. And after he became the father of Arphaxad, Shem lived 500 years and had other sons and daughters.

When Arphaxad had lived 35 years, he became the father of Shelah. And after he became the father of Shelah, Arphaxad lived 403 years and had other sons and daughters.

When Shelah had lived 30 years, he became the father of Eber. And after he became the father of Eber, Shelah lived 403 years and had other sons and daughters.

When Eber had lived 34 years, he became the father of Peleg. And after he became the father of Peleg, Eber lived 430 years and had other sons and daughters.

When Peleg had lived 30 years, he became the father of Reu. And after he became the father of Reu, Peleg lived 209 years and had other sons and daughters.

When Reu had lived 32 years, he became the father of Serug. And after he became the father of Serug, Reu lived 207 years and had other sons and daughters.

When Serug had lived 30 years, he became the father of Nahor. And after he became the father of Nahor, Serug lived 200 years and had other sons and daughters.

When Nahor had lived 29 years, he became the father of Terah. And after he became the father of Terah, Nahor lived 119 years and had other sons and daughters.

After Terah had lived 70 years, he became the father of Abram, Nahor and Haran.

This is the account of Terah.

Terah became the father of Abram, Nahor and Haran. And Haran became the father of Lot. While his father Terah was still alive, Haran died in Ur of the Chaldeans, in the land of his birth. Abram and Nahor both married. The name of Abram's wife was Sarai, and the name of Nahor's wife was Milcah; she was the daughter of Haran, the father of both Milcah and Iscah. Now Sarai was barren; she had no children.

Terah took his son Abram, his grandson Lot son of Haran, and his daughter-in-law Sarai, the wife of his son Abram, and together they set out from Ur of the Chaldeans to go to Canaan. But when they came to Haran, they settled there.

Terah lived 205 years, and he died in Haran.

The Lord said to Abram, "Leave your country, your people and your father's household and go to the land I will show you. I will make you into a great nation and I will bless you; I will make your name great and you will be a blessing. I will bless those who bless you, and whoever curses you I will curse; and all peoples on earth will be blessed through you."

So Abram left, as the Lord had told him; and Lot went with him. Abram was seventy-five years old when he set out from Haran. He took his wife Sarai, his nephew Lot, all the possessions they had accumulated and the people they had acquired in Haran, and they set out for the land of Canaan, and they arrived there.

Abram traveled through the land as far as the site of the great tree of Moreh at Shechem. At that time the Canaanites were in the land. The Lord appeared to Abram and said, "To your offspring I will give this land." So he built an altar there to the Lord, who had appeared to him.

From there he went toward the hills east of Bethel and pitched his tent, with Bethel on the west and Ai on the east. There he built an altar to the Lord and called on the name of the Lord. Then Abram set out and continued toward the Negev.

Now there was a famine in the land, and Abram went down to Egypt to live there for a while because the famine was severe.

*   *   *

Jacob and Esau

When Isaac was old and his eyes were so weak that he could no longer see, he called for Esau his older son and said to him, "My son."

"Here I am," he answered.

Isaac said, "I am now an old man and don't know the day of my death. Now then, get your weapons—your quiver and bow—and go out to the open country to hunt some wild game for me. Prepare me the kind of tasty food I like and bring it to me to eat, so that I may give you my blessing before I die."

Now Rebekah was listening as Isaac spoke to his son Esau. When Esau left for the open country to hunt game and bring it back, Rebekah said to her son

Jacob, "Look, I overheard your father say to your brother Esau, 'Bring me some game and prepare me some tasty food to eat, so that I may give you my blessing in the presence of the Lord before I die.' Now, my son, listen carefully and do what I tell you: Go out to the flock and prepare some tasty food for your father, just the way he likes it. Then take it to your father to eat, so that he may give you his blessing before he dies."

Jacob said to Rebekah his mother, "But my brother Esau is a hairy man, and I'm a man with smooth skin. What if my father touches me? I would appear to be tricking him and would bring down a curse on myself rather than a blessing."

His mother said to him, "My son, let the curse fall on me. Just do what I say; go and get them for me."

So he went and got them and brought them to his mother, and she prepared some tasty food, just the way his father liked it. Then Rebekah took the best clothes of Esau her older son, which she had in the house, and put them on her younger son Jacob. She also covered his hands and the smooth part of his neck with the goatskins. Then she handed to her son Jacob the tasty food and the bread she had made.

He went to his father and said, "My father."

"Yes, my son," he answered. "Who is it?"

Jacob said to his father, "I am Esau your firstborn. I have done as you told me. Please sit up and eat some of my game so that you may give me your blessing."

Isaac asked his son, "How did you find it so quickly, my son?"

"The Lord your God gave me success," he replied.

Then Isaac said to Jacob, "Come near so I can touch you, my son, to know whether you really are my son Esau or not."

Jacob went close to his father Isaac, who touched him and said, "The voice is the voice of Jacob, but the hands are the hands of Esau." He did not recognize him, for his hands were hairy like those of his brother Esau; so he blessed him. "Are you really my son Esau?" he asked.

"I am," he replied.

Then he said, "My son, bring me some of your game to eat, so that I may give you my blessing."

Jacob brought it to him and he ate; and he brought some wine and he drank. Then his father Isaac said to him, "Come here, my son, and kiss me."

So he went to him and kissed him. When Isaac caught the smell of his clothes, he blessed him and said, "Ah, the smell of my son is like the smell of a field that the Lord has blessed. May God give you of heaven's dew and of earth's richness—and abundance of grain and new wine. May nations serve you and peoples bow down to you. Be lord over your brothers, and may the sons of your mother bow down to you. May those who curse you be cursed and those who bless you be blessed."

After Isaac finished blessing him and Jacob had scarcely left his father's presence, his brother Esau came in from hunting. He too prepared some tasty food and brought it to his father. Then he said to him, "My father, sit up and eat some of my game, so that you may give me your blessing."

His father Isaac asked him, "Who are you?"

"I am your son," he answered, "your firstborn, Esau."

Isaac trembled violently and said, "Who was it, then, that hunted game and brought it to me? I ate it just before you came and I blessed him—and indeed he will be blessed!"

When Esau heard his father's words, he burst out with a loud and bitter cry and said to his father, "Bless me—me too, my father!"

But he said, "Your brother came deceitfully and took your blessing."

Esau said, "Isn't he rightly named Jacob? He has deceived me these two times: He took my birthright, and now he's taken my blessing!" Then he asked, "Haven't you reserved any blessing for me?"

Isaac answered Esau, "I have made him lord over you and have made all his relatives his servants, and I have sustained him with grain and new wine. So what can I possibly do for you, my son?"

Esau said to his father, "Do you have only one blessing, my father? Bless me too, my father!" Then Esau wept aloud.

His father Isaac answered him, "Your dwelling will be away from the earth's richness, away from the dew of heaven above. You will live by the sword and you will serve your brother. But when you grow restless, you will throw his yoke from off your neck."

Esau held a grudge against Jacob because of the blessing his father had given him. He said to himself, "The days of mourning for my father are near; then I will kill my brother Jacob."

When Rebekah was told what her older son Esau had said, she sent for her younger son Jacob and said to him, "Your brother Esau is consoling himself with the thought of killing you. Now then, my son, do what I say: Flee at once to my brother Laban in Haran. Stay with him for a while until your brother's fury subsides. When your brother is no longer angry with you and forgets what you did to him, I'll send word for you to come back from there. Why should I lose both of you in one day?"

QUESTIONS TO CONSIDER

1. How does each of these passages portray the Hebrew people and their relationship to God?
2. Where is the line between "myth" and "history" in this work?
3. How might these tales be used for both political and religious purposes? Can one separate these elements from one another?

FOR FURTHER READING

Albright, W. F. *From the Stone Age to Christianity*. 2nd ed. Garden City, NY: Doubleday, 1957.

Bright, John. *A History of Israel*. 2nd ed. Philadelphia: Westminster, 1972.

Friedman, Richard E. *Who Wrote the Bible?* New York: Summit, 1987.

Guthrie, Donald, and J. A. Motyer, eds. *The New Bible Commentary, Revised.* Grand Rapids, MI: Eerdmans, 1970.

Halpern, Baruch. *The First Historians: The Hebrew Bible and History.* New York: Harper and Row, 1988.

Leach, Edmund. *Genesis as Myth and Other Essays.* London: Jonathan Cape, 1969.

Miller, J. Maxwell, and John H. Hays. *A History of Ancient Israel and Judah.* Philadelphia: Westminster, 1986.

NOTES

1. *The Holy Bible, New International Version* (Grand Rapids, MI: Zondervan, 1984), Genesis 1:1–2:3, 11:10–12:20, 27:1–45. Used by permission of the International Bible Society.

CHAPTER 6

Homer

Epic Poet

Homer reciting the Iliad
© 1995 North Wind Pictures

The great epic poems of Homer, the *Iliad* and the *Odyssey*, have intrigued and entertained for more than 2500 years. The episodes, the characters, and the values they reflected shaped Greek, Roman, and later western European cultures. Many ancient thinkers wondered how much of what Homer recounted was historically accurate. The fifth-century BCE Greek Herodotus rejected much of it as woman-stealing myth.

The poems were composed in oral form shortly after 800 BCE. Scholars debate whether they were compiled by an individual or a group. The *Iliad* recounts events that occurred during the siege and sack of Troy by the Achaians (Greeks). It focuses on the warlike deeds and conflicts of a few heroes on both sides. The *Odyssey* tells of the prolonged, adventure-filled return of Odysseus, a minor character in the *Iliad*, to his home in Ithaca. The poems are an amalgamation of many shorter songs that date from different centuries. Some of them, no doubt, survived from a time contemporaneous with the Trojan War.

The question that has intrigued students of history is: How much is historically accurate? In general, no one thinks the Homeric poems are one hundred percent historically accurate, and no one assumes they are absolutely fictitious or completely distorted. Much scholarly debate focuses on the historical accuracy of particular episodes and incidents. For example, the catalogue of ships in Book 2 of the *Iliad* shows knowledge of locations in Greece that were inhabited in Mycenaean times (ca. 1400–1100 BCE) but abandoned thereafter until rediscovered by archeological digs in the nineteenth and twentieth centuries. A recent article even argues that the description of battlefield tactics in the *Iliad*—a description that has often been advanced to illustrate how Homer misunderstood the material he was using—in fact accurately portrays Mycenaean open formation tactics. On the other hand, literary scholars note that the poems were designed to entertain an audience and it is their charm as storytelling, rather than any historical accuracy, that accounts for their continued popularity. The following selections are two among the many memorable passages from the *Iliad*.

The Iliad[1]

Book One

Sing, goddess, the anger of Peleus' son Achilleus
and its devastation, which put pains thousandfold upon the Achaians
hurled in their multitudes to the house of Hades strong souls
of heroes, but gave their bodies to be the delicate feasting
of dogs, of all birds, and the will of Zeus was accomplished
since that time when first there stood in division of conflict
Atreus' son the lord of men and brilliant Achilleus.

What god was it then set them together in bitter collision?
Zeus' son and Leto's, Apollo, who in anger at the king drove
the foul pestilence among the host, and the people perished,
since Atreus' son had dishonoured Chryses, priest of Apollo,
when he came beside the fast ships of the Achaians to ransom
back his daughter, carrying gifts beyond count and holding
in his hands wound on a staff of gold the ribbons of Apollo
who strikes from afar, and supplicated all the Achaians,
but above all Atreus' two sons, the marshals of the people:
'Sons of Atreus and you other strong-greaved Achaians,
to you may the gods grant who have their homes on Olympos
Priam's city to be plundered and a fair homecoming thereafter,
but may you give me back my own daughter and take the ransom,
giving honour to Zeus' son who strikes from afar, Apollo.'

*   *   *

Book Two

Tell me now, you Muses who have your homes on Olympos.
For you, who are goddesses, are there, and you know all things,
and we have heard only the rumour of it and know nothing.
Who then of those were the chief men and the lords of Danaans?
I could not tell over the multitude of them nor name them,
not if I had ten tongues and ten mouths, not if I had
a voice never to be broken and a heart of bronze within me,
not unless the Muses of Olympia, daughters
of Zeus of the aegis, remembered all those who came beneath Ilion.
I will tell the lords of the ships, and the ships numbers.

Leïtos and Peneleos were leaders of the Boiotians,
with Arkesilaos and Prothoenor and Klonios;
they who lived in Hyria and in rocky Aulis,
in the hill-bends of Eteonos, and Schoinos, and Skolos,
Thespeia and Graia, and in spacious Mykalessos;
they who dwelt about Harma and Eilesion and Erythrai,
they who held Eleon and Hyle and Peteon,

with Okalea and Medeon, the strong-founded citadel,
Kopai, and Eutresis, and Thisbe of the dove-cotes;
they who held Koroneia, and the meadows of Haliartos,
they who held Plataia, and they who dwelt about Glisa,
they who held the lower Thebes, the strong-founded citadel,
and Onchestos the sacred, the shining grove of Poseidon;
they who held Arne of the great vineyards, and Mideia,
with Nisa the sacrosanct and uttermost Anthedon.
Of these there were fifty ships in all, and on board
each of these a hundred and twenty sons of the Boiotians.

But they who lived in Aspledon and Orchomenos of the Minyai,
Askalaphos led these, and Ialmenos, children of Ares,
whom Astyoche bore to him in the house of Aktor
Azeus' son, a modest maiden; she went into the chamber
with strong Ares, who was laid in bed with her secretly.
With these two there were marshalled thirty hollow vessels.

Schedios and Epistrophos led the men of Phokis,
children of Iphitos, who was son of great-hearted Naubolos.
These held Kyparissos, and rocky Pytho, and Krisa
the sacrosanct together with Daulis and Panopeus;
they who lived about Hyampolis and Anamoreia,
they who dwelt about Kephisos, the river immortal,
they who held Lilaia beside the well springs of Kephisos.
Following along with these were forty black ships,
and the leaders marshalling the ranks of the Phokians set them
in arms on the left wing of the host beside the Boiotians.

Swift Aias son of Oileus led the men of Lokris,
the lesser Aias, not great in size like the son of Telamon,
but far slighter. He was a small man armoured in linen,
Yet with the throwing spear surpassed all Achaians and Hellenes
These were the dwellers in Kynos and Opoeis and Kalliaros,
and in Bessa, and Skarphe, and lovely Augeiai,
in Thronion and Tarphe and beside the waters of Boagrios.
Following along with him were forty black ships
of the Lokrians, who dwell across from sacred Euboia.

They who held Euboia, the Abantes, whose wind was fury,
Chalkis and Eretria, the great vineyards of Histiaia,
and seaborne Kerinthos and the steep stronghold of Dion,
they who held Karystos and they who dwelt about Styra,
of these the leader was Elephenor, scion of Ares,
son of Chalkodon and lord of the great-hearted Abantes.
And the running Abantes followed with him, their hair grown
long at the back, spearmen furious with the out-reached ash spear
to rip the corselets girt about the chests of their enemies.
Following along with him were forty black ships.

But the men who held Athens, the strong-founded citadel,
the deme of great-hearted Erechtheus, whom once Athene
Zeus' daughter tended after the grain-giving fields had born him
and established him to be in Athens in her own rich temple;
there as the circling years go by the sons of the Athenians
make propitiation with rams and bulls sacrificed;
of these men the leader was Peteos' son Menestheus.
Never on earth before had there been a man born like him
for the arrangement in order of horses and shielded fighters.
Nestor alone could challenge him, since he was far older.
Following along with him were fifty black ships.

Out of Salamis Aias brought twelve ships and placed them
next to where the Athenian battalions were drawn up.

They who held Argos and Tiryns of the huge walls,
Hermione and Asine lying down the deep gulf,
Troizen and Eionai, and Epidauros of the vineyards,
they who held Aigina and Mases, sons of the Achaians,
of these the leader was Diomedes of the great war cry
with Schenelos, own son of the high-renowned Kapaneus
and with them as a third went Euryalos, a man godlike,
son of Mekisteus the king, and the scion of Talaos;
but the leader of all was Diomedes of the great war cry.
Following along with these were eighty black ships.

But the men who held Mykenai, the strong-founded citadel,
Korinth the luxurious, and strong-founded Kleonai;
they who dwelt in Orneai and lovely Araithyrea,
and Sikyon, where of old Adrestos had held the kingship;
they who held Hyperesia and steep Gonoëssa
they who held Pellene and they who dwelt about Aigion,
all about the sea-shore and about the wide headland of Helike,
of their hundred ships the leader was powerful Agamemnon,
Atreus' son, with whom followed far the best and bravest
people; and among them he himself stood armoured in shining
bronze, glorying, conspicuous among the great fighters,
since he was greatest among them all, and led the most people.

*   *   *

Now all those who dwelt about Pelasgian Argos,
those who lived by Alos and Alope and at Trachis,
those who held Phthia and Hellas the land of fair women,
who were called Myrmidons and Hellenes and Achaians,
of all these and their fifty ships the lord was Achilleus.
But these took no thought now for the grim clamour of battle
since there was no one who could guide them into close order,
since he, swift-footed brilliant Achilleus, lay where the ships were,

angered over the girl of the lovely hair, Briseis,
Whom after much hard work he had taken away from Lyrnessos
after he had sacked Lyrnessos and the walls of Thebe
and struck down Epistrophos and Mynes the furious spearmen,
children of Euenos, king, and son of Selepios.
For her sake he lay grieving now, but was soon to rise up.

* * *

These then were the leaders and the princes among the Danaans
Tell me then, Muse, who of them all was the best and bravest,
of the men, and the men's horses, who went with the sons of Atreus.

Best by far among the horses were the mares of Eumelos
Pheres' son, that he drove, swift-moving like birds, alike in
texture of coat, in age, both backs drawn level like a plumb-line.
These Apollo of the silver bow had bred in Pereia,
mares alike, who went with the terror of the god of battle.
Among the men far the best was Telamonian Aias
while Achilleus stayed angry, since he was far best of all of them,
and the horses also, who carried the blameless son of Peleus.
But Achilleus lay apart among his curved sea-wandering
vessels, raging at Agamemnon, the shepherd of the people,
Atreus' son; and his men beside the break of the sea-beach
amused themselves with discs and with light spears for throwing
and bows; and the horses, standing each beside his chariot,
champed their clover and the parsley that grows in wet places,
resting, while the chariots of their lords stood covered
in the shelters, and the men forlorn of their warlike leader
wandered here and there in the camp, and did no fighting.

* * *

Book Twenty

He [Achilleus] spoke, and leapt back into the ranks, and urged each man on:
'No longer stand away from the Trojans, o great Achaians,
but let each one go to face his man, furious to fight him.
It is a hard thing for me, for all my great strength, to harry
the flight of men in such numbers or to fight with all of them.
Not Ares, who is a god immortal, not even Athene
could take the edge of such masses of men and fight a way through them.
But what I can do with hands and feet and strength I tell you
I will do, and I shall not hang back even a little
but go straight on through their formation, and I think that no man
of the Trojans will be glad when he comes within my spear's range.'

He spoke, urging them on, but glorious Hektor called out
in a great voice to the Trojans, and was minded to face Achilleus:
'Do not be afraid of Peleion, o high-hearted Trojans.

I myself could fight in words against the immortals,
but with the spear it were hard, since they are far stronger than we are.
Even Achilleus will not win achievement of everything
he says. Part he will accomplish, but part shall be baulked halfway done.
I am going to stand against him now, though his hands are like flame,
though his hands are like flame and his heart like the shining of iron.'

He spoke, urging the Trojans, and they lifted their spears to face them.
Their fury gathered into bulk and their battle cry rose up.
But now Phoibos Apollo stood by Hektor and spoke to him:
'Hektor, do not go out all alone to fight with Achilleus,
but wait for him in the multitude and out of the carnage
lest he hit you with the spear or the stroke of the sword from close in.'

He spoke, and Hektor plunged back into the swarm of the fighting
men, in fear, when he heard the voice of the god speaking.
But Achilleus, gathering the fury upon him, sprang on the Trojans
with a ghastly cry, and the first of them he killed was Iphition
the great son of Otrynteus and a lord over numbers of people,
born of a naiad nymph to Otrynteus, sacker of cities,
under the snows of Tmolos in the rich countryside of Hyde.
Great Achilleus struck him with the spear as he came in fury,
in the middle of the head, and all the head broke into two pieces.
He fell, thunderously. Great Achilleus vaunted above him:
'Lie there, Otrynteus' son, most terrifying of all men.
Here is your death, but your generation was by the lake waters
of Gyge, where is the allotted land of your fathers
by fish-swarming Hyllos and the whirling waters of Hermos.'

He spoke, vaunting, but darkness shrouded the eyes of the other,
and the running-rims of Achaian chariots cut him to pieces
in the van of the onrush. Next, after him, facing Demoleon
lord defender of battle and son of Antenor,
Achilleus stabbed him in the temple through the brazen sides of the helmet,
and the brazen helmet could not hold, but the bronze spearhead
driven on through smashed the bone apart, and the inward
brain was all spattered forth. So he beat him down in his fury.
Next he stabbed with a spear-stroke in the back Hippodamas
as he fled away before him and sprang from behind his horses.
He blew his life away, bellowing, as when a bull
bellows as he is dragged for Poseidon, lord of Helike,
and the young men drag him. In such bulls the earth shaker glories.
Such was the bellowing as the proud spirit flitted from his bones.
Next he went with the spear after godlike Polydoros,
Priam's son, whom his father would not let go into battle
because he was youngest born of all his sons to him, and also
the most beloved, and in speed of his feet outpassed all the others.

But now, in his young thoughtlessness and display of his running
he swept among the champions until thus he destroyed his dear life.
For as he shot by swift-footed brilliant Achilleus hit him
with a spear thrown in the middle of the back where the clasps of the war
    belt
were golden and came together at the joining halves of the corselet.
The spearhead held its way straight on and came out by the navel,
and he dropped, moaning, on one knee as the dark mist gathered
about him, and sagged, and caught with his hands at his bowels in front of
    him.

But now when Hektor saw Polydoros, his own brother,
going limp to the ground and catching his bowels in his hands,
the mist closed about his eyes also, he could stand no longer
to turn there at a distance, but went out to face Achilleus
hefting his sharp spear, like a flame. Seeing him Achilleus
balanced his spear in turn, and called out to him, and challenged him:
'Here is the man who beyond all others has troubled my anger,
who slaughtered my beloved companion. Let us no longer
shrink away from each other along the edgeworks of battle.'

He spoke, and looking darkly at brilliant Hektor spoke to him:
'Come nearer, so that sooner you may reach your appointed destruction.'

But with no fear Hektor of the shining helm answered him:
'Son of Peleus, never hope by words to frighten me as if I were a baby.
I myself understand well enough
how to speak in vituperation and how to make insults.
I know that you are great and that I am far weaker than you are.
Still, all this lies upon the knees of the gods; and it may be
that weaker as I am I might still strip the life from you
with a cast of the spear, since my weapon too has been sharp before this.'

He spoke, and balanced the spear and let it fly. But Athene
blew against it and turned it back from renowned Achilleus
with an easy blast. It came back again to glorious Hektor
and dropped to the ground in front of his feet. Meanwhile Achilleus
made a furious charge against him, raging to kill him
with a terrible cry, but Phoibos Apollo caught up Hektor
easily, since he was a god, and wrapped him in thick mist.
Three times swift-footed brilliant Achilleus swept in against him
with the brazen spear. Three times his stroke went into the deep mist.
But as a fourth time, like something more than a man, he charged in,
Achilleus with a terrible cry called in winged words after him:
'Once again now you escaped death, dog. And yet the evil
came near you, but now once more Phoibos Apollo has saved you,
he to whom you must pray when you go into the thunder of spears thrown.
Yet I may win you, if I encounter you ever hereafter,

if beside me also there is some god who will help me.
Now I must chase whoever I can overtake of the others.'

* * *

As inhuman fire sweeps on in fury through the deep angles
of a drywood mountain and sets ablaze the depth of the timber
and the blustering wind lashes the flame along, so Achilleus
swept everywhere with his spear like something more than a mortal
harrying them as they died, and the black earth ran blood.
Or as when a man yokes male broad-foreheaded oxen
to crush white barley on a strong-laid threshing floor, and rapidly
the barley is stripped beneath the feet of the bellowing oxen,
so before great-hearted Achilleus the single-foot horses
trampled alike dead men and shields, and the axle under
the chariot was all splashed with blood and the rails which encircled
the chariot, struck by flying drops from the feet of the horses,
from the running rims of the wheels. The son of Peleus was straining
to win glory, his invincible hands spattered with bloody filth.

QUESTIONS TO CONSIDER

1. Homer calls upon the muses and goddesses at several points throughout his recitation. What function might this have served?
2. Why does Homer go on at such length with his catalogue of leaders and ships?
3. What values can you infer from Homer's account?
4. How is this text similar in its presentation and content to the Sundiata epic (Chapter 4)?

FOR FURTHER READING

Clark, Howard. *Homer's Readers: A Historical Introduction to the "Iliad" and the "Odyssey."* Newark: University of Delaware Press, 1981.
Finley, M. I. *The World of Odysseus.* Harmondsworth, U.K.: Penguin, 1979.
Lorimer, H. L. *Homer and the Monuments.* London: Macmillan, 1950.
Page, D. L. *History and the Homeric "Iliad."* Berkeley, CA: University of California Press, 1959.
Van Wees, Hans. "The Homeric Way of War: The *Iliad* and the Hoplite Phalanx." *Greece and Rome* 41 (1994): 1–18.

NOTES

1. Homer, *The Iliad of Homer*, Trans. Richmond Lattimore (Chicago: University of Chicago Press, 1951), 59, 89–91, 94, 96, 413–16, 417.

CHAPTER 7

Scholars of Zhou

History as Ethics

Confucius
© *North Wind Pictures*

China, the civilization with the longest unbroken history, stretches back at least to the Shang dynasty, nearly three and a half millenia ago. For most of that time, China has been the dominant power in East Asia and, indeed, one of the most sophisticated civilizations in the world.

One of the reasons we know quite a bit about ancient Chinese history is that the Chinese started writing records very early. A script of five thousand characters, ancestors to modern Chinese writing, was used in divination ceremonies as early as the fourteenth century BCE, carved on scapular bones and tortoise shells. In that same era, the Chinese passed down orally tales of their people and their leaders. People also began to make records of everyday matters and affairs of state and preserve them on bronze, pottery, and skins (paper was invented in China in the first century CE).

In the eleventh century BCE the Shang was replaced by the Zhou dynasty, which for most of its history was a loose collection of principalities under a nominal emperor. Starting between the ninth and the sixth centuries BCE, the scholars at the royal court, along with those in several principalities, brought together court records and oral traditions that gradually coalesced into five collections of documents. The oldest of these, the *I Ching* or *Book of Changes*, comprises directions and interpretations from Shang oracle bones. The second volume is the *Shu Ching* or *Book of History*, selections from which follow. The *Shih Ching* or *Book of Odes* collected three hundred poems, some very ancient and some contemporary to the collectors. The *Li Chi* or *Book of Rites* comprised philosophical statements and rules for everyday living. The *Ch'un Ch'iu* or *Spring and Autumn Annals* included a brief history of the state of Lu down to the fifth century BCE, together with explanatory material.

Nearly as old as these five classics are the writings attributed to Kongzi, "Master Kong," a sixth-century BCE teacher known in the West as Confucius. His words of wisdom, collected in the *Analects*, constitute one of the great repositories of ethical ideas, and form the basis for much of the Chinese value system to this day. Confucianism was a backward-looking ethical system that held up the ancient people depicted in the Classics as models of right behavior and their era as a golden age. Chinese people down to modern times regarded the events described in the *Book of History* as true and their authorship as very ancient. In recent decades scholars have suggested that some pieces were in fact written late in the Zhou dynasty or even into the first Han dynasty (206 BCE to CE 24).

The pieces of the *Book of History* reproduced here are generally thought to be of ancient origin, and they show the ethical concern of the compilers. The first selection deals with the Emperor Yao and his successor Shun, who were thought to have lived around 2200 BCE, during the Xia dynasty, of which we know little. It holds Yao and Shun up as models of gentility, moderation, and filial piety, and shows very early on the Chinese rulers' intense interest in calendars and astronomy as key items in their stewardship of the good of the people. In the second selection, Kao Yao, a minister under Emperor Shun, sets forth the enduring Confucian doctrines that the Chinese emperor is the Son of Heaven and that the well-being of the country—indeed, of all humankind—

depends on his virtue. The third piece, a speech by the Duke of Shao, is intended to bolster the Zhou dynasty's claim to legitimacy. It asserts that the Mandate of Heaven—another important Chinese political concept—had passed from Xia and Shang to Zhou hands because of the superior piety of the Zhou rulers. Like the tellers of the Hopi origin tale and of the Bible, this author uses an old story to legitimize the rule of the victors.

Book of History[1]

The Canon of Yao

Examining into antiquity, we find the sovereign Yao was styled Fang Hsün. He was reverent, intelligent, accomplished, and thoughtful—naturally and without effort. He was sincerely courteous and capable of all complaisance. The bright influence of these qualities extended through the four quarters of the land and reached to heaven above.

He distinguished the able and virtuous, and thence proceeded to the love of all in the nine classes of his kindred, who thus became harmonious. He also regulated and polished the people of his domain, who all became brightly intelligent. Finally, he united and harmonized the myriad states [those of the princes beyond the imperial domain]. And so the black-haired people were transformed. The result was universal concord.

He commanded the brothers Hsi and the Brothers Ho, in reverent accord with their observation of the wide heavens, to calculate and delineate the movements and appearances of the sun, the moon, the stars, and the zodiacal spaces [houses], and so to deliver respectfully the seasons to be observed by the people.

He separately commanded the second brother Hsi to reside at Yü-i, in what was called the Bright Valley, there respectfully to receive as a guest the rising sun, and to adjust and arrange the labors of the spring. "The day," said he, "is of the medium length and the star is in Niao. You may thus exactly determine mid-spring. The people are dispersed in the fields and birds and beasts breed and copulate."

He further commanded the third brother Hsi to reside at Nan-chiao, in what was called the Brilliant Capital, to adjust and arrange the transformations of the summer, and respectfully to observe the exact limit of the shadow. "The day," said he, "is at its longest, and the star is in Huo. You may thus exactly determine mid-summer. The people are more dispersed; the birds and beasts have their feathers and hair thin and change their coats."

He separately commanded the second brother Ho to reside in the west, in what was called the Dark Valley, there respectfully to convoy the setting sun and to adjust and arrange the harvest labors of the autumn. "The night," said he, "is of medium length and the star is in Hsü. You may thus exactly determine mid-autumn. The people feel at ease, and birds and beasts have their coats in good condition."

He further commanded the third brother Ho to reside in the northern region, in what was called the Somber Capital, and there to adjust and examine the changes of the winter. "The day," said he, "is at its shortest, and the star is in Mao. You may thus exactly determine mid-winter. The people keep in their houses, and the coats of birds and beasts are downy and thick."

The sovereign said, "Ah! you brothers Hsi and you brothers Ho, a round year consists of three hundred, sixty, and six days. By means of the intercalary month, you are to fix the four seasons and complete the determination of the period of a year. Thereafter, the various officers being regulated in accord with this, all the work of the seasons will be fully performed."

The sovereign said, "Who will search out for me a man according to the times, whom I can raise and employ?"

Fang Ch'i said, "Your heir-son Chu is highly intelligent."

The sovereign said, "Alas! he is insincere and quarrelsome. Could he do?"

The sovereign said, "Who will search out for me a man equal to the exigency of my affairs?"

Huan Tou said, "Oh! the merits of the minister of Works have just been displayed on a wide scale."

The sovereign said, "Alas! when all is quiet, he talks; but when employed, his actions turn out differently. He is respectful only in appearance. See! the floods assail the heavens!"

The sovereign said, "Oh! Chief of the Four Mountains, the waters of the inundation are destructive in their overflow. In their fastness they embrace the hills and overtop great heights, threatening the heavens with their floods. The lower people groan and murmur! Is there a capable man to whom I can assign the correction of this calamity?"

All in the court said, "Ah! is there not Kun?"

The sovereign said, "Alas! how perverse is he! He is disobedient to orders and tries to injure his peers."

The Chief of the Four Mountains said, "Well, but try him—to see if he can accomplish the work."

Accordingly, Kun was employed.

The sovereign said to him, "Go; be reverent!"

For nine years Kun labored. But the work was not accomplished.

The sovereign said, "Oh! Chief of the Four Mountains, I have been on the throne for seventy years. You can carry out my commands. I will resign my throne to you."

The Chief said, "I have not the virtue; I should disgrace the imperial seat."

The sovereign said, "Show me someone among the illustrious, or set forth one from among the poor and mean."

All then said to the sovereign, "There is an unmarried man among the lower people called Shun of Yü."

The sovereign said, "Yes, I have heard of him. What have you to say about him?"

The Chief said, "He is the son of a blind man. His father was obstinately unprincipled; his stepmother was insincere; his half brother Hsiang was arrogant. Shun has been able, however, by his filial piety to live in harmony with them and to lead them gradually to self-government, so that they no longer proceed to great wickedness."

The sovereign said, "I will try him; I will wive him and thereby see his behavior with my two daughters."

Accordingly he prepared and sent down his two daughters to the north of the Kuei, to be wives in the family of Shun in Yü. The sovereign said to his daughters, "Be reverent!"

* * *

The Counsels of Kao Yao

Examining into antiquity, we find that Kao Yao said, "If the sovereign sincerely pursues the course of his virtue, the counsels offered to him will be intelligent and the admonitions he receives will be harmonious."

Yü said, "Yes, but explain yourself."

Kao Yao said, "Oh! let him be careful about his personal cultivation, with thoughts that are far-reaching; thus he will effect a generous kindness and nice observance of distinctions among the nine branches of his kindred. Also, all the intelligent will exert themselves in his service. In this way from what is near the sovereign will reach to what is distant."

Yü did reverence to the excellent words and said, "Yes."

Kao Yao continued, "Oh! it lies in knowing men and giving repose to the people."

Yü said, "Alas! to attain these things was a difficulty even to Yao. When a sovereign knows men, he is wise and can put every one into the office for which he is fit. When he gives repose to the people, his kindness is felt and the black-haired race cherish him in their hearts. When a sovereign can be thus wise and kind, what occasion will he have for anxiety about a Huan Tou or removing a lord of Miao? What has he to fear from insincere words, insinuating appearance, and great artfulness?"

Kao Yao said, "Oh! there are in all nine virtues to be discovered in conduct. When we say that a man possesses any virtue, it is as much as to say he does such and such a thing." Yü asked, "What are the nine virtues?"

Kay Yao replied, "Affability combined with dignity, mildness with firmness, bluntness with respectfulness, aptness for government with reverence, docility with boldness, straightforwardness with gentleness, an easy negligence with discrimination, boldness with sincerity, and valor with righteousness. When these qualities are continuously displayed, have we not the good officer? When there is a daily display of three of these virtues, their possessor could early and late regulate and brighten the clan of which he was made chief. When there is a daily severe and reverent cultivation of six virtues, their possessor could brilliantly conduct the affairs of the state to which he was constituted ruler. When such men are all received and advanced, the possessors of those nine virtues will be employed in the public service. The men of a thousand and men of a hundred will be in their offices; the various ministers will emulate one another; all the officers will accomplish their duties at the proper times, observant of the seasons and the elements predominating in them; thus their various duties will be fully accomplished.

"Let not the Son of Heaven set the example of indolence or dissoluteness to the rulers of states. Let him be wary and fearful, remembering that in one day or two days there may occur ten thousand springs of things. Let not his various officers obstruct their places. The work is Heaven's; men must act for it!

"From Heaven are the social relationships with their several duties. To us it is given to enforce those five duties. Lo, then we have the five courses of generous conduct. From Heaven are the social distinctions with their several ceremonies; from us proceed the observances of those five ceremonies; and lo! they then appear in regular practice. When sovereign and ministers show a common reverence and united respect for these ceremonies do they not harmonize the moral nature of the people? Heaven graciously distinguishes the virtuous: are there not the five ceremonial robes with the five decorations? Heaven punishes the guilty; are there not the five punishments for that purpose? The business of government! Ought we not to be earnest in it? Ought we not to be earnest in it?

"Heaven hears and sees as our people hear and see; Heaven brightly approves and displays its terrors as our people brightly approve and would fear; such connection is there between the upper and lower worlds. How reverent ought the masters of the earth to be!

"My words are in accord with reason and may be put in practice."

Yü said, "Yes, your words may be put in practice and crowned with success."

Kay Yao said, "As to that I do not know; but I wish daily to be helpful. May the government be perfected!"

* * *

The Announcement of the Duke of Shao

In the second month, on the day *yi-wei*, six days after full moon, the king went in the morning from Chou to Feng. Thence the Grand Guardian preceded the duke of Chou to survey the locality of the new capital. In the third month, on the day *wu-shen*, the third day after the first appearance of the moon on *ping-wu*, he came in the morning to Lo. He divined by the tortoise shell about the several localities and, having obtained favorable indications, he set about laying out the plan of the city. On *keng-hsü*, the third day after, he led the people of Yin to prepare the various sites on the north of the Lo. This work was completed on *chia-yin*, the fifth day after.

On *yi-mao*, the day following, the duke of Chou came in the morning to Lo and thoroughly inspected the plan of the new city. On *ting-ssu*, the third day after, he offered two bulls as victims in the northern and southern suburbs. On the morrow, *wu-wu*, at the altar to the spirit of the land in the new city, he sacrificed a bull, a ram, and a boar. After seven days, on *chia-tzu* in the morning, he gave their several orders to the people of Yin, and the presiding chiefs of the princes from the Hou, Tien, and Nan domains, from his written specifications. When the people of Yin had thus received their orders they arose and entered with vigor on their work.

When the work was drawing to a completion, the Grand Guardian went out with the hereditary princes of the various states to bring their offerings for the king. When he returned he gave them to the duke of Chou, saying, "With my hands to my head and my head to the ground, I present these to his Majesty and your Grace. Announcements for the information of the multitudes of Yin must come from you, with whom is management of affairs.

"Oh! God dwelling in the great heavens has changed his decree respecting his great son and the great dynasty of Yin. Our king has received that decree. Unbounded is the happiness connected with it, and unbounded is the anxiety. Oh! how can he be other than reverent?

"When Heaven rejected and made an end of the decree in favor of the great dynasty of Yin, there were many of its former wise kings in Heaven. The king, however, who had succeeded to them, the last of his race, from the time of his entering into their appointment, proceeded in such a way as to keep the wise in obscurity and the vicious in office. The poor people in such a case, carrying their children and leading their wives, made their moan to Heaven. They even fled, but were apprehended again. Oh! Heaven had compassion on the people of the four quarters; its favoring decree lighted on our earnest founders. Let the king sedulously cultivate the virtue of reverence.

"Examining the men of antiquity, there was Yü, founder of the Hsia dynasty. Heaven guided his mind, allowed his descendants to succeed him, and protected them. He acquainted himself with Heaven, and was obedient to it. But in process of time the decree in his favor fell to the ground. So also is it now when we examine the case of Yin. There was the same guiding of its founder T'ang, who corrected the errors of Hsia, and whose descendants enjoyed the protection of Heaven. He also acquainted himself with Heaven, and was obedient to it. But not the decree in favor of him has fallen to the ground. Our king has not come to the throne in his youth. Let him not slight the aged and experienced, for it may be said of them that they have studied the virtuous conduct of the ancients and have matured their counsels in the sight of Heaven.

"Oh! although the king is young, yet he is the eldest son of Heaven. Let him effect a great harmony with the lower people and that will be the blessing of the present time. Let not the king presume to be remiss in this but continually regard and stand in awe of the perilous uncertainty of the people's attachment.

"Let the king come here as the vice-regent in this center of the land. Tan said, 'Now that this great city has been built, from henceforth he may be the mate of great Heaven, and reverently sacrifice to the spirits above and below; henceforth he may from this central spot administer successful government.' Thus shall the king enjoy the favoring regard of Heaven all complete, and the government of the people will now be prosperous.

"Let the king first bring under his influence those who were the managers of affairs under Yin, associating them with the managers of affairs for our Chou. This will regulate their perverse natures and they will make daily advancement. Let the king make reverence the resting place of his mind; he must maintain the virtue of reverence.

"We should by all means survey the dynasties of Hsia and Yin. I do not presume to know and say, 'The dynasty of Hsia was to enjoy the favoring decree of Heaven just for so many years,' nor do I presume to know and say, 'It could not continue longer.' The fact was simply that, for want of the virtue of reverence, the decree in its favor prematurely fell to the ground. Similarly,

I do not presume to know and say, 'The dynasty of Yin was to enjoy the favoring decree of Heaven just for so many years,' nor do I presume to know and say, 'It could not continue longer.' The fact simply was that, for want of the virtue of reverence, the decree in its favor fell prematurely to the ground. The king has now inherited the decree—the same decree, I consider, which belonged to those two dynasties. Let him seek to inherit the virtues of their meritorious sovereigns; let him do this especially at this commencement of his duties.

"Oh! it is as on the birth of a son, when all depends on the training of his early life through which he may secure his wisdom in the future, as if it were decreed to him. Now Heaven may have decreed wisdom to the king; it may have decreed good fortune or bad; it may have decreed a long course of years; we only know that now is the commencement of his duties. Dwelling in this new city, let the king now sedulously cultivate the virtue of reverence. When he is fully devoted to this virtue, he may pray to Heaven for a long-abiding decree in his favor.

"In the position of king let him not, because of the excesses of the people in violation of the laws, presume also to rule by the violent infliction of death; when the people are regulated gently, the merit of government is seen. It is for him who is in the position of king to overtop all with his virtue. In this case the people will imitate him throughout the kingdom and he will become still more illustrious.

"Let the king and his ministers labor with a mutual sympathy, saying, 'We have received the decree of Heaven and it shall be great as the long-continued years of Hsia; yea, it shall not fail of the long-continued years of Yin.' I wish the king, through the attachment of the lower people, to receive the long-abiding decree of Heaven."

The duke of Shao then did obeisance with his hands to his head and his head to the ground, and said, "I, a small minister, presume with the king's heretofore hostile people and all their officers, and with his loyal friendly people, to maintain and receive his majesty's dread command and brilliant virtue. That the king should finally obtain the decree all complete, and that he should become illustrious—this I do not presume to labor for. I only bring respectfully these offerings to present to his majesty, to be used in his prayers to Heaven for its long-abiding decree."

QUESTIONS TO CONSIDER

1. According to the scholars of Zhou, what are the characteristics of a virtuous ruler?
2. How might the ethical concerns of these historians have shaped the narrative presented here?
3. How might political concerns have shaped the narrative presented here?

FOR FURTHER READING

DeBary, Wm. Theodore, Wing-tsit Chan, and Burton Watson. *Sources of Chinese Tradition.* Vol. I. New York: Columbia University Press, 1960.

Gernet, Jacques. *A History of Chinese Civilization.* Trans. J. R. Foster. Cambridge: Cambridge University Press, 1982.

Legge, James. *The Chinese Classics.* 5 vols. Hong Kong: Hong Kong University Press, 1960.

Li, Dun J. *The Civilization of China.* New York: Scribner's, 1975.

Pound, Ezra. *The Confucian Odes.* New York: New Directions, 1959.

Waley, Arthur, trans. *The Analects of Confucius.* London: George Allen & Unwin, 1938.

_____ . *Three Ways of Thought in Ancient China.* Garden City, NY: Doubleday, 1956.

_____ . *The Book of Songs.* New York: Grove, 1960.

Wang Bi. *The I Ching: The Classic of Changes.* New York: Columbia University Press, 1994.

NOTES

1. Clae Waltham, *Shu Ching: Book of History: A Modernized Edition of the Translations of James Legge* (Chicago: Regnery, 1971), 4–7, 26–29, 161–66.

PART TWO

Early Historians

The foregoing chapters are history, but not formal history. Each recounts the past but does so in an oral or literary mode, often for aesthetic or political aims. The world's formal historical traditions built on such material, but transformed it to present more closely the real past. Such formal history began in some parts of the world with the introduction of writing; in other places it emerged somewhat later. The selections in Part 2 of this anthology each are typical of the early work in several world civilizations: Greek, Chinese, Roman, Christian, Muslim, Indian, and Aztec.

As can be seen from the passages we have chosen, these traditions saw history differently. They differed, for example, in the way they viewed time. The Greco-Roman view of time was cyclical, and saw events as guided by Fate. Christian historians, on the other hand, saw history as linear and directional, starting from creation and heading for a big bang at the end. They also saw it as directed by an infinite personal God, or at least Providence, not something so impersonal as Fate. The Chinese view of time was both cyclical—emphasizing recurrent patterns in

dynastic cycles, for example—and backward-looking, to an early Golden Age. Some Muslim historians similarly looked on early Islam as a time of perfection, though they also inherited a linear sense from Judaism and Christianity. In those periods when Indian writers were Hindus or Buddhists, they tended to take cyclical views of history; when Muslims predominated, the views were more linear. Early Aztec history was annalistic, though governed in the long term by complex calendrical notions that do not show up in such passages as the one we have excerpted here.

The different traditions also differed in the aspects of the past that they found important. Indian writers generally focused on kings and dynasties; Kalhana's Rajatarangini means "the river of kings" and is exactly that: a record of succession extending back (so Kalhana tells us) over 2,000 years. While still largely literary, it cares about dates and time order, and so deserves its renown as the first real work of history in the Indian tradition. Similarly Herodotus was the first Greek to write prose history whose primary goal was accurately to depict the past. He combined first-hand observation with travelers' accounts and research in written sources to portray events and the patterns of daily life in the different societies of the Eastern Mediterranean. Appropriately, in the West he was called the father of history; as he does not limit himself to kings and politics, he could as justifiably be called the father of Western anthropology.

Later Greeks (Thucydides) and Romans (Tacitus) narrowed their scope to pure political history— concerns that have been primary in the West. The "parents" of Chinese history—the Sima and Ban families— similarly wrote about dynastic events, though they included a more detailed portrayal of court life than is found in their Western counterparts. Early Muslim and Christian historians, on the other hand, concerned themselves more with the history of their faiths than with political events or the patterns of daily life. Each of these dominant themes lived on in the major traditions, in some cases to the present day.

Historians sometimes have a tendency to read their current concerns back onto the past. German historians of the mid-nineteenth century, for example, tried to establish history on a scientific basis, and so dictated that historical work should always heavily use written records of the past to corroborate the material records that may remain. They also insisted that events have causes and ruled out all but the naturalistic ones. Annalistic lists were not seen as real history, and stories of gods, miracles, and so on were relegated to folklore. Scanning the past, they noted that Herodotus used records and emphasized natural causes; they

thus called him the "first historian" and thought the history writing of other civilizations inferior. Critics have noted that this identification of naturalistic history with the West conveniently forgets that the Christian carriers of Western civilization saw God as history's motive force—as non-naturalistic a power as one can imagine. Be that as it may, the constellation of concerns—written sources, cause-and-effect reasoning, natural causes, and doing research to verify accounts—dominates the modern Western historical tradition. It has close parallels in several other traditions as well.

This is especially true of the use of written records. Much can be inferred about past human society from material remains; we can make solid generalizations about life-style patterns, for example. Archaeological digs into ancient cities and garbage heaps can tell us about what people ate, their housing, their tools, even their trade with other communities and migration patterns. The art work and monuments that survive give us some clues about what was important to past groups. What written records preserve, however— and what distinguishes history from archaeology and the other social sciences—are specificity and nonmaterial realities. How else would we know the specific year the battle of Marathon occurred but for the written records? Would we know the names of the peoples in conflict at this battle without a written account? Would we know the names of the individual leaders, Miltiades and Hippias? Could we have inferred the reason it took place? (Herodotus said it was the Athenian resistance to the re-establishment of tyranny.) Material remains rarely record the thoughts and ideas of people, especially if those ideas are abstract.

Reliance on written records has significant dangers as well, however. Many records seem to have survived by chance and we cannot know how representative they are (the same concern, of course, applies to the survival of material remains). Historians spend much of their energy trying to ascertain the trustworthiness of the written witnesses that have survived. Although the aforementioned nineteenth-century Germans were concerned with this, modern historians are more apt to question both their sources' biases and their own. That is, historians have become increasingly aware that they, too, see the world through culturally specific lenses. Much ink has been spilled in quarreling over the extent of such biases in particular historical interpretations.

A bias toward natural causation also shows up in several of the world's historical traditions, though not so early (nor so briefly) as among the Greeks. There is a good reason for this. For Herodotus, as for Sima Qian in China, Tacitus in Rome, and many subsequent historians, history was intended to be a practical study that could teach lessons, especially to leaders and statesmen. Thus, though religion and the supernatural were important parts of the human experience, the very fact that these involved areas beyond human control and understanding made them of limited explanatory use to the historian. By the modern period, even historians who were committed believers did not function as such in their writing and their historical analysis.

Likewise, every tradition has emphasized historical research. The Greek word *historie* means "researches" and, appropriately, that name has been given to the whole discipline. The specific skills that distinguish historians from other learned folk are found in this area (the subject matter of history, change over time, also distinguishes it). These are the skills taught in a history curriculum and particularly stressed in the research seminar: finding sources of information, checking out the accounts, not accepting hearsay at face value, recording or reconciling discrepant accounts, on the spot investigation, interviewing eyewitnesses, and developing a hypothesis to explain the evidence. Though not all these elements appear in every case, the fact that historians in all eras and traditions went to some lengths to distinguish their work from what they regarded as the errors of other historians shows that this concern is neither modern nor Western. It appears worldwide and in all periods.

Most modern American academic historians follow their nineteenth-century German forebears in emphasizing written records, cause-and-effect reasoning, naturalistic causation, and detailed critical research. As the following passages show, not all early Western historians cared about all these elements. And many historians of other traditions did care about them, though they arranged them in different constellations. The following selections from several major historical traditions show us how early historians from several of the world's traditions worked.

CHAPTER 8

Herodotus

The Founder of Western History

Herodotus
© 1992 North Wind Pictures

The keepers of the flame of Western historiography call Herodotus the "Father of History," and rightly so, for that tradition begins with him. He was the first Greek to write with an eye to accuracy, causation, and accountability to sources. But he is also the father of Western geography and anthropology. His "research" (*historie* in Greek) reflects observations he made while traveling around the Aegean and eastern Mediterranean seas in the fifth century BCE.

The writing of Herodotus is the earliest extended Greek prose. Previous literary work, such as the writing of Homer, was done in verse, for that which was written was first performed orally, and verse was easier to remember. Herodotus' history is studded with digressions—often fascinating tales that the reader enjoys fully as much as the central narrative—perhaps remnants of the earlier, storyteller's tradition. Another such holdover is Herodotus' habit of creating speeches for his characters, having them say in dramatic language what he felt was called for by their circumstances.

Herodotus established many of the traditions that have been followed by Western historians for many centuries. His primary subjects were war, diplomacy, and politics. His history proceeded in roughly chronological order. He made note of the sources of his information; he told his reader whether he obtained a particular fact from an interview, from reading the writings of others, from personal observation, from archeology, and so forth (oral sources were the most prominent). He advocated a multifaceted view of causation; the Greek war with Persia resulted, in his account, not just from woman-stealing or fate, but from a wide variety of interactions and foreign entanglements, which he tried to lay out with some subtlety. Herodotus showed wide-ranging interests in what we now call social sciences—geography, ethnography, anthropology, demography, and economics—and used them all to construct and explain his history. Some commentators would even go so far as to say that Herodotus was responsible for the perennial tendency of Europeans and North Americans to cast international conflicts as part of a titanic East-West struggle over fundamental values and definitions of civilization, a struggle between western democrats and eastern despots.

On the other hand, Herodotus showed traits that were not picked up by his successors in the main line of the Western historiographical tradition. He frequently told several alternative versions of a story so the reader could decide for herself which was closest to the truth; most later writers regarded that as untidy and lacking in conviction. He treated the conspicuous involvement of the divine and the miraculous in human affairs in a matter-of-fact way (for example, the attention paid to oracles and to dreams). And Herodotus ascribed to women a prominent role—far more prominent than that voiced by other writers of his time and culture, indeed, of any time or culture before the present generation.

We do not know much about Herodotus the man. He was born about 480 BCE on the eastern shore of the Aegean. Following a local political squabble, he fled with his family into exile. He appears to have traveled extensively about the eastern Mediterranean, some think as a merchant. On one of those trips he seems to have conceived of a grand task: to write a history of the Greeks' wars with Persia, and therein to explain and celebrate Greek freedom. He did his research while traveling. Those travels took him at least as far as Egypt and Babylon, and perhaps farther to the south and east. He was in Athens periodically and seems to have been an acquaintance of the playwright Sophocles there. Eventually, Herodotus joined an international pan-Hellenic venture at Thurii in southern Italy. He died there sometime after 424 BCE.

The Persian Wars[1]

In this book, the result of my inquiries into history, I hope to do two things: to preserve the memory of the past by putting on record the astonishing achievements both of our own and of the Asiatic peoples; secondly, and more particularly, to show how the two races came into conflict.

Persian historians put the responsibility for the quarrel on the Phoenicians. These people came originally from the coasts of the Indian Ocean; and as soon as they had penetrated into the Mediterranean and settled in that part of the country where they are today, they took to making long trading voyages. Loaded with Egyptian and Assyrian goods, they called at various places along the coast, including Argos, in those days the most important of the countries now called by the general name of Hellas.

Here in Argos they displayed their wares, and five or six days later when they were nearly sold out, it so happened that a number of women came down to the beach to see the fair. Amongst these was the king's daughter, whom Greek and Persian writers agree in calling Io, daughter of Inachus. These women were standing about near the vessel's stern, buying what they fancied, when suddenly the Phoenician sailors passed the word along and made a rush at them. The greater number of them got away; but Io and some others were caught and bundled aboard the ship, which cleared at once and made off for Egypt.

This, according to the Persian account (the Greeks have a different story), was how Io came to Egypt; and this was the first in a series of provocative acts.

Later on some Greeks, whose name the Persian historians fail to record—they were probably Cretans—put into the Phoenician port of Tyre and carried off the king's daughter Europa, thus giving them tit for tat.

For the next outrage it was the Greeks again who were responsible. They sailed in an armed merchantman to Aea in Colchis on the river Phasis, and, not content with the regular business which had brought them there, they abducted the king's daughter Medea. The king sent to Greece demanding reparations and his daughter's return; but the only answer he got was that the Greeks had no intention of offering reparation, having received none themselves for the abduction of Io from Argos.

The accounts go on to say that some forty or fifty years afterwards Paris, the son of Priam, was inspired by these stories to steal a wife for himself out of Greece, being confident that he would not have to pay for the venture any more than the Greeks had done. And that was how he came to carry off Helen.

The first idea of the Greeks after the rape was to send a demand for satisfaction and for Helen's return. The demand was met by a reference to the seizure of Medea and the injustice of expecting satisfaction from people to whom they themselves had refused it, not to mention the fact that they had kept the girl.

Thus far there had been nothing worse than woman-stealing on both sides; but for what happened next the Greeks, they say, were seriously to blame; for it was the Greeks who were, in a military sense, the aggressors. Abducting young women, in their opinion, is not, indeed, a lawful act; but it is stupid after the event to make a fuss about it. The only sensible thing is to take no notice; for it is obvious that no young woman allows herself to be abducted if she does not wish to be. The Asiatics, according to the Persians, took the seizure of the women lightly enough, but not so the Greeks: the Greeks, merely on account of a girl from Sparta, raised a big army, invaded Asia and destroyed the empire of Priam. From that root sprang their belief in the perpetual enmity of the Grecian world towards them—Asia with its various foreign-speaking peoples belonging to the Persians, Europe and the Greek states being, in their opinion, quite separate and distinct from them.

Such then is the Persian story. In their view it was the capture of Troy that first made them enemies of the Greeks.

As to Io, the Phoenicians do not accept the Persians' account; they deny that they took her to Egypt by force. On the contrary, the girl while she was still in Argos went to bed with the ship's captain, found herself pregnant, and, ashamed to face her parents, sailed away voluntarily to escape exposure.

So much for what Persians and Phoenicians say; and I have no intention of passing judgement on its truth or falsity. I prefer to rely on my own knowledge, and to point out who it was in actual fact that first injured the Greeks; then I will proceed with my history, telling the story as I go along of small cities no less than of great. . . .

* * *

The Lydians who were to bring the presents to the temples were instructed by Croesus to ask the oracles if he should undertake the campaign against Persia, and if he should strengthen his army by some alliance. On their arrival, therefore, they offered the gifts with proper ceremony and put their question in the following words: "Croesus, King of Lydia and other nations, in the belief that these are the only true oracles in the world, has given you gifts such as your power of divination deserves, and now asks you if he should march against Persia and if it would be wise to seek an alliance." To this question both oracles returned a similar answer; they foretold that if Croesus attacked the Persians, he would destroy a great empire, and they advised him to find out which of the Greek states was the most powerful, and to come to an understanding with it.

Croesus was overjoyed when he learnt the answer which the oracles had given, and was fully confident of destroying the power of Cyrus. To express his satisfaction he sent a further present to Delphi of two gold staters for every man, having first inquired how many men there were. The Delphians in return granted in perpetuity to Croesus and the people of Lydia the right of citizenship for any who wished, together with exemption from dues, front seats at state functions and priority in consulting the oracle.

When Croesus had given the Delphians their presents, he consulted the oracle a third time, for one true answer had made him greedy for more. On this occasion he asked if his reign would be a long one. The Priestess answered:

When comes the day that a mule shall sit on the Median throne,
Then, tender-footed Lydian, by pebbly Hermus
Run and abide not, nor think it shame to be a coward. . . .

"Master," Croesus answered, "you will please me best if you let me send these chains to the god of the Greeks, whom I most honoured, and ask him if he is accustomed to cheat his benefactors." Cyrus asked the reason for this request, whereupon Croesus repeated the whole story of what he had hoped to accomplish and of the answers of the oracles, and dwelt at length upon the rich gifts he had sent and on how his belief in the prophecies had emboldened him to invade Persia. Then he ended by repeating his request for permission to reproach Apollo for his deceit. Cyrus laughed, and told Croesus he should have what he wanted, and anything else he might ask for, no matter when. Croesus, therefore, sent to Delphi, and instructed his messengers to lay the chains on the threshold of the temple; then, pointing to the chains, they were to ask the god if, when such things were the fruits of war, he was not ashamed to have encouraged Croesus by his oracles to invade Persia in the confident hope of destroying the power of Cyrus. And they were also to ask if it was the habit of Greek gods to be ungrateful.

It is said that when the Lydian messengers reached Delphi and asked the questions they had been told to ask, the Priestess replied that not God himself could escape destiny. As for Croesus, he had expiated in the fifth generation the crime of his ancestor, who was a soldier in the bodyguard of the Heraclids, and, tempted by a woman's treachery, had murdered his master and stolen his office, to which he had no claim. The God of Prophecy was eager that the fall of Sardis might occur in the time of Croesus' sons rather than in his own, but he had been unable to divert the course of destiny. Nevertheless what little the Fates allowed, he had obtained for Croesus' advantage: he had postponed the capture of Sardis for three years, so Croesus must realize that he had enjoyed three years of freedom more than was appointed for him. Secondly, the god had saved him when he was on the pyre. As to the oracle, Croesus had no right to find fault with it: the god had declared that if he attacked the Persians he would bring down a mighty empire. After an answer like that, the wise thing would have been to send again to inquire which empire was meant, Cyrus' or his own. But as he misinterpreted what was said and made no second inquiry, he must admit the fault to have been his own. Moreover, the last time he consulted the oracle he failed also to understand what Apollo said about the mule. The mule was Cyrus, who was the child of parents of different races—a nobler mother and a baser father. His mother was a Mede and daughter of Astyages, king of Media; but his father was a Persian, subject to the Medes, and had married his queen to whom he was in every way inferior.

When the Lydians returned to Sardis with the Priestess' answer and reported it to Croesus, he admitted that the god was innocent and he had only himself to blame. . . .

*   *   *

No one has any accurate information about what lies beyond the region I am now discussing, and I have never met anyone who claims first-hand acquaintance with it. Even Aristeas, whom I have just mentioned, does not pretend in his poem to have gone further than the country of the Issedones, and admits that his account of what lies beyond is mere hearsay, founded on tales which the Issedones told him. I will, nevertheless, put down everything which careful inquiry about these remote parts has brought to my notice. West of the seaport at the mouth of the Borysthenes (Dnieper)—which lies in the middle of the Scythian coastline—the first people are the Graeco-Scythian tribe called Callipidae, and their neighbours to the eastward are the Alizones. Both these people resemble the Scythians in their way of life, and also grow grain for food, as well as onions, leeks, lentils, and millet. . . . Northward again, so far as we can tell, there is utter desert without trace of human life. Eastward of the Scythians who lived off the land, and on the other side of the Panticapes, are the nomadic Scythians, who know nothing of agriculture. All this region with the exception of Hylaea is treeless. The nomadic tribes are to be found over a stretch of country extending eastward fourteen days' journey as far as the river Gerrhus, on the further side of which lies what is called the country of the Kings, and the Royal Scythians, who are the most warlike and numerous section of their race, and look upon the others as their slaves. . . .

Further to the north and east lives another Scythian tribe, which moved into these parts after some trouble with the Royal Scythians to which it originally belonged. As far as this, the country I have been describing is a level plain with good deep soil, but further on it becomes rugged and stony; beyond this region, which is of great extent, one comes to the foothills of a lofty mountain chain, and a nation of bald men. They are said to be bald from birth, women and men alike, and to have snub noses and long chins; they speak a peculiar language, dress in the Scythian fashion, and live on the fruit of a tree called ponticum—a kind of cherry—which is about the size of a fig-tree and produces a stoned fruit as large as a bean. They strain the ripe fruit through cloths and get from it a thick dark-coloured juice which they call *aschy*. They lap the juice up with their tongues, or mix it with milk for a drink, and make cakes out of the thick sediment which it leaves. They have but few sheep, as the grazing is poor. Every man lives under his ponticum-tree, which he protects in winter with bands of thick white felt, taking them off in the summer. These people are supposed to be protected by a mysterious sort of sanctity; they carry no arms and nobody offers them violence; they settle disputes amongst their neighbours, and anybody who seeks asylum amongst them is left in peace. They are called Argippaei.

As far as the bald men, a great deal is known of the country and of the people to the south and west from the reports, which are easy enough to come by, of Scythians who visit them, and of Greeks who frequent the port on the Dnieper and other ports along the Black Sea coast. The Scythians who penetrate as far as this do their business through interpreters in seven languages. Beyond the Argippaei, however, lies a region of which no one can give an accurate account, for further progress is barred by a lofty and impassable range of mountains. The bald men themselves tell the improbable tale that the mountains are inhabited by a goat-footed race, beyond which, still further north, are men who sleep for six months in the year—which to my mind is utterly incredible. . . .

Having described the natural resources of the country, I will go on to give some account of the people's customs and beliefs. The only gods the Scythians worship are Hestia (their chief deity), Zeus, and Earth (whom they believe to be the wife of Zeus), and, as deities of secondary importance, Apollo, Celestial Aphrodite, Heracles, and Ares. These are recognized by the entire nation; the Royal Scythians also offer sacrifices to Poseidon. . . .

As regards war, the Scythian custom is for every soldier to drink the blood of the first man he kills. The heads of all enemies killed in battle are taken to the king; a head being a sort of ticket by which a soldier is admitted to his share of the loot—no head, no loot. He strips the skin off the head by making a circular cut round the ears and shaking out the skull; he then scrapes the flesh off the skin with the rib of an ox, and when it is clean works it in his fingers until it is supple, and fit to be used as a sort of handkerchief. He hangs these handkerchiefs on the bridle of his horse, and is very proud of them. The finest fellow is the man who has the greatest number. . . .

When the king of Scythia falls sick, he sends for three of the most reputable soothsayers, who proceed to practise their arts in the way I have described; more often than not they declare that such and such a person (whose name they mention) has sworn falsely by the king's hearth—it being customary in Scythia to use this form of oath for the most solemn purposes. The supposed culprit is at once arrested and brought into the king's presence, where he is charged by the soothsayers, who tell him that their powers of divination have revealed that he has sworn by the king's hearth and perjured himself, and that his perjury is the cause of the king's sickness. The man, of course, denies the charge, and makes a great fuss, whereupon the king sends for more soothsayers—six this time instead of three—who also bring their skill to bear. Should they convict the accused of perjury, he is beheaded without more ado, and his property is divided by lot amongst the first three soothsayers; if, however, the next six acquit him, more are brought in, and, if need be, still more again, and if, in the final result, the majority declare for the man's innocence, the law is that the three original ones should be executed. . . .

*   *   *

To Marathon, therefore, Hippia directed the invading army, and the Athenians, as soon as the news arrived, hurried to meet it. . . . It was this Miltiades who was now in command of the Athenian troops. He had recently escaped from the Chersonese and twice nearly lost his life—once when the Phoenicians chased him as far as Imbros in their anxiety to catch him and take him to Darius, and again when, after escaping that danger and getting home to what looked like safety, he found his enemies waiting for him and was prosecuted in the courts for his unconstitutional and despotic government in the Chersonese. But he was not caught this time either, and after the trial was appointed, by popular vote, to the command.

Before they left the city, the Athenian generals sent off a message to Sparta. The messenger was an Athenian named Pheidippides, a trained runner still in the practice of his profession. . . . [H]e reached Sparta the day after he left Athens. At once he delivered his message to the Spartan government. "Men of Sparta" (the message ran) "the Athenians ask you to help them, and not to stand by while the most ancient city of Greece is crushed and enslaved by a foreign invader. Already Eretria is destroyed, and her people in chains, and Greece is the weaker by the loss of one fine city." The Spartans, though moved by the appeal, and willing to send help to Athens, were unable to send it promptly because they did not wish to break their law. It was the ninth day of the month, and they said they could not take the field until the moon was full. So they waited for the full moon, and meanwhile Hippias, the son of Pisistratus, guided the Persians to Marathon. . . .

The Athenian troops were drawn up on a piece of ground sacred to Heracles, when they were joined by the Plataeans, who came to support them with every available man. . . . Amongst the Athenian commanders opinion was divided: some were against risking a battle, on the ground that the Athenian force was too small to stand a chance of success; others—and amongst them Miltiades—urged it. It seemed for a time as if the more faint-hearted policy would be adopted—and so it would have been but for the action of Miltiades. In addition to the ten commanders, there was another person entitled to a vote, namely the polemarch, or War Archon, an official appointed in Athens not by vote but by lot. This office (which formerly carried an equal vote in military decisions with the generals) was held at this time by Callimachus of Aphidne. To Callimachus, therefore, Miltiades turned. "It is now in your hands, Callimachus," he said, "either to enslave Athens, or to make her free and to leave behind you for all future generations a memory more glorious than ever Harmodius and Aristogeiton left. Never in the course of our long history have we Athenians been in such peril as now. If we submit to the Persian invader, Hippias will be restored to power in Athens—and there is little doubt what misery must then ensue; but if we fight and win, then this city of ours may well grow to pre-eminence amongst all the cities of Greece. If you ask me how this can be, and how the decision rests with you, I will tell you: we commanders are ten in number, and we are not agreed upon what action to take; half of us are for a battle, half against it. If we refuse to fight, I have little doubt that the result will be the rise in Athens of bitter political dissension; our purpose will be shaken, and we shall submit to Persia. But if we fight before the rot can show itself in any of us, then, if God gives us fair play, we can not only fight but win. Yours is the decision; all hangs upon you; vote on my side, and our country will be free—yes, and the mistress of Greece. But if you support those who have voted against fighting, that happiness will be denied you—you will get the opposite."

Miltiades' words prevailed. The vote of Callimachus the War Archon was cast on the right side, and the decision to fight was made.

The generals exercised supreme command in succession, each for a day; and those of them who had voted with Miltiades, offered, when their turn for duty came, to surrender to him. Miltiades accepted the offer, but would not fight until the day came when he would in any case have had the supreme command. When it did come, the Athenian army moved into position for the coming struggle. The right wing was commanded by Callimachus—for it was the regular practice at that time in Athens that the War Archon should lead the right wing; then followed the tribes, one after the other, in an unbroken line; and, finally, on the left wing, was the contingent from Plataea. Ever since the battle of Marathon, when the Athenians offer sacrifice at their quadrennial festival, the herald links the names of Athens and Plataea in the prayer for God's blessing.

One result of the disposition of Athenian troops before the battle was the weakening of their centre by the effort to extend the line sufficiently to cover the whole Persian front; the two wings were strong, but the line in the centre was only a few ranks deep. The dispositions made, and the preliminary sacrifice promising success, the word was given to move, and the Athenians advanced at a run towards the enemy, not less than a mile away. The Persians, seeing the attack developing at the double, prepared to meet it confidently enough, for it seemed to them suicidal madness for the Athenians to risk an assault with so small a force—at the double, too, and with no support from either cavalry or archers. Well, that was what they imagined; nevertheless, the Athenians came on, closed with the enemy all along the line, and fought in a way not to be forgotten. They were the first Greeks, so far as I know, to charge at a run, and the first who dared to look without flinching at Persian dress and the men who wore it; for until that day came, no Greek could hear even the word Persian without terror.

The struggle at Marathon was long drawn out. In the centre, held by the Persians themselves and the Sacae, the advantage was with the foreigners, who were so far successful as to break the Greek line and pursue the fugitives inland from the sea; but the Athenians on one wing and the Plataeans on the other were both victorious. Having got the upper hand, they left the defeated Persians to make their escape, and then, drawing the two wings together into a single unit, they turned their attention to the Persians who had broken through in the centre. Here again they were triumphant, chasing the routed enemy, and cutting them down as they ran right to the edge of the sea. Then, plunging into the water, they laid hold of the ships, calling for fire. It was in this phase of the struggle that the War Archon Callimachus was killed, fighting bravely, and also Stesilaus, the son of Thrasylaus, one of the commanders; Cynegirus, too, the son of Euphorion, had his hand cut off with an axe as he was getting hold of a ship's stern, and so lost his life, together with many other well-known Athenians. Nevertheless the Athenians secured in this way seven ships; the rest managed to get off, and the Persians aboard them. . . .

In the battle of Marathon some 6400 Persians were killed; the losses of the Athenians were 192. . . .

*   *   *

Thus it was that the confederate troops, by Leonidas' orders, abandoned their posts and left the pass, all except the Thespians and the Thebans who remained with the Spartans. The Thebans were detained by Leonidas as hostages very much against their will—unlike the loyal Thespians, who refused to desert Leonidas and his men, but stayed, and died with them. They were under the command of Demophilus the son of Diadromes.

In the morning Xerxes poured a libation to the rising sun, and then waited till about the time of the filling of the market-place, when he began to move forward. This was according to Ephialtes' instructions, for the way down from the ridge is much shorter and more direct than the long and circuitous ascent. As the Persian army advanced to the assault, the Greeks under Leonidas, knowing that the fight would be their last, pressed forward into the wider part of the pass much further than they had done before; in the previous days' fighting they had been holding the wall and making sorties from behind it into the narrow neck, but now they left the confined space and battle was joined on more open ground. Many of the invaders fell; behind them the company commanders plied their whips, driving the men remorselessly on. Many fell into the sea and were drowned, and still more were trampled to death by their friends. No one could count the number of the dead. The Greeks, who knew that the enemy were on their way round by the mountain track and that death was inevitable, fought with reckless desperation, exerting every ounce of strength that was in them against the invader. By this time most of their spears were broken, and they were killing Persians with their swords.

In the course of that fight Leonidas fell, having fought like a man indeed. Many distinguished Spartans were killed at his side—their names, like the names of all the three hundred, I have made myself acquainted with, because they deserve to be remembered. Amongst the Persian dead, too, were many men of high distinction—for instance, two brothers of Xerxes, Habrocomes and Hyperanthes, both of them sons of Darius by Artanes' daughter Phratagune.

There was a bitter struggle over the body of Leonidas; four times the Greeks drove the enemy off, and at last by their valour succeeded in dragging it away. So it went on, until the fresh troops with Ephialtes were close at hand; and then, when the Greeks knew that they had come, the character of the fighting changed. They withdrew again into the narrow neck of the pass, behind the walls, and took up a position in a single compact body—all except the Thebans—on a little hill at the entrance to the pass, where the stone lion in memory of Leonidas stands today. Here they resisted to the last, with their swords, if they had them, and, if not, with their hands and teeth, until the Persians, coming on from the front over the ruins of the wall and closing in from behind, finally overwhelmed them.

Of all the Spartans and Thespians who fought so valiantly on that day, the most signal proof of courage was given by the Spartan Dieneces. It is said that before the battle he was told by a native of Trachis that, when the Persians shot their arrows, there were so many of them that they hid the sun. Dieneces, however, quite unmoved by the thought of the terrible strength of the Persian army, merely remarked: "This is pleasant news that the stranger from Trachis brings us: for if the Persians hide the sun, we shall have our battle in the shade." He is said to have left on record other sayings, too, of a similar kind, by which he will be remembered. After Dieneces the greatest distinction was won by the two Spartan brothers, Alpheus and Maron, the sons of Orsiphantus; and of the Thespians the man to gain the highest glory was a certain Dithyrambus, the son of Harmatides.

The dead were buried where they fell, and with them the men who had been killed before those dismissed by Leonidas left the pass. Over them is this inscription, in honour of the whole force:

Four thousand here from Pelops' land
Against three million once did stand.

QUESTIONS TO CONSIDER

1. Herodotus presents both Greek and Persian versions of the conflict that resulted in the battle of Marathon. Why does he do this?
2. Why does Herodotus spend so much time talking about the prophecies of oracles?
3. What does Herodotus' story of the land of the bald-headed people tell us about his view of the role of historical fact?
4. Contrast Herodotus's account of Scythians, whom he knew from the reports of others, with his account of the battle of Marathon, the site of which he had visited.

FOR FURTHER READING

Evans, J. A. S. *Herodotus.* Boston: Twayne, 1982.
Finley, Moses. *Ancient History: Evidence and Models.* London: Chatto and Windus, 1985.
Grant, Michael. *The Ancient Historians.* New York: Scribner's, 1970.
Hunter, Virginia. *Past and Process in Herodotus and Thucydides.* Princeton, NJ: Princeton University Press, 1982.
Lateiner, Donald. *The Historical Method of Herodotus.* Toronto: University of Toronto Press, 1989.
Myres, J. L. *Herodotus, Father of History.* Oxford: Clarendon, 1953.

NOTES

1. Herodotus, *The Persian Wars,* trans. Aubrey de Selincourt (Baltimore: Penguin, 1954), 13–15, 32–33, 50–51, 248–50, 260, 262–63, 492–94.

CHAPTER 9

Thucydides

Democracy, War, and Politics

Thucydides
The Granger Collection, New York

Herodotus' successor, Thucydides (460?–404? BCE), further developed the art of Greek historical writing and set precedents followed by many historians since. Thucydides' subject was the Peloponnesian War between Athens and Sparta from 431 to 404 BCE. Born into a well-connected Athenian family, Thucydides was well educated and apparently set on a political career. He was old enough to understand the significance of the Peloponnesian War at the beginning and participated on the Athenian side. Elected as one of the ten Athenian military leaders for 424 BCE, a high honor, he was exiled by Athenian citizens disappointed in his failure to hold a strategic city against a Spartan onslaught. His position as an exile gave him opportunity to observe the war from the Spartan side and to travel relatively freely—extremely important for his research on the war. He lived long enough to see Athens defeated and conquered by the Spartans in 404, but not long enough to complete the revision of his text, which ends rather abruptly covering the events of fall 411.

In contrast to Herodotus, Thucydides was writing contemporary history, recording and analyzing events shortly after they occurred. As a result, he revised constantly as later events transformed the meaning and importance of previous ones. Historical analysts have found three stages of composition within the work itself: notes, a chronicle of events stage, and the final polished version. Thucydides used a rigid chronology based on the military campaign season (Greeks traditionally fought only in the summer dry season). The style is compressed and tight and in some ways defies translation. At the same time, Thucydides was highly analytical in his narrative, much less of the pure storyteller than Herodotus. The beauty of Thucydides' work lies in the clarity and brilliance of his analysis. In contrast to Herodotus, Thucydides gave us only his conclusions, not the sources of alternatives for his analysis. As a result, his view of the Peloponnesian War is the major one that has survived. On the other hand, wherever archaeological and other materials have surfaced, Thucydides' efforts have largely been borne out as accurate.

Thucydides' theme focused on the inevitability of the conflict between powerful, conservative, land-based Sparta and up-and-coming, sea-based, radical Athens. Thucydides everywhere portrayed the Athenians as dashing, innovative, and sometimes brilliant, and the Spartans as stodgy, plodding, and crafty. Yet the Spartans won the war because of the over-confidence and fickleness of the democratic Athenian mobs.

Thucydides influenced later Western historians by laying out his assumptions and historical methods early in the narrative (he eschewed supernatural explanations, for example). In a pattern used by historians of many traditions, he first criticized his predecessors for accepting mythological explanations or for pandering to the public with good stories. Then he explained why his work was needed to provide a more accurate account. He frequently cited as evidence his own personal observations of things or the accounts of eyewitnesses. He acknowledged that the speeches he records were not verbatim but reconstructed from his own and others' memories. Yet, since many of his audience would have heard the original speeches, we should assume he could not alter significantly their thrust.

The first piece that follows is Thucydides' statement about the purpose of history. The second records the events near Corcyra—an island off the west coast of Greece—that triggered the war, a fine piece of military and diplomatic reporting. The third segment describes the still-unknown disease that erupted in Athens in 429 BCE, killing one third of the population and changing the course of the war.

History of the Peloponnesian War[1]

In investigating past history, and informing the conclusion which I have formed, it must be admitted that one cannot rely on every detail which has come down to us by way of tradition. People are inclined to accept all stories of ancient times in an uncritical way—even when these stories concern their own native countries. Most people in Athens, for instance, are under the impression that Hipparchus, who was killed by Harmodius and Aristogeiton, was tyrant at the time, not realizing that it was Hippas who was the eldest and the chief of the sons of Pisistratus, and that Hipparchus and Thessalus were his younger brothers. What happened was this: on the very day that had been fixed for their attempt indeed at the very last moment, Harmodius and Aristogeiton had reason to believe that Hippias had been informed of the plot by some of the conspirators. Believing him to have been forewarned, they kept away from him, but, as they wanted to perform some daring exploit before they were arrested themselves, they killed Hipparchus when they found him by the Leocorium organizing the Panathenaic procession.

The rest of the Hellenes, too, make many incorrect assumptions not only about the dimly remembered past, but also about contemporary history. For instance there is a general belief that the kings of Sparta are each entitled to two votes, whereas in fact they have only one; and it is believed, too, that the Spartans have a company of troops called 'Pitane.' Such a company has never existed. Most people, in fact, will not take trouble in finding out the truth, but are much more inclined to accept the first story they hear.

However, I do not think that one will be far wrong in accepting the conclusions I have reached from the evidence which I have put forward. It is better evidence than that of the poets, who exaggerate the importance of their themes, or of the prose chroniclers, who are less interested in telling the truth than in catching the attention of their public, whose authorities cannot be checked, and whose subject-matter, owing to the passage of time, is mostly lost in the unreliable streams of mythology. We may claim instead to have used only the plainest evidence and to have reached conclusions which are reasonably accurate, considering that we have been dealing with ancient history. As for this present war, even though people are apt to think that the war in which they are fighting is the greatest of all wars and, when it is over, to relapse again into themselves, one will see that this was the greatest war of all.

In this history I have made use of set speeches some of which were delivered just before and others during the war. I have found it difficult to remember the precise words used in the speeches which I listened to myself and my various informants have experienced the same difficulty; so my method has been, while keeping as closely as possible to the general sense of the words that were actually used, to make the speakers say what, in my opinion, was called for by each situation.

And with regard to my factual reporting of the events of the war I have made it a principle not to write down the first story that came my way, and not even to be guided by my own general impressions; either I was present myself at the events which I have described or else I heard of them from eye-witnesses whose reports I have checked with as much thoroughness as possible. Not that even so the truth was easy to discover: different eye-witnesses give different accounts of the same events, speaking out of partiality for one side or the other or else from imperfect memories. And it may well be that my history will seem less easy to read because of the absence in it of a romantic element. It will be enough for me, however, if these words of mine are judged useful by those who want to understand clearly the events which happened in the past and which (human nature being what it is) will, at some time or other and in much the same ways, be repeated in the future. My work is not a piece of writing designed to meet the taste of an immediate public, but was done to last forever.

The Dispute Over Corcyra

In Corinth tempers were running high over the war with Corcyra. All through the year following the sea battle and in the year after that the Corinthians were building ships and doing everything possible to increase the efficiency of their navy. Rowers were collected from the Peloponnese itself, and good terms were offered to bring them also from the rest of Hellas.

In Corcyra the news of the preparations provoked alarm. They had no allies in Hellas, since they had not enrolled themselves either in the Spartan or in the Athenian league. They decided, therefore, to go to Athens, to join the Athenian alliance, and see whether they could get any support from that quarter.

When the news of this move reached Corinth, the Corinthians also sent representatives to Athens, fearing that the combined strength of the navies of Athens and Corcyra would prevent them from having their own way in the war with Corcyra. An assembly was held and the arguments on both sides were put forward. The representatives of Corcyra spoke as follows:

"Athenians, in a situation like this, it is right and proper that first of all certain points should be made clear. We have come to ask you for help, but cannot claim that this help is due to us because of any great services we have done to you in the past or on the basis of any existing alliance. We must therefore convince you first that by giving us this help you will be acting in your own interests, or certainly not against your own interests; and then we must show that our gratitude can be depended upon. If on all these points you find our arguments unconvincing, we must not be surprised if our mission ends in failure.

"Now Corcyra has sent us to you in the conviction that in asking for your alliance we can also satisfy you on these points. What has happened is that our policy in the past appears to have been against our own present interests, and at the same time makes it look inconsistent of us to be asking help from you. It certainly looks inconsistent to be coming here to ask for help when in the past we have deliberately avoided all alliances; and it is because of this very policy that we are now left entirely alone to face a war with Corinth. We used to think that our neutrality was a wise thing, since it prevents us being dragged into danger by other people's policies; now we see it clearly as a lack of foresight and as a source of weakness.

"It is certainly true that in the recent naval battle we defeated the Corinthians single-handed. But now they are coming against us with a much greater force drawn from the Peloponnese and from the rest of Hellas. We recognize that, if we have nothing but our own national resources, it is impossible for us to survive, and we can imagine what lies in store for us if they overpower us. We are therefore forced to ask for assistance, both from you and from everyone else; and it should not be held against us that now we have faced the facts and are reversing our old policy of keeping ourselves to ourselves. There is nothing sinister in our action; we merely recognize that we made a mistake.

"If you grant our request, you will find that in many ways it was a good thing that we made it at this particular time. First of all, you will not be helping aggressors, but people who are the victims of aggression. Secondly, we are now in extreme peril, and if you welcome our alliance at this moment you will win our undying gratitude. And then, we are, after you, the greatest naval power in Hellas. You would have paid a lot of money and still have been very grateful to have us on your side. Is it not, then, an extraordinary stroke of good luck for you (and one which will cause heartburning among your enemies) to have us coming over voluntarily into your camp, giving ourselves up to you without involving you in any dangers or any expense? It is a situation where we, whom you are helping, will be grateful to you, the world in general will admire you for your generosity, and you yourselves will be stronger than you were before. There is scarcely a case in history where all these advantages have been available at the same time, nor has it often happened before that a power looking for an alliance can say to those whose help it asks that it can give as much honour and as much security as it will receive.

* * *

"The whole thing can be put very shortly, and these few words will give you the gist of the whole argument why you should not abandon us. There are three considerable naval powers in Hellas—Athens, Corcyra, and Corinth. If Corinth gets control of us first and you allow our navy to be united with hers, you will have to fight against the combined fleets of Corcyra and the Peloponnese. But if you receive us into your alliance, you will enter upon the war with our ships as well as your own."

After this speech from the Corcyraean side, the representative of Corinth spoke as follows: "These Corcyraeans have not confined their argument to the question of whether or not you should accept alliance. They have named us as aggressors and have stated that they are the victims of an unjust war. Before, therefore, we go on to the rest of our argument, we must deal first with these two points. Our aim will be to give you a clear idea of what exactly we are claiming from you, and to show that there are good reasons why you should reject the appeal of Corcyra.

" 'Wisdom' and 'Moderation' are the words used by Corcyra in describing her old policy of avoiding alliances. In fact the motives were entirely evil, and there was nothing good about them at all. She wanted no allies because her actions were wrong, and she was ashamed of calling in others to witness her own misdoings. The geographical situation of Corcyra gives its inhabitants a certain independence. The ships of other states are forced to put in to their harbours much more often than Corcyraean ships visit the harbours of other states. So in cases where a Corcyraean has been guilty of injuring some other national, the Corcyraeans are themselves their own judges, and there is no question of having the case tried by independent judges appointed by treaty. So this neutrality of theirs, which sounds so innocent, was in fact a disguise adopted not to preserve them from having to share in the wrong-doings of others, but in order to give them a perfectly free hand to do wrong themselves, making away with other people's property by force, when they are strong enough, cheating them, whenever they can manage to do so, and enjoying their gains without any vestige of shame. Yet if they really were the honourable people they pretend to be, this very independence of theirs would have given them the best possible opportunity of showing their good qualities in the relations of common justice.

"In fact they have not acted honourably either towards us or towards anyone else. Though they are colonists of ours, they have never been loyal to us and are now at war with us. They were not sent out in the first place, they say, to be ill treated. And we say that we did not found colonies in order to be insulted by them, but rather to retain our leadership and to be treated with proper respect. At all events our other colonies do respect us, and indeed they treat us with affection. It is obvious then, that if the majority are pleased with us, Corcyra can have no good reason for being the only one that is dissatisfied; and that we are not making war unreasonably, but only as the result of exceptional provocation. Even if we were making a mistake, the right thing would be for them to give in to us, and then it would be a disgrace to us if we failed to respect so reasonable an attitude. As it is, their arrogance and the confidence they feel in their wealth have made them act improperly towards us on numerous occasions, and in particular with regard to Epidamnus, which belongs to us. When this place was in distress, they took no steps towards bringing it under their control; but as soon as we came to relieve it, they forcibly took possession of it, and still hold it.

                                    *   *   *

"The right course, surely, is either for you to preserve a strict neutrality or else to join us against them. . . .

                                    *   *   *

". . . No, you should deal with us as we have dealt with you, and you should be conscious that we are in one of those critical situations where real friendship is to be gained from helping us and real hostility from opposing us. Do not go against us by receiving these Corcyraeans into your alliance. Do not aid and abet them in their crimes. Thus you will be acting as you ought to act and at the same time you will be making the wisest decision in your own interests."

This was the speech of the Corinthian delegation. The Athenians, after listening to both sides, discussed the matter at two assemblies. At the first of these, opinion seemed to incline in favour of the Corinthian arguments, but at the second there was a change, and they decided on entering into some kind of alliance with Corcyra. This was not to be a total alliance involving the two parties in any war which either of them might have on hand; for the Athenians realized that if Corcyra required them to join in an attack on Corinth, that would constitute a breach of their treaty with the Peloponnese. Instead the alliance was to be of a defensive character and would only operate if Athens or Corcyra or any of their allies were attacked from outside.

The general belief was that, whatever happened, war with the Peloponnese was bound to come. Athens had no wish to see the strong navy of Corcyra pass into the hands of Corinth. At the same time she was not averse from letting the two Powers weaken each other by fighting together; since in this way, if war did come, Athens herself would be stronger in relation to Corinth and to the other naval Powers. Then, too, it was a fact that Corcyra lay very conveniently on the coastal route to Italy and Sicily.

So, with these considerations in mind, Athens made her alliance with Corcyra. The Corinthian representatives returned to Corinth, and soon afterwards Athens sent ten ships as a reinforcement to Corcyra.

* * *

Then, after the signals had been hoisted on both sides, they joined battle. The fighting was of a somewhat old-fashioned kind, since they were still behindhand in naval matters, both sides having numbers of hoplites aboard their ships, together with archers and javelin throwers. But the fighting was hard enough in spite of the lack of skill shown: indeed, it was more like a battle on land than a naval engagement. When the ships came into collision it was difficult for them to break away clear, because of the number engaged and of their close formation. In fact both sides relied more for victory on their hoplites, who were on the decks and who fought a regular pitched battle there while the ships remained motionless. No one attempted the manoeuvre of encirclement; in fact it was a battle where courage and sheer strength played a greater part than scientific methods. Everywhere in the battle confusion reigned, and there was shouting on all sides.

The Athenian ships would come up in support of the Corcyraeans whenever they were hard pressed and would so help to alarm their enemies, but they did not openly join the battle, since the commanders were afraid of acting contrary to the instructions they had received at Athens.

* * *

The reasons that each side had for claiming the victory and setting up a trophy were as follows. The Corinthians had had the upper hand in the fighting until night fall: thus they had brought in most of the disabled ships and their own dead: they held at least 1,000 prisoners and they had sunk about seventy enemy ships. The Corcyraeans had destroyed about thirty ships and, after the arrival of the Athenians, they had recovered off their coast their own dead and their disabled vessels. Then on the day after the battle the Corinthians, on seeing the Athenians had arrived, had not come out from Sybota to fight. So both sides claimed the victory.

On their voyage home the Corinthians took Anactorium, at the mouth of the Ambracian Gulf. It was a place in which both Corinth and Corcyra had rights and it was given up to the Corinthians by treachery. Before sailing home the Corinthians put settlers of their own into Anactorium. They sold 800 of the Corcyraean prisoners who were slaves, and they kept in captivity 250 whom they treated with great consideration hoping that a time would come when they would return and win over the island of Corinth. Most of them were in fact people of great power and influence in Corcyra.

So Corcyra remained undefeated in her war with Corinth and the Athenian fleet left the island. But this gave Corinth her first cause for war against Athens, the reason being that Athens had fought against her with Corcyra although the peace treaty was still in force.

The Plague

. . . They had not been many days in Attica before the plague first broke out among the Athenians. Previously attacks of the plague had been reported from many other places in the neighbourhood of Lemnos and elsewhere, but there was no record of the disease being so virulent anywhere else or causing so many deaths as it did in Athens. At the beginning the doctors were quite incapable of treating the disease because of their ignorance of the right methods. In fact mortality among the doctors was the highest of all, since they came more frequently in contact with the sick. Nor was any other human art or science of any help at all. Equally useless were prayers made in the temples, consultation of oracles, and so forth; indeed, in the end people were so overcome by their sufferings that they paid no further attention to such things.

The plague originated, so they say, in Ethiopia in upper Egypt, and spread from there into Egypt itself and Libya and much of the territory of the King of Persia. In the city of Athens it appeared suddenly, and the first cases were among the population of Piraeus, where there were no wells at that time, so that it was supposed by them that the Peloponnesians had poisoned the reservoirs. Later, however, it appeared also in the upper city, and by this time the deaths were greatly increasing in number. As to the question of how it could first have come about or what causes can be found adequate to explain its powerful effect on nature, I must leave that to be considered by other writers, with or without medical experience. I myself shall merely describe what it was like and set down symptoms, knowledge of which will enable it to be recognized, if it should ever break out again. I had the disease myself and saw others suffering from it.

That year, as is generally admitted, was particularly free from all other kinds of illness, though those who did have any illness previously all caught the plague in the end. In other cases, however, there seemed to be no reason for the attacks. People in perfect health suddenly began to have burning feelings in the head; their eyes became red and inflamed; inside their mouths there was bleeding in the throat and tongue, and the breath became unnatural and unpleasant. The next symptoms were sneezing and horseness of voice, and before long the pain settled on the chest and was accompanied by coughing. Next the stomach was affected with stomach-aches and with vomitings of every kind of bile that has been given a name by the medical profession, all this being accompanied by great pain and difficulty. In most cases there were attacks of ineffectual retching, producing violent spasms; and sometimes ended with this stage of the disease, but sometimes continued long afterwards. Externally the body was not very hot to the touch, nor was there any pallor: the skin was rather reddish and livid, breaking out into small pustules and ulcers. But inside there was a feeling of burning, so that people could not bear the touch even of the lightest linen clothing, but wanted to be completely naked, and indeed most of all would have liked to plunge into cold water. Many of the sick who were uncared for actually did so, plunging into the water-tanks in an effort to relieve a thirst which was unquenchable; for it was just the same with them whether they drank much or little. Then all the time they were afflicted with insomnia and the desperate feeling of not being able to keep still.

In the period when the disease was at its height, the body, so far from wasting away, showed surprising powers of resistance to all the agony, so that there was still some strength left on the seventh or eighth day, which was the time when, in most cases, death came from the internal fever. But if people survived this critical period, then the disease descended to the bowels, producing violent ulceration and uncontrollable diarrhoea, so that most of them died later as a result of the weakness caused by this. For the disease, first settling in the head, went on to affect every part of the body in turn, and even when people escaped its worst effects, it still left its traces on them by fastening upon the extremities of the body. It affected the genitals, the fingers, and the toes, and many of those who recovered lost the use of these members; some, too, went blind. There were some also who, when they first began to get better, suffered from a total loss of memory, not knowing who they were themselves and being unable to recognize their friends.

Words indeed fail one when one tries to give a general picture of this disease; and as for the sufferings of individuals, they seemed almost beyond the capacity of human nature to endure. Here in particular is a point where this plague showed itself to be something quite different from ordinary disease: though there were many dead bodies lying about unburied, the birds and animals that eat human flesh either did not come near them or, if they did eat the flesh, died of it afterwards. Evidence for this may be found in the fact there was a complete disappearance of all kinds of prey: they were not to be seen either round the bodies or any where else. But dogs, being domestic animals, provided the first opportunity of observing this effect of the plague.

. . . The most terrible thing of all was the despair into which people fell when they realized that they had caught the plague; for they would immediately adopt an attitude of utter hopelessness and by giving in this way, would lose their powers of resistance. Terrible, too, was the sight of people dying like sheep through having caught the disease as a result of nursing others. This indeed caused more deaths than anything else. For when people were afraid to visit the sick, then they died with no one to look after them; indeed, there were many houses in which all the inhabitants perished through lack of any attention. When, on the other hand they did visit the sick, they lost their own lives, and this was particularly true of those who made it a point of honour to act properly. Such people felt ashamed to think of their own safety and went into their friends' houses at times when even the members of the household were so overwhelmed by the weight of their calamities that they had actually given up the usual practice of making laments for the dead. Yet still the ones who felt most pity for the sick and the dying were those who had had the plague themselves and had recovered from it. They knew what it was like and at the same time felt themselves to be safe, for no one caught the disease twice, or, if he did, the second attack was not fatal. Such people were congratulated on all sides, and they themselves were so elated at the time of their recovery that they first imagined that they could never die of any other disease in the future.

QUESTIONS TO CONSIDER

1. How does Thucydides' vision of history differ from that of Herodotus (Chapter 8)?
2. Thucydides consistently puts words in the mouths of his characters. Does this make his history more or less accurate?
3. Modern physicians are able to recognize no disease that displays the symptoms that Thucydides describes during the plague at Athens. Should we assume, therefore, that Thucydides was mistaken in his description?

FOR FURTHER READING

Adcock, F. E. *Thucydides and His History.* Hamden, CT: Archon Books, 1973.
Cogan, Marc. *The Human Thing: The Speeches and Principles of Thucydides' History.* Chicago: University of Chicago Press, 1981.
Connor, W. Robert. *Thucydides.* Princeton, NJ: Princeton University Press, 1984.
Finley, J. H. *Thucydides.* Cambridge, MA: Harvard University Press, 1942.
Gomme, A. W., et al. *A Historical Commentary on Thucydides.* 5 vols. Oxford: Clarendon Press, 1945–1981.
Hornblower, Simon. *Thucydides.* Baltimore: Johns Hopkins University Press, 1987.
_____ . *A Commentary on Thucydides.* Vol. 1. Oxford: Oxford University Press, 1991.
Proctor, Dennis. *The Experience of Thucydides.* Warminster, U. K.: Aris and Phillips, 1980.
Rawlings, Hunter R. *The Structure of Thucydides' History.* Princeton, NJ: Princeton University Press, 1981.

NOTES

1. Thucydides, *History of the Peloponnesian War,* trans. Rex Warner (Harmondsworth, U.K.: Penguin, 1954), 23–25, 30–31, 33–40, 43, 123–126.

CHAPTER 10

Sima Tan and Sima Qian

Founding the Chinese Historical Tradition

Emperor Wu
Museum of Fine Arts Boston

wo great family projects undertaken during the Han dynasties set the standard for Chinese historical writing for nearly two thousand years. The first of these was the *Shi zhi,* or *Records of the Historian,* by Sima Tan and Sima Qian. The Chinese have been an unusually historically minded people for millenia. The earliest Chinese dynasties—Xia, Shang, and Zhou, stretching back past 1800 BCE—employed their own court historians and prized the historians' task. Those early historians' duties verged on the sacramental, as they shaded over into astronomy and divination. Historians were the tutors and counselors of emperors.

Sima Tan (d. 110 BCE) was appointed Grand Historian by the Han Emperor Wu, shortly after the emperor's assumption of the throne in 141 BCE. Like earlier court historians, Sima Tan seems to have devoted himself to his tutorial, advisory, and ritual functions. But he also began to collect materials for a history of China and its neighbors from the beginning of memory down to his own time. When Sima Tan died, the Emperor Wu appointed his son, Sima Qian (145–c.90 BCE), to the post of Grand Historian, with a dying charge from his father to continue the work. Twenty-seven years later, Sima Qian completed the task.

The *Shi zhi* comprises 130 chapters on the history of China and of all the surrounding peoples of which China had knowledge, from the earliest times to the late second century BCE. The Simas divided their account not chronologically or geographically, but in thematic sections that became the standard for Chinese histories: "Basic Annals," one on each of the dynasties, and one on each ruler within the Han dynasty; "Chronological Tables" that listed important events and their dates; "Treatises" on subjects such as astronomy, religion, and economics; "Hereditary Houses," which described certain ancient feudal states; and—the largest section—"Biographies" of famous people.

The Simas' purpose was didactic: to show examples of moral individuals, especially rulers, for others to emulate. Unlike earlier Chinese writers, they expressed little interest in the supernatural, and much interest in the lives and characters of individuals. In these aspects they resembled the great historians of ancient Greece and Rome, Herodotus, Thucydides, and Tacitus. They resembled the Mediterraneans, too, in that they freely created speeches and put them in their characters' mouths, in order to describe and comment on events and personalities. With the Simas, even more than with the Greeks and Romans, the narrative was carried by speech and action, without much intrusion by a narrator. The Simas told great stories of the Chinese ruling class from earliest times down to the middle of the Han dynasty.

The Han dynasty was not one dynasty but two: the Former Han, lasting from 202 BCE to 9 CE, and the Later Han, from 25 to 220 CE. The Former Han dynasty, during which the Sima family wrote, set the pattern for Chinese government and society. It was the Former Han that expanded China to something like its modern geographical limits; that adopted Confucianism as the official orthodoxy; that designed a government of scholar-bureaucrats trained in the Confucian classics and selected by standardized tests; that created countless other features of social life that came to be standard for two millenia. The Former Han dynasty was so important that the new dynasty that came to power in 25 CE called itself the Later Han. It was so important that Chinese people from the second century BCE to this day have referred to themselves as "Han people." It was the Former Han court that hired the people—the Sima family—who wrote the first formal Chinese history.

The selections reproduced here show two of the types of writing that the Simas made standard in the Chinese historical tradition: biography and annals. The first, "The Biography of Po Yi and Shu Ch'i," sets forth the Simas' ideas on the historian's role and their thoughts on historical reliability, even as they tell a story of exemplary men—one of their passionate themes. The second is an excerpt from "The Basic Annals of Emperor Kao-tsu." It tells of the origins of the man who rose to found the Former Han Dynasty.

Records of the Historian[1]

The Biography of Po Yi and Shu Ch'i

While a degenerate age scrambled for profit, they alone hastened to righteousness, relinquishing a state, starving to death, and for this the whole world praised them. Thus I made The Biography of Po Yi and Shu Ch'i.

Although in the world of learning there exist a large number and variety of books and records, their reliability must always be examined in the light of the Six Classics [*Annalects, Book of History,* etc.]. In spite of deficiencies in the *Odes* [*Annalects*] and *Documents* [*Book of History*], we can nevertheless know something about the culture of the times of Emperor Shun and the Hsia dynasty. When, for instance, Emperor Yao wished to retire from his position, he yielded the throne to Shun, and Shun in turn yielded it to Yü. But in each case the high court officials first unanimously recommended these men for the position and they were given the throne for a period of trial. Only after they had discharged the duties of the imperial office for twenty or thirty years, and their merit and ability had become manifest, was the rule finally ceded to them. This proves that the empire is a precious vessel, its ruler part of a great line of succession, and that its transmission is a matter of extreme gravity. Yet there are theorists who say that Yao tried to yield the empire to Hsü Yu and that Hsü Yu was ashamed and would not accept it but instead fled into hiding. Again, for the time of the Hsia dynasty we have similar stories of men called Pien Sui and Wu Kuang. Where do people get stories like this?

The Grand Historian remarks: When I ascended Mount Chi I found at the top what is said to be the grave of Hsü Yu. Confucius, we know, eulogizes the ancient sages and men of wisdom and virtue, and quite specifically mentions such figures as T'ai-po of Wu and Po Yi. Now I am told that Hsü Yu and Wu Kuang were men of the highest virtue, and yet in the Classics there appears not the slightest reference to them. Why would this be?

Confucius said, "Po Yi and Shu Ch'i never bore old ills in mind and hence seldom had any feelings of rancor." "They sought to act virtuously and they did so; what was there for them to feel rancor about?"

I am greatly moved by the determination of Po Yi. But when I examine the song that has been attributed to him, I find it very strange.

The story of these men states that Po Yi and Shu Ch'i were elder and younger sons of the ruler of Ku-chu. Their father wished to set up Shu Ch'i as his heir but, when he died, Shu Ch'i yielded in favor of his elder brother Po Yi. Po Yi replied that it had been their father's wish that Shu Ch'i should inherit the throne and so he departed from the state. Shu Ch'i likewise, being unwilling to accept the rule, went away and the people of the state set up a middle brother as ruler. At this time Po Yi and Shu Ch'i heard that Ch'ang, the Chief of the West, was good at looking after old people, and they said, "Why not go and follow him?" But when they had gone they found that the Chief of the West was dead and his son, King Wu, had taken up the ancestral tablet of his father, whom he honored with the posthumous title of King Wen, and was marching east to attack the emperor of the Yin dynasty. Po Yi and Shu Ch'i clutched the reins of King Wu's horse and reprimanded him, saying, "The mourning for your father not yet completed and here you take up shield and spear—can this conduct be called filial? As a subject you seek to assassinate your sovereign—can this conduct be called humane?" The king's attendants wished to strike them down, but the king's counselor, T'ai-kung, interposed, saying, "These are righteous men," and he sent them away unharmed.

After this, King Wu conquered and pacified the people of the Yin and the world honored the house of Chou as its ruler. But Po Yi and Shu Ch'i were filled with outrage and considered it unrighteous to eat the grain of Chou. They fled and hid on Shou-yang Mountain, where they tried to live by gathering ferns to eat. When they were on the point of starvation, they composed a song:

> We climb this western hill
> and pick its ferns;
> replacing violence with violence,
> he will not see his own fault.
> Shen Nung, Yü, and Hsia,
> great men gone so long ago—
> whom shall we turn to now?
> Ah—let us be off,
> for our fate has run out!

They died of starvation on Shou-yang Mountain. When we examine this song, do we find any rancor or not?

Some people say, "It is Heaven's way to have no favorites but always to be on the side of the good man." Can we say then that Po Yi and Shu Ch'i were good men or not? They piled up a record for goodness and were pure in deed, as we have seen, and yet they starved to death.

Of his seventy disciples, Confucius singled out Yen Hui for praise because of his diligence in learning, yet Yen Hui was often in want, never getting his fill of even the poorest food, and in the end he suffered an untimely death. Is this the way Heaven rewards the good man?

Robber Chih day after day killed innocent men, making mincemeat of their flesh. Cruel and willful, he gathered a band of several thousand followers who went about terrorizing the world, but in the end he lived to a ripe old age. For what virtue did he deserve this?

These are only the most obvious and striking examples. Even in more recent times we see that men whose conduct departs from what is prescribed and who do nothing but violate the taboos and prohibitions enjoy luxury and wealth to the end of their lives, and hand them on to their heirs for generations without end. And there are others who carefully choose the spot where they will place each footstep, who "Speak out only when it is time to speak," who "walk no bypaths" and expend no anger on what is not upright and just, and yet, in numbers too great to be reckoned, they meet with misfortune and disaster. I find myself in much perplexity. Is this so-called Way of Heaven right or wrong?

Confucius said, "Those whose ways are different cannot lay plans for one another." Each will follow his own will. Therefore he said, "If the search for riches and honor were sure to be successful, though I should become a groom with whip in hand to get them, I would do so. But as the search might not be successful, I will follow after that which I love." "When the year becomes cold, then we know that the pine and cypress are the last to lose their leaves." When the whole world is in muddy confusion, then is the man of true purity seen. Then must one judge what he will consider important and what unimportant.

"The superior man hates the thought of his name not being mentioned after his death." As Chia Yi has said:

> The covetous run after riches,
> the impassioned pursue a fair name;
> the proud die struggling for power,
> and the people long only to live.

Things of the same light illumine each other; things of the same class seek each other out. Clouds pursue the dragon; the wind follows the tiger. The sage arises and all creation becomes clear.

Po Yi and Shu Ch'i, although they were men of great virtue, became, through Confucius, even more illustrious in fame. Though Yen Hui was diligent in learning, like a fly riding the tail of a swift horse, his attachment to Confucius made his deeds renowned. The hermit-scholars hiding away in their caves may be ever so correct in their givings and takings, and yet the names of them and their kind are lost and forgotten without receiving a word of praise. Is this not pitiful? Men of humble origin living in the narrow lanes strive to make perfect their actions and to establish a name for themselves, but if they do not somehow attach themselves to a great man, a "man of the blue clouds," how can they hope that their fame will be handed down to posterity?

The Basic Annals of Emperor Kao-tsu

Hsiang Yü was violent and tyrannical, while the king of Han practiced goodness and virtue. In anger he marched forth from Shu and Han, returning to conquer the three kingdoms of Ch'in. He executed Hsiang Yü and became an emperor, and all the world was brought to peace. He changed the statutes and reformed the ways of the people. Thus I made The Basic Annals of Emperor Kao-tsu.

Kao-tsu was a native of the community of Chung-yang in the city of Feng, the district of P'ei. His family name was Liu and his polite name Chi. His father was known as the "Venerable Sire" and his mother was "Dame Liu."

Before he was born, Dame Liu was one day resting on the bank of a large pond when she dreamed that she encountered a god. At this time the sky grew dark and was filled with thunder and lightning. When Kao-tsu's father went to look for her, he saw a scaly dragon over the place where she was lying. After this she became pregnant and gave birth to Kao-tsu.

Kao-tsu had a prominent nose and a dragonlike face, with beautiful whiskers on his chin and cheeks; on his left thigh he had seventy-two black moles. He was kind and affectionate with others, liked to help people, and was very understanding. He always had great ideas and paid little attention to the business the rest of his family was engaged in.

When he grew up he took the examination to become an official and was made village head of Ssu River. He treated all the other officials in the office with familiarity and disdain. He was fond of wine and women and often used to go to Dame Wang's or old lady Wu's and drink on credit. When he got drunk and lay down to sleep, the old women, to their great wonder, would always see something like a dragon over the place where he was sleeping. Also, whenever he would drink and stay at their shops, they would sell several times as much wine as usual. Because of these strange happenings, when the end of the year came around the old women would always destroy Kao-tsu's credit slips and clear his account.

Kao-tsu was once sent on *corvée* labor to the capital city of Ysien-yang and happened to have an opportunity to see the First Emperor of Ch'in. When he saw him he sighed and said, "Ah, this is the way a great man should be."

There was a man of Shan-fu, one Master Lü, who was a friend of the magistrate of P'ei. In order to avoid the consequences of a feud, he accepted the hospitality of the magistrate and made his home in P'ei. When the officials and the wealthy and influential people of P'ei heard that the magistrate had a distinguished guest, they all came to pay their respects. Hsiao Ho, being the director of officials, was in charge of gifts and informed those who came to call that anyone bringing a gift of less than one thousand cash would be seated below the main hall. Kao-tsu, who as a village head was in the habit of treating the other officials with contempt, falsely wrote on his calling card: "With respects—ten thousand cash," though in fact he did not have a single cash. When his card was sent in, Master Lü was very surprised and got up and came to the gate to greet him. Master Lü was very good at reading people's faces and when he saw Kao-tsu's features he treated him with great honor and respect and led him in to a seat. "Liu Chi," remarked Hsiao Ho, "does a good deal of fine talking, but so far has accomplished very little." But Kao-tsu, disdaining the other guests, proceeded to take a seat of honor without further ado.

When the drinking was nearly over, Master Lü glanced at Kao-tsu in such a way as to indicate that he should stay a while longer, and so Kao-tsu dawdled over his wine. "Since my youth," said Master Lü, "I have been fond of reading faces. I have read many faces, but none with signs like yours. You must take good care of yourself, I beg you. I have a daughter whom I hope you will do me the honor of accepting as your wife."

When the party was over, Dame Lü was very angry with her husband. "You have always idolized this girl and planned to marry her to some person of distinction," she said. "The magistrate of P'ei is a friend of yours and has asked for her, but you would not give your consent. How can you be so insane as to give her to Liu Chi?"

"This is not the sort of thing women and children can understand!" replied Master Lü. Eventually he married the girl to Kao-tsu, and it was this daughter of Master Lü who became Empress Lü and gave birth to Emperor Hui and Princess Yüan of Lu.

When Kao-tsu was acting as village head he once asked for leave to go home and visit his fields. Empress Lü at the time was in the fields weeding with her two children. When an old man passed by and asked for something to drink, Empress Lü accordingly gave him some food. The old man examined her face and said, "Madam will become the most honored woman in the world." She asked him to examine her children. Looking at her son, he said, "It is because of this boy that madam will obtain honor," and when he examined the girl, he said that she too would be honored.

After the old man had gone on, Kao-tsu happened to appear from an outhouse nearby. Empress Lü told him all about how the traveler had passed by and, examining her and her children, had predicted great honor for all of them. When Kao-tsu inquired where the man was, she replied, "He cannot have gone very far away!"

Kao-tsu ran after the old man and, overtaking him, questioned him. "The lady and the little children I examined a while ago," he replied, "all resemble you. But when I examine your face, I find such worth that I cannot express it in words!"

Kao-tsu thanked him, saying, "If it is really as you say, I will surely not forget your kindness!" But when Kao-tsu finally became honored he could never find out where the old man had gone.

When Kao-tsu was acting as village head, he fashioned a kind of hat out of sheaths of bamboo and sent his "thief-seeker" [a subordinate official] to the district of Hsieh to have some made up for him, which he wore from time to time. Even after he became famous he continued to wear these hats. These are the so-called Liu family hats.

As village head Kao-tsu was ordered to escort a group of forced laborers from the district of P'ei to Mount Li. On the way, however, so many of the laborers ran away that Kao-tsu began to suspect that by the time he reached his destination they would all have disappeared. When they had reached a place in the midst of a swamp west of Feng, Kao-tsu halted and began to drink. That night he loosened the bonds of the laborers he was escorting and freed them, saying, "Go, all of you! I too shall go my own way from here."

Among the laborers were ten or so brave men who asked to go with him. Kao-tsu, full of wine, led the men in the night along a path through the swamp, sending one of them to walk ahead. The man who had gone ahead returned and reported, "There is a great snake lying across the path ahead. I beg you to turn back!"

"Where a brave man marches what is there to fear?" replied Kao-tsu drunkenly and, advancing, drew his sword and slashed at the snake. After he had cut the snake in two and cleared the path, he walked on a mile or so and then lay down to sleep off his drunkenness.

When one of the men who had lagged behind came to the place where the snake lay, he found an old woman crying in the night. He asked her why she was crying and she answered, "I am crying because someone has killed my son."

"How did your son come to be killed?" he asked.

"My son was the son of the White Emperor," said the old woman. "He had changed himself into a snake and was lying across the road. Now he has been cut in two by the son of the Red Emperor, and therefore I weep."

The man did not believe the old woman and was about to accuse her of lying, when suddenly she disappeared. When the man caught up with Kao-tsu, he found him already awake and reported what had happened. Kao-tsu was very pleased in his heart and set great store by the incident, while his followers day by day regarded him with greater awe.

QUESTIONS TO CONSIDER

1. What does the frequent reference to the moral qualities of historical figures indicate about the purposes of history as the Sima family wrote it?
2. What is the role of the supernatural in this writing? Does it serve a historical or a moral purpose?
3. What do we learn about the lives of ordinary Chinese people from this account? What do we learn about politics, religion, or other matters?

FOR FURTHER READING

Fang, Achilles. *The Chronicle of the Three Kingdoms (A.D. 220–265).* 2 vols. Cambridge, MA: Harvard University Press, 1962–65.

Giles, H. A. *The Travels of Fa Hsien.* Cambridge, MA: Cambridge University Press, 1923.

Kierman, Frank Algerton. *Ssu-ma Ch'ien's Historiographical Attitude as Reflected in Four Late Warring States Biographies.* Wiesbaden: O. Harrassowitz, 1962.

Li, Dun, trans. *The Civilization of China.* New York: Scribner's, 1975.

Loewe, Michael. *Records of Han Administration.* 2 vols. Cambridge, U.K.: Cambridge University Press, 1967.

Ssu-ma Ch'ien [and Ssu-ma T'an]. *Statesman, Patriot, and General in Ancient China: Three Biographies of the China Dynasty.* Trans. Derk Bodde. New Haven, CT: American Oriental Society, 1940.

————. *Records of the Grand Historian of China.* Trans. Burton Watson. New York: Columbia University Press, 1961.

————. *Records of the Historian: Chapters from the Shih Chi of Ssu-ma Ch'ien.* Trans. Burton Watson. New York: Columbia University Press, 1969.

Watson, Burton. *Ssu-ma Ch'ien: Grand Historian of China.* New York: Columbia University Press, 1958.

NOTES

1. Ssu-ma Ch'ien [and Ssu-ma T'an], *Records of the Historian: Chapters from the Shih Chi of Ssu-ma Ch'ien,* trans. Burton Watson (New York: Columbia University Press, 1969), 11–15, 105–109.

CHAPTER 11

Ban Gu and Ban Zhao

Dynastic Historians

Court Lady of the Han Dynasty
© *Christie's Images, Inc.*

T he other great early Chinese history was also a family project. Ban Biao (3–54 CE) served the Later Han dynasty as Sima Tan had the Former: as historian to the court of the emperor. He inherited the Simas' books and many of their source materials and endeavored to carry their narrative down through the rest of the Former Han dynasty. It is unclear how far Ban Biao got with that project before his death in 54 CE. His son Ban Gu (32–92 CE) succeeded him as court historian and recast the project as a comprehensive history of the Former Han dynasty alone, the *Han shu* or *History of the Former Han Dynasty*. Using both written materials and oral tradition, Ban Gu adopted the thematic structure of the Simas but filled it with different material. Because he focused on a single dynasty, he gave much more detail about the lives of individuals. At the same time, he adopted an almost scientific objectivity, eschewing the passion and personality that the Simas brought to their writing. This set the style for all the succeeding centuries of imperial Chinese historical writing: focused on the doings of notable people, organized by theme rather than chronology, devoted to the purpose of producing moral rulers, realistic in content, detached in tone.

The project was yet unfinished at Ban Gu's death. His younger sister, Ban Zhao (c.45–c.120), completed the *Han shu*. Ban Zhao was the foremost woman of Chinese letters from her time to the twentieth century. The extent of her contribution to the *Han shu* is unclear. She may have simply added a few mechanically written chronologies, or she may have edited the entire manuscript and produced several chapters of her own. Since the largest section of the *Han shu* is devoted to biographies, and since (unlike other dynastic histories) many of the subjects are women sympathetically portrayed, one may suppose that Ban Zhao's contribution was substantial. The selections that follow, from Chapter 97, "Accounts of the Families Related to the Emperors by Marriage," show vividly the lives and careers of court women in ancient China. Chinese people drew moral lessons from these stories, and poets recounted their personalities and echoed their themes throughout the rest of Chinese history.

History of the Former Han Dynasty[1]

Madam Li, Concubine of Emperor Wu

Madam Li, a concubine of Emperor Wu the filial, originally entered service in the palace as an entertainer. Her elder brother Li Yen-nien, who had an innate understanding of music, was skilled at singing and dancing and Emperor Wu took a great liking to him. Whenever he presented some new song or musical composition, there were none among his listeners who were not moved to admiration. Once when he was attending the emperor, he rose from his place to dance and sing this song:

> Beautiful lady in a northern land,
> standing alone, none in the world like her,
> a single glance and she upsets a city,
> a second glance, she upsets the state!
> Not that I don't know she upsets states and cities,
> but one so lovely you'll never find again!

The emperor sighed and said, "Splendid!—but I doubt there's anyone that beautiful in the world." The emperor's elder sister Princess P'ing-yang then informed him that Li Yen-nien had a little sister, and he forthwith had her summoned and brought before him. She was in fact strikingly beautiful and skilled at dancing as well, and because of this she won his favor.

She bore him a son, known posthumously as King Ai of Ch'ang-i, but died shortly afterwards at a very young age. The emperor, filled with grief and longing, had a portrait of her painted at the Palace of Sweet Springs. Later, Empress Wei was removed from the position of empress, and four years afterwards, when Emperor Wu passed away, the general in chief Ho Kuang, following what he knew to have been the emperor's wishes, had sacrifices performed to Madam Li in the emperor's mortuary temple as though she had been his official consort, posthumously honoring her with the title "Empress of Emperor Wu the Filial."

Earlier, when Madam Li lay critically ill, the emperor came in person to inquire how she was, but she pulled the covers over her face and, apologizing, said, "I have been sick in bed for a long time and my face is thin and wasted. I cannot let Your Majesty see me, though I hope you will be good enough to look after my son the king and my brothers."

"I know you've been very sick, and the time may come when you never rise again," said the emperor. "Wouldn't you feel better if you saw me once more and asked me face to face to take care of the king and your brothers?"

"A woman should not appear before her lord or her father when her face is not properly made up," she said. "I would not dare let Your Majesty see me in this state of disarray."

"Just let me have one glimpse of you!" said the emperor. "I'll reward you with a thousand pieces of gold and assign your brothers to high office!"

But Madam Li replied, "It is up to Your Majesty to assign offices as you please—it does not depend on one glimpse of me."

When the emperor continued to insist on one last look at her, Madam Li, sobbing, turned her face toward the wall and would not speak again. The emperor rose from his seat in displeasure and left.

Madam Li's sisters berated her, saying, "Why couldn't you let him have one look at you and entreat him face to face to take care of your brother! Why should you anger him like this!"

"The reason I didn't want the emperor to see me," she said, "was so I could make certain he would look after my brothers! It was because he liked my looks that I was able to rise from a lowly position and enjoy the love and favor of the ruler. But if one has been taken into service because of one's beauty, then when beauty fades, love will wane, and when love wanes, kindness will be forgotten. The emperor thinks fondly and tenderly of me because he remembers the way I used to look. Now if he were to see me thin and wasted, with all the old beauty gone from my face, he would be filled with loathing and disgust and would do his best to put me out of his mind. Then what hope would there be that he would ever think kindly of me again and remember to take pity on my brothers?"

When Madam Li died, the emperor had her buried with the honors appropriate to an empress. After that, he enfeoffed her eldest brother Li Kuang-li, the Sutrishna general, as marquis of Hai-hsi, and appointed her brother Li Yen-nien as a chief commandant with the title "Harmonizer of the Tones."

The emperor continued to think longingly of Madam Li and could not forget her. A magician from Ch'i named Shao-weng, announcing that he had the power to summon spirits, one night lit torches, placed curtains around them, and laid out offerings of wine and meat. He then had the emperor take his place behind another curtain and observe the proceedings from a distance. The emperor could see a beautiful lady who resembled Madam Li circling within the curtains, sitting down and then rising to walk again. But he could not move closer to get a good look and, stirred more than ever to thoughts of sadness, he composed this poem:

> Is it she?
> Is it not?
> I stand gazing from afar:
> timid steps, soft and slow,
> how long she is in coming!

He then ordered the experts of the Music Bureau to devise a string accompaniment and make it into a song.

He also composed a work in *fu* or rhyme-prose form to express his grief at the loss of Madam Li; it read as follows:

> Beauty soft and yielding, matchless grace,
> A life cut off forever, to thrive no more—
> We decked the new temple, waited to greet you, [refers to a seance]
> But firmly you declined to return to your old home.
> Grieving in the thicket, rank and weed grown,

Hiding in a dark place, harboring your pain,
You left your horse and carriage at the crest of the hill,
To tarry in that long night that knows no dawn.
Autumn's breath is sad and sharp with chill,
The limbs of the cassia fall and fade away.
Your spirit, lonely, pines for those far off,
Your soul wanders restless to the borders and beyond.
Consigned to sunken darkness for long ages to come,
I pity these lush flowers cut off half way;
Reflecting that for all time you'll return no more,
I recall how you came and went in beauty's prime,
Petals clustered about a center, unfurled to wait the wind,
Blossoms heaped and jumbled in increasing radiance,
Shining serenely, elegantly fair,
Pleasing in gentleness, yet more grave than before.
At leisure, unconstrained, you leaned against a column,
Lifted moth eyebrows, cast your glance around the room.
But when you'd roused my heart to follow after,
You hid your rosy face and shone no more.
Forced to part after intimate joys,
At night I start from dreams, dazed and lost.
So sudden that change from which you'll never return,
Your soul set free to fly far off;
In such perplexity your sacred spirit,
Roaming in grief and consternation;
But the days are many since you took to that road,
And in the end, hesitant, you said goodby,
Traveling ever westward, quickly out of sight.
I am sunk in longing, silent and dumb,
With thoughts that surge like waves, and pain in my heart.

   Reprise:
Beauty wreathed in splendor,
A crimson flower fell.
(Those other jealous wretches,
How could they compare?)
In days of greatest glory,
Cut off before your time!
Your son and brothers sobbing,
Bathed in tears of woe,
Wailing, lamenting,
Unable to cease their cries,
But such cries must go unanswered—
Let there be an end!
Thin and worn with sighing,
You grieved for the future of your little boy,

And though sorrow left you speechless,
You trusted to the favor you had once known.
No vows are needed among good men,
Much less between those who love!
Though you've gone and will never return,
I repeat once more my pledge to be true!
You left the sunny brightness,
Went to realms of dark,
And though you descended to our new temple,
You come no more to the gardens of old.
Ah, alas,
I dream of your soul!

Later, Li Yen-nien and his younger brother Li Chi were tried on charges of immoral behavior with women in the palace, and Li Kuang-li, the eldest brother, surrendered to the Hsiung-nu [Huns]. As a result, all the members of the Li family were put to death.

* * *

Lady Wang, Consort of the Imperial Grandson Shih

Lady Wang, the consort of the imperial grandson Shih, was the mother of Emperor Hsuan. Her name was Weng-hsu. During the *t'ai-shih* period (96–93 B.C.) she gained favor with the imperial grandson Shih. The imperial grandson's wife and concubines did not have any titles; all were referred to simply as "daughters of commoners."

In the second year of *cheng-ho* (91 B.C.), Lady Wang gave birth to the future Emperor Hsuan, and a few months later the heir apparent, Emperor Wu's son by Empress Wei, and the imperial grandson Shih met their downfall. The imperial grandson's wife and concubines were all arrested and put to death—there was not even anyone left to gather up the bodies and bury them. Only the future Emperor Hsuan was allowed to live. After he came to the throne, he posthumously honored his mother Lady Wang with the title Consort of Tao and his father's mother the Good Companion Shih with the title Consort of Li. Both were moved to new graves, with funerary parks and villages set up and officials appointed to guard and maintain them. (A discussion will be found in the Biography of the Heir Apparent Li.)

In the third year of *ti-chieh* (67 B.C.), Emperor Hsuan finally succeeded in locating his mother's mother, known as Dame Wang. Dame Wang, along with her sons Wu-ku and Wu, accompanied the imperial envoy who had located them and together journeyed to the capital to appear before the ruler. Dame Wang and her sons made the trip in a cart pulled by a yellow ox, and the common people therefore referred to her as "the old lady of the yellow ox."

Earlier, when Emperor Hsuan first came to the throne, he several times sent out envoys to search for the members of his mother's family, but since so many years had gone by, although the officials were often able to locate persons who seemed at first to fit the description, they were never the real ones. When at last Dame Wang was found, the emperor ordered the palace counselor Jen Hsuan, along with various officials attached to the offices of the chancellor and the imperial secretary, to conduct a careful cross-examination of the villagers who were acquainted with her. The villagers all testified that she was in fact Dame Wang.

Dame Wang herself reported that her name was Wang-jen and that her home was originally in P'ing Village of Li-wu in Cho Province. When she was fourteen she married a man named Wang Keng-te of the same village; after his death, she married again, this time a man named Wang Nai-shih of the district of Kuang-wang, bearing him two sons named Wu-ku and Wu and a daughter named Weng-hsu.

When Weng-hsu was eight or nine, she went to stay for a time in the house of Liu Chung-ch'ing, a younger son of Marquis Chieh of Kuang-wang. Liu Chung-ch'ing said to Weng-hsu's father, "Give me Weng-hsu and I will raise her myself." Weng-hsu's mother accordingly made an unlined silk robe for the girl and sent her off to the home of Liu Chung-ch'ing. Liu Chung-ch'ing taught her to sing and dance, and she was allowed to visit her parents and to return home to fetch winter and summer clothes.

After she had lived at Liu Chung-ch'ing's house for four or five years, she came home one time and said to her mother, "There is a merchant from Han-tan named Chang-erh who is looking for singers and dancers and I think Chung-ch'ing wants to give me to him!" Dame Wang immediately took her daughter and fled with her to P'ing Village. Liu Chung-ch'ing came looking for them in a carriage, bringing the girl's father with him. Dame Wang, flustered and at a loss to know what to do, brought her daughter back home, but she said to Liu Chung-ch'ing, "Though the child has been living in your house, my lord, we have never been given so much as a single cash for her! What right have you now to give her to someone else?" Liu Chung-ch'ing, however, hypocritically protested, "I would never do such a thing!"

A few days later, Weng-hsu passed the gate of her mother's house in a horse-drawn carriage belonging to the merchant Chang-erh. As she passed the gate, she called out, "They are taking me away after all! We are headed for Liu-su!" Dame Wang and her husband followed her to Liu-su and managed to get to see her, both parents and daughter bursting into tears when they met. Dame Wang said, "I'll bring a law suit against them for this!" but Weng-hsu replied, "Never mind, mother. Whatever house I go to I'll manage to get along. It wouldn't do any good to try to sue."

Dame Wang and her husband returned home to get more money and provisions and then resumed their journey, following Weng-hsu as far as Lu-nu in the state of Chung-shan. There they located her in a group of five singers and dancers who were all staying at the same place. Dame Wang spent the night with her daughter and the following day, leaving her husband there to keep watch on Weng-hsu, she went home once more to get together more money, intending to follow Weng-hsu all the way to Han-tan. But before she had finished selling grain to raise money and buying what she needed for the trip, her husband Nai-shih returned home, announcing, "Weng-hsu has already gone. I didn't have any money to follow her." According to Dame Wang, they completely lost track of Weng-hsu and had never heard anything more of her till the present day.

The merchant Chang-erh's wife Cheng and his assistant Shih Sui reported that twenty years earlier a retainer of the heir apparent named Hou Ming had come from Ch'ang-an looking for singers and dancers, and had asked for Weng-hsu and others, five persons in all. Chang-erh had accordingly ordered Shih Sui to escort them to Ch'ang-an, and all of them had become members of the heir apparent's household. The elder of Kuang-wang Keng Shih, Liu Chung-ch'ing's wife Ch'i, and others, forty-five persons in all, testified to the truth of these reports. The emperor's envoy Jen Hsuan accordingly submitted a memorial stating that it was absolutely certain that Dame Wang was the mother of Lady Wang, the consort of the imperial grandson Shih.

The emperor, as has been stated, summoned Dame Wang and the others to an audience in the capital and enfeoffed Dame Wang's sons Wu-ku and Wu as marquises within the Pass. Within the space of a month he handed out gifts and rewards to them worth countless sums of money.

The emperor then commanded the imperial secretary to bestow on his grandmother the title of Lady Po-p'ing, assigning to her the two districts of Po-p'ing and Li-wu with their eleven thousand households to be her bath-town. He also enfeoffed his uncle Wu-ku as marquis of P'ing-ch'ang and his uncle Wang Wu as marquis of Lo-ch'ang, each to enjoy the revenue from a town of six thousand households.

The emperor's grandfather Wang Nai-shih had died of illness earlier in the fourth year of *pen-shih* (70 B.C.), three years before Dame Wang was discovered and the family became rich and eminent, he was given the posthumous title of Ssu-ch'eng Marquis and orders were issued to Cho Province to repair his grave and set up a funerary park and village of four hundred households with officials to guard and maintain it according to the law. A year or so later, the emperor's grandmother passed away and was given the posthumous title Lady of the Ssu-ch'eng Marquis. Orders were given to have the body of the Ssu-ch'eng Marquis exhumed and buried along with that of his wife just south of the funerary temple of Feng-ming Ku-ch'eng, where their daughter was interred; a funerary park and village was set up with officials to tend it. The funerary park that had earlier been established for the Ssu-ch'eng Marquis in Cho Province was accordingly done away with.

Two members of the Wang family were enfeoffed as marquises, Wang Wu-ku and Wang Wu. Wang Wu-ku's son Wang Chieh became grand marshal and carriage and cavalry general. Wang Wu's son Wang Shang rose to the post of chancellor and has his own biography.

QUESTIONS TO CONSIDER

1. How does the Ban family's dynastic history differ from the Sima family's universal history (Chapter 10) in subject matter and approach?

2. Ban Zhao takes us behind the scenes at the Chinese court. In what ways might court women see Chinese politics differently from men?

3. What role does poetry play in this account?

FOR FURTHER READING

Fang, Achilles. *The Chronicle of the Three Kingdoms (A.D. 220–265).* 2 vols. Cambridge, MA: Harvard University Press, 1962–65.

Giles, H. A. *The Travels of Fa Hsien.* Cambridge, U.K.: Cambridge University Press, 1923.

Li, Dun, ed. *The Civilization of China.* New York: Scribner's, 1975.

Loewe, Michael. *Records of Han Administration.* 2 vols. Cambridge, U.K.: Cambridge University Press, 1967.

Pan Ku [and Pan Chao]. *China in Central Asia.* Trans. A. F. P. Hulsewe. Leiden, Netherlands: E. J. Brill, 1979.

———. *Courtier and Commoner in Ancient China: Selections from the History of The Former Han.* Trans. Burton Watson. New York: Columbia University Press, 1974.

———. *Food and Money in Ancient China.* Trans. Nancy Lee Swan. Princeton, NJ: Princeton University Press, 1950.

———. *History of the Former Han Dynasty.* Trans. Homer H. Dubs. 3 vols. Baltimore: Waverly Press and American Council of Learned Societies, 1938–1955.

Swann, Nancy Lee. *Pan Chao: Foremost Woman Scholar of China.* New York: Century, 1932.

NOTES

1. Pan Ku [and Pan Chao], *Courtier and Commoner in Ancient China,* trans. Burton Watson (New York: Columbia University Press, 1974), 247–51, 253–57.

CHAPTER 12

Josephus

Jewish Historian, Roman Historian

Josephus
The Granger Collection, New York

The works of Josephus provide us with the clearest portrait of first-century Judaism. By no means an uninvolved observer, Josephus participated in many of the events he recorded, and overtly indicated his preferences and perspectives in that process. Nonetheless, he could not resist telling a good story or showing off what he knew, and so he recorded innumerable details of the era that would otherwise be lost. His work is important for historians interested in the development of Judaism, the roots and context for Christianity, and the relation of both of these to Roman military power and Hellenistic cultural dominance.

Flavius Josephus (Joseph ben Matthias, 37–100?) grew up in a priestly family as a very religious Jew. After spending three years in the wilderness Josephus became a member of the Pharisees, the faction that focused on the moral laws rather than the ceremonial laws of Judaism. In CE 64, a trip to Rome impressed him with the glory and, especially, the military prowess of the Romans. There he also made friends high in the Roman elite. In 66, the Jewish revolt broke out in Palestine. Josephus found himself reluctantly drawn into military leadership of the rebels in Galilee. Josephus dutifully fortified the towns in Galilee, but the Roman commander (and future Emperor) Vespasian captured him after a long siege. Josephus prophesied that Vespasian would soon become Roman Emperor. When that came true, Vespasian freed Josephus, who accompanied him and his son Titus on campaigns in Palestine as adviser. Josephus sought to mediate between the Jews and Romans, but both sides mistrusted him so he accomplished little. In honor of Vespasian's patronage, Josephus took his family name Flavius. After the capture of Jersusalem in 70, Josephus lived in Rome, associated with the imperial court and wrote books to explain the Romans to the Jews and vice versa.

Josephus first produced *The Jewish War* in the Aramaic language of Palestine and then oversaw its translation into Greek for the non-Jewish audience. His eyewitness account explained many details of the war and showed him to be an astute observer of Roman battle tactics and military procedures. He stressed Roman invincibility, possibly in an attempt to dissuade Jews throughout the Mediterranean world from attempting to renew the revolt. Late in 93, he brought forth the *Antiquities of the Jews*, an account of Jewish history from the Creation to just before the revolt in 66. In this work, he portrayed Judaism in its most rational form to appeal to the biases of the Hellenistic elite. This work is less accurate than *The Jewish War*, but it preserves many sources for postbiblical Jewish history that would otherwise be lost.

Like the Greek historian Thucydides, Josephus in *The Jewish War* stressed the value of contemporary history written by eyewitnesses to the events, but in his use of anecdotes and compelling digressions, he more nearly resembled Herodotus. Relatively uncritical of his sources, Josephus held consistent biases: against the leaders of the Jewish rebels, in favor of the Romans as the hand of God, especially Vespasian and his son Titus, and in favor of his own behavior as being wise and honorable despite appearances to the contrary. He excelled at describing architecture and geographic features so that his work now serves as a kind of handbook to Palestinian archeology. In addition to his personal observations, Josephus clearly used a variety of written sources of uneven reliability. He used the Hebrew Old Testament sparingly, relying more heavily on the Targum (Aramaic version) and the Greek Septuagint translation. He preserved for us much Midrash, traditional rabbinic interpretation and elaboration on biblical passages and Jewish history. Echoes and references to Greek and Roman classics appear frequently. Some have suggested he modeled *The Jewish War* on Caesar's *Gallic War* and modeled *Jewish Antiquities* on the work of Dionysius of Halicarnassus, *Roman Antiquities*. Others believe Josephus's Greek assistants contributed the Hellenistic cultural references. Much of his work appears to be based on the *Universal History* of Nicolas of Damascus, a long history, now lost. However his compositions were put together, Josephus's style is for the most part engaging and lively enough that it easily served as the basis for the movie *Masada* in the early 1980s.

The first selection that follows is Josephus's introduction to *The Jewish War*, where he expressed his purpose for writing. Then, two scenes from his description of the siege and destruction of Jerusalem in 70 display his skill at empathy and melodrama.

The Jewish War[1]

The war of the Jews against the Romans grew the greatest conflict—not only of our time, but of most all other recorded conflicts—between cities or nations, and so it has not lacked historians.

Inadequacy of previous histories. Among them one can distinguish two types of writers: those who were not present at the events and rarely recorded, in rhetorical style, casual and contradictory tales collected from hearsay, and others who wrote on a basis of personal experience, and whose recounting of the facts was influenced by excessive flattery of the Romans or hatred of the Jews. Consequently, these works were characterized either by invective or fault finding, but not by accurate factual history. Thus, I Josephus, son of Matthias, a Hebrew by race and a priest from Jerusalem—having personally fought against the Romans in the early stage of the war, and an unwilling witness of the ensuing event—propose to reveal the facts to the people of the Roman Empire by translating into Greek the work that I previously wrote in my native tongue for circulation among the Barbarians.

Crucial years for the Roman Empire. The upheaval, as I said, was indeed of the greatest magnitude; and at the time it overtook us, Rome was in a most unsettled state and beset by internal dissensions. The Jewish revolutionary party, whose numbers and fortunes had greatly increased, reached its peak during the general disturbance; insurrections broke out as agitation increased. So widespread had the violence become that the Empire's eastern possessions wavered in the balance. The rebellious Jews were filled with high hopes of acquiring these lands, whereas the Romans feared losing their hold over them. The Jews were confident that their fellow country men living beyond the Euphrates would join them in their revolt while the Romans were involved with the neighboring Gauls and restive Celts. Moreover, there was general confusion after Nero's death, and several men considered the time propitious to aspire to the throne; the military leaders hoped that a transference of power would greatly improve their fortunes.

I therefore considered it altogether inexcusable for the truth to be misrepresented and disregarded when such momentous issues were involved. The Parthians, the Babylonians, and the remote peoples of Arabia, as well as our country-men beyond the Euphrates and the people of Adiabene, were accurately informed through my diligent work of the origin of the war, the chain of calamities it brought in its wake, and its tragic end. It was unforgivable that the Greeks and the Romans, apart from those who took part in the war, should not be told the truth and be exposed solely to flattering and fictitious accounts.

Though these historians claim to be writing history, they do not, in my opinion, impart sound information and miss their target completely. They are bent on representing the Romans as a great nation, while they constantly disparage and decry the behavior of the Jews. But I fail to see why the conquerors of a feeble nation should be regarded as great. Furthermore, these writers do not take into account the duration of the war, nor the vast numbers of Roman troops that were involved; or they deprecate the ability of the commanders whose strenuous endeavors during the seige of Jerusalem will bring them little glory in the writers' eyes if their achievements are belittled.

The author's feelings in the matter. However, it is not my intention to emulate those who praise Roman might by magnifying the heroism of my countrymen: I will accurately report the actions of both combatants; but in tracing the course of events I cannot hide my personal feelings nor refrain from bewailing my country's tragic fate. The fact that it was being ruined by civil strife, that the tyrannical Jewish leaders were those who drew the might of the unwilling Roman army to the holy sanctuary, and the flames that subsequently consumed it, is attested to by Titus Caesar himself, who ravaged the city. Throughout the hostilities he pitied the people who were left to the mercy of the rebellious parties and delayed the capture of the city time and again; for by prolonging the siege he gave the guilty a chance to repent. But should anyone criticize me for condemning the tyrants and the crimes committed by their gangs of bandits, or for lamenting my country's disaster, I beg indulgence for my natural compassion, which is not customary for a historian. For of all the cities in the Roman domain, ours had attained the highest level of expansion and prosperity, and has now been reduced to the lowest level of misery. Indeed, I can hardly compare the misfortunes of all other nations since the beginning of time, with the calamities that have befallen the Jews; and though we cannot blame a foreign nation for all these misfortunes, it is more than I can do to restrain my grief. Should any critic be too stern for pity, let him credit history with the facts and this historian with the lamentations.

Superiority of the historian of contemporary events over compilers of ancient history. I could also justly censure the Greek scholars, in whose days events of such magnitude took place as to overshadow the wars of antiquity, and who sit in judgment on these current events and deprecate those who make them their special study, historians whose principles they lack even if they show greater literary judgment and merit. The ancient historians chose the histories of the Assyrian and Median empires as their themes, implying that the chronicles of the ancient historians were not good enough. The truth is that they are inferior to them in both literary judgement and merit. The ancient historians had set themselves exclusively to record the history of their own times. Their connections with contemporary events added clarity to their writings, and any misrepresentations on their part could have been detected and denounced by their contemporaries. Indeed, a historian who writes of events of his own time should serve as a model and is worthy of the highest praise. A diligent writer is not one who edits the material and arrangement of other authors, but who contributes fresh data and constructs a historical edifice of his own. As for me, though I am a foreigner, I have gone to great pains and expense to present a memorial of these great achievements to the Greeks and Romans. As for the native Greeks, their mouths are agape and their tongues loosened soon enough where any material advantage or legal dispute is involved; but where the writing of history is concerned, with its requisite for veracity and careful collection of facts, they remain mute and leave the task of recording the exploits of their rulers to the inferior and ill-informed writers among them. Let us then honor historical truth, since it is disregarded by the Greeks.

* * *

Simon's attack on the other ramps; the Jews' invasion of the Roman camp. Two days later Simon's forces launched a further attack on the other embankments, for the Romans had brought up the ramps on that side and were already battering the wall. A certain Gephthaeus who came from Garis, a town in Galilee, and Magassarus, a soldier of the king and one of the henchmen of Mariamme, along with the son of a certain Nabataeus from Adiabene, nicknamed Ceagiras which means "lame," because of his disability, snatched up torches and rushed at the engines. In the whole course of the war the city produced no one more heroic than these three nor were there any who inspired greater terror, sallying out of town. As though running toward friends rather than the enemy ranks, they neither hesitated nor shrank back, but charged through the midst of the enemy and set the engines on fire. Attacked with shots and swords from every quarter, nothing could move them from their perilous course until the fire had caught hold of the engines. With the flames already towering aloft, the Romans came rushing from the encampments to the rescue, while the Jews obstructed them from the ramparts and, utterly disregarding their personal danger, struggled hand-to-hand with those who were endeavoring to extinguish the flames. On the one side were the Romans attempting to drag the battering-engines out of the fire while their wicker shelters blazed; on the other side the Jews, surrounded by flames, pulled the other way, clutching the red-hot iron and refusing to relinquish the rams. From the engines the fire spread to the embankments, out-stripping the defenders. Thereupon the Romans, enveloped in flames and despairing of saving their handiwork, beat a retreat to their camps; while the Jews pursued them hard, their numbers constantly swelled by fresh reinforcements from the city and emboldened by their success, pressed on with uncontrolled impetuosity right up to the [Roman] entrenchments, finally grappling with the sentries. There is a line of troops, periodically relieved, which occupies a position in front of every camp and is subject to the very drastic Roman law that he who quits his post under any pretext whatsoever must be executed. These men, preferring an heroic death to capital punishment, stood their ground and at their desperate plight many of the fugitives returned ashamed. Posting the quick-firers along the camp wall, they kept at bay the masses who, without a thought for safety or personal defense, were pouring out of the city. The Jews grappled with any who stood in their path, and unguardedly flinging their very bodies against the enemy's spear points, would strike at their antagonists. But their advantage lay less in deeds than in daring, and the Romans yielded rather to intrepidity than to their own bosses.

The attack repulsed by Titus; the Jews' withdrawal into the city. Now at last Titus appeared from the Antonia, where he had gone to choose a site for fresh embankments. He severely reprimanded his troops, who after capturing the enemy's fortifications, endangered their own, and had put themselves in the position of the besieged by freeing the Jews from their prison house; then he himself at the head of his picked men attacked the enemy in the flank; but though assailed from the front as well, they turned around and resolutely resisted him. In the confusion of the battle, blinded by the dust and deafened by the din, neither side could distinguish friend from foe. The Jews still stood firm not so much through prowess now as from despair of salvation, while the Romans were braced by respect for their honor and their arms, especially with Caesar in the forefront of the danger. Such was the fury of the Romans that the struggle, I imagine, would have ended in the capture of the entire Jewish host, had they not forestalled the turn of the battle by retreating into the city. The Romans, however, with their embankments destroyed, were downhearted, having lost the fruits of their long labors in one hour, and many felt that through the use of conventional weaponry they would never capture the city.

Titus' council of war. Titus held a council of war with his officers. The more sanguine were for bringing up the entire force and attempting a full-scale assault; for hitherto only separate fractions of their forces had been engaged with the Jews; whereas, if they advanced *en masse*, the Jews would yield to their onslaught, for they would be overwhelmed by the hail of missiles. Of the more cautious some urged that the embankments be reconstructed. Others advised abandoning these and resorting to a blockade, merely preventing the inhabitants from making sorties and bringing in food, thus leaving the city to starve and refraining from combat; for there was no battling with desperate men who prayed to die by the sword, and for whom—if that was denied them—a more horrible fate was in store. Titus thought it undignified to let so large a force remain idle, while there was no point in fighting those who would soon destroy each other. He pointed out that throwing up embankments was a hopeless task, with materials so scarce, and to prevent sorties was still more difficult. For, to form a ring of men around so big a city, and over such difficult terrain, was no easy matter, and would expose them to the risk of enemy attacks. They might block the obvious outlets, but the Jews by necessity and local knowledge would contrive secret ways out; and if provisions were smuggled in, the siege would be prolonged still further. He feared, moreover, that the luster of success would be dimmed by the delay, for, given time, anything could be accomplished, but haste was essential to win renown. If they wanted to combine speed with safety, they must throw a dyke around the whole city; that was the only way to block every exit, and only thus would the Jews abandon their last hope of survival and surrender the city, or, wasted by famine, fall an easy prey. He himself would not sit still, but would once more turn his attention to the embankments when he had an enfeebled foe to obstruct him. And if anyone considered this a difficult operation, he ought to remember that trivial tasks did not suit the Romans, and that without toil nothing great could easily be achieved by any man.

* * *

The deadly impact of the unbroken famine; the neglect of burial. When all exits were closed to the Jews, every hope of escape was eliminated and the famine, strengthening its hold, devoured the people, houses and families, one after another. The roofs were full of women and infants in the last stages of exhaustion, the alleys with the corpses of the aged; children and young men, swollen with hunger, haunted the market places and collapsed wherever faintness overcame them. Those who were ill had not the strength to bury their kinsfolk, and those who were still fit hesitated to do so because of the multitude of the dead and the uncertainty of their own fate. Many, as they buried the fallen, fell dead themselves, while others set out for their graves before their fate was upon them. And throughout these calamities, no weeping or lamentation was heard: hunger stifled emotion; and with dry eyes and grinning mouths those who were slow to die watched those whose end came sooner. Deep silence blanketed the city, and night laden with death was in the grip of a yet fiercer foe—the brigands. They broke as tomb-plunderers into the houses, rifled the deceased and stripped the coverings from their bodies, then departed laughing; they tried the points of their swords on the corpses, even transfixed some of the wretches who lay prostrate but still living, to test the steel, and any who implored them to employ their hand and sword-thrust to end their misery, they disdainfully left to perish of hunger. And each victim breathed his last with his eyes transfixed on the Temple, turning his gaze from the rebels he was leaving alive. The latter at first ordered these bodies to be buried at public expense, for they found the stench intolerable; later, when this proved impossible, they flung them from the ramparts into the ravines.

* * *

The Temple burned despite Titus' orders. Titus retired to the Antonia, intending to launch a full scale attack the following day at dawn and take possession of the Temple. The sanctuary, however, had long before been condemned by God to the flames; and now, after the passing of the years, the fated day was at hand, the tenth of the month of Lous—the very date when centuries before it had been burned by the King of Babylon. But now it was their own people who had caused and started the conflagration. For when Titus had withdrawn, the rebels shortly after attacked the Romans again, and a clash followed between the guards of the sanctuary and the troops who were putting out the fire inside the inner court; the latter routed the Jews and followed in hot pursuit right up to the Temple itself. Then one of the soldiers, without awaiting any orders and with no dread of so momentous a deed, but urged on by some supernatural force, snatched a blazing piece of wood and, climbing on another soldier's back, hurled the flaming brand through a low golden window that gave access, on the north side, to the rooms that surrounded the sanctuary. As the flames shot up, the Jews let out a shout of dismay that matched the tragedy; they flocked to the rescue, with no thought of sparing their lives or husbanding their strength; for the sacred structure that they constantly guarded with such devotion was vanishing before their eyes.

The ferocity of the Roman army. A runner brought the news to Titus while he rested in his tent after the battle. Leaping up as he was, he ran to the Temple to extinguish the conflagration. He was followed by all his generals, and these, in turn, by the excited legionaries, with the shouting and confusion characteristic of a disorganized rush by such a large force. Caesar, both through voice and a raised hand, waved to the combatants to put out the fire; but his shouts were not heard, as their ears were deafened by the overwhelming din, and his beckoning hand went unheeded amid the distractions of the fight and the avenging fury. No exhortation or threat could now restrain the impetuosity of the legions; for passion was in supreme command. Crowded together around the entrances, many were trampled down by their companions; others, stumbling on the smoldering and smoke-filled ruins of the porticoes, died as miserably as the defeated. As they drew closer to the Temple, they pretended not even to hear Caesar's orders, but urged the men in front to throw in more firebrands. The rebels were powerless to help; carnage and flight spread throughout. Most of the slain were peaceful citizens, weak and unarmed, and they were butchered where they were caught. The heap of corpses mounted higher and higher about the altar; a stream of blood flowed down the Temple's steps, and the bodies of those slain at the top slipped to the bottom.

Caesar's vain attempt to save the Temple. When Caesar failed to restrain the fury of his frenzied soldiers, and the fire could not be checked, he entered the building with his generals and looked at the holy place of the sanctuary and all its furnishings, which exceeded by far the accounts current in foreign lands and fully justified their splendid repute in our own. As the flames had not yet penetrated the inner sanctum, but were consuming the chambers that surrounded the sanctuary, Titus assumed correctly that there was still time to save the structure; he ran out and by personal appeals he endeavored to persuade his men to put out the fire, instructing Liberalisus, a centurion of his bodyguard of lancers, to club any of the men who disobeyed his orders. But their respect for Caesar and their fear of the centurion's staff who was trying to check them were overpowered by their rage, their detestation of the Jews, and an utterly uncontrolled lust for battle. Most of them were spurred on, moreover, by the expectation of loot, convinced that the interior was full of money and dazzled by observing that everything around them was made of gold. But they were forestalled by one of those who had entered into the building, and who, when Caesar dashed out to restrain the troops, pushed a firebrand, in the darkness, into the hinges of the gate. Then, when the flames suddenly shot up from the interior, Caesar and his generals withdrew, and no one was left to prevent those outside from kindling the blaze. Thus, in defiance of Caesar's wishes, the Temple was set on fire.

The Temple destroyed on the anniversary of the previous conflagration. Deeply as one must mourn the destruction of the most wonderful edifice ever seen or spoken of, whether for its structure, size, and lavish perfection of detail, or the repute of its holy places, yet we may find very real comfort in the thought that fate is inexorable, not only in regard to living beings but also in regard to structures and places. We may wonder, too, at the accuracy of the cycle of fate; for it awaited, as I said, the very month and day on which the Temple had been burned by the Babylonians. From its first foundation by King Solomon to its present destruction, which occurred in the second year of

Vespasian's reign, was a period of one thousand one hundred and thirty years, seven months, and fifteen days; from its rebuilding in the second year of the reign of Cyrus, for which Haggai was responsible, to its capture under Vespasian, was six hundred and thirty-nine years and forty-five days.

The scenes of horror and massacre attending the fire. While the Temple was ablaze, the attackers plundered it, and countless people who were caught by them were slaughtered. There was no pity for age and no regard was accorded rank; children and old men, laymen and priests, alike were butchered; every class was pursued and crushed in the grip of war, whether they cried out for mercy or offered resistance. Through the roar of the flames streaming far and wide, the groans of the falling victims were heard; such was the height of the hill and the magnitude of the blazing pile that the entire city seemed to be ablaze; and the noise—nothing more deafening and frightening could be imagined. There were the war cries of the Roman legions as they swept onwards en masse, the yells of the rebels encircled by fire and sword, the panic of the people who, cut off above, fled into the arms of the enemy, and their shrieks as they met their fate. The cries on the hill blended with those of the multitudes in the city below; and now many people who were exhausted and tongue-tied as a result of hunger, when they beheld the Temple on fire, found strength once more to lament and wail. Peraea and the surrounding hills, added their echoes to the deafening din. But more horrifying than the din were the sufferings. The Temple Mount everywhere enveloped in flames, seemed to be boiling over from its base; yet the blood seemed more abundant than the flames and the numbers of the slain greater than those of the slayers. The ground could not be seen anywhere between the corpses; the soldiers climbed over heaps of bodies as they chased the fugitives. The rebel horde managed with difficulty to push through the Romans, and to break through the outer courts of the Temple Mount and from there to the city, while the surviving populace took refuge on the outer porticoes. Some of the priests at first tore out from the Temple roof the spikes with their lead sockets and hurled them at the Romans; but subsequently, as they did not achieve anything and the flames leaped towards them, they withdrew to the wall, which was eight cubits wide, and stayed there. However, two men of note, who were in a position either to save their lives by going over to the Romans or to stay there and face the same fate as the others, threw themselves into the fire and were consumed with the Temple; they were Meirus son of Belgas, and Josephus son of Dalaeus.

Burning of the surrounding area and destruction of the people. The Romans, deeming it useless to spare the surrounding buildings now that the Temple was in flames, set fire to them all, both of what remained of the porticoes and all the gates, except two, one of the east gates and the southern gate, both of which were later demolished. They burned also the treasury chambers, which contained huge sums of money, vast quantities of raiment, and other precious belongings; here, in fact, was the general depository of Jewish wealth, where the rich had brought the contents of their dismantled homes for safe keeping. They now reached the last surrounding portico of the outer court, on top of which poor women and children of the populace and a mixed multitude, numbering six thousand, had found refuge. Before Caesar could reach any decision or give any orders to his officers as regards these people, the soldiers, carried away by their fury, set fire to the porticoes from below; consequently, many were killed as they threw themselves out of the flames, while others were consumed by the blaze; of all that multitude not a soul escaped.

QUESTIONS TO CONSIDER

1. What advantages and disadvantages are there for historians to write about events in which they participated as leaders?
2. Josephus and Thucydides (Chapter 9) both participated in the wars about which they wrote. How do their presentations differ?
3. What do we learn about Jewish and Roman life and warfare from Josephus's account?

FOR FURTHER READING

Cornfeld, Gaalya, ed. and trans. *Josephus: The Jewish War*. Grand Rapids, MI: Zondervan, 1982.

Feldman, Louis, and Gohei Hata, eds. *Josephus, Judaism and Christianity*. Detroit, MI: Wayne State University Press, 1987.

_____. *Josephus, the Bible and History*. Detroit, MI: Wayne State University Press, 1989.

Mason, Steve. *Josephus and the New Testament*. Peabody, MA: Hendrickson Publishers, 1992.

Rajak, Tessa. *Josephus, the Historian and His Society*. Philadelphia: Fortress Press, 1984.

Thackeray, H. St. J. *Josephus the Man and Historian*. New York: Ktav, 1929.

_____, et al., trans. *Josephus: Jewish Antiquities*. 6 vols. London: Heineman, 1930–65.

Williamson, G. A. *The World of Josephus*. Boston: Little, Brown 1964.

_____, trans. *Josephus: The Jewish War*. Harmondsworth, U.K.: Penguin, 1970.

NOTES

1. Gaalya Cornfeld, et al., eds., *Josephus: The Jewish War* (Grand Rapids, MI: Zondervan, 1982), 8–10, 391–95, 421–27.

CHAPTER 13

Tacitus

History in the Roman Mode

Cornelius Tacitus
The Bettmann Archive

The work of Cornelius Tacitus is our chief source for the history of the Roman Empire in the first century CE. His picture of the emperors dominates historical interpretation of this extremely important period, when the foundations were laid for the 500-year span of the Roman Empire, when Greco-Roman culture spread into Western Europe, and when Christianity developed—the roots of Western civilization. In addition, Tacitus's Latin style influenced Latin prose composition for 1,500 years after his death.

What little biographical information we have for Tacitus comes from his own works. Probably born around 56 CE to a senatorial (that is, aristocratic) family, he pursued an expected career in public service. He made a very good political and social connection in 77 when he married the daughter of Agricola, a distinguished senator near the peak of his career, who served that year in the highly honored post of consul. Tacitus himself proceeded in the normal career path for his social status, serving in a variety of civil and military posts until he achieved the consulship in 97. Shortly after this he began writing an adulatory biography of his father-in-law, who had been Roman governor in Britain and fought frontier wars against the Britons and Picts. Tacitus followed with an account of the German tribes, contrasting the simple virtues of the Germans with the decadent sophistication of the Romans—a recurrent theme in his works and in many later histories of Rome. Tacitus's *Histories*, an account of the Emperors between 68 and 96, he composed before 109. Of its original twelve or fourteen books, only four and fragments survived into the modern era. This was a great loss since it covered events that Tacitus witnessed as a contemporary. Tacitus served as governor of the important province of Asia in 112–13 and with that added perspective completed the work of his maturity, *The Annals*, which recounted the history of the Julio-Claudian dynasty of Roman emperors from 14 to 68 CE. Internal evidence suggests that he completed this work after 117 so that we can assume that Tacitus died sometime after that date. *The Annals* too survived only in fragments.

Tacitus shared and employed the historical perspective of the senatorial order and of Roman historians generally. By such people, the past was deemed better than the present. In particular he decried the moral and political decay that came from elevating one man (or at least one family) to autocratic power. Monarchy disguised as a republic—the form of the Roman government in his era—fooled no one. Only the Roman historian Sallust, almost a century earlier, saw anything good in the populist tendencies (the twentieth century might call them demagogic) that led to the imperial system. Tacitus painted a dark picture of the emperors, not by misrepresenting their deeds, but by word choice, innuendo, and asserting malevolent motives for their actions. Thus, we can usually depend on the accuracy of his facts, less often on his interpretations. Most modern scholars believe that Tacitus projected the recent evil behavior of the Emperor Domitian (81–96) onto past emperors and presumed that all emperors, of necessity, were like him.

Like most ancient Western historians, Tacitus was interested in history for the lessons it could teach. He focused on the individual and on individual motivation, partly because autocracy made the emperor's personality vital and determinative. Tacitus followed convention and used speeches to set forth the situation or express the point of view of someone, not to record what was said verbatim. He rarely told the reader about his sources except in criticism of the obsequious way previous historians had treated the emperors. For much of what he recorded, his is the sole surviving witness. Despite his somber theme, Tacitus's writing and characterization were so lively that they formed the basis for a novel by Robert Graves and later for a television series, *I Claudius,* on the BBC in recent decades.

In selections that follow, Tacitus relates some perspectives on the duty of the historian and writing imperial history. The account of Tiberius's accession illustrates how he used innuendo to censure the emperor. His description of the Great Fire of Rome under Nero reveals his cynicism as well as his dramatic flair.

The History[1]
Book I

January–March, A.D. 69

I begin my work with the time when Servius Galba was consul for the second time with Titus Vinius for his colleague. Of the former period, the 820 years dating from the founding of the city, many authors have treated; and while they had to record the transactions of the Roman people, they wrote with equal eloquence and freedom. After the conflict at Actium, and when it became essential to peace that all power should be centered in one man, these great intellects passed away. Then too the truthfulness of history was impaired in many ways; at first, through men's ignorance of public affairs, which were now wholly strange to them, then through their passion for flattery, or, on the other hand, their hatred of their masters. And so between the enmity of the one and the servility of the other, neither had any regard for posterity. But while we instinctively shrink from a writer's adulation, we lend a ready ear to detraction and spite, because flattery involves the shameful imputation of servility, whereas malignity wears the false appearance of honesty. I myself knew nothing of Galba, of Otho, or of Vitellius, either from benefits or from injuries. I would not deny that my elevation was begun by Vespasian, augumented by Titus, and still further advanced by Domitian; but those who profess inviolable truthfulness must speak of all without partiality and without hatred. I have reserved as an employment for my old age, should my life be long enough, a subject at once more fruitful and less anxious in the reign of the Divine Nerva and the empire of Trajan, enjoying the rare happiness of times, when we think what we please, and express what we think.

I am entering on the history of a period rich in disasters, frightful in its wars, torn by civil strife, and even in peace full of horrors. Four emperors perished by the sword. There were three civil wars; there were more with foreign enemies; there were often wars that had both characters at once. There was success in the East, and disaster in the West. There were disturbances in Illyricum; Gaul wavered in its allegiance; Britain was thoroughly subdued and immediately abandoned; the tribes of the Suevi and the Sarmata rose in concert against us; the Dacians had the glory of inflicting as well as suffering defeat; the armies of Parthies were all but set in motion by the cheat of a counterfeit Nero. Now too Italy was prostrated by disasters either entirely novel, or that recurred only after a long succession of ages; cities in Campania's richest plains were swallowed up and overwhelmed; Rome was wasted by conflagrations, its oldest temples consumed, and the Capitol itself fired by the hands of citizens. Sacred rites were profaned; there was profligacy in the highest ranks; the sea was crowded with exiles, and its rocks polluted with bloody deeds. In the capital there were yet worse horrors. Nobility, wealth, the refusal or the acceptance of office, were grounds for accusation, and virtue ensured destruction. The rewards of the informers were no less odious than their crimes; for while some seized on consulships and priestly offices, as their share of the spoil, others on procuratorships, and posts of more confidential authority, they robbed and ruined in every direction amid universal hatred and terror. Slaves were bribed to turn against their masters, and freedmen to betray their patrons; and those who had not an enemy were destroyed by friends.

Yet the age was not so barren in noble qualities, as not also to exhibit examples of virtue. Mothers accompanied the flight of their sons; wives followed their husbands into exile; there were brave kinsmen and faithful sons in law; there were slaves whose fidelity defied even torture; there were illustrious men driven to the last necessity, and enduring it with fortitude; there were closing scenes that equalled the famous deaths of antiquity. Besides the manifold vicissitudes of human affairs, there were prodigies in heaven and earth, the warning voices of the thunder, and other intimations of the future, auspicious or gloomy, doubtful or not to be mistaken. Never surely did more terrible calamities of the Roman People, or evidence more conclusive, prove that the Gods take no thought for our happiness, but only for our punishment.

The Annals of Imperial Rome[2]

The only proposals in the senate that I have seen fit to mention are particularly praiseworthy or particularly scandalous ones. It seems to me a historian's foremost duty to ensure that merit is recorded, and to confront evil deeds and words with the fear of posterity's denunciations. But this was a tainted, meanly obsequious age. The greatest figures had to protect their positions by subserviency; and, in addition to them, all ex-consuls, most ex-praetors, even many junior senators competed with each other's offensively sycophantic proposals. There is a tradition that whenever Tiberius left the senate-house he exclaimed in Greek, 'Men fit to be slaves!' Even he, freedom's enemy, became impatient of such abject servility.

* * *

I am aware that much of what I have described, and shall describe, may seem unimportant and trivial. But my chronicle is quite a different matter from histories of early Rome. Their subjects were great wars, cities stormed, kings routed and captured. Or, if home affairs were their choice, they could turn freely to conflicts of consuls with tribunes, to land- and corn-laws, feuds of conservatives and commons. Mine, on the other hand, is a circumscribed, inglorious field. Peace was scarcely broken—if at all. Rome was plunged in gloom. The ruler uninterested in expanding the empire.

Yet even apparently insignificant events such as these are worth examination. For they often cause major historical developments. This is so whether a country (or city) is a democracy, an oligarchy, or an autocracy. For it is always one or the other—a mixture of the three is easier to applaud than to achieve, and besides, even when achieved, it cannot last long. When there was democracy, it was necessary to understand the character of the masses and how to control them. When the senate was in power, those who best knew its mind—the mind of the oligarchs—were considered the wisest experts on contemporary events. Similarly, now that Rome has virtually been transformed into an autocracy, the investigation and record of these details concerning the autocrat may prove useful. Indeed, it is from such studies— from the experience of others—that most men learn to distinguish right and wrong, advantage and disadvantage. Few can tell them apart instinctively.

So these accounts have their uses. But they are distasteful. What interests and stimulates readers is a geographical description, the changing fortunate of a battle, the glorious death of a commander. My themes on the other hand concern cruel orders, unremitting accusations, treacherous friendships, innocent men ruined—a conspicuously monotonous glut of down falls and their monotonous causes. Besides, whereas the ancient historian has few critics— nobody minds if he over-praises the Carthaginian (or Roman) army—the men punished or disgraced under Tiberius have numerous descendants living today. And even when the families are extinct, some will think, if their own habits are similar, that the mention of another's crimes is directed against them. Even glory and merit makes enemies—by showing their opposites in too sharp and critical relief.

* * *

From Augustus to Tiberius

When Rome was first a city, its rulers were kings. Then Lucius Junius Brutus created the consulate and free Republican institutions in general. Dictatorships were assumed in emergencies. A Council of Ten did not last more than two years; and then there was a short-lived arrangement by which senior army officers—the commanders of contingents provided by the tribes— possessed consular authority. Subsequently Cinna and Sulla set up autocracies, but they too were brief. Soon Pompey and Crassus acquired predominant positions, but rapidly lost them to Caesar. Next, the military strength which Lepidus and Antony had built up was absorbed by Augustus. He found the whole state exhausted by internal dissensions, and established over it a personal regime known as the principate.

Famous writers have recorded Rome's early glories and disasters. The Augustan Age, too, had its distinguished historians. But then the rising tide of flattery exercised a deterrent effect. The reigns of Tiberius, Gaius, Claudius, and Nero were described during their lifetimes in fictitious terms, for fear of the consequences; whereas the accounts written after their deaths were influenced by raging animosities. So I have decided to say a little about Augustus, with special attention to his last period, and then go on to the reign of Tiberius and what followed. I shall write without indignation or partisanship: in my case the customary incentives to these are lacking.

The violent deaths of Brutus and Cassius left no Republican forces in the field. Defeat came to Sextus Pompeius in Sicily, Lepidus was dropped, Antony killed. So even the Caesarian party had no leader left except the 'Caesar' himself, Octavian. He gave up the title of Triumvir, emphasizing instead his position as consul; and the powers of a tribune, he proclaimed, were good enough for him—powers for the protection of ordinary people.

He seduced the army with bonuses, and his cheap food policy was successful bait for civilians. Indeed, he attracted everybody's goodwill by the enjoyable gift of peace. The he gradually pushed ahead and absorbed the functions of the senate, the officials, and even the law. Opposition did not exist. War or judicial murder had disposed of all men of spirit. Upper-class survivors found that slavish obedience was the way to succeed, both politically and financially. They had profited from the revolution, and so now they liked the security of the existing arrangement better than the dangerous uncertainties of the old regime. Besides, the new order was popular in the provinces. There, government by Senate and People was looked upon skeptically as a matter of sparring dignitaries and extortionate officials. The legal system had provided no remedy against these, since it was wholly incapacitated by violence, favouritism, and—most of all—bribery.

                                          *   *   *

Then two pieces of news became known simultaneously: Augustus was dead, and Tiberius was in control.

The new reign's first crime was the assassination of Agrippa Postumus. He was killed by a staff-officer—who found it a hard task, though he was a persevering murderer and the victim taken by surprise unarmed. Tiberius said nothing about the matter in the senate. He pretended that the orders came from Augustus, who was alleged to have instructed the colonel in charge to kill Agrippa Postumus as soon as Augustus himself was dead. It is true that Augustus' scathing criticisms of the young man's behavior were undoubtedly what had prompted the senate to decree his banishment. But the emperor had never been callous enough to kill any of his relations, and that he should murder his own grandchild to remove the worries of a stepson seemed incredible. It would be nearer the truth to suppose that Tiberius because he was afraid, and Livia through stepmotherly malevolence, loathed and distrusted the young Agrippa Postumus and got rid of him at the first opportunity. But when the staff-officer reported in military fashion that he had carried out his orders, Tiberius answered that he had given no orders and that what had been done would have to be accounted for in the senate.

This came to the notice of Tiberius' confidant, Gaius Sallustius Crispus. It was he who had sent instructions to the colonel, and he was afraid that the responsibility might be shifted to himself—in which case either telling the truth or lying would be equally risky. So he warned Livia that palace secrets, and the advice of friends, and services performed by the army, were best undivulged; and Tiberius must not weaken the throne by referring everything to the senate. The whole point of autocracy, Crispus observed, is that the accounts will not come right unless the ruler is their only auditor.

Meanwhile at Rome consuls, senate, knights, precipitately became servile. The more distinguished men were, the greater their urgency and insincerity. They must show neither satisfaction at the death of one emperor, nor gloom at the accession of another: so their features were carefully arranged in a blend of tears and smiles, mourning and flattery. The first to swear allegiance to Tiberius Caesar were the consuls Sextus Pompeius (II) and Sextus Appuleius; then in their presence the commander of the Guard, Lucius Seius Strabo, and the controller of the corn-supply, Gaius Turranius; next the senate, army, and public. For Tiberius made a habit of always allowing the consuls the initiative, as though the Republic still existed and he himself were uncertain whether to take charge or not. Even the edict with which he summoned the senate to its House was merely issued by virtue of the tribune's power which he had received under Augustus. His edict was brief, and very unpretentious. In it he proposed to arrange his father's last honours, and stay by the side of his body. This, he said, was the only state business which he was assuming.

*   *   *

But Nero profited by his country's ruin to build a new palace. Its wonders were not so much customary and commonplace luxuries like gold and jewels, but lawns and lakes and faked rusticity—woods here, open spaces and views there. With their cunning, impudent artificialities, Nero's architects and engineers, Serverus and Celer, did not balk at effects which Nature herself had ruled out as impossible.

They also fooled away an emperor's riches. For they promised to dig a navigable canal from lake Avernus to the Tiber estuary, over the stony shore and mountain barriers. The only water to feed the canal was in the Pontine marshes. Elsewhere, all was precipitous or waterless. Moreover, even if a passage could have been forced, the labour would have been unendurable and unjustified. But Nero was eager to perform the incredible; so he attempted to excavate the hills adjoining Lake Avernus. Traces of his frustrated hopes are visible today.

In parts of Rome unfilled by Nero's palace, construction was not—as after the burning by Gauls—without plan or demarcation. Street-fronts were of regulated alignment, streets were broad, and houses built round courtyards. Their height was restricted, and their frontages protected by colonnades. Nero undertook to erect these at his own expense, and also to clear debris from building-sites before transferring them to their owners. He announced bonuses, in proportion to rank and resources, for the completion of houses and blocks before a given date. Rubbish was to dumped in the Ostian marshes by corn-ships returning down the Tiber.

A fixed proportion of every building had to be massive, untimbered stone from Gabii or Alba (these stones being fireproof). Furthermore, guards were ensured a more abundant and extensive public water-supply, hitherto diminished by irregular private enterprise. Householders were obliged to keep fire-fighting apparatus in an accessible place; and semi-detached houses were forbidden—they must have their own walls. These measures were welcomed for their practicality, and they beautified the new city. Some, however, believed that the old town's configuration had been healthier, since its narrow streets and high houses had provided protection against the burning sun, whereas now the shadowless open spaces radiated a fiercer heat.

So much for human precautions. Next came attempts to appease heaven. After consultation of the Sibylline books, prayers were addressed to Vulcan,

Ceres, and Proserpine. Juno, too, was propitiated. Women who had been married were responsible for the rites—first on the Capital, then at the nearest sea-board, where water was taken to sprinkle her temple and statue. Women with husbands living also celebrated ritual banquets and vigils.

But neither human resources, nor imperial munificence, nor appeasement of the gods, eliminated sinister suspicions that the fire had been instigated. To suppress this rumour, Nero fabricated scapegoats—and punished with every refinement the notoriously depraved Christians (as they were popularly called). Their originator, Christ, had been executed in Tiberius' reign by the governor of Judea, Pontius Pilatus. But in spite of this temporary setback the deadly superstition had broken out afresh, not only in Judaea (where the mischief had started) but even in Rome. All degraded and shameful practices collect and flourish in the capital.

First, Nero had self-acknowledged Christians arrested. Then, on their information, large numbers of others were condemned—not so much for incendiarism as for their anti-social tendencies. Their deaths were made farcical. Dressed in wild animals' skins, they were torn to pieces by dogs, or crucified, or made into torches to be ignited after dark as substitutes for daylight. Nero provided his Gardens for the spectacle, and exhibited displays in the Circus, at which he mingled with the crowd—or stood in a chariot, dressed as a charioteer. Despite their guilt as Christians, and the ruthless punishment it deserved, the victims were pitied. For it was felt that they were being sacrificed for one's brutality rather than to the national interest.

QUESTIONS TO CONSIDER

1. How does Tacitus's choice of words betray his sympathies in Roman politics?
2. Tacitus chooses to describe only the "particularly praiseworthy or particularly scandalous" actions of the Roman senate. How might such an approach have shaped his treatment? How might a more inclusive approach have brought different results?
3. Which parts of Tacitus's account seem to come from his own direct observations and which from documentary sources? How do his treatments of these materials differ?
4. Most Roman historians believed the history of their own times showed a decline compared with the glory of the Roman past. What examples of this do you find in Tacitus?

FOR FURTHER READING

Benario, Herbert W. *An Introduction to Tacitus.* Athens, GA: University of Georgia Press, 1975.

Luce, T. J., and A. J. Woodman, eds. *Tacitus and the Tacitean Tradition.* Princeton, NJ: Princeton University Press, 1993.

Martin, Ronald H. *Tacitus*. Berkeley, CA: University of California Press, 1981.

Mellor, Ronald. *Tacitus*. New York: Routledge, 1992.

Mendell, Clarence Whittlesey. *Tacitus, the Man and his Work*. New Haven, CT: Yale University Press, 1957.

Syme, Ronald. *Tacitus*. Oxford: Clarendon, 1958.

NOTES

1. Moses Hadas, ed., *The Complete Works of Tacitus*, trans. A. J. Church and W. J. Brodribb (New York: Modern Library, 1942), 419–21.

2. Tacitus, *The Annals of Imperial Rome*, trans. Michael Grant (Harmondsworth, U.K.: Penguin, 1973), 31–35, 150, 172–73, 364–66.

CHAPTER 14

Luke

Historian of Early Christianity

Luke
© North Wind Pictures

Christian tradition uniformly regards Luke as the writer of two biblical books, the third gospel and the more historically constructed *Acts of the Apostles*, although neither work names a composer. Acts and Luke's gospel are joined both in their dedication to a certain Theophilus and in their language and style. Luke probably accompanied the apostle Paul on some of his missionary journeys in the first century CE and so was an eyewitness to some of the events he narrates. Paul referred to Luke as a physician in Colossians 4:14, and Luke's name clearly suggests that he was a Gentile Greek at least in education and language.

The preface to Luke's gospel, intended for *Acts* as well, bespeaks a purpose to strengthen converts' religious conviction; at the same time it offers a vivid description of the task of the narrative historian, clearer and more succinct than what we have seen in the Greeks, to whose tradition Luke was an heir:

> Many have undertaken to draw up an account of the things that have been fulfilled among us, just as they were handed down to us by those who from the first were eyewitnesses and servants of the word. Therefore, since I myself have carefully investigated everything from the beginning, it seemed good also to me to write an orderly account for you, most excellent Theophilus, so that you may know the certainty of the things you have been taught. (Luke 1:1–4)

Luke did his own personal research, checking previous accounts and interviewing eyewitnesses. He proposed to write an orderly narrative, essentially chronological (he cited several chronological guideposts, e.g. when Quirinius was governor of Syria, in the fifteenth regnal year of Roman emperor Tiberius), starting at the beginning (the background to Jesus's life), and continuing past Jesus's death to describe the early decades of the Christian church. Like most historians, Luke implied that previous accounts had not been as accurate as he hoped to be, so that, after hearing Luke's account, Theophilus could be certain of the things he had been taught.

Luke is regarded by some scholars as having witnessed much of what was recorded in Acts. The detailed descriptions of places in Palestine seem to assume that the readers would be unfamiliar with the eastern end of the Mediterranean, so many scholars believe Acts was composed in Rome or the West, with a Gentile audience in mind. This book, then, was part of the process that made Christianity a universally available religion, rather than remaining a small sect within Judaism. Like many later Christian historians, at least until the Enlightenment, Luke freely believed in a world filled with evil spirits and in the active hand of God to counteract them and to protect God's people.

The selections presented here describe three events in the life of the Christian church in the years after Jesus's death: (1) a speech by the apostle Peter on the occasion of Pentecost; (2) a council of church leaders held at Jerusalem that allowed Gentiles as well as Jews to join the church and so laid the way for it to broaden from a Jewish sect to a world religion; and (3) the appearance of the apostle Paul before the Roman governor Felix. Throughout, Luke offers a naturalistic narrative with lots of care as to descriptive detail.

The Acts of the Apostles[1]

When the day of Pentecost came, they were all together in one place. Suddenly a sound like the blowing of a violent wind came from heaven and filled the whole house where they were sitting. They saw what seemed to be tongues of fire that separated and came to rest on each of them. All of them were filled with the Holy Spirit and began to speak in other tongues as the Spirit enabled them.

Now there were staying in Jerusalem God-fearing Jews from every nation under heaven. When they heard this sound, a crowd came together in bewilderment, because each one heard them speaking in his own language. Utterly amazed, they asked: "Are not all these men who are speaking Galileans? Then how is it that each of us hears them in his own native language? Parthians, Medes and Elamites; residents of Mesopotamia, Judea and Cappadocia, Pontus and Asia, Phrygia and Pamphylia, Egypt and the parts of Libya near Cyrene; visitors from Rome (both Jews and converts to Judaism); Cretans and Arabs—we hear them declaring the wonders of God in our own tongues!" Amazed and perplexed, they asked one another, "What does this mean?"

Some, however, made fun of them and said, "They have had too much wine."

Then Peter stood up with the Eleven, raised his voice and addressed the crowd: "Fellow Jews and all of you who live in Jerusalem, let me explain this to you; listen carefully to what I say. These men are not drunk, as you suppose. It's only nine in the morning! No, this is what was spoken by the prophet Joel:

> In the last days, God says, I will pour out my Spirit on all people. Your sons and daughters will prophesy, your young men will see visions, your old men will dream dreams. Even on my servants, both men and women, I will pour out my Spirit in those days, and they will prophesy. I will show wonders in the heaven above and signs on the earth below, blood and fire and billows of smoke. The sun will be turned to darkness and the moon to blood before the coming of the great and glorious day of the Lord. And everyone who calls on the name of the Lord will be saved.

"Men of Israel, listen to this: Jesus of Nazareth was a man accredited by God to you by miracles, wonders and signs, which God did among you through him, as you yourselves know. This man was handed over to you by God's set purpose and foreknowledge; and you, with the help of wicked men, put him to death by nailing him to the cross. But God raised him from the dead, freeing him from the agony of death, because it was impossible for death to keep its hold on him."

*   *   *

When the people heard this, they were cut to the heart and said to Peter and the other apostles, "Brothers, what shall we do?"

Peter replied, "Repent and be baptized, every one of you, in the name of Jesus Christ for the forgiveness of your sins. And you will receive the gift of the Holy Spirit. The promise is for you and your children and for all who are far off—for all whom the Lord our God will call."

With many other words he warned them; and he pleaded with them. "Save yourselves from this corrupt generation." Those who accepted his message were baptized, and about three thousand were added to their number that day.

*   *   *

Some men came down from Judea to Antioch and were teaching the brothers: "Unless you are circumcised, according to the custom taught by Moses, you cannot be saved." This brought Paul and Barnabas into sharp dispute and debate with them. So Paul and Barnabas were appointed, along with some other believers, to go up to Jerusalem to see the apostles and elders about this question. The church sent them on their way, and as they traveled through Phoenicia and Samaria, they told how the Gentiles had been converted. This news made all the brothers very glad. When they came to Jerusalem, they were welcomed by the church and the apostles and elders, to whom they reported everything God had done through them.

Then some of the believers who belonged to the party of the Pharisees stood up and said, "The Gentiles must be circumcised and required to obey the law of Moses."

The apostles and elders met to consider this question. After much discussion, Peter got up and addressed them: "Brothers, you know that some time ago God made a choice among you that the Gentiles might hear from my lips the message of the gospel and believe. God, who knows the heart, showed that he accepted them by giving the Holy Spirit to them, just as he did to us. He made no distinction between us and them, for he purified their hearts by faith. Now then, why do you try to test God by putting on the necks of the disciples a yoke that neither we nor our fathers have been able to bear? No! We believe it is through the grace of our Lord Jesus that we are saved, just as they are."

The whole assembly became silent as they listened to Barnabas and Paul telling about the miraculous signs and wonders God had done among the Gentiles through them. When they finished, James spoke up: "Brothers, listen to me. Simon [i.e., Peter] has described to us how God at first showed his concern by taking from the Gentiles a people for himself. The words of the prophets are in agreement with this, as it is written:

> After this I will return and rebuild David's fallen tent. Its ruins I will rebuild, and I will restore it, that the remnant of men may seek the Lord, and all the Gentiles who bear my name, says the Lord, who does these things that have been known for ages.

"It is my judgment, therefore, that we should not make it difficult for the Gentiles who are turning to God. Instead we should write to them, telling them to abstain from food polluted by idols, from sexual immorality, from the meat of strangled animals and from blood. For Moses has been preached in every city from the earliest times and is read in the synagogues on every Sabbath."

The apostles and elders, with the whole church, decided to choose some of their own men and send them to Antioch with Paul and Barnabas. They chose Judas (called Barsabbas) and Silas, two men who were leaders among the brothers. With them they sent the following letter:

> The apostles and elders, your brothers,
> To the Gentile believers in Antioch, Syria and Cilicia:
> Greetings.
>   We have heard that some went out from us without our authorization and disturbed you, troubling your minds by what they said. So we all agreed to choose some men and send them to you with our dear friends Barnabas and Paul—men who have risked their lives for the name of our Lord Jesus Christ. Therefore we are sending Judas and Silas to confirm by word of mouth what we are writing. It seemed good to the Holy Spirit and to us not to burden you with anything beyond the following requirements: You are to abstain from food sacrificed to idols, from blood, from the meat of strangled animals and from sexual immorality. You will do well to avoid these things.
>   Farewell.

The men were sent off and went down to Antioch, where they gathered the church together and delivered the letter. The people read it and were glad for its encouraging message. Judas and Silas, who themselves were prophets, said much to encourage and strengthen the brothers. After spending some time there, they were sent off by the brothers with the blessing of peace to return to those who had sent them. But Paul and Barnabas remained in Antioch, where they and many others taught and preached the word of the Lord.

* * *

Five days later the high priest Ananias went down to Caesarea with some of the elders and a lawyer named Tertullus, and they brought their charges against Paul before the governor. When Paul was called in, Tertullus presented his case before Felix: "We have enjoyed a long period of peace under you, and your foresight has brought about reforms in this nation. Everywhere and in every way, most excellent Felix, we acknowledge this with profound gratitude. But in order not to weary you further, I would request that you be kind enough to hear us briefly.

"We have found this man to be a trouble-maker, stirring up riots among the Jews all over the world. He is a ringleader of the Nazarene sect and even tried to desecrate the temple; so we seized him. By examining him yourself you will be able to learn the truth about all these charges we are bringing against him."

The Jews joined in the accusation, asserting that these things were true.

When the governor motioned for him to speak, Paul replied: "I know that for a number of years you have been a judge over this nation; so I gladly make my defense. You can easily verify that no more than twelve days ago I went up to Jerusalem to worship. My accusers did not find me arguing with anyone at the temple, or stirring up a crowd in the synagogues or anywhere else in the city. And they cannot prove to you the charges they are now making against me. However, I admit that I worship the God of our fathers as a follower of the Way, which they call a sect. I believe everything that agrees with the Law and that is written in the Prophets, and I have the same hope in

God as these men, that there will be a resurrection of both the righteous and the wicked. So I strive always to keep my conscience clear before God and man.

"After an absence of several years, I came to Jerusalem to bring my people gifts for the poor and to present offerings. I was ceremonially clean when they found me in the temple courts doing this. There was no crowd with me, nor was I involved in any disturbance. But there are some Jews from the province of Asia, who ought to be here before you and bring charges if they have anything against me. Or these who are here should state what crime they found in me when I stood before the Sanhedrin—unless it was this one thing I shouted as I stood in their presence: 'It is concerning the resurrection of the dead that I am on trial before you today.'"

Then Felix, who was well acquainted with the way, adjourned the proceedings. "When Lysias the commander comes," he said, "I will decide your case." He ordered the centurion to keep Paul under guard but to give him some freedom and permit his friends to take care of his needs.

Several days later Felix came with his wife Drusilla, who was a Jewess. He sent for Paul and listened to him as he spoke about faith in Christ Jesus. As Paul discoursed on righteousness, self-control and the judgment to come, Felix was afraid and said, "That's enough for now! You may leave. When I find it convenient, I will send for you." At the same time he was hoping that Paul would offer him a bribe, so he sent for him frequently and talked with him.

When two years had passed, Felix was succeeded by Porcius Festus, but because Felix wanted to grant a favor to the Jews, he left Paul in prison.

QUESTIONS TO CONSIDER

1. How should historians deal with accounts that report supernatural events, such as the tongues of fire on the Christians?
2. What can we learn about controversies within the early Christian community from Luke's account of the preaching of Barnabus and Paul?
3. How might this account have looked different if it had been written by a Roman or Jewish historian?

FOR FURTHER READING

Barrett, Charles Kingsley. *Luke the Historian in Recent Study*. Philadelphia: Fortress Press, 1970.

Brawley, Robert L. *Luke-Acts And The Jews: Conflict, Apology, and Conciliation*. Atlanta, GA: Scholars Press, 1987.

Franklin, Eric. *Luke: Interpreter of Paul, Critic of Matthew*. Sheffield, U.K.: JSOT Press, 1994.

Jervell, Jacob. *The Unknown Paul: Essays On Luke-Acts and Early Christian History*. Minneapolis, MN: Augsburg, 1984.

Marshall, I. Howard. *Luke: Historian And Theologian*. Exeter, U.K.: Paternoster Press, 1970.

Neyrey, Jerome H., ed. *The Social World Of Luke-Acts: Models for Interpretation.*
    Peabody, MA: Hendrickson, 1991.
Walaskay, Paul W. *"And So We Came To Rome": The Political Perspective of St. Luke.*
    New York: Cambridge University Press, 1983.

NOTES

1. *The Holy Bible, New International Version* (Grand Rapids, MI: Zondervan, 1984), Acts 2:1–24, 37–41, 15:1–35, 24:1–27. Used by permission of the International Bible Society.

CHAPTER 15

Eusebius

Ecclesiastical Chronicler

Eusebius
The Bettmann Archive

E usebius (260–339?) is regarded as the father of church history. He lived at a time of great transition for Christians, when the Roman government changed from persecuting and killing them to a policy favoring Christians and seeking their advice. Roman policy from about CE 70 to 313 was to execute confessed Christians as enemies of the state, although the edict was sporadically and irregularly enforced. Especially in the Greek-speaking eastern end of the Roman Empire, Christians often flourished and practiced their religion openly for several generations, especially after 270. Under such conditions, Eusebius studied and worked at Caesarea in Palestine under the patronage of Pamphilius, a learned Christian. Here also Eusebius had access to an extensive library, which served him well in his historical task. In 303 a great empirewide persecution of Christians broke out, and visible and prominent Christians were particularly sought. Eusebius's mentor Pamphilius was imprisoned and eventually executed. It is likely that Eusebius himself was imprisoned for a while, and scholars believe he began his historical work amidst the persecution. After the persecution ended (in 311 in the east, 313 in the west), Eusebius became bishop of Caesarea. His life was busy thereafter. He had to deal with a church rapidly growing in numbers because of toleration and even favor by the Emperor Constantine. Christians soon became embroiled in doctrinal controversies over the relationship within the Trinity between Christ and the Creator known as the Arian controversy. Eusebius tried unsuccessfully to mediate between extreme positions in this debate. He came to the Council of Nicaea in 325 under suspicion of Arianism but ended up as the chief theological adviser to the Emperor Constantine. The bishops defined the relationship within the Godhead as one of equality among God the Father, Jesus the Son, and the Holy Spirit—a position Eusebius later upheld. Eusebius was an enthusiastic supporter of Constantine and his goal to unify the empire and bring peace, and he tried to get Constantine to rule as a Christian ruler. Eusebius's overzealous championing of the emperor caused him grief when Constantine died and his sons were less amenable to Eusebius's influence. Eusebius died about three years after Constantine, in about 339.

Eusebius was well suited to write church history. In addition to the aforementioned library at Caesarea, he had developed a system of chronology as a foundation for accurate history. This *Chronicon* has not survived in its Greek form but other translations show it to be a table of columns of world events starting from the beginning of time. It probably was done before 303 and so preceded his church history. The plan of the *History* must have been laid in 311, for Eusebius spoke of the end of the martyrdoms in his own time. The work went through several editions, adding events that happened after 311 and removing some embarrassingly adulatory comments about Constantine's co-emperor Licinius when he later was perceived as a traitor.

Eusebius relies on a variety of written sources and often cites the location of a quotation or source—relatively unusual in premodern writers. In addition to the Bible, he relies heavily on Josephus, a first-century CE Jewish general and historian (see Chapter 11); Philo of Alexandria, a first-century Jewish philosopher; Clement of Alexandria, a second-century Christian bishop; Justin Martyr,

a second-century philosopher converted to Christianity; Irenaeus, a defender
of the Christian faith; a variety of minor Christian authors; and a number of
works that no longer exist, known to us only by their titles and authors.
Where it is possible to check Eusebius, his quotations and references are quite
accurate and reflect fairly the ideas of his sources.

Eusebius did have a bias, however, one that continues to influence writers
of Christian history to this very day. Eusebius both assumed and sought to
prove that the ideas and doctrines of the church developed in unbroken
succession from the time of the apostles to his present, and that any deviation
from that tradition was heresy and required correction. This led Eusebius to
downplay the dissent within the church and to exaggerate the evil intent of
heretics (while the cliché that the winners write history is grossly simplistic,
there is some truth in it).

A second problem stems from the fact that Eusebius enthusiastically
appreciated the toleration for Christians first granted by Emperor Galerius
(d. 311) in the east and then extended to the whole empire by Constantine in
CE 313. This caused his overarching judgment of historical figures to be based
mainly on whether they helped or hindered the church. Thus, Galerius—
perpetrator of the most violent persecutions of Christians—ended up being
judged favorably because he relented and gave Christians legal tolerance. And
Constantine and his father Constantius were deemed pious for belated
clemency toward Christians.

The first passage that follows shows Eusebius' attitude toward a couple of
early postapostolic heresies, the Ebionites and the Nicolaïtians. The second is
his interpretation of the victory by Constantine over his more able rival
Maxentius near Rome in CE 312. Eusebius clearly believed that the hand of
God was at work in this unexpected victory.

The Ecclesiastical History[1]

Let us now continue the narrative. Menander succeeded Simon Magus and showed himself as a weapon of the devil's power not inferior to his predecessor. He, too, was a Samaritan, progressed to the highest point of sorcery not less than his master, and abounded in greater wonders. He said of himself that he was the saviour who had been sent from above for the salvation of men from invisible aeons and taught that no one, not even of the angels who made the world, could survive unless they were first rescued through the magic art which was transmitted by him and through the baptism which he delivered, for those who were vouchsafed it would obtain a share of eternal immortality in this life itself, no longer mortal but remaining here, destined to everlasting and ageless immortality. This point can also be easily studied from the writings of Irenaeus. Justin, too, in the same way after mentioning Simon continues his account of him by saying, "We also know that a certain Menander, who also was a Samaritan from the village of Caparataea, became a disciple of Simon and being similarly stimulated by the demons appeared in Antioch and deceived many by magical arts. He persuaded those who followed him that they would not die, and there are still some of his followers who believe this."

It was assuredly at the instigation of the devil that the name of Christian was adopted by such sorcerers to calumniate by magic the great mystery of religion and through them to destroy the teaching of the Church on the immortality of the soul and the resurrection of the dead. Those who termed these Saviours fell from the true hope. But others the wicked demon, when he could not alienate them from God's plan in Christ, made his own, when he found them by a different snare. The first Christians gave these the suitable name of Ebionites because they had poor and mean opinions concerning Christ. They held him to be a plain and ordinary man who had achieved righteousness merely by the progress of his character and had been born naturally from Mary and her husband. They insisted on the complete observation of the Law, and did not think that they would be saved by faith in Christ alone and by a life in accordance with it. But there were others besides these who have the same name. These escaped the absurd folly of the first mentioned, and did not deny that the Lord was born of a Virgin and the Holy Spirit, but nevertheless agreed with them in not confessing his pre-existence as God, being the Logos and Wisdom. Thus they shared in the impiety of the former class, especially in that they were equally zealous to insist on the literal observance of the law. They thought that the letters of the Apostle [Paul] ought to be wholly rejected and called him an apostate from the Law. They used only the Gospel called according to the Hebrews and made little account of the rest. Like the former they used to observe the Sabbath and the rest of the Jewish ceremonial, but on Sundays celebrated rites like ours in commemoration of the Saviour's resurrection. Wherefore from these practices they have obtained their name, for the name of Ebionites indicates the poverty of their intelligence, for this name means "poor" in Hebrew.

We have received the tradition that at the time under discussion Cerinthus founded another heresy. Gaius, whose words I have quoted before, in the inquiry attributed to him writes as follows about Cerinthus. "Moreover, Cerinthus, who through revelations attributed to the writing of a great apostle, lyingly introduces portents to us as though shown him by angels, and says that after the resurrection the kingdom of Christ will be on earth and that humanity living in Jerusalem will again be the slave of lust and pleasure. He is the enemy of the scriptures of God and in his desire to deceive says that the marriage feast will last a thousand years." Dionysius, too, who held the bishopric of the diocese of Alexandria in our time, in the second book of his Promises makes some remarks about the Apocalypse of John as though from ancient tradition and refers to the same Cerinthus in these words, "Cerinthus too, who founded the Cerinthian heresy named after him, wished to attach a name worthy of credit to his own invention, for the doctrine of his teaching was this, that the kingdom of Christ would be on earth, and being fond of his body and very carnal he dreamt of a future according to his own desires, given up to the indulgence of the flesh, that is, eating and drinking and marrying, and to those things which seem a euphemism for these things, feasts and sacrifices and the slaughter of victims."

Dionysius said this and Irenaeus in his first book *Against Heresies* quoted some of his more abominable errors, and in the third book has committed to writing a narrative, which deserves not to be forgotten, stating how, according to the tradition of Polycarp, the apostle John once went into a bath-house to wash, but when he knew that Cerinthus was within leapt out of the place and fled from the door, for he did not endure to be even under the same roof with him, and enjoined on those who were with him to do the same, saying, "Let us flee, lest the bath-house fall in, for Cerinthus, the enemy of the truth, is within."

At this time, too, there existed for a short time the heresy of the Nicolaïtans of which the Apocalypse of John also makes mention. These claimed Nicolas, one of the deacons in the company of Stephen who were appointed by the Apostles for the service of the poor. Clement of Alexandria in the third book of the *Stromata* gives the following account of him. "He had, they say, a beautiful wife; but after the ascension of the Saviour he was accused of jealousy by the apostles, and brought her forward and commanded her to be mated to anyone who wished. They say that this action was in consequence of the injunction 'it is necessary to abuse the flesh,' and that by following up what had been done and said with simplicity and without perversion those who follow his heresy lead a life of unrestrained license. But I have learned that Nicolas had nothing to do with any other woman beside her whom he married, and that of his children the daughters reached old age as virgins, and that the son remained uncorrupted. Since this is the case it is clear that the exposure of the wife of whom he was jealous in the midst of the disciples was the abandonment of passion, and that teaching the abuse of the flesh was continence from the pleasures which he had sought. For I think that according to the command of the Saviour he did not wish to serve two masters—pleasure and the Lord. They also say that this was the teaching of Matthias, to slight the flesh and abuse it, yielding nothing to it for pleasure, but to make the soul grow through faith and knowledge." Let this suffice concerning the attempts made during this period to triumph against the truth which were, nevertheless, extinguished forever more quickly than it takes to tell.

Clement, whose words we cited recently in the context of the previous quotation, enumerates, on account of those who reject marriage, those of the Apostles who were married, saying, "Or will they disapprove even of the Apostles? For Peter and Philip begat children, and Philip even gave his daughters to husbands, while Paul himself does not hesitate in one of his letters to address his wife whom he did not take about with him in order to facilitate his mission." Since we have made these quotations there is no harm in adducing another memorable narrative of Clement which he wrote down in the seventh book of the *Stromata,* and narrates as follows: "They say that the blessed Peter when he saw his own wife led out to death rejoiced at her calling and at her return home and called out to her in true warning and comfort, addressing her by her name, 'Remember the Lord.' Such was the marriage of the blessed and the perfect disposition of those dearest to them." Let this, cognate to the present subject, suffice for the moment.

* * *

Such were the wages received for the proud boasting of Maximin and for the petitions presented by the cities against us; while the proofs of the Christians' zeal and piety in every respect were manifest to all the heathen. For example, they alone in such an evil state of affairs gave practical evidence of their sympathy and humanity: all day long some of them would diligently persevere in performing the last offices for the dying and burying them (for there were countless numbers, and no one to look after them); while others would gather together in a single assemblage the multitude of those who all throughout the city were wasted with the famine, and distribute bread to them all, so that their action was on all men's lips, and they glorified the God of the Christians, and, convinced by the deeds themselves, acknowledged that they alone were truly pious and God-fearing.

After these things were thus accomplished, God, the great and heavenly champion of the Christians, when He had displayed His threatening and wrath against all men by the aforesaid means, in return for their exceeding great attacks against us, once again restored to us the bright and kindly radiance of His providential care for us. Most marvellously, as in a thick darkness, He caused the light of peace to shine upon us from Himself, and made it manifest to all the God Himself had been watching over our affairs continually, at times scourging and in due season correcting His people by means of misfortunes, and again on the other hand after sufficient chastisement showing mercy and goodwill to those who fix their hopes on Him.

Thus in truth Constantine, who, as aforesaid, was Emperor and sprung from an Emperor, pious and sprung from a most pious and in every respect most prudent father, and Licinius, who ranked next to him—both honoured for their understanding and piety—were stirred up by the King of Kings, God of the universe and Saviour, two men beloved of God, against the two most impious tyrants; and when war was formally engaged, God proved their ally in the most wonderful manner, and Maxentius fell at Rome at the hands of Constantine; while he of the East did not long survive him, for he too perished by most disgraceful death at the hands of Licinius, who had not yet become mad.

But to resume. Constantine, the superior of the Emperors in rank and dignity, was the first to take pity on those subjected to tyranny at Rome; and, calling in prayer upon God who is in heaven, and His Word, even Jesus Christ the Saviour of all, as his ally, he advanced in full force seeking to secure for the Romans their ancestral liberty. Maxentius, to be sure, put his trust rather in devices of magic than in the goodwill of his subjects, and in truth did not dare to advance even beyond the city's gates, but with an innumerable multitude of heavy-armed soldiers and countless bodies of legionaries secured every place and district and city that had been reduced to slavery by him in the environs of Rome and in all Italy. The Emperor, closely relying on the help that comes from God, attacked the first, second and third of the tyrant's armies, and capturing them all with ease advanced over a large part of Italy, actually coming very near to Rome itself. Then, that he might be compelled because of the tyrant to fight against Romans, God Himself as if with chains dragged the tyrant far away from the gates; and those things which were inscribed long ago in the sacred books against wicked men—to which as a myth very many gave no faith, yet were they worthy of faith to the faithful—now by their very clearness found faith, in a word, with all, faithful and faithless, who had the miracle before their eyes. As, for example, in the days of Moses himself and the ancient and godly race of the Hebrews, "Pharaoh's chariots and his host hath he cast into the sea, his chosen horsemen, even captains, they were sunk in the Red Sea, the deep covered them"; in the same way also Maxentius and the armed soldiers and guards around him "went down into the depths like a stone," when he turned his back before the God-sent power that was with Constantine, and was crossing the river that lay in his path, which he himself had bridged right well by joining of boats, and so formed into an engine of destruction against himself. Wherefore one might say: "He hath made a pit, and digged it, and shall fall into the ditch which he made. His work shall return upon his own head, and his wickedness shall come down upon his own pate."

Thus verily, through the breaking of the bridge over the river, the passage across collapsed, and down went the boats all at once, men and all, into the deep; and first of all he himself, that most wicked of men, and then also the shield-bearers around him, as the divine oracles foretell, sank as lead in the mighty waters. So that suitably, if not in words, at least in deeds, like the followers of the great servant Moses, those who had won the victory by the help of God might in some sort of hymn the very same words which were uttered against the wicked tyrant of old, and say: "Let us sing unto the Lord, for gloriously hath he been glorified: the horse and his rider hath he thrown into the sea. The Lord is my strength and protector, he is become my salvation"; and "Who is like unto thee, O Lord, among the gods? Who is like thee, glorified in saints, marvellous in praises, doing wonders?" These things, and such as are akin and similar to them, Constantine by his very deeds sang to God the Ruler of all and Author of the victory; then he entered Rome with hymns of triumph, and all the senators and other persons of great note, together with women and quite young children and all the Roman people, received him in a body with beaming countenances to their very heart as a ransomer, saviour and benefactor, with praises and insatiable joy. But he, as one possessed of natural piety towards God, was by no means stirred by their shouts nor uplifted by their praises, for well he knew that his help was from God; and straightway he gave orders that a memorial of the Saviour's Passion should be set up in the hand of his own statue; and indeed when they set him in the most public place in Rome holding the Saviour's sign in his right hand, he bade them engrave this very inscription in these words in the Latin tongue: "By this salutary sign, the true proof of bravery, I saved and delivered your city from the yoke of the tyrant; and moreover I freed and restored to their ancient fame and splendour both the senate and the people of the Romans."

And after this Constantine himself, and with him the emperor Licinius, whose mind was not yet deranged by the madness into which he afterwards fell, having propitiated God as the Author of all their good fortune, both with one will and purpose drew up a most perfect law in the fullest terms on behalf of the Christians; and to Maximin, who was still ruler of the provinces of the East and playing at being their friends, they sent on an account of the marvellous things that God had done for them, as well as of their victory over the tyrant, and the law itself.

QUESTIONS TO CONSIDER

1. How do Eusebius' own commitments in theology and church politics shape his account?
2. Outside of biblical revelation, how do historians in the Christian tradition represent the "hand of God" in historical events?
3. What should historians do with accounts that are clearly tendentious when those accounts are all that we have available for many events?

FOR FURTHER READING

Attridge, Harold W., and Gohei Hata, eds. *Eusebius, Christianity, and Judaism.* Detroit, MI: Wayne State University Press, 1992.
Barnes, Timothy D. *Constantine and Eusebius.* Cambridge, MA: Harvard University Press, 1981.
Grant, Robert McQueen. *Eusebius as Church Historian.* Oxford: Clarendon Press, 1980.
McIntire, C. T., ed. *God, History, and Historians.* New York: Oxford University Press, 1977.
Stevenson, James. *Studies in Eusebius.* Cambridge, U. K.: The University Press, 1929.
Wallace-Hadrill, D. S. *Eusebius of Caesarea.* Westminster, MD: Canterbury Press, 1961.

NOTES

1. Eusebius, *The Ecclesiastical History,* trans. Kirsopp Lake and J. E. L. Oulton (London: Heinemann, 1926–42), 1:259–69, 2:357–65.

CHAPTER 16

Al-Tabari

Founder of Muslim Historiography

An illustrated page of the Koran on display in Tehran.
© Corbis

T he founding of Islam was arguably the most important event in the West
between the fall of Rome and Columbus's voyages to the "New World."
Muhammad and his successors not only created a religion and an Arab
empire; they created a civilization. Islam absorbed what had gone before it:
Greek philosophy, Persian and Roman forms of government, Jewish and
Christian moral codes. But it transformed these, imbued them with a new
spirit, and welded them into a unique whole.

This was as true for history writing as it was for other parts of life. Greeks,
Romans, Persians, Jews, and Christians all wrote histories, which Muslim
historians read and preserved. But Muslims created their own pattern. This
pattern reached its height in the tenth-century work of al-Tabari. A vast
annalistic compilation, his *History of the Prophet and Kings* set the standard by
which Muslim historians were measured for the next several centuries.

Muhammad ibn Jarir al-Tabari (there is some disagreement about the
number and nature of his names) was born about 839 in Tabaristan, a Persian
province just south of the Caspian Sea. His father supposedly dreamed that
his son was destined for greatness, and so arranged for him to study in Egypt,
Damascus, and Baghdad. He eventually settled in the latter city, where he
followed the traditional career of a Muslim scholar until his death in 923. He
wrote on many subjects: the law, theology, and Qur'anic interpretation as well
as history. He is said to have written forty folios a day for forty years—a
prodigious output. Modern scholars should note that his father's wealth made
such production possible, giving him free time with no teaching or court
responsibilities. Unfortunately, many of his twenty-eight major works have
been lost. His lengthy *History* and a thirty-volume treatise on the Qur'an are
the principal ones to survive.

Al-Tabari's *History* looks strange to modern eyes. First, he does not sift his
sources for information out of which to construct an account of the past.
Instead, he presents events exactly as his sources report them, giving us two,
three, or more versions where his sources disagree. Second, he organizes
events by years rather than continuously, splitting up longer events into
several episodes. Both these techniques were derived from traditional
Qur'anic scholarship or *hadith*. Al-Tabari's innovation was to apply them to
historical material.

Both make sense in the Islamic context. Early Islam saw eyewitness
description as the best criterion of truth, so long as those who see and report
an event are of good character. The Qur'an is true because it recounts the
words of the angel Gabriel exactly as they were uttered to a man of great
character—Muhammad. He then transmitted the Qur'an to others, who are
themselves unimpeachable. This chain of authorities (*isnad*) assures us of the
veracity of what we now read. By quoting his sources directly and listing the
isnad from which they derive, al-Tabari is treating events as Qur'anic scholars
treated their holy book. He establishes the truth of events by establishing the
reliability of their transmitters.

Similarly, the episodic, annalistic approach matches the Qur'an's aphoris-
tic nature. Though it contains narratives, the Qur'an is more a collection of

proof texts and less a collection of stories than are the Hebrew and Christian Bibles that it in part absorbed. In imitation, al-Tabari highlights isolated events to the detriment of the context in which those events are found. He again applied a Qur'anic approach to history, reinforcing similar moves by his predecessors.

Despite these peculiarities, al-Tabari's *History* is still our best source for the first three hundred years of Islam—from the time of the prophet to al-Tabari's own day. Its multiple versions of events and its record of what previous authors wrote are invaluable for reconstructing this early era, not the least because most of his sources have been lost. On the other hand, though his work claims to be a universal history, it is not. Its description of the world before Islam follows the Qur'an rather mechanically. Later sections focus on political events and on the development of Islam, leaving social and cultural history aside. The last sections focus quite closely on the Baghdad in which al-Tabari lived. The first two of these limits set the pattern for later Muslim histories, though some of these came to be organized by rulerships or dynasties, rather than by years.

The following passage is typical of both al-Tabari's method and the substance of his work. It recounts events from Muhammad's years in Mecca, reports the various stories that have been passed down about them, and gives their chains of transmission. The result may seem odd to us; yet it exemplifies the Muslim historiography of its time quite well.

The History of Prophets and Kings[1]
The Beginning of the Prophetic Mission

Abu Ja'far (al-Tabari): Quraysh's rebuilding of the Ka'bah was fifteen years after the Sacrilegious War. There were twenty years between the Year of the Elephant and the Year of the Sacrilegious War. The early authorities differ as to the age of the Messenger of God when he became a prophet. Some say that it was five years after the Quraysh rebuilt the Ka'bah, when his fortieth birthday had passed.

Those who say this:

Muhammad b. Khalaf al-'Asqalani—Adam—Hammad b. Salamah—Abu Jamrah al-Duba'i—Ibn 'Abbas: The Messenger of God commenced his mission at the age of forty.

'Amr b. 'Ali and Ibn al-Muthanna—Yahya b. Muhammad b. Qays—Rabi'ah b. Abi 'Abd al-Rahman—Anas b. Malik: The Messenger of God commenced his mission at the beginning of his fortieth year.

Al-'Abbas b. al-Walid—his father al-Awza'i—Rabi'ah b. Abi 'Abd al-Rahman—Anas b. Malik: The Messenger of God commenced his mission at the beginning of his fortieth year.

Ibn 'Abd al-Rahim al-Barqi—'Amr b. Abi Salamah—al-Awza'i—Rabi'ah b. Abi 'Abd al-Rahman—Anas b. Malik: The Messenger of God commenced his mission at the beginning of his fortieth year.

Abu Shurahbil al-Himsi—Abu al-Yaman—Isma'il b. 'Ayyash—Yahya b. Sa'id—Rabi'ah b. Abi 'Abd al-Rahman—Anas b. Malik: The Messenger of God received the revelation when he was aged forty.

Ibn al-Muthanna—al-Hajjaj b. al-Minhal—Hammad—'Amr b. Dinar—Urwah b. al-Zubayr: The Messenger of God commenced his mission when he was aged forty.

Ibn al-Muthanna—al-Hajjaj—Hammad—'Amr-Yahya b. Ja'dah: The Messenger of God said to Fatimah, "(Gabriel) has reviewed the Qur'an with me once a year, but this year he has reviewed it with me twice, and I fancy that my time has come. You are the nearest to me of my kin. Whenever a prophet has been sent, his mission has lasted for a period of half his predecessor's lifetime. Jesus was sent for a period of forty years, and I was sent for twenty."

'Ubayd b. Muhammad al-Warraq—Rawh b. 'Ubadah—Hisham—'Ikrimah—Ibn 'Abbas: The Messenger of God commenced his mission at the age of forty, and remained in Mecca for thirteen years.

Abu Kurayb—Abu Usamah and Muhammad b. Maymun al-Za'farani—Hisham b. Hassan—'Ikrimah—Ibn 'Abbas: The Messenger of God commenced his mission and received the revelation when he was aged forty, and remained in Mecca for thirteen years.

Others say that he became a prophet when he was aged forty-three.

Those who say this:

Ahmad b. Thabit al-Razi—Ahmad—Yahya b. Sa'id—Hisham—Ikrimah—Ibn 'Abbas: The Prophet received the revelation when he was aged forty-three.

Ibn Humayd—Jarir—Yahya b. Sa'id—Sa'id al-Musayyab: The Messenger of God received the revelation when he was aged forty-three.

Ibn al-Muthanna—'Abd al-Wahhab—Yahya b. Sa'id—Sa'id, that is, Ibn al-Musayyab: The Messenger of God received the revelation when he was aged forty-three.

* * *

Signs of the Approach of Prophethood

Abu Ja'far (al-Tabari): Before Gabriel appeared to him to confer on him his mission as Messenger of God, it is said that he used to see signs and evidences indicating that God wished to ennoble him and to single him out for his favor. One of these is the account which I have previously given of the two angels who came to him, opened his breast, and removed the hatred and the impurity which were in it. This was when he was with his foster-mother, Halimah. Another is that it is said that whenever he passed along a road and passed by a tree or a stone, it would greet him.

Al-Harith b. Muhammad—Muhammad d. Sa'd—Muhammad b.'Umar—'Ali b. Muhammad b. 'Ubaydallah b. 'Abdallah b. 'Umar b. al-Khattab—Mansur b. 'Abd al-Rahman—his mother Barrah bt. Abi Tajrah: When God willed that Muhammad should be ennobled and should enter upon prophethood, it came about that whenever he went out to attend his business he would go a great distance, out of sight of houses, and into the ravines and wadi-beds; and then every stone and tree he passed would say, "Peace be upon you, Messenger of God." He would turn to the right and the left and turn around, but could not see anyone.

* * *

The Manner in Which the Qur'an Was First Revealed

We now return to an account of the condition of the Prophet of God at the time when God began to ennoble him by sending Gabriel to him bearing the revelation.

Abu Ja'far (al-Tabari): We have mentioned previously some of the stories related to the first occasion on which Gabriel brought our prophet Muhammad the revelation from God and how old the prophet was at that time. We shall now describe the manner in which Gabriel began to come to him and to appear to him bringing the revelation of his Lord.

Ahmad b. 'Uthman, known as Abu al-Jawza—Wahb b. Jarir—his father—al-Nu'man b. Rashid—al-Zuhri—'Urwah—'A'ishah: The first form in which the revelation came to the messenger of God was true vision; this used to come to him like the break of dawn. After that, he grew to love solitude and used to remain in a cave on Hira' engaged in acts of devotion for a number of days before returning to his family. Then he would return to his family and supply himself with provisions for a similar number of days. This continued until the Truth came to him unexpectedly, and said 'Muhammed, you are the Messenger of God.'" (Describing what happened next,) the Messenger of God said, "I had been standing, but fell to my knees; and crawled away, my shoulders trembling. I went to Khadijah and said, 'Wrap me up! Wrap me up!' When the terror had left me, he came to me and said, 'Muhammed, you are the messenger of God.' "

He (Muhammed) said: I had been thinking of hurling myself down from a mountain crag, but he appeared to me, as I was thinking about this and said, "Muhammed, I am Gabriel and you are the Messenger of God." Then he said, "What shall I recite?" He took me and pressed me three times tightly until I was nearly stifled and was utterly exhausted; then he said: "Recite in the name of your Lord who created," and I recited it. Then I went to Khadijah and said, "I have been in fear for my life." When I told her what had happened, she said, "Rejoice, for God will never put you to shame, for you treat your kinsfolk well, tell the truth, deliver what is entrusted to you, endure fatigue, offer hospitality to the guest, and aid people in misfortune."

Then she took me to Waraqah b. Nawfal b. Asad and said to him "Listen to your brother's son." He questioned me and I told him what had happened. He said, "This is the Namus which was sent down to Moses, son of 'Imaran. Would that I were a young man now, and would that I could be alive when your people drive you out!" I said, "Will they drive me out?" "Yes," he said. "No man has ever brought the message which you have brought without being met with enmity. If I live to see that day, I shall come firmly to your aid."

The first parts of the Qur'an to be revealed to me after Iqra' were:

> Nun. By the pen, and that which they write. You are not, through your Lord's favor to you, a madman. Yours will be a reward unfailing, and you are of a great nature. You shall see and they shall see.

and:

> O you enveloped in your cloak, arise and warn!

and:

> By the forenoon, and by the night when it is still.

Yunus b. 'Abd al-A 'la—Ibn Wahb—Yunus—Ibn Shihabb—'Urwah—'A'ishah: A similar account, but omitting the last part from the words "The first parts of the Qur'an. . . ."

Muhammad b. 'Abd al-Malik b. Abi al-Shawarib—'Abd al-Wahid b. Ziyad—Sulayman al-Shaybani—'Abd Allah b. Shaddad: Gabriel came to Muhammad and said, "O Muhammad, recite!" He said, "I cannot recite." Gabriel was violent towards him and then said again, "O Muhammad recite!" He said, "I cannot recite," and Gabriel again used violent words towards him. A third time he said, "O Muhammad, recite!" He said, "What shall I recite?" and he said:

> Recite in the name of your Lord who creates! He creates man from a clot of blood.
> Recite: And your Lord is the most Bountiful, He who teaches by the pen, teaches man what he knew not.

Then he went to Khadijah and said, "Khadijah, I think that I have gone mad." "No, by God," she said. "Your Lord would never do that to you. You have never committed a wicked act." Khadijah went to Waraqah b. Nawfal and told him what had happened. He said, "If what you say is true, your husband is a prophet. He will meet adversity from his people. If I live long enough, I shall believe in him."

After this, Gabriel did not come to him for a while, and Khadijah said to him, "I think that your Lord must have come to hate you." Then God revealed to him:

> By the forenoon, and by the night when it is still, your Lord has not forsaken you, nor does he hate you.

Ibn Humayd—Salamah—Muhammad b. Ishaq—Wahb b. Kaysan the *mawla* of the family of al-Zubayr: I heard 'Abdallah b. al-Zubayr saying to 'Ubayd, b. 'Umayr b. Qatadah al-Laythi, "Relate to us, 'Ubayd, what the beginning of the Messenger of God's prophetic mission was like when Gabriel came to him." I was present as 'Ubayd related the following account to 'Abdallah b. al-Zubayr and those with him. He said, "The Messenger of God used to spend one month in every year in religious retreat on Hira'." This was part of the practice of *tahannuth* in which Quraysh used to engage during the Jahiliyyah. *Tahannuth* means self-justification. (Mentioning this practice) Abu Talib said, "By those ascending Hira' and those descending."

The Messenger of God used to spend this month in every year in religious retreat, feeding the poor who came to him. When he had completed his month of retreat the first thing which he would do on leaving, even before going home, was to circumbulate the Ka'bah seven times, or however many times God willed; then he would go home.

When the month came in which God willed to ennoble him, in the year in which God made him his Messenger, this being the month of the Ramadan, the Messenger of God went out as usual to Hira' accompanied by his family. When the night came on which God ennobled him by making him his Messenger and thereby showed mercy to his servants, Gabriel brought him the command of God. The Messenger of God said, "Gabriel came to me as I was sleeping with a brocade cloth in which was writing. He said, "Recite!" and I said, "I cannot recite." He pressed me tight and almost stifled me, until I thought that I should die. Then he let me go, and said, "Recite!" I said, "What shall I recite?" only saying that in order to free myself from him, fearing that he might repeat what he had done to me. He said:

> Recite in the name of your Lord who creates! He creates man from a clot of blood.
> Recite: And your Lord is the Most Bountiful, He who teaches by the pen, teaches man what he knew not.

I recited it, and then he desisted and departed. I woke up, and it was as though these words had been written on my heart. There was no one of God's creation more hateful to me than a poet or a madman; I could not bear to look at either of them. I said to myself, "Your humble servant (meaning himself) is either a poet or a madman, but Quraysh shall never say this of me. I shall take myself to a mountain crag, hurl myself down from it, kill myself, and find relief in that way."

I went out intending to do that, but when I was halfway up the mountain I heard a voice from heaven saying, "O Muhammad, you are the Messenger of God, and I am Gabriel." I raised my head to heaven, and there was Gabriel in the form of a man with his feet set on the horizon, saying, "O Muhammad, you are the Messenger of God and I am Gabriel." I stood looking at him and this distracted me from what I had intended, and I could go neither forward nor back. I turned my face away from him to all points of the horizon, but wherever I looked I saw him in exactly the same form. I remained standing there, neither going forward nor turning back, until Khadijah sent her messengers to look for me. They went as far as Mecca and came back to her, while I was standing in the same place. At last Gabriel left me and I went back to my family. When I came to Khadijah, I sat down with my thigh next to hers, and she said to me, "Abu al-Qasim, where have you been? I sent messengers to look for you all the way to Mecca and back." I said to her, "I am either a poet or a madman," but she answered, "May God save you from that, Abu al-Qasim! God would not do that to you considering what I know of your truthfulness, your great trustworthiness, your good character, and your good treatment of your kinsfolk. It is not that, cousin. Perhaps you did see something." "Yes," I said, and then told her what I had seen. "Rejoice, cousin, and stand firm," she said. "By Him is whose hand is Khadijah's soul, I hope that you may be the prophet of this community." Then she rose up, gathered her garments around her, and went to Waraqah b. Nawfal b. Asad, who was her paternal cousin. He had become a Christian, read the Scriptures, and learned from the people of the Torah and the Gospel. She told him what the Messenger of God had told her that he had seen and heard. Waraqah said, "Holy, Holy! By Him in whose hand is the soul of Waraqah, if what you say is true, Khadijah, there has come to him the greatest Namus—meaning by Namus, Gabriel—he who came to Moses (That means that) Muhammad is the prophet of this community. Tell him to stand firm."

Khadijah went back to the Messenger of God and told him what Waraqah had said, and this relieved his anxiety somewhat. When he had completed his retreat he went back to Mecca and, as was his usual practice, went first to the Ka'bah and circumambulated it. Waraqah b. Nawfal met him as he was doing this and said, "Son of my brother, tell me what you saw or heard." The Messenger of God did so, and Waraqah said to him, "By Him in whose hand is my soul, you are the prophet of this community, and there has come to you the greatest Namus, he who came to Moses. They will call you a liar, molest you, drive you out, and fight you. If I live to see that, I will come to God's assistance in a way which he knows." Then he brought his head close and kissed the top of his head. The Messenger of God went home with his resolve strengthened by what Waraqah had said and with some of his anxiety relieved.

Ibn Humayd—Salamah—Muhammad b. Ishaq—Isma'il b. Abi Hakiim the *mawla* of the family of al-Zubayr: He was told that Khadijah said to the

Messenger of God, to keep him steadfast in the prophethood with which God had ennobled him, "Cousin, can you tell me when this companion of yours who visits you comes?" He replied, "Yes," and she said, "Tell me then, when he comes." Gabriel came to him as before, and the Messenger of God said to Khadijah, "Kahdijah, here is Gabriel who has come to me." She said, "Yes? Come and sit by my left thigh cousin." He came and sat by her and she said, "Move around and sit by my right thigh." He did so, and she said, "Can you see him?" He replied, "Yes," and she said, "Move around and sit in my lap." He did so, and she said, "Can you see him?" He replied yes and she was grieved, and flung off her veil while the Messenger of God was sitting in her lap. Then she said, "Can you see him?" and he replied, "No." At that she said, "Cousin, be steadfast and rejoice. By God, this being is an angel and no devil."

Ibn Humayd—Salamah—Muhammad b. Ishaq: I related this tradition (*hadith*) to 'Abdallah b. al-Hasan, and he said, "I heard my mother Fatimah bt. al-Husayn relating this *Hadith* on the authority of Khadijah, except that I heard her saying that Khadijah put the Messenger of God inside her shift next to her body, and that thereupon Gabriel departed. Then she said, 'This being is an angel and no devil.'"

Ibn al-Muthanna—'Uthman b. 'Umar b. Faris—'Ali b. al-Mubarak—Yahya, that is, Ibn Ani Kathir: I asked Abu Salamah which part of the Qur'an had been revealed first, and he replied:

> "O you enveloped in your cloak, arise and warn!"

Muhammad b. 'Abd al-A'la—Ibn Thawr—Ma'mar—al-Zuhri: The inspiration ceased to come to the Messenger of God for a while, and he was deeply grieved. He began to go to the tops of mountain crags, in order to fling himself from them; but every time he reached the summit of a mountain, Gabriel appeared to him and said to him, " You are the Prophet of God." Thereupon his anxiety would subside and he would come back to himself.

The Prophet used to relate this story as follows: "I was walking one day when I saw the angel who used to come to me at Hira' on a throne between heaven and earth. I was terror-stricken by him, and I went back to Khadijah and said, "Wrap me up!" So we wrapped him up (*zammalnahu*), that is, enveloped him in a cloak (*daththarnahu*), and God revealed:

> O you enveloped in your cloak, arise and warn! Your Lord magnify, your raiment purify.

Al-Zuhri: The first thing to be revealed to him was "Recite in the name of your Lord who creates . . ." as far as the words "what he knew not."

Yunus b. 'Abd al-A'la—Ibn Wahb—Yunus—Ibn Shihab—Abu Salamah b. 'Abd al-Rahman—Jabir b. 'Abdallah al-Ansari: The Messenger of God said, relating the story of the interruption or gap in the revelation, "As I was walking, I heard a voice from heaven. I looked up, and suddenly saw the angel who came to me at Hira' seated on a throne between heaven and earth. I was terror-stricken and went (to Khadijah) and said "Wrap me up! Wrap me up!" They enveloped me in my cloak, and God revealed, "O you enveloped in your cloak, arise and warn . . ." as far as "and pollution shun."

After that, the revelation came in regular succession.

QUESTIONS TO CONSIDER

1. What kinds of events does al-Tabari report as most significant? What classes of events does he leave out?
2. What are the benefits of organizing events by years rather than narratively? What does this approach to history miss?
3. Al-Tabari consistently refuses to choose between or among the various versions of events handed down to him. What does this say about his view of objective historical truth?
4. Can you think of ways in which we, like al-Tabari, value the testimonies of people of "good character" over more objective evidence?

FOR FURTHER READING

Al-Tabari. *The History of Al-Tabari.* Trans. Franz Rosenthal. 38 vols. Albany, NY: State University of New York Press, 1985– .

Duri, A. A. *The Rise of Historical Writing Among the Arabs.* Princeton, NJ: Princeton University Press, 1983.

Rosenthal, Franz. *A History of Muslim Historiography.* 2nd ed. Leiden, Netherlands: E. J. Brill, 1968.

NOTES

1. Abu Ja'far Muhammad al-Tabari, *The History of al-Tabari,* trans. W. Montgomery Watt and M. V. McDonald (Albany, NY: State University of New York Press, 1988), 6:60–61, 63–64, 67–76.

CHAPTER 17

Kalhana

Poet of the Kashmiri Past

An example of a siva (shiva)
The Bettman Archive

India is an ancient civilization with much history. It has also had many historians. Until the Muslim invasions of the fourteenth century, however, most of these did not write history as we now think about it. Early Indian historiography was not well separated from literature, not even from fiction. For centuries historical events, myths, poems, and so on were combined to make morally instructive epics. Accuracy took a back seat to edification and other values.

The *Mahabharata*, for example, which recounts a civil war in the Bharata or Paurava Dynasty, may contain some historical elements from its era (possibly c. 900 BCE). Though typical of the traditional Indian use of the past, it is not history except to the credulous. It is more akin to myth, standing somewhere between the *Kumulipo* and the *Sundiata Epic* of the previous section. And it is so acknowledged. Traditional Indian "history" was written with other aims in mind than accurately recording past events.

Yet some work is different. The Jain philosopher Hemacandra, for example, wrote a history of the Mahavira, Jainism's founder, which valued accuracy somewhat more than do traditional Indian works. But India's acknowledged first historian is Kalhana, a twelfth-century Kashmiri aristocrat. His *Rajatarangini*—"the River of Kings"—turns a critical eye toward the received traditions. Though still steeped in myth, it gives real events more attention than had authors before.

The *Rajatarangini* is a regional history of Kashmir, now a province on the border between present day India and Pakistan. Then a meeting ground between Hindus and Buddhists—as it is now between Hindus and Muslims—Kashmir was one of the many regional states that filled the Indian subcontinent. The text traces Kashmiri history from around 1200 BCE to Kalhana's day. It is set in verse—Kalhana, too, wanted to edify and entertain—and divided into eight cantos or *tarangas*, the first six of which come down to us in better condition than do the last two. The passages that follow come from the first *taranga*.

We do not know much about Kalhana's life beyond what we can infer from his massive epic poem. Internal evidence dates him to the first half of the twelfth century, a time of dynastic chaos in Kashmir. He was apparently independently wealthy, for his critical remarks about his rulers show him to be no court historian, dependent on royal patronage. He signs each of the *tarangas* "Kalhana, son of the noble Lord Canpaka, the great Kashmiri minister." His father was thus in government service. Kalhana identifies him in the text as a chief officer in King Harsha's government—a somewhat Neronian ruler whose fall ushered in the time of strife. Most likely Canpaka either had or attained the land or wealth that made his son independent. We can thus place Kalhana among the Kashmiri elite, though not in the portion of the elite involved in politics after Harsha's death. The text shows Kalhana had no love for Harsha, but neither did he favor his fellow aristocrats; he criticized their greed and their failure to protect their subjects.

In fact, the *Rajatarangini* is as much a morality play as is any other traditional Indian writing. Kalhana praises the good and condemns the wicked. The former are shown ascending like gods at death; he presumes the latter to pay for their misdeeds. Indeed, various supernatural beings reinforce his judgments, appearing and disappearing as aids to his plot. As critical as he is about the errors of other historians, he is no secularist. History for him is the plaything of nature and supernature, both conspiring to give us moral examples.

Yet despite this moralizing, and despite his attention to the art of history writing—his poetry is exceedingly fine as the following translation suggests— Kalhana put considerable effort into getting the main outlines of the story right. He particularly wanted to locate kings and dynasties in their proper order, and did so with some precision. For example, he located the reign of Durlabhavardhana in the Kashmiri equivalent of our early seventh century—a fact confirmed by the writings of Hieun Tsiang, a Chinese visitor who published a memoir of his trip across the Himalayas. His record of successions matches much, but not all, of the evidence from coins, inscriptions, and other historians. He just provides a fuller list—one that becomes less and less mythological as it approaches Kalhana's own day.

Unfortunately, we do not have a very accurate text of these later eras, especially those of his own time. Like all histories before the advent of printing, the *Rajatarangini* had to be copied by hand. Few copies have survived, the most prominent being made by Rajanaka Ratnakantha, a good seventeenth-century scholar with bad handwriting. His script is difficult to read, but accurately leaves blank the places where the birchbark original had worn away. These are more common in the later *tarangas*; the first six are relatively complete. Kalhana's poetry makes filling these blanks difficult, as does his specific references to the Kashmiri landscape. Indeed, early transla- tions of the work made little sense of these; it was not until translators familiar with Kashmir took up the task that a credible English text emerged. Here, then, is the earliest reliable history in the Indian tradition.

Rajatarangini[1]

To Siva charming with the collective iridescence of jewels on the heads of snakes which adorn him—a salutation; in him who is like the wishing tree of paradise are absorbed those who have been liberated. Her forehead is marked with saffron, pendant from the ear she wears sportively a cluster of earrings for display, the beauty of her white throat has the semblance of the ocean-born conch, the bosom is garbed in a faultless brassiére; his forehead is marked with the fiery flame, close to the ear he carries a collection of snakes who playfully open their mouths, the lustre of his throat gleams white despite the nuance of the ocean-born poison, the chest has for armour the lord of the snakes; may the part of Siva, half of whom is united with his wife, be for your glory whether it is the left or the right.

Worthy of homage is the indescribable insight of a gifted poet which excels the stream of ambrosia since through it is achieved a permanent embodiment of glory by the poet and others as well.

Who else is capable of making vivid before one's eyes pictures of a bygone age barring the poet and the Creator who create naturally delightful productions?

Were he not to have the awareness, through intuition, of existences which he is about to reveal to everyone what other indication would there be of the divine perception of the poet?

Although owing to the exigency of the length of the narrative a variety of events have not been set down in detail, there should still be in this poem enough material for the delectation of the rightminded.

That man of merit alone deserves praise whose language, like that of a judge, in recounting the events of the past has discarded bias as well as prejudice.

Without hearkening to the reason why the theme, which has been treated already by our predecessors, has once again been dealt with, it will not be fair on the part of the discriminate to turn away their faces.

When they, who had pieced together the history of the kings, each one as he saw it, had gone to their rest, what kind of skill is it on the part of those born in later times that they should add to the narrative? Hence my endeavour will be in this narrative of past events to repair by all manner of means where there is error.

The voluminous works in fragments containing the early history of the kings were epitomized in Suvrata's composition so that they may be remembered.

The style of Suvrata being irksome, owing to the fault of pedantry, his composition, although it has acquired celebrity, is lacking in the art of the exposition of the theme.

While owing to an incomprehensible lack of care in the work of Ksemendra, known as the List of Kings, even a portion is not free from error, although it is the composition of a poet.

Moreover, eleven works of former savants containing the annals of royalty have been scrutinised by me as well as the views of the Sage Nila.

By the inspection of ordinances of former kings relating to religious foundations and grants, laudatory inscriptions as well as written records, all wearisome error has been set at rest.

Fifty-two kings had, through lack of tradition, passed into oblivion; out of these have been discovered by me from the Nilamata the four, namely Gonanda and others.

Formerly by the Brahman Helaraja, a professing Pasupata, a work had been composed called Panthivavali, containing twelve thousand verses. Padmamihira, having studied his work, adopted in his own composition the list of eight kings, Lava and his successors who preceded Asoka and others.

Also the five kings, beginning with Asoka, whom the illustrious Chavillakara mentions, they are from among the fifty-two, for his verse is as follows:

"From Asoka to Abhimanyu the five, who have been enumerated as kings, were taken from the very fifty-two by the ancients."

This saga which is properly made up should be useful for kings as a stimulant or as a sedative, like a physic, according to time and place.

And in any case what man of culture is there, to whose heart such a connected narrative dealing with innumerable incidents of the remote past will not appeal?

And when he has finished contemplating the ephemeral duration of the spark in living beings, may he record a finding that the crowning sentiment of this poem is the inner poise.

Now, gentle friend! drink freely, your ears serving as the mother of pearl glasses, of this River of Kings delightful with the flow of its sustaining sentiment.

Once upon a time there was the lake of Sati; and from the beginning of the Kalpas the land in the womb of the Himalayas was filled with waters during the intervening period of six Manus.

Now when the present period of Vaivasvata Manu had come, the Prajapati Kasyapa induced the gods Druhina, Upendra, Rudra and others to descend and, having caused Jalodbhava, who resided in it, to be slain, founded, upon the site of the lake, the kingdom of Kasmir.

It is the territory which is under the protection of Nila, supreme lord of all the Nagas, whose parasol is the swelling Nila Kunda with the flowing waters of the Vitasta for its staff.

Where Parvati, who adores Guha and whose copious milk is drunk by the elephant-faced Ganesa, although she has converted herself into the Vitasta, which turns her face towards low-lying lands and whose abundant waters are drunk in mouthfuls by the Nagas, does not abandon her natural impulse.

It is the resort of the Nagas, prominent among whom are Sankha and Padma, like the city of the Giver of Wealth, of the guardians of treasure.

It has, forsooth, stretched forth on their back its arms in the guise of its mountain ramparts for the safeguarding of the Nagas who had approached from terror of Garuda.

Where, within the sanctuary of Papasudana, those who touch the husband of Uma in wooden form secure for reward the pleasures of life and liberation.

Where, on a waterless hill, the goddess of Twilight is in possession of water which is the ocular demonstration of the presence of piety and the absence of sin.

Where the self-originating Fire, emerging from the womb of the Earth, accepts with many arms of flame the votive offering of the sacrificers.

Where the goddess Sarasvati herself may be seen in the form of a swan in a lake on the peak of the Bheda mountain which is hallowed by the rise of the Ganga.

Where in the shrine of the residence of Siva at Nandiksetra are to be seen, to this day, the drops of the votive sandal emollient offered by the celestials.

Where by visiting the goddess Sarada one gets in a moment to the river Madhumati and the Sarasvati adored by the poets.

In that country adorned by Cakrabhrt, Vijayesa, Adikesava and Isana there is not even so much land as can be covered by a sesamum seed which is profane.

Such is Kasmir, the country which may be conquered by the force of spiritual merit but not by armed force; where the inhabitants in consequence fear more the next world; where there are hot baths in winter, comfortable landing places on the river-banks, where the rivers being free from aquatic animals are without peril; where, realizing that the land created by his father is unable to bear heat, the hot-rayed sun honours it by bearing himself with softness even in summer. Learning, high dwelling houses, saffron, iced water, grapes and the like—what is a commonplace there, is difficult to secure in paradise.

In the three worlds of the Earth, the producer of jewels, is worthy of praise and on it the North, the direction of the lord of wealth; there again the mountain, the father of Parvati, and within it, the country of Kasmir.

In Kasmir, the contemporaries of the Kauravas and Pandavas—in the Kali era—up to Gonanda, fifty-two kings have passed into oblivion.

In that age, owing to the former misdeeds of those kinds, surely no creative poets existed who could have embodied them in glory.

Renowned kings, in the shelter of whose arms this Earth wearing the girdle of the oceans had rested as if in the shade of a forest and enjoyed peace and security from hostile attack, would not even be remembered without its favour—to the art of the poet which is sublime in its nature, we offer salutation.

Even those who, in the past, had rested their feet on the forehead of elephants, those too, who had acquired glory, in whose mansions resided young ladies who were like day-moons—those kings, the ornaments of the world, have been ignored by the people as if they had no existence even in dreams; O brother! the work of a gifted poet! why praise thee a hundredfold? Without thee the world were in darkness.

In the Kali era Gonanda and other kings ruled in Kasmir for twenty-two hundred sixty-eight years. Some have been deluded by the tradition that the

Mahabharata had taken place at the end of Dvapara and have erroneously made this calculation of time.

When the number of years of the kings is calculated, the period of whose sovereignty is known, after deducting them, there is no remainder left of the period hitherto passed of Kali itself as follows:

When six hundred fifty-three years had elapsed there lived on the surface of the earth the Kauravas and the Pandavas.

Of the laukika era in the twenty-fourth year at present one thousand seventy years of the Saka era have gone by.

Roughly, commencing from Gonanda III, two thousand three hundred thirty autumns have now elapsed.

Twelve hundred sixty-six years is the duration of time which, it is believed, to be that of the fifty-two kings.

From one Naksatra to another, the Great Bear moves in a hundred years, such being its course, the author of the *Brhat-samihita* has furnished a solution on this point.

The Great Bear stood in the constellation Magha when king Yudhisthira ruled the earth; two thousand five hundred twenty-six years prior to the Saka era was the epoch of his reign.

To the mighty Gonanda, king of Kasmir, the North, of which the dazzling Kailasa is the smile and the tossing Ganga the scarf, rendered homage.

Having abandoned Sesa, as if dreading his venom, the earth took refuge in the king's arms marked by the jewels sacred to Garuda.

The aid of this king having been sought by Jarasandha he laid siege to Mathura, the city of the enemy of Kamsa, with large forces.

When he pitched his camp on the banks of the Yamuna, he caused the fame of the warriors together with the jewels of the Yadava ladies to fade.

On one occasion, to save his army which was broken up on all sides, he who had the plough as the emblem on his banner encountered him fighting in battle.

During the combat of the two warriors of equal prowess having remained too long in the hand of the goddess of victory owing to the uncertainty of the issue, one might well ask if the triumphal garland had withered away.

Eventually, with his limbs wounded by weapons in the battlefield, the king of Kasmir embraced the earth while the Yadava king embraced the goddess of victory.

When that true Ksatriya had gone the way which the very brave find it easy, his exalted son Darnodara began to support the earth.

Although he had obtained a kingdom furnished in plenitude with life's enjoyments, that proud king brooding over the death of his father had not been at peace.

At this time the haughty king, whose arms were powerful like trees, heard that in the region of the Indus the Gandharas had made preparations for the Svayamvara of the princess, to which the Yadavas had been specially invited.

Then, when they were not far off, he marched against them with impetuosity so that the dust of his cavalry regiments swallowed up the vault of the heavens.

In that battle the bride, who was about to choose her bridegroom yearning, for the wedding languished while the heavenly damsels held a Svayamvara in the land of the Gandharas.

Then, surrounded by an array of his enemies, this brave king of kings went to heaven, in the battle, by way of the edge of the battle-disc of Krsna.

*   *   *

Then became king that son Jalauka, leader of men and of the gods, who with the nectar of his glory rendered gleaming white the cosmic world.

The tales of those whose divine power, when they reached their ears, indeed held the very gods spell-bound.

Having gained the elixir which could transform essences of substances he, no doubt, with gifts of gold, was capable of removing the void from the cavity of the firmament.

Having made the waters rigid he entered the interior of the lakes of the Nagas and carried to perfection the youth of the Naga maidens by the joys of love.

That king had for his spiritual adviser one erudite philosopher, who had defeated an assembly of puffed up Buddhist debators, who were powerful in those days.

That veracious king had vowed that he would ever worship Vijayesvara and Jyesthesa in Nandisa-ksera.

In every village horses had been posted to gallop; disallowing this a certain Naga, out of friendliness, bore him always on his person.

Having expelled the Mlecchas, who had overrun the land, the king of mighty valour conquered in his victorious campaigns the earth which wears the girdle of the oceans.

The place where the king crushed the invading Mleccha horde is called by the people Ujjhatadimba even to this day.

Having conquered territories including Kanhakubja, he settled in his own country the four castes from there as well as upright men with legal experience.

Not having attained development as it should have by means of trade, wealth and the like, the administration of the kingdom was like that of any ordinary state at this time.

The Chief Justice, the Superintendent of Revenue, the Treasurer, the Chief of the Army, the Envoy, the Pontiff and the Astrologer—had been the seven functionaries of the state.

Having created eighteen traditional departments of state, the king, from that time, inaugurated the constitutional system of Yudhisthira.

With the wealth he had acquired by his martial exploits and energy this king of conspicuous intelligence founded the Agraharas of Varabala and others.

At the frontier and other regions were founded, by his august queen Isanadevi, Matrcakas which were bright with spiritual power.

The king, having heard the *Nandipurana* expounded by a disciple of Vyasa, began to worship at Sodara and other places as vying with Nandisa.

While he was installing Jyestha Rudra in Srinagara, he realized that it could not, without the Sodara spring, vie with Nandisa.

One day, the king being occupied in state affairs forgot his daily observance and having failed to bathe in Sodara, which was situated at a distance, he became uneasy in mind. He observed in a waterless spot water suddenly welling up which in colour, taste and other respects was indistinguishable from that of Sodara.

Then he had a dip in that sacred spring which had appeared of itself and the proud king achieved the fulfillment of his ambition to vie with Nandirudra.

On one occasion to test this he cast into Sodara an empty gold pitcher with its mouth closed with the lid; after two and a half days when it rose to the surface in the spring at Srinagara it dispelled the misgivings of the king.

Indeed it seemed as if he were Nandisa himself who had descended upon the earth to enjoy the pleasures of life; the realization of such a miracle could not have happened otherwise.

Once, when the king was proceeding to Vijayesvara, a frail woman, standing in the middle of the road, begged food of him.

The king having promised to give such food as she desired she, assuming a hideous form, revealed her longing for human flesh.

When he, who abstained from killing living beings, had granted her permission to take for her enjoyment the flesh from his own body she then spoke to him in this wise:

"You are some Bodhisattva, O protector of the land! whose mind has been ennobled by upright conduct, hence, O high-minded one! you have such deep tenderness for living creatures."

Unfamiliar with Buddhist phraseology, being a devotee of Siva, the king then asked her "for what Bodhisattva, good lady! do you take me?"

She, however, said to the king, "You should hear the reason why I have been raised by the Buddhists whom you have antagonized by your wrath."

"Residents of the environs of Mount Lokaka we are the Krtyakas of darkness. Having taken refuge solely in Bodhisattva, we long for the destruction of darkness."

"In this world beginning from the blessed Lord of the worlds some few persons have conquered sorrow; know them to be Bodhisattvas."

"Against even a wrong-doer they do not grow angered but, through forgiveness, return good for evil; they who desire enlightenment not for self alone, are bent on the salvation of the world."

"By the sound of the clarions of the Viharas when formerly you had been kept awake, being instigated by wicked persons you, in anger, had ordered the demolition of the Viharas."

"The King being a Mahasakya cannot be hurt by you; on the other hand, O good lady! when you have the sight of him, for you there will be an end of darkness. We exhort you to induce him, who has been misled by the wicked, to build Viharas by giving up his own horde of gold. When that is carried out, the sin of the demolition of the Viharas will not have been incurred and atonement by him and his instigators will have been done. The Buddhists who were furious having thought of me, I had rushed forth to kill you but had been recalled by the Bodhisattvas at that time and was instructed in such wise."

"And so through disguise in this way, I tested your transcendent merit and having to-day become free from sin I now depart. All hail to you."

While the king vowed to rebuild the Viharas, the Krtyadevi, with eyes glistening with exceeding joy, vanished from sight.

Then the king built a Vihara named Krtyasrama and on that very spot founded an image of Krtyadevi who had been redeemed from darkness.

Having founded a temple of stone in Nandiksatra for Bhutesa, that king offered with his treasures due worship consisting of precious stones.

In the sanctuary of Ciramocana that pious king, by practising penance for many a night, sitting in the Brahma posture with his body moveless in meditation, after a long time made blunt his anxious desire for touching Nandisa on account of the Kanaka-Vahini river.

Through rising ecstasy he presented to Jyestharudra a hundred of the ladies of the royal household who had got up to dance at the hour of dancing and singing.

After enjoying sovereignty he eventually entered Ciramocana together with his wife and attained communion with the lord of Parvati.

QUESTIONS TO CONSIDER

1. What is the point of Kalhana's long introduction?
2. Contrast the deeds of kings Yudhisthira and Jalauka. Why does Kalhana deem Jalauka the more worthy?
3. What kinds of events does Kalhana recount (and thus think are important)? What kinds of events might a modern historian wish to recount about the same era?

FOR FURTHER READING

Dhar, Somnath. *Kalhana.* New Delhi: Sahitya Akademi, 1978.

Kalhana. *Kalhana's Rajatarangini: Chronicle of the Kings of Kashmir: Sanskrit Text with Critical Notes.* Ed. M. A. Stein. New Delhi: Motilal Banarsidass, 1988; orig. 1892.

_____ . *Rajatarangini: Saga of the Kings of Kashmir.* Trans. Ranjit Sitaram Pandit. New Delhi: Sahitya Akademi, 1968; orig. 1935.

Warder, A. K. *An Introduction to Indian Historiography.* Bombay: Popular Prakashan, 1972.

NOTES

1. Kalhana, *Rajatarangini: The Saga of the Kings of Kasmir,* trans. Ranjit Sitaram Pandit (New Delhi: Sahitya Akademi, 1935), 1–17, 21–26.

CHAPTER 18

Annals of Cuauhtitlan

Aztec History

Aztec Picture Writing
© North Wind Pictures

The Valley of Mexico, in that country's central highlands, has been occupied for nearly ten thousand years. Shortly after the beginning of the Christian era, it became the seat of empires. Over the next fifteen centuries, various of its cities rose to prominence: Teotihuacan, Tollan, Colhuacan, Cuauhtitlan, Tepaneca, Tetzcoco, and finally Tenochtitlan. The last was the seat of the Mexica, more commonly known as Aztecs.

These successive empires wrote histories. Lacking an alphabet, they painted theirs in stylized pictures on reed paper. Certain glyphs represented years: 1-Reed, 2-Flint, 3-House, 4-Rabbit, and so on through their 52-year calendrical cycle. Other pictures stood for common events: for example, an arrow through a temple meant an invasion, and footprints meant a journey. Still others used sounds: for example, the place name Cuauhnahuac was represented by an eagle—*cuauhtli* in the Nahuatl language. More complicated events were depicted graphically.

These painted manuscripts or codices were not read by ordinary citizens. At special times, priests unfolded them and recited them aloud, embellishing certain points with stories passed down orally. The result was midway between a written year-count and an oral history. Reciting this history was a political event; the manuscript was a mnemonic prompt for a public storytelling session.

The Aztecs consolidated their power over their neighbors about 1430. Their rule eventually stretched to the Gulf of Mexico and to present-day Guatemala. Tribute of all sorts—gold, shells, turquoise, feathers, food, and slaves—flowed in, making their capital one of the richest cities of the world. Like many conquerors, they rewrote history. Their fourth king, Itzcóatl, collected most of the extant manuscripts and burned them. He then ordered them rewritten to glorify Aztec exploits and lineage. Some survived, but most were revised to suit the needs of the victors.

The Aztec capital Tenochtitlan fell to Spanish invaders under Cortés in 1521 (Chapter 29 presents the native view of that conquest). Unfortunately for us, the Spanish carried out a second book-burning soon after they had subjugated the region. They destroyed most of the painted manuscripts as "instruments of the devil." Only about two dozen survived. Some of these are histories; others describe the gods, rituals, astronomy, and so on. Vast amounts of native knowledge disappeared.

Yet not all was lost. Luckily, some of the Spanish clergy worked hard to preserve native thought and culture. By the late 1520s, they had taught members of the Aztec nobility to read and write Nahuatl using Spanish script. At mid-century, Franciscans like Fray Bernardino de Sahagún were collecting histories from learned elders. His native students Tezozómoc, Ixtlixóchitl, and Chimalpain blended the surviving manuscripts from the various Nahuatl city-states into histories that are as close as we can get to the picture-manuscript tradition. As the following example from the *Annals of Cuauhtitlan* shows, events listed by years are interspersed with longer stories, most likely taken from oral sources. Because these stories were told in public rituals, they are apt to be more stable than are other oral traditions.

The *Annals* manuscript has an interesting history. It is written in Nahuatl (in Spanish script), and forms the first part of the *Codex Chimalpopoca*. The latter two parts of that book are an essay on native rites in Spanish and the Nahuatl *Legend of the Suns,* recounting native origin myths. These three unrelated works were copied together onto forty-two leaves of parchment in the 1570s, possibly by the aforementioned Ixtlixóchitl. The *Codex* passed through various hands until it found a home at the Mexican National Anthropology Museum. It vanished from there about 1949. Fortunately, a version in German and Nahuatl was published in 1938, and an exact photocopy was made about 1945. These form the basis for the current translation.

Cuauhtitlan was one of the key towns in the Valley of Mexico. Motolinía described it among the finest towns of his time (the 1530s), and fourth among the towns of the Aztec empire. The *Annals* are centered on the town's history. They chronicle its relationships with its neighbors, from its hundred-year war against Xaltocan (ca. 1297–1395) to its decline at the hands of Tepanecan assassins (1408). Some of that history is mythological: the world is said to have begun in the year 1-Reed, which the author correlates with CE 635. But its later years match parts of other documents, making it reliable for the two or three centuries before the Spanish conquest.

Of course, like all histories, it has a point of view. Most noteworthy is its claim of a close relationship between Cuauhtitlan and Tenochtitlan, the Aztec (Mexica) capital. Though it portrays other towns as hostile to the Mexica newcomers, it claims that the Cuauhtitlancalque were friendly to them. This may reflect the Aztec's 1430 rewriting of history, or it may show a desire on the part of later writers to curry favor with the new capital.

The following passage describes the Tepaneca War in the early fifteenth century. It begins with a description of the cruelties of Tezozomoctli, the ruler of Azcapotzalco. He ordered his assassins to kill many of the surrounding rulers, a policy his sons continued. After describing his rule and his death, the narrator inserts the story of Nezahualcoyotl, the young son of one of his victims. First, the boy finds refuge among the Mexica to avoid his father's assassins. Then he grows up to rule Tetzcoco with the help of his mentor Coyohua, who also helps him ward off his father's fate. Though this part of the story ends with him in prison, waiting execution, we later learn that he escapes and leads the joint Mexican/Tetzcocan armies that defeat the Tepaneca.

Two minor points are worth mentioning about this account. First, in noting a change of rulers in Tenochtitlan, the narrator remarks that the residents of Tetzcoco "say it truthfully" and that the residents of Colhuacan "say it in their year count." He has clearly consulted other now-vanished memoirs of this event. Second, the Nezahualcoyotl story both reinforces the tyrannical image of the Tepaneca and links the Tetzcocan war hero to that city's prewar ruling family. In an earlier passage, the author makes a similar (and more fabulous) connection between the ousted rulers of Colhuacan and the rulers of Cuauhtitlan in its glory days. Such connections apparently lent legitimacy to native rulers, much as they have to rulers in all parts of the world.

Annals of Cucuhtitlan[1]

[The Fall of Colhuacan: 1298–1348 CE]

1 Rabbit [1298].

2 Reed [1299]. This was when the Cuauhquecholteca were defeated for the second time. They were surrounded again, just as was told above.

3 Flint [1300] was when the Colhuacan ruler Xihuitltemoctzin died. Then Coxcox Teuctli was inaugurated and ruled in Colhuacan.

4 House.

5 Rabbit [1302] was when Epcoatzin, ruler of Tizic Cuitlahuac, died. Quetzalmichin Teuctli was inaugurated.

6 Reed [1303] In that year it happened one day that the ruler of Cuauhtitlan, who was Huactzin, went hunting, and he met a young woman at the place called Tepolco. But he did not know whether this young woman was a lady.

Finally he asked her. He said, "Who are you? Whose daughter are you? Where do you come from?"

She answered him, saying, "My lord, I live in Colhuacan, and my father is the king, Coxcox Teuctli."

"And what does he call you?" he asked. "What is your name?"

"My name is Itztolpanxochi," she replied.

Well, when Huactli heard this, he took her home with him and made her his wife. And Huactli had children with her. The first was called Cuauhtliipantemoc. The second was Iztactototl. They were born the grandchildren of the Colhuacan ruler, Coxcoxtzin Teuctli.

7 Flint. 8 House. 9 Rabbit. 10 Reed. 11 Flint. 12 House. 13 Rabbit. 1 Reed. 2 Flint.

3 House [1313] This was when Quetzalmichin Teuctli died. Then Cuauhtlotli Teuctli was inaugurated and ruled in Cuitlahuac Tizic.

4 Rabbit. 5 Reed. 6 Flint.

7 House [1317] This was when Cuauhtlotli Teuctli died. Then Mamatzin Teuctli was inaugurated and ruled in Cuitlahuac Tizic.

8 Rabbit [1318] This was the year that Mexico Tenochtitlan got started. As yet the Mexitin built only a few stray huts. There was only a wilderness of sedges all around when they made their settlement.

9 Reed.

10 Flint [1320] In that year the Cuauhtitlan ruler Huactli gave the order for his son Iztactototl to lead a war party at Xaltocan Acpaxapocan. He summoned his messengers and said to them, "Go tell my captains Acatzin, Tlacuatzin, Xochipan, and Mecellotl, who are in charge there at Acahuacan Tepeyacac. Give them this message: 'You are no longer in power here at Cuahuacan. Let that boy Iztactototzin be surrounded someplace or other. But he mustn't be thrown to the enemy, he mustn't be captured. Let them give heed to this. I beseech all my captains.' "

Then the message was brought to the Chichimecs who were in charge at Tepeyacac. And when they had heard it, they said, "Our ruler has favored us. Let us do what we can."

And right away these Chichimecs sent to Coacalco, taking a message to the Tepaneca. They had just come to settle there, in Coacalco, where a certain Xochmitl was governing, and when Xochmitl heard the Chichimecs' command that they were to [go] with them [and] accompany the ruler's son Iztactototl into battle, then he authorized his Tepanec charges to go to war with this son of the ruler Huactzin.

And it was done. They followed the ruler's son Iztactototl to Acpaxapocan, where the Xaltocameca were in the habit of making payment.

Now, when they had appeared, they came forth and made the payment, though indeed it was as they usually came, always dressed for war. Immediately Iztactototl made a take, and as soon as he had gotten his prisoner, there was a battle. And on account of it the Chichimecs Acatzin and Tlacuatzin died, along with eight of the Tepaneca that Xochmitl had sent from Coacalco.

And it was all by himself that Iztactototl had taken the prisoner.

When he had gotten his prisoner, the news was brought to the ruler Huactli, and they told him now ten had died because of it.

This upset him, and he gave orders for the war to be intensified, for the Chichimecs to fight hard and not let the Xaltocameca go free.

Now, when Iztactototl had gotten his prisoner, he sent word to his mother. And then she said to him, "Go see your grandfather, Coxcox Teuctli, the ruler of Colhuacan. Give him greetings and show him that you have taken a prisoner in Xaltocan."

And Iztactototl heeded his mother, for she was a princess of Colhuacan.

Then he went with his prisoner to inspire his grandfather, and his Chichimec captains went along as his guards. When he got there, he presented himself, offered greetings, and explained that he was his grandson.

"O lord, O ruler," he said, "I have come from Cuauhtitlan to bring you greetings, for I have heard what perhaps is true, that you may have lost a daughter, the departed Itztolpanxochi." He continued: "She is my mother, and she has told me that it was you who sired her. And so today I have come before you to bring you inspiration. My father, Huactzin, had a war in Xaltocan. And I went there and took a prisoner."

He said to him, "Welcome, my child. It is true that I lost a daughter, from whom you have sprung. Sit down, for you are my grandson. Such as I am, I am old and must die. Here in Colhuacan it is you who will be ruler. You will be ruler of the Colhuaque."

And to Iztactototl he was a little like an oracle the way he spoke. And after hearing his speech, he said nothing.

Finally the ruler Coxcox Teuctli withdrew. From within his chamber he sent back a messenger to inform him that he was never to come again, and he was told he would definitely become ruler, succeeding his grandfather.

Well, after he had heard these words, he laughed and said, "Whose ruler would I be? For the Colhuacan nation is not to endure. It is to be destroyed and broken up. But I say give this message to the king, my grandfather: Probably it will not happen in his lifetime, and when it does, some could go to our capital and become our followers there. For our land is so big that from there to Cuauhtepetl here, takes a whole day, so wide is the expanse. And the ruler is my father, Huactzin."

Then they took the message to the ruler Coxcox Teuctli. When he heard it, he was angry and insulted. He said, "That little boy, that baby, what is he saying? Ask him what it is that would happen to our nation and who would destroy us. Is this a death that is not native? How would it rise against us? Pox, bloody diarrhea, coughing sickness, fever, and consumption are here, of course. And of course we know that the sun might be eaten or the earth might shake or we might have to perform sacrifices. How is our nation to be destroyed and broken up? What is the boy saying? Let him tell it plainly."

And then the messengers came back. In anger and amazement they questioned him.

And he answered them. "What is the king worried about?" he said. "Give him this message: It is not by war that the nation will be destroyed, no one will bother him, no one will make fun of him anymore. The way it will happen is that lords and nobles will simply become agitated and rebel, and their vassals will be scattered in foreign lands. The nation will become deserted. And that is why I say, when you are destroyed, go to our capital, which lies beyond Cuauhtepetl here. The ruler, I say, is my father. He will be waiting for you, and he will give you land."

They took the message to the ruler and with that he fell silent, etc.

11 House. 12 Rabbit. 13 Reed.

1 Flint [1324] This was when the Colhuacan ruler Coxcoxtli died. Then Acamapichtli was inaugurated and ruled in Colhuacan.

2 House [1325] According to what the Cuitlahuaca know, this was when the elder Ixtlilxochitl of Tetzcoto was born.

3 Rabbit. 4 Reed. 5 Flint. 6 House. 7 Rabbit.

8 Reed [1331] Cuitlahuaca say that at this time Tezozomoctli was inaugurated as ruler in Tlalhuacpan.

9 Flint. 10 House. 11 Rabbit. 12 Reed.

13 Flint [1336] This was the year that Achitometl killed Acamapichtli, who was ruler of Colhuacan. And having killed him, Achitometl was inaugurated as ruler. This was also when the ruler Achitometl spoke craftily to the Mexitin. Also it was when the elder Tezozomoctli was inaugurated as ruler in Azcapotzalco.

1 House [1337] was when the ruler of Cuitlahuac Tizic, Mamatzin Teuctli, died. Then Pichatzin Teuctli was inaugurated.

2 Rabbit.

3 Reed [1339] was when the Cuauhquecholteca were again defeated, and it was the Huexotzinca who defeated them, campaigning against them unaided. This was when Xayacamachan was ruling in Huexotzinco.

The year 3 Reed is when the Chalco ruler Tozpquihua died. Then a lord named Xipemetztli was inaugurated as ruler.

And it was in 3 Reed that Tezozomoctli of Tlalhuacpan started his war in Techichco, which was filled with Chalca—the people of Techichco were counted as Chalco. That's where the Chalca boundary, or frontier, was, there in Colhuacan. And this war of Tezozomoctli's lasted thirty-seven years. As yet the Tepanecatl was acting on his own when he set out for Techichco Colhuacan. As yet the Mexitin were not included.

4 Flint. 5 House. 6 Rabbit.

7 Reed [1343] was when the Totomihuaque were defeated. The Huexotzinca campaigned against them unaided, in the time that Xayacamachan was ruler.

8 Flint. 9 House.

10 Rabbit [1346] This 10 Rabbit is when Ilancueitl and the ladies who accompanied her went to Coatlichan to get Acamapichtli, who had been sent there to be brought up.

11 Reed [1347] That was the year it came to pass that the Colhuaque were destroyed, were scattered and dispersed in foreign lands, when the people went off in all directions.

When the Colhuaque had been destroyed, their temple and their city sprouted grass.

In the year 12 [Flint: 1348] Achitometl, who had been ruler of Colhuacan, met his death. As soon as he died, the Colhuaque were destroyed.

These Colhuaque were not conquered: the way they were destroyed is that they just agitated each other. That's how they were destroyed.

And that's when the Colhuaque, accompanied by the Mexicatzinca, came here to Cuauhtitlan. It was said that the Colhuacan nation was dispersed when Achitometl died.

[The Founding of the City of Cuauhtitlan: 1348 CE and Later]

Now, when the Colhuaque were newly arrived here in Cuauhtitlan, it was during [the fifteen "months"] called:

1. Huei Tecuilhuitl. 2. Tlaxochimaco. 3. Xocotl Huetzi. 4. Ochpaniztli. 5. Teotl Eco. 6. Tepeilhuitl. 7. Quecholli. 8. Panquetzaliztli. 9. Atemoztli. 10. Tititl. 11. Izcalli. 12. Cuauhitl Ehua. 13. Tlacaxipehualiztli. 14. Tozoztontli. 15. Huei Tozoztli.

Thus the Colhuaque stayed for 300 days [for fifteen twenty-day "months", mid-July through mid-May].

And also at this time, when the Colhuaque had started making themselves an earth altar, the incoming elders Cuauhnochtli, Atempanecatl, Xiloxochcatl, Mexicatl, and Tetec Tlamacazqui set up their gods, known as Toci and Chiucnauhozomatli and Xochiquetzal.

Now, when these Colhuaque had built their earth altar, they petitioned the Chichimec princes called Totmatlatzin and Cuauhtzoncaltzin, who governed in Chichimecacuicoyan, sending them a message, telling them, "We have made our settlement at the waterside where you allowed us to settle, there in your territory. But what can we take? For we are asking, please, won't you help us out with something like one little rabbit, a little snake, with which we might have just a bit of a dedication ceremony for the little earth altar we have made for our gods?"

And when the Chichimecs heard this, they got together and said, "Ah, that's where they're supposed to be. We believe that where they've come to settle they'll eventually be swept away by the water. Indeed, when we allowed them to settle there, we said, 'Here's your rampart,' for these are the people who make war on the Mexitin and chased them away. Now, what are we going to tell them? Should we give them this rabbit, this snake that they're asking for? They would get used to hunting in our gardens. That's impossible. But there's this: we have a war going on nearby in Xaltocan. Let's tell them to go get captives there, so that they can become worthy of receiving our daughters and our lands."

And then the Chichimecs told this to the Colhuaque. Indeed, the Chichimecs said, "What would a snake or a rabbit be? Indeed, we have a war nearby. Go there, to Xaltocan. Is it far? Whoever takes captives wins our daughters. We'll present them to you along with our lands. Give heed to this. It's how you'll have your dedication ceremony."

And then the Colhuaque went off and made war in Xaltocan. And when the Colhuaque had gotten three captives, the Chichimecs took a great liking to the Colhuaque, and they all became friends. So the Chichimecs gave them their daughters. Also they were given land.

When it was Toxcatl, the Colhuaque came and celebrated the feast in Cuauhtitlan for the first time. They came and made human sacrifices.

As yet the Chichimecs were not doing this, not making human sacrifices before their gods. Although they were taking captives and would eat them, they just killed them. It wasn't before their gods. They did not use them for dedication ceremonies, and as yet they had no temples.

It was at this time that the Colhuaque and the Chichimecs began to build themselves temples. It was then that the town that there is today got started and had its beginning.

And that's why the town lies in an out-of-the-way spot, because the Chichimecs had been driving the Colhuaque to desperation, thinking, when they settled the Colhuaque there, that eventually they would be flooded and would become weary and would perhaps go off somewhere. [But] it was not possible. In that very spot the town of Cuauhtitlan grew up where it is today.

Well, when the Colhuaque were finally settled, the river was still there, and when the water would come, it would spread out. Later, however, the river was relocated, because a hundred households were swept away. Those who perished were Toltitlancalque. And so the waterway was relocated when Ayactlacatzin came in as ruler. It was he who relocated the waterway.

And finally, as for those Chichimecs who had no temples, what they had were just arrows that they set up in beds of hay. They would make an earth altar and set up white plume-banners there, and each one would dress himself as Mixcoatl. Thus they remembered what the devil Itzpapalotl taught them. They always remembered it during [the feast] called Quecholli.

And as for the above-mentioned Colhuaque who went off in all directions, this was when they were scattered and dispersed in alien lands, some going to Azcapotzalco, Coatlichan, Huexotla, and Cuauhtitlan.

[The Massacre of the Chichimecs: 1349 CE and Later]

13 [House: 1349] This was the year that Huactli, who had been ruler of Cuauhtitlan, died. Then a stand-in, or substitute, came to be inaugurated in his place. Soon the Colhuaque got themselves a ruler: They wanted to install [Iztactototl,] son of the ruler Huactli, since they knew he was the grandson of the above-mentioned Coxcox Teuctli, who had been ruler of Colhuacan. At this time they sheltered him where the house of the devil Mixcoatl was. As yet Mixcoatl had the ruler Iztactototl with him in his calpulli temple [put him in a rude straw hut]. But eventually the Colhuaque supported him with great honor, honored the ruler Iztactototl. And they made many arrangements.

And furthermore, they introduced all the different manufactures, ceramic ware, matting, pots, bowls, and all the rest.

And it was they who built the town of Cuauhtitlan. And they provided it with lands, for the Chichimecs just kept being pushed back.

And it was they who brought all the idolatry. They brought their many gods.

And when they had become quite mingled with the Chichimecs, then they began to make milpa. And at last, peacefully, they began to mark off boundaries of fields, laying out their calpulli lands.

And in later times, when all the people had become god worshippers, when Itzcoatzin was ruling in Tenochtitlan, still there were many Chichimecs. And then the Colhuaque went to Mexico to lodge charges against them, because they refused to worship the gods, refused to observe the so-called arrow fast. In those days the arrow fast was customary.

On account of it, they were captured. Indeed, they were prisoners to Mexico. And those Chichimecs were these: a certain Xiuhcac from Toltepec, which is now called Xiuhcacco; then Pitzallotl's grandchildren in Tlalcozpan Hueitoctitlan; then Cocotl from Cocotitlan, and Pipilo, who was also from there, toward Tzictla; and others besides.

Those people went to their death in Mexico. So then they were stripped of their lands, which therefore are known today as Acxoteca lands, Mexica lands. And it was the same with their other servant communities.

Indeed, Maxtlaton of Xallan was likewise killed, and his lands too are now known as Acxotlan lands, Mexica lands.

It was the same with all of Zoltepec and Cuauhtepec, and others as well that were Mexica lands.

And during this time the Chichimecs, who were being killed off, who were gradually disappearing and going to their destruction, slipped away little by little and settled in Motozahuican and Tlachco.

QUESTIONS TO CONSIDER

1. What does this history tell you about the lives of the nobility in the fourteenth century?

2. Do you think that Iztactotatl actually uttered the prophesies attributed to him in the year 10 Flint (1320)? If not, why do they appear in the story?
3. Which rulers and peoples does this chronicle support? Which does it denigrate? What would be the probable political impact of this account on the hearer?

FOR FURTHER READING

History and Mythology of the Aztecs: The Codex Chimalpopoca. Trans. John Bierhorst. Tucson, AZ: University of Arizona Press, 1992.

León-Portilla, Miguel. *Aztec Thought and Culture: A Study of the Ancient Nahuatl Mind.* Trans. Jack Emory Davis. Norman: University of Oklahoma Press, 1963.

Popol Vuh: The Book of Counsel. trans. Dennis Tedlock. New York: Simon and Schuster, 1985.

Sahagún, Fray Bernardino de. *Florentine Codex: General History of the Things of New Spain.* Trans. Arthur J. O. Anderson and Charles E. Dibble. Salt Lake City, UT: University of Utah Press, 1982.

Sten, María. *The Mexican Codices and their Extraordinary History.* Illus. Rafael López Castro. Trans. Carolyn B. Czitrom. Mexico City: Ediciones Lara, S.A. 1974.

NOTES

1. *History and Mythology of the Aztecs: The Codex Chimalpopoca,* trans. John Bierhorst (Tucson, AZ: University of Arizona Press, 1992), 63–71.

PART THREE

Evolving Traditions

*T*his section surveys the further development of the historical traditions that emerged in various parts of the world as described in Part 2. European Renaissance scholars called the era from 500 to 1500 the "Middle Ages" to distinguish it from the world of ancient Greece and Rome that they admired so much and from their own "modern" era. Although medieval Europe was not the dark and barbarous place that the Italian humanists imagined, the focus of world civilization in that period was indeed elsewhere—in the cities of the Muslim Middle East and Africa, in India, and in China. In all parts of the writing world, including Europe, historical writing continued. Some historians worked within the framework of a tradition, while others developed original approaches and subjects.

The writers selected for this section come from a variety of times and cultures. Three are distinctly Christian in their approach. Three come from Muslim cultures. Two are from northern Europe, two from Mediterranean lands, two from India, one from China, and one from Japan.

In Bede and Gregory of Tours we see a continuation of the emphasis on Christian ecclesiastical history started by Eusebius (see Chapter 15) with less of the careful documentation that Eusebius showed. Miracles abounded and the deeds of kings and rulers were important primarily in the way they abetted or hindered the spread of Christianity. Anna Comnena, though equally explicitly Christian, reversed the pitch and reported on ecclesiastical and doctrinal issues as they reflected on her primarily political concerns: the great deeds of her father the Byzantine Emperor Alexius. Comnena modeled her work on Thucydides but modified it on the basis of Christian and Roman tradition.

The three Muslim writers came from opposite ends of the Muslim world—Ibn Khaldûn from Morocco and Algeria and Abu'l Fazl and Gulbadan from India—about a century apart. They came at a time when the great cultural achievements of Islam had peaked and begun a slow, self-aware decline. The tenets of Islam were taken for granted among their intended audience, and these writers were much less explicitly Muslim than the Christian writers were Christian. The Muslim writers differed from each other in focus: Ibn Khaldûn looked beyond and beneath politics to the geographical and social determinants of civilization. Abu'l Fazl concentrated on the remarkable military and political achievements of his patron, the Mughal Emperor Akbar. Gulbadan, a woman even closer to the seats of power, told the human dramas of the Indian court and politics.

Sima Guang took the tradition of the dynastic cycle in China (see Ban Gu and Ban Zhao, Chapter 11) and made it a more universal descriptive pattern for a broad sweep of Chinese history—the 16 dynasties from 403 BCE to 959 CE. He continued the focus on political narrative and the central role of the emperor but improved the critical approach to the documentary evidence.

Arai Hakuseki deviated more widely from the Chinese dynastic model, writing near the end of Japan's feudal era (1657–1725). The absence of a strong emperor in Japan made the Chinese pattern awkward to apply to Japanese feudal politics, so Arai Hakuseki discarded the dynastic model. He worked at the court of the Shogun and he supported the Shogunate, but not uncritically. He retained a political and military focus in his work and critically delved into documentary sources. In doing so, he anticipated many of the developments of slightly later European historical writing.

Thus did the traditions evolve.

CHAPTER 19

Gregory of Tours

Medieval European

Gregory of Tours
The Granger Collection, New York

G regory of Tours witnessed the change from Roman civilization to the "barbarian" kingdom of the Franks, the beginning of the Middle Ages in western Europe. In recording his observations, he preserved much of the intellectual attitude of the early Middle Ages—an era very alien to twentieth-century people, one that seems soaked with superstition and credulity. From Gregory, we can infer the decay of institutions and attitudes we associate with civility as well as the new mores and customs brought by the Germanic barbarians. In other words, his writing allows us to see one side of the collapse of classical civilization that so fascinated other historians such as Edward Gibbon (see Chapter 31).

Gregory (538–94) lived most of his life in the Loire valley, which marked the southern frontier of Frankish settlement in Gaul. From a Gallo-Roman senatorial family, Gregory occupied an ideal spot geographically and socially to observe most of the events he recounted. Tours was both an important junction on the north-south trade routes in Gaul and the leading objective for pilgrims who came to the healing shrine of St. Martin. Eventually most people of importance passed through Tours and most stayed for a while. This gave an interested inquirer like Gregory access to many sources of information from various parts of Gaul. Gregory's works give evidence that he was well read in Christian authors, but he himself noted that he was not liberally educated in the pagan classics. He wrote in vulgar Latin—that is, the spoken language—with a large vocabulary (especially church jargon) and rather clumsy gram-mar. Most of the time he wrote in a plain style that can seem abrupt, as when he bluntly described deaths and tortures in a brutal and bloody age.

The History of the Franks focused on the Merovingian dynasty of Frankish kings. The bulk of the events discussed in the book occurred within Gregory's lifetime, especially after he became bishop of Tours (573). He relied on written sources for much that happened before his lifetime (he handled history from the creation of the world to about 500 CE in 12 pages of one English translation). At Tours, he had frequent contact with other bishops in Gaul and visitors to the shrine of St. Martin. In addition, he had personal ties to four of the Merovingian kings whose deeds he described. Like any historian, Gregory had his prejudices. His particular viewpoint was not pro-Roman or pro-Frank in the cultural conflict that marked his period, but rather he was pro-church, especially favorable to the authority of bishops. Gregory was disgusted by war and saw one of his roles as bishop to be a peacemaker. Gregory understood history in terms of spiritual warfare and was convinced of the power of both demons and sacred relics in human military conflicts. Thus his judgment of political leaders mostly reflected how they dealt with the Catholic church; the good helped the church, the bad hindered Catholics or aided pagans and Arian heretics. Yet within that context, Gregory clearly understood political power and its uses and dynamics. Modern thinkers are sometimes frustrated by the shrewdness of his political judgment juxtaposed with his abject credulity about supernatural things. Yet Gregory's own accounts indicate that most people shared his understanding of the interaction of the supernatural with human history. In fact this assumption underlay

European historical writing throughout the Middle Ages, though often in a less extreme form than Gregory displayed.

In the passages that follow Gregory explains his reasons for writing history, and the methods and models he used. He describes the conversion of Clovis (d. 511), king of the Franks, to Catholic Christianity (significant since most other German tribes were Arian Christians considered heretics by Romans). Gregory recounts Clovis's conquest of Gaul by expelling the occupying Arian Visigoths in alliance with the Gallo-Roman majority and by dominating other Frankish tribal kingdoms. Finally, his assessment of the character of Chilperic (d. 584) shows quite clearly the values that Gregory used in judging the behavior of kings.

History of the Franks[1]

Here Begins Gregory's First Preface

With liberal culture on the wane, or rather perishing in the Gallic cities, there were many deeds being done both good and evil: the heathen were raging fiercely; kings were growing more cruel; the church, attacked by heretics, was defended by Catholics; while the Christian faith was in general devoutly cherished, among some it was growing cold; the churches also were enriched by the faithful or plundered by traitors—and no grammarian skilled in the dialectic art could be found to describe these matters either in prose or verse; and many were lamenting and saying: "Woe to our day, since the pursuit of letters has perished from among us and no one can be found among the people who can set forth the deeds of the present on the written page." Hearing continually these complaints and others like them I [have under-taken] to commemorate the past, in order that it may come to the knowledge of the future; and although my speech is rude, I have been unable to be silent as to the struggles between the wicked and the upright; and I have been especially encouraged because, to my surprise, it has often been said by men of our day, that few understand the learned words of the rhetorician but many the rude language of the common people. I have decided also that for the reckoning of the years the first book shall begin with the very beginning of the world, and I have given its chapters below.

* * *

Here Begins the Second Book

Following the order of time we shall mingle together in our tale the miraculous doings of the saints and the slaughters of the nations. I do not think that we shall be condemned thoughtlessly if we tell of the happy lives of the blessed together with the deaths of the wretched, since it is not the skill of the writer but the succession of times that has furnished the arrangement. The attentive reader, if he seeks diligently, will find in the famous histories of the kings of the Israelites that under the just Samuel the wicked Phineas perished, and that under David, whom they called Strong-hand, the stranger Goliath was destroyed. Let him remember also in the time of the great prophet Elias, who prevented rains when he wished and when he pleased poured them on the parched ground, who enriched the poverty of the widow by his prayer, what slaughters of the people there were, what famine and what thirst oppressed that wretched earth. Let him remember what evil Jerusalem endured in the time of Hezekiah, to whom God granted fifteen additional years of life. Moreover under the prophet Elisha, who restored the dead of life and did many other miracles among the peoples, what butcheries, what miseries crushed the very people of Israel. So too Eusebius, Severus and Jerome in their chronicles, and Orosius also, interwove the wars of kings and the miracles of the martyrs. We have written in this way also, because it is thus easier to perceive in their entirety the order of the centuries and the system of the years down to our day. And so, leaving the histories of the writers who have been mentioned above, we shall describe at God's bidding what was done in the later time.

*   *   *

After these events Childeric died and Clovis his son reigned in his stead. In the fifth year of his reign Siagrius, king of the Romans, son of Egidius, had his seat in the city of Soissons which Egidius, who was mentioned before, once held. And Clovis came against him with Ragnachar, his kinsman, because he used to possess the kingdom, and demanded that they make ready a battle-field. And Siagrius did not delay nor was he afraid to resist. And so they fought against each other and Siagrius, seeing his army crushed, turned his back and fled swiftly to king Alaric at Toulouse. And Clovis sent to Alaric to send him back, otherwise he was to know that Clovis would make war on him for his refusal. And Alaric was afraid that he would incur the anger of the Franks on account of Siagrius, seeing it is the fashion of the Goths to be terrified, and he surrendered him in chains to Clovis' envoys. And Clovis took him and gave orders to put him under guard, and when he had got his kingdom he directed that he be executed secretly. At that time many churches were despoiled by Clovis' army, since he was as yet involved in heathen error. Now the army had taken from a certain church a vase of wonderful size and beauty, along with the remainder of the utensils for the service of the church. And the bishop of the church sent messengers to the king asking that the vase at least be returned, if he could not get back any more of the sacred dishes. On hearing this the king said to the messenger: "Follow us as far as Soissons, because all that has been taken is to be divided there and when the lot assigns me that dish I will do what the father asks." Then when he came to Soissons and all the booty was set in their midst, the king said: "I ask you, brave warriors, not to refuse to grant me in addition to my share, yonder dish," that is, he was speaking of the vase just mentioned. In answer to the speech of the king those of more sense replied: "Glorious king, all that we see is yours, and we ourselves are subject to your rule. Now do what seems well-pleasing to you; for no one is able to resist your power." When they said this a foolish, envious and excitable fellow lifted his battle-ax and struck the vase, and cried in a loud voice: "You shall get nothing here except what the lot fairly bestows on you." At this all were stupefied, but the king endured the insult with the gentleness of patience, and taking the vase he handed it over to the messenger of the church, nursing the wound deep in his heart. And at the end of the year he ordered the whole army to come with their equipment of armour, to show the brightness of their arms on the field of March. And when he was reviewing them all carefully, he came to the man who struck the vase, and said to him: "No one has brought armor so carelessly kept as you; for neither your spear nor sword nor ax is in serviceable condition." And seizing his ax he cast it to the earth, and when the other had bent over somewhat to pick it up, the king raised his hands and drove his own ax into the man's head. "This," said he, "is what you did at Soissons to the vase." Upon the death of this man, he ordered the rest to depart, raising great dread of himself by this action. He made many wars and gained many victories. In the tenth year of his reign he made war on the Thuringi and brought them under his dominion.

Now the king of the Burgundians was Gundevech, of the family king Athanaric the persecutor, whom we have mentioned before. He had four sons; Gundobad, Godegisel, Chilperic and Godomar. Gundobad killed his brother Chilperic with the sword, and sank his wife in water with a stone tied to her neck. His two daughters he condemned to exile; the older of these who became a nun, was called Chrona, and the younger Clotilda. And as Clovis often sent embassies to Burgundy, the maiden Clotilda was found by his envoys. And when they saw that she was of good bearing and wise, and learned that she was of the family of the king, they reported this to King Clovis, and he sent an embassy to Gundobad without delay asking her in marriage. And Gundobad was afraid to refuse, and surrendered her to the men, and they took the girl and brought her swiftly to the king. The king was very glad when he saw her, and married her, having already by a concubine a son named Theodoric.

He had a first-born son by queen Clotilda, and as his wife wished to consecrate him in baptism, she tried unceasingly to persuade her husband, saying: "The gods you worship are nothing, and they will be unable to help themselves or anyone else. For they are graven out of stone or wood or some metal. And the names you have given them are names of men and not of gods, as Saturn, who is declared to have fled in fear of being banished from his kingdom by his son; as Jove himself, the foul perpetrator of all shameful crimes, committing incest with men, mocking at his kinswomen, not able to refrain from intercourse with his own sister as she herself says: Jovisque et soror et conjunx. What could Mars or Mercury do? They were endowed rather with the magic arts than with the power of the divine name. But he ought rather to be worshipped who created by his word heaven and earth, the sea and all that in them is out of a state of nothingness, who made the sun shine, and adorned the heavens with stars, who filled the waters with creeping things, the earth with living things and the air with creatures that fly, at whose nod the earth is decked with growing crops, the trees with fruit, the vines with grapes, by whose hand mankind was created, by whose generosity all that creation serves and helps man whom he created as his own." But though the queen said this the spirit of the king was by no means moved to belief, and he said: "It was at the command of our gods that all things were created and came forth, and it is plain that your God has no power and, what is more, he is proven not to belong to the family of the gods." Meantime the faithful queen made her son ready for baptism; she gave command to adorn the church with hangings and curtains, in order that he who could not be moved by persuasion might be urged to belief by this mystery. The boy, whom they named Ingomer, died after being baptized, still wearing the white garments in which he became regenerate. At this the king was violently angry, and reproached the queen harshly, saying: "If the boy had been dedicated in the name of my gods he would certainly have lived; but as it is, since he was baptized in the name of your God, he could not live at all." To this the queen said: "I give thanks to the omnipotent God, creator of all, who has judged me not wholly unworthy, that he should deign to take to his kingdom one born from my womb. My soul is not stricken with grief for his sake, because I know that, summoned from this world as he was in his baptismal garments, he will be fed by the vision of God."

After this she bore another son, whom she named Chlodomer at baptism; and when he fell sick, the king said: "It is impossible that anything else should happen to him than happened to his brother, namely, that being baptized in the name of your Christ, he should die at once." But through the prayers of his mother, and the Lord's command, he became well.

The queen did not cease to urge him to recognize the true God and cease worshiping idols. But he could not be influenced in any way to this belief, until at last a war arose with the Alamanni, in which he was driven by necessity to confess what before he had of his free will denied. It came about that as the two armies were fighting fiercely, there was much slaughter, and Clovis's army began to be in danger of destruction. He saw it and raised his eyes to heaven, and with remorse in his heart he burst into tears and cried: "Jesus Christ, whom Clotilda asserts to be the son of the living God, who art said to give aid to those in distress, and to bestow victory on those who hope in thee, I beseech the glory of thy aid, with the vow that if thou wilt grant me victory over these enemies, and I shall know that power which she says that the people dedicated in thy name have had from thee, I will believe in thee and be baptized in thy name. For I have invoked my own gods, but, as I find, they have withdrawn from aiding me; and therefore I believe that they possess no power, since they do not help those who obey them. I now call upon thee, I desire to believe thee, only let me be rescued from my adversaries." And when he said this, the Alamanni turned their backs, and began to disperse in flight. And when they saw that their king was killed, they submitted to the dominion of Clovis, saying: "Let not the people perish further, we pray; we are yours now." And he stopped the fighting, and after encouraging his men, retired in peace and told the queen how he had had merit to win the victory by calling on the name of Christ. This happened in the fifteenth year of his reign.

Then the queen asked saint Remi, bishop of Rheims, to summon Clovis secretly, urging him to introduce the king to the word of salvation. And the bishop sent for him secretly and began to urge him to believe in the true God, maker of heaven and earth, and to cease worshiping idols, which could help neither themselves nor any one else. But the king said: "I gladly hear you, most holy father; but there remains one thing: the people who follow me cannot endure to abandon their gods; but I shall go and speak to them according to your words." He met with his followers, but before he could speak the power of God anticipated him, and all the people cried out together: "O pious king, we reject our mortal gods, and we are ready to follow the immortal God whom Remi preaches." This was reported to the bishop, who was greatly rejoiced, and bade them get ready the baptismal font. The squares were shaded with tapestried canopies, the churches adorned with white curtains, the baptistery set in order, the aroma of incense spread, candles of fragrant odor burned brightly, and the whole shrine of the baptistery was filled with a divine fragrance: and the Lord gave such grace to those who stood by that they thought they were placed amid the odors of paradise. And the king was the first to ask to be baptized by the bishop. Another Constantine advanced to the baptismal font, to terminate the disease of ancient leprosy and wash away with fresh water the foul spots that had long been borne. And when he entered to be baptized, the saint of God began with ready speech: "Gently bend your neck, Sigamber; worship what you burned; burn what you worshipped." The holy bishop Remi was a man of excellent wisdom and especially trained in rhetorical studies, and of such surpassing holiness that he equalled the miracles of Silvester. For there is extant a book of his life which tells that he raised a dead man. And so the king confessed all-powerful God in the Trinity, and was baptized in the name of the Father, Son and holy Spirit, and was anointed with the holy ointment with the sign of the cross of Christ. And of his army more than 3000 were baptized. His sister also, Albofled, was baptized, who not long after passed to the Lord. And when the king was in mourning for her, the holy Remi sent a letter of consolation which began in this way: "The reason of your mourning pains me, and pains me greatly, that Albofled your sister, of good memory, has passed away. But I can give you this comfort, that her departure from the world was such that she ought to be envied rather than mourned." Another sister also was converted, Lanthechild by name, who had fallen into the heresy of the Arians, and she confessed that the Son and the holy Spirit were equal to the Father, and was anointed.

*   *   *

Now when Alaric, king of the Goths, saw Clovis conquering nations steadily, he sent envoys to him saying: "If my brother consents, it is the desire of my heart that with God's favor we have a meeting." Clovis did not spurn this proposal but went to meet him. They met in an island of the Loire which is near the village of Amboise in the territory of Tours, and they talked and ate and drank together, and plighted friendship and departed in peace. Even at the time many of the Gauls desired greatly to have the Franks as masters.

Whence it happened that Quintian, bishop of Rodez, was driven from his city through ill-will on this account. For they said: "It is your desire that the rule of the Franks be extended over this land." A few days later a quarrel arose between him and the citizens, and the Goths who dwelt in the city became suspicious when the citizens charged that he wished to submit himself to the control of the Franks; they took counsel and decided to slay him with the sword. When this was reported to the man of God he rose in the night and left the city of Rodez with his most faithful servants and went to Clermont. There he was received kindly by the holy bishop Eufrasius, who had succeeded Aprunculus of Dijon, and he kept Quintian with him, giving him houses as well as fields and vineyards, and saying: "The wealth of this church is enough to keep us both; only let the charity which the blessed apostle preaches endure among the bishops of God." Moreover the bishop of Lyons bestowed upon him some of the possessions of the church which he had Auvergne. And the rest about the holy Quintian, both the plottings which he endured and the miracles which the Lord deigned to work through him, are written in the book of his life.

Now Clovis the king said to his people: "I take it very hard that these Arians hold part of the Gauls. Let us go with God's help and conquer them and bring the land under our control." Since these words pleased all, he set his army in motion and made for Poitiers where Alaric was at that time. But since part of the host was passing through Touraine, he issued an edict out of respect to the blessed Martin that no one should take anything from that country except grass for fodder, and water. But one from the army found a poor man's hay and said: "Did not the king order grass only to be taken, nothing else? And this," said he, "is grass. We shall not be transgressing his command if we take it." And when he had done violence to the poor man and taken his hay by force, the deed came to the king. And quicker than speech the offender was slain by the sword, and the king said: "And where shall our hope of victory be if we offend the blessed Martin? It would be better for the army to take nothing else from this country." The king himself sent envoys to the blessed church saying: "Go, and perhaps you will recieve some omen of victory from the holy temple." Then giving them gifts to set up in the holy place, he said: "If thou, O Lord, art my helper, and hast determined to surrender this unbelieving nation, always striving against thee, into my hands, consent to reveal it propitiously at the entrance to the church of St. Martin, so that I may know that thou wilt deign to be favorable to the servant." Clovis' servants went on their way according to the king's command, and drew near to the place, and when they were about to enter the holy church, the first singer, without any prearrangement, sang this response: "Thou hast girded me, O Lord, with strength unto the battle; thou has subdued under me those that rose up against me, and has made mine enemies turn their backs unto me, and thou hast utterly destroyed them that hated me." On hearing this singing they thanked the Lord, and paying their vow to the blessed confessor they joyfully made their report to the king. Moreover, when he came to the river Vienne with his army, he did not know where he ought to cross. For the river had swollen from the rains. When he had prayed to the Lord in the night to show him a ford where he could cross, in the morning by God's will a hind of wonderful size entered the river before them and when it passed over the people saw where they could cross. When the king came to the neighborhood of Poitiers and was encamped some distance off he saw a ball of fire come out of the church of Saint Hilarius and pass, as it were, over him, to show that, aided by the light of the blessed confessor Hilarius, he should more boldly conquer the heretic armies, against which the same bishop had often fought for the faith. And he made it known to all the army that neither there nor on the way should they spoil any one or take any one's property.

There was in these days a man of praiseworthy holiness, the abbot Maxentius, who had become a recluse in his own monastery in Poitou because of his fear of God. We have not put the name of the monastery in this account because the place is called to the present day *Cellula sancti Maxentii*. And when his monks saw a division of the host approaching the monastery, they prayed to the abbot to come forth from his cell to consult with them. And as he stayed, they were panic-stricken and opened the door and dragged him from his cell. And he hastened boldly to meet the enemy to ask for peace. And one of them drew out his sword to launch a stroke at his head, and when he had raised his hand to his ear it became rigid and the sword fell. And he threw himself at the feet of the blessed man, asking pardon. And the rest of them seeing this returned in great fear to the army, afraid that they should all perish together. The man's arm the holy confessor rubbed with consecrated oil, and made over it the sign of the cross and restored it to soundness. And owing to his protection the monastery remained uninjured. He worked many other miracles also, and if any one diligently seeks for them he will find them all in reading the book of his life. In the twenty-fifth year of Clovis.

Meantime king Clovis met with Alaric, king of the Goths, in the plain of Vouille at the tenth mile-stone from the Poitiers, and while the one army was for fighting at a distance the other tried to come to close combat. And when the Goths had fled as was their custom, king Clovis won the victory by God's aid. He had to help him the son of Sigibert the lame, named Chloderic. This Sigibert was lame from a wound in the leg, received in a battle with the Alemanni near the town of Zulpich. Now when the king had put the Goths to flight and slain king Alaric, two of the enemy suddenly appeared and struck at him with their lances, one on each side. But he was saved from death by the help of his coat of mail, as well as by his fast horse. At that time there perished a very great number of the people of Auvergne, who had come with Apollinaris and the leading senators. From this battle Amalaric, son of Alaric, fled to Spain and wisely seized his father's kingdom. Clovis sent his son Theodoric to Clermont by way of Albi and Rodez. He went, and brought under his father's dominion the cities from the boundaries of the Goths to the limit of the Burgundians. Alaric reigned twenty-two years. When Clovis had spent the winter in Bordeaux and taken all the treasures of Alaric at Toulouse he went to Angouleme. And the Lord gave him such grace that the walls fell down of their own accord when he gazed at them. Then he drove the Goths out and brought the city under his own dominion. Thereupon after completing his victory he returned to Tours, bringing many gifts to the holy church of the blessed Martin.

Clovis received an appointment to the consulship from the emperor Anastasius, and in the church of the blessed Martin he clad himself in the purple tunic and chlamys, and placed a diadem on his head. Then he mounted his horse, and in the most generous manner he gave gold and silver as he passed along the way which is between the gate of the entrance [of the church of St. Martin] and the church of the city, scattering it among the people who were there with his own hand, and from that day he was called consul or Augustus. Leaving Tours he went to Paris and there he established the seat of his kingdom. There also Theodoric came to him.

[Licinius was bishop of Tours at the time of Clovis' visit. His travels.]

When King Clovis was dwelling at Paris he sent secretly to the son of Sigibert saying: "Behold your father has become an old man and limps in his weak foot. If he should die," said he, "of due right his kingdom would be yours together with our friendship." Led on by greed the son plotted to kill his father. And when his father went out from the city of Cologne and crossed the Rhine and was intending to journey through the wood Buchaw, as he slept at midday in his tent his son sent assassins in against him, and killed him there, in the idea that he would get his kingdom. But by God's judgment he walked into the pit that he had cruelly dug for his father. He sent messengers to king Clovis to tell about his father's death, and to say: "My father is dead, and I have his treasures in my possession, and also his kingdom. Send men to me, and I shall gladly transmit to you from his treasures whatever pleases you." And Clovis replied: "I thank you for your good will, and I ask that you show the treasures to my men who come, and after that you shall possess all yourself." When they came, he showed his father's treasures. And when they were looking at the different things he said: "It was in this little chest that my father used to put his gold coins." "Thrust in your hand," said they, "to the bottom, and uncover the whole." When he did so, and was much bent over, one of them lifted his hand and dashed his battle-ax against his head, and so in a shameful manner he incurred the death which he had brought on his father. Clovis heard that Sigibert and his son had been slain, and came to the place and summoned all the people, saying: "Hear what has happened. When I," said he, "was sailing down the river Scheldt Cloderic, son of my kinsman, was in pursuit of his own father, asserting that I wished him killed. And when his father was fleeing through the Forest of Buchaw, he set highwaymen upon him, and gave him over to death, and slew him. And when he was opening the treasures, he was slain himself by some one or other. Now I know nothing at all of these matters. For I cannot shed the blood of my own kinsmen, which it is a crime to do. But since this has happened, I give you my advice, if it seems acceptable; turn to me, that you may be under my protection." They listened to this, and giving applause with both shields and voices, they raised him on a shield, and made him king over them. He received Sigibert's kingdom with his treasures, and placed the people, too, under his rule. For God was laying his enemies low every day under his hand, and was increasing his kingdom, because he walked with an upright heart before him, and did what was pleasing in his eyes.

QUESTIONS TO CONSIDER

1. How does Gregory justify his "mingling miracles and slaughters"?
2. Gregory uses parallels with Biblical events and the works of earlier Christian historians. What cultural and literary background do we need to know to be able to understand his text?

3. What should historians do with the portents that Gregory interprets as showing God's favor to Clovis (the deer indicating the ford, the fireball emitted from the chapel)?

FOR FURTHER READING

Goffart, Walter A. *The Narrators of Barbarian History (A.D. 550–800): Jodanes, Gregory of Tours, Bede, and Paul the Deacon.* Princeton, NJ: Princeton University Press, 1988.

Gregory, Saint, Bishop of Tours, 538–594. *The History of the Franks.* Trans. Lewis Thorpe. New York: Penguin Books, 1974.

Nie, Giselle de. *Views from a Many-windowed Tower: Studies of Imagination in the Works of Gregory of Tours = Waarnemingen vanuiteen toren met vele vensters: studien over verbeelding in de werken van Gregorius van Tours.* Amsterdam: Rodopi, 1987.

NOTES

1. Gregory, Bishop of Tours, *History of the Franks,* trans. Ernest Brehaut (New York: Norton, 1969), 1, 21, 36–41, 44–49.

CHAPTER 20

Bede

Venerable Briton

Venerable Briton Bede
The Bettmann Archive

B ede (673–735), often called Venerable Bede, wrote a history that was widely distributed among literate Europeans (mostly monks) in the Middle Ages. His *Historia ecclesiastica gentis Anglorum* (*Ecclesiastical History of the English People*) lays the foundation for the study of English history from the time of raids by Julius Caesar (55 BCE) to CE 731. Bede focused intensely on church history, but the complex interplay of religion and political power sheds occasional light on other aspects of English society. His works popularized the European practice of dating events according to the Christian era (BC, AD) which prevailed for centuries in much of the world (although like many twentieth-century writers we use BCE and CE—Before Common Era and Common Era).

Bede spent his entire life in what is now northern England, most of it in the monastery at Jarrow where he was educated and ordained as a deacon and priest. He wrote many books of biblical commentary and literary analysis, as well as works on chronology, primarily dealing with the proper date for the celebration of Easter, an issue of considerable dispute in the early Christian centuries. He listed 37 distinct works in a chapter appended to his *Ecclesiastical History*, so he was well experienced as a writer before he began the monumental task of compiling a history of the conversion of England.

Bede's *Ecclesiastical History* has a framework dealing with the eventual triumph of Roman Catholic Christianity over both Anglo-Saxon pagan religion and the Celtic form of Christianity in England. Bede traced the decline and persecution of Romano-British Christians under the invasion by the pagan Anglo-Saxons in the fifth century CE, efforts to evangelize the Anglo-Saxons sponsored by Pope Gregory I starting from Canterbury in 597, and the simultaneous efforts in the north by Celtic missionaries from Ireland and Scotland. Both efforts focused initially on converting the political leaders of the Anglo-Saxon kingdoms, so much of Bede's account reflects the political intrigues needed to keep unbelieving heirs true to their fathers' commitments or the struggles of one potential heir with another. Once a veneer of Christianity had been laid, there was a less dramatic, but nonetheless intense, struggle between advocates of the Roman and the Celtic rituals and practices. Issues such as the proper style of shaving clergy heads and the correct date for celebrating Easter, which seem minor in the twentieth century even to Christian believers, occupied much time and energy. Eventually, the Roman rite prevailed and tied England more closely to continental Europe and the spiritual authority of the pope for the rest of its history.

Bede worked carefully as a historian. His work is an outstanding achievement, for he dealt with seven centuries of material, much of it from oral sources, and still managed to fit it together into a coherent and compelling whole. For one isolated at very nearly the end of the world, Bede had access to remarkable sources. Copies of letters from the Vatican archives relating to the Roman missions to the Anglo-Saxons were available to him. He wrote that he sought out any living witnesses to the events he recounted, as well as exploring traditions of the several Anglo-Saxon kingdoms, especially the traditions associated with the royal families of Northumbria. In his preface,

Bede lists all the sources he used for his composition—a courtesy that later historians truly appreciate. As his translator assesses, "Bede's *History* contains relatively few errors, and modern research has confirmed the accuracy of most of his statements."

Bede thought that the Roman tradition was the right one in the conflict among the Christians, but he also extolled the virtues of the Celtic saints whose stories he recounted, and he gave us a good look at the vibrant, scholarly faith of Irish and Scottish Christians in the era just prior to his own. Bede submitted his work to others for checking and correction. Post-Enlightenment readers are often dismayed by the number of miracles attributed to the saints in Bede's text. But Bede was not wholly credulous. One of his criteria for including a miraculous happening was the credibility of the witnesses. Some tales, however, Bede recounted because they would edify.

Bede's stated purpose in writing the *Ecclesiastical History* was to inform Ceolwulf, King of Northumbria, of the doings and sayings of great men of the past. Bede wrote that history had a didactic purpose—to teach us to imitate the good deeds of good people and to avoid the sinful and perverse deeds of the wicked. Yet he insisted that he had first to record the deeds accurately in order for the lesson to have its best effect.

Ecclesiastical History of the English People[1]

To the Most Glorious King Ceolwulf, Bede the Priest and Servant of Christ

Some while ago, at Your Majesty's request, I gladly sent you the history of the Church in England which I had recently completed, in order that you might read it and give it your approval. I now send it once again to be transcribed, so that Your Majesty may consider it at greater leisure. I warmly welcome the diligent zeal and sincerity with which you study the words of Holy Scripture, and your eager desire to know something of the doings and sayings of great men of the past, and of our own nation in particular. For if history records good things of good men, the thoughtful hearer is encouraged to imitate what is good: or if it records evil of wicked men, the good, religious listener or reader is encouraged to avoid all that is sinful and perverse, and to follow what he knows to be good and pleasing to God. Your Majesty is well aware of this; and since you feel so deeply responsible for the general good of those over whom divine Providence has set you, you wish that this history may be better known both to yourself and to your people.

But in order to avoid any doubts as to the accuracy of what I have written in the minds of yourself or of any who may listen to or read this history, allow me briefly to state the authorities upon whom I chiefly depend. My principal authority and adviser in this work has been the most reverend Abbot Albinus, an eminent scholar educated in the church of Canterbury by Archbishop Theodore and Abbot Hadrian, both of them respected and learned men. He carefully transmitted to me verbally or in writing through Nothelm, a priest of the church of London, anything he considered worthy of mention that had been done by disciples of the blessed Pope Gregory in the province of Kent or the surrounding regions. Such facts he ascertained either from records or from long established traditions. Nothelm himself later visited Rome, and obtained permission from the present Pope Gregory (II) to examine the archives of the holy Roman Church. He found there letters of Pope Gregory (I) and other Popes, and when he returned, the reverend father Albinus advised him to bring them to me for inclusion in this history. So from the period at which this volume begins until the time when the English nation received the Faith of Christ, I have drawn extensively on earlier writers. But from that time until the present, I owe much of my information about what was done in the See of Canterbury by the disciples of Pope Gregory and their successors, and under what kings events occurred, to the remarkable industry of Abbot Albinus made known to me through Nothelm. They also provided some of my information about the bishops and kings under whom the provinces of the East and West Saxons, the East Angles, and the Northumbrians received the grace of the Gospel. Indeed, it was due to the persuasion of Albinus that I was encouraged to begin this work. Also the most reverend Bishop Daniel of the West Saxons sent to me in writing certain facts about the history of the Church in his province, in the adjoining province of the South Saxons, and in the

Island of Vectis. I am indebted to the brethren of Lastingham monastery for their careful account of the conversion of the province of Mercia to Christ by the holy priests Cedd and Ceadda, their founders; of how the province of the East Saxons rejected and recovered the Faith; and of how their holy fathers lived and died. In addition, I have traced the progress of the Church in the province of the East Angles, partly from old traditions and writings, and partly from the account given by the most reverend Abbot Esi. The growth of the Christian Faith and Succession of bishops in the province of Lindsey I have learned either from the letters of the most reverend Bishop Cynebert, or by word of mouth from other reliable persons. But with regard to events in the various districts of the province of Northumbria, from the time that it received the Faith of Christ up to the present day, I am not dependent on any one author, but on countless faithful witnesses who either know or remember the facts, apart from what I know myself. In this connexion, it should be noted that whatever I have written concerning our most holy father and Bishop Cuthbert, whether in this book or in my separate account of his life and doings, I have in part taken and accurately copied from a Life already compiled by the brethren of the Church of Lindisfarne; and I have carefully added to this whatever I could learn from the reliable accounts of those who knew him. Should the reader discover any inaccuracies in what I have written, I humbly beg that he will not impute them to me, because, as the laws of history require, I have laboured honestly to transmit whatever I could ascertain from common report for the instruction of posterity.

I earnestly request all who may hear or read this history of our nation to ask God's mercy on my many failings of mind and body. And in return for the diligent toil that I have bestowed on the recording of memorable events in the various provinces and places of greater note, I beg that their inhabitants may grant me the favour of frequent mention in their devout prayers.

*   *   *

Book I, Chapter 22: The Britons enjoy a respite from foreign invasions, but exhaust themselves in civil war and plunge into serious crimes.

Meanwhile Britain enjoyed a rest from foreign, though not from civil wars. Amid the wreckage of deserted cities destroyed by the enemy, the natives who had survived the enemy now attacked each other. So long as there remained any kings, priests, nobles, and private individuals who remembered the former disasters, these kept their proper rank. But when they died, there grew up a generation who knew nothing of these things, and had experienced only the present peaceful order. Then were all restraints of truth and justice so utterly abandoned that no trace of them remained, and very few of the people even recalled their existence. Among other unspeakable crimes, recorded with sorrow by their own historian Gildas, they added this—that they never preached the Faith to the Saxons who dwelt with them in Britain. But God in his goodness did not utterly abandon the people whom he had chosen, for he remembered them, and sent this nation more worthy preachers of truth to bring them to the Faith.

Chapter 23: The holy Pope Gregory sends Augustine and other monks to preach to the English nation, and encourages them in a letter to persevere in their mission [CE 596].

In the year of our Lord 582, Maurice, fifty-fourth successor to Augustus, became Emperor, and ruled for twenty-one years. In the tenth year of his reign, Gregory, an eminent scholar and administrator, was elected Pontiff of the apostolic Roman see, and ruled it for thirteen years, six months, and ten days. In the fourteenth year of this Emperor, and about the one hundred and fiftieth year after the coming of the English to Britain, Gregory was inspired by God to send his servant Augustine with several other God-fearing monks to preach the word of God to the English nation. Having undertaken this task at the Pope's command and progressed a short distance on their journey, they became afraid, and began to consider returning home. For they were appalled at the idea of going to a barbarous, fierce, and pagan nation, of whose very language they were ignorant. They unanimously agreed that this was the safest course, and sent back Augustine—who was to be consecrated bishop in the event of their being received by the English—so that he might humbly request the holy Gregory to recall them from so dangerous, arduous, and uncertain a journey. In reply, the Pope wrote them a letter of encouragement, urging them to proceed on their mission to preach God's word, and to trust themselves to his aid. This letter ran as follows:

Gregory, Servant of the servants of God, to the servants of God. My very dear sons, it is better never to undertake any high enterprise than to abandon it when once begun. So with the help of God you must carry out this holy task which you have begun. Do not be deterred by the troubles of the journey or by what men say. Be constant and zealous in carrying out this enterprise which, under God's guidance, you have undertaken: and be assured that the greater the labour, the greater will be the glory of your eternal reward. When Augustine your leader returns, whom We have appointed your abbot, obey him humbly in all things, remembering that whatever he directs you to do will always be to the good of your souls. May Almighty God protect you with His grace, and grant me to see the result of your labours in our heavenly home. And although my office prevents me from working at your side, yet because I long to do so, I hope to share in your joyful reward. God keep you safe, my dearest sons.

"Dated the twenty-third of July, in the fourteenth year of the reign of our most devout lord Maurice Tiberius Augustus, and the thirteenth year after the Consulship of our said Lord. The fourteenth indiction."

*   *   *

Chapter 25: Augustine reaches Britain, and first preaches in the Isle of Thanet before King Ethelbert, who grants permission to preach in Kent [CE 597].

Reassured by the encouragement of the blessed father Gregory, Augustine and his fellow-servants of Christ resumed their work in the word of God, and arrived in Britain. The King of Kent at this time was the powerful King Ethelbert, whose domains extended northwards to the river Humber, which forms the boundary between the north and south Angles. To the east of Kent lies the large island of Thanet, which by English reckoning is six hundred hides in extent; it is separated from the mainland by a waterway about three furlongs broad called the Wantsum, which joins the sea at either end, and is fordable only in two places. It was here that God's servant Augustine landed with companions, who are said to have been forty in number. At the direction of blessed Pope Gregory, they had brought interpreters from among the Franks, and they sent these to Ethelbert, saying that they came from Rome bearing very glad news, which infallibly assured all who would receive it of eternal joy in heaven, and an everlasting kingdom with the living and true God. On receiving this message, the king ordered them to remain in the island where they had landed, and gave directions that they were to be provided with all necessaries until he should decide what action to take. For he had already heard of the Christian religion, having a Christian wife of the Frankish royal house named Bertha, whom he had received from her parents on condition that she should have freedom to hold and practise her faith unhindered with Bishop Liudhard whom they had sent as her chaplain.

After some days, the king came to the island, and sitting down in the open air, summoned Augustine and his companions to an audience. But he took precautions that they should not approach him in a house, for he held an ancient superstition that if they were practisers of magical arts, they might have opportunity to deceive and master him. But the monks were endowed with power from God, not from the Devil, and approached the king carrying a silver cross as their standard, and the likeness of our Lord and Saviour painted on a board. First of all they offered prayer to God, singing a litany for the eternal salvation both of themselves and of those for whose sake they had come. And when, at the king's command, Augustine had sat down and preached the word of life to the king and his court, the king said: "Your words and promises are fair indeed, but they are new and strange to us, and I cannot accept them and abandon the age-old beliefs of the whole English nation. But since you have travelled far, and I can see that you are sincere in your desire to instruct us in what you believe to be true and excellent, we will not harm you. We will receive you hospitably, and take care to supply you with all that you need; nor will we forbid you to preach and win any people you can to your religion." The king then granted them a dwelling in the city of Canterbury, which was the chief city of all his realm, and in accordance with his promise, he allowed them provisions and did not withdraw their freedom to preach. Tradition says that as they approached the city, bearing the holy cross and the likeness of our great King and Lord Jesus Christ as was their custom, they sang in unison this litany: "We pray Thee, O Lord, in all Thy mercy, that Thy wrath and anger may be turned away from this city and from Thy holy house, for we are sinners. Alleluia."

Chapter 26: The life and doctrine of the primitive Church are followed in Kent: Augustine establishes his episcopal see in the king's city.

As soon as they had occupied the house given to them they began to emulate the life of the apostles and the primitive Church. They were constantly at prayer; they fasted and kept vigils; they preached the word of life to whomsoever they could. They regarded worldly things as of little importance, and accepted only necessary food from those they taught. They practised what they preached, and were willing to endure any hardship, and even to die for the Faith which they proclaimed. A number of heathen, admiring the simplicity of their holy lives and the comfort of their heavenly message, believed and were baptized. On the east side of the city stood an old church, built in honour of Saint Martin during the Roman occupation of Britain, where the Christian queen went to pray. Here they first assembled to sing the psalms, to pray, to say Mass, to preach, and to baptize, until the king's own conversion to the Faith enabled them to preach openly, and to build and restore churches everywhere.

At length the king and others, edified by the pure lives of these holy men and their gracious promises, the truth of which they confirmed by many miracles, believed and were baptized. Thenceforward great numbers gathered each day to hear the word of God, forsaking their heathen rites, and entering the unity of Christ's holy Church as believers. While the king was pleased at their faith and conversion, he would not compel anyone to accept Christianity, for he had learned from his instructors and guides to salvation that the service of Christ must be accepted freely and not under compulsion; nevertheless, he shows greater favour to believers, because they were fellow-citizens of the kingdom of Heaven. And it was not long before he granted his teachers a property of their own in his capital of Canterbury, and gave them possessions of various kinds to supply their wants.

*   *   *

Book 3, Chapter 25: Controversy arises with the Scots over their observance of Easter [CE 664]

. . . About this time there arose a great and recurrent controversy on the observance of Easter, those trained in Kent and Gaul maintaining that the Scottish observance was contrary to that of the universal Church. The most zealous protagonist of the true Easter was a Scot named Ronan, who had been trained in theology and law in Gaul and Italy. He disputed against Finan and convinced many, or at least persuaded them to make more careful enquiry into the truth. But he entirely failed to move Finan, a hot-tempered man whom reproof made more obstinate, and openly hostile to the truth. James, formerly the deacon of the venerable Archbishop Paulinus, of whom I have spoken, kept the true and Catholic Easter with all whom he could persuade to adopt the right observance. Also Queen Eanfleda and her court, having as chaplain a Kentish priest named Romanus who followed the Catholic customs, observed the customs she had seen in Kent. It is said that the confusion in those days was such that Easter was kept twice in one year, so that when the King had ended Lent and was keeping Easter, the Queen and her attendants were still fasting and keeping Palm Sunday. During Aidan's lifetime these differences of Easter observance were partially tolerated by everyone, for it was realized that although he was in loyalty bound to retain the customs of those who sent him, he nevertheless laboured diligently to cultivate the faith, piety, and love that marks out God's saints. He was therefore rightly loved by all, even by those who differed from his opinion on Easter, and was held in high respect not only by ordinary folk, but by Honorius of Canterbury and Felix of East Anglia.

When Finan, who followed Aidan as bishop, died, he was succeeded by an Irishman, Colman, under whom an even more serious controversy arose about Easter and the rules of Church discipline. This dispute began to trouble the minds and consciences of many people, who feared that they might have received the name of Christian in vain. . . . [I]t was decided to hold a synod to put an end to this dispute. . . . When Wilfred had received the king's permission to speak, he said: "Our Easter customs are those that we have seen universally observed in Rome, where the blessed Apostles Peter and Paul lived, taught, suffered, and are buried. We have also seen the same customs generally observed throughout Italy and Gaul when we travelled through these countries for study and prayer. Furthermore, we have found them to be observed in many different countries and languages at the same time, in Africa, Asia, Egypt, Greece, and throughout the world wherever the church of Christ has spread. The only people who are stupid enough to disagree with the whole world are these Scots and their obstinate adherents the Picts and Britons, who inhabit only a portion of these two islands in the remote ocean." In reply to this statement, Colman answered: "It is strange that you call our customs stupid when they rest on the authority of so great an Apostle [John], who was considered worthy to lean on our Lord's breast, and whose great widsom is acknowledged throughout the world." . . . [T]he king concluded: "Then, I tell you, Peter is guardian of the gates of heaven, and I shall not contradict him. I shall obey his commands in everything to the best of my knowledge and ability; otherwise, when I come to the gates of heaven, he who holds the keys may not be willing to open them."

All present, both high and low, signified their agreement with what the king had said, and abandoning their imperfect customs, readily accepted those which they had learned to be better.

QUESTIONS TO CONSIDER

1. What audience was Bede addressing in his writing? What did he expect his audience to know?
2. Bede accepts some miracles as genuine and rejects others. What criteria does he use?
3. Granted that we can often learn vicariously from the praiseworthy and blameworthy actions of our predecessors, can history itself have a didactic moral purpose?

FOR FURTHER READING

Blair, Peter Hunter. *Bede's Ecclesiastical History of the English People and Its Importance Today.* The Jarrow Lecture, 1959.
_____ . *The World of Bede.* Cambridge, U.K.: Cambridge University Press, 1990.
Brown, George Hardin. *Bede, the Venerable.* Boston: Twayne, 1987.
Carroll, T. A. *Venerable Bede: His Spiritual Teachings.* Washington, DC: Catholic University of America Press, 1946.
Wallace-Hadrill, J. M. *Bede's Ecclesiastical History of the English People: A Historical Commentary.* New York: Oxford University Press, 1988.
Ward, Benedicta. *The Venerable Bead.* Harrisburg, PA: Morehouse, 1990.

NOTES

1. Bede, *A History of the English Church and People,* trans. Leo Sherley-Price (Baltimore: Penguin, 1955), 33–35, 65–71, 182–83, 184–85, 188.

CHAPTER 21

Anna Comnena

Loyal Daughter

The family of Anna Comnena: her father, Emperor Alexius
(right) and her brother, Emperor John II (left).
The Granger Collection, New York

The first woman historian in Europe was a Byzantine princess, Anna Comnena (1083–after 1148), who wrote an account of her father, the Emperor Alexius (reigned 1081–1118). His reign saw a resurgence of Byzantine strength against the Turks in Asia Minor and coincided with the excursion of western Christians to the Holy Land in the First Crusade.

Anna was well placed to do her work. She was her father's eldest child and seems to have been his favorite. Highly educated, she had access to the written documents of her father's reign as well as to the oral accounts of his fellow soldiers and commanders. Betrothed at a very young age to the designated heir to the throne, Anna developed lifelong animosity against her younger brother John who eventually replaced her fiancé as heir. She was later married to another man against her will, but the marriage turned loving and lasted forty years. Her husband's family was almost as well connected politically as her own, so she was never far from the center of imperial power in the Byzantine court.

Anna wrote in the archaized Attic Greek style that characterized most Byzantine authors. She consciously echoed Homer, Herodotus, and Thucydides in much that she wrote, but with the added element of deeply held Christian piety. Anna's perspective was entirely elitist, focusing on war and political power in its highest reaches; the common people do not appear in her account. She was relatively good at describing and understanding science and military technology (especially Greek fire, a Byzantine incendiary secret weapon), but vague on geography and battle tactics. Her chronology is sometimes confusing to the reader. Her prose is florid. Her tone is sad; lamentations about her father's death and her husband's intermingle with praise for their deeds. Anna's prejudices are not hidden or subtle. Her father was restoring the Byzantine Empire to its former greatness and virtue. Non-Byzantines were barbarous to various degrees, whether westerners ("Latins"), Muslims, Armenians, or followers of the Pope. She hated heretics and delighted in their tortures and deaths. Her brother John could do little right in her eyes.

The history of the work itself is important. It was cited in Byzantium for about 100 years after her death, but then disappeared from mention until about 1610 when a printed version caught the interest of Renaissance humanists in the West. Edward Gibbon's misogynistic assessment that "an elaborate affectation of rhetoric and science betrays in every page the vanity of a female author. The genuine character of Alexius is lost in a vague constellation of virtues; and the perpetual strain of panegyric and apology awakens our jealously to question the veracity of the historian and the merit of the hero . . ." discouraged interest in it until the revival by Byzantine studies in the twentieth century.

In the passages that follow, Anna declares her purpose in writing history and her qualifications to do so. The crusaders made a not altogether favorable impression on her, especially the Norman Bohemond. Her satisfaction with the punishments of the heretic Bogomils shows something of the depth and obstinacy of her Orthodox faith.

The Alexiad[1]

Preface

The stream of Time, irresistible, ever moving, carries off and bears away all things that come to birth and plunges them into utter darkness, both deeds of no account and deeds which are mighty and worthy of commemoration; as the playwright says, it 'brings to light that which was unseen and shrouds from us that which was manifest.' Nevertheless, the science of History is a great bulwark against this stream of Time; in a way it checks this irresistible flood, it holds in a tight grasp whatever it can seize floating on the surface and will not allow it to slip away into the depths of Oblivion.

I, Anna, daughter of the Emperor Alexius and the Empress Irene, born and bred in the Purple, not without some acquaintance with literature— having devoted the most earnest study to the Greek language in fact, and being not unpractised in Rhetoric and having read thoroughly the treatises of Aristotle and the dialogues of Plato, and having fortified my mind with the Quadrivium of sciences (these things must be divulged, and it is not self-advertisement to recall what Nature and my own zeal for knowledge have given me, nor what God has apportioned to me from above and what has been contributed by Opportunity); I, having realized the effects wrought by Time, desire now by means of my writings to give an account of my father's deeds, which do not deserve to be consigned to Forgetfulness nor to be swept away on the flood of Time into an ocean of Non-Remembrance; I wish to recall everything, the achievements before his elevation to the throne and his actions in the service of others before his coronation.

I approach the task with no intention of flaunting my skill as a writer; my concern is rather that a career so brilliant should not go unrecorded in the future, since even the greatest exploits, unless by some chance their memory is preserved and guarded in history, vanish in silent darkness. My father's actions themselves prove his ability as a ruler and show too, that he was prepared to submit to authority, within just limits.

* * *

The main reason why I have to write the account of my father's deeds is this: I was the lawful wife of the Caesar Nicephorus, who was descended from the Bryennii, an extremely handsome man, very intelligent, and in the precise use of words far superior to his contemporaries. . . . [H]e chose in particular to write the history of the Emperor Alexius, my father (on the orders of the empress), and to record the events of his reign in several books, when a brief lull in the warfare gave him the chance to turn his attention to historical and literary research. He did indeed begin the history. . . . However, he was disappointed in his hopes and the history was not completed. After carrying on the account to the times of the Emperor Nicephorus Botaniates he stopped writing because circumstances prevented any further progress, to the detriment of the history itself and the sorrow of its readers. That is why I have chosen to record the full story of my father's deeds myself, so that future generations may not be deprived of knowledge about them.

* * *

The Caesar's untimely death and the suffering it brought about touched my heart deeply and the pain of it affected the innermost part of my being. . . . But I see that I have been led astray by these thoughts from my subject; the Caesar stood over me and his sorrow provoked heavy sorrow in me too. I will wipe away the tears from my eyes, recover from my grief and continue my story, earning thereby a double share of tears, as the playwright says, for one disaster recalls another. To put before the public the life-history of such an emperor reminds me of his supreme virtue, his marvelous qualities—and the hot tears fall again as I weep with all the world. When I remember him and make known the events of his reign, it is for me a theme of lamentation; the others will be reminded of their loss. However, this is where I must begin the history of my father, at the point where it is better to begin, where the narrative will become at once clearer and more accurate.

*   *   *

The First Crusade

Bohemond and all the counts met at a place from which they intended to sail across the Kibotos, and with Godfrey they awaited the arrival of Saint-Gilles who was coming with the emperor. Thus with their forces united they would set out along the road to Nicaea. However, their numbers were so immense that further delay became impossible—the food-supplies were deficient. So they divided their army in two: one group drove on through Bithynia and Nicomedia towards Nicaea; the other crossed the strait to Kibotos and assembled in the same area later. Having approached Nicaea in this manner they allotted towers and intervening battlements to certain sections. The idea was to make the assault on the walls according to this disposition; rivalry between the various contingents would be provoked and the siege pressed with greater vigour. The area allotted to Saint-Gilles was left vacant until he arrived. At this moment the emperor reached Pelekanum, with his eye on Nicaea (as I have already pointed out). The barbarians inside the city meanwhile sent repeated messages to the sultan asking for help, but he was still wasting time and as the seige had already gone on for many days, from sunrise right up to sunset, their condition was obviously becoming extremely serious. They gave up the fight, deciding that it was better to make terms with the emperor than to be taken by the Kelts. Under the circumstances they summoned Boutoumites, who had often promised in a never-ending stream of letters that this or that favour would be granted by Alexius, if only they surrendered to him. He now explained in more detail the emperor's friendly intentions and produced written guarantees. He was gladly received by the Turks, who had despaired of holding out against the overwhelming strength of their enemies; it was wiser, they thought, to cede Nicaea voluntarily to Alexius and share in his gifts, with honourable treatment, than to become the victims of war to no purpose. Boutoumites had not been in the place more than two days before Saint-Gilles arrived, determined to make an attempt on the walls without delay; he had siege engines ready for the task. Meanwhile a rumour spread that the sultan was on his way. At this news the Turks, inspired with courage again, at once expelled Boutoumites. As for the sultan, he sent a detachment of his forces to observe the Frankish offensive, with orders to fight if they met any Kelts. They were seen by Saint-Gilles's men from a distance and a battle took place—but it went ill for the Turks, for the other counts and Bohemond himself, learning of the engagement, set aside up to 200 men from each company, thus making up a considerable army, and sent them immediately to help. They overtook the barbarians and pursued them till nightfall. Nevertheless, the sultan was far from downcast at this setback; at sunrise the next morning he was in full armour and with all his men occupied the plain out-side the walls of Nicaea. The Kelts heard about it and they too armed themselves for battle. They descended on their enemies like lions. The struggle that then ensued was ferocious and terrible. All through the day it was indecisive, but when the sun went down the Turks fled. Night had ended the contest. On either side many fell and most of them were killed; the majority of the fighters were wounded. So the Kelts won a glorious victory. The heads of many Turks they stuck on the ends of spears and came back carrying these like standards, so that the barbarians, recognizing afar off what had happened and being frightened by this defeat at their first encounter, might not be so eager for battle in future. So much for the ideas and actions of the Latins. The sultan, realizing how numerous they were and after this onslaught made aware of their self-confidence and daring, gave a hint to the Turks in Nicaea: 'From now on do just what you consider best.' He already knew that they preferred to deliver up the city to Alexius than to become prisoners of the Kelts. Meanwhile Saint-Gilles, setting about the task allotted to him, was constructing a wooden tower, circular in shape; inside and out he covered it with leather hides and filled the centre with intertwined wicker-work. When it was thoroughly strengthened, he approached the so-called Gonatas Tower. His machine was manned by soldiers whose job was to batter the walls and also by expert sappers, equipped with iron tools to undermine them from below; the former would engage the defenders on the ramparts above, while the latter worked with impunity below. In place of the stones they prised out, logs of wood were put in and when their excavations reached the point where they were nearly through the wall and a gleam of light could be seen from the far side, they set light to these logs and burnt them. After they were reduced to ashes, Gonatas inclined even more, and merited its name even more than before. The rest of the walls were surrounded with a girdle of battering-rams and 'tortoises'; in the twinkling of an eye, so to speak, the outer ditch was filled with dust, level with the flat parts on either side of it. Then they proceeded with the siege as best they could.

* * *

The emperor was still in the vicinity of Pelekanum. He wished those counts who had not yet sworn allegiance to give him pledges in person. Written instructions were issued to Boutoumites to advise all counts not to begin the march to Antioch before doing homage to the emperor; this would be an opportunity for them to accept even greater gifts. Hearing of money and gifts, Bohemond was the first to obey Boutoumites' advice. He immediately counselled all of them to return. Bohemond was like that—he had an uncontrollable lust for money. The emperor welcomed them with great splendor at Pelekanum. He was most sedulous in promoting their welfare. Finally he called them together and spoke: 'Remember the oath you have all sworn to me and if you really intend not to transgress it, advise any others you know, who have not sworn, to take this same oath.' They at once sent for these men and all, with the exception of Tancred, Bohemond's Nephew, assembled to pay homage. Tancred, a man of independent spirit, protested that he owed allegiance to one man only, Bohemond, and that allegiance he hoped to keep till his dying day. He was pressed by the others, including even the emperor's kinsmen. With apparent indifference, fixing his gaze on the tent in which the emperor held the seat of honour (a tent more vast than any other in living memory) he said, 'If you fill it with money and give it to me, as well as the sums you have given to all the other counts, then I too will take the oath.' Palaeologus, zealous on the emperor's behalf and finding Tancred's words insufferable and hypocritical, pushed him away with contempt. Tancred recklessly darted towards him, whereupon Alexius rose from his throne and intervened. Bohemond, for his part, calmed down his nephew, telling him it was improper to behave with disrespect to the emperor's relatives. Tancred, ashamed now of acting like a drunken lout before Palaeologus and to some extent convinced by the arguments of Bohemond and the others, took the oath. When all had taken their leave of the emperor, Taticius (at that time Great Primicerius) and the forces under his command were ordered to join the Franks; Taticius' duty would be to help and protect them on all occasions and also to take over from them any cities they captured, if indeed God granted them that favour. Once more therefore the Kelts made the crossing on the next day and all set out for Antioch. Alexius assumed that not all their men would necessarily follow the counts; he accordingly notified Boutoumites that all Kelts left behind were to be hired to guard Nicaea. Taticius, with his forces, and all the counts, with their numberless hosts, reached Leukai in two days. At his own request Bohemond was in charge of the vanguard, while the rest followed in column of march at a slow pace. When some Turks saw him moving rather fast on the plain of Dorylaeum they thought they had chanced upon the whole Keltic army and treating it with disdain they at once attacked. That crazy idiot, Latinus, who had dared to seat himself on the imperial throne, forgetting the emperor's advice stupidly rode out in front of the rest (he was on the extreme end of Bohemond's line). Forty of his men were killed then and he himself was seriously wounded. He turned in flight and hurried back to the centre—visible proof, although he would not admit it in words, of Alexius' wise counsel. Bohemond, seeing the ferocity of the Turks, sent for reinforcements, which quickly arrived. From then on the battle was hotly contested, but the terrible conflict ended in a victory for the Romans and Kelts. After that the march continued, but with the contingents in touch with one another. They were met near Hebraike by the Sultan Tanisman and Hasan, who alone commanded 80,000 fully-armed infantry. It was hard-fought battle, not only because of the vast numbers involved, but also because neither side would give way. However, the Turks were fighting with more spirit and Bohemond, commanding on the right wing, realized this. So, detaching himself from the rest of the army, he made a headlong onslaught on Kilij Arslan himself, charging 'like a lion exulting in his might,' as the poet says. This had a terrifying effect on the enemy and they fled. The Kelts, remembering the emperor's instructions, did not pursue them very far, but they occupied the Turkish entrenchment and rested there for a short time. They again fell in with the Turks near Augustopolis, attacked and routed them completely. After that the barbarians faded away. The survivors from the battle were scattered in all directions, leaving behind their women and children and making certain of their own safety in flight; in future they had not even the strength to look the Latins in the face.

* * *

Later, in the . . . year of Alexius' reign there arose an extraordinary 'cloud of heretics,' a new, hostile group, hitherto unknown to the Church. For two doctrines, each known to antiquity and representative of what was most evil, most worthless, now coalesced: one might say that the impiety of the Manichaeans (also known as the Paulician heresy) and the loathsome character of the Massalians were united in the Bogomils, for the dogma of the latter was an amalgam of Manichaean and Massalian teaching. Apparently it was in existence before my father's time, but was unperceived (for the Bogomils' sect is most adept at feigning virtue). No worldly hairstyles are to be seen among Bogomils: their wickedness is hidden beneath cloak and cowl. Your Bogomil wears a sombre look; muffled up to the nose, he walks with a stoop, quietly muttering to himself—but inside he's a ravening wolf. This unpleasant race, like a serpent lurking in its hole, was brought to the light and lured out by my father with secret magical incantations. He had recently freed himself of most of his cares in east and west, and was now turning his attention to things more spiritual. (For he was in everything superior to all his contemporaries: as a teacher he surpassed the educational experts, as a soldier and a general he excelled the professionals who were most admired.) The fame of the Bogomils had by now spread to all parts, for the impious sect was controlled with great cunning by a certain monk called Basil. He had twelve followers whom he called 'apostles' and also dragged along with him certain female disciples, women of bad character, utterly depraved. In all quarters he made his wicked influence felt and when the evil, like some consuming fire, devoured many souls, the emperor could no longer bear it. He instituted a thorough inquiry into the heresy. Some of the Bogomils were brought to the palace; without exception they denounced as their master, the protagonist of their heresy, a certain Basil. One of them, Diblatius, was imprisoned. Since under interrogation he was unwilling to confess, he was subjected to torture. He then admitted that Basil was the leader and he named the 'apostles' whom Basil had chosen. Several men were accordingly given the task of finding him. Basil, Archisatrap of Satanael, was brought to light, dressed in monkish garb, austere of face, with a thin beard, very tall. At once the emperor, wishing to discover from him the man's innermost thoughts, tried compulsion, but with a show of persuasion: he invited him to the palace on some righteous pretext. He even rose from his seat when Basil came in, made him sit with him and share his own table. The whole line was run out for the catch, with all kinds of tempting bait on the hooks for this voracious monster to swallow; the monk, so practised in villainy, was by every means urged to gulp down the whole treacherous offering. Alexius feigned a desire to become his disciple and maybe he was not alone in this: his brother, the Sebastocrator Isaac, also led Basil on. Alexius pretended to regard all his sayings as some divine oracle and gave way to every argument; his one hope, he said, was that the wretched Basil would effect his soul's salvation. 'I, too, most reverend father,' said he (for he smeared the cup's rim with honey sweetness, so that the other in his lunacy might vomit forth his dark beliefs), 'I too admire you for your virtue. I pray you make me understand in some degree the doctrines that your Honour teaches, for those of our Church are all but worthless, in no way conducive to virtue.' At first Basil was coy; he wrapped close about him the lion's skin—he who was in reality an ass—and at the emperor's words shied away. Nevertheless he was filled with conceit by Alexius' praises—he had even invited Basil to share his meal. At all times Isaac was at his brother's side, play-acting with him. Finally Basil did vomit forth Bogomil doctrine. It happened thus: a curtain divided the women's quarters from the room where the brothers were, as this loathsome creature belched out and plainly declared all his heart's secrets; meanwhile a secretary behind the curtain recorded what was said. The fool, to all appearances, was the teacher, while the emperor played the part of learner and the lesson was committed to writing by the secretary. The accursed fellow strung everything together, lawful and unlawful alike; no jot of his blasphemous doctrine was held back. Worse than that, he looked askance at our doctrine of the Divine Nature of Christ and wholly misinterpreted His human nature. He even went so far as to call the holy churches the temples of demons and treated as of little importance what among us is believed to be the consecrated Body and Blood of our first High Priest and Sacrifice. The reader will wish to know the sequel to this. Well, the emperor threw off his pretence and drew back the curtain. Then a conference was summoned of all the senate, the chief army commanders and the elders of the Church. The hateful teachings of the Bogomil were read aloud. The proof was incontestable. Indeed, the accused made no attempt to dispute the charge, but at once proceeded without a blush to counterattack, promising that he was ready to undergo fire and scourgings, to die a thousand deaths. These misguided Bogomils are persuaded, you see, that they can endure any punishment without feeling pain, for angels (they think) will pluck them from the funeral pyre itself. And although all threatened him and reproached him his irreverence—even those who had shared in his ruin—he was still the same Basil, inexorable, a true Bogomil. Despite the burning and other tortures held over him, he clung with all his might to his devil, holding fast to his Satanael. He was sent to prison. Many times Alexius sent for him, many times called upon him to abjure his wickedness; but to all the emperor's pleadings he remained as deaf as ever. I must now relate the extraordinary thing which happened to this Basil before the emperor had begun to take sterner measures against him. After he had confessed his impiety, he retired temporarily to a small house newly built for him quite near the imperial palace. It was the evening after the meeting of the Synod; the stars above were shining in a cloudless sky and the moon was bright. When about midnight the monk had entered his cell, stones were thrown against it in the manner of hailstorm. Now the stones fell automatically: they were hurled by no hand and no man was to be seen stoning this devilish abbot. Seemingly it was an act of vengeance—Satanael's demons were wrathful, outraged no doubt at the betrayal of their secrets to the emperor and the notable persecution of their heresy which followed it. Parasceviotes, the appointed guard of the diabolical old man (Basil), whose duty it was to prevent him talking with others and contaminating them with his own filth, swore with the most frightful oaths that he had heard the clatter of the stones as they were hurled on the ground and on the roof-tiles; he had seen them falling in thick showers, one after another; but he had no glimpse anywhere of a thrower. The fall of stones was followed by a sudden earthquake which rocked the ground and the roof-tiles had rattled. Nevertheless Parasceviotes, before he realized that this was devils' work, had (according to his story) been unafraid; but when he saw that the stones were raining down, as it were, from heaven and that the wretched old heresiarch had slunk inside and closed the door behind him, he decided that this was indeed the doing of demons and knew not what to make of it.

I will say no more about that miracle. It was my intention to expound the whole Bogomilian heresy, but 'modesty,' as the lovely Sappho somewhere remarks, 'forbids me'; historian I may be, but I am also a woman, born in the Porphyra, most honoured and first-born of Alexius' children; what was common hearsay had better be passed over in silence. Despite my desire to give a full account, I cannot—for if I did my tongue would be sullied. However, those who would like to know all are referred to the so-called *Dogmatic Panoply*, a book compiled on my father's orders. He sent for a monk named Zygabenus, known to my grandmother on the maternal side and to all the clergy, who had a great reputation as a grammarian, was not unversed in rhetoric and had an unrivalled knowledge of dogma. Zygabenus was commanded to publish a list of all heresies, to deal with each separately and append in each case the refutation of it in the texts of the holy fathers. The Bogomilian heresy was included, just as the impious Basil had interpreted it. This book Alexius named the *Dogmatic Panoply* and the volumes are so called to this day. But we must return to Basil's downfall. From all over the world the emperor summoned Basil's disciples and fellow mystics, in particular the 'twelve apostles'; their opinions were tested and their loyalty to Basil was unimpeachable. In fact the evil had deep roots: it had penetrated even the greatest houses and enormous numbers were affected by this terrible thing. Alexius condemned the heretics out of hand: chorus and chorus-leader alike were to suffer death by burning. When the Bogomils had been hunted down and brought together in one place, some clung to the heresy, but others denied the charges completely, protesting strongly against their accusers and rejecting the Bogomilian heresy with scorn. The emperor was not inclined to believe them and to prevent possible errors of identification he devised a novel scheme, making sure that real Christians should not be destroyed. (There was a chance that Christians might be confused with Bogomils and a Bogomil might be mistaken for a Christian and so escape.) On the next day he took his seat on the imperial throne. Many of the senators were present on this occasion, together with members of the Holy Synod and certain picked Naziraeans noted for their learning. All those prosecuted for their Bogomilian beliefs were made to stand trial before this assembly; Alexius ordered them to be examined for a second time, one by one. Some admitted that they were Bogomils and vigorously clung to their heresy; others absolutely denied this and called themselves Christians. When they were challenged, they retracted nothing. The emperor glared at them and said, 'Two pyres will have to be lit today. By one a cross will be planted firmly in the ground. Then a choice will be offered to all: those who are prepared to die for their Christian faith will separate themselves from the rest and take up position by the pyre with the cross; the Bogomilian adherents will be thrown on the other. Surely it is better that even Christians should die than live to be hounded down as Bogomils and offend the conscience of the majority. Go away, then, all of you, to whichever pyre you choose.' This declaration to the Bogomils seemingly closed the case. Accordingly they were seized and led away at once. A huge crowd gathered and stood all about them. Fires were then lit, burning seven times more fiercely than usual (as the lyric poet says) in the place called Tzykanisterin. The flames leapt to the heavens. By one pyre stood the cross. Each of the condemned was given his choice, for all were to be burnt. Now that escape was clearly impossible, the orthodox to a man moved over to the pyre with the cross, truly prepared to suffer martyrdom; the godless adherents of the abominable heresy went off to the other. Just as they were about to be thrown on the flames, all the bystanders broke into mourning for the Christians; they were filled with indignation against the emperor (they did not know of his plan). But an order came from him just in time to stop the executioners. Alexius had in this way obtained firm evidence of those who were really Bogomils. The Christians, who were victims of calumny, he released after giving them much advice; the rest were committed once again to prison, but the 'apostles' were kept apart. Later he sent for some of these men every day and personally taught them, with frequent exhortations to abandon their abominable cult. Certain church leaders were told to make daily visits to the rest, to instruct them in the orthodox faith and advise them to give up their heretical ideas. And some did change for the better and were freed from prison, but others died in their heresy, still incarcerated, although they were supplied with plentiful food and clothing.

QUESTIONS TO CONSIDER

1. What is Anna Comnena's purpose in writing? How does it shape her account?
2. What can we learn about the varieties of people in the Byzantine world and the relationships among them from Comnena's account?

3. Is Gibbon correct when he asserts that this work "betrays the vanity of a female author"? Is there something distinctive to the writings of a woman historian like Anna Comnena?

FOR FURTHER READING

Buckler, Georgina. *Anna Comnena: A Study.* Oxford: Clarendon, 1929.
Dalven, Rae. *Anna Comnena.* New York: Twayne, 1972.
Sewter, E. R. A., trans. *The Alexiad of Anna Comnena.* Harmondsworth, U.K.: Penguin, 1969.

NOTES

1. E. R. A. Sewter, trans., *The Alexiad of Anna Comnena* (Harmondsworth, U.K.: Penguin, 1969), 17–21, 333–42, 360–64, 496–505.

CHAPTER 22

Sima Guang

History in the Confucian Mode

Emperor Wen-Ti, founder of the Sui Dynasty
Museum of Fine Arts Boston

S inologists are fond of proclaiming that "China possesses a wealth of historical writing unequalled by any other country before modern times" (Beasley and Pulleyblank, 135), and they are right. No empire or people on earth possessed so elaborate a set of historical institutions as did imperial China. From at least the Han dynasty forward, the court employed a small army of official historians to keep records of the past as well as to write the history of the current dynasty. All these historians were highly trained in the Confucian classics. Like other government officials, they held their positions by virtue of their knowledge of the *Analects*, the *Book of Changes*, and so forth, and by their ability to write elegant essays on those ancient books.

The official historians followed Ban Gu and Ban Zhao rather than Sima Qian. That is, they wrote the histories of particular dynasties, not histories covering longer periods like Sima Qian's *Shi zhi*. Not until Sima Guang (1019–1086) did any official attempt a more universal history again. The dynastic historians concentrated on politics; it is only incidentally that the reader learns from them anything of the life of the Chinese people. The emperor was the center of concern, especially his place in the dynastic cycle.

Chinese historians from the first Han dynasty down to the end of the imperial era in 1911 used dynasties and the reigns of sovereigns as their chronological units of analysis, and the moral qualities of rulers as their theme. Each of the thirty dynasties they interpreted on a common cyclical pattern. The cycle began with the rise of a vigorous and virtuous ruler who united the country by force of arms, whereupon there followed a steady increase in the nation's power and prosperity under a succession of enlightened emperors and efficient bureaucrats. Thereafter, corruption set into the bureaucracy and the emperors neglected their religious duties, floods and famine and astronomical oddities plagued the country, peasants rebelled, outside barbarians attacked, and the dynasty collapsed. The dynastic cycle theory resembles in some ways Ibn Khaldûn's four generations of prestige (see Chapter 23). The dynastic cycle brought order to Chinese historians' and leaders' understanding of their past, but it obscured much of the change—economic, social, cultural, even bureaucratic—that went on beneath the political surface.

Sima Guang embraced the bureaucratic historians' political emphasis and their fixation on the dynastic cycle as an interpretive model. He did not break new ground as a researcher. What he did do that was unusual was make sense of a very large part of Chinese history and bring a critical eye to the evaluation of his sources.

Sima was a *jin-shi*, a scholar-official who had passed the highest level of official exams. He served many posts in government, starting at age 20 and continuing until he was made prime minister in his 60s. He was well versed in the Confucian classics, music, and astronomy. He wrote 32 books totaling 886 volumes.

The most widely celebrated of these was the *Zi-zhi tong-jian (Comprehensive Mirror for Aid in Government)*, which he wrote between 1072 and 1084. Sima and his assistants combed all the records they could find: dynastic

histories, unofficial accounts, biographies, over 300 novels, and odd papers
they found here and there. They organized them chronologically, weighed
their accuracy, drew lessons for rulers, and condensed it all into a single
narrative of the rise and fall of 16 dynasties between 403 BCE and CE 959, from
the Warring States period down to just before the founding of the Song
dynasty. Despite the immense scope of the overall work, Sima's focus on
personalities and his feel for narrative make the *Comprehensive Mirror* a
pleasure to read.

   This broad, sweeping view of Chinese history, Confucian attention to how
best to run government, careful weighing of numerous documents, and vivid
storytelling are the hallmarks of Sima Guang's writing. He was influenced by
his contemporary Ou-yang Xiu (1007–1072), and in turn he influenced
thinkers throughout East Asia, among them the Japanese historian Hayashi
Razan and the Neo-Confucian philosophers Zhu Xi of China and Ogyu Sorai
of Japan. The following selection, from the 185th chapter of the *Comprehensive
Mirror,* shows the moral decline of the emperor at the end of the dynastic cycle
and the treachery of the coup d'etat that ended the Sui dynasty. It contains
some of the most vivid characters in Chinese historical writing.

Comprehensive Mirror for Aid in Government[1]

The Last Days of Sui Yang-ti

As the empire continued to disintegrate, Sui Yang-ti could not but feel insecure about himself. After each conference with his ministers, he often changed into casual attire and, carrying a cane in his hand, strolled in the palace compound and wandered from one building to another. He would not stop wandering until dusk, as if every tour of his might be his last. He had taught himself the art of divination and loved to speak in the Wu dialect. With a wine cup in his hand while looking up at the stars, he would say to Empress Hsiao: "Many people outside this palace wish to harm me, but I shall have no worry. Even when the worst arrives, I can still be another Duke Ch'angch'eng and you another Queen Shen. Why should I worry? Let us drink and enjoy life to the fullest." Needless to say, he became drunk again after each remark of this kind. Observing himself in the mirror, he once said: "What a beautiful head! I am wondering who will have the privilege of cutting it off." Looking at his wife's shocked expression, he merely burst into laughter. "Happiness and sorrow take turns governing the life of a man," he responded. "What is wrong with my stating the obvious?"

Seeing that North China had plunged into chaos and war, Sui Yang-ti thought seriously of not returning to the north. He had in mind the permanent move of his capital to Tanyang, thus enabling him to hold the Lower Yangtze even after the loss of North China to the rebels. He ordered his ministers to stage a debate on this issue but was surprised to see the division it caused. One group, headed by Yü Shih-chi, was in favor, while another group, headed by General Li Ts'ai, was vigorously opposed and recommended instead that the emperor should return to Ch'angan immediately. The debate was so heated that Yü Shih-chi and Li Ts'ai continued to exchange angry words as they left the conference. Li T'ung, an official in the Second Secretariat, stated: "South China is damp and mountainous and does not have the resources to support the court and the army. The people will be taxed beyond endurance and in that case chaos and war will inevitably occur as they have already occurred in the north." Li T'ung was censored, however, after having made these remarks, as his critics accused him of having deliberately undermined an established policy of the government. Other officials, sensing the trend, began to say what the emperor had wanted to hear. "The people of South China have waited for Your Majesty's presence for a long time," they stated. "Your Majesty will be most enthusiastically received, as the Great Yü once was, should he decide to pass across the Yangtze River to rule and comfort them." An order was then issued to build palaces at Tanyang where the new capital was supposed to be.

Meanwhile the food supply in Yangchow was about to be exhausted. Most of the soldiers who had accompanied the emperor on his southern tour were natives of Kuanchung and, having been in the south for a long time, were homesick and anxious to return home. Now that the emperor had decided to stay in the south, they plotted to return by themselves. One contingent of troops, led by Colonel Tou Hsien, deserted their ranks and moved westward. The emperor, furious, ordered his cavalry elite to pursue them. When captured, said the emperor, these deserters were to be killed on the spot. The number of deserters continued to increase, however, despite the government's stringent measures to stop them.

As the number of deserters multiplied, General Ssu-ma Teh-k'an, a longtime favorite of the emperor's who was then commanding a crack contingent stationed in the eastern section of the city, approached his friends Generals Yüan Li and P'ei Ch'ien-t'ung and spoke to them as follows: "What should we do, now that the soldiers are deserting their ranks one after another? If we report all these happenings to the emperor, we will certainly be held responsible and severely punished. If we do not, not only we ourselves but also all members of our families will be in serious difficulties when the emperor finds out the truth himself. As you recall, after Li Hsiao-chung had switched sides in the losing battle against the rebels in Kuanchung, the emperor threw his two younger brothers into jail and proposed to try them for treason. Do you not think that we should be equally concerned, since our families are still in the north?"

Generals Yüan Li and P'ei Ch'ien-t'ung were frightened upon hearing these remarks. "What should we do?" they asked.

"Since our soldiers are deserting us," Ssu-ma Teh-k'an replied, "we may as well desert with them."

The two men approved this idea and began to contact others for the same purpose. Among those who were contacted and agreed to become participants in a coup were Yüan Min, Chao Hsing-ch'u, Meng Ping, Niu Fang-yü, Hsü Hung-jen, Hsüeh Shih-liang, T'ang Feng-yi, Chang K'ai, and Yang Shih-lan, all of whom held important positions with the government. They met day and night and pledged not to betray one another. They aired their sentiments of rebellion even in public, as if they had nothing to be afraid of.

One of the court women reported the conspiracy to Empress Hsiao but was advised to report directly to the emperor, "if you so desire." Hearing the report, the emperor ordered the poor woman to be put to death on the grounds that the conspiracy, if there was one, was none of her business. When other court women continued to make the same report, Empress Hsiao only sighed with resignation. "The state of the empire has so deteriorated that nothing you and I can do will make any difference," she replied. "Telling him the truth only worries him more, with no difference in the end whatsoever." From then on no court woman even mentioned the plot any more. . . .

General Yü-wen Hua-chi, who had never been known for his daring or audacity, was understandably shocked and perspired profusely when informed by the plotters that he had been designated as their leader to stage a coup against the emperor. Nevertheless, after some hesitation, he agreed to serve as their leader. Having thus secured the general's consent, Ssu-ma Teh-k'an sent Hsü Hung-jen and Chang K'ai to the palace to inform everyone they knew as follows: "His Majesty has heard that the northern soldiers intend to stage a rebellion and has therefore ordered their execution by poison. The poison will be placed in the wine during a banquet which His Majesty is scheduled to give in their honor. Having had all of the northern soldiers killed, His Majesty will then feel safe with the southerners." The rumor spread by these two men yielded its desired result, as the northern soldiers could hardly wait for the coup to begin.

On the day of Yi-mao [10 April 618] Ssu-ma Teh-k'an gathered all of the officers of the northern army and instructed them in what to do. "We will do whatever you say, sir," they responded unanimously."

It was a windy and cloudy day, and darkness shrouded the city even at noon. Shortly after 6 P.M. Ssu-ma Teh-k'an arrived at the royal stable, taking control of the horses and ordering all present to ready themselves for the battle. Meanwhile Yüan Li and P'ei Ch'ien-t'ung led their men to the palace compound on the pretense of providing additional strength to safeguard the life of the emperor. T'ang Feng-yi, whose official duty was to guard all of the city gates, secretly communicated to P'ei Ch'ien-t'ung that all the gates would not be bolted on that particular evening.

By midnight, after he had gathered more than forty thousand men in the eastern section of the city, Ssu-ma Teh-k'an ordered the burning of houses as a signal to the allied troops outside the city wall that they should proceed with their part of the plan. In the palace, meanwhile, the emperor was questioning P'ei Ch'ien-t'ung about the fire he saw and the noise he heard. "It is nothing, sir," P'ei Ch'ien-t'ung replied. "Some of the haylofts have caught fire, and people are fighting it." By this time the communication between the palace and the outside world had been totally cut off; the emperor, consequently, had no way of knowing what was going on outside.

Outside the city wall Yü-wen Chih-chi and Meng Ping, commanding approximately one thousand men, launched a sudden attack upon a contingent headed by Feng P'u-yüeh, captain of the city patrol, and captured him alive. Their mission completed, the men were ordered to guard the nearby side streets.

Having sensed that a coup had already begun, Prince T'an of Yen [a grandson of Sui Yang-ti's] secretly entered the city, in the darkness of the night, through an aqueduct next to the Fang-lin Gate. When he was stopped at the Hsüan-wu Gate that led to the palace compound, he told the guards that he had suddenly suffered a stroke, would die soon, and must see the emperor to bid him farewell. P'ei Ch'ien-t'ung, instead of reporting his presence to the emperor, ordered him to be arrested.

Shortly before dawn on the next morning Ssu-ma Teh-k'an ordered the troops under P'ei Ch'ien-t'ung's command to replace the imperial guards as sentries at all the gates leading to the palace compound. Meanwhile P'ei Ch'ien-t'ung himself, commanding several hundred cavalrymen, headed for the Ch'eng-hsiang Palace. When the imperial guards stationed in the palace discovered the intruders' presence, P'ei Ch'ien-t'ung ordered all the gates to be closed immediately, with the exception of the Eastern Gate, through which the imperial guards were ordered to get out. The guards, surprised and overwhelmed, dropped their weapons and hurried out as ordered. Only the commander, a man named Tu-hu Sheng, decided to put up a fight. "Who do you think you are?" said he to P'ei Ch'ien-t'ung. "What do you think you are doing?"

"We have already made the move," P'ei Ch'ien-t'ung replied. "What we are doing today has nothing to do with you. Please stay where you are and do not do anything foolish."

"You old thief," Tu-hu Sheng scolded as loudly as he could. "What kind of talk is this?" Without even bothering to put on his armor, he ordered his immediate followers, who numbered no more than fifteen, to rush into battle. In the ensuing fight all of them, including Tu-hu Sheng, were killed by the rebel soldiers. . . .

Previously, in anticipation of unusual developments, Sui Yang-ti had selected several hundred public slaves, known officially as servitors-at-large, to be stationed at the Hsüan-wu Gate on an around-the-clock basis. These servitors-at-large were chosen for their physical strength and military skill and were treated so well that the emperor even married many of them to the court women he owned. What the emperor did not realize was that Wei Shih, the royal chamberlain in charge of the palaces, had already joined the conspirators and agreed to do whatever he could to facilitate the coup from the inside. Shortly before the coup, Wei Shih, in a forged decree, ordered the servitors-at-large to leave their posts and go to the city to amuse themselves. Thus, when Ssu-ma Teh-k'an arrived with his men at the Hsüan-wu Gate, there was not a single servitor-at-large on guard.

The emperor, finally convinced that the rebels were indeed storming his palace, quickly changed into civilian clothes and ran toward the Western Pavilion. Meanwhile two of the conspirators, P'ei Ch'ien-t'ung and Yüan Li, were pounding the gate that led to the Left Pavilion. Wei Shih opened the gate from the inside and the conspirators, together with their men, found themselves in a narrow corridor. "Where is His majesty?" they asked. One of the emperor's concubines, who happened to be in the corridor at this time, pointed out the direction in which the emperor had fled.

Lieutenant Ling-hu Hsing'teh unsheathed his sword and ran straight to the Western Pavilion. The emperor, hiding part of his face behind a window curtain, said to Ling-hu Hsing-teh, "Are you going to kill me?"

"How can your servant dare to do a thing like that?" the conspirator replied. "We only wish to obtain Your Majesty's consent to return to North China." Having said this, he helped the emperor down the steps from the Western Pavilion.

Before the coup P'ei Ch'ien-t'ung had been one of the emperor's most trusted lieutenants, dating to the days when the emperor was still a crown prince. Imagine the emperor's shock when he was brought face to face with the conspirator. "Are you not an old friend of mine?" the emperor asked. "What have I done to you that makes you betray me?"

"It is not your servant's intention to stage a rebellion," P'ei Ch'ien-t'ung replied. "The officers and men are homesick and want to go home. They would like very much to have the privilege of escorting Your Majesty back to the capital [Ch'ang-an]."

"I would like to return to the north too," said the emperor. "The reason for the delay is that the rice ships from the Upper Yangtze have not yet arrived. If you insist, I am going with you now." Despite his consent to return to the north, the emperor remained a captive, as P'ei Ch'ien-t'ung ordered his men to keep constant watch over him.

As soon as the day broke, Meng Ping dispatched several cavalrymen to escort General Yü-wen Hua-chi to the palace compound. The general, trembling and speechless, had to be assisted to his mount. Whenever someone came near to pay his respects, he merely raised his head, crouched forward against the saddle, and kept murmuring: "What a shame! What a shame!" At the city gate he was met by Ssu-ma Teh-k'an who subsequently escorted him to the Hall of Audience. As soon as he was inside the hall, the general was proclaimed prime minister.

In the palace, meanwhile, P'ei Ch'ien-t'ung was preparing the emperor to proceed to the Hall of Audience to meet with the leaders of the coup. "All the ministers are ready," he said. "Your Majesty must go there to comfort them in person." A mount was brought in, but the emperor, reluctant to leave, complained about the shabbiness of the saddle. The saddle was changed, and the emperor, having no more excuses, had to mount. P'ei Ch'ien-t'ung led the emperor out of the palace by the horse's reins, while brandishing a sword. Rebel soldiers on both sides of the road, watching the emperor pass by, shouted with joy.

Yü-wen Hua-chi, the newly proclaimed prime minister, did not relish the idea of meeting the emperor face to face. "Why does he have to be taken out of the palace?" he shouted. "Why can he not be finished off quickly where he is?" The emperor, consequently, was returned to his palace.

Having returned to the palace, P'ei Ch'ien-t'ung and Ssu-ma Teh-k'an seated the emperor in a chair, while they themselves, with swords in their hands, stood behind him.

"What have I done to deserve a fate like this?" the emperor asked.

"Plenty," Ma Wen-chu, one of the rebel leaders, replied. "Your Majesty deserted his ancestral temple and conducted endless tours of pleasure. He indulged in military adventures abroad, while living an extravagant, licentious life at home. Consequently millions of men died in war and millions of women were left helpless in the gutter. Millions of others lost their means of livelihood, while banditry and riots mushroomed all over the country. He trusted nobody except those who knew how to flatter; he protected the guilty and punished the innocent. How can he say that he has done nothing to deserve punishment?"

"I may have betrayed the common people," the emperor replied. "But certainly I have not done anything wrong to men like you who enjoy honor and wealth on account of me. How can you possibly do this thing to me? Who, may I ask, is in charge of today's events?"

"The whole world has grievances against you," Ssu-ma Teh-k'an replied. "Yet you are talking to only one person."

Yü-wen Hua-chi sent Feng Teh-yi to enumerate the emperor's crimes. "You are a scholar," said the emperor. "Scholars do not degrade themselves by doing things like this." With a reddened face, Feng Teh-yi withdrew without completing his enumeration of crimes.

During the exchange of accusing words, Prince K'ao, a lad of eleven and the emperor's most beloved child, was leaning against his father and crying incessantly. Annoyed by the crying and yet unable to stop him, Ssu-ma Teh-k'an cut the boy's head off with one swipe of his sword, causing blood to spatter over the emperor's clothes. "A Son of Heaven must die with dignity, and beheading is not the proper way to end his life," said the emperor, when Ssu-ma Teh-k'an was about to slay him too. "I would appreciate a cup of poisoned wine."

Ma Wen-chu, supported by others, turned down the emperor's request for poison; instead, he ordered Ling-hu Hsing-teh to push the emperor hard against the chair. The emperor, knowing the end was near, untied his silk belt and handed it over to Ling-hu Hsing-teh. The latter strangled him to death on the chair.

Previously, in anticipation of a situation similar to that described above, Sui Yang-ti had prepared a jar of poisoned wine which accompanied him wherever he went. "If traitors show up," he instructed his favorite concubines, "you ladies drink this wine first before I do it myself." When the anticipated moment arrived, all of his favorite concubines had already fled and he could not even find the poisoned wine.

QUESTIONS TO CONSIDER

1. According to Sima Guang's interpretation, where in the dynastic cycle is China at the time of the events recorded here?
2. What does this passage suggest about the relative value Sima Guang assigned to historical accuracy, presenting a moral lesson, and telling a good story?
3. What aspects of Chinese life and politics does an account of this sort leave out?

FOR FURTHER READING

"Achievements in the Writing of History." In *Sources of Chinese Tradition,* edited by Wm. Theodore DeBary, Wing-tsit Chan, and Burton Watson, Vol. I, 436–54. New York: Columbia University Press, 1960.

Beasley, W. G., and E. G. Pulleyblank, eds. *Historians of China and Japan.* Oxford: Oxford University Press, 1961.

Chan, Wing-tsit, ed. *Chu Hsi and Neo-Confucianism.* Honolulu, HI: University of Hawaii Press, 1986.

Liu, James T. C. *Ou-yang Hsiu: An Eleventh-Century Neo-Confucianist.* Stanford, CA: Stanford University Press, 1967.

Ssu-ma Kuang. *The Chronicle of the Three Kingdoms.* Trans. Achilles Fang, ed. Glen W. Baxter. 2 vols. Cambridge, MA: Harvard University Press, 1952, 1965.

Twitchett, Denis. *The Writing of Official History Under the T'ang.* New York: Cambridge University Press, 1992.

NOTES

1. Ssu-ma Kuang, "The Last Days of Sui Yang-ti," in *The Civilization of China*, trans. Dun J. Li (New York: Scribner's, 1975), 153–60.

CHAPTER 23

Ibn Khaldûn

Observer of Historical Forces

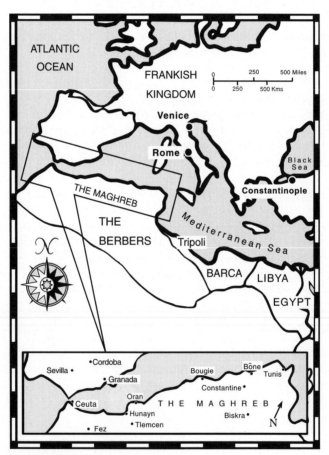

The Maghreb
© Gary Olsen

All great civilizations have nurtured historians. The Muslim civilization of the Middle East was no exception. After its founding in 622 by Muhammad, Islam spread outward from the Arabian Peninsula as far as Persia and India in the east and Spain in the west. Had it not been for the Frankish victory at the battle of Tours in 732, Europe today might be Muslim rather than Christian. As it was, the centers of learning in the West before 1400 were Baghdad, Egypt, and Muslim Spain, not Paris or Rome. Europe was a cultural and political backwater. History—and historians—were centered elsewhere.

'Abd-ar-Rahmân Abû Zaid Walî-ad-Dîn Ibn Khaldûn was born in 1332 in Tunis. His family was of Arab Yemenite origin. They had joined the Muslim conquest of Spain before moving to the Maghreb—the Arab-dominated sector of northwest Africa (present-day Morocco, Algeria, Tunisia, and Libya). By Ibn Khaldûn's time, the Maghreb was no longer politically unified (as it had been earlier in the Muslim era). Instead, it was divided between several fractious kingdoms, whose shifting alliances made the region a political minefield. Ibn Khaldûn spent the first half of his life as a politician and administrator for various of these kingdoms. This experience not only gave him a keen sense of the role of history in creating politics. It also led him to seek the underlying causes of that history—a key element of his contribution as a historian. His search for the causes of history in social forces anticipated the work of Ranke, Marx, and Braudel five and six centuries later.

As a boy in Tunis, Ibn Khaldûn was trained in the Qur'an and in the Malikite school of Islamic law. He studied philosophy, science, and some mysticism, as well as the political traditions of the Arab ruling families. His father and grandfather were minor court officials and scholars. On his family's death in the plague epidemic of 1348–49, Ibn Khaldûn followed his teachers to Morocco. He pursued a life of court service and political intrigue in Morocco, Spain, and finally Algeria. There he wrote the first draft of *Kitâb al-'Ibar* (of which *The Muqadimmah* is the introduction). At the age of 50, Ibn Khaldûn left the Maghreb for good. After a pilgrimage to Mecca, he settled in Egypt, where he taught, wrote, and engaged in minor court posts. He continued to revise his *Al-'Ibar* until his death in 1406.

Underlying Ibn Khaldûn's political adventures were two intersecting visions: one Islamic and the other classically Greek. Like most Muslims, he saw the early years of Islam as a golden era. Then, the faithful had been unified and pure. Seven centuries later, they were corrupt and divided. As an idealistic young politican, Ibn Khaldûn tried to serve rulers whom he thought could restore Arab unity—to the Maghreb if not to the Islamic world as a whole. Following Plato and Aristotle, whose works he had studied, he believed that wise rulership comes from studying philosophy. As a scholar-courtier like Confucius he tried to educate his masters. Through his efforts, he hoped they would govern well.

Time and again, though, his hopes were dashed: rulers proved fickle; they became petty tyrants; or they were virtuous, but overthrown. Gradually, Ibn Khaldûn came to see that other factors were at work, factors strong enough to frustrate his designs. His failure as a politician led directly to his greatness as a historian: it led him to look to the social forces that govern the lives of peoples. As he tried to understand the politics of the Maghreb, he came to see deeper patterns at work. Yes, history is made by individuals. But the character of individual rulers as well as of the people they rule is formed by forces more powerful than mere learning. It is those forces Ibn Khaldûn sought to expose in his history.

Several key concepts underlie Ibn Khaldûn's work. First, he distinguishes between nomadic and sedentary peoples. The former, because of the rigors of their life, are brave and filled with *Al 'Assabiyya* (translated in the following passage as "group feeling"). They are, however, rude and cruel, and they lack civilization. Sedentary peoples, on the other hand, are refined and cultured— traits made possible by their wealth. Yet they rely on laws rather than on loyalties to achieve order, and this weakens their character. Lacking group feeling, sedentary societies inevitably decline. Ibn Khaldûn saw the history of the Maghreb as made up of successive waves of conquest by vigorous nomads. For a few generations, these nomads unify the land they conquer. To rule, however, they must take on the laws and sedentary habits of their subjects—losing their vigor in the process. They decline, making way for the next set of invaders.

The concept of "group feeling"—something like ethnic identity—is probably Ibn Khaldûn's greatest contribution. History is, for him, not just made by great persons. Rather, it develops from the changing character of social ties. In some circumstances, the group is held together by "blood" loyalty to a leader or a clan. In other circumstances, economic factors provide the glue. Individuals act differently, depending on the ties that bind them to others. History is the sum of these actions. Thus the historian must understand group feeling, in order to understand why events occur.

Two other forces, not treated in the passages that follow, deserve mention. First, Ibn Khaldûn saw religion as an independent force in history. The rise of the Arabs, he believed, came not only from their well-developed group feeling and from the decline of the settled peoples who had previously ruled them. It also came from Islam. This religion not only made it possible for the Arabs to unite but also gave them a reason to expand beyond the Arabian peninsula. Second, Ibn Khaldûn recognized the multi-ethnic nature of Muslim society. The Maghreb contained Berbers as well as Arabs, plus Jews and a few Christians. Residents of Tunis and Fez saw themselves as different from their neighbors—a perception that made them so. History results from interactions between the *'assabiyya* of various groups.

The disunity of the Maghreb, for Ibn Khaldûn, was the result of a complex interplay between nomadic invasions and sedentary declines, between a unifying religion and fractionating ethnicities. All this he set in the context of an environment offering particular opportunities and tribulations. In his vision, the ability of the wise person to influence history is therefore quite limited.

The first part of the following passage comes from *The Muqaddimah*, and illustrates Ibn Khaldûn's approach to history. The second part comes from chapter 2 of book 1 of the *Kitâb al-'Ibar*. It shows how Ibn Khaldûn used his central concepts to help understand historical events.

The Muqaddimah[1]

History is a discipline widely cultivated among nations and races. It is eagerly sought after. The men in the street, the ordinary people, aspire to know it. Kings and leaders vie for it.

Both the learned and the ignorant are able to understand it. For on the surface history is no more than information about political events, dynasties, and occurrences of the remote past, elegantly presented and spiced with proverbs. It serves to entertain large, crowded gatherings and brings to us an understanding of human affairs. (It shows) how changing conditions affected (human affairs), how certain dynasties came to occupy an ever wider space in the world, and how they settled the earth until they heard the call and their time was up.

The inner meaning of history, on the other hand, involves speculation and an attempt to get at the truth, subtle explanation of the causes and origins of existing things, and deep knowledge of the how and why of events. (History,) therefore, is firmly rooted in philosophy. It deserves to be accounted a branch of (philosophy).

* * *

The (writing of history) requires numerous sources and greatly varied knowledge. It also requires a good speculative mind and thoroughness. (Possession of these two qualities) leads the historian to the truth and keeps him from slips and errors. If he trusts historical information in its plain transmitted form and has no clear knowledge of the principles resulting from custom, the fundamental facts of politics, the nature of civilization, or the conditions governing human social organization, and if, furthermore, he does not evaluate remote or ancient material through comparison with near or contemporary material, he often cannot avoid stumbling and slipping and deviating from the highroad of truth. Historians, Qur'an commentators and leading transmitters have committed frequent errors in the stories and events they reported. They accepted them in the plain transmitted form, without regard for its value. They did not check them with the principles underlying such historical situations, nor did they compare them with similar material. Also, they did not probe (more deeply) with the yardstick of philosophy, with the help of knowledge of the nature of things, or with the help of speculation and historical insight. Therefore, they strayed from the truth and found themselves lost in the desert of baseless assumptions and errors.

* * *

For example, al-Mas'ûdî and many other historians report that Moses counted the army of the Israelites in the desert. He had all those able to carry arms, especially those twenty years and older, pass muster. There turned out to be 600,000 or more. In this connection, (al-Mas'ûdî) forgets to take into consideration whether Egypt and Syria could possibly have held such a number of soldiers. Every realm may have as large a militia as it can hold and support, but no more. This fact is attested by well-known customs and familiar conditions. Moreover, an army of this size cannot march or fight as a unit. The whole available territory would be too small for it. If it were in battle formation, it would extend two, three, or more times beyond the field of vision. How, then, could two such parties fight with each other, or one battle formation gain the upper hand when one flank does not know what the other flank is doing! The situation at present day testifies to the correctness of this statement. The past resembles the future more than one (drop of) water another.

* * *

A hidden pitfall in historiography is disregard for the fact that conditions within the nations and races change with the change of periods and the passing of days. This is a sore affliction and is deeply hidden, becoming noticeable only after a long time, so that rarely do more than a few individuals become aware of it.

* * *

Often, someone who has learned a good deal of past history remains unaware of the changes that conditions have undergone. Without a moment's hesitation, he applies his knowledge (of the present) to the historical information and measures the historical information by the things he has observed with his own eyes, although the difference between the two is great. Consequently, he falls into an abyss of error.

This may be illustrated by what the historians report concerning the circumstances of Al-Hajjâj. They state that his father was a schoolteacher. At the present time, teaching is a craft and serves to make a living. It is a far cry from the pride of group feeling. Teachers are weak, indigent, and rootless. Many weak professional men and artisans who work for a living aspire to positions for which they are not fit but which they believe to be within their reach. They are misled by their desires, a rope which often slips from their hands and precipitates them into the abyss of ruinous perdition. They do not realize that what they desire is impossible for men like them to attain. They do not realize that they are professional men and artisans who work for a living. And they do not know that at the beginning of Islam and during the (Umayyad and 'Abbâsid) dynasties, teaching was something different. Scholarship, in general, was not a craft in that period. Scholarship was transmitting statements that people had heard the Lawgiver (Muhammad) make. It was teaching religious matters that were not known, by way of oral transmission. Persons of noble descent and people who shared in the group feeling (of the ruling dynasty) and who directed the affairs of Islam were the ones who taught the Book of God and the Sunnah of the Prophet, (and they did so) as one transmits traditions, not as one gives professional instruction. (The Qur'ân) was their Scripture, revealed to the Prophet in their midst. It constituted their guidance, and distinguished them from the other nations and ennobled them. They wished to teach it and make it understandable to the Muslims. They were not deterred by censure coming from pride, nor were they restrained by criticism coming from arrogance. This is attested by the fact that the Prophet sent the most important of the men around him with his embassies to the Arabs, in order to teach them the norms of Islam and the religious laws he brought. He sent his ten companions and others after them on this mission.

Then, Islam became firmly established and securely rooted. Far-off nations accepted Islam at the hands of the Muslims. With the passing of time, the situation of Islam changed. Many new laws were evolved from the (basic) texts as the result of numerous and unending developments. A fixed norm was required to keep (the process) free from error. Scholarship came to be a habit. For its acquisition, study was required. Thus, scholarship developed into a craft and profession. This will be mentioned in the chapter on scholarship and instruction.

The men who controlled the group feeling now occupied themselves with directing the affairs of the royal and governmental authority. The cultivation of scholarship was entrusted to others. Thus, scholarship became a profession that served to make a living. Men who lived in luxury and were in control of the government were too proud to do any teaching. Teaching came to be an occupation restricted to weak individuals. As a result, its practitioners came to be despised by the men who controlled the group feeling and the government.

Now, Yûsuf, the father of Al-Hajjâj, was one of the lords and nobles of the Thaqîf, well known for their share in the Arab group feeling and for their rivalry with the nobility of the Quraysh. Al-Hajjâj's teaching of the Qur'ân was not what teaching of the Qur'ân is at this time, namely, a profession that serves to make a living. His teaching was teaching as it was practiced at the beginning of Islam and as we have just described it.

*   *   *

It should be known that history, in matter of fact, is information about human social organization, which itself is identical with world civilization. It deals with such conditions affecting the nature of civilization as, for instance, savagery and sociability, group feelings, and the different ways by which one group of human beings achieves superiority over another. It deals with royal authority and the dynasties that result (in this manner) and with the various ranks that exist within them. (It further deals) with the different kinds of gainful occupations and ways of making a living, with the sciences and crafts that human beings pursue as part of their activities and efforts, and with all the other institutions that originate in civilization through its very nature.

Kitâb al-'Ibar²

[1] Both Bedouins [desert nomads] and sedentary people are natural groups.

It should be known that differences of condition among people are the result of the different ways in which they make their living. Social organization enables them to co-operate toward that end and to start with the simple necessities of life, before they get to conveniences and luxuries.

Some people adopt agriculture, the cultivation of vegetables and grains, (as their way of making a living). Others adopt animal husbandry, the use of sheep, cattle, goats, bees, and silkworms, for breeding and for their products.

Those who live by agriculture or animal husbandry cannot avoid the call of the desert, because it alone offers the wide fields, acres, pastures for animals, and other things that the settled areas do not offer. It is therefore necessary for them to restrict themselves to the desert. Their social organization and co-operation for the needs of life and civilization, such as food, shelter, and warmth, do not take them beyond the bare subsistence level, because of their inability (to provide) for anything beyond those (things). Subsequent improvement of their conditions and acquisition of more wealth and comfort than they need, cause them to rest and take it easy. Then, they co-operate for things beyond the (bare) necessities. They use more food and clothes, and take pride in them. They build large houses, and lay out towns and cities for protection. . . . Here, now, (we have) sedentary people. "Sedentary people" means the inhabitants of cities and countries, some of whom adopt the crafts as their way of making a living, while others adopt commerce. They earn more and live more comfortably than Bedouins, because they live on a level beyond the level of (bare) necessity, and their way of making a living corresponds to their wealth.

It has thus become clear that Bedouins and sedentary people are natural groups which exist by necessity, as we have stated.

*   *   *

[6] The reliance of sedentary people upon laws destroys their fortitude and power of resistance.

Not everyone is master of his own affairs. Chiefs and leaders who are masters of the affairs of men are few in comparison with the rest. As a rule, man must by necessity be dominated by someone else. If the domination is kind and just and the people under it are not oppressed by its laws and restrictions, they are guided by the courage or cowardice that they possess in themselves. They are satisfied with the absence of any restraining power. Self-reliance eventually becomes a quality natural to them. They would not know anything else. If, however, the domination with its laws is one of brute force and intimidation, it breaks their fortitude and deprives them of their power of resistance as a result of the inertness that develops in the souls of the oppressed, as we shall explain.

'Umar forbade Sa'd (b. Abî Waqqâs) to exercise such (arbitrary power) when Zuhrah b. Hawiyah took the spoils of al-Jâlinûs. The value of the spoils was 75,000 gold pieces. (Zuhrah) had followed al-Jâlinûs on the day of al-Qâdisîyah, killed him, and taken his spoils. Sa'd took them away from him and said, "Why did you not wait for my permission to follow him?" He wrote to 'Umar and asked 'Umar for permission (to confiscate the spoils). But 'Umar replied, "Would you want to proceed against a man like Zuhrah, who already has borne so much of the brunt (of battle), and while there still remains so much of the war for you (to finish)? Would you want to break his strength and morale?" Thus 'Umar confirmed (Zuhrah) in possession of the spoils.

When laws are (enforced) by means of punishment, they completely destroy fortitude, because the use of punishment against someone who cannot defend himself generates in that person a feeling of humiliation that, no doubt, must break his fortitude.

For this (reason), greater fortitude is found among the savage Arab Bedouins than among people who are subject to laws. Furthermore, those who rely on laws and are dominated by them from the very beginning of their education and instruction in the crafts, sciences, and religious matters, are thereby deprived of much of their own fortitude. They can scarcely defend themselves at all against hostile acts. This is the case with students, whose occupation it is to study and to learn from teachers and religious leaders, and who constantly apply themselves to instruction and education in very dignified gatherings. This situation and the fact that it destroys the power of resistance and fortitude must be understood.

It is no argument against the (statement just made) that men around Muhammad observed the religious laws, and yet did not experience any diminution of their fortitude, but possessed the greatest possible fortitude. When the Muslims got their religion from the Lawgiver (Muhammad), the restraining influence came from themselves, as a result of the encouragement and discouragement he gave them in the Qur'an. It was not a result of technical instruction or scientific education. (The laws) were laws and precepts of the religion, which they received orally and which their firmly rooted (belief in) the truth of the articles of faith caused them to observe. Their fortitude remained unabated, and it was not corroded by education or authority. 'Umar said, "Those who are not educated (disciplined) by the religious law are not educated (disciplined) by God." (This statement expresses) 'Umar's desire that everyone should have his restraining influence on himself. It also expresses his certainty that the Lawgiver (Muhammad) knew best what is good for mankind.

(The influence of) religion, then, decreased among men, and they came to use restraining laws. The religious laws became a branch of learning and a craft to be acquired through instruction and education. People turned to sedentary life and assumed the character trait of submissiveness to law. This led to a decrease in their fortitude.

* * *

The restraining influence among Bedouin tribes comes from their *shaykhs* and leaders. It results from the great respect and veneration they generally enjoy among the people. The hamlets of the Bedouins are defended against outside enemies by a tribal militia composed of noble youths of the tribe who are known for their courage. Their defense and protection are successful only if they are a closely-knit group of common descent. This strengthens their stamina and makes them feared, since everybody's affection for his family and his group is more important (than anything else). Compassion and affection for one's blood relations and relatives exist in human nature as something God put into the hearts of men. It makes for mutual support and aid, and increases the fear felt by the enemy.

This may be exemplified by the story in the Qur'an about Joseph's brothers. They said to their father: "If the wolf eats him, while we are a group, then, indeed, we have lost out." This means that one cannot imagine any hostile act being undertaken against anyone who has his group feeling to support him.

*   *   *

[9] Purity of lineage is found only among the savage Arabs of the desert and other such people.

This is on account of the poor life, hard conditions, and bad habits that are peculiar to the Arabs. . . . No member of any other nation was disposed to share their conditions. No member of any other race felt attracted to them. . . . Therefore, their pedigrees can be trusted not to have been mixed up and corrupted. They have been preserved in unbroken lines. This is the case, for instance, with Mudar tribes such as the Quraysh, the Kinânah, the Thaqîf, the Banû Asad, the Hudhayl, and their Khuzâ'ah neighbors. They lived a hard life in places where there was no agriculture or animal husbandry. They lived far from the fertile fields of Syria and the 'Irâq, far from the sources of seasonings and grains. How pure have they kept their language! These are unmixed in every way, and are known to be unsullied.

Other Arabs lived in the hills and at the sources of fertile pastures and plentiful living. Among these Arabs were the Himyar and the Kahlân, such as the Lakhm, the Judhâm, the Ghassân, the Tayy, the Qudâ'ah, and the Iyâd. Their lineages were mixed up, and their groups intermingled. It is known that people (genealogists) differ with respect to each one of these families. This came about as the result of intermixture with non-Arabs. They did not pay any attention to preserving the (purity of) lineage of their families and groups. This was done only by (true) Arabs. 'Umar said: "Study genealogy, and be not like the Nabataeans of the Mesopotamian lowlands. When one of them is asked about his origin, he says: 'From such and such a village.' " Furthermore, the Arabs of the fertile fields were affected by the general human trend toward competition for the fat soil and the good pastures. This resulted in intermingling and much mixture of lineages. Even at the beginning of Islam, people occasionally referred to themseves by their places of residence. They referred to the Districts of Qinnasrîn, of Damascus, of the 'Awâsim (the border region of northern Syria). This custom was then transferred to Spain. It happened not because the Arabs rejected genealogical considerations, but because they acquired particular places of residence after the conquest. They eventually became known by their places of residence. These became a distinguishing mark, in addition to the pedigree, used by (the Arabs) to identify themselves in the presence of their amirs. Later on, sedentary (Arabs) mixed with Persians and other non-Arabs. Purity of lineage was completely lost, and its fruit, the group feeling, was lost and rejected. The tribes, then, disappeared and were wiped out, and with them, the group feeling was wiped out. But the (earlier situation) remained unchanged among the Bedouins.

God inherits the earth and whomever is upon it.

*   *   *

[11] Leadership over people who share in a given group feeling cannot be vested in those not of the same descent.

This is because leadership exists only through superiority, and superiority only through group feeling, as we have mentioned before. Leadership over people, therefore, must, of necessity, derive from a group feeling that is superior to each individual group feeling. Each individual group feeling that becomes aware of the superiority of the group feeling of the leader is ready to obey and follow (that leader).

Now, a person who has become attached to people of a common descent usually does not share the group feeling that derives from their common descent. He is merely attached to them. The firmest connection he has with the group is as a client and ally. This in no way guarantees him superiority over them. Assuming that he has developed close contact with them, that he has mixed with them, that the fact that he was originally merely attached to them has been forgotten, and that he has become one of their skin and is addressed as one having the same descent as they, how could he, or one of his forebears, have acquired leadership before that process had taken place, since leadership is transmitted in one particular branch that has been marked for superiority through group feeling? The fact that he was merely attached to the tribe was no doubt known at an earlier stage, and at the time prevented him (or rather, his forebears) from assuming leadership. Thus, it could not have been passed on by (a man) who was still merely attached (to the tribe). Leadership must of necessity be inherited from the person who is entitled to it, in accordances with the fact, which we have stated, that superiority results from group feeling.

Many leaders of tribes or groups are eager to acquire certain pedigrees. They desire them because persons of that particular descent possessed some special virtue, such as bravery, or nobility, or fame, however this may have come about. They go after such a family and involve themselves in claims to belong to a branch of it. They do not realize that they thus bring suspicion upon themselves with regard to their leadership and nobility.

Such things are frequently found among people at this time. Thus, the Zantah in general claim to be Arabs. The Awlâd Rabâb, who are known as the Hijâzis and who belong to the Banû 'Amir, one of the branches of the Zughbah, claim that they belong to the Banû Sulaym and, in particular, to the Sharîd, a branch of the Banû Sulaym. Their ancestor is said to have joined the Banû 'Amir as a carpenter who made biers. He mixed with them and developed a close contact with them. Finally, he became their leader. He was called by them al-Hijâzî.

Similarly, the Banû 'Abd-al-Qawû b. al-'Abbâs of the Tûjîn claim to be descendants of the al-'Abbâs b. 'Abd-al-Muttalib, because they want to have noble descent (from the family of the Prophet), and hold a mistaken opinion concerning the name of al-'Abbâs b. 'Atîyah, the father of 'Abd-al-Qawî. It is not known that any 'Abbâsid ever entered the Maghrib. From the beginning of the 'Abbâsid dynasty and thereafter, the Maghrib was under the influence of the Idrîsids and the 'Ubaydid (-Fâtimids), 'Alid enemies of the 'Abbâsids. No 'Abbâsid would have become attached to a Shî'ah.

Similarly, the Zayyânids, the 'Abd-al-Wâdid rulers (of Tlemcen), claim to be descendants of al-Qâsim b. Idrîs, basing their claim on the fact that their family is known to have descended from al-Qâsim. In their own Zanâtah dialect, they are called Ait al-Qâsim, that is Banû l-Qâsim. They claim that the Qâsim (after whom they were named) was al-Qâsim b. Idrîs, or al-Qâsim b. Muhammad b. Idrîs. If that were true, all that can be said concerning the Qâsim is that he fled his own realm and attached himself to (the Zanâtah group of the 'Abd-al-Wâd). How, then, could he have gained complete leadership over them in the desert? The story is an error resulting from the name of al-Qâsim, which is very frequent among the Idrîsids. (The Zayyâ-nids), therefore, thought that their Qâsim was an Idrîsid. (But after all,) they hardly need so spurious a genealogy. They gained royal authority and power through their group feeling, not through claims to 'Alid, 'Abbâsid, or other descent.

* * *

The connection of the Mahdî of the Almohads with the 'Alid family should not be considered a case of this type. The Mahdî did not belong to the leading family among his people, the Harghah. He became their leader after he had become famous for his knowledge and religion, and by virtue of the fact that the Masmûdah tribe followed his call. Yet he belonged to a (Harghah) family of medium rank.

* * *

[26] *The transformation of the caliphate into royal authority*

When 'Umar b. al-Khattâb [the third Caliph] went to Syria and was met by Mu'âwiyah in full royal splendor as exhibited both in the number (of Mu'âwiyah's retinue) and his equipment, he disapproved of it and said: "Are these royal Persian manners, O Mu'âwiyah?" Mu'âwiyah replied: "O Commander of the Faithful, I am in a border region facing the enemy. It is necessary to vie with (the enemy) in military equipment." 'Umar was silent and did not consider Mu'âwiyah to be wrong. He had used an argument that was in agreement with the intentions of the truth and of Islam. If the intention (implied in 'Umar's remark) had been to eradicate royal authority as such, 'Umar would not have been silenced by the answer with which Mu'âwiyah (excused) his assumption of royal Persian manners. He would have insisted that Mu'âwiyah give them up altogether. 'Umar meant by "royal Persian manners" the attitude of the Persian rulers, which consisted in doing worthless things, constantly practicing oppression, and neglecting God. Mu'âwiyah replied that he was not interested in royal Persian manners as such, or in the worthlessness connected with them, but his intention was to serve God. Therefore, ('Umar) was silent. . . .

When the Messenger of God [Muhammad] was about to die, he appointed Abû Bakr as his representative to (lead the) prayers, since (praying) was the most important religious activity. People were, thus, content to accept (Abû Bakr) as caliph, that is, as the person who causes the great mass to act according to the religious laws. No mention was made of royal authority, because royal authority was suspected of being worthless, and because at that time it was the prerogative of unbelievers and enemies of Islam. Abû Bakr discharged the duties of his office in a manner pleasing to God, following the Sunnah of his master (Muhammad). He fought against apostates until all the Arabs were united in Islam. He then appointed 'Umar his successor. 'Umar followed Abû Bakr's example and permitted the Arabs to appropriate the worldly possessions of (those nations) and their royal authority, and the Arabs did that.

(The caliphate), then, went to 'Uthmân b. 'Affân and 'Alî. All (these caliphs) renounced royal authority and kept apart from its ways. They were strengthened in this attitude by the low standard of living in Islam and the desert outlook of the Arabs. The world and its luxuries were more alien to them than to any other nation, on account of their religion, which inspired asceticism where the good things of life were concerned, and on account of the desert outlook and habitat and the rude, severe life to which they were accustomed. No nation was more used to a life of hunger than the Mudar. In the Hijâz, the Mudar inhabited a country without agricultural or animal products. They were kept from the fertile plains, rich in grain, because the latter were too far away and were monopolized by the Rabî'ah and Yemenites who controlled them. They had no envy of the abundance of (those regions). They often ate scorpions and beetles. They were proud to eat *'ilhiz*, that is, camel hair ground with stones, mixed with blood, and then cooked. The Quraysh were in a similar situation with regard to food and housing.

Finally, the group feeling of the Arabs was consolodated in Islam through the prophecy of Muhammad with which God honored them. They then advanced against the Persians and Byzantines, and they looked for the land that God had truthfully promised and destined to them. They took away the royal authority of (the Persians and Byzantines) and confiscated their worldly possessions. They emassed enormous fortunes. It went so far that one horseman obtained, as his share in one of the raids, about 30,000 gold pieces. . . . Still, they kept to their rude way of life. . . . Such were the gains people made. Their religion did not blame them for (amassing so much), because, as booty, it was lawful property. They did not employ their property wastefully but in a planned way in (all) their conditions, as we have stated. Amassing worldly property is reprehensible, but it did not reflect upon them, because blame attaches only to waste and lack of planning, as we have indicated. Since their expenditures followed a plan and served the truth and its ways, the amassing (of so much property) helped them along the path of truth and served the purpose of attaining the other world.

Soon, the desert attitude of the Arabs and their low standard of living approached its end. The nature of royal authority—which is the necessary consequence of group feeling as we have stated—showed itself, and with it, their came (the use of) superiority and force. . . .

When trouble arose between 'Alî and Mu'wâiyah as a necessary consequence of group feeling, they were guided in (their dissention) by the truth
and by independent judgment. They did not fight for any worldly purpose or
over preferences of no value, or for reasons of personal enmity. This might be
suspected, and heretics might like to think so. However, what caused their
difference was their independent judgment as to where the truth
lay. . . . Even though 'Alî was in the right, Mu'âwiyah's intentions were not
bad ones. He wanted the truth, but he missed (it). Each was right in so far as
his intentions were concerned. Now, the nature of royal authority requires
that one person claim all the glory for himself and appropriate it to himself. It
was not for Mu'âwiyah to deny (the natural requirement of royal authority) to
himself and his people. (Royal authority) was a natural thing that group
feeling, by its very nature, brought in its train. Even the Umayyds and those of
their followers who were not after the truth like Mu'âwiyah felt that. They
banded together around him and were willing to die for him. Had Mu'âwiyah
tried to lead them on another course of action, had he opposed them and not
claimed all the power for (himself and them), it would have meant the
dissolution of the whole thing that he had consolidated. It was more
important to him to keep it together than to bother about (a course of action)
that could not entail much criticism.

QUESTIONS TO CONSIDER

1. What is the substance of Ibn Khaldûn's distinction between nomadic and
   sedentary peoples? On what does this distinction seem to be based? How
   does it affect his account?
2. What are the "group feelings" that glue together each of these peoples, and
   how do they affect the history that Ibn Khaldûn recounts?
3. What are Ibn Khaldûn's criticisms of other historians? Does he avoid the
   weaknesses he ascribes to them?

FOR FURTHER READING

Issawi, Charles. *An Arab Philosophy of History.* New York: Paragon Book Gallery, 1969.
Khaldûn, Ibn. *The Muqaddimah.* 3 vols. Trans. Franz Rosenthal. Princeton, NJ:
    Princeton University Press, 1958.
Mahdi, Muhsin. *Ibn Khaldûn's Philosophy of History.* Chicago: University of Chicago
    Press, 1964.
Rosenthal, Franz. *A History of Muslim Historiography.* 2nd ed. Leiden, Netherlands:
    E. J. Brill, 1968.

NOTES

1. Ibn Khaldûn, *The Muqaddimah,* trans. Franz Rosenthal (Princeton NJ:
   Princeton University Press, 1958), 1:6, 15–17, 56–60, 89.
2. Ibn Khaldûn, *The Muqaddimah,* 1:249–50, 258–60, 262–62, 265–67, 269–71,
   417–22.

CHAPTER 24

Shaikh Abu'l Fazl

History as Politics, Politician as Historian

Emperor Akbar
The Granger Collection, New York

T he reign of the Emperor Akbar (1542–1605) stands at the pinnacle of India's Muslim civilization. After reconquering the throne of Delhi, from which his father had been driven, Akbar extended his sway across north India. At his death his empire stretched from the Himalayas to the Deccan, and from present-day Pakistan to Bangladesh.

Like all successful rulers, Akbar wanted his deeds remembered. He ordered his court historians to record what he and his ancestors had accomplished. He gave their reports to one of his courtiers, Shaikh Abu'l Fazl, who crafted from them a history of Akbar's triumphs. The resulting *Akbar-Nama* is similar in many ways to other Indian court histories. It recounts Akbar's climb, focusing on the campaigns and battles by which his victory was won. Yet it rises above ordinary court histories, both because Abu'l Fazl used better sources and because he tried to portray the institutional underpinnings of Akbar's reign. Though he fawns too much for modern tastes, his history was as objective as Akbar's patronage and Abu'l Fazl's court position allowed. His choice of sources and topics set the standard for court histories throughout the Mughal era. Indeed, Peter Hardy has argued that the kind of history that the *Akbar-Nama* represents continued to be the favored style among historians of India, with few exceptions, down to the present century.

Shaikh Abu'l Fazl 'Allami (1551–1602) was the younger son of Shaikh Mubarak, one of the most learned men of his time. Mubarak was a religious liberal. Orthodox in his personal commitments, he nevertheless tolerated Islamic sects and even other religions. The Jesuits who visited Akbar's court about 1570, for example, remembered his kindness. Mubarak trained his sons in his erudite and freethinking ways. This aroused the wrath of the Ulema—the religious court that enforced Muslim orthodoxy. Faced with intrigue and possible death, Mubarak and his sons called on Akbar for protection. Akbar chose to help them, partly because he was himself a freethinker, and partly because of his regard for the poetry of Abu'l Faiz, one of Abu'l Fazl's brothers. Abu'l Faiz was the most popular Persian-language poet of his day; his poems are still held in high esteem.

Under Akbar's protection, Abu'l Fazl rose rapidly through the ranks of court officialdom. He aided Akbar's efforts to undercut the Ulema—successfully enough that its leaders were soon exiled. He assumed a variety of minor administrative posts. For a time, for example, he oversaw the wool trade; at another point he was co-governor of Delhi. All available records, however, show that the Emperor's favor was bestowed more for Abu'l Fazl's personal and intellectual merits than for his bureaucratic services. He himself wrote that he was promoted to high office without having accomplished much. And Akbar did not at this point think him much of a soldier, the usual route by which courtiers advanced.

Abu'l Fazl's rise won him enemies. Other courtiers grew jealous, and Akbar's son, Prince Salim, looked on him with scorn. About 1598, Salim and the others prevailed upon the Emperor to send Abu'l Fazl to the Deccan, supposedly to fetch Prince Murad to the court. All witnesses agree that this was a sign of Akbar's displeasure. This exile proved fortunate, however. While there, Abu'l Fazl used newfound diplomatic and military skill to bring that region back under Akbar's control. Akbar amply rewarded him for his accomplishments, to the consternation of those who had intrigued against him.

By the turn of the century, Akbar's hold on his empire was crumbling. Several of the princes were in open revolt, and Abu'l Fazl was kept busy suppressing them. Even Prince Salim defied his father's authority, setting up his own court at Allahabad. Akbar sent for Abu'l Fazl, hoping that his advice would help him win back his son. To reach the Emperor, Abu'l Fazl had to pass near the domain of Raja Bir Singh Bundela, one of Salim's allies. The Raja's troops overwhelmed his small escort, and Abu'l Fazl was killed. Prince Salim received his head as a gift—and then promptly made up with his father.

The *Akbar-Nama*, Abu'l Fazl's monumental work, was to have filled five volumes: four of narrative, and a fifth, the *A'in-i-Akbari*, about the institutional aspects of Akbar's rule. He only finished three: two narratives and the *A'in*. The first volume traced the history of the world from Adam to the seventeenth year of Akbar's reign. The second continued the saga to Akbar's forty-sixth regnal year. Because Abu'l Fazl died in the forty-seventh year, and Akbar a few years later, the original plan was not carried out. Later court historians divided the first volume in two and appended a *Supplement* covering Akbar's final years. The manuscripts we have are thus in four volumes: three of narrative plus the *A'in*.

As noted, Abu'l Fazl wrote in the tradition of Indian court historians. The *Akbar-Nama* is mainly a narrative of political events: battles and campaigns, intrigues, dethronements, and ascensions. Other things appear, but only tangentially, yet the *Akbar-Nama* stands out from the ordinary run of court histories. He consulted official documents, read histories and memoirs, and talked with participants in the events he tried to relate. Where he found contradictions, he accepted the points common to all and depended—in his words—"on prudence, truth-speaking and caution" to discern among the rest. Now and then he bent the truth, especially to justify Akbar's growing control over religious life. Given his own role in Akbar's fight with the Ulema, this is understandable, though it makes his account suspect in other areas as well.

The narrative volumes of the *Akbar-Nama* follow a distinct pattern. Abu'l Fazl presents Akbar's reign as the high point of human history; thus all previous events point toward it. He rushes from Adam to the earliest Mughals with little attempt to separate fact from legend. Only Akbar's reign and those of his immediate predecessors matter much to him. He organizes his account of those predecessors by reign, as if everything stopped when one emperor died and another ascended. Similarly, he arranges his account of Akbar's rule by years, stopping ongoing tales to insert contemporaneous but unrelated events in the proper time order. He does, however, pick up the stories again, relating them both to the lives of the individuals involved and to certain moral truths that he thinks they illustrate. These truths often show up the Emperor's wisdom, a feature later court historians borrowed.

In this regard—and in this regard only—did Abu'l Fazl venture beyond political history. Yet even here, the *Akbar-Nama* embodied the elite point of view. Abu'l Fazl wrote history from the top, as it appeared to an imperial court that saw itself as the center of the moral and political universe. He did nothing to dissuade it of its pretensions. And yet, his work epitomizes a style of history that has been much seen in the world.

The Akbar-Nama[1]

March Against Bengal

In the year 941 [Islamic reckoning] Humayun turned his attention to the conquest of the eastern countries, and marched to subdue Bengal. When he arrived at the town of Kinar, near Kalpi, he was informed that Sultan Bahadur of Gujarat had laid siege to the fort of Chitor: and had detached a large force under the command of Tatar Khan, who had very ambitious projects in his head; so in the month of Jumada-l awwal Humayun fell back to resist his enemies.

Tatar Khan pressed his delusive advice upon Sultan Bahadur, and strongly urged that he might be sent towards the Imperial dominions, representing Humayun's army to be given up to pleasure and indolence. Sultan Bahadur took measures to forward the views of the rebels. Having fitted out Tatar Khan, he sent twenty krors of the old Gujarat coinage, equal to forty of the ordinary Dehli standard, to the fort of Rantambhor, there to be expended by Tatar Khan in raising forces. He sent Sultan 'Alau-d-din, father of Tatar Khan, in command of a strong force, against Kalinjar, to increase the rebellious feeling in that neighbourhood. Burhanu-l Mulk Bunyani was sent with a force of Gujaratis through Nagor to make a demonstration against the Panjab. Under the idea that the Imperial army would now disperse, he divided his own army, and although wise and experienced counsellors advised him to keep his army together, their words had no effect. When Tatar Khan marched on his wild enterprise against Dehli, Sultan Bahadur himself proceeded to invest the fort of Chitor. . . . Tatar Khan, employing the money at his disposal, gathered a force of nearly forty thousand horse, of Afghans and others, with which he advanced and took Bayana. While this was going on, Humayun was engaged in his invasion of the east country; but on receiving the intelligence of it, he hastened back to Agra. Mirzas 'Askari and Hindal and Yadgar Nasir Mirza and . . . were sent with eighteen thousand horse to meet the chief army of insurgents, which was marching against Dehli, for it was deemed expedient to defeat this army first. When the Imperial army approached the insurgents, numbers of the latter deserted every day, until the force dwindled down to three thousand horse. The men collected with so much trouble, and at so great an expense, had neither the heart to advance nor the spirit to fight. At length he (Tartar Khan), washing his hands of life, fought with all the strength he could muster, at Mandrail, and was there killed.

Campaign Against Sultan Bahadur

Humayun left Agra on this expedition against Gujarat, in the beginning of Jumada-I awwal, 941 H. When he encamped near the fort of Raisin, the commandant sent large presents with a message, saying that the fort was His Majesty's, and the men of the garrison were the servants of His Majesty, and they would hold the fort till Sultan Bahadur's business was settled. As the Emperor was intent upon the conquest of Gujarat, he did not delay here, but marched on to Malwa, and encamped at Sarangpur. Sultan Bahadur was engaged in the siege of Chitor; and when he heard of the Emperor's advance, he held a council with his officers, the majority of whom were for raising the siege, and marching against the Emperor. But Sadr Khan, a wise and prudent councillor, urged that the fort was upon a point of surrender, and that they should press the siege to a conclusion, for no Muhammadan king would attack while they were engaged in war with infidels. This advice was followed, and on the 3rd Ramazan, 941 H., the fort of Chitor was taken.

Flight Of Bahadur

On the 21st of Shawwal Sultan Bahadur lost all hope. He ordered all the large guns and mortars to be filled with powder, and to be fired till they burst. When night came on, he, along with Miran Muhammad Shuja' and five or six of his personal associates, went out from the back of the camp towards Agra, and afterwards turned towards Mandu. Sadr Khan and 'Imadu-I Mulk went off with 20,000 horse direct to Mandu, and Muhammad Zaman Mirza with another body went off towards Lahore to raise disturbances. Great cries and clamour arouse on that night from the Gujarati camp; but the facts of the matter were not known to the Imperial army. The Emperor mounted and remained under arms till morning. It was not till one watch of the day had passed, that Sultan Bahadur's flight became known. The troops then entered the camp, and obtained great plunder. Khudawand Khan, the tutor and minister of Sultan Bahadur, was taken prisoner. He was very graciously treated, and taken into the Emperor's service. Yadgar Nasir Mirza, Kasim Sultan, and Hindu Beg were sent in pursuit of the fugitives. . . . Sadr Khan and 'Imadu-I Mulk went straight to Mandu, and Humanyun followed, and encamped before the fort. Rumi Khan deserted from the Gujaratis, and came in to the Emperor, who bestowed a robe upon him. On the 14th (?), Sutan Bahadur entered the fort, and the question of peace came to be debated, and it was proposed that Gujarat and Chitor should remain in the hands of Sultan Bahadur, and that Mandu should be given up to the Emperor. These terms were finally agreed upon by the negotiators on both sides. But on that night the garrison of the fort relaxed their guard, and a party of about two hundred soldiers of the Imperial army went to the back of the fortress, and scaled the walls by means of ladders and ropes. Jumping down from the walls, they opened the gate, and brought in their horses, and others followed. Mallu 'Khan, the commander of the batteries, a native of Mandu, who had the title of Kadir Shadi, learnt what was passing, seized a horse, and went to Sultan Bahadur. He was asleep, but the cries of Mallu Khan aroused him, and he rushed out with three or four attendants. On his way he met Bhupat Rai, son of Silhadi, one of his councillors, with about twenty horse, whom he joined. On reaching the gate at the top of the *maidan,* they encountered a party of about 200 of the Imperial cavalry. Sultan Bahadur was the first to attack them. He was followed by some others, and he cut his way through and went off with Mallu Khan and another attendant to the fort of Sungar. He had his horses let down (the precipice of the town) by ropes. He himself followed through a thousand difficulties, and took the road to Gujarat. Kisim Husain Khan (an Imperial officer) was stationed near the fort, and an Uzbek servant of his, named Bori, who had previously been in Sultan Bahadur's service, recognized his old master, and told Kasim Husain, but he took no notice of it. So Sultan Bahadur escaped to Champanir, being joined on the way by about 1,500 men.

* * *

Death Of Sultan Bahadur

When Humayun returned to Agra, Bhupal Rai, the ruler of Bijagarh, finding the fort of Mandu empty, came up boldly and took possession of it. Kadir Shah also returned there, and Miran Muhammad Faruki also came up from Burhanpur. Sultan Bahadur remained a fortnight at Champanir, and then returned to Div. . . . Upon reaching the port, he found the Portuguese commander had arrived there with his sailors and fighting men. The Portuguese chief was apprehensive that as the Sultan was no longer in want of assistance, he mediated some treachery. So he sent to inform the Sultan that he had come as requested, but that he was ill and unable to go on shore, so that the interview must be deferred until he got better. The Sultan, quitting the royal road of safety, proceeded on the 3rd Ramazan, 943 H; with a small escort, on board a boat to visit the Governor. As soon as he reached the vessel, he discovered that it was a mere pretence of sickness, and he was sorry he had come. He sought to return directly; but the Portuguese were unwilling that such prey should escape them and hoped that by keeping him prisoner, they might obtain some more ports. The governor came forward and asked the Sultan to stay a little while, and examine some curiosities he had to present. The Sultan requested that they might be sent after him and turned quickly towards his own boat. A European *kazi* (priest?) placed himself in the Sultan's way and bade him stop. The Sultan, in exasperation, drew his sword, and cleft him in twain; then he leaped into his own boat. The Portuguese vessels which were around drew together round the Sultan's boat, and a fight began. The Sultan and Rumi Khan threw themselves into the water. A friend among the Portuguese stretched a hand to Rumi Khan, and saved him; but the Sultan was drowned in the waves. His companions also perished.

* * *

Reign of the Emperor Akbar

At this time (first year of the reign of Akbar) there was a great scarcity in Hindustan. In some districts, and especially in the province of Dehli, it reached a most alarming height. If men could find money, they could not get sight of corn. Men were driven to the extremity of eating each other, and some formed themselves into parties to carry off lone individuals for their food.

Destruction of Himu's Family: Alwar and Ajmir

Akbar was now informed that Haji Khan, a *ghulam* of Sher Khan Afghan (Sher Shah), a brave and able general, was setting up pretensions to rule in Alwar, and that Himu's father and wife, and all his property and wealth, were in that country. So the Emperor sent Nasiru-I Mulk (Pir Mahammad Sarwani) with a select force to attack him. Haji Khan, in dread of the Imperial army, fled before it arrived. Alwar and all the territory of Mewat thus came into the Imperial power. The fugitives proceeded to Dewati-majari, a strong place, which was Himu's family home. Much resistance and fighting followed. Himu's father was taken alive, and brought before Nasiru-I Mulk, who tried to convert him to the faith; but the old man said, "For eighty years I have worshipped God in the way of my own religion; how can I now forsake my faith? Shall I, through fear of death, embrace your religion without understanding it?" Maulana Pir Muhammad treated his question as unheard but gave him an answer with the tongue of the sword. He then returned with much spoil and fifty elephants to the Emperor. Haji Khan, when he left Alwar, proceeded to Ajmir, deeming that a secure refuge for his family, and prepared his soldiers for battle. The Rana, who was a great zamindar, was the son of that rana who had acted improperly towards the late Emperor Humanyun, and had suffered defeat at his hands. Haji Khan made demands upon him, and grievously troubled him, so that a battle was fought between them in the vicinity of Ajmin. Haji Khan and Muzaffar Khan Sarwani, his *vakil*, exhibited conspicuous gallantry in the fight and the Rana, who was too confident in the number of his forces, was defeated. Haji Khan then took possession of Ajmir and Nagor and all those parts. When this success of Haji Khan's was reported to the Emperor, he appointed Saiyid Muhammad Kasim Khan Naishapuri and . . . to march against him. . . . Intelligence was now brought that Haji Khan was so strong as to offer resistance to the forces sent against him; so the Emperor determined to proceed to Hisar, and to send reinforcements from thence. After visiting the tomb of his father at Sirhind, he proceeded to Hisar, accompanied by Bairam Khan. . . . When intelligence of this reached Haji Khan, his forces dispersed. Every man went to his own place, and Haji Khan himself hastened to Gujarat. Muhammad Kasim Khan was sent by the Emperor to take charge of Ajmir. Saiyi Muhammad Barha and Shah Kuli Khan Mahram were sent out with a force to capture Jitasaran, and they killed a great many Rajputs, and made themselves masters of the fort.

* * *

Sixth Year Of The Reign
Adham Khan

The folly and wilfulness of Adham Khan were well known. His mother, Maham Anka, had charge of the royal harem, and he now conspired with some of his mother's servants to carry off two of the beauties of Baz Bahadur, who had lately been presented to the Emperor. When every one was engaged in preparing for the march, and little heed was paid to what was going on, the abduction was effected. When this disgraceful action was made known to the Emperor, he sent two fast riders after the fugitives, who exerted themselves so well that they overtook them, and brought them back. Maham Anka, lest these two women should be brought into the presence of the Emperor, and expose her conduct and the villainy of her son, had the two poor innocent girls put to death, for dead people tell no tales. His Majesty had not yet torn the veil from his eyes, so he passed over this heinous crime.

Seventh Year Of The Reign

Prisoners of War Not to be Made Slaves

One of the gracious acts of His Majesty in this (seventh) year of his reign was the prohibition against making slaves of prisoners taken in war. It had been the custom of the royal troops, in their victorious campaigns in India, to forcibly sell or keep in slavery the wives, children, and dependents of the natives. But His Majesty, actuated by his religious, prudent, and kindly feelings, now issued an order that no soldier of the royal army should act in this manner; for although evil-disposed men might follow senseless courses, and taking up arms against the Emperor might suffer defeat, the children and people belonging to them were to be secure from all molestation from the royal troops, and no one, small or great, was to be made a slave. All were to be free to go as they pleased to their own houses or to the houses of their relatives; for although the repression and destruction of insolent opponents and the chastisement and coercion of rebels are among the duties of the ruling power, and are approved by lawyers and men of justice, still the punishment of their innocent wives and children is a transgression of the law. For if the husband pursues an evil course, what fault is it of the wife? and if the father rebels, how can the children be blamed?

Murder of Shamsu-d Din Muhammad Atka by Adham Khan

Adham Khan, the youngest son of that pattern of chastity Maham Anka, who had neither a well-ordered mind nor a good temper, in the rashness of youth and intoxication of prosperity, was very envious of Shamsu-d din Atka Khan. The Khankhanan Mun'im Khan was also under the influence of the same feeling, and exhibited it constantly in ways that no one of lower dignity could have done. He irritated and excited Adham Khan, until at last, on the 12th Ramazan, a great outrage was committed. Mun'im Khan, Atka Khan, Sahabu-d din Ahmad Khan, and other nobles, were sitting in the royal audience chamber engaged in business of state. Adham Khan came violently in with a party of ruffians more violent than himself. Those who were present in the court rose up, to show their respect, and Atka Khan also half stood up. As soon as he entered, Adham Khan clapped his hand to his dagger in a menacing way, and faced Atka Khan. He then cast an angry look upon

Khiusham Uzbek, one of his officers, and upon the other graceless wretches who had joined him in his outrageous business, as if to ask them why they hesitated. The truculent Khusham Uzbek then drew his dagger, and inflicted a terrible wound in the bosom of the minister. Atka Khan, in the greatest terror, rushed off towards the apartments of the Emperor and had nearly reached them when he received two sword cuts, and fell dead in the court yard of the palace. Dismay come upon all present, and a great outcry arose.

The blood-stained murderer, with that demented presumption which marked his proceedings, now directed his steps to the private apartments where His Majesty was sleeping. He mounted, sword in hand, to the parapet (*suffah*) which surrounds the palace on all sides about the height of a man and a half, and endeavoured to force his way inside. A eunuch who was near shut the door and locked it, and refused to open it for all the menaces of the assassin. The attendants of the royal court were greatly to be blamed that they did not at once inflict merited punishment on the murderer, and put a stop to his proceedings. But this want of resolution was probably ordained so that the courage and justice of the Emperor might become manifest to all, both small and great. The noise awoke him, and he inquired what was the matter, but no one of the inside attendants could inform him. He then went out himself to ascertain the facts. One of the old officers of the palace made known what had happened.

Amazed at the horrible statement, His Majesty inquired what it all meant, and the attendant then confirmed his words by pointing to the blood-stained corpse. When the Emperor realized the actual state of affairs, his anger blazed forth, and by a sudden inspiration he rushed out by another door, and not by that to which the assassin had fled in his vain hope. As he went forth, one of his attendants placed a sword in his hand without being asked for it. He took it and went on. On turning a corner of the parapet, he perceived the ungrateful culprit. Addressing him by an opprobrious epithet, he asked what he had done. The presumptuous villain then rushed forward, and seizing both the hands of the Emperor, besought him to inquire into and reflect upon the matter, and not to condemn him without investigation. The Emperor, letting go his sword, delivered himself from the grasp of the culprit, and endeavoured to seize his sword. But the wretched man loosed his hold of the Emperor, and endeavoured to retain his sword. Relinquishing his attempt to get the sword, the Emperor struck him a blow in the face with his fist, which brought him senseless to the ground. Farhat Khan and Sangram Hoshnak were there present, and the Emperor with angry looks demanded why they stood there looking on. He ordered them to bind the mad-brained fellow, and they and some others did so. He then gave his just command for them to cast him down headlong from the parapet. The stupid men showed tenderness where want of tenderness would have been a thousand times better, and did not hurl him down as they ought to have done, and he was only half killed. They were then ordered to bring him up and cast him down again. So they dragged him back by the hair, and throwing him down more carefully, his neck was broken and his brains knocked out. So that the criminal received the just reward of his deed. The vigorous hand of the Emperor had dealt him such a blow that those who were not aware of the fact supposed it to have been given with a mace.

Mun'im Khan Khan-khanan and Shagabu-d din Ahamad Khan, who were near at hand, recoiled before the Emperor's anger, and took to flight. Yusuf Muhammad Khan, the eldest son of Atka Khan, when he was informed of the fate of his father, assembled the Atka khail in arms, and blocked the road against Adham Khan and Maham Anka. They were as yet unaware of the just retribution inflicted by His Majesty, who had paid no regard to his connection (*nisbat*) with Miham Anka. . . . But one of their number went and saw the punishment the culprit had received at the hands of the Emperor, and their anger was then appeased.

Maham Anka was at her own home, stretched upon the bed of sickness. She had heard of her son's outrageous conduct, and that the Emperor had put him in confinement. Moved by her maternal affection, she arouse and went to the Emperor hoping to obtain release of her son. When the Emperor saw her he told her that Adham had killed his *atka*, and that he had inflicted the retaliatory punishment. Maham Anka did not understand from this that her son was dead, so she replied that His Majesty had done well. But the *takhta-begi*, one of the ladies of the Court, then told her the truth, that he had been killed, and that he bore upon his face the marks of a blow with a mace—these marks being, in fact, those made by His Majesty's fist.

Maham Anka's good sense so far restrained her that she said nothing disrespectful to the Emperor, but she was greatly distressed. Her heart received a thousand wounds and the colour forsook her face. She wished to go and see the body of her son, but His Majesty would not allow her, and he endeavoured to console and comfort her with kind and gentle words. On the same day the two corpses were sent to Dehli, and the Emperor after doing his utmost to console Maham Anka, gave her permission to return home. That wise and grief-stricken woman respectfully took her departure. She then resigned herself to the divine decree, and passed her days in grief and sorrow. The disease with which she was afflicted increased, and forty days afterwards she died. His Majesty was deeply grieved at the death of this pattern of chastity. Her body was sent to Dehli with all respect and honour, and the Emperor himself followed it for some steps. The nobles and officers of the state all testified their respect, and the Emperor ordered a splendid monument to be erected over her and her son.

QUESTIONS TO CONSIDER

1. What kind of events does Abu'l Fazl find most important? What kinds are missing from this chronicle?
2. Where do the preceding passages show Abu'l Fazl's need to exalt his patron Akbar?
3. According to Abu'l Fazl, what makes a ruler strong? How does he show this?

FOR FURTHER READING

Abu'l Fazl 'Allami. *The A'in-i Akbari.* Trans. H. Blochmann. New Delhi: Oriental
Books Reprint Corporation, 1977.

Hardy, Peter. *Historians of Medieval India: Studies in Indo-Muslim Historical Writing.*
Westport, CT: Greenwood Press, 1960.

Mukhia, Harbans. *Historians and Historiography During the Reign of Akbar.* New Delhi:
Vikas Publishing House, 1976.

NOTES

1. Abu'l Fazl, *Akbar-Nama* (Lahore: Hafiz Press, 1975), 11–19, 21–30.

CHAPTER 25

Gulbadan Bagam

Mughal Princess

Emperor Babar, father of Gulbadan Bagam
© *Explorer/SuperStock*

Among the reminiscences from which Abu'l Fazl constructed his Akbar-nama, one deserves special mention. Gulbadan Begam, "Princess Rose-body," was Akbar's aunt, who saw much in the course of her 80 years. With the rest of the royal women, she had followed Akbar's grandfather and father as they won, then lost, the empire he was later to rebuild. She saw their wars and campaigns from a woman's vantage point. Through her, we see court life as well as politics. We see the women rejoicing in their men's triumphs, fearful for their safety, but glad when they return home to peace.

Gulbadan was born about 1523 CE, the youngest surviving daughter of Babar, Akbar's grandfather, the founder of India's Mughal empire. Babar was descended on his mother's side from Jenghiz Khan, and on his father's from Timur-the-Lame, or Tamerlane. At twelve, he inherited a tiny kingdom in present-day Turkmenistan, but had to spend the next several years defending it from his relatives. He took Samarkand, lost it, retook it, and lost it again, this time along with his own throne. He then took Kabul, and from there built an empire that stretched into India.

Gulbadan was born just before Babar set out to conquer Hindustan, a conquest that lasted with one break until the British banished the Emperor Bahadur Shah 330 years later. She did not see him for several years, until he moved his capital to Agra and sent for his wives, daughters, and aunts. She reported a glorious and heartfelt reunion, shattered by his death from fever a few months later. Her older brother Humayun ascended the throne.

Humayun was a beloved, but not a strong, leader. He seems to have taken his father's admonition to protect his family too literally. His brothers repeatedly rebelled against him, but he always forgave them, leaving them enough power to rebel again. The worst of them, Kamran, took Kabul while Humayun was losing Hindustan to Sher Shah; Humayun needed an alliance with the Persian Shah Tahmasp to eject both. Gulbadan was in the thick of things, as active as a woman could then be. Alternately a bystander, a hostage, and a go-between, she decried Kamran's treacheries as she welcomed Humayun's reconquests. But she did not have long to celebrate them. Humayun died in 1556 soon after retaking Delhi, and his son Akbar ascended the throne.

We do not know much of Gulbadan during Akbar's reign, other than her pilgrimage to Mecca from 1575 to 1582. Sometime between 1587 and 1590, she was asked to write what she knew of her father's and brother's reigns so that Abu'l Fazl could compile a history culminating in Akbar's accomplishments. She did so quite simply, beginning with her father's accession and ending with Humayun's final victory over his brother Kamran. (There appears to have been more to her manuscript, but it has been lost.) Akbar may not have thought much of the result; the *Humayun-nama* has little of the flowery court flattery to which he was accustomed, and it presents his predecessors as persons in themselves, not as mere heralds of Akbar's coming. It also gives us what seems to be a more rounded picture of Mughal life, with everyday scenes as well as the honorific events that Akbar thought worth remembering. Abu'l Fazl apparently liked it, though: he lifted sections of it for his own history, without, however, attributing their prose to Gulbadan's hand.

Later historians continued this neglect. Gulbadan's death in 1603 is mentioned, as is the fact that Akbar helped carry her funeral bier. Her manuscript was only copied three times. Two of these disappeared, and the third was lost until the mid-1800s, when it was found among some thousand manuscripts gathered by Colonel Hamilton in Lucknow and Delhi. It now lies in the British Museum. It lacks an ending, one folio is out of place, and it has been badly rebound. The translator, Annette Beveridge, tells us that a Dr. Rieu identified it as the most significant manuscript in the Hamilton Collection. Her translation was not an easy task, as Gulbadan's Persian is mixed with many Turkic words (Persian was the Mughal court language; Turkic the language of her childhood). Though published in English in 1901, historians have only gradually begun to see the treasure here.

Gulbadan constructed her history from two types of sources. The first was her own experience of court life, of which she had seen much. Though court women usually lived in their own quarters, political events were much discussed among them, especially among those who, like Gulbadan, had been educated. Her second source was the histories and reminiscences of others, which allowed her to fill in the events she did not see first hand. The first passage below is built from the accounts of others, supplemented by her own knowledge. The second is built from her memories and from the first-hand reports she received.

Gulbadan's history is unusual, both for her tradition and for her times. Like other Mughal histories, *The Humayun-nama* focuses on politics: wars, court intrigues, diplomatic slights made, rebuked, and forgiven—in short, it is a standard "history from above." Yet we see more human life in her writing than we do in most. She shows us not just how women lived, but how men lived when they were not consumed by wars and battles. We see them rest from politics, and how they were pulled from that rest, often against their wills. We see details of battles and occupations that only women would know—powerless as they were to direct events, pawns that they so often were in men's quarrels. She shows us men's pride, but also their weaknesses. And she does all this with a simplicity not to be found in Abu'l Fazl and the court history tradition he exemplified.

In the case of her brother Humayun, it is for those weaknesses that she revered him. A devout Muslim, she valued the gentleness and the willingness to forgive that she felt showed his Muslim character. She knew that these qualities, which Akbar lacked, hindered his reign. But they were, to her, worth preserving, as was his memory. Gulbadan's *Humayun-nama* is also worth preserving, and worth introducing to a wider audience.

The Humayun-nama[1]

In the name of God, the Merciful, the Compassionate!

There had been an order issued, 'Write down whatever you know of the doings of Firdaus-makani and Jannat-ashyani' [the posthumous names of her father Babar and her half-brother Humayun, respectively].

At the time when his Majesty Firdaus-makani passed from this perishable world to the everlasting home, I, this lowly one, was eight years old, so it may well be that I do not remember much. However, in obedience to the royal command, I set down whatever there is that I have heard and remember.

First of all, by way of invoking a blessing [on my work], and in pious commemoration, a chapter is written about my royal father's deeds, although these are told in his memoirs.

From his Majesty Sahib-qirani [known to Westerners as Timur or Tamer-lane] down to my royal father there was not one of the bygone princes who laboured as he did. He became king in his twelfth year, and the *khutba* was read in his name on June 10th, 1494, in Andijan, the capital of Farghana.

For eleven full years his wars and struggles against the Chaghatai and Timurid and Uzbeg princes in Mawara'u-n-nahr [Transoxiana] were such that the tongue of the pen is too feeble and weak to recount them.

The toils and perils which in the ruling of kingdoms befell our prince, have been measured out to few, and of few have been recorded the manliness, courage and endurance which he showed in battle-fields and dangers. Twice he took Samarqand by force of the sword. The first time my royal father was twelve years old, the second nineteen, the third time he was nearly twenty-two [when he conquered it without fighting]. For six months he was besieged [in Samarqand], and neither Sultan Husain Mirza Bayqra, his paternal uncle, who [ruled] in Khurasan, nor Sultan Mahmud Khan, his maternal uncle, who ruled in Kashghar, sent him help. When none came from any quarter, he grew desperate.

At this difficult time, Shahi Beg Khan sent to say: 'If you would marry your sister Khanzada Begam to me, there might be peace and a lasting alliance between us.' At length it had been done; he gave the begam to the khan and came out himself [from Samarqand]. With 200 followers on foot, wearing long frocks on their shoulder and peasants' brogues on their feet, and carrying clubs in their hands,—in this plight, unarmed, and relying on God, he went towards the lands of Badakhshan and Kabul.

Khusrau Shah's people and army were in Kunduz and the Badakhshanat. He came and paid his respects to his Majesty, my father, who, being as he was manly and kind and generous, did not in any way touch the question of retaliation, although Khusrau Shah had committed such crimes as the martyr-dom of Bayasanghar Mirza and the blinding of Sultan Mas'ud Mirza, both of whom were sons of my royal father's paternal uncle. In addition to this, when in the early days of the forays, his Majesty chanced to cross his country, he was watched and rudely driven out. Now he was pleased to command that Khusrau Shah should take whatever his heart desired of his [own] jewels and golden vessels, and so he got leave to go to Khurasan in kindness and safety, and took with him five or six strings of camels and five or six of baggage mules.

His Majesty now set out for Kabul, which was occupied by Muhammad Muqim, a son of Zu'l-nun Arghun, and grandfather of Nahid Begam. He had captured it after Ulugh Beg Mirza's death from Mirza 'Abdu-r-razzaq, son of his Majesty's paternal uncle [Ulugh Beg].

His Majesty reached Kabul in safety. Muhammad Muqim kept command for a few days, and then by pact and agreement made over charge to the royal servants, and went off with goods and chattels to his father in Qandahar. This was in the last ten days of Rabi II., 910H [1504 CE]. Being now master of Kabul, his Majesty went to Bangash, took it at a blow, and returned to Kabul.

Her Highness, the khanam, his Majesty's mother, had fever for six days, and then departed from this fleeting world to the eternal home. They laid her in the New Year's Garden. His Majesty paid 1,000 coined *misqal* to his kinsmen, the owners of the garden, and laid her there.

At this time urgent letters arrived from Sultan Husain Mirza, saying: 'I am planning a war against the Uzbegs. It would be excellent if you came too.' My royal father sought counsel of God. At length he set out to join the mirza. On the way news came that the mirza was dead. His Majesty's amirs represented that, this being so, it was advisable to return to Kabul, but he replied: 'As we have come so far, we will carry our condolences to the princes.' In the end he went on towards Khurasan.

When the princes heard of the royal visit, they one and all set out to give him honourable meeting, except Badi'u-z-zaman Mirza, who did not go because Baranduq Beg and Zu'l-nun Beg—amirs of Sultan Husain Mirza— said, in effect, that as his Majesty was fifteen years younger than Badi'u-z-zaman Mirza, it was right that he should be first to bow, and they should then embrace one another. Qasim Beg rejoined: 'Younger he is by years, but by the *tura* [court rules], he has precedence because he has more than once taken Samarqand by force of the sword.' At length they agreed that his Majesty should bow on coming in, and that Badi'u-z-zaman should then advance to show him honour, and they should embrace. The mirza was not attending when his Majesty came in at the door; Qasim Beg clutched my royal father's girdle and pulled it, and said to Baranduq Beg and Zu'l-nun Beg: 'The agreement was that the mirza would come forward and that they should embrace one another.' The prince then advanced in great agitation and they embraced.

As long as his Majesty was in Khurasan, each one of the princes showed him hospitality, and feasts were arranged, and excursions to all the gardens and places of interest. They set forth to him the inconvenience of winter, and said: 'Wait till it is over, and we will fight the Uzbegs.' But they could not in any way settle about the war. Eighty years long had Sultan Husain Mirza kept Khurasan safe and sound, but the mirzas could not fill their father's palace for six months. When his Majesty saw that they were careless about his expenses and revenue, he went to Kabul on the pretext of seeing the place he had assigned to himself. Much snow had fallen that year. They took the wrong road. His Majesty and Qasim Beg chose one because of its shortness, but the amirs had given other advice, and when this was not taken, they all left him without a thought for him. He and Qasim Beg and his sons made a road in two or three days by removing snow, and the people of the army followed. So they reached Ghurband. Some Hazara rebels having met his Majesty here, there was fighting; and cattle and sheep and goods without number belonging to the Hazara fell into the hands of his people. Then they started for Kabul with their enormous booty.

At the skirts of Minar Hill they heard that Mirza Khan and Mirza Muhammad Husain Gurkan had rebelled and were holding Kabul. His Majesty sent a comforting and cheering letter [to his friends in the fort], and said: 'Be of good heart! I too am here. I will light a fire on the Hill of the Moon-faced Lady; do you light one on the Treasury, so that I may be sure you know of our coming. In the morning we will fall on the enemy, you from that side and we from this.' But he had fought and won before the people of the fort came out.

Mirza Khan hid himself in his mother's house; she was his Majesty's maternal aunt. Mirza Muhammad Husain was in his wife's house. She was his Majesty's younger maternal aunt. He flung himself down on a carpet, and in fear of his life cried to a servant, 'Fasten it up!' His Majesty's people heard of this. They took him out of the carpet and brought him to the presence. In the end, his Majesty forgave the mirzas their offences, for the sake of his aunts. He used to go, in his old fashion, in and out of his aunts' houses, and showed them more and more affection, so that no mist of trouble might dim their hearts. He assigned them places and holdings in the plain-country.

God the most High, having freed Kabul from the power of Mirza Khan, committed it to my royal father's care. He was then twenty-three years old and had no child and greatly desired one. In his seventeenth year a girl had been born to him by Ayisha Sultan Begam, a daughter of Sultan Ahmad Mirza, but she died in a month. The most high God blessed the taking of Kabul, for after it eighteen children were born. (1.) Of my Lady [Akam] who was Maham Begam there was born his Majesty the Emperor Humayun, and Barbul Mirza, and Mihr-jan Begam, and Ishan-daulat Begam, and Faruq Mirza.

(2.) Ma'suma Sultan Begam, daughter of Sultan Ahmad Mirza, died in childbed. The mother's name they gave to the daughter.

(3.) Of Gul-rukh Begam was born Kamran Mirza, and Askari Mirza, and Shah-rukh Mirza, and Sultan Ahmad Mirza, and Gul-'izar Begam.

(4.) Of Dil-dar Begam were born Gul-rang Begam, and Gul-chihra Begam, and Hindal Mirza, and Gulbadan Begam [the author], and Alwar Mirza.

In short, in taking Kabul he got a good omen. All his children were born there except two begams who were born in Khost, viz., Mihr-jan Begam, a daughter of Maham Begam, and Gul-rang, a daughter of Dil-dar Begam.

*   *   *

[During The Reign of Humayun]

The victorious Emperor dismounted in triumph in the Bala-i-hisar when five hours of the night of Ramzan 12th had passed,—prosperously and with safety and good luck. All those followers of Mirza Kamran who had been promoted to the royal service, entered Kabul with drums beating [November, 1545].

On the 12th of the same month, her Highness my mother, Dil-dar Begam, and Gul-chihra Begam, and this lowly person paid our duty to the Emperor. For five years we had been shut out and cut off from this pleasure, so now when we were free from the toil and pain of separation, we were lifted up by our happiness in meeting this Lord of beneficence again. Merely to look at him eased the sorrow-stricken heart and purged the blear-eyed vision. Again and again we joyfully made the prostration of thanks. There were many festive gatherings, and people sat from evening to dawn, and players and singers made continuous music. Many amusing games, full of fun, were played. Amongst them was this: Twelve players had each twenty cards and twenty *shahrukhis*. Whoever lost, lost those twenty *shahrukhis*, which would make five *misqals*. Each player gave the winner his twenty *shahrukhis* to add to his own.

To widows and orphans, and kinsfolk of men who had been wounded or killed at Chausa and Kanauj, or Bhakkar, or who were in the royal service during those intermissions, he gave pension, and rations, and water, and land, and servants. In the days of his Majesty's good fortune, great tranquillity and happiness befell soldiers and peasants. They lived without care, and put up many an ardent prayer for his long life.

A few days later he sent persons to bring Hamida-banu Begam from Qandahar. When she arrived, they celebrated the feast of the circumcision of the Emperor Jalalu-d-din Muhammad Akbar. Preparations were made, and after the New Year they kept splendid festivity for seventeen days. People dressed in green, and thirty or forty girls were ordered to wear green and come out to the hills. On the first day of the New Year they went out to the Hill of the Seven Brothers and there passed many days in ease and enjoyment and happiness. The Emperor Muhammad Akbar was five years old when they made the circumcision feast in Kabul. They gave it in the same large Audience Hall Garden. They decorated all the bazars. Mirza Hindal and Mirza Yadgar-nasir, and the sultans and amirs, decorated their quarters beautifully, and in Bega Begam's garden the begams and ladies made theirs quite wonderful in a new fashion.

All the sultans and amirs brought gifts to the Audience Hall Garden. There were many elegant festivities and grand entertainments, and costly *khi'lats* and head-to-foot dresses were bestowed. Peasants and preachers, the pious, the poor and the needy, noble and plebeian, low and high,—everybody lived in peace and comfort, passing the days in amusement and the nights in talk.

Then the Emperor went to Fort Victory [Qila'-i-zafar]. In it was Mirza Sulaiman, who came out to fight but could not stand face to face with his Majesty and so decided to run away. The Emperor then entered the fort safe and sound. Then he went to Kishm, where, after a little while, an illness attacked his blessed frame and he slept day and night. When he came to his senses, he sent Mun'im Khan's brother, Faza'il Beg, to Kabul, and said: 'Go! comfort and reassure the people of Kabul. Set them at ease in various ways. Let them not quarrel. Say: "It began ill, but has ended well."'

When Faza'il Beg had gone, he [Humayun] went one day nearer Kabul.

False news having been sent to Mirza Kamran in Bhakkar, he set out post-haste for Kabul. In Ghazni he killed Zahid Beg and then came on. It was morning; the Kabulis were off their guard; the gates had been opened in the old way, and water-carriers and grass-cuts were going in and out, and the mirza passed into the fort with all these common people. He at once killed Uncle Muhammad Ali who was in the hot bath. He alighted at the college of Mulla 'Abdu-l-khaliq.

When the Emperor was starting for Qila'-i-zafar, he placed Naukar at the door of the *haram*. Mirza Kamran must have asked: 'Who is in the Bala-i-hisar?' and someone must have said: 'It is Naukar.' Naukar heard of this and at once put on a woman's dress and went out. The mirza's people laid hands on the doorkeeper of the fort, and took him to Mirza Kamran, who ordered him to be imprisoned. The mirza's people went into the Bala-i-hisar, and plundered and destroyed innumerable things belonging to the *haram*, and they made settlement for them in Mirza Kamran's court. He put the great begams into Mirza 'Askari's house and there he shut up a room with bricks and plaster and dung-cakes, and they used to give the ladies water and food from over the four walls.

In what was once Mirza Yadgar-nasir's house he put Khwaja Mu'azzam and ordered his own wives and family to stay in the palace where the royal *haram* and the begams once lived. He behaved very ill indeed to the wives and families of the officers who had left him for the Emperor, ransacking and plundering all their houses and putting each family into somebody's custody.

When the Emperor heard that Mirza Kamran had come from Bhakkar and was acting in this way, he returned from Qila'-i-zafar and Andar-ab safe and sound to Kabul. Qila'-i-zafar he gave to Mirza Sulaiman.

When he came near to Kabul, Mirza Kamran sent for her Highness my mother and for me from the house, and gave my mother orders to reside in the armourer's house. To me he said: 'This is your house as well as mine. You stay here.' 'Why,' I asked, 'should I stay here? I will stay with my mother.' He then went on: 'Moreover, write to Khizr Khwaja Khan and tell him to come and join me and to keep an easy mind, for just as Mirza 'Askari and Mirza Hindal are my brothers, so is he. Now is the time to help.' I answered: 'Khizr Khwaja Khan has no way of recognizing a letter from me. I have never written to him myself. He writes to me when he is away, by the tongue of his sons. Write yourself what is in your mind.' At last he sent Mahdi Sultan and Shir 'Ali to fetch the khan. From the first I had said to the khan: 'Your brothers may be with Mirza Kamran, [but] God forbid that you should have the thought of going to him and joining them. Beware, a thousand times beware of thinking of separating yourself from the Emperor.' Praise be to God! the khan kept to what I said.

When the Emperor heard that Mirza Kamran had sent Mahdi Sultan and Shir 'Ali to fetch Khizr Khwaja Khan, he himself despatched Qambar Beg, the son of Mirza Haji, to the khan, who was then in his own *jagir*, and said: 'Beware, a thousand times beware! Let there be no joining Mirza Kamran.

Come and wait on me.' The result of this auspicious message was that the khan set out at once for court, and came to the 'Uqabain [Hill of the two eagles] and paid his respects.

When the Emperor passed Minar Hill, Mirza Kamran sent forward all his well-ordered soldiers under Shir Afkan, the father of Shiroya, so that they might go out and fight. We saw from above how he went out with his drums beating, out beyond Baba Dashti, and we said, 'God forbid you should fight,' and we wept. When he reached the Afghans' village, the two vanguards came face to face. The royal advance-guard at once drove off the mirza's and, having taken many prisoners, brought them to the Emperor. He ordered the Mughals to be cut to pieces. Many of the mirza's men who had gone out to fight were captured and some of them were killed and some were kept prisoners. Amongst them was Juki Khan, one of Mirza Kamran's amirs.

In triumph and glory and to the sound of music, the Emperor entered the 'Uqabain, with Mirza Hindal in attendance and a splendid cavalcade. He set up for himself tents and pavilions and an audience hall. He gave Mirza Hindal charge of the Mastan bridge, and stationed the amirs one after another. For seven months he kept up the blockade.

It happened one day that Mirza Kamran went from his own quarters to the roof [of the citadel], and that someone fired a gun from the 'Uqabain. He ran and took himself off. Then he gave this order about the Emperor Akbar: 'Bring him and put him in front.' Someone let his august Majesty [Humayun] know that Mirza Muhhamad Akbar was being kept on the front, so he forbade the guns to be fired and after that none were aimed at the Bala-i-hisar. Mirza Kamran's men used to fire from the tower upon the Emperor on the 'Uqabain. The royal soldiers put Mirza 'Askari to stand right in front and make fun of him.

Mirza Kamran's men also used to make sallies from the fort, and on both sides many were killed. The royal troops were often the victors and then the others had not courage to come out. For the sake of his wives and children and the begams and the household, etc., the Emperor did not have the cannon fired nor did he place the large houses in difficulty.

When the long siege was ended, they [i.e., the ladies] sent Khwaja Dost Khawand to his Majesty to say: 'For God's sake, do whatever Mirza Kamran asks, and save the servants of God from molestation.'

The Emperor sent for their use from outside nine sheep, seven flasks of rose-water, one of lemonade, and seven sets of nine dress-lengths and some made-up jackets. He wrote: 'For their sakes, I could not use force against the citadel, lest I should give an advantage to their enemies.'

During the siege Jahan Sultan Begam who was two years old, died. His Majesty wrote: 'Some time or other, if we had used force against the citadel, Mirza Muhammad Akbar would have disappeared.'

To finish the story: There were always people in the Bala-i-hisar from evening prayer till dawn, and there was a continuous uproar. The night Mirza Kamran went away, prayer-time passed and indeed bedtime came, and there was no noise at all.

There was a steep stair by which people came up from below. When all the city was asleep, there suddenly sounded [on the stairs] a clashing and clinking of armour so that we said to one another: 'What a noise!' Perhaps a thousand people were standing in front [of the fort]. We were afraid, but all at once, without warning, off they went. Qaracha Khan's son Bahadur brought us word that the mirza had fled.

Having thrown a rope, they [or he] brought up Khwaja Mu'azzam by way of the wall.

Our people and the begam's people and the rest who were outside, took away the door which had kept us fastened in. Bega Begam urged: 'Let us go to our own houses.' I said: 'Have a little patience. We should have to go by the lane and perhaps too someone will come from the Emperor.' At that moment 'Ambar Nazir came and said: 'This is the royal order: "They are not to leave that place until I come."' In a little while the Emperor came and embraced Dil-dar Begam and me, and then Bega Begam and Hamida-banu Begam, and said: 'Come quickly out of this place. God preserves His friends from such a house, and let such be the portion of His foes.' He said to Nazir: 'Guard one side,' and to Tardi Beg Khan: 'Guard the other, and let the begams pass out.' All came out, and we spent the evening of that day with the Emperor in perfect content till night became morning. We embraced Mah-chuchak Begam and Khanish *agha* and those of the *haram* who had been with the Emperor on the campaign.

In Badakhshan Mah-chuchak had a daughter born. On the same night the Emperor had this dream: 'Fakhru-n-nisa', my nanny, and Daulat-bakht came in by the door, and brought something or other, and then left me alone.' Consider it as he might, he could only ask: 'What does this dream mean?' Then it occurred to him that, as a daughter had just been born, he would call her after the two, and taking *nisa'* from one, and *bakht* from the other, would run them together into *Bakht-nisa'*.

Mah-chuchak had four daughters and two sons,—Bakht-nisa' Begam, and Sakina-banu Begam, and Amina-banu Begam, and Muhammad Hakim Mirza, and Farrukh-fal Mirza. She was with child when the Emperor went to Hindustan [1554], and bore a son in Kabul, whom they named Farrukh-fal Mirza. A little later Khanish *agha* had a son whom they named Ibrahim Sultan Mirza.

The Emperor spent a full year and a half in Kabul, prosperously and happily, and in comfort and sociability.

QUESTIONS TO CONSIDER

1. What kind of events does Gulbadan find most important? What kinds does she leave out?
2. Gulbadan admits to not having witnessed much of her father's reign. What sources might she have consulted?

3. Though richer in detail than Abu'l Fazl's history, Gulbaden's work still concentrates on the Mughal nobility. What do you suppose the lives of common people were like during this period?

FOR FURTHER READING

Godden, Rumer. *Gulbadan: Portrait of a Rose Princess at the Mughal Court.* New York: Viking, 1980.
Gul-Badan Begam. *The History of Humayun (Humayun-Nama).* Trans. Annette S. Beveridge. Delhi: Idarah-i Adabiyat-i Delli, 1901; repr. 1972.

NOTES

1. Gul-Badan Begam, *The History of Humayun (Humayun-nama)*, trans. Annette S. Beveridge (Delhi: Idarah-i Adabiyat-i Delli, 1901; repr. 1972), 83–90, 178–88.

Arai Hakuseki

The First Modern Historian

Shogun Tokugawa Hidetada
© SuperStock

Murasaki Shikibu (975?–1031?) was the author of *The Tale of Genji*, widely regarded as the world's first novel. Another Japanese, Arai Hakuseki (1657–1725), might well be accorded the title of the world's first modern historian. His empirical research methods, his attempt at scholarly detachment, and his concern for rational causation were far in advance of any historian up to his time, in Japan or anywhere else.

Before Arai, Japanese historical writing—like Japan's government, its written language, and its capital city architecture—tried to follow models set by China, the dominant power in East Asia. The earliest Japanese historical account was the *Kojiki (Record of Ancient Things)*. It was a proto-history and origin myth like those found in Part 1 of this volume, written down in Chinese characters based on oral traditions and imperial family documents, beginning in the sixth century and finishing in 712. The *Kojiki* was followed in the eighth century by the *Nihongi (Chronicles of Japan)*, a chronicle modelled on the Chinese annals of Sima Qian, Ban Gu, and others. Sima Guang's *Comprehensive Mirror* (see Chapter 22) was copied by the *Okagami* (Great Mirror) and several lesser mirrors in the eleventh to fourteenth centuries.

As the central government lost control of the countryside in the twelfth and thirteenth centuries, Japan came to resemble the fragmented polity of feudal Europe more than the bureaucratic majesty of imperial China. Power passed from the imperial court to the Shogun, a military ruler atop a pyramid of *daimyo* (lords) and *bushi* or *samurai* (warriors). The ill fit between Chinese institutions and Japanese reality became apparent to many. Chinese models began to lose prestige in many parts of Japanese society, including among historians. The *Jinno Shotoki (Records of the True Descent of the Divine Emperors)*, written by Kitabatake Chikafusa in 1340, was the first history to begin to diverge from Chinese models. It was concerned less with a past golden age and the dynastic cycle than with reestablishing a strong role for the emperor, by stressing his ancestral links with the gods who formed Japan, and by delineating the proper relationship between the emperor and the Shogun.

Arai Hakuseki's departure from Chinese models was more complete, and marked the beginning of a separate Japanese historiographical tradition. Arai was a minor samurai made leaderless by the flux of feudal politics. He lived at the end of the feudal period, when the Tokugawa family was transforming the Shogun from a military chieftain to the head of a fairly strong centralized government, ruling always in the name of the emperor, who retained his title but was practically powerless. Arai took a job as a Confucian scholar-advisor to Tokugawa Tsunatoyo, a junior member of the family who eventually was elevated to Shogun and who brought Arai with him. Thus Arai spent much of his career shaping public policy. But he also took time to write treatises on politics, history, Europe, his own life, and other subjects. Almost all of these can be construed as providing intellectual supports for the Tokugawa house and for the policies Arai advocated.

Arai wrote three major historical works: the *Hankampu (Account of the Feudal Domains*, 1702); the *Koshitsu (Survey of Ancient History*, 1716); and the *Tokushi Yoron (Lessons from History*, 1712–24). The *Koshitsu* was a revisionist

monograph, reviewing what was presented in the standard histories, weighing their evidence, and coming up with new interpretations based on the
political issues of Arai's own time. The *Koshitsu* enunciated clearly Arai's
philosophy of history: like Ranke (see Chapter 38), he professed to want just
the facts, even as he pursued a moral purpose. "History," Arai wrote, "is the
science of describing historical events based on actual facts, which give lessons
to readers and call for their sincere reflection." He repudiated the mythical age
of the gods that stood as the foundation stone of earlier Japanese histories and
proclaimed, "gods are nothing but men." He called for scholars to investigate
widely and delve deeply, comparing Japanese records with their Chinese and
Korean counterparts. He asked them to listen carefully to the language of their
sources, strip away the accreted interpretations of the centuries, and search for
their original meanings. He developed a system of footnotes (not reproduced
in this chapter) to inform his reader about his sources. He advocated empirical
investigation, framing periodization from the documents rather than from a
predetermined philosophical schema. He perceived history as dynamic, ever
changing. He was less concerned with cycles or with some past golden
age—key elements of Chinese historiography and its Japanese imitators—than
with noting links of causation. In all these, Arai Hakuseki was a modern
historian, before any such historian appeared anywhere else in the world.

At the same time as all this rationalism, and like Ranke and other modern
historians, Arai had a moral or didactic purpose near the heart of his work.
The *Tokushi Yoron* was his masterwork, presented in draft form as lectures to
the Shogun in 1712. Arai spent the rest of his life revising it for posterity. Its
focus was on politics, on the shift of power from the imperial house to the
Shogun, and then from one shogunal house to another. Arai offered the
Shogun lessons from the triumphs and mistakes of his predecessors. He also
offered a defense of the shogunal system, as the inevitable result of imperial
incompetence, and of the Tokugawa house, on account of the weakness of
earlier Shoguns. But as a Confucian scholar, Arai saw the rulers' incompetence
as not merely political but also ethical, and he took pains to examine both
political and moral failings. The selection below is taken from the final
chapters of the *Tokushi Yoron*, where Arai discusses the reign of Oda
Nobunaga, a predecessor of the Tokugawa shoguns.

Tokushi Yoron[1]

The Administration of Oda Nobunaga

In the eighth month of the first year of Tensho [1573] Oda Nobunaga set out for Echizen Province, overthrew Asakura Yoshikage, and finally reaching Omi Province, subjugated Asai Nagamasa and his father, Shimotsuke-no-Kami Hisamasa; and when he attacked (Uemon-no-Kami) Sasaki Yoshisuke's castle at Namazue, Yoshisuke took to flight, so that the House of Sasaki was also destroyed. In the eleventh month of the fourth year [1576, Nobunaga] killed Kitabatake Tomonori and two of his sons, and took [his eldest son], Nobumasa, prisoner.

Earlier, Nobunaga had taken by force the eight districts of north Ise Province, and in the eleventh year of Eiroku [1568], having made peace with Shimosa-no-Kami Kambe [Tomomori], had him adopt into his family his third son, Nobutaka, then eleven years old. That year also, Nobunaga had made his younger brother Sanjuro the heir of the House of Nagano and had married him to a younger sister of Kambe Kurodo, giving him the name Kozuke-no-Suke Nagano Nobukane. Then, after gaining the support of the warriors within [Ise] province, he attacked the provincial governor [Kitabatake] Tomonori's castle at Okochi and within a short time arranged a treaty of peace. In the twelfth year of the same era [1569] he had married his second son, Nobukatsu (aged twelve), to the daughter of [Kitabatake] Nobumasa (son of Tomonori), making this son the heir of that House.

On the twenty-fifth day of the eleventh month of the fourth year of Tensho [1576] Nobunage killed [Kitabatake] Tomonori by a trick, as well as his second son, "Nagano-Gosho" [Fujinori], his third son, Shikibu-no-Sho, two other small sons aged three years and one year, Hyogo-no-Kami Sakauchi (Kitabatake's son-in-law), the whole of the Okochi family, the whole of the Sakauchi family (all relatives of the Kitabatake family), and thirteen other members of the Kitabatake family besides, in various places. He spared Nobumasa's life and made him prisoner. The Kitabatake family, which had continued for a total of nine generations and 240-odd years from Chikafusa's third son, Akiyoshi, through Akiyasu, Mitsumasa, Noritomo, Mastomo, Murachika, Harutomo, Tomonori to Nobumasa, was destroyed over night. (At this time Tomonori was forty-nine years old, Nobumasa twenty-five, and Nobukatsu nineteen.)

In the spring of the fifth year [1577] Nobunaga pacified Kii Province. In the tenth month he captured Shigi [san] Castle in Yamato Province. Matsunaga Hisahide and his son Hisamichi committed suicide. Earlier, Matsunaga with Miyoshi Yoshitsugu had overthrown Hatakeyama Takamasa. When Nobunaga went to Hatakeyama's help, Hisahide shut himself up in Shigi[san Castle], and Hisamichi in Tamon Castle, but in the spring of the first year of Tensho [1573] Hisahide surrendered together with his son. That year Hisahide pitched camp at the Tennoji Temple to attack the stronghold at Osaka [the Ishiyama-Honganji Temple] but withdrew to Shigi[san]. Though he won over the Ikko mons of the Honganji Temple and the garrison in Saiga fort and revolted against Nobunaga, he was overthrown by [Nobunaga's eldest son,] Nobutada.

> Comment: The Miyoshi were descended from Ogasawara Nagakiyo's second son, Magojiro Nagafus. [One of them] became Shugo of Awa Province and was the first to remove from Shinano Province and live in a place called Miyoshi, whence he took his name. It is said that this was Shinano-no-Kami Yoshinaga, a descendant in the eighth generation of [Ogasawara] Nagafus. During the Ashikaga shogunate the Hosokawa held Shikoku, so the Miyoshi attached themselves to them. Miyoshi Jirozaemonnojo Yukinaga served [Hosokawa] Mochimoto but died prematurely. His son Tarozaemonnjo Yuki-yoshi was attached to the service of Hosokawa Katsumoto and Masamoto. Yukiyoshi's son was Chikuzen-no-Kami Nagateru Nyudo Kiun. Nagateru's eldest son was Shimosa-no-Kami Nagahide. Nagahide's son was Satsuma-no-Kami [Nagamoto, at first] Motonaga Nyudo Kaiun. Nagamoto's eldest son was Shuri-Daibu [Norinaga] Chokei; his second son Bungo-no-Kami Yukitora (also called Yukiyasu [or Motoyasu] Nyudo Jikkyu; his third son Settsu-no-Kami Ataka [or Ataki] Fuyuyasu; his fourth son Mimbu-no-Sho Sogo Ka-zunori; and his fifth son Noguchi Fuyunaga. The Ataka [or Ataki] and Noguchi in Awaji Province, the Ichinomiya and Izawa in Awa Province, and the Sogo in Sanuki Province were all relatives of the Miyoshi. As Chokei's son Yoshinaga died, Sogo Kazunori's son was made his heir. This was Sakyo-no-Daibu Yoshitsugu. The man known as Nyudo Sosan was Nagateru's fifth son, and was [at first] called Shingoro Masanaga. [Masanaga's] eldest son, Shimotsuke-no-Kami Sadakiyo, took the Buddhist name Chokansai, and his second son, Inaba-no-Kami Kazuto, turned priest, being called Isan. There were also the younger brothers of Kaiun, who were called Isan. Hyuga-no-Kami Masafusa and Yamashiro-no-Kami Yasunaga Nyudo Shogan. Alto-gether, in the senior line of the Miyoshi the five generations Kiun, Nagahide, Kaiun, Chokei, and Yoshitsugu appear. The rest—Sosan, Shogan, and Jikkyu—are well known.
> Matsunaga [Hisahide] (born in Nishioka in Kyoto) was a retainer of Chokei, and he was one of the worst villains of the time. At first he helped Chokei and so made a name for himself, but when Chokei was in his dotage, [Matsunaga] poisoned [Chokei's son] Yoshinaga and brought about the death of [Chokei's younger brother] Fuyuyasu by slander finally, together with [Chokei's adopted son] Yoshitsugu, assassinated the Shogun Yoshiteru. How-ever, Nobunaga, espousing Ashikaga Yoshiaki's cause, issued a declaration that he would put this rebel [Matsunaga] to death, and finally he accom-plished the capitulation of Miyoshi Yoshitsugu and Matsunaga Hisahide; but he granted them provinces and districts, and himself expelled Yoshiaki, and did not investigate their crime [in killing Yoshiteru].
> Yoshitsugu and Matsunaga then rebelled against Nobunaga, but Matsu-naga quickly surrendered again, and a second time Nobunaga accepted his surrender. Yoshitsugu was finally put to death by his retainers, and since Matsunaga rebelled a third time Nobunaga executed him. The destruction of these two men was not due merely to the crimes they had committed against Nobunaga.
> Nobunaga, at the head of an army of retainers who had revolted against their own lords, swore loyalty to Yoshiaki, and Yoshiaki, without inquiring into their crimes, accepted as his retainers men whom he should have

regarded as his deadly enemies. Thus, in a disturbed age like this, was morality overthrown. Since this had come to be the pattern of society, it had reached the point where even though a man might have slain his lord or father, he would yet be valued for his courage on the battlefield. And thus Oda Nobunaga was eventually slain by his retainer Akechi Mitsuhide, and Nobunaga's son Nobutaka, too, was killed by Toyotomi Hideyoshi and Nobukatsu also was overthrown by Hideyoshi. These were dastardly deeds.

In the month in which Matsunaga was killed, Nobunaga gave Hideyoshi Harima Province. Although Hideyoshi had hoped that Nobunaga would give him the whole of the Chugoku region, this was denied him. When Hideyoshi subjugated Tajima Province he was at last permitted to the Chugoku region. In the sixth year [of Tensho, 1578] Nobunaga put down the rebellion of Settsu-no-Kami Araki Murashige in Settsu. In the seventh year [1579] Tamba Province was subjugated. In the eighth year [1580] Harima Province was subjugated. This year, owing to an imperial decree, Kosa, Monzeki of the [Ishiyama-] Honganji Temple in Osaka, made peace and moved to Saiga [fort] in Kii Province.

Comment: Above all else, Nobunaga brought peace to the country within the eleven years between the outbreak [of the revolt of the Ikko sectaries of the Ishiyama-Honganji Temple] in Osaka in the first year of Genki [1570] and this year [1580]. He was unable to accomplish this by his military might alone, so finally he obtained an imperial decree and by this means achieved his aim.

Earlier [the Ikko monks] who held Nagashima [Castle] in Owari province rose up in arms, but within four years Nobunaga was victorious. Those slain were numberless, including Nobunaga's elder brother Osumi-no-Kami [Oda-] Tsuda Nobuhiro, his younger brother Hanzaemonnojo Hidenari, his cousin Ichi-no-Suke [Oda-] Tsuda Nobunari, Hitachi-no-Suke Ujiie Nyudo Bokuzen, and Hayashi Shinzaburo [Mitsutoki]. Shibata Katsuie and Iga-no-Kami Iga were wounded. And before that the House of Togashi-no-Suke [Masachika] in Kaga Province was destroyed by the monks of the Ikko sect. Asakura [Yoshikage] of Echizen Province, too, was frequently harassed by the Ikko monks of Kaga Province. In more recent times, also, the country was brought almost to ruin by these monks. Therefore, at the beginning of his administration, our Divine Ancestor divided this sect into [two branches] east and west and was able to suppress their power a little, but even though they had no land, the wealth of these two branches was comparable to that of a lord. This may be a fact to which we should give very careful attention.

In the third month of the tenth year [1582] Nobunaga subjugated Kai Province and overthrew Takeda Katsuyori (aged thirty-seven) and his son Nobukatsu (aged sixteen). On the first day of the sixth month he was assassinated (at the age of forty-nine) by his retainer Hyuga-no-Kami Akechi Mitsuhide. [His eldest son, Oda] Nobutada, committed suicide in Nijo Castle (at the age of twenty-six).

Comment: One of the hereditary houses of the Kanryo of the Ashikaga shogunate, the House of Buei [Shiba], held the office of Shugo of Owari Echizen, and Totomi provinces. Of these the eight districts of Owari, Echizen, and Totomi provinces. Of these the eight districts of Owari Province had been divided into two, the four southern districts coming under the control of Yamato-no-Kami Oda [Tatsukatsu] stationed in Kiyosu Castle with his suzerain [Yoshitatsu], a member of the Shiba family and the four northern districts under that of Ise-no-Kami Oda Nobuyasu, in Castle. (The Oda were one of the six chief vassals of the Shiba family.) Under Tatsukatsu there were three Bugyo. They were Inaba-no-Kami [Tatsuhiro], Tozaemon [Hirokore], and Danjo-no-Jo [Nobuhide]. All these bore the name of Oda. Danjo-no-Jo [Nobuhide] was later called Bingo-no-Kami. He was the father of Nobunaga. Nobunaga's grandfather [Nobusada] was called Getsugan. His five sons were Bingo-no-Kami [Nobuhide], Yojiro [Nobuyasu], Magosaburo [Nobumitsu], Shirojiro [Nobuzane], and Uemon-no-Jo [Nobutsugu]. Nobunaga was [Nobuhide's] second son, and altogether he had ten brothers.

When Nobunaga was sixteen, his father, Nobuhide, died. Nobunaga succeeded to his share of [Nobuhide's] estates and, killing [Oda] Hikogoro [Nobutomo], the [adopted] son of Inaba-no-Kami [Tatsuhiro Nyudo Joyu], by a trick, seized his castle at Kiyosu [actually, 1555] and lived there. (Earlier, Nobuhide had built Nagoya Castle and established Nobunaga there, himself living in Furuwatari.) The following year (the third of Koji [1557]) Nobunaga killed his younger brother Kanjuro Nobuyuki by a trick and seized the whole of his father's estates. He overthrew the House of Ise-no-Kami [Oda Nobukata] and took possession of their castle at Iwakura. At the age of twenty-six he fought with Imagawa Yoshimoto and slew him. Thereafter his military power increased greatly. He pacified the whole of Owari Province and shortly afterward also annexed Mino Province. After that, at the request of the Shogun Yoshiaki, he pacified the whole country.

The lands he held numbered twenty-eight, comprising: the five home provinces; in the Tokaido region Iga, Ise, Shima Owari, and Kai provinces; in the Tosando region, [Omi], Mino, Hida, Shinano, and Kozuke provinces; in the Hokurikudo region, Wakasa, Echizen, Kaga, Noto, and Etchu provinces; in the San'indo region, Tamba, Tango, Tajima, and Inaba provinces; in the Sanyodo region, Harima, Bizen, and Bitchu provinces; and Kii Province in the Nankaido region.

Thus, those families which had enjoyed prominence since ancient times but were destroyed by Nobunaga were innumerable. First, leaving aside the Ashikaga, the [Kitabatake family, which held the office of] provincial governor of Ise; the Sasaki-Rokkaku; the two branches of Takeda family of Wakasa and Kai provinces; the [Anegakoji, who held the office of] provincial governor of Hida, and the Asakura [of Echizen] had all been famous daimyos for generations. Others again, like the Miyoshi and Matsunaga of Awa Province, the Saito of Mino Province, the Bessho of Harima Province, and the Asai the Wada, and the Araki of Omi Province, were still more numerous. In everything he did, Nobunaga had a cruel nature, and he achieved his ambitions by tricks. So his meeting with a violent death was his own fault and not simply due to misfortune.

The reason why Nobunaga won fame in the empire was that he supported the Shogun Yoshiaki. But it seems clear that after he had realized his ambiiton he conceived the plan of destroying him. After Nobunaga had established Yoshiaki in Kyoto, he soon rebuilt the Imperial Palace and restored the houses of the court nobles which had come to an end. Moreover, it is recorded that in the first of Nobunaga's "Seventeen Articles" rebuking

Yoshiaki, he said, "Since "Kogon'in Dono" [the Shogun Yoshiteru] was negligent in attending at the Imperial Palace, divine assistance was denied him and there is no need to recapitulate [the many misfortunes he suffered during his life]. You have already completely forgotten that when I first set you up as shogun I warned you never to be negligent in this throughout your whole reign. In recent years you have completely neglected it, which is the height of discourtesy to the emperor." This letter of admonition does not at all appear to show deep loyalty to Yoshiaki. Rather it seems to have been aimed at publishing his shortcomings to the world. The result was that Yoshiaki, [perceiving Nobunaga's real intentions and] unable to contain his anger, issued a call to arms. Does this not at once expose Nobunaga's plot to control the emperor and rule the empire? Hideyoshi made use of this old trick to seize supreme power and laboured for the advantage of his own House. And so Nobunaga's support of Yoshiaki, and Hideyoshi's support of Nobutada's son "Gifu Dono" [Hidenobu], were both temporary devices, in order to make use of their names [as their sponsors].

If we survey Nobunaga's whole career, we see that he first deceived his own mother, slew his younger brother [Nobuyuki] and seized the whole of his father's estates; and after that he made his son [Nobukatsu] destroy his whole family. Then, making his younger brother Nobukane and his third son, Nobutaka, the adopted sons of Nagano and Kambe, he seized their lands. Then, by marrying his own younger sister to Asai, he overthrew him. Then he married his daughter to "Okazaki Dono" [Tokugawa Nobuyasu] and slandered and killed him. In order to induce Takeda [Harunobu Nyudo Shingen] to relax his military vigilance, he was a man totally lacking in filial or fraternal sentiments. He accomplished the downfall of [Yoshiaki, whom], he had honoured as his suzerain. Against men like Sado-no-Kami Hayashi [Michikatsu], Iga-no-Kami Iga, and Uemon-no-Jo Sakuma [Nobumori], who had won wide fame for many years, he nursed inveterate hatred and got rid of them. This [sort of conduct] was the cause of the rebellion of [Akechi] Mistuhide. And this was also because he did not understand the proper relationship between lord and subject. Worse, under the pretext that he was punishing the rufians who had slain the Shogun Yoshiteru, he first accomplished the surrender of Miyoshi Yoshitsugu and Matsunaga Hisahide, and then granted them fiefs. But when Sasaki-Rokkaku Yoshisuke of Omi Province, and Asakura Yoshikage of Echizen Province lacked the military might to assist Yoshiaki, he destroyed them on the grounds that they were disloyal subjects. This showed no regard for due punishment or reward.

There must be some reason why, though this evil man only temporarily achieved his ambitions, his descendants continue to survive. Traditional accounts suggest that Nobunaga was a descendant of "Komatsu Naifu" [Taira] Shigemori. If that is true, it must have been due to Shigemori's accumulated merit. This was the first reason why his descendants survive. After the Onin War [1467–77], because of their love of warfare, day by day the strength of the [military classes] deteriorated, and day by day economic conditions worsened. [Nobunaga's father] Bingo-no-Kami Oda Nobuhide, however, was possessed by a wealthy ancestral fief, and concentrating on increasing its wealth and power of promoting agriculture and waging war, he built up both his military and financial resources. Nobunaga took over his task and, recruiting heroic fighters, won victories in many battles. This was the second reason. His province was at the hub of the country's communications network, and close to Kyoto. Moreover, Nobunaga [in supporting Yoshiaki] rose by borrowing the prestige of the many generations of the Ashikaga shogunate and in this way won renown in the empire. This was the third reason. When Hideyoshi cheated Nobunaga's [infant grandson], the fatherless [Hidenobu], and seized control of the country, those in league with him were all old retainers of Nobunaga, hence it was naturally impossible for him to destroy Nobunaga's descendants entirely. Later, when our Divine Ancestor replaced Hideyoshi, since he did not forget his former friendship [with Oda Nobunaga], even today [Oda's] descendants are still in possession of fiefs. This was the fourth reason. In all the disturbances since the Onin War, if Oda Nobunaga had not by harsh measures mobilized the military resources of the empire so that they could be utilized by our Divine Ancestor, we would not be enjoying the peace we have today. Those who rank as daimyos and hold large fiefs at the present time are all of them men who rose under Nobunaga. This was the fifth reason. It is owing to these circumstance that, although Nobunaga only temporarily achieved his ambition, his descendants yet survive.

Now, it is generally said that Nobunaga and Hideyoshi were excellent judges of men, but with this I do not agree. Hideyoshi was not nearly as good a judge as Nobunaga, and even Nobunaga did not always show such remarkable ability in his judgements. Hideyoshi and Mitsuhide both turned out to have had designs on the empire, and Nobunaga himself was killed by Mitsuhide, while his grandson was destroyed by Hideyoshi. Can it be said that his judgement was good here? But men like Niwa [Nagahide], Shibata [Katsuie], Takigawa [Kazumasu], Sasa [Narimasa], Maeda [Toshiie], Ikeda [Terumasa], Hori [Naomasa], Mori [Yoshinari], Kuroda [Yoshitaka], and Yamanouchi [Katsutoyo] all rose from being Nobunaga's vassals, and in most cases their descendants are now daimyos with hereditary fiefs, so there is up to a point some reason for crediting him with good judgement of men. But after all, Shibata [Katsuie] and Sasa [Narimasa] were the only two who sacrificed their lives and their houses on behalf of Nobunaga's sons after his death. The rest all supported Hideyoshi and later put an end to [Nobunaga's] progeny. It is even doubtful whether Shibata and Sasa were loyal to Nobunaga. For Shibata was originally a retainer of Nobunaga's younger brother Musashi-no-Kami [Nobuyuki] but went over to Nobunaga and slew his own lord; and Sasa afterward submitted to Hideyoshi but in the end was put to death by him.

The men employed by Hideyoshi were Asano [Nagamasa and his son Yukinaga], Fukushima [Masanori], and the two Kato [Kiyomasa and Yoshiaki]. Besides these, there were the Five Bugyo [Masuda Nagamori, Maeda Toshiie, Asano Nagamasa, Nagatsuka Masaie, and Ishida Mitsunari]. Leaving aside Asano and the rest for a while, men like the Five Bugyo were only underlings whom it is not necessary to consider. It can only be said that he had the talent to lead heroes but at the time there were no true heroes [to lead]. Both lord and vassals were what might be called unprincipled rascals who took advantage of the disturbed state of society. How can they be compared to our Divine Ancestor's retainers, who were all loyal vassals?

But the accounts that have come down to us have been written by people who, having heard that Nobunaga and Hideyoshi gave many provinces to those who had performed meritorious service, think that our Divine Ancestor was inferior to them [and that he was only interested in getting possession of provinces but was not prepared to share them among his followers]. They were quite unaware that our Divine Ancestor had given deep and far-sighted thought to this problem. In the state of Ch'i people praised prowess, so overlords ruling by force were able to arise; but in the state of Lu, on the contrary, people praised wisdom and humanity, and hence in that state there were many virtuous kings. The so-called rejoicing of the subjects of the man who holds the hegemony, and the deep contentment of the subjects of the man who holds the royal dignity proceed from these attitudes. The reason for this can be clearly understood from the reply given by the Divine Ancestor during the Komaki campaign when Nobukatsu was about to reward Nagai [Naokatsu's] meritorious service in taking Ikeda [Nobuteru's] head. When we consider the intention of the Divine Ancestor, there are points of resemblance to Kuang-wu-ti, founder of the Later Han Dynasty, and he even surpasses Chao K'uang-yin, founder of the Sung Dynasty.

The man who holds the hegemony is described as the chief; he is the man who makes himself the chief of all the other princes and manipulates the emperor and issues the orders. He cannot do this if he does not have a strong state and great military power. So when Kuan Chung assisted Duke Huan of Ch'i, he appears to have adopted that policy. But the reason why Nobunaga succeeded seems to have been because he was very cunning and pretended to be merciful.

If we consider the intention of Minamoto Yoritomo's government, we see it was based on the policy of the man who seizes the hegemony, but under the situation at that time there were no princes [i.e., daimyos] of whom he could become the chief.

Ashikaga Takauji also manipulated the emperor as he pleased and issued orders, and so his rule resembled a hegemony, but since the daimyos of that time all bestowed lands on those who had served them well, his rule was not like a hegemony of ancient times.

Nobunaga was originally a sub-vassal of the shogunate government, but after temporarily supporting the shogun, and performing meritorious services, he turned against him and immediately began to manipulate the emperor and issue orders, but his plans were aborted when only half-way to fruition. We may regard this as an attempt on his part to seize the hegemony, but he could not achieve it.

Hideyoshi was probably the only one who genuinely aimed at establishing a hegemony, and who really succeeded in doing so. Hideyoshi in everything he did made use of Nobunaga's old tricks, but perhaps because he wanted to achieve supremacy quickly, unlike Nobunaga, he did not destroy all the ancient magnates, great and small. Instead he left those who submitted to his military might in possession of their lands, and finally he destroyed only one, the Hojo of Sagami Province. So immediately there was proof of his military might. The letters he sent to Shimazu Yoshifusa and Hojo Ujimasa were all entitled decrees. This was nothing else but treating the emperor as his puppet. But at this time no one cared about the emperor's decrees. Therefore, Shimazu and Hojo completely ignored Hideyoshi's letters. It was like putting on a devil's mask in order to frighten children, and was thoroughly ridiculous.

It is quite impossible to compare it to our Divine Ancestor's subjugation of the empire by his divine might.

Nobunaga himself became Dainagon and Taisho, and his son Nobutada was appointed Akita-Jo-no-Suke. His retainer Toyotomi Hideyoshi was appointed Chikuzen-no-Kami, Kawajiri Yohei [Hidetaka] was appointed Hizen-no-Kami, and Hanawa Kurozaemon [Naomasa] was appointed Bitchu-no-Kami Harada. Yanada Saemon-Taro was appointed Ukon-no-Shogen, and changed his name to Bekki.

It is generally said that Nobunaga wished to unify the whole country. I say he had no such intention. We can probably judge his contrivances by his actions in connection with this matter. As it was then the very middle of the civil war period, the roads between east and west were blocked, and it was difficult to pass back and forth. People only knew the barest outline of what was happening at that time by hearsay. For example, when people of the Shikoku, Kyushu, and Chugoku regions heard from merchants of Kyoto and Sakai on their travels that his son [Nobutada] had been appointed Akita-Jo-no-Suke, they thought that perhaps Nobunaga had already subjugated as far as Mutsu Province. Also, when people of the eastern provinces listened to the stories that those who sold horses and hawks in Kyoto told on their return about Nobunaga's giving all his retainers the names of the ancient houses of Kyushu and appointing them to their offices, they must have thought that Nobunaga had probably already annexed the territory of Kyushu. And so it is said that to the people of the western provinces he sent hawks and horses from the eastern provinces, and to the people of the eastern region he sent the products of China. This was nothing but a plan to intimidate people by advance propaganda and was no different from terrifying babies by dressing up like a devil. Hideyoshi's subjugation of Korea was the same sort of thing.

QUESTIONS TO CONSIDER

1. What is the effect of the interplay between separate sections of chronicle and commentary in Arai's writing?
2. How may Arai's position as an employee of the Tokugawa clan have shaped this narrative?
3. In what sense does this passage reveal Arai Hakuseki to be "the world's first modern historian"?

FOR FURTHER READING

Arai Hakuseki. *The Armour Book in Honcho-Gunkiko.* Trans. Y. Otsuka. Ed. H. Russell Robinson. Rutland, VT: C. E. Tuttle, 1964.

———. *Lessons from History: The Tokushi Yoron.* Trans. Joyce Ackroyd. St. Lucia, Australia: University of Queensland Press, 1982.

———. *Told Round a Brushwood Fire.* Trans. Joyce Ackroyd. Princeton, NJ: Princeton University Press, 1980.

Beasley, W. G., and E. G. Pulleyblank, eds. *Historians of China and Japan*. London: Oxford University Press, 1961.

Kitabatake Chikafusa. *A Chronicle of Gods and Sovereigns: Jinno Shotoki*. Trans. H. Paul Varley. New York: Columbia University Press, 1980.

Murasaki Shikibu. *Tale of Genji*. Trans. Edward Seidensticker. New York: Knopf, 1976.

Philippi, Donald L., trans. *Kojiki*. Princeton, NJ: Princeton University Press, 1969.

NOTES

1. Arai Hakuseki, *Lessons from History: The Tokushi Yoron*, trans. Joyce Ackroyd (St. Lucia, Australia: University of Queensland Press, 1982), 290–301.

PART FOUR

Growth of the West

*T*he growth of the West—Europe and North America—to dominate the globe is the most important development of modern history. Before about 1450, Europe was a cultural backwater: a remote, not very heavily populated part of the globe, marginal to the world's great civilizations in India, China, Persia, and elsewhere. At one time, Rome, a quasi-European civilization, had risen to considerable wealth, power, extent, and cultural glory. But, as the ancient Greeks and such modern historians as Martin Bernal have observed, Greece was not primarily European but rather a civilization of the Eastern Mediterranean. Rome can be seen as little more than a temporary, albeit powerful, westward extension of Greek culture that receded after the fifth century, despite later attempts by various popes and German princes to rekindle Rome's glory on a distinctly European base. After the decline of Rome, Europeans were left largely to their own devices. Lots of interesting things were happening in Europe before the modern era from the Europeans' point of view, but not much that people cared about anywhere else in the world.

It was a shock, therefore, when Europe leapt on the world stage in the fifteenth century, beginning a process that has dominated human affairs for the last five centuries. First Portuguese sailors went exploring, then they and others began to trade. Soon European armies and diseases were conquering the peoples of the New World and knocking on the gates of Asia. Historians have presented a variety of interpretations of this massive event. Karl Marx emphasized the role of economics, specifically the influx of gold from the New World and its role in enabling the rise of the bourgeoisie. Paul Kennedy highlighted the development of warfare. Immanuel Wallerstein concentrated on the formation of an international market system. Frederick Merk thought ideological issues were the key. Alfred Crosby stressed the role of diseases, animals, and plants. These and many other historians presented valid interpretations of European and later North American imperial adventures around the globe. For present purposes, we do not need to choose among them. Suffice it to say that the Industrial Revolution of the eighteenth and nineteenth centuries gave added impetus and power to the undertaking. In the nineteenth century, it was often said that the sun never set on the British flag; in the late twentieth, the same can be said of McDonald's.

Along the way, various European writers built an ideology of European cultural—even biological—superiority to justify, or at least to explain, colonialism. These explanations ranged from the lofty ideals of bringing civilization and a better life to the rest of the world expressed by Lord Balfour (see Chapter 56) to crass pseudoscientific racial theories. Just as there were varied European explanations for this expansion, so there were various responses by the peoples whose territories were expanded upon. Some responded by trying to imitate on their colonial masters. Others rejected European dominance both politically and culturally.

Part 4 is about historians experiencing this expansion from both sides. Machiavelli and Guicciardini were part of the first dawnings of the modern imagination in Europe at the time of the Renaissance. William Bradford took part in and recorded the early spread of one European people abroad: tentative, not yet dominating, but with an embryonic sense of moral certitude, even divine chosenness. Voltaire and Gibbon exemplify the building European self-confidence in the glory of France and the celebration of Rome. Macaulay and Martineau express the power of England at its peak. The Aztec and Mayan chroniclers responded to European expansion in its early, most brutal phase. Dutt and Johnson, writing later, had absorbed many European tools and much European culture, as they observed the impact of Europe on their peoples. Fukuzawa, Liang, and Hu tried to build strategies by which their nations might use European culture and technology to make themselves strong. All these historians, then, were bound up in that most powerful development of modern history, the growth of Western hegemony.

FOR FURTHER READING

Bernal, Martin. *Black Athena: The Afroasiatic Roots of Classical Civilization*. Vol. 1, *The Fabrication of Ancient Greece, 1785–1985*. London: Free Association Books, 1987.

Crosby, Alfred W. *Ecological Imperialism: The Biological Expansion of Europe, 900–1900*. New York: Cambridge University Press, 1986.

Kennedy, Paul. *The Rise and Fall of Great Powers: Economic Change and Military Conflict from 1500 to 2000*. New York: Random House, 1988.

Merk, Frederick. *Manifest Destiny and Mission in American History*. New York: Vintage, 1963.

Wallerstein, Immanuel. *The Modern World-System*. 3 vols. New York: Academic Press, 1974–89.

CHAPTER 27

Machiavelli and Guicciardini

Renaissance Humanists

Machiavelli
© North Wind Pictures

D ionysius of Halicarnassus said that history is philosophy teaching by example. That is a sentiment to which the most famous historian of the European Renaissance, Niccolò Machiavelli (1469–1527), could have sub-scribed. Although Machiavelli wrote history, he was fundamentally a political scientist and an intense patriot who used historical data to illustrate his points. The son of a Florentine lawyer, Machiavelli was a well-respected public servant in the republican phase of that city-state's history, from 1498 to 1512. When the Medici family came back to power, Machiavelli was arrested, imprisoned, tortured, and then sent to exile on a farm in the mountains outside Florence.

The rest of Machiavelli's life was spent writing about history and politics, and trying to regain a position of influence. His first book, *The Prince* (1513), became his most famous. It was a series of pithy maxims on the most efficient means by which a prince may wield power, contemplating such questions as "Whether It Is Better to be Loved or Feared." Each piece of advice was illustrated by recounting a tale from Roman, Italian, or other history that would have been well known to his audience. *The Prince* was remarkable for its apparent amorality. Machiavelli, focusing on the human, was concerned only with the machinations of power, not with ethics or the will of God—a far cry from medieval European histories. *The Prince* can be viewed either as a set of serious propositions for leadership or as satire; in either case, it was also an attempt to convince Lorenzo the Magnificent to employ its author as an adviser. Lorenzo declined the honor, but politicians have learned from Machiavelli's wisdom ever since.

Machiavelli's next historical work was the *Discourses upon the First Ten Books of Livy* (1517 or 1518). Here again, Machiavelli focused on lessons to be learned, this time as he compared the lasting glory of the Roman republic and the fleeting, half-realized glory of the Florentine. Belatedly, a few people in high places began to heed Machiavelli's words. In 1520 he was commissioned by Cardinal Giulio de Medici (later Pope Clement VII) to write a history of his home city; that history took the rest of his life. A Renaissance humanist to the core, Machiavelli followed Roman models in constructing his *Florentine Histories*. He started with general description and worked his way down to detailed descriptions. He concentrated on politics and military adventures, giving detailed, stylized accounts of political debates, diplomatic encounters, and battles. Throughout, he was as concerned to instruct as to get the story straight. The section reproduced here tells disparagingly of the Duke of Athens conquering Florence in 1342, and of the heroic (in Machiavelli's eyes) resistance of the Florentine people.

Machiavelli knew a younger Florentine politician, Francesco Guicciardini (1483–1540), who is less famous today but is generally regarded as a better historian. Guicciardini was also a more facile politician. Son of a wealthy family allied to the Medici, Guicciardini nonetheless served in the Republic and again under his patrons when they returned to power. He was ambassa-dor to the court of Ferdinand of Aragon, and acquired from his experiences a more cosmopolitan view than Machiavelli's. Where Machiavelli never reached beyond the history of the Florentine city-state except for the occasional example, Guicciardini came to see Florence in the context of Italy, and Italy in the context of Europe. His *History of Florence* points outward from the city-state to the entire peninsula. The *History of Italy* deals with the relationships between Italy and France, Germany, Spain, and England, with mention as well of the Swiss, the Turks, the Reformation, the spice trade with Asia, and the discovery of the New World.

Guicciardini remained as focused on the political and military as Machiavelli. Yet the reader can see in Guicciardini's work the beginning of a modern critical consciousness. He spent years mining family archives and the archives of the pope. Where Machiavelli accepted stories from ancient historians and from local lore as he received them, Guicciardini was scrupulous and detailed in checking such accounts against available documentary evidence. He was less concerned than his older contemporary with presenting a vivid story or neatly crafted argument, and much more concerned with factual accuracy. The selection reproduced here, from Book Nine of the *History of Italy*, tells of the attempt of the warrior-pope Julius II to expel the French barbarians from Italy in 1511, and shows Guicciardini's attention to detail and to judgments regarding moral character.

Florentine Histories[1]

Machiavelli

Now that the duke had acquired lordship, so as to take away the authority of those who were accustomed to being defenders of freedom, he prohibited the Signori from gathering at the palace and consigned them to a private house. He took away the ensigns from the Gonfaloniers of the companies of the people; he removed the orders of justice against the great, freed the prisoners from the jails, had the Bardi and the Frescobaldi returned from exile, forbade anyone to carry arms; and to defend himself better from those inside, he made himself a friend to those outside. He greatly benefited the Aretines, therefore, and all others subject to the Florentines; he made peace with the Pisans, even though he had been made prince so as to make war on them; he canceled the bills of those merchants who had lent money to the republic in the war against Lucca, increased the old taxes and created new ones, took all authority away from the Signori and sought advice from Messer Baglione da Perugia and Messer Guglieomo d'Assisi, his rectors, and Messer Cerrettieri Bisdomini. The assessments he levied on citizens were heavy and his sentences unjust, and the severity and humanity that he had feigned were converted into arrogance and cruelty, whence many great citizens and popular nobles were either fined or killed, or tortured in new modes. And, lest he behave better outside than inside, he ordered six rectors for the countryside, who beat and despoiled the peasants. He kept the great under suspicion even though he had been benefited by them and had returned to many of them their fatherland, for he could not believe that the generous spirits usually found in the nobility could be content in obedience to him; and so he turned to benefiting the plebs, thinking that with their favors and with foreign arms he could preserve the tyranny. Therefore, when the month of May came, a time in which peoples are wont to celebrate, he made more companies of the plebs and the lesser people, to which, honored with splendid titles, he gave ensigns and money: so one part of them went about the city celebrating and the other accepted the celebrations with very great pomp. As the fame of his new lordship spread, many of French blood came to seek him out, and he gave them all positions as his most trusted men, so that Florence in a short time became subject not only to the French but to their customs and their dress; for the men and women imitated them without any regard to civil life or to any shame. But above all else, what displeased was the violence that he and his men did, without any respect, to the women.

Thus did citizens live full of indignation as they saw the majesty of their state ruined, the orders laid waste, the laws annulled, every decent being corrupted, all civil modesty eliminated; for those accustomed to not seeing any regal pomp were unable to meet him without sorrow, surrounded by his armed satellites on foot and on horse. For when they saw their shame nearer, they were compelled of necessity to honor the one they especially hated. To this was added fear as they saw the frequent deaths and continuing assessments with which he impoverished and consumed the city. Such indignation and fears were known to the duke and feared by him; nonetheless, he wished to show everyone he believed himself loved. Thus it happened that when Matteo di Morozzo, either to ingratiate himself with him or to free himself from danger, revealed to him that the Medici family with some others had conspired against him, the duke not only did not investigate the thing but had the discloser put to death miserably. With this course he took away spirit from those who might seek to warn him for his safety and gave it to those who might wish his ruin. He also had the tongue of Bettone Cini cut out with such cruelty that he died of it, for having censured the assessments that were levied on the citizens. This increased the indignation of the citizens and their hatred of the duke, for the city was accustomed to do and to speak about everything and with every license and could not bear to have its hands tied and its mouth sealed. Thus the indignation and hatred grew to such a degree that they would have inflamed not only the Florentines, who do not know how to maintain freedom and are unable to bear slavery, but any servile people to recover their freedom. Wherefore many citizens of every quality resolved to lose their lives or get back their freedom; and in three parties of three sorts of citizens three conspiracies were made: the great, the people, and the artisans. They were moved, apart from universal causes, because it appeared to the great that they were not getting back the state; to the people, that they had lost it; and to the artisans, that they were losing their earnings.

The archbishop of Florence, Messer Agnolo Acciaiuoli, had already exalted the deeds of the duke in his sermons and had got great favors from the people for him. But after he saw him a lord and recognized his tyrannical ways, it appeared to him that he had deceived his fatherland; and to amend the error he had committed, he thought he had no other remedy than to have the hand that had inflicted the wound heal it. He made himself head of the first and strongest conspiracy, in which were the Bardi, Rossi, Frescobaldi, Scali, Altoviti, Magalotti, Strozzi, and Mancini. Messers Manno and Corso Donati were princes of one of the other two, and with them were the Pazzi, Cavicciuli, Cerchi, and Albizzi. In the third, Antonio Adimari was the first, and with him were the Medici, Bordoni, Rucellai, and Aldobrandini. These men thought about killing the duke in the house of the Albizzi, where they believed he might go on the day of San Giovanni to see the horse races, but since he did not go, they did not succeed. They thought of attacking him as he went for a walk in the city, but they saw that this mode was difficult because he went about well accompanied and armed and always varied his route so that there could be no certain place to wait for him. They reasoned about killing him at the councils, but it appeared to them that even if they killed him they would be left at the discretion of his forces. While these things were being discussed among the conspirators, Antonio Adimari revealed himself to some of his Sienese friends so as to get men from them by showing them a part of the conspirators and affirming that the whole city was prepared to free itself. Whereupon one of them passed the thing along to Messer Francesco Brunelleschi, not to expose it but in the belief that he too was one of the conspirators. Messer Francesco, either out of fear for himself or out of the hatred he bore for the others, revealed everything to the duke; hence Pagolo del Mazzeca and Simone da Monterappoli were taken. They frightened the duke by revealing the quality and quantity of the conspirators, and he was advised to summon them rather than arrest them, because if they should flee, it would be possible to secure himself against them without scandal by their exile. So the duke had Antonio Adimari summoned, who, trusting in his companions, immediately appeared. He was detained. The duke was advised by Messer Francesco Brunelleschi and Messer Uguccione Buondelmonte to ride through the town armed and to have those who had been arrested put to death, but this was not agreeable to him as it appeared to him that for so many enemies his forces were small. Yet he took another course by which, if it had succeeded, he would have secured himself against his enemies and provided himself with forces. The duke was accustomed to summon citizens to advise him on current cases; so having sent outside to provide men, he made a list of three hundred citizens and had his sergeants summon them under color of wanting to consult with them. Then, when they would have been brought together, he planned to eliminate them either by death or by prison. The capture of Antonio Adimari and the sending for men, which could not be done secretly, had frightened the citizens, especially the guilty ones, hence the boldest refused to obey. And because each had read the list, they sought each other out and inspired each other to take up arms, preferring to die like men, arms in hand, than to be led like cattle to the slaughterhouse. Thus, in a few hours, all three conspiracies were revealed to each other and they resolved to start a tumult in the Mercato Vecchio on the following day, which was the 26th of July, 1343, and after that to arm themselves and to call the people to freedom.

History of Italy[2]

Julius at the Siege of Mirandola

Guicciardini

The beginning of the new year [1511] was made memorable by an unexpected occurrence, something unheard of throughout the centuries. For, the attack against Mirandola seeming in Julius' eyes to be proceeding slowly; and attributing this partly to the inexperience and partly to the perfidy of his captains, and especially his nephew, and blaming them for what largely was the result of many difficulties, he decided to speed up the campaign by his own presence. Setting the importunity and violence of his mind above all other considerations, Julius was not restrained by the consideration of how unworthy it was for the majesty of so high a position, that the Roman pontiff should lead armies in person against Christian towns; nor how dangerous this was, scorning the reputation and judgment that the entire world would make of him, and lending apparent reason and almost justification to those who were seeking to convoke the Council and arouse the princes of Christendom against him, on the grounds primarily that his rule was pernicious to the Church and his failings scandalous and incorrigible. Such were the words resounding throughout the papal court; everyone was astonished; everyone criticized him to the utmost, the Venetian ambassadors no less than the others; the cardinals begged him with the greatest insistence not to go. But all these pleas were in vain, and vain everyone's persuasions.

Julius departed on the second day of January from Bologna, accompanied by three cardinals. When he arrived at the camp he lodged in a farmer's hut lying within reach of the enemy artillery, no farther than twice an ordinary crossbow's shot from the walls of Mirandola. And there, wearying and exercising his body no less than his mind and his authority, Julius rode almost continually here and there throughout the camp, ordering the proper place-ment of the artillery pieces, of which only a small part had been placed until that day; for almost all military operations were impeded by the bitter weather and almost steady snowfall, and because no amount of diligence was sufficient to keep the artillerymen from fleeing, since besides the bitter weather they were under a great deal of cannon fire from the defenders. Therefore, since it was necessary to build new ramparts and call up new artillerymen to the camp in the places where the artillery had to be set, the Pope went, while these things were being carried out, to Concordia in order not to suffer the hardships of the army during this time. At Concordia, Alberto Pio came to him at the commission of Chaumont [Charles d'Amboise, Marshal of Chaumont, and King Louis XII's governor at Milan] proposing various offers of agreement; but all these were in vain (despite the many goings and comings on both sides) either because of the Pope's usual obdurance, or because Alberto, more suspected all the time, was not carrying out the negotiations with a convincing show of sincerity.

Julius remained at Concordia for a few days; his inveterate impatience bringing him back to the camp: that same ardor whose fires were not in the lightest chilled by the heavy snow which continued to fall from the sky during his march, nor by the bitter cold which his soldiers could scarcely endure. He took lodging in a little church near his artillery and even closer to the wall than had been his former lodging, nor was he satisfied with anything that had been done or was being done, and complained violently about all his captains except Marcantonio Colonna, whom he had summoned again from Modena. And he continued with no less energy moving through the camp, now shouting at this one, now comforting another and acting in all his words and deeds like a military leader, promising his soldiers that if they went about their tasks like men, he would not accept any pact in taking Mirandola, but leave the city for them to sack. And it was certainly a notable thing and very new in men's eyes, that the King of France, a secular prince, still young and very healthy, trained in handling arms, should at that time be reposing in his chambers, and leaving a war waged principally against him, to be led by his captains; and on the other side to see the highest Pontiff, Vicar of Christ on earth, old and infirm and accustomed to comfort and pleasures, personally conducting a war stirred up by him against Christians, and camping in a miserable countryside; where as a leader of soldiers he exposed himself to hardships and perils, retaining of his pontificate nothing but the garb and the name.

By his extreme diligence, by his complaints, promises, and threats, things moved ahead with greater celerity than otherwise; and yet, many difficulties opposing him, they were proceeding slowly withal, what with the small number of sappers and an insufficiency of artillery pieces in the Pope's army (nor were those of the Venetians very large), and also because the gunpowder could accomplish its usual task only with difficulty as a result of the wetness of the season. Those within the walls defended themselves valiantly, led by Alessandro da Trivulzio with four hundred foreign footsoldiers, who supported all dangers with greater resolution because they hoped for help promised by Chaumont. He had been ordered by his King not to permit the Pope to take that town, and had therefore sent for all the Spanish infantrymen who were at Verona, and levied his men from everywhere, continually enlisting footsoldiers. And inducing the Duke of Ferrara to do the same, Chaumont promised to assault the enemy camp before the twentieth of January. But many things made this plan difficult and dangerous: the very limited time he had to gather so many provisions, the opportunity given the enemy to fortify their camp, the difficulty of bringing up artillery, munitions and provisions in so cold a season through terrible roads and the worst snow of many years. And he who should have mitigated these hardships by alertly making up for lost time, augmented them instead. For Chaumont rode suddenly by post to Milan, claiming that he was going there to more swiftly raise money and other necessary provisions; but it was divulged and believed that he had been induced to this sudden departure rather by the love of a Milanese lady; and this sudden departure of his, although he returned quickly, abated the spirits of his soldiers and the hopes of those defending Mirandola. Wherefore many people said openly that Chaumont's hatred against Gianiacopo da Trivulzio was no less harmful perhaps than his negligence or baseness; and that therefore his own passions (as often happens) weighing more with him than his King's welfare, he was pleased that [Trivulzio's] nephews should be deprived of that state [Mirandola].

On the other hand, the Pope spared nothing to gain his victory, roused to greater fury because two of his men had been slain in his kitchen by a cannon shot fired out of the town. This danger caused the Pope to leave that lodging, and then because he could not forebear returning there the next day, he was constrained by new dangers to take the tent of the Cardinal Regino; and those within the walls knowing by chance that the Pope had transferred to that place, directed a big artillery piece against it, not without danger to his life. Finally, the defendants having entirely lost hope of help, the artillery having done great damage, and besides this, the water in the ditches frozen so hard that it could hold up the soldiers, and fearing that they would not be able to resist at the first battle which had been ordered to begin within two days, they sent, on the same day in which Chaumont had promised to join them, ambassadors to the Pope to surrender on condition that everyone's goods and lives be spared.

Although at the beginning, Julius replied that he did not wish to be obliged to spare the lives of the soldiers, yet at last, conquered by the entreaties of all his advisers, he accepted the surrender under the conditions proposed; except that Alesandro da Trivulzio with several of his captains of footsoldiers should remain his prisoners, and that the town should pay him a certain amount of money as recompense for the sack which had been promised the soldiers. Nevertheless, since the soldiers felt that they were due what had been promised them, it was no easy task for the Pope to keep them from sacking it.

This done, the gates being rammed up, the Pope had himself drawn up onto the wall, and from there he descended into the town. The castle yielded at the same time, permission being granted to the Countess to depart with all her goods.

QUESTIONS TO CONSIDER

1. What are Machiavelli's purposes in constructing a history of Florence?
2. How does Guicciardini's greater care with his sources and with historical detail show through in this account of the warrior-pope?
3. To what uses might these two varieties of historical writing be put?

FOR FURTHER READING

Bonadella, Peter E. *Machiavelli and the Art of Renaissance History.* Detroit, MI: Wayne State University Press, 1973.

Gilbert, Felix. *Machiavelli and Guicciardini: Politics and History in Sixteenth-Century Florence.* Princeton, NJ: Princeton University Press, 1965.

Guicciardini, Francesco. *History of Italy and History of Florence.* Trans. Cecil Grayson. New York: Twayne, 1964.

_____ . *Selected Writings.* Trans. Margaret Grayson. Ed. Cecil Grayson. New York: Oxford University Press, 1965.

Jensen, De Lamar. *Machiavelli: Cynic, Patriot, or Political Scientist?* Boston: D. C. Heath, 1960.

Machiavelli, Niccolo. *Discourses on the First Ten Books of Titus Livius.* Trans. Christian E. Detmold. New York: Random House, 1950.

_____ . *Florentine Histories.* Trans. Laura F. Banfield and Harvey C. Mansfield, Jr. Princeton, NJ: Princeton University Press, 1988.

_____ . *The Prince.* Trans. Luigi Ricci. Rev. E. R. P. Vincent. New York: Penguin, 1980; orig. 1952.

Prezzolini, Giuseppe. *Machiavelli.* New York: Farrar, Straus and Giroux, 1967.

NOTES

1. Niccolò Machiavelli, *Florentine Histories*, trans. Laura F. Banfield and Harvey C. Mansfield, Jr. (Princeton, NJ: Princeton University Press, 1988), 94–97.
2. Francesco Guicciardini, *The History of Italy*, trans. Sidney Alexander (New York: Macmillan, 1969), 212–15.

CHAPTER 28

William Bradford

Historian of a Godly Community Overseas

William Bradford
The Granger Collection, New York

E uropeans as they went abroad recorded their adventures for posterity. Bernal Diaz de Castillo immortalized the Spanish conquest of the Aztec civilization. Bartolomé de las Casas told the story of the destruction of America's indigenous population by the Spanish. Manuel de Faria e Sousa wrote of the Portuguese explorations and trade in Africa and Asia. Richard Hakluyt entranced the European peoples with accounts of many people's voyages to the New World. Samuel de Champlain left a widely read record of his own travels. (Chapter 29 gives two accounts by subjected peoples in the Americas).

One of the fine contemporary historians of the European overseas venture was William Bradford (1590–1657), the first permanent resident of British North America to write history (Captain John Smith of Virginia wrote first, but he went back to England). Bradford was a farmer in Nottinghamshire who adopted the radical convictions of a Protestant sect who came to call themselves Pilgrims. Fleeing persecution in England, the sect made its way in 1609 to Holland, a country whose people shared the members' Calvinist convictions. Within a few years they were back in England, then off to the New World in 1620 in search of a safe haven, a place where they might build a model Christian commonwealth. In the New World the group gathered themselves under the Mayflower Compact. In 1621 they elected William Bradford their governor, on the basis of his spiritual devotion, moral probity, and general good sense; they reelected him 30 times. Bradford began *Of Plymouth Plantation* in 1630 and continued writing until 1650, as a record of God's hand at work in the life of his community.

Bradford was both a medieval and a modern Western historian. He referred constantly to God, and to the sense of mission the Pilgrims felt as they moved from England to Holland, back to England, and then to Plymouth Colony in what is now Massachusetts. In this explicit sense of God's hand at work in history (leading God's people and combatting the evil of Satan and his minions), Bradford was not unlike Bede, Luke, or Eusebius. But he was also part of the broader Calvinist movement, which radically remade medieval notions of Christianity. One feels underneath the surface of his account an intimate, personal connection between God and God's people. Unlike medieval writers, there is little sense of the hand of the institutional church in human affairs in any positive sense (the pope is present merely as a foil for those whom Bradford regards as true Christians). What there is, instead of a church universal, is a covenanted community of individual believers— America's first voluntary association.

The form of Bradford's narrative is a chronicle. The sources of information are Bradford's notebooks and his memory. The language is simple and straightforward, giving an intimate feel for the Pilgrims' lives. The following selections tell of the beginnings of the sect, their early persecutions, the voyage of their ship *Mayflower,* and their arrival on the coast of North America.

Of Plymouth Plantation[1]

First I will unfold the causes that led to the foundation of the New Plymouth
Settlement, and the motives of those concerned in it. In order that I may give
an accurate account of the project, I must begin at the very root and rise of it;
and this I shall endeavor to do in a plain style and with singular regard to the
truth, at least as my slender judgment can attain to it.

As is well known, ever since the breaking out of the light of the gospel in
England, which was the first country to be thus enlightened after the gross
darkness of popery had overspread the Christian world, Satan has maintained
various wars against the Saints, from time to time, in different ways—
sometimes by bloody death and cruel torment, at other times by imprison-
ment, banishment, and other wrongs—as if loth that his kingdom should be
overcome, the truth prevail, and the churches of God revert to their ancient
purity, and recover their primitive order, liberty, and beauty. But when he
could not stifle by those means the main truths of the gospel, which began to
take root in many places, watered by the blood of martyrs and blessed from
heaven with a gracious increase, he reverted to his ancient stratagems, used of
old against the first Christians. For when, in those days, the bloody and
barbarous persecutions of the heathen emperors could not stop and subvert
the course of the gospel, which speedily overspread the then best known parts
of the world, he began to sow errors, heresies, and discord amongst the clergy
themselves, working upon the pride and ambition and other frailties to which
all mortals, and even the Saints themselves in some measure, are subject.
Woeful effects followed; not only were there bitter contentions, heart-
burnings, and schisms, but Satan took advantage of them to foist in a number
of vile ceremonies, with many vain canons and decrees, which have been
snares to many poor and peaceable souls to this day.

So, in the early days, Christians suffered as much from internal dissension
as from persecution by the heathen and their emperors, true and orthodox
Christians being oppressed by the Arians [who believed God and Christ were
essentially different from each other] and their heretical accomplices. Socrates
[a fifth-century theologian and historian] bears witness to this in his second
book. His words are these: "Indeed, the violence was no less than that
practiced of old towards the Christians when they were compelled to sacrifice
to idols; for many endured various kinds of torment—often racking and
dismemberment of their joints, confiscation of their goods, or banishment
from their native soil."

Satan has seemed to follow a like method in these later times, ever since the
truth began to spring and spread after the great defection of that man of sin, the
Papal Antichrist. Passing by the infinite examples throughout the world as well
as in our country, when that old serpent found that he could not prevail by fiery
flames and the other cruel torments which he had put in use everywhere in the
days of Queen Mary and before, he then went more closely to work, not merely
to oppress but to ruin and destroy the kingdom of Christ by more secret and
subtle means, and by kindling flames of contention and sowing seeds of strife and
bitter enmity amongst the reformed clergy and laity themselves.

Mr. Foxe records that besides those worthy martyrs and confessors who were burned and otherwise tormented in Queen Mary's days, as many as 800 students and others fled out of England, and formed separate congregations at Wesel, Frankfort, Basel, Emden, Marburg, Strasbourg, Geneva, etc.

Among these bodies of Protestant reformers—especially among those at Frankfort—arose a bitter war of contention and persecution about the ceremonies and the service book and other such popish and anti-Christian stuff, the plague of England to this day. Such practices are like the high places in Israel, which the prophets cried out against; and the better part of the reformers sought to root them out and utterly abandon them, according to the purity of the gospel; while the other part, under veiled pretenses, sought as stiffly to maintain and defend them, for their own advancement. This appears in the account of these contentions published in 1575—a book that deserves to be known.

The one part of reformers endeavored to establish the right worship of God and the discipline of Christ in the Church according to the simplicity of the gospel and without the mixture of men's inventions, and to be ruled by the laws of God's word dispensed by such officers as pastors, teachers, elders, etc., according to the Scriptures.

The other party—the episcopal—under many pretenses, endeavored to maintain the episcopal dignity after the popish manner—with all its courts, canons, and ceremonies; its livings, revenues, subordinate officers, and other means of upholding their anti-Christian greatness, and of enabling them with lordly and tyrannous power to persecute the poor servants of God. The fight was so bitter that neither the honor of God, the persecution to which both parties were subjected, nor the mediation of Mr. Calvin and other worthies, could prevail with the episcopal party. They proceeded by all means to disturb the peace of this poor persecuted church of dissenters, even so far as to accuse (very unjustly and ungodly, yet prelate-like) some of its chief members with rebellion and high treason against the Emperor, and other such crimes.

* * *

Those reformers who saw the evil of these things, and whose hearts the Lord had touched with heavenly zeal for His truth, shook off this yoke of anti-Christian bondage and as the Lord's free people joined themselves together by covenant as a church, in the fellowship of the gospel to walk in all His ways, made known, or to be made known to them, according to their best endeavors, whatever it should cost them, the Lord assisting them. And that it cost them something, the ensuing history will declare.

These people became two distinct bodies of churches and congregated separately; for they came from various towns and villages about the borders of Nottinghamshire, Lincolnshire, and Yorkshire. One of these churches was led by Mr. John Smyth, a man of able gifts, and a good preacher, who was afterwards made pastor; but later, falling into some errors in the Low Countries, most of its adherents buried themselves and their names. To the other church, which is the subject of this discourse, belonged besides other worthy men, Mr. Richard Clyfton, a grave and reverend preacher, who by his pains and diligence had done much good, and under God had been the means of the conversion of many; also that famous and worthy man, Mr. John Robinson, who was afterwards their pastor for many years, till the Lord took him away; also Mr. William Brewster, a reverend man, who was afterwards chosen an elder of the church, and lived with them till old age.

But after the events referred to above, they were not long permitted to remain in peace. They were hunted and persecuted on every side, until their former afflictions were but as fleabitings in comparison. Some were clapped into prison; others had their houses watched night and day, and escaped with difficulty; and most were obliged to fly, and leave their homes and means of livelihood. Yet these and many other even severer trials which afterwards befell them, being only what they expected, they were able to bear by the assistance of God's grace and spirit. However, being thus molested, and seeing that there was no hope of their remaining there, they resolved by consent to go into the Low Countries, where they heard there was freedom of religion for all; and it was said that many from London and other parts of the country, who had been exiled and persecuted for the same cause, had gone to live at Amsterdam and elsewhere in the Netherlands. So after about a year, having kept their meeting for the worship of God every Sabbath in one place or another, notwithstanding the diligence and malice of their adversaries, seeing that they could no longer continue under such circumstances, they resolved to get over to Holland as soon as they could—which was in the years 1607 and 1608.

*   *   *

These troubles being over, and all being together in the one ship, they put to sea again on September 6th [1620] with a prosperous wind, which continued for several days and was some encouragement to them, though, as usual, many were afflicted with seasickness. I must not omit to mention here a special example of God's providence. There was an insolent and very profane young man—one of the sailors, which made him the more overbearing—who was always harassing the poor people in their sickness, and cursing them daily with grievous execrations, and did not hesitate to tell them that he hoped to help throw half of them overboard before they came to their journey's end. If he were gently reproved by anyone, he would curse and swear most bitterly. But it pleased God, before they came half seas over, to smite the young man with a grievous disease, of which he died in a desperate manner, and so was himself the first to be thrown overboard. Thus his curses fell upon his own head, which astonished all his mates for they saw it was the just hand of God upon him.

After they had enjoyed fair winds and weather for some time, they encountered cross winds and many fierce storms by which the ship was much shaken and her upper works made very leaky. One of the main beams amidships was bent and cracked, which made them afraid that she might not be able to complete the voyage. So some of the chief of the voyagers, seeing that the sailors doubted the efficiency of the ship, entered into serious consultation with the captain and officers, to weigh the dangers betimes and rather to return than to cast themselves into desperate and inevitable peril.

Indeed there was great difference of opinion among the crew themselves. They wished to do whatever could be done for the sake of their wages, being now half way over; on the other hand they were loth to risk their lives too desperately. But at length all opinions, the captain's and the others' included agreed that the ship was sound under the water-line, and as for the buckling of the main beam, there was a great iron screw the passengers brought out of Holland, by which the beam could be raised into its place; and the carpenter affirmed that with a post put under it, set firm in the lower deck, and otherwise fastened, he could make it hold. As for the decks and upper works, they said they would calk them as well as they could; and though with the working of the ship they would not long keep stanch, yet there would otherwise be no great danger, if they did not overpress her with sail.

So they committed themselves to the will of God, and resolved to proceed. In several of these storms the wind was so strong and the seas so high that they could not carry a knot of sail, but were forced to hull for many days. Once, as they thus lay at hull in a terrible storm, a strong young man, called John Howland, coming on deck was thrown into the sea; but it pleased God that he caught hold of the topsail halliards which hung overboard and ran out at length; but he kept his hold, though he was several fathoms under water, till he was hauled up by the rope, and then with a boathook helped into the ship and saved; and though he was somewhat ill from it he lived many years and became a profitable member both of the church and commonwealth. In all the voyage only one of the passengers died, and that was William Button, a youth, servant to Samuel Fuller, when they were nearing the coast. But to be brief, after long beating at sea, on November 11th they fell in with a part of the land called Cape Cod, at which they were not a little joyful. After some deliberation among themselves and with the captain, they tacked about and resolved to stand for the southward, the wind and weather being fair, to find some place near Hudson's River for their habitation. But after they had kept that course about half a day, they met with dangerous shoals and roaring breakers, and as they conceived themselves in great danger—the wind falling—they resolved to bear again for the Cape, and thought themselves happy to get out of danger before night overtook them, as by God's providence they did. Next day they got into the bay, where they rode in safety.

*   *   *

Having found a good haven and being brought safely in sight of land, they fell upon their knees and blessed the God of Heaven who had brought them over the vast and furious ocean, and delivered them from all the perils and miseries of it, again to set their feet upon the firm and stable earth, their proper element. And no marvel that they were thus joyful, when the wise Seneca was so affected with sailing a few miles on the coast of his own Italy that he affirmed he had rather taken twenty years to make his way by land, than to go by sea to any place in however short a time—so tedious and dreadful it was to him.

But here I cannot but make a pause, and stand half amazed at this poor people's present condition; and so I think will the reader, too, when he considers it well. Having thus passed the vast ocean, and that sea of troubles before while they were making their preparations, they now had no friends to welcome them, nor inns to entertain and refresh their weatherbeaten bodies, nor houses—much less towns—to repair to.

It is recorded in Scripture (Acts, xxviii) as a mercy to the Apostle and his shipwrecked crew, that the barbarians showed them no small kindness in refreshing them; but these savage barbarians when they met with them (as will appear) were readier to fill their sides full of arrows than otherwise! As for the season, it was winter, and those who have experienced the winters of the country know them to be sharp and severe, and subject to fierce storms, when it is dangerous to travel to known places—much more to search an unknown coast. Besides, what could they see but a desolate wilderness, full of wild beasts and wild men; and what multitude there might be of them they knew not! Neither could they, as it were, go up to the top of Pisgah, to view from this wilderness a more goodly country to feed their hopes; for which way soever they turned their eyes (save upward to the heavens!) they could gain little solace from any outward objects. Summer being done, all things turned upon them a weatherbeaten face; and the whole country, full of woods and thickets, presented a wild and savage view.

If they looked behind them, there was the mighty ocean which they had passed, and was now a gulf separating them from all civilized parts of the world. If it be said that they had their ship to turn to, it is true; but what did they hear daily from the captain and crew? That they should quickly look out for a place with their shallop, where they would be not far off; for the season was such that the captain would not approach nearer to the shore till a harbor had been discovered which he could enter safely; and that the food was being consumed apace, but he must and would keep sufficient for the return voyage. It was even muttered by some of the crew that if they did not find a place in time, they would turn them and their goods ashore and leave them.

Let it be remembered, too, what small hope of further assistance from England they had left behind them, to support their courage in this sad condition and the trials they were under; for how the case stood between the settlers and the merchants [who had bankrolled the venture] has already been described. It is true, indeed, that the affection and love of their brethren at Leyden towards them was cordial and unbroken; but they had little power to help them or themselves.

What, then, could now sustain them but the spirit of God, and His grace? Ought not the children of their fathers rightly to say: Our fathers were Englishmen who came over the great ocean, and were ready to perish in this wilderness; but they cried unto the Lord, and He heard their voice, and looked on their adversity. . . . Let them therefore praise the Lord, because He is good, and His mercies endure forever. Yea, let them that have been redeemed of the Lord, show how He hath delivered them from the hand of the oppressor. When they wandered forth into the desert wilderness, out of the way, and found no city to dwell in, both hungry and thirsty, their soul was overwhelmed in them. Let them confess before the Lord His loving kindness, and His wonderful works before the sons of men!

QUESTIONS TO CONSIDER

1. How does Bradford convey the European sense of godly mission in his account of Plymouth Plantation?
2. How does Bradford's sense of Christianity differ from the earlier Christian writers we have encountered?
3. How might a Native American witness have described the Pilgrims' arrival in North America?

FOR FURTHER READING

Champlain, Samuel de. *Voyages and Explorations of Samuel de Champlain, 1604–1616.* Trans. Annie Nettlebone Bourne. New York: Allerton, 1922.

Diaz de Castillo, Bernal. *The Discovery and Conquest of Mexico, 1517–1521.* Trans. A. P. Maudslay. New York: Farrar, Straus and Cudahy, 1956.

Faria e Sousa, Manuel de. *The Portuguese Asia.* 3 vols. Trans. John Stevens. Farnborough, U.K.: Gregg, 1971.

Gay, Peter. *A Loss of Mastery: Puritan Historians in Colonial America.* Berkeley, CA: University of California Press, 1966.

Hakluyt, Richard. *Voyages and Documents.* New York: Oxford University Press, 1958.

Las Casas, Bartolomé. *In Defense of the Indians.* Trans. Stafford Poole. DeKalb, IL: Northern Illinois University Press, 1992.

Miller, Perry. *The New England Mind: From Colony to Province.* Cambridge, MA: Harvard University Press, 1954.

———. *The New England Mind: The Seventeenth Century.* Cambridge, MA: Harvard University Press, 1954.

Simpson, Alan. *Puritanism in Old and New England.* Chicago: University of Chicago Press, 1952.

Smith, John. *The General Historie of Virginia, New-England and the Summer Isles.* 1624.

NOTES

1. William Bradford, *Of Plymouth Plantation,* trans. Harold Paget (Toronto: Van Nostrand, 1948), 3–6, 10–12, 82–87.

CHAPTER 29

Aztec and Mayan Chronicles

The Victims Speak

Aztec and Mayan Chronicles
© 1993 North Wind Pictures

Columbus discovered America in 1492. Or, to take another perspective, a group of Native Americans found him wandering lost on their shores, jabbering about "Cipangu" (Japan) and the riches of the East. We all know who won this encounter and who suffered from it. Until recently, though, we have only seen history through the winners' eyes. Victors always write the official histories, but victims, too, have their ways of seeing. How did the Spanish conquest look to the native peoples of the Americas?

For a conquest it was. The poorly organized tribes of the Caribbean stood no chance against the invaders. Stone fled before steel, bows and arrows fell before cannon and musket, foot soldiers quailed before horses and armor. Within a generation, brutality and disease had wiped out the island population so thoroughly that the Spanish had to import African slaves to work their plantations. Thus began a second European conquest, of Africa, that culminated three centuries later in the colonial partition of that continent.

Yet the militaristic societies of Mexico and Peru also fell to this attack, and more quickly than any could have imagined. Cortés conquered the Aztecs with but six hundred men—supported, it is true, by many of the Aztecs' rebellious subjects. Inca resistance was crushed by Pizarro's tiny band of cutthroats, without much outside aid. Pedro de Alvarado decimated the Mayan kingdoms, partly by pitting one against another, and partly by murdering key Mayan leaders, thus demoralizing the population.

Disease also played a part. New World peoples had been isolated from the Old World for some 10,000 years, long enough to have lost any immunity to Old World infections. The world's greatest biological exchange sent maize, potatoes, and other crops eastward to feed the Europeans; it also sent smallpox, measles, and influenza westward, to kill the Indians. Perhaps 14 epidemics swept through Mexico between 1520 and 1600; as many as 17 hit Peru. The Spanish chronicler Motolinía claimed that in many areas of Mexico more than half the population died. A Mayan resident of the Yucatan wrote in the *Book of Chilam Balam* that before the Spanish came, "There was then no sickness; they had no aching bones; they had then no high fever; they had then no smallpox; they had then no burning chest. . . . At that time the course of humanity was orderly. The foreigners made it otherwise when they arrived here."

Between disease and barbarity, scholars today estimate that the population of central Mexico dropped from about 25 million to 16.8 million within 10 years of the conquest. The Caribbean was almost totally depopulated. Figures are harder to obtain from areas such as Peru, where uncountable thousands died in an epidemic just a few years before Pizarro's invasion. The impact was enormous everywhere. Indigenous societies melted before the onslaught.

Not all the invaders sought riches, though most did. Christian friars came with them, to save souls. Some defended the natives, protesting their ill treatment to the crown. Fray Bartolomé de las Casas, for example, urged the king to control the *conquistadores* and to take the remaining Indians under his personal protection. More often, though, the friars destroyed native temples and holy places, burned their manuscripts, and persecuted their religious leaders. A contemporary said of Fray Diego de Landa, for example, that "Instead of doctrine, the Indians have been given miserable tortures; instead of revealing God to them, they have been driven to despair."

We do not have to rely on the Spanish for our picture of the invasion. We have native words as well. Despite the Spanish attempt to snuff out Indian culture, some pre-Conquest manuscripts survive. As was explained in Chapter 18, the earliest of these are in picture-writing: glyphic histories of the pre-Columbian era. Only a few escaped the Spanish flames. But the Spanish themselves taught the native elites to write their own languages with Spanish script. Dozens of manuscripts in Nahuatl, Quiché, Cakchiquel, and other languages stem from these times.

Not all of these manuscripts are histories; and not all the histories present an Indian point of view. The Spanish, after all, colonized the Indians' minds as much as they colonized their lands. Most did not want their disciples to put forth independent ideas.

Yet some did, and some manuscripts see things through native eyes. Fray Bernardino de Sahagún, for example, helped his Indian acolytes interview those who saw Cortés's invasion and organize their memories into a native history. Written between 1555 and 1575, it appeared as Book 12 of his *General History of the Things of New Spain*. Scholars know this work as *Florentine Codex* because the best preserved copy is in the Biblioteca Medicea-Laurenziana in Florence, Italy. Other copies of the book were made, though most have been lost. The first of the following passages comes from that *Codex*.

A similar account comes from Guatemala. A group of Indians wrote it in the late 1500s in Cakchiquel using Spanish script. For many years it lay in the village of Sololá, in the highlands overlooking Lake Atitlán. It passed through various hands until the mid-nineteenth century, when the French Abbé Brasseur de Bourbourg acquired it. He translated it into French, but badly. At his death, a North American scholar brought it to the University of Pennsylvania museum, where it now resides.

Both accounts describe the Spanish invasion from native points of view, show the wonder with which the Aztecs and Mayans viewed the Spanish, and depict the latter's greed and cruelty. They do not paint a pretty picture of the Spanish conquest, but for the natives, there was little positive to portray. These accounts tell of the deaths of two proud civilizations at the hands of barbarians.

The Fall of México[1]

Fifth Chapter

Here is related what came to pass when the messengers of Moctezuma went aboard the boat of Don Hernando Cortés.

Thereupon they climbed up. They bore in their arms the array [of the gods]. When they had proceeded to go up into the boat, each in his turn disposed himself to kiss the earth before the Captain. Having done so, they besought and said unto him:

"Let the god deign to hear: for his vassal, Moctezuma, who guardeth over Mexico for him, prayeth to him. For [so] he speaketh: 'The god hath suffered, he is weary [from travel].' "

Upon this, they adorned the Captain himself; they put on him the turquoise mosaic serpent mask; with it went the quetzal feather head fan; and with it went—in it they had set and with it went hanging—the green stone ear plugs in the form of serpents. And they clad him in the sleeveless jacket; they put the sleeveless jacket upon him. And they put the necklace upon him: the plaited green stone neck band in the midst of which lay the golden disc. With this they bound, on the small of his back, the mirror for the small of the back. Also with it they laid upon his back the cape named *tzitzilli*. And about [the calf of] his leg they placed the green stone band with the golden shells. And they gave him, and placed upon his arm, the shield with lines of gold and shells crossing, on whose [lower] rim went spread quetzal feathers and a quetzal feather flag. And before him they set the obsidian sandals.

And the other three sets of adornment, the array of the gods, they only laid in rows and placed in order before him.

And when this had been done, the Captain said to them: "Are these perchance all your gifts, your greetings?"

They answered: "This is all with which we came, O our lord."

Then the Captain commanded that they be bound. They fastened irons about their ankles and necks. This done, then they shot the great lombard gun. And the messengers then, verily, fainted and swooned. One by one, they fell to the deck; swaying they went down, and knew no more. And the Spaniards lifted and raised them up so that they sat, and made them drink wine. Thereupon they served them food and made them eat, that they might catch their breath and revive.

And when this had come to pass, then the Captain said to them: "Hearken: I have known and heard it said that these Mexicans are very strong, exceedingly brave, and great victors. Supposedly, one Mexican can pursue, overpower, conquer, and rout even ten, even twenty of his foes. And now I would satisfy my doubts. I would behold and test how strong and powerful you are."

Then he gave them leather shields, and iron swords, and iron lances.

"And this, early in the morning, at dawn, will come to pass: we shall fight and join the fray among ourselves, and try our strength among ourselves, [to see] who will fall."

They answered the Captain and said to him: "Let the lord hear: his vassal Moctezuma hath not thus commanded us [to act]. We have come to do only this one thing—to greet and salute [our lord]. It is not our charge [to do] what the lord requireth. For if we do so, Moctezuma would therefore be wroth, and might destroy us for it."

Then the Captain said: "Nay, for it must be [as I say]. I wish to see and marvel [at your prowess]. For this is known in Castile; it is told that you are very powerful and valiant. Early in the morning shall ye eat. I also shall eat. [Then] verily shall you gird yourselves [for combat]."

Sixth Chapter

Here is told how the messengers of Moctezuma returned here to Mexico and came to relate to Moctezuma that which they had seen.

Thereupon [Cortés] dismissed them, and let them descend to their boats. And when they had climbed down into the boats, they rowed with great force. Mightily did they ply their oars. Some paddled with their hands.

Fleeing with all their force, they came saying to one another: "O warriors, [use] all your strength! Row with haste, lest something here overtake us—lest something here befall us!"

Speedily they hastened to reach by water the place called Xicalanco; there they no more than quickly caught their breath, that once again they might with energy hasten on. Then they came to reach Tecpan tlayacac, whereupon they also hastened and hurried on, and soon came to reach Cuetlaxtlan. [From there] they likewise departed in haste, [having] in this place taken some rest.

And [those] of Cuetlaxtlan said to them: "Rest yet but a brief day; catch your breath!"

But they replied to them: "Nay, we may only go on swiftly. We must give the news to the lord, the ruler Moctezuma. We must tell him what we have seen, which is terrifying—the like of which hath never been seen. Had you, perchance, already, ere now, heard of it?"

Then they speedily departed from there and soon came to reach Mexico. It was deep night when they went reaching [the city]; they came in here quite by night.

And when this was happening, [Moctezuma] could enjoy no sleep, no good. Never could one speak to him. That which he did [was] only as if it were in vain. Ofttimes he sighed; he was spent, downcast. He felt delight in no savory morsel, joy, or pleasure.

Wherefore he said: "What will now become of us? Who, forsooth, standeth [in command]? Alas, until now, I. In great torment is my heart, as if run through with chili water, so that it burneth and smarteth. Where, in truth, [may we turn], O our lord ?"

Then [the messengers] commanded those who watched; they said to those at the head of the guard "Even though he sleepeth, tell him: 'Lo, they who thou hast sent over the water have come!' "

And when they went to tell him, then he replied "I shall not hear it here; I shall hear it in the Coacalli. There let them go." And he commanded and said: "Let two captives be covered with chalk."

And then the messengers went to the Coacalli and also the noble Moctezuma himself.

Thereupon, before them, were slain the captives; they slashed open their breasts; they sprinkled the messengers with their blood. For this reason did they so do: that they had traveled into very perilous places; that they had gone to see—had looked in the faces and at the heads of, and had verily spoken to—the gods.

Seventh Chapter

In which is related the account by which the messengers informed Moctezuma of the boat which they had gone to see.

And after this, they then informed Moctezuma; they told him how they had gone in astonishment; and they showed him what their food was like.

And when he had heard how the messengers reported, he was exceeding fearful and terror-struck. And much did he marvel at their food.

Yet more was he frightened when he heard how [the shot] discharged, at [the Spaniards'] command, from the gun; how it resounded like thunder when it went off. Indeed, it overpowered one; it deafened our ears. And when it discharged, something like a round pellet came forth from within. Fire went scattered forth; sparks showered forth. And its smoke smelled very foul; it had a fetid odor which, verily, wounded the head. And when [the pellet] struck [a] mountain, [it was] as if it fell apart and crumbled. And when it struck a tree, it splintered, seeming to vanish as if someone blew it away.

All iron was their war array. They clothed themselves in iron. They covered their heads with iron. Iron were their swords. Iron were their crossbows. Iron were their shields. Iron were their lances.

And their deer, which bore them upon their backs, were as high as roof-tops.

And they covered all parts of their bodies. Alone to be seen were their faces very white. They had eyes like chalk; they had yellow hair, although the hair of some was black. Long were their beards, and also yellow; they were yellow-bearded. [The hair of the Negroes] was kinky and curly.

And their food was like lords' food—very large, and white; not heavy like [tortillas, but] like the stalks of maize plants—as if of ground maize stalks; it tasted a little sweet, a little honeyed—it tasted honeyed, it tasted sweet.

And their dogs were very large. They had ears doubled over: great hanging jowls; blazing eyes—flaming yellow, fiery yellow eyes; thin flanks, with ribs showing; and gaunt stomachs. [They were] very tall and fierce. They went about panting, with tongues hanging. They were spotted like ocelots; they had spots.

And when Moctezuma heard this, he was filled with a great dread, as if he were swooning. His soul was sickened, his heart was anguished.

Eighth Chapter

In which is told how Moctezuma sent the magicians, wizards, and soothsayers so that they might do something to the Spaniards.

Then Moctezuma sent emissaries. He dispatched various evil men—soothsayers and magicians. And he sent the constables, hardy [warriors], chieftains, to purvey [to the Spaniards] all they might need of food: turkeys, eggs, white tortillas, and all they might ask for as well as whatsoever might satisfy their hearts' desire. They were to watch them well. He sent captives, so that they might be prepared if perchance [the Spaniards] would drink their blood. And just so did the messengers do.

And when [the Spaniards] beheld this, their stomachs turned. They spat; they blinked; they shut their eyes and shook their heads. For the food, which they had sprinkled and spattered with blood, sickened and revolted them. For strongly did it reek of blood.

And thus had Moctezuma provided, for he thought them gods; he took them for gods; he paid them reverence as gods. For they were called and named "gods come from the heavens." And the black ones were said to be black gods.

*   *   *

And it is told why Moctezuma sent magicians and soothsayers—that they might behold what kind [of men] they were, and that perchance they might bewitch and cast a spell over them. Perhaps they might blow them away, or enchant them. Mayhap they might cast something at them, or they might with some words of the Evil One, utter an incantation over them, so that they might sicken and die, or else because of it turn back.

But these, when they performed their charge and commission upon the Spaniards, were at once powerless. Nothing could they do.

Then they quickly returned and came to tell Moctezuma what they were like and how strong they were: "We cannot contend against them; we are as nothing."

Then Moctezuma commanded sternly, charged, enjoined, and ordered on pain of death, that the stewards and all the noblemen and constables should see to it that [the Spaniards] be cared for in all that they might need.

And when [the Spaniards] had crossed over to the land, when finally they came, when already they moved, proceeded, and marched ahead, they were well cared for; they were honored. They passed from hand to hand as they took their way. Much was done for them.

*   *   *

Twenty-ninth Chapter

Here is related how the plague came, named smallpox, of which the natives died, when the Spaniards set forth from Mexico.

And [even] before the Spaniards had risen against us, a pestilence first came to be prevalent: the smallpox. It was [the month of] Tepeilhuitl when it began, and it spread over the people as great destruction. Some it quite covered [with pustules] on all parts—their faces, their heads, their breasts, etc. There was great havoc. Very many died of it. They could not walk; they only lay in their resting places and beds. They could not move; they could not stir; they could not change position, nor lie on one side, nor face down, nor on their backs. And if they stirred, much did they cry out. Great was its destruction. Covered, mantled with pustules, very many people died of them. And very many starved; there was death from hunger, [for] none could take care of [the sick]; nothing could be done for them.

And on some the pustules were widely separated; they suffered not greatly, neither did many [of them] die. Yet many people were marred by them on their faces; one's face or nose was pitted. Some lost their eyes; they were blinded.

At this time, this pestilence prevailed sixty days, sixty day signs. When it left, when it abated, when there was recovery and the return of life, the plague had already moved toward Chalco, whereby many were disabled—not, however, completely crippled. When it came to be prevalent, [it was the month of] Teotl eco. And when it went, weakened, it was Panquetzaliztli. Then the Mexicans, the chieftains, could revive.

And after this, then the Spaniards came; they marched from Texcoco. By way of Quauhtitlan they set out, and quartered themselves at Tlacopan. There then the task was divided; their routes were there separated. Pedro de Alvarado's charge became the road leading into Tlatilulco. And the Marquis went to and established quarters at Coyoacan, and it became the Marquis' charge—as well as the road from Acachinanco which led into Tenochtitlan; for the Marquis knew that those of Tenochtitlan were great warriors, great chieftains.

And at Nextlatilco, or Iliacac, there in truth first came the fighting, when they quickly came to and reached Nonoalco. The chieftains came pursuing them. None of the Mexicans died. Then the Spaniards turned back. The chieftains, who fought valiantly by boat, the warboatmen, shot darts at them. Their darts rained upon the Spaniards. They then entered [Nonoalco]. And the Marquis thereupon threw himself upon those of Tenochtitlan; he proceeded along the Acachinanco road. Many times, in truth, there was battle, and the Mexicans contended against him.

The Annals of the Cakchiquels[2]

The Arrival of the Spaniards at Xetulul

During this year the Spaniards arrived. Forty-nine years ago the Spaniards came to Xepit and Xetulul.

On the day 1 Ganel [February 20, 1524] the Quichés were destroyed by the Spaniards. Their chief, he who was called Tunatiuh Avilantaro [Pedro de Alvarado], conquered all the people. Their faces were not known before that time. Until a short time ago the wood and the stone were worshiped.

Having arrived at Xelahub, they defeated the Quichés; all the Quiché who had gone out to meet the Spaniards were exterminated. Then the Quichés were destroyed before Xelahub.

Then [the Spaniards] went forth to the city of Gumarcaah, where they were received by the kings, the Ahpop and the Ahpop Qamahay, and the Quichés paid them tribute. Soon the kings were tortured by Tunatiuh.

On the day 4 Qat [March 7, 1524] the kings Ahpop and Ahpop Qamahay were burned by Tunatiuh. The heart of Tunatiuh was without compassion for the people during the war. Soon a messenger from Tunatiuh came before the [Cakchiquel] kings to ask them to send him soldiers: "Let the warriors of the Ahpozotzil and the Ahpoxahil come to kill the Quichés," the messenger said to the kings. The order of Tunatiuh was instantly obeyed, and two thousand soldiers marched to the slaughter of the Quichés.

Only men of the city went; the other warriors did not go down to present themselves before the kings. The soldiers went three times only to collect tribute from the Quichés. We also went to collect it for Tunatiuh, oh my sons.

How They Came to Yximché

On the day 1 Hunahpu [April 12, 1524] the Spaniards came to the city of Yximché; their chief was called Tunatiuh. The kings Belehe Qat and Cahi Ymox went at once to meet Tunatiuh. The heart of Tunatiuh was well disposed toward the kings when he came to the city. There had been no fight and Tunatiuh was pleased when he arrived at Yximché. In this manner the Castilians arrived of yore, oh, my sons! In truth they inspired fear when they arrived. Their faces were strange. The lords took them for gods. We ourselves, your father, went to see them when they came into Yximché.

Tunatiuh slept in the house of Tzupam. On the following day the chief appeared, frightening the warriors, and went toward the residence where the kings were. "Why do you make war upon me when I can make it upon you?" he said. And the kings answered: "It is not so, because in that way many men would die. You have seen the remains there in the ravines." And then he entered the house of the chief Chicbal.

Then Tunatiuh asked the kings what enemies they had. The kings answered: "Our enemies are two, oh, Lord: the Zutuhils and [those of] Panatacat. Thus the kings said to him. Only five days later Tunatiuh left the city. The Zutuhils were conquered then by the Spaniards. On the day 7 Camey [April 18, 1524] the Zutuhils were destroyed by Tunatiuh.

Twenty-five days after his arrival in the city, Tunatiuh departed for Cuzcatan, destroying Atacat on the way. On the day 2 Queh [May 9] the Spaniards killed those of Atacat. All the warriors and their Mexicans went with Tunatiuh to the conquest.

On the day 10 Hunahpu [July 21, 1524] he returned from Cuzcatan; it was two months after he left for Cuzcatan when he arrived at the city. Tunatiuh then asked for one of the daughters of the king and the lords gave her to Tunatiuh.

The Demand for Money

Then Tunatiuh asked the kings for money. He wished them to give him piles of metal, their vessels and crowns. And as they did not bring them to him immediately, Tunatiuh became angry with the kings and said to them: "Why have you not brought me the metal? If you do not bring with you all of the money of the tribes, I will burn you and I will hang you," he said to the lords.

Next Tunatiuh ordered them to pay twelve hundred pesos of gold. The kings tried to have the amount reduced and they began to weep, but Tunatiuh did not consent, and he said to them: "Get the metal and bring it within five days. Woe to you if you do not bring it! I know my heart!" Thus he said to the lords.

They had already delivered half of the money to Tunatiuh when a man, an agent of the devil, appeared and said to the kings: "I am the lightning. I will kill the Spaniards; by the fire they shall perish. When I strike the drum, depart [everyone] from the city, let the lords go to the other side of the river. This I will do on the day 7 Ahmak [August 26, 1524]." Thus that demon spoke to the lords. And indeed the lords believed that they should obey the orders of that man. Half of the money had already been delivered when we escaped.

Then We Fled from the City

On the day 7 Ahmak we accomplished our flight. Then we abandoned the city of Yximché because of the agent of the devil. Afterwards the kings departed. "Tunatiuh will surely die at once," they said. "Now there is no war in the heart of Tunatiuh, now he is satisfied with the metal that has been given him."

Thus it was that, because of the wicked man, we abandoned our city on the day 7 Ahmak, oh, my sons!

But Tunatiuh knew what the kings had done. Ten days after we fled from the city, Tunatiuh began to make war upon us. On the day 4 Camey [September 5, 1524] they began to make us suffer. We scattered ourselves under the trees, under the vines, oh, my sons! All our tribes joined in the fight against Tunatiuh. The Spaniards began to leave at once, they went out of the city, leaving it deserted.

Then the Cakchiquels began hostilities against the Spaniards. They dug holes and pits for the horses and scattered sharp stakes so that they should be killed. At the same time the people made war on them. Many Spaniards perished and the horses died in the traps for horses. The Quichés and the Zutuhils died also; in this manner all the people were destroyed by the Cakchiquels. Only thus did the Spaniards give them a breathing spell, and thus also all the tribes made a truce with them [the Spaniards].

In the ninth month after our flight from Yximché, the twenty-ninth year was ended.

On the day 2 Ah [February 19, 1525] the twenty-ninth year after the revolution was ended.

During the tenth year [of the second cycle] the war with the Spaniards continued. The Spaniards had moved to Xepau. From there, during the tenth year, they made war on us and killed many brave men.

Then Tunatiuh left Xepau and began hostilities against us because the people did not humble themselves before him. Six months had passed of the second year of our flight from the city, or [from the time] when we abandoned it and departed, when Tunatiuh came to it in passing and burned it. On the day 4 Camey [February 7, 1526] he burned the city; at the end of the sixth month of the second year of the war he accomplished it and departed again.

On the day 12 Ah [March 26, 1526] ended the thirtieth year after the revolution.

During the course of this year our hearts had some rest. So also did the kings Cahà Ymox and Belehé Qat. We did not submit to the Spaniards, and we were living in Holom Balam, oh, my sons!

One year and one month had passed since Tunatiuh razed [the city], when the Spaniards came to Chij Xot. On the day 1 Caok [March 27, 1527] our slaughter by the Spaniards began. The people fought them, and they continued to fight a prolonged war. Death struck us anew, but none of the people paid the tribute. The thirty-first year after the revolution had almost ended when they arrived at Chij Xot.

On the day 9 Ah [April 30, 1527] ended the thirty-first year after the revolution.

During this year, while we were busy with the war against the Spaniards, they abandoned Chij Xot and went to live at Bulbuxya.

During that year the war continued. And none of the people paid the tribute.

QUESTIONS TO CONSIDER

1. How did the Aztecs and Mayas explain the European conquest? What reasons did they give for their civilizations' fall?
2. Why were the European invaders so cruel? What might have motivated them to destroy so much?
3. How are these stories different from the accounts Europeans told? Are there any ways to judge which point of view is "right"?

FOR FURTHER READING

Adorno, Roleno, ed. *From Oral to Written Expression: Native Andean Chronicles of the Early Colonial Period.* Syracuse, NY: Maxwell School of Citizenship and Public Affairs, Syracuse University, 1982.

Annals of the Cakchiquels. Trans. Adrián Recinos and Delia Goetz. Norman, OK: University of Oklahoma Press, 1953.

The Book of Chilam Balam of Chumayel. Ed. and trans. Ralph L. Roy. Washington, DC: Carnegie Institution of Washington, 1933.

Crosby, Alfred W., Jr. *The Columbian Exchange: Biological and Cultural Consequences of 1492.* Westport, CT: Greenwood, 1972.

Díaz del Castillo, Bernal. *The Bernal Díaz Chronicles: The True Story of the Conquest of Mexico.* Trans. Albert Idell. Garden City, NY: Doubleday, 1962.
León-Portilla, Miguel. *The Broken Spears: The Aztec Account of the Conquest of Mexico.* Trans. Lysander Kemp. Expanded and updated version. Boston: Beacon, 1990.
Popol Vuh. Trans. Ralph Nelson. Boston: Houghton Mifflin, 1976.

NOTES

1. Fray Bernardino do Sahagún, *General History of the Things of New Spain [The Florentine Codex: Book 12 — The Conquest of Mexico,* trans. from the Aztec by Arthur J. O. Anderson and Charles E. Dribble (Santa Fe, NM: School of American Research, 1955), 15–23, 81–82.
2. *The Annals of the Cakchiquels,* trans. Adrián Recinos and Delia Goetz (Norman, OK: University of Oklahoma Press, 1953), 119–35.

CHAPTER 30

Voltaire

Philosophe

Voltaire
© 1995 North Wind Pictures

Francois-Marie Arouet (1694–1778) took the pen name Voltaire in young manhood to mark his success as a dramatist. His claim to fame comes from being the foremost popularizer and propagandist of the ideas of European intellectuals of his era, often called the Enlightenment, rather than from any originality on his own part. A veritable polymath, he wrote plays, satires, poetry, essays, and novels as well as history. He has been properly called the father of modern Western historiography in that he articulated the conventions and rules of historical work that still prevail. He was the first European historian to consider the history of non-Europeans in China and India as instructive in its own right. In turn, his life and career reflect vividly the impact of the Enlightenment on European intellectual life.

Voltaire was born to a bourgeois family, but we know little of his home life. His godfather and intellectual mentor was the free thinking Abbé de Chateauneuf. Voltaire attended a Jesuit school and absorbed the classics, but not the religion, he found there. He eventually focused on literature as his career but was mistakenly imprisoned for a poem he had not composed mocking the Regent of France. With aplomb, Voltaire penned a humorous account of the event after he was released from the Bastille. Shortly after this, his plays brought him great recognition and success and established a literary reputation. Voltaire lived in protective exile in England (1726–29) after a tangle with an aristocrat; the sojourn was decisive in forming his views. He admired the relative freedom of speech and inquiry found in England and the advancement of science following the work of Newton. But he believed French tragedy superior to English and returned to France to continue his participation in the theater. In 1731 he first ventured into history with an account of Charles XII of Sweden, whose reign had ended only 13 years earlier. Voltaire used extensive manuscript sources and interviews in assembling this account but also captured something of the drama of the life of the Swedish Napoleon. Voltaire continued writing plays throughout his life, but later ventured into philosophy and political theory in various formats (letters, essays, the novel *Candide*). He also did scientific experiments in his own laboratory and wrote essays on a variety of topics. His letter writing was also prodigious and influenced many of the intellectual elite in Europe. Everywhere Voltaire spread the ideas of the Enlightenment: the law-abiding universe revealed by Newton; the empiricism and vision of limited government of John Locke; the dispassionate, unconcerned Creator of the English Deists; the hope that science would eventually discover the laws of human nature and society in order to accelerate human progress. In 1751 he published *The Age of Louis XIV,* the fruit of almost 20 years' gestation. Until his death in 1778, Voltaire continued publishing works urging reforms in many areas of life, including one on agriculture. His impact on the intelligentsia of his era was immense.

Since Voltaire was a popularizer, we should not expect him to be systematic or consistent in his views. Nowhere is that truer than in his approach to history, which he addressed in a variety of essays, letters, and books. The *bon mot* "history is philosophy teaching by example" (which Voltaire stole from Thucydides via a Latin intermediary) expresses a key focus of Voltaire—he believed that ideas are the primary stuff of history. The purpose of history is to teach citizenship and virtue by showing us the folly and criminality of the past. In his view of historical causation, Voltaire was an absolute naturalist. He believed that historians must disregard any evidence which does not reflect the regular flow of natural law and of common sense. No miracles and no providence shaped the course of human events in his writing.

Second, Voltaire assumed a universal human nature that underlay all the peculiarities of human culture and which, if it were unalloyed, would very much resemble that of an enlightened French gentleman of the eighteenth century, rational and tolerant. The course of history reflected the natural struggle within the human psyche between self-love and the desire for justice and order. The major influences shaping the human mind are climate, government, and religion. The combination and variability of these result in the ideas that characterize an era. Consistent with his hopes for human enlightenment, Voltaire wanted history to be established on a scientific foundation. But he also recognized that historical fact could never be established empirically (in the sense that it could not be replicated in a controlled laboratory setting), so historians need to aim for increasing the probability of ascertaining the truth about an event. In different places, Voltaire asserted several rules for historical analysis that are still tacitly assumed among historians in the West. Historical evidence must not contradict reason or common sense. Witnesses cannot be assumed to be reliable, rather the contrary. We should accept as strong evidence only what witnesses from opposite perspectives aver in common. Voltaire hated anecdotes and gossip as derogatory of the dignity of history. "Tell posterity nothing but what is worthy of posterity," he wrote. Character ought to be revealed by the actions of the individual, not by a sketch or portrait. Voltaire also warned historians to concentrate on the main themes of the work and to select carefully which data to include in writing so as not to confuse the reader with tangential material.

The passages that follow illustrate some of Voltaire's pronouncements on the writing of history and also illustrate that he did not always abide by his own rules. The first is the introduction to *The Age of Louis XIV.* The second is Voltaire's account of the Fronde, a very confusing episode of civil strife early in Louis's reign.

The Age of Louis XIV[1]

It is not merely the life of Louis XIV, that we propose to write; we have a wider aim in view. We shall endeavour to depict for posterity, not the actions of a single man, but the spirit of men in the most enlightened age the world has ever seen.

Every age has produced its heroes and statesmen; every nation has experienced revolutions; every history is the same to one who wishes merely to remember facts. But the thinking man, and what is still rarer, the man of taste, numbers only four ages in the history of the world; four happy ages when the arts were brought to perfection and which, marking an era of the greatness of the human mind, are an example to posterity.

The first of these ages, to which true glory belongs, is that of Philip and Alexander, or rather of Pericles, Demosthenes, Aristotle, Plato, Apelles, Phidias, Praxiteles; and the rest of the known world being in a barbarous state.

The second age is that of Caesar and Augustus, distinguished moreover by the names of Lucretius, Cicero, Livy, Virgil, Horace, Ovid, Varro and Vitruvius.

The third is that which followed the taking of Constantinople by Mahomet II. The reader may remember that the spectacle was then witnessed of a family of mere citizens in Italy accomplishing what should have been undertaken by the kings of Europe. The scholars whom the Turks had driven from Greece were summoned by the Medici to Florence; it was the hour of Italy's glory. The fine arts had already taken on new life there; and the Italians honoured them with the name of virtue as the early Greeks had characterized them with the name of wisdom. Everything conduced to perfection. The arts, for ever transplanted from Greece to Italy, fell on favourable ground, where they flourished immediately. France, England, Germany and Spain, in their turn, desired the possession of these fruits; but either they never reached these countries or they degenerated too quickly.

Francis I. encouraged scholars who were scholars and nothing else: he had architects, but neither a Michael Angelo nor a Palladio; it was in vain that he endeavoured to found Schools of Painting, for the Italian painters whom he employed made no French disciples. A few epigrams and fables made up the whole of our poetry. Rabelais was the only prose writer in fashion in the age of Henry II.

In a word, the Italians alone possessed everything, if one except music, which had not yet been brought to perfection, and experimental philosophy, equally unknown everywhere, and which Galileo at length brought to men's knowledge.

The fourth age is that which we call the age of Louis XIV.; and it is perhaps of the four the one which most nearly approaches perfection. Enriched with the discoveries of the other three it accomplished in certain departments more than the three together. All the arts, it is true, did not progress further than they did under the Medici, under Augustus or under Alexander; but human reason in general was brought to perfection.

Rational philosophy only came to light in this period; and it is true to say that from the last years of Cardinal Richelieu to those which followed the death of Louis XIV., a general revolution took place in our arts, minds and customs, as in our government, which will serve as an eternal token of the true glory of our country. This beneficent influence was not merely confined to France; it passed over into England, and inspired a profitable rivalry in that intellectual and fearless nation; it imported good taste into Germany, and the sciences into Russia; it even revived Italy, who had begun to languish, and Europe has owed both her manners and the social spirit to the court of Louis XIV.

It must not be assumed that these four ages were exempt from misfortunes and crimes. The attainment of perfection in those arts practised by peaceful citizens does not prevent princes from being ambitious, the people from being mutinous, nor priests and monks from becoming sometimes turbulent and crafty. All ages resemble one another in respect of the criminal folly of mankind, but I only know of these four ages so distinguished by great attainments.

Prior to the age which I call that of Louis XIV., and which began almost with the founding of the *Académie française,* the Italians looked upon all those north of the Alps as barbarians; it must be confessed that to a certain extent the French deserved the insult. Their fathers joined the romantic courtesy of the Moors to Gothic coarseness. They practised scarcely any of the fine arts, which proves that the useful arts were neglected; for when one has perfected the necessary things, one soon discovers the beautiful and agreeable; and it is not to be wondered at that painting, sculpture, poetry, oratory and philosophy were almost unknown to a nation which, while possessing ports on the Atlantic Ocean and the Mediterranean, yet had no fleet, and which, though inordinately fond of luxury, had but a few coarse manufactures.

The Jews, the Genoese, the Venetians, the Portuguese, the Flemish, the Dutch, the English, in turn carried on the trade of France, who was ignorant of its first principles. When Louis XIII. ascended the throne he did not possess a ship; Paris did not contain four hundred thousand inhabitants, and could not boast of four fine buildings; the other towns of the kingdom resembled those market towns one sees south of the Loire. The whole of the nobility, scattered over the country in their moat-surrounded castles, oppressed the people, who were engaged in tilling the land. The great highways were well-nigh impassable; the towns were without police, the state without money, and the government nearly always without credit among foreign nations. The fact must not be concealed that after the decadence of Charlemagne's descendants France had continued more or less in this state of weakness simply because she had hardly ever enjoyed good government.

If a state is to be powerful, either the people must enjoy a liberty based on its laws, or the sovereign power must be affirmed without contradiction. In France, the people were enslaved until the time of Philip Augustus; the nobles were tyrants until the time of Louis XI., and the kings continually engaged in upholding their authority over that of their vassals had neither the time to think of the welfare of their subjects nor the power to make them happy.

Louis XI. did a great deal for the royal power, but nothing for the happiness and glory of the nation. Francis I. inaugurated commerce, navigation, letter and arts; but he did not succeed in making them take root in France, and they all perished with him. Henri-Quatre was about to redeem France from the calamities and barbarity into which she had been plunged by twenty years of dissension, when he was assassinated in his capital, in the midst of the people to whom he was on the point of bringing prosperity. Cardinal Richelieu, occupied with the humbling of the House of Austria, Calvinism and the nobles, did not possess a sufficiently secure position to reform the nation; but at least he inaugurated the auspicious work.

Thus for nine hundred years the genius of France had almost continually been cramped under a gothic government, in the midst of partitions and civil wars, having neither laws nor fixed customs, and changing every two centuries a language ever uncouth; her nobles undisciplined and acquainted solely with war and idleness; her clergy living in disorder and ignorance; and her people without trade, sunk in their misery.

The French also had no share in the great discoveries and wonderful inventions of other nations; printing, gunpowder, glassmaking, telescopes, the proportional compass, pneumatic machines, the true system of the universe—in such things they had no concern; they were engaged in tournaments while the Portuguese and Spaniards discovered and conquered new worlds to the east and west. Charles V. was already lavishing on Europe the treasures of Mexico before a few subjects of Francis I. discovered the uncultivated regions of Canada; but even from the slight accomplishments of the French at the beginning of the sixteenth century, one could see what they are capable of when they are led.

We propose to show what they became under Louis XIV. Do not let the reader expect here, more than in the description of earlier centuries, minute details of wars, of attacks on towns taken and retaken by force of arms, surrendered and given back by treaties. A thousand events interesting to contemporaries are lost to the eyes of posterity and disappear, leaving only to view great happenings that have fixed the destiny of empires. Every event that occurs is not worth recording. In this history we shall confine ourselves to that which deserves the attention of all time, which paints the spirit and the customs of men, which may serve for instruction and to counsel the love of virtue, of the arts and of the fatherland.

The state of France and the other European States before the birth of Louis XIV. has already been described: we shall here relate the great political and military events of his reign. The internal government of the kingdom, the most important matter for the people at large, will be treated separately. To the private life of Louis XIV., to the peculiarities of his court and of his reign, a large part will be devoted. Other chapters will deal with the arts, the sciences, and the progress of the human mind in this age. Finally, we shall speak of the

Church, which has been joined to the government for so long a period, sometimes disturbing it, at other times invigorating it, and which, established for the teaching of morality, often surrenders herself to politics and the passions of mankind.

*   *   *

Civil War

Anne of Austria, now become absolute regent, had made Cardinal Mazarin France's master and her own. He had such dominion over her as a clever man may well have over a woman born with sufficient weakness to be ruled and sufficient obstinacy to persist in her choice.

One reads in certain memoirs of that period that the queen placed her confidence in Mazarin only after the complete failure of Potier, Bishop of Beauvais, whom she had first chosen as her minister. This bishop is represented as being an incompetent man; it is probable that he was, and that the queen only used him for a certain time as a lay figure, in order not to alarm the nation by the immediate choice of another cardinal, who was moreover a foreigner.

But it is unbelievable that Potier inaugurated his ministry by declaring to the Dutch "that they would have to become Catholics if they wished to remain the allies of France." He would have had to make the same stipulation to the Swedes. This absurdity is related by nearly all historians, because they have read it in the memoirs of courtiers and *frondeurs*. There are openly too many facts in these memoirs that are either corrupted by prejudice or based upon popular rumour. What is obviously puerile should not be quoted, just as what is obviously absurd cannot be believed. All goes to show that for a long time, perhaps even during the life of Louis XIII., the queen had decided in her own mind upon Cardinal Mazarin as her minister; indeed, it cannot be doubted when one has read the Memoirs of La Porte, first gentleman of the bedchamber of Anne of Austria. Subordinates who are witnesses of the inner working of the court, know things of which parliaments and even the leaders of parties are unaware or do no more than suspect.

At first Mazarin used his power with moderation. One must have lived a long time with a minister to portray his character, to say what degree of courage or weakness he possessed, how far he was either prudent or crafty. Accordingly, we will merely say what Mazarin did, without attempting to guess what he was. At the outset of his greatness he affected as much simplicity as Richelieu had previously displayed haughtiness. Far from surrounding himself with guards and travelling with royal pomp, he was accompanied at first by the most unpretending suite; where his predecessor had displayed an unbending arrogance, he revealed an affability of nature sometimes approaching to weakness. The queen was eager that her regency and her person should be loved by court and people alike, and she succeeded in both. Gaston, Duke of Orleans, brother of Louis XIII., and the Prince de Conde upheld her power, and had no other rivalry but that of how best to serve the state.

Taxes were needed for the maintenance of the war against Spain and the Emperor. Since the death of the great Henry IV, France's exchequer had been as badly managed as that of Spain and Germany. The administration of taxes was in a state of chaos; ignorance was extreme; brigandage was at its height, although not directed to such large ends as it is today. The national debt was one-eighth of what it is now; there were no armies of two hundred thousand men to keep up, no immense subsidies to pay, no naval war to maintain. In the first years of the regency state revenues amounted to nearly seventy-five million livres of the period. Had the ministry practised economy all would have been right; but in 1646 and 1647 new means of raising revenue became necessary. The comptroller at that time was a Siennese peasant, by name Particelli Emeri, whose mind was even lower than his birth, and whose pomp and dissoluteness aroused the whole country's indignation. This man invented burdensome and ridiculous expedients. He created the posts of controllers of faggots, jurors for the selling of hay, king's councillors to act as criers of wine; he also sold letters of nobility. Paris municipal stocks at that time amounted only to close upon eleven millions. A few quarters were re-divided among the *rentiers,* custom duties were increased; posts were created for masters of petitions, and pay to the extent of eighty thousand crowns was withheld from the magistrates.

It is easy to conjecture how the minds of men were stirred up against the two Italians, both of whom had come penniless to France, and who had enriched themselves at the expense of the nation over which they had so great a hold. The parliament of Paris, the masters of petitions, the other courts, the *rentiers*—all rebelled. In vain did Mazarin deprive his favourite, Emeri, of the comptrollership and dismiss him to one of his estates; indignation was felt that this man should still possess estates in France, and Cardinal Mazarin was regarded with detestation, although at the very time he was concluding the great work at the peace of Munster; for it should be noted that that famous treaty and the barricades belong to the same year, 1648.

The civil wars began in Paris as they had begun in London, over the question of a little money.

(1647) The parliament of Paris, possessing as it did the right of inspecting the decrees of taxes, vehemently opposed the new edicts and gained the confidence of the people by the continued opposition with which it harassed the ministry.

Revolution did not come at once; men's minds are provoked and become bold only by degrees. The populace may at once rush to arms and choose a leader, as they did at Naples; but magistrates and statesmen proceed with more caution and at first observe a certain decorum, so far as a partisan spirit allows them.

Cardinal Mazarin had thought that by skillfully dividing the magistracy he could prevent all disturbance; but they met his subtletly with inflexibility. He kept back four years' pay from all the higher courts, meanwhile granting them exemption from the *paulette,* that is to say, exempting them from payment of the tax devised by Paulet under Henri IV., which secured to them the ownership of their offices. This remission was not wrong, but he allowed parliament to keep their four years' pay, thinking thus to appease its members. Parliament, however, scorned a favour which exposed it to the reproach of preferring its own interest to that of other bodies in the state.

(1648) The offer accordingly did not prevent it from issuing its decree of union with the other courts of justice. Mazarin, who had never been able to pronounce French properly, said that the *arret d'ognon* (i.e. the "onion" decree) was unlawful, and having had it annulled by the council, this word "onion" alone was sufficient to make him ridiculous; and as one does not submit to those one despises, parliament became still more venturesome.

It boldly demanded the dismissal of all the commissaries, regarded by the people as extortioners, and the abolition of the new type of magistracy, which had been established under Louis XIII. without the usual apparatus of legal formulary; such a project pleased the nation as much as it annoyed the court. It claimed that in accordance with ancient laws no citizen should be imprisoned without the proper judges being informed of the fact within twenty-four hours; nothing appeared more just.

Parliament did more; it abolished (14 May, 1648) the commissaries by a decree, ordering the local king's attorneys to take proceedings against them.

Thus hatred of the minister, aided by ardour for the public welfare, threatened the court with a revolution. The queen gave way; she offered to dismiss the commissaries, asking only that she might be allowed to retain three: this demand was refused.

(20 August, 1648) While these troubles were brewing, the Prince de Conde won the famous victory of Lens, the crowning point of his glory. The king, who was then only ten years of age, exclaimed: "Parliament will be very grieved at this." These words were sufficient to show that the court at that time looked upon the parliament of Paris as merely a body of rebels.

The Cardinal and his courtiers gave it indeed no other name. The more that members of parliament had to complain of being treated like rebels, the more they resisted.

Queen and cardinal determined to remove three of the most obstinate magistrates in parliament, Novion Blancmenil, Chief Justice, as he was called; Charton, President of a chamber of Common Pleas, and Broussel, formerly Clerk Councillor of the grand chamber.

They were not themselves the party leaders, but their tools. Charton, a very narrow-minded man, was known by the nickname of President *Je dis ca* ("That's what I say") because he always began and ended his speeches with these words. Broussel had only his white locks to commend him, his hatred of the ministry, and the reputation of always raising his voice against the court on whatever subject was brought up. His colleagues thought little of him, but the populace idolised him.

Instead of removing them quietly in the silence of the night, the cardinal thought to overawe the people by arresting them in broad daylight, while the *Te Deum* was being sung in Notre-Dame for the victory of Lens, and the Swiss guards were bearing in the seventy-three standards taken from the enemy. It was precisely this that caused the rising of the whole kingdom. Charton escaped, Blancmenil was taken without any trouble, but with Broussel matters were very different. A solitary old serving-woman seeing her master forced into a carriage by Comminges, a lieutenant of the lifeguards, stirs up the people; they surround the carriage and break it open, but the French Guards come to the rescue and the prisoner is escorted on the road to Sedan. So far from intimidating the people, his abduction irritates and encourages them. Shops are closed, and the large iron chains that were at that time stretched at the entrance to the principal streets are hung up; some barricades are erected, and four hundred thousand voices cry *Liberty and Broussel.*

It is difficult to reconcile all the details given by the Cardinal de Retz, Mme. de Motteville, the Solicitor-General, Talon, and many others, but all agree on the principal points.

During the night that followed the riot, the queen called up about two thousand troops quartered some leagues from Paris to defend the king's palace. Chancellor Segnier was already on his way to parliament, preceded by a lieutenant and several archers, for the purpose of annulling all decrees and even, it was said, of suspending parliament itself. But on the same night, the rebels had assembled at the house of the Coadjutor of Paris, so well known as the Cardinal de Retz, and everything was arranged for putting the city under arms.

QUESTIONS TO CONSIDER

1. How does Voltaire demonstrate his conviction that ideas are the primary stuff of history?
2. What kinds of things appear in this account? What is left out?
3. How does Voltaire's view of the person and office of the king differ from those of Anna Comnena (Chapter 21) and Abu'l Fazl (24)?

FOR FURTHER READING

Black, J. B. *The Art of History: A Study of Four Great Historians of the Eighteenth Century.* New York: Russell and Russell, 1965.
Brumfitt, J. H. *Voltaire: Historian.* London: Oxford University Press, 1958.
Gay, Peter. *Voltaire's Politics.* 2nd ed. New Haven, CT: Yale University Press, 1959.
Lanson, Gustave. *Voltaire.* Trans. Robert A. Wagoner. New York: Wiley, 1966.

NOTES

1. Voltaire, *The Age of Louis XIV,* trans. Martyn P. Pollack (New York: Dutton, 1961), 1–5 25–40.

CHAPTER 31

Edward Gibbon

Enlightenment Skeptic

Edward Gibbon
© North Wind Pictures

E dward Gibbon (1737–1794) typifies the breezy intellectual arrogance of the Enlightenment. In all things the skeptic, he analyzed the decline and fall of the Roman Empire as the "triumph of religion and barbarism." The elegance of his language and the grace of his balanced and periodic sentences have rendered him among the most quotable of English historians. His massive erudition made him one of the most important.

Gibbon's preparation for his great work was out of the ordinary and encouraged his independent turn of mind. Because of ill health, he rarely attended formal school but read desultorily and omnivorously in his aunt's library. From age 12 he knew he was intensely interested in history. At 15 he converted to Roman Catholicism after reading some disputations about the nature of the early church. That meant virtual outlawry in England, so his father sent him to Lausanne, Switzerland, to study with a Calvinist pastor. Within 18 months Gibbon renounced his Catholicism but became a vague Christian or Deist rather than a fervent Protestant. Meanwhile the pastor tutored him extensively in Latin and French literature and honed Gibbon's study habits and self-discipline for five years. Gibbon betrothed a local woman, but his father ordered him to break the engagement. Dutiful son, he did so and returned to England, never to marry. From 1760 to 1763 he served as captain in the Hampshire Militia defensive unit during the Seven Years War with France. Though he saw no combat, the experience contributed to his understanding of military operations and tactics.

When the war ended, he went on a tour of the continent, first spending time amidst the *philosophes* and *salons* of France but eventually reaching Rome in 1764. Here one afternoon, seated among the remains of ancient imperial Rome, he conceived his grand scheme: to understand and analyze how such a great city had fallen into ruin. Later he expanded his vision to comprehend the decline and fall of the entire Roman Empire. Over the next 23 years, Gibbon worked at his monumental task while pursuing an active life. When completed, he had six volumes and thousands of pages of well-wrought prose. Meanwhile, Gibbon served in Parliament from 1744 to 1783. Although he gave no speeches, he did write a defense of Britain's treatment of the North American colonies in 1779. The first volume of his *Decline* came out in 1776 and was immediately very popular and widely read. His subsequent volumes were eagerly anticipated and well received, and the work was finished in 1787. After he left Parliament, he spent much time at Lausanne and in other travels, but his writing continued. He died in 1794.

The History of the Decline and Fall of the Roman Empire has remained popular for two hundred years. *Books in Print* lists eight versions of the work currently available in English. The title itself has shown up in many paraphrases and parodies (*The Rise and Fall of the Third Reich, The Decline and Fall of Practically Everybody*). The work covers the history of the Roman Empire both in the east (Byzantium) and the west from the second century CE to the surrender of Constantinople to the Ottoman Turks in 1453. Thus, more than half deals with the Byzantines and their neighbors. Yet the famous parts are those that relate to classical Roman culture and its alteration.

Essentially, Gibbon viewed Roman imperial history as a continual and unwavering decay from the glories of the Republic (when political and intellectual freedom prevailed) to the triumph by Christianity (otherworldly values) and barbarism (the Germanic peoples) that produced the Middle Ages in western Europe. The material decay of the Roman world paralleled the decay of Roman moral virtues (patriotism, military discipline, self-sacrifice, severity toward enemies) and their replacement by Christian virtues such as meekness and kindness. While many would argue that this general pattern works for the West, few would say it fits the Byzantine experience, so Gibbon often contradicted himself when he tried to force Byzantine history into this pattern.

Gibbon read all the relevant material that was available in published form in his era—a remarkable achievement itself. He was one of the first European historians to use footnotes to document his sources, as had Arai Hakuseki in Japan a century earlier. Gibbon's style and even his tone are strongly influenced by the Roman historian Tacitus (see Chapter 13). When the first volume was published, Gibbon was immediately attacked for being anti-Christian, but modern readers, perhaps more used to having institutions criticized, find only that his ironic appraisal touches all aspects of human experience. Gibbon was a stylist: he strove as much for esthetic beauty in his sentences and paragraphs as he did for historical accuracy. Occasionally, euphony triumphs over strict truth when items that may be a hundred years apart in the historical record are joined in a paragraph for the sake of coherence. Gibbon appealed even less to his audience's emotions and feelings than had other Enlightenment writers. Very little sympathy for his characters shows through. His esthetics and his humor are primarily intellectual. The passage that follows is a part of Gibbon's account of the siege and sack of the city of Rome in 410 by the Visigoths under Alaric, one of the blows that symbolized the end of Roman power in the West.

The Decline and Fall of the Roman Empire[1]

Third Siege and Sack of Rome by the Goths

... Alaric advanced within three miles of Ravenna to press the irresolution of the imperial ministers, whose insolence soon returned with the return of fortune. His indignation was kindled by the report that a rival chieftain—that Sarus, the personal enemy of Adolphus, and the hereditary foe of the House of Balti—had been received into the palace. At the head of three hundred followers, that fearless barbarian immediately sallied from the gates of Ravenna, surprised and cut in pieces a considerable body of Goths, re-entered the city in triumph, and was permitted to insult his adversary by the voice of a herald, who publicly declared that the guilt of Alaric had forever excluded him from the friendship and alliance of the emperor.[2] The crime and folly of the court of Ravenna were expiated a third time by the calamities of Rome. The King of the Goths, who no longer dissembled his appetite for plunder and revenge, appeared in arms under the walls of the capital; and the trembling senate, without any hopes of relief, prepared by a desperate resistance to delay the ruin of their country. But they were unable to guard against the secret conspiracy of their slaves and domestics, who either from birth or interest were attached to the cause of the enemy. At the hour of midnight the Salarian gate was silently opened, and the inhabitants were awakened by the tremendous sound of the Gothic trumpet. Eleven hundred and sixty-three years after the foundation of Rome, the imperial city, which had subdued and civilized so considerable a part of mankind, was delivered to the licentious fury of the tribes of Germany and Scythia.[3]

The proclamation of Alaric, when he forced his entrance into a vanquished city, discovered, however, some regard for the laws of humanity and religion. He encouraged his troops boldly to seize the rewards of valor, and to enrich themselves with the spoils of a wealthy and effeminate people; but he exhorted them, at the same time to spare the lives of the unresisting citizens, and to respect the churches of the apostles St. Peter and St. Paul as holy and inviolable sanctuaries. Amidst the horrors of nocturnal tumult, several of the Christian Goths displayed the fervor of a recent conversion; and some instances of their uncommon piety and moderation are related, and perhaps adorned, by the zeal of ecclesiastical writers.[4] While the barbarians roamed through the city in quest of prey, the humble dwelling of an aged virgin, who had devoted her life to the service of the altar, was forced open by one of the powerful Goths. He immediately demanded, though in civil language, all the gold and silver in her possession, and was astonished at the readiness with which she conducted him to a splendid hoard of massy plate of the richest materials and the most curious workmanship. The barbarian viewed with wonder and delight this valuable acquisition, till he was interrupted by a serious admonition, addressed to him in the following words: "These," said she, "are the consecrated vessels belonging to St. Peter; if you presume to touch them, the sacrilegious deed will remain on your conscience. For my part, I dare not keep what I am unable to defend." The Gothic captain, struck with reverential awe, despatched a messenger to inform the king of the treasure which he had discovered, and received a peremptory order from Alaric that all the consecrated plate and ornaments should be transported, without damage or delay, to the church of the apostle. From the extremity, perhaps, of the Quirinal Hill to the distant quarter of the Vatican, a numerous detachment of Goths, marching in order of battle through the principal streets, protected with glittering arms the long train of their devout companions who bore aloft on their heads the sacred vessels of gold and silver, and the martial shouts of the barbarians were mingled with the sound of religious psalmody. From the adjacent houses a crowd of Christians hastened to join this edifying procession; and a multitude of fugitives, without distinction of age or rank, or even of sect, had the good fortune to escape to the secure and hospitable sanctuary of the Vatican. The learned work concerning the *City of God* was professedly composed by St. Augustine to justify the ways of Providence in the destruction of the Roman greatness. He celebrates with peculiar satisfaction this memorable triumph of Christ, and insults his adversaries by challenging them to produce some similar example of a town taken by storm, in which the fabulous gods of antiquity had been able to protect either themselves or their deluded votaries.[5]

In the sack of Rome some rare and extraordinary examples of barbarian virtue have been deservedly applauded. But the holy precincts of the Vatican and the apostolic churches could receive a very small proportion of the Roman people; many thousand warriors, more especially of the Huns who served under the standard of Alaric, were strangers to the name, or at least to the faith, of Christ; and we may suspect, without any breach of charity or candor, that in the hour of savage license, when every passion was inflamed and every restraint was removed, the precepts of the Gospel seldom influenced the behavior of the Gothic Christians. The writers the best disposed to exaggerate their clemency have freely confessed that a cruel slaughter was made of the Romans,[6] and that the streets of the city were filled with dead bodies, which remained without burial during the general consternation. The despair of the citizens was sometimes converted into fury; and whenever the barbarians were provoked by opposition, they extended the promiscuous massacre to the feeble, the innocent, and the helpless. The private revenge of forty thousand slaves was exercised without pity or remorse; and the ignominious lashes which they had formerly received were washed away in the blood of the guilty or obnoxious families. The matrons and virgins of Rome were exposed to injuries more dreadful, in the apprehension of chastity, than death itself; and the ecclesiastical historian has selected an example of female virtue for the admiration of future ages.[7] A Roman lady of singular beauty and orthodox faith had excited the impatient desires of a young Goth, who according to the sagacious remark of Sozomen, was attached to the Arian heresy. Exasperated by her obstinate resistance, he drew his sword, and, with the anger of a lover, slightly wounded her neck. The bleeding heroine still continued to brave his resentment and to repel his love, till the ravisher desisted from his unavailing efforts, respectfully conducted her to the sanctuary of the Vatican, and gave six pieces of gold to the guards of the church on condition that they should restore her inviolate to the arms of her husband. Such instances of courage and generosity were not extremely common. The brutal soldiers satisfied their sensual appetites without consulting either the inclination or the duties of their female captives; and a nice question of casuistry was seriously agitated, whether those tender victims who had inflexibly refused their consent to the violation which they sustained had lost, by their misfortune, the glorious crown of virginity.[8]

There were other losses, indeed, of a more substantial kind and more general concern. It cannot be presumed that all the barbarians were at all times capable of perpetrating such amorous outrages; and the want of youth or beauty or chastity protected the greatest part of the Roman women from the danger of a rape. But avarice is an insatiate and universal passion, since the enjoyment of almost every object that can afford pleasure to the different tastes and tempers of mankind may be procured by the possession of wealth. In the pillage of Rome a just preference was given to gold and jewels, which contain the greatest value in the smallest compass and weight; but after these portable riches had been removed by the more diligent robbers, the palaces of Rome were rudely stripped of their splendid and costly furniture. The sideboards of massy plate, and the variegated wardrobes of silk and purple, were irregularly piled in the wagons that always followed the march of a Gothic army. The most exquisite works of art were roughly handled or wantonly destroyed. Many a statue was melted for the sake of the precious materials; and many a vase, in the division of the spoil, was shivered into fragments by the stroke of a battle-axe. The acquisition of riches served only to stimulate the avarice of the rapacious barbarians, who proceeded by threats, by blows, and by tortures to force from their prisoners the confession of hidden treasure.[9] Visible splendor and expense were alleged as the proof of a plentiful fortune; the appearance of poverty was imputed to a parsimonious disposition; and the obstinacy of some misers, who endured the most cruel torments before they would discover the secret object of their affection, was fatal to many unhappy wretches, who expired under the lash for refusing to reveal their imaginary treasures. The edifices of Rome, though the damage has been much exaggerated, received some injury from the violence of the Goths. At their entrance through the Salarian gate they fired the adjacent houses to guide their march and to distract the attention of the citizens. The flames, which encountered no obstacle in the disorder of the night, consumed many private and public buildings; and the ruins of the palace of Sallust[10] remained in the age of Justinian a stately monument of the Gothic conflagration.[11] Yet a contemporary historian has observed that fire could scarcely consume the enormous beams of solid brass, and the strength of man was insufficient to subvert the foundations of ancient structures. Some truth may possibly be concealed in his devout assertion that the wrath of Heaven supplied the imperfections of hostile rage, and that the proud Forum of Rome, decorated with the statues of so many gods and heroes, was levelled in the dust by the stroke of lightning.[12]

Whatever might be the numbers of equestrian or plebian rank who perished in the massacre of Rome, it is confidently affirmed that only one senator lost his life by the sword of the enemy.[13] But it was not easy to compute the multitudes who, from an honorable station and prosperous fortune, were suddenly reduced to the miserable condition of captives and exiles. As the barbarians had more occasion for money than for slaves, they fixed at a moderate price the redemption of their indigent prisoners; and the ransom was often paid by the benevolence of their friends or the charity of strangers.[14] The captives, who were regularly sold, either in open market or by private contract, would have legally regained their native freedom, which it was impossible for a citizen to lose or to alienate.[15] But as it was soon discovered that the vindication of their liberty would endanger their lives, and that the Goths, unless they were tempted to sell, might be provoked to murder, their useless prisoners, the civil jurisprudence had been already qualified by a wise regulation—that they should be obliged to serve the moderate term of five years till they had discharged by their labor, the price of there redemption.[16] The nations who invaded the Roman empire had driven before them into Italy, whole troops of hungry and affrighted provincials, less apprehensive of servitude than of famine. The calamities of Rome and Italy dispersed the inhabitants to the most lonely, the most secure, the most distant places of refuge. While the Gothic cavalry spread terror and desolation along the sea-coast of Campania and Tuscany, the little island of Igilium, separated by a narrow channel from the Argentarian promontory, repulsed or eluded their hostile attempts; and at so small a distance from Rome, great numbers of citizens were securely concealed in the thick woods of that sequestered spot.[17] The ample patrimonies which many senatorian families possessed in Africa invited them, if they had time and prudence to escape from the ruin of their country, to embrace the shelter of that hospitable province. The most illustrious of these fugitives was the noble and pious Proba,[18] the widow of the praefect Petronius. After the death of her husband, the most powerful subject of Rome, she had remained at the head of the Anician family, and successively supplied, from her private fortune, the expense of the consulships of her three sons. When the city was besieged and taken by the Goths, Proba supported with Christian resignation the loss of immense riches; embarked in a small vessel, from whence she beheld, at sea, the flames of her burning palace; and fled with her daughter Laeta and her granddaughter, the celebrated virgin Demetrias, to the coast of Africa. The benevolent profusion with which the matron distributed the fruits or the price of her estates contributed to alleviate the misfortunes of exile and captivity. But even the family of Proba herself was not exempt from the rapacious oppression of Count Heraclian, who basely sold, in the matrimonial prostitution, the noblest maidens of Rome to the lust or avarice of the Syrian merchants. The Italian fugitives were dispersed through the provinces, along the coast of Egypt and Asia, as far as Constantinople and Jerusalem; and the village of Bethlehem, the solitary residence of

St. Jerome and his female converts, was crowded with illustrious beggars of either sex and every age, who excited the public compassion by the remembrance of their past fortune.[19] This awful catastrophe of Rome filled the astonished empire with grief and terror. So interesting a contrast of greatness and ruin disposed the fond credulity of the people to deplore, and even to exaggerate, the afflictions of the Queen of Cities. The clergy, who applied to recent events the lofty metaphors of Oriental prophecy, were sometimes tempted to confound the destruction of the capital and the dissolution of the globe.

There exists in human nature a strong propensity to depreciate the advantages and to magnify the evils of the present time. Yet, when the first emotions had subsided and a fair estimate was made of the real damage, the more learned and judicious contemporaries were forced to confess that infant Rome had formerly received more essential injury from the Gauls than she had now sustained from the Goths in her declining age.[20] The experience of eleven centuries has enabled posterity to produce a much more singular parallel; and to affirm with confidence that the ravages of the barbarians whom Alaric had led from the banks of the Danube were less destructive than the hostilities exercised by the troops of Charles the Fifth, a Catholic prince, who styled himself Emperor of the Romans.[21] The Goths evacuated the city at the end of six days; but Rome remained above nine months in the possession of the imperialists, and every hour was stained by some atrocious act of cruelty, lust, and rapine. The authority of Alaric preserved some order and moderation among the ferocious multitude which acknowledged him for their leader and king; but the Constable of Bourbon had gloriously fallen in the attack of the walls, and the death of the general removed every restraint of discipline from an army which consisted of three independent nations—the Italians, the Spaniards, and the Germans. In the beginning of the sixteenth century, the manners of Italy exhibited a remarkable scene of the depravity of mankind. They united the sanguinary crimes that prevail in an unsettled state of society with the polished vices which spring from the abuse of art and luxury; and the loose adventurers, who had violated every prejudice of patriotism and superstition to assault the palace of the Roman pontiff, must deserve to be considered as the most profligate of the *Italians*. At the same era the *Spaniards* were the terror both of the Old and the New World; but their high-spirited valor was disgraced by gloomy pride, rapacious avarice, and unrelenting cruelty. Indefatigable in the pursuit of fame and riches, they had improved, by repeated practice the most exquisite and effectual methods of torturing their prisoners. Many of the Castilians who pillaged Rome were familiars of the Holy Inquisition; and some volunteers, perhaps, were lately returned from the conquest of Mexico. The *Germans* were less corrupt than the Italians, less cruel than the Spaniards; and the rustic or even savage aspect of those *Tramontane* warriors often disguised a simple and merciful disposition. But they had imbibed, in the first fervor of the Reformation, the spirit as well as the principles of Luther. It was their favorite amusement to insult or destroy the consecrated objects of Catholic superstition; they indulged, without pity or remorse, a devout hatred against the clergy of every denomination and degree who form so considerable a part of the inhabitants of modern Rome; and their fanatic zeal might aspire to subvert the throne of Antichrist, to purify with blood and fire the abominations of the spiritual Babylon.[22]

NOTES

1. Edward Gibbon, *The History of the Decline and Fall of the Roman Empire* (Chicago: Great Books, 1952), chapter 31, pp 508–512. Footnotes renumbered to fit abridgment.

2. Zosimus, 1., vi. [c 13] [.384. Sozomen, 1. ix. c. 9. Philostorgius, 1. xii. c. 3]. In this place the text of Zosimus is mutilated, and we have lost the remainder of his sixth and last book, which ended with the sack of Rome. Credulous and partial as he is, we must take our leave of that historian with some regret.

3. Adest Alaricus, trepidam Romam obsidet, turbat, irrumpit.—Orosius, 1. vii. c. 39, p 573. He dispatches this great event in seven words; but he employs whole pages in celebrating the devotion of the Goths. I have extracted from an improbable story of Procopius the circumstances which had an air of probability. Procop. de Bell. Vandal. 1. i. c. 2 [tom. i. p. 315, edit. Bonn]. He supposes that the city was surprised while the senators slept in the afternoon; but Jerome, with more authority and more reason, affirms that it was in the night, "nocte Moab capta est; nocte cecidit murus ejus," tom. i. p. 121, ad Principiam [Epist. cxxvii. c. 12, tom. i. p. 953, edit. Vallars.].

4. Orosius (I. vii. c. 39, p. 573–576) applauds the piety of the Christian Goths without seeming to perceive that the greatest part of them were Arian heretics. Jornandes (c. 30, p. 653 [p. 86, edit. Lugd. B. 1597]) and Isidore of Seville (Chron. p. 714, edit. Grot.), who were both attached to the Gothic cause, have repeated and embellished these edifying tales. According to Isidore, Alaric himself was heard to say that he waged war with the Romans, and not with the apostles. Such was the style of the seventh century; two hundred years before, the fame and merit had been ascribed, not to the apostles, but to Christ.

5. See Augustine, De Civitate Dei, 1. i. c. 1–6. He particularly appeals to the examples of Troy, Syracuse, and Tarentum.

6. Jerome (tom. i. p. 121, ad Principiam [Ep. cxxvii. tom. i. p. 953, edit. Vallars.]) has applied to the sack of Rome all the strong expressions of Virgil:

> Quis cladem illius noctis, quis funera fando,
> Explicet, etc.

Procopius (I. i. c. 2 [tom. i. p. 316, edit. Bonn]) positively affirms that great numbers were slain by the Goths. Augustine (De Civ. Dei, 1. i. c. 12, 13) offers Christian comfort for the death of those whose bodies *(multa corpora)* had remained *(in tanta strage)* unburied. Baronius, from the different writings of the Fathers, has thrown some light on the sack of Rome. Annal. Eccles. A.D. 410, No. 16–44.

7. Sozomen, 1. ix. c. 10. Augustine (De Civitate Dei, 1. i. c. 17) intimates that some virgins or matrons actually killed themselves to escape violation; and though he admires their spirit, he is obliged by this theology to condemn their rash presumption. Perhaps the good Bishop of Hippo was too easy in the belief, as well as too rigid in the censure, of this act of female heroism. The twenty maidens (if they ever existed) who threw themselves into the Elbe when Magdeburg was taken by storm have been multiplied to the number of twelve hundred. See Harte's History of Gustavus Adolphus, vol. i. p. 308.

8. See Augustine, De Civitate Dei, 1. i. c. 16–18. He treats the subject with remarkable accuracy; and, after admitting that there cannot be any crime where there is no consent, he adds, "Sed quia non solum quod ad dolorem, verum etiam quor ad libidinem, pertinet, in corpore alieno perpetrari potest; quicquid tale factum fuerit, etsi retentamconstantissimo animo pudicitiam non excutit, pudorem tamen incutit, ne credatur factum cum mentis etiam voluntate, quod fiere fortasse sine carnis aliqua voluptate non potuit." In c. 18 he makes some curious distinctions between moral and physical virginity.

9. Marcella, a Roman lady, equally respectable for her rank, her age, and her piety, was thrown on the ground and cruelly beaten and whipped, "caesam fustibus flagellisque," etc. Jerome, tom. i. p. 121, ad Principiam [Ep. cxxvii. c. 13, tom. i. p. 953, edit. Vallars.]. See Augustine, De Civ. Dei, 1. i. c. 10. The modern Sacco di Rome, p. 208, gives an idea of the various methods of torturing prisoners for gold.

10. The historian Sallust, who usefully practised the vice which he has so eloquently censured, employed the plunder of Numidia to adorn his palace and gardens on the Quirinal Hill. The spot where the house stood is now marked by the Church of St. Susanna, separated only by a street from the baths of Diocletian, and not far distant from the Salarian gate. See Nardini, Roma Antica, p. 192, 193, and the great Plan of Modern Rome, by Nolli.

11. The expressions of Procopius are distinct and moderate (De Bell. Vandal. 1. i. c. 2 [tom i. p. 316, edit. Bonn]). The chronicle of Marcellinus speaks too strongly, "partem urbis Romae cremavit"; and the words of Philostorgius ([Greek omitted in abridgment], 1. xii. c. 3) convey a false and exaggerated idea. Bargaeus has composed a particular dissertation (see tom. iv. Antiquit. Rom. Graev.) to prove that the edifices of Rome were not subverted by the Goths and Vandals.

12. Orosius, 1. ii. c. 19, p. 143. He speaks as if he disapproved *all* statues: "vel Deum vel hominem mentiuntur." They consisted of the kings of Alba and Rome from Aeneas, the Romans illustrious either in arms or arts, and the deified Caesars. The expression which he uses of *Forum* is somewhat ambiguous, since there existed *five* principal *Fora*; but as they were all contiguous and adjacent, in the plain which is surrounded by the Capito-

line, the Quirinal, the Esquiline, and the Donatus, p. 162–201, and the Roma Antica of Nardini, p. 212–273. The former is more useful for the ancient descriptions, the latter for the actual topography.

13. Orosius (1. ii. c. 19, p. 142) compares the cruelty of the Gauls and the clemency of the Goths. "Ibi vix quemquam inventum senatorem, qui vel abseus evaserit; hic vix quemquam requiri, qui forte ut latens perierit." But there is an air of rhetoric, and perhaps of falsehood, in this antithesis; and Socrates (1. vii. c. 10) affirms, perhaps by an opposite exaggeration, that *many* senators were put to death with various and exquisite tortures.

14. "Multi . . . . Christiani captivi ducti sunt" (Augustine, De Civ. Dei, 1. i. c. 14); and the Christians experienced no peculiar hardships.

15. See Heineccius, Antiquitat. Juris Roman. tom. i. p. 96.

16. Appendix Cod. Theodos. xvi. in Sirmond. Opera, tom. i. p. 735. This edict was published on the 11th of December, A.D. 408, and is more reasonable than properly belonged to the ministers of Honorius.

17.   Eminus lgilii sylvosa cacumina miror;
                      Quem fraudare nefas laudis honore suae.
                  Haed proprios nuper tutata est insula saltus;
                      Sive loci ingenio, seu domini genio.
                  Gurgite cum modico victricibus obstitit armis,
                      Tanquam longinquo dissociata mari.
                  Haec multos lacera suscepit ab urbe fugatos,
                      Hic fessis posito certa timore salus.
                  Plurima terreno populaverat aequora bello,
                      Contra naturam classe timendus qeues:
                  Unum, mira fides, vario discrimine portum!
                      Tam propre Romanis, ram procul esse Getis.
                              Rutilius, in Itinerar. 1. i. 325.

The island is not called Giglio. See Cluver. Ital. Antiq. 1. ii. p. 502.

18. As the adventures of Proba and her family are connected with the life of St. Augustine, they are diligently illustrated by Tillemont, Mém. Ecclés. tom. xiii. p. 620–635. Some time after their arrival in Africa, Demetrias took the veil and made a vow of virginity, an event which was considered of the highest importance to Rome and to the world. All the *saints* wrote congratulatory letters to her; that of Jerome is still extant (tom. i. p. 62–73, ad Demetriad. de servanda Virginitat. [Epist. cxxx. tom. i. p. 969, edit. Vallars.]), and contains a mixture of absurd reasoning, spirited declamation, and curious facts, some of which relate to the siege and sack of Rome.

19. See the pathetic complaint of Jerome (tom. v. p. 400) in his preface to the second book of his Commentaries on the prophet Ezekiel.

20. Orosius, though with some theological partiality, states this comparison, 1. ii. c. 19, p. 142, 1. vii. c. 39, p. 575. But in the history of the taking of Rome by the Gauls everything is uncertain, and perhaps fabulous. See Beaufort sur l'Incertitude, etc., de l'Histoir Romaine, p. 356; and Melot, in the Mém. de l'Académie des Inscript. tom. xv. p. 1–21.

21. The reader who wishes to inform himself of the circumstances of this famous event may peruse an admirable narrative in Dr. Robertson's History of Charles V, vol. ii. p. 283, or consult the Annali d'Italia of the learned Muratori, tom. xiv. p. 230–244, octavo edition. If he is desirous of examining the originals, he may have recourse to the eighteenth book of the great but unfinished history of Guicciardini. But the account which most truly deserves the name of the authentic and original is a little book entitled II Sacco di Roma, composed, within less than a month after the assault of the city, by the *brother* of the historian Guicciardini, who appears to have been an able magistrate and a dispassionate writer.

22. The furious spirit of Luther, the effect of temper and enthusiasm, has been forcibly attacked (Bossuet, Hist. des Variations des Églises Protestantes, livre i. p. 20–36) and feebly defended (Seckendorf, Domment. de Lutheranismo, especially 1. i. No. 78, p. 120, and 1. iii. No. 122, p. 556).

QUESTIONS TO CONSIDER

1. How does Gibbon portray Roman officialdom in this passage? What does this say about his views of the origins of Roman weakness?
2. How does Gibbon portray Alaric? What does this indicate about his view of the proper character of leaders?
3. What is the purpose of Gibbon's footnotes? Do they add to our understanding or to our confidence regarding the accuracy of what we read?

FOR FURTHER READING

Black, J. B. *The Art of History: A Study of Four Great Historians of the Eighteenth Century.* New York: Russell and Russell, 1965.

Craddock, Patricia B. *Edward Gibbon: Luminous Historian, 1772–1794.* Baltimore: Johns Hopkins University Press, 1989.

CHAPTER 32

Thomas Babington Macaulay

British Nationalist

Thomas Babington Macaulay
© *North Wind Pictures*

In England a hundred years ago the works of Thomas Babington Macaulay (1800–1859) were read as widely as those of his contemporary Charles Dickens. A man of political action as well as of letters, Macaulay enmeshed himself in the movements for political and social reform of the early nineteenth century. He typified and popularized the Whig interpretation of history that still characterizes the best-selling works of popular history: the emphases are on politics, personality, and progress, with the nineteenth-century British held up as the pinnacle of human excellence. As a consequence, his ideas have influenced millions of people who have never heard his name.

Macaulay grew up in an atmosphere permeated by reform politics and religious sincerity. His father was a leader in the antislavery movement in England and had been one of the first governors of the colony of Sierra Leone in Africa, founded by slaves freed in British dominions. A general concern for the downtrodden characterized the evangelical wing of the Church of England, associated with William Wilberforce, which dominated the neighborhood and family circles in which Macaulay was reared. A precocious child, he launched plans to write a universal history at age eight and penned epic verse for his family's amusement. He memorized masses of written poetry easily and read with great speed and comprehension.

A prize student at Cambridge, Macaulay was admitted to the bar in 1826 but never practiced law, concentrating instead on writing and politics. He served in the House of Commons from 1830 to 1847 and from 1852 to 1856, representing various ridings (mostly Edinburgh) while also pursuing a productive literary career. He first spoke in favor of a bill to remove political disabilities from Jews in Britain—sounding the theme of reform that characterized his Whig politics. With Wilberforce and other evangelicals, Macaulay was a lead orator in favor of the Reform Act of 1832 that led to more equitable representation in Parliament. He was appointed Commissioner of the Board of Control for India in 1832 to oversee the transition from East India Company control to direct rule by the British government. In India from 1833 to 1838, Macaulay helped construct an Indian penal code that recognized the equality of Indians and Britons before the law. He also laid ground to guarantee a free press in India.

In 1839 Macaulay became Secretary-at-War in the cabinet and began work on his *History of England*. The government resigned in 1841, and he resumed intense activity on the *History* and other literary projects while maintaining his parliamentary seat. Defeated in the general election of 1847, he brought out the first two volumes of the *History* in 1848; they were instant best sellers. In 1852 Macaulay was reelected to Parliament, but he suffered a heart attack and resigned his seat in 1856. Meanwhile, volumes three and four were published, to continuing accolades. In 1859 Macaulay was ennobled as Baron Macaulay of Rothely; later that same year he died. His sister Hannah edited and published a fifth volume of the *History* in 1861. Macaulay's influence in English historiography continued for almost a century in the writing of his nephew Otto Trevelyan and grandnephew Hugh Trevelyan, both famous historians.

Originally, Macaulay had planned to write a history of England from 1688 to 1820, but he only finished the section up to 1703. Nonetheless, the span from 1688 to 1702 was sufficient to display the fundamental outline of the Whig interpretation of history: the triumph of evangelical and reform values with the surpemacy of Parliament that was achieved in the Glorious Revolution of 1688. At heart, Macaulay shared with many of his Victorian contemporaries the view that the peak of human civilization had been reached in England after the Reform Act of 1832, and that the values and tastes of respectable English people of the Victorian era were self-evidently superior to those of other peoples in other times and places. Thus, whatever events or movements led toward the extension of widespread manhood suffrage, powerful representative assemblies, an end to slavery, and compassionate treatment of the less fortunate, were good; whatever led to autocracy, arbitrary elitism, religious intolerance, suppression of one group by another, or disdain for the poor, was evil. Macaulay used these criteria to evaluate English history, and they gave form to his narrative. Macaulay believed not only in the superiority of Britain but also in progress—not just material progress such as machines but also moral and intellectual progress, which he identified with trends in Britain in his own day. In all these respects, Macaulay was not unlike the most prominent American historians of his era, writers such as Francis Parkman, George Bancroft, and Henry Adams, who were similarly confident in the culture, values, and destiny of the United States.

Macaulay's style derived much from oratory, with short sentences (compared to such as Gibbon) and self-contained paragraphs. He wrote narrative history, in a soaring style that affected historians writing in English for a century after his death. Macaulay consumed popular novels uncritically and sought to bring something of the effect of the novel into his narration. His subject was primarily politics, although he used a wide range of sources and tried to illuminate social history as well.

The passages that follow are intended to give the reader a sampling of Macaulay's narrative style. The first is the introduction to the *History of England,* where Macaulay states his purpose. The second is a part of his description of England in 1685. The third summarizes the Whig understanding of history in a concrete way.

The History of England[1]

I purpose to write the history of England from the accession of King James the Second down to a time which is within the memory of men still living. I shall recount the errors which, in a few months, alienated a loyal gentry and priesthood from the House of Stuart. I shall trace the course of that revolution which terminated the long struggle between our sovereigns and their parliaments, and bound up together the rights of the people and the title of the reigning dynasty. I shall relate how the new settlement was, during many troubled years, successfully defended against foreign and domestic enemies; how, under that settlement, the authority of law and the security of property were found to be compatible with a liberty of discussion and of individual action never before known; how, from the auspicious union of order and freedom, sprang a prosperity of which the annals of human affairs had furnished no example; how our country, from a state of ignominious vassalage, rapidly rose to the place of umpire among European powers; how her opulence and her martial glory grew together; how, by resolute good faith, was gradually established a public credit fruitful of marvels which, to the statesmen of any former age, would have seemed incredible; how a gigantic commerce gave birth to a maritime power, compared with which every other maritime power, ancient or modern, sinks into insignificance; how Scotland, after ages of enmity, was at length united to England, not merely by legal bonds, but by indissoluble ties of interest and affection; how, in America, the British colonies rapidly became far mightier and wealthier than the realms which Cortes and Pizarro had added to the dominions of Charles the Fifth; how, in Asia, British adventurers founded an empire not less splendid, and more durable than that of Alexander.

Nor will it be less my duty faithfully to record disasters mingled with triumphs, and great national crimes and follies far more humiliating than any disaster. It will be seen that even what we justly account our chief blessings were not without alloy. It will be seen that the system which effectually secured our liberties against the encroachments of kingly power gave birth to a new class of abuses, from which absolute monarchies are exempt. It will be seen that, in consequence partly of unwise interference, and partly of unwise neglect, the increase of wealth and the extension of trade produced, together with immense good, some evils from which poor and rude societies are free. It will be seen how, in two important dependencies of the crown, wrong was followed by just retribution; how imprudence and obstinacy broke the ties which bound the North American colonies to the parent state; how Ireland, cursed by the domination of race over race, and of religion over religion, remained indeed a member of the empire, but a withered and distorted member, adding no strength to the body politic, and reproachfully pointed at by all who feared or envied the greatness of England.

Yet, unless I greatly deceive myself, the general effect of this checkered narrative will be to excite thankfulness in all religious minds, and hope in the breasts of all partiots. For the history of our country during the last hundred and sixty years is eminently the history of physical, of moral, and of intellectual improvement. Those who compare the age on which their lot has fallen with a golden age which exists only in their imagination, may talk of degeneracy and decay; but no man who is correctly informed as to the past will be disposed to take a morose or desponding view of the present.

I should very imperfectly execute the task which I have undertaken, if I were merely to treat of battles and seiges, of the rise and fall of administrations, of intrigues in the palace, and of debates in the parliament. It will be my endeavor to relate the history of the people as well as the history of the government; to trace the progress of useful and ornamental arts; to describe the rise of religious sects and the changes of literary tastes; to portray the manners of successive generations; and not to pass by with neglect even the revolutions which have taken place in dress, furniture, repasts, and public amusements. I shall cheerfully bear the reproach of having descended below the dignity of history, if I can succeed in placing before the English of the nineteenth century a true picture of the life of their ancestors.

* * *

I intend, in this chapter, to give a description of the state in which England was at the time when the crown passed from Charles the Second to his brother. Such a description, composed from scanty and dispersed materials, must necessarily be very imperfect. Yet it may perhaps correct some false notions which would render the subsequent narrative unintelligible or uninstructive.

If we would study with profit the history of our ancestors we must be constantly on our guard against that delusion which the well-known names of families, places, and offices naturally produce, and must never forget that the country of which we read was a very different country from that in which we live. In every experimental science there is a tendency towards perfection. In every human being there is a wish to ameliorate his own condition. These two principles have often sufficed, even when conteracted by great public calamities and by bad institutions, to carry civilization rapidly forward. No ordinary misfortune, no ordinary misgovernment, will do so much to make a nation wretched, as the constant progress of physical knowledge and the constant effort of every man to better himself will do to make a nation prosperous. It has often been found that profuse expenditure, heavy taxation, absurd commercial restrictions, corrupt tribunals, disastrous wars, seditions, persecutions, conflagrations, inundations, have not been able to destroy capital so fast as the exertions of private citizens have been able to create it. It can easily be proved that in our own land the national wealth has, during at least six centuries, been almost uninterruptedly increasing; that it was greater under the Tudors than under the Plantagenets; that it was greater under the Stuarts than under the Tudors; that, in spite of battles, sieges and confiscations, it was greater on the day of the Restoration than on the day when the Long Parliament met; that, in spite of maladministration, of extravagance, of public bankruptcy, of two costly and unsuccessful wars, of the pestilence and of the fire, it was greater on the day of the death of Charles the Second than on the day of his restoration. This progress, having continued during many ages, became at length, about the middle of the eighteenth century, portentously rapid, and has proceeded during the nineteenth with accelerated velocity. In consequence, partly of our geographical and partly of our moral position, we have, during several generations, been exempt from evils which have elsewhere impeded the efforts and destroyed the fruits of industry. While every part of the Continent, from Moscow to Lisbon, has been the theatre of bloody and devastating wars, no hostile standard has been seen here but as a trophy. While revolutions have taken place all around us our government has never once been subverted by violence. During a hundred years there has been in our island no tumult of sufficient importance to be called an insurrection. The law has never been borne down either by popular fury or by regal tyranny. Public credit has been held sacred. The administration of justice has been pure. Even in times which might by Englishmen be justly called evil times, we have enjoyed what almost every other nation in the world would have considered as an ample measure of civil and religious freedom. Every man has felt entire confidence that the State would protect him in the possession of what had been earned by his diligence and hoarded by his self-denial. Under the benignant influence of peace and liberty science has flourished and has been applied to practical purposes on a scale never before known. The consequence is that a change to which the history of the whole world furnishes no parallel has taken place in our country. Could the England of 1685 be, by some magical process, set before our eyes, we should not know one landscape in a hundred, or one building in ten thousand. The country gentleman would not recognize his own fields. The inhabitant of the town would not recognize his own street. Everything has been changed, but the great features of nature, and a few massive and durable works of human art. We might find out Snowdon and Windermere, the Cheddar Cliffs and Beachy Head. We might find out here and there a Norman minster, or a castle which witnessed the Wars of the Roses. But, with such rare exceptions, everything would be strange to us. Many thousands of square miles which are now rich corn land and meadow, intersected by green hedgerows, and dotted with villages and pleasant country seats, would appear as moors overgrown with furze, or fens abandoned to wild ducks. We should see straggling huts built of wood and covered with thatch where we now see manufacturing towns and seaports renowned to the farthest ends of the world. The capital itself would shrink to dimensions not much exceeding those of its present suburb on the south of the Thames. Not less strange to us would be the garb and manners of the people, the furniture and the equipages, the interior of the shops and dwellings. Such a change in the state of a nation seems to be at least as well entitled to the notice of an historian as any change of the dynasty or of the ministry.

*   *   *

Still more important is the benefit which all orders of society, and especially the lower orders, have derived from the mollifying influence of civilization on the national character. The groundwork of that character has indeed been the same through many generations, in the sense in which the groundwork of the character of an individual may be said to be the same when he is a rude and thoughtless schoolboy and when he is a refined and accomplished man. It is pleasing to reflect that the public mind of England has softened while it has ripened, and that we have, in the course of ages, become not only a wiser but also a kinder people. There is scarcely a page of the history or lighter literature of the seventeenth century which does not contain some proof that our ancestors were less humane than their posterity. The discipline of workshops, of schools, of private families, though not more efficient than at present, was infinitely harsher. Masters, well born and bred, were in the habit of beating their servants. Pedagogues knew no way of imparting knowledge but by beating their pupils. Husbands, of decent station, were not ashamed to beat their wives. The implacability of hostile factions was such as we can scarcely conceive. Whigs were disposed to murmur because Stafford was suffered to die without seeing his bowels burned before his face. Tories reviled and insulted Russell as his coach passed from the tower to the scaffold in Lincoln's Inn Fields.

As little mercy was shown by the populace to sufferers of a humbler rank. If an offender was put into the pillory, it was well if he escaped with life from the shower of brickbats and paving stones. If he was tied to the cart's tail, the crowd pressed round him, imploring the hangman to give it the fellow well, and make him howl. Gentlemen arranged parties of pleasure to Bridewell on court days for the purpose of seeing the wretched women who beat hemp there whipped. A man pressed to death for refusing to plead, a woman burned for coining, excited less sympathy than is now felt for a galled horse or an overdriven ox. Fights compared with which a boxing match is a refined and humane spectacle were among the favorite diversions of a large part of the town. Multitudes assembled to see gladiators hack each other to pieces with deadly weapons, and shouted with delight when one of the combatants lost a finger or an eye. The prisons were hells on earth, seminaries of every crime and of every disease. At the assizes the lean and yellow culprits brought with them from their cells to the dock an atmosphere of stench and pestilence which sometimes avenged them signally on bench, bar, and jury. But on all this misery society looked with profound indifference. Nowhere could be found that sensitive and restless compassion which has, in our time, extended a powerful protection to the factory child, to the Hindoo widow, to the negro slave, which pries into the stores and watercasks of every emigrant ship, which winces at every lash laid on the back of a drunken sailor, which will not suffer the thief in the hulks to be ill fed or overworked, and which has repeatedly endeavored to save the life even of the murderer. It is true that compassion ought, like all other feelings, to be under the government of reason, and has, for want of such government, produced some ridiculous and some deplorable effects. But the more we study the annals of the past, the more shall we rejoice that we live in a merciful age, in an age in which cruelty is abhorred, and in which pain, even when deserved, is inflicted reluctantly and from a sense of duty. Every class doubtless has gained largely by this great moral change: but the class which has gained most is the poorest, the most dependent, and the most defenseless.

The general effect of the evidence which has been submitted to the reader seems hardly to admit of doubt. Yet, in spite of evidence, many will still image to themselves the England of the Stuarts as a more pleasant country than the England in which we live. It may at first sight seem strange that society, while constantly moving forward with eager speed, should be constantly looking backward with tender regret. But these two propensities, inconsistent as they may appear, can easily be resolved into the same principle. Both spring from our impatience of the state in which we actually are. That impatience, while it stimulates us to surpass preceding generations, disposes us to overrate their happiness. It is, in some sense, unreasonable and ungrateful in us to be constantly discontented with a condition which is constantly improving. But, in truth, there is constant improvement precisely because there is constant discontent. If we were perfectly satisfied with the present we should cease to contrive, to labor, and to save with a view to the future. And it is natural that, being dissatisfied with the present, we should form a too favorable estimate of the past.

In truth we are under a deception similar to that which misleads the traveller in the Arabian desert. Beneath the caravan all is dry and bare: but far in advance, and far in the rear, is the semblance of refreshing waters. The pilgrims hasten forward to find nothing but sand where an hour before they had seen a lake. They turn their eyes and see a lake where, an hour before, they were toiling through sand. A similar illusion seems to haunt nations through every stage of the long progress from poverty and barbarism to the highest degree of opulence and civilisation. But if we resolutely chase the mirage backward, we shall find it recede before us into the regions of fabulous antiquity. It is now the fashion to place the golden age of England in times when noblemen were destitute of comforts the want of which would be intolerable to a modern footman, when farmers and shopkeepers breakfasted on loaves the very sight of which would raise a riot in a modern workhouse, when to have a clean shirt once a week was a privilege reserved for the higher class of gentry, when men died faster in the purest country air than they now die in the more pestilential lanes of our towns, and when men died faster in the lanes of our towns than they now die on the coast of Guiana. We too shall, in our turn, be outstripped, and in our turn envied. It may well be, in the twentieth century, that the peasant of Dorsetshire may think himself miserably paid with twenty shillings a week; that the carpenter at Greenwich may receive ten shillings a day; that laboring men may be as little used to dine without meat as they now are to eat rye bread; that sanitary police and medical discoveries may have added several more years to the average length of human life; that numerous comforts and luxuries which are now unknown, or confined to a few, may be within the reach of every diligent and thrifty working man. And yet it may then be the mode to assert that the increase of wealth and the progress of science have benefitted the few at the expense of the many, and to talk of the reign of Queen Victoria as the time when England was truly merry England, when all classes were bound together by brotherly sympathy, when the rich did not grind the faces of the poor, and when the poor did not envy the splendor of the rich.

QUESTIONS TO CONSIDER

1. What reasons does Macaulay give for writing this history?
2. How does passage three reflect the "Whig interpretation of history"? Compare Macaulay's vision of industrial progress to Thompson's depiction of the weaver's lives (chapter 51).
3. In what sense might this writing "betray the vanity of a male author" (to paraphrase Gibbon's dismissal of Anna Comnena)? Is there something distinctive to the writing of a male historian like Macaulay?

FOR FURTHER READING

Adams, Henry. *History of the United States During the Jefferson and Madison Administrations.* 9 vols.

Bancroft, George. *History of the Colonization of the United States.* 15th ed. Boston, 1852.

_____ . *History of the United States.* 6 vols. 1834–1882.

Butterfield, Herbert. *The Whig Interpretation of History.* New York: Norton, 1965; orig. 1931.

Callcott, George H. *History in the United States, 1800–1860: Its Practice and Purpose.* Baltimore, 1970.

Clive, John. *Macaulay: The Shaping of the Historian.* New York: Knopf, 1973.

Cruikshank, Margaret. *Thomas Babington Macaulay.* Boston: Twayne, 1978.

Jacobs, Wilbur R. *Francis Parkman, Historian as Hero.* Austin, TX: University of Texas Press, 1991.

Millgate, Jane. *Macaulay.* London: Routledge and Kegan Paul, 1973.

Parkman, Francis. *France and England in North America.* 7 vols. Boston: Little, Brown, 1865–92.

NOTES

1. Thomas Babington Macaulay, *The History of England*, vol. 1 (New York: Allison, 1887), 1–3, 218–20, 330–33.

CHAPTER 33

Harriet Martineau

Victorian Polymath

Harriet Martineau
The Granger Collection, New York

I t is instructive to contrast Macaulay's career with that of Harriet Martineau (1802–1877). Both were enormously popular historians and people of letters in mid-nineteenth-century Britain. Both expressed the national self-confidence of the British at the height of Victoria's empire. Both were careful scholars who wrote vivid prose. Macaulay was male, and a political career was open to him to go with his literary achievements; Martineau was female and so limited to literature. Macaulay was held up to later generations of British students as the historian *par excellence;* Martineau was forgotten.

Had Martineau been male, perhaps today we would celebrate her wide learning and her keen insights into such matters as the growth of British industrialism and the plight of its lower classes. We would likely read her analysis of British rule in India and her history of England's "thirty years of peace" (1816–1846). Probably we would study her account of American society, which in its time was deemed second only to Alexis de Tocqueville's still famous work.

Yet nineteenth-century England gave intellectual women neither status nor social role. Martineau had to work without institutional support, private fortune, or public career. Still, she managed to become one of her era's major pundits, at various times a historian, a social critic, a writer, a public educator, and a journalist. Her histories, popular pamphlets, novels, travelogues, and newspaper commentaries gave her both a readership and an income. Yet they spread her so thin that our own more specialized age is only now beginning to acquaint itself with her genius.

And a genius she was. Despite frequent bouts of ill health, she wrote over 70 books, scores of journal articles, and nearly 2,000 newspaper pieces. The last were particularly impressive in an age when the papers often ran articles of 20 pages or more—far longer than the snippets that now appear. She was, in short, a grand dame of English letters, friend to such now better-remembered figures as Thomas Carlyle, William Wordsworth, Charlotte Brontë, J. S. Mill, Florence Nightingale, and Matthew Arnold. Arnold praised her for her independence of mind and for the originality of her prose.

Her work fits no ordinary mold. Born sixth of eight children to a Norwich textile manufacturer, Harriet Martineau was forced to take up her pen after the crash of 1827 destroyed her father's business. She found herself too independent to accept marriage, and deafness prevented her from becoming a governess, the other main career open to middle-class women. Her first successful work was a series of fictional illustrations of the principles of laissez-faire economics. Each sold tens of thousands of copies, and the series made her reputation. She then traveled to the United States and wrote a well-received analysis of American society—the first to show the importance of women's everyday roles to the rest of social life.

After several novels and a book on household economy, Martineau wrote a historically informed travel book on Egypt and the Middle East, a social history of England in the early 1800s, and some books on American slavery. She translated and condensed Auguste Comte's *Cours de Philosophie Positive,* a highly influential treatise on scientific progress. Comte founded scientific sociology, and like him, Martineau believed that science could solve all social ills. The educated of the world—and by this she meant upper-class Europeans and Americans—had a duty to spread science to the lower orders and to people of other lands. She thus believed in imperialism, though she preferred it more enlightened than it often was in practice. With proper guidance, she held, all the world's peoples could make progress from superstition to true knowledge. In this way, they could improve their lives.

Martineau's faith in science and in enlightened European rule are now out of style. Her regard for women's social roles and her analysis of the plight of the poor and downtrodden are the parts of her work that are the most timely today. They have, indeed, led to her recent honor among feminists and sociologists. But they are only examples of her general sensitivity to history's social side. For her, history was not a list of political events, nor the sayings of great men. It was, instead, the story of everyday social progress, often halting, toward the fulfillment of human potential. Martineau believed that such potential could only be met by understanding social history and its laws.

These themes are evident in the passage that follows. Martineau wrote *British Rule in India: A Historical Sketch* in 1857 to inform the public about the circumstances behind the Sepoy Rebellion of that year. In her view, despite good intentions and an honest effort to govern in a humane and scientific manner, the British rulers of India did not understand Indian social life. Their laws ran afoul of Indian customs and social structures. Not that Martineau particularly liked such customs. She thought many of them evil, and needlessly harsh toward the peasantry. But it was foolish, she held, not to take them into account. Successful social engineering needed sure knowledge of the social landscape—a fact that Britain's leaders ignored at their peril. Note that Martineau did not advocate abandoning India. She believed that her countrymen had a role to play there, and that European settlement was the best cure for native ills. Like Comte, whose disciple she remained, she believed that progress required constant effort and great wisdom.

British Rule in India[1]

Beginning Of A Revenue System: 1793

. . . It is very interesting to follow the fortunes of the British in India, as their dominion extended by war and diplomacy; and especially when they were forced into war by the aggressions of their neighbours—-as in the instance of the Mysore usurpers, Hyder and Tippoo; but our real position and contemporary prospects cannot be understood without some observation of the measures introduced by Lord Cornwallis as reforms in the internal administration of the country. These measures have affected the destinies of the native inhabitants to an incalculable extent; and they have been the subject of controversy among statesmen and economists from their first promulgation to this day. No picture of the English in India can therefore be faithful in which features of so much importance are not sketched, however meagerly.

Horace Walpole said of Lord Cornwallis that he was "as cool as Conway, and as brave; he was indifferent to everything but being in the right; he held fame cheap, and smiled at reproach." This noble eulogium indicates the faults as well as the virtues of the statesman; for a man of such qualities could hardly have any other faults than those which were the shady side of his virtues. So it was, as every part of his eventful life proved, and especially the seven years of his rule in India. He went out with fixed ideas as to the principles and characteristics of a paternal government; and he proceeded to institute from Calcutta a system founded on those ideas. There was another great and humane man at Madras, equally devoted to the work of good government; and his aspirations took form in a scheme the exact opposite of that of Lord Cornwallis. The subsequent controversy has related to the rival schemes of Lord Cornwallis and Sir Thomas Munro. We must look at the outlines of both, as both were tried in different districts.

The revenue of the Company at that time was derived from the land to the extent of more than two-thirds, the monopolies of salt and opium supplying two-thirds of the remainder. The land tenures, and the method of drawing revenue from them, were, therefore, the first object of interest and care to a good government. Lord Cornwallis believed that nothing could well be worse than the condition of the whole agricultural population, as he and his predecessors found it, and that his duty clearly was to remodel the whole system on incontrovertible principles. He held that a steady emanation of capital from land would sustain, and was the only means of sustaining, an upper class, by which the mass would ultimately be raised in their intellectual and material condition; that such capital would create commerce; that such commerce would create knowledge and enlightenment; and that thus the ends of good government would ultimately be answered. It should be added, in justice to him and to Sir Thomas Munro, that both anticipated with entire confidence the speedy colonization of India as the consequence of the free trade which they supposed to be near at hand. Every assumption of new political and territorial power by the Company was, in their eyes, an outgrowing of the original commercial function, which must soon, as they calculated, be vacated altogether. The failure of that calculation explains a part of such ill-success as attended both schemes. Lord Cornwallis arrived from England full of the constitutional supposition that an industrial people had their lot in their own hands, when once they were furnished with good laws and methods. He was so far from perceiving that clear and abundant knowledge of the people to be legislated for was requisite, that he and his helpers volunteered an explanation that they knew very little of the residents and their ways and notions, adding that the knowledge would come in time, and give the means of working the new system more and more effectually. The good-natured conceit of this notion is so like that which at once institutes and damages most philanthropic experiments, that there is no need to enlarge upon it: nor need to be added that Lord Cornwallis's view of our duty to India was that we should Europeanize it as thoroughly and rapidly as possible. India was, from the earliest times discernible by us, studded over with villages, the land being divided into minute portions, which were jointly and severally, in each village liable for the whole rent and taxes. However long such a system might have lasted if it had been left to itself, it was thoroughly dislocated by the Mussulman intrusion. The tyranny which under Mogul rule crushed the peasantry, made the soil change hands; and in one place several holders depended on one portion, while in another several portions were in the hands of one man. Where the Mussulman had not penetrated there were complications quite as difficult to deal with. The original method seems to have everywhere sprung out of the primary necessity every community was under to defend itself against enemies, brute or human; and as it permitted no inequality of fortune, it was sure to give way in some point or another, and to lapse into special customs quite as important in the people's eyes as any principles or laws whatever. All these facts and considerations were ignored by Lord Cornwallis in instituting his celebrated "permanent settlement."

He found ready-made to his hand a class called zemindars, who were so full of complaints and so eager in their claims, that they formed a very prominent object in his view of Indian life. Many of these were Hindoo princes of very ancient families; and no small number boasted of having held their property since a long date before the Mogul conquest. It was natural for the British to regard the order as a sort of nobles, and for Lord Cornwallis to suppose that he had only to endow them with certain powers to obtain the upper class on which the future enlightenment and elevation of the country depended. Whereas in the parts of India which then concerned us (a limitation which must be borne in mind) the zemindars were the class responsible for the payment of the land revenue, and virtually, therefore, the masters of the cultivators and the land. The community of the villages was one of liability and not of possessions; and the zemindars were regarded practically as the landowners of society, when they were theoretically only the middlemen, whose function was to levy the revenue, and pay it over to the sovereign. This account of the zemindars should be accompanied by the warning that their precise character and function are still a matter of dispute between the advocates of opposite systems, some considering them as genuine landowners, and others as mere officers of Government, making their own fortunes out of their office, and at the expense of the ryots or cultivators from whom they levied the revenue. What Lord Cornwallis proposed to do with them was this:

In 1793 he made proclamation of a definitive settlement of the land revenues in Bengal. The Government gave up all claim to an increased revenue in future. The zemindars were to be the proprietors of the soil, but under the restriction that they could not displace any ryot who paid the then existing amount of rent. The difference between what the zemindar received and what he paid to Government was supposed to be one-third; and he had a further means of improving his fortunes in the waste lands, which were handed over to the class as a gift. These lands amounted to at least a third of the whole area. The method of equal division was imposed as the law of inheritance. All this might look well on paper on the Governor-general's desk; but a multitude of difficulties rose up at the first hour of its enforcement. Zemindars and ryots could not agree about rent and other claims; there were endless contradictions about ownership of lands: and as soon as there were courts ready to try causes arising under the new system, the amount and hopeless intricacy of the business might have dismayed any but the stoutest heart. Opinions vary still as to the results of the method on the whole. Where it fails, some lay the blame on Lord Wellesley's passive reception of the policy, which he did not try to amend; and it is certain that the official successors of Lord Cornwallis were too full of their wars and their diplomacy to give proper attention to a scheme which involved the vital interests of nearly the whole population. Complaints abounded, certainly; but it may be true that these complaints were a sign of reviving life, as far preferable to the previous apathy of the ryot class as the screams of a resuscitated patient under the pains of a returning circulation are better than the insensibility of a drowning man under water. On the one hand, again, the rise in the value of land, soon apparent at sales, seemed to show that the plan worked well; while, on the other, it is alleged that such rise was not only capricious where the settlement extended, but that it exactly corresponded with the increased value of the nearest lands which were not subject to the "permanent settlement." It could hardly be alleged that the lot of the ryot was improved, while the landowner could find means of involving him in difficulty, and then turning him out, in order to make way for a tenant who would pay more. In six years from the first promulgation, a former power was restored to the zemindars, on their complaint that they could not obtain payment from the ryots, and on their showing that many of them had lost their ancient estates, and been ruined. They gained their point partly by showing that the ruined zemindars gave place to a new set of landowners more oppressive than themselves. They were allowed, as of old, to eject the ryots, and then the ryots found themselves thrown into a worse purgatory than that from which they had been ostensibly rescued. It was under this regime that Rammohun Roy came over, and gave us his opinion, which was that the system worked well for the Company, well for the zemindars, and most wretchedly for the ryots. Bengal paid better than

Madras, which was under the other system: but then, the North-West provinces, which were not under the settlement, paid as well as Bengal. The prosperity of the zemindars was owing not only to the legitimate resources of the waste lands, but to that exaction of increased rents which it was the main object of the whole scheme to preclude. As for the depressed millions, the testimony of Rammohun Roy was very striking. He said that one might take one's stand anywhere in the country, and find that within a circle of a hundred miles there was probably not one man, outside the landholding class, who was in independent circumstances, or even in possession of the comforts of life. No doubt matters have greatly improved in the quarter of a century that has elapsed since this testimony was recorded; but the existence of so low an average of welfare in 1830 proves that Lord Cornwallis's plan was not adapted for remedying the evils inherent in the Asiatic social system—such as we found it. Lord Wellesley, however, had no misgivings about it, but extended it to conquered and ceded provinces, till it had a very wide area for the trial of its powers.

Sir Thomas Munro's scheme, called the Ryotwar system, had its trial and its failures too. It set out from the premises the very opposite of those of Lord Cornwallis. Society in India, we were told, was successful, powerful, civilized, orderly, and refined, clothed in bright shawls and fine muslins, while the Britons wore hides and painted themselves for battle; and the inhabitants of such a country, descendants of such ancestors, must know better than any upstart strangers what social methods were most suitable to their constitution and environment. The object should therefore be to make Indian society as intensely Asiatic as possible. It was not suggested that, for such an aim, the legislating and executive authority ought to be Asiatic too; but the absurdity and peril of subjecting fifty millions of people to the ideas of European closet-statesmen, who admitted their own ignorance of native history, was emphatically exhibited by the advocates of the Ryotwar system. On their part, however, they fell into the mistake of imposing a truly Asiatic repression on the industrial classes. Sir Thomas Munro swept away all intervention between the Government and the taxpayer. He demolished the intermediate function of the zemindars altogether. Every ryot was to have his field surveyed and assessed; a deduction for errors was to be made in each group of assessments, and then he was to pay the annual rent direct to the State; that rent being fixed for ever at the amount first settled. The waste land, after being surveyed and classed, was to be taken in hand by the ryots at their own pleasure; and they were at liberty to give up any portions of their lands, after the assessment had once determined the value. This looked well at first, like the scheme it was intended to supersede; and the more because Munro proposed the most liberal terms that could be offered to the ryots. But the working was immediately encompassed with difficulties. Alarmed zemindars showed that certain fields had paid rent to their fathers, in money or in kind, for many generations; there were many cases in which the ryots were virtually tenants at will; and in such instances the plan was either oppressive or impracticable. By sweeping away the landholders, the only chance of a thinking and lettered order of society was destroyed. The plan of survey, minute and meddlesome, let loose an army

of rapacious native agents upon the poor ryots, who were accustomed to
suppose that nothing could be done without bribes. According to Sir Thomas
Munro himself, not more than five per cent of subordinate officials were
innocent of peculation. As for the collection of the small installments of rent
(or tax, whichever it is called), it afforded more opportunity for oppression
and corruption than the power of any constitutionally intermediate body.
Upon one pretence or another, the lower functionaries of the State might
interfere with the ryot almost every day. Nor could the class, or any members
of it, rise in fortune and independence. Where there is no middle class, or only
one class, such elevation never happens. In this case the impossibility was
strengthened by the remarkable arrangement that bad seasons and other
accidents should make no difference in the payments. As a bad year or two
might thus ruin the most thrifty and industrious cultivator, the temptation
was irresistible—to live from hand to mouth, and be satisfied with what
chance might send. Thus a whole series of districts sank down to the condition
of the few which had before no zemindars, and which were noted for their
depression. According to the accounts transmitted of the district Coimbatore,
where the Ryotwar system worked best, the ryot paid, in 1828, about 1£.13s.
per annum out of a gross produce averaging 5£. It seems almost incredible
that the cultivator should be expected to thrive on 3 £.7s. a year for himself
and his family, allowing him as much cattle as he could keep in consistency
with his tillage. It is not surprising that the revenue under the Ryotwar system
should fall far below that raised in Bengal under the Permanent Settlement.
And it is rather surprising if we do not perceive that the elevation of society in
India must depend on something else than arbitrary assortment of ranks and
orders, and ingenious inventions for assigning land and collecting revenue. In
as far as the people are higher and happier than under native anarchy, it is
from the moral power with which we are invested in their eyes (and especially
through the improvement visible in the character and conduct of our officials
in India), and from the moral vitality which we are thus able to impart to
them. Political systems must always be weak or useless means of social
advancement till the advancement has itself proceeded a long way. Hence we
may acknowledge the failure, on the whole, of both the schemes proposed for
the redemption of native society, without losing hope of final success, or
denying such beneficial consequences as arose from each. Under the one there
was, no doubt, a considerable extension of tillage, and improved industrial
animation. Under the other, the peasantry felt an immediate relief from the
heavy hand of the landholder. For the rest, other influences were necessary
than belong to any land revenue scheme.

The crowning glory of Lord Cornwallis's plan was supposed to be the
wide diffusion of equal justice. For the first time, the peasantry saw the
collectors of the revenue subject to laws which could be read to the people in
a way which they could understand; and they were told that if anybody
attempted to charge them more than the amount settled on the institution of
the new plan, they had only to apply to the courts to get justice. The courts
were presently overwhelmed with applications, which it was found impracticable to deal with from the intricacy of claims and of the evidence brought on

behalf of them. Matters were worse when the power of ejectment was restored to the zemindars against the ryots; and at the end of a few years it was evident that, whatever the law might say to it, the ryots were made to pay higher rents than the settlement authorized, and that they could not obtain justice when they appealed against the hardship.

Under the Ryotwar system there was even less chance of justice. Sir Thomas Munro believed that the old laws, as well as the old customs of the region must be adopted; and he therefore preserved, as an essential provision of the common law of India in civil matters, the Punchayet, or method of arbitration. No native, he said, would ever believe that justice could be had without resort to it. The people, however, abandoned it as soon as they perceived that courts on the European method involved less delay and expense. In three years' time even the courts in which only native judges sat to administer European law, were resorted to in preference to the Punchayet, which might have preserved society in India (as Sir James Mackintosh declared that it did) before any European authority was established, but which was soon to be confined to those localities where the people had never seen an Englishman, nor heard of the new plans which were on trial throughout the land. The benefits of the Ryotwar scheme, such as they were, were soon almost neutralized by the corruption of the judicial part of the plan. The collectors were found so entirely unable to levy the revenue, that it was considered necessary to make magistrates of them, and give them the control of the police. This was a return to the old grievance of the officers of Government sitting in judgment on their own acts, and employing the police to execute their own purposes. More and more power was given to the native collectors under the Madras Government, till, in a quarter of a century, they were authorized not only to impose fines but stripes. In 1826, the Directors sent over a strong protest against unchecked powers being confided to a class of men who were under constant temptation to apply them tyrannically. On the whole it is clear that benevolent and just-minded men had failed in discovering means of carrying justice within reach of the whole people. For many years the headman of the village was still the main hope of the inhabitants, and his traditional authority was worth more to them than any new judicial system; and the Brahmins and heads of castes did more to preserve order and reconcile differences in their communities than the best men who worthily placed themselves under the orders of the pure-hearted Cornwallis.

In reviewing the operation of the Permanent Settlement and the Ryotwar system, it is (as was observed before) necessary to bear in mind that complement of both schemes which was, after all, never introduced—a free trade, inducing an ample colonization of the country from Europe. When Lord Wellesley made a progress through the upper provinces, in 1801, he was delighted by the signs of improvement which were visible in such agricultural districts as were fertile enough to invite experiment. His suite had rare sport among the wild beasts which were disturbed by clearances in the jungle; and the ryots were improving their tillage in the confidence that their rent would not be immediately increased. It is true there were not a few old and opulent zemindar families, now reduced to poverty, weeping along the roadside, having lost the estates which their fathers had held for centuries. It is true these were succeeded, too often, by rapacious strangers, who used the restored powers of ejectment very harshly in regard to the ryots; but the great point seemed to be gained in the bringing new lands into cultivation. Such increased production would stimulate commerce when trade was thrown open; and commerce would bring capitalists; and the capitalists would make roads and canals, opening new markets, and, through the markets, further production still. Each village would no longer be all in all to itself—in good seasons glutted with food while poor in clothing; and in bad seasons pressed by famine because there was no access to any granaries. Each village was at all times like the hamlets of lower Bengal in a flood, cut off from access to every other, and subsisting as best it might; but the hope of the legislators of the time was that capital, industry, and commerce would unite the settlements into a prosperous community. This did not happen; and allowance must be made accordingly in estimating the Permanent Settlement. It was not till 1834 that the commercial monopoly was broken up; and it is only recently that public works of the most essential character have been even begun. If India had been freely thrown open and colonized *pari passu* with the growth of free trade opinion at home, the whole country would by this time have been so attached to English rule, and so retained on the side of peaceful industry and commerce, that the Mussulmans would not have constituted an eighth part of the population; and the Mohammedan element, whether greater or smaller, would have been powerless at this day amidst the prevalent loyalty to British supremacy. As this did not happen, we must suppose that it could not happen; but when we remember how confidently the benevolent legislators of sixty years ago expected it, and what have been the consequences of the disappointment, allowance must be made for very bitter grief, though it may be more natural than philosophical.

QUESTIONS TO CONSIDER

1. What are Martineau's sympathies relative to British colonial domination of India, and how might they have shaped her account?
2. Why does Martineau focus her attention on laws regulating Indian land ownership? Why does she not concentrate on political events?
3. Why does Martineau criticize both Cornwallis and Munro? What does she say was wrong with each of their approaches to administering India?

FOR FURTHER READING

Hoecker-Drysdale, Susan. *Harriet Martineau: First Woman Sociologist.* Oxford: Berg, 1992.

Martineau, Harriet. *The History of England During the Thirty Year's Peace, 1816–1846.* 2 vols. London: Charles Knight, 1849.

_____ . *A History of the American Compromises*. London: John Chapman, 1856.
_____ . *Society in America*. 3 vols. London: Saunders and Otley, 1837. Condensed ed., Garden City, NY: Doubleday Anchor, 1962.
Webb, Robert K. *Harriet Martineau: A Radical Victorian*. New York: Columbia University Press, 1960.

NOTES

1. Harriet Martineau, *British Rule in India: A Historical Sketch* (London: Smith, Elder, 1857), 170–85.

CHAPTER 34

Romesh Chunder Dutt

Indian Nationalist

Romesh Chunder Dutt
The British Library

The British justified their control of India on the grounds of cultural superiority. The West alone, so the argument ran, had escaped from backwardness and superstition. It ruled the East in order to spread enlightenment and economic progress. Its management would, so it was claimed, allow less fortunate "Orientals" (see Chapter 56) to gain the benefits of modernity: peace, prosperity, liberty, and the scientific temperament in whose soil these grew.

Many colonized peoples, of course, resented this slur on their abilities and heritage. Some rebelled politically, as in the Indian Rebellion of 1857. Others rebelled culturally and continue to do so, as demonstrated by the passage by Edward Said that ends this volume. Both responses undercut Western conceit.

Yet the moderate Indian nationalists of the late nineteenth and early twentieth centuries took another tack. While welcoming many aspects of British administration, they questioned its altruism. They appreciated its efficiency and its suppression of communal conflict, while arguing that it had, in fact, created many of the problems that it claimed to be trying to solve. Chief among these critics was Romesh C. Dutt (1848–1909). A writer and statesman of the turn-of-the-century Bengali renaissance, Dutt provided the first Indian critique of the economic consequences of British imperialism. His work is important, both for the questions it raised and for its influence on the Indian independence movement.

Romesh Dutt was born in Calcutta into a family with a history of government service and learning. One grandfather had been a prominent Anglicist in the eighteenth century; an uncle was the first principal of the Sanskrit College. His father was a deputy collector in the Bengali government, charged with surveying the rural population. Traveling with him, Dutt saw firsthand India's rural poverty, which affected him greatly. After studying law and government in London, he worked for 26 years in the Indian Civil Service, rising to the post of district commissioner. This was the highest level attained by an Indian up to that time. He wrote extensively while off duty: four historical novels, a book on Bengali peasant life, a translation of the *Rig Veda* into Bengali, a somewhat pedestrian *History of Civilisation in Ancient India* based on Sanskrit texts. In 1893 he founded an association to encourage Bengali literature. Toward the end of that decade he translated two Indian classics—the *Mahabharata* and the *Ramayana*—into English.

Dutt was keenly aware of the discrimination permeating the Civil Service, which kept Indians from using their talents for the benefit of their countryfolk. This, and his increasing loss of faith in the British imperial system, led him to retire from the Service in 1897. He taught Indian history at University College, London, for a short time while exploring Colonial Office records. He used these as the basis of his most significant work: an economic critique of British rule.

Dutt criticized the British on several grounds, some of which appear in the passages that follow. He especially faulted the heavy taxes on Indian agriculture, the discouragement of Indian industry, and the British practice of overcharging India for administrative costs. All these put a severe burden on the Indian populace. He believed that, were it not for that burden, which fell most harshly on the peasants, India would have been making economic progress. As it was, India suffered famine and want on an ever increasing scale. Dutt was the first Indian historian to draw a detailed causal connection between British administrative policies and such concrete social problems.

Dutt used Britain's own parliamentary inquiries and official statistics to prove his case, essentially creating an Indian economic history where none had existed before. Though his economic interpretations have been challenged—some say he did not fully appreciate the positive effect of investment in railroads, for example—his work was widely read by nationalist leaders such as Gandhi and Nehru. His moderate critique of the British fed their radical one, a sign of the importance of his work.

In the last five years of his life, Dutt had a chance to follow his own recommendations. He joined the administration of the Gaekwar of Baroda, an Indian-run state in Gujarat. There, he began reforming the rural land taxes so as better to reward the peasantry. Here, too, he was frustrated by his inability to put good policies into action. He had just attained the rank of Prime Minister when he died in 1909.

Two passages from Dutt's economic histories follow. The first comes from the preface to his *Economic History of India Under Early British Rule*. It gives us an overview of his approach. The second comes from his *Economic History of India in the Victorian Age*. Here we see the kinds of materials he used to make his points.

The Economic History of India[1]

Excellent works on the military and political transactions of the British in India have been written by eminent historians. No history of the people of India, of their trades, industries, and agriculture, and of their economic condition under British administration, has yet been compiled.

Recent famines in India have attracted attention to this very important subject, and there is a general and widespread desire to understand the condition of the Indian people—the sources of their wealth and the causes of their poverty. A brief Economic History of British India is therefore needed at the present time.

Englishmen can look back on their work in India, if not with unalloyed satisfaction, at least with some legitimate pride. They have conferred on the people of India what is the greatest human blessing—Peace. They have introduced Western Education, bringing an ancient and civilised nation in touch with modern thought, modern sciences, modern institutions and life. They have built up an Administration which, though it requires reform with the progress of the times, is yet strong and efficacious. They have framed wise laws, and have established Courts of Justice, the purity of which is as absolute as in any country on the face of the earth. These are results which no honest critic of British work in India regards without high admiration.

On the other hand, no open-minded Englishman contemplates the material condition of the people of India under British rule with equal satisfaction. The poverty of the Indian population at the present day is unparalleled in any civilised country; the famines which have desolated India within the last quarter of the nineteenth century are unexampled in their extent and intensity in the history of ancient or modern times. By a moderate calculation, the famines of 1877 and 1878, of 1889 and 1892, of 1897 and 1900, have carried off fifteen millions of people. The population of a fair-sized European country has been swept away from India within twenty-five years. A population equal to half of that of England has perished in India within a period which men and women, still in middle age, can remember.

What are the causes of this intense poverty and these repeated famines in India? Superficial explanations have been offered one after another, and have been rejected on close examination. It was said that the population increased rapidly in India and that such increase must necessarily lead to famines; it is found on inquiry that the population has never increased in India at the rate of England, and that during the last ten years it has altogether ceased to increase. It was said that the Indian cultivators were careless and improvident, and that those who did not know how to save when there was plenty, must perish when there was want; but it is known to men who have lived all their lives among these cultivators, that there is not a more abstemious, a more thrifty, a more frugal race of peasantry on earth. It was said that the Indian money-lender was the bane of India, and by his fraud and extortion kept the tillers of the soil in a chronic state of indebtedness; but the inquiries of the latest Famine Commission have revealed that the cultivators of India are forced under the thraldom of money-lenders by the rigidity of the Government revenue demand. It was said that in a country where the people depended almost entirely on their crops, they must starve when the crops failed in years of drought; but the crops in India, as a whole, have never failed, there has never been a single year when the food supply of the country was insufficient for the people, and there must be something wrong, when failure in a single province brings on a famine, and the people are unable to buy their supplies from neighbouring provinces rich in harvests.

* * *

It is, unfortunately, a fact which no well-informed Indian official will ignore, that, in many ways, the sources of national wealth in India have been narrowed under British rule. India in the eighteenth century was a great manufacturing as well as a great agricultural country, and the products of the Indian loom supplied the markets of Asia and of Europe. It is, unfortunately, true that the East Indian Company and the British Parliament, following the selfish commercial policy of a hundred years ago, discouraged Indian manufacture in the early years of British rule in order to encourage the rising manufactures of England. Their fixed policy, pursued during the last decades of the eighteenth century and the first decades of the nineteenth, was to make India subservient to the industries of Great Britain, and to make the Indian people grow raw produce only, in order to supply material for the looms and manufactories of Great Britain. This policy was pursued with unwavering resolution and with fatal success; orders were sent out, to force Indian artisans to work in the Company's factories; commercial residents were legally vested with extensive powers over villages and communities of Indian weavers; prohibitive tariffs excluded Indian silk and cotton goods from England; English goods were admitted into India free of duty or on payment of a nominal duty.

The British manufacturers, in the words of the historian H. H. Wilson, "employed the arm of political injustice to keep down and ultimately strangle a competitor with whom he could not have contended on equal terms"; millions of Indian artisans lost their earnings; the population of India lost one great source of their wealth. It is a painful episode in the history of British rule in India; but it is a story which has to be told to explain the economic condition of the Indian people, and their present helpless dependence on agriculture. The invention of the power-loom in Europe completed the decline of the Indian industries; and when in recent years the power-loom was set up in India, England once more acted towards India with unfair jealousy. An excise duty has been imposed on the production of cotton fabrics in India which disables the Indian manufacturer from competing with the manufacturer of Japan and China, and which stifles the new steam-mills of India.

Agriculture is now virtually the only remaining source of national wealth in India, and four-fifths of the Indian people depend on agriculture. But the Land Tax levied by the British Government is not only excessive but, what is worse, it is fluctuating and uncertain in many provinces.

It will appear from the facts stated above that the Land Tax in India is not only heavy and uncertain, but that the very principle on which it is raised is different from the principle of taxation in all well-administered countries. In such countries the State promotes the accumulation of wealth, helps the people to put money into their pockets, likes to see them prosperous and rich, and then demands a small share of their earnings for the expenses of the State. In India the State virtually interferes with the accumulation of wealth from the soil, intercepts the incomes and gains of the tillers, and generally adds to its land revenue demand at each recurring settlement, leaving the cultivators permanently poor. In England, in Germany, in the United States, in France and other countries, the State widens the income of the people, extends their markets, opens out new sources of wealth, identifies with the nation, grows richer with the nation. In India, the State has fostered no new industries and revived no old industries for the people; on the other hand, it intervenes at each recurring land settlement to take what it considers its share out of the produce of the soil. Each new [land tax] settlement in Bombay and in Madras is regarded by the people as a wrangle between them and the State as to how much the former will keep and how much the latter will take. It is a wrangle decided without any clear limits fixed by the law—a wrangle in which the opinion of the revenue officials is final, and there is no appeal to judges or Land Courts. The revenue increases and the people remain destitute.

Taxation raised by a king, says the Indian poet, is like the moisture of the earth sucked up by the sun, to be returned to the earth as fertilising rain; but the moisture raised from the Indian soil now descends as fertilising rain largely on other lands, not on India. Every nation reasonably expects that the proceeds of the taxes raised in the country should be mainly spent in the country. Under the worst governments that India had in former times, this was the case. The vast sums which Afghan and Moghal Emperors spent on their armies went to support great and princely houses, as well as hundreds of thousands of soldiers and their families. The gorgeous palaces and monuments they built, as well as the luxuries and displays in which they indulged, fed and encouraged the manufacturers and artisans of India. Nobles and Commanders of the army, Subadars [provincial governors], Dewans [chief ministers], and Kazis [judges], and a host of inferior officers in every province and every district, followed the example of the Court; and mosques and temples, roads, canals and reservoirs, attested to their wide liberality, or even to their vanity. Under wise rulers as under foolish kings, the proceeds of taxation flowed back to the people and fructified their trade and industries.

* * *

For one who has himself spent the best and happiest years of his life in the work of Indian administration, it is an ungracious and a painful task to dwell on the weak side of that administration, the financial and economic policy of the Indian government. I have undertaken this duty because at the present moment the economic story of British India has to be told, and the deep-seated cause of the poverty of the Indian people has to be explained. Place any other country under the same condition, with crippled industries, with agriculture subject to a heavy and uncertain Land Tax, and with financial arrangements requiring one-half of its revenues to be annually remitted out of the country, and the most prosperous nation on earth will soon know the horrors of famine. A nation prospers if the sources of its wealth are widened, and if the proceeds of taxation are spent among the people, and for the people. A nation is impoverished if the sources of its wealth are narrowed, and the proceeds of taxation are largely remitted out of the country. These are plain, self-evident economic laws, which operate in India, as in every other country, and the Indian statesman and administrator must feel that the poverty of India cannot be removed until Indian industries are revived, until a fixed and intelligible limit is placed on the Indian Land Tax, and until the Indian revenues are more largely spent in India.

*   *   *

Land Settlements in Bombay[2]

The British frontier in Western India rapidly advanced under the Marquis of Hastings, and the whole of the Deccan came under British rule in 1817, after the last Mahratta War. Valuable reports on the newly-acquired territories were submitted, first by Mountstuart Elphinstone in 1819, and then by Chaplin in 1821 and 1822. And these reports throw much light on the state of agriculture, and the condition of the peasantry, under the Mahratta rule.

The first and most important feature of the Mahratta Government in the Deccan, wrote Elphinstone, was the division of the country into townships or Village Communities. "These Communities contain in miniature all the materials of a State within themselves, and are almost sufficient to protect their members if all other governments are withdrawn." The Patel or head of the Village Community, wrote Captain Robertson of Poona, "was, and is still, a magistrate by the will of the community as well as by the appointment of Government; he enforces the observance of what in England would be termed the bye-laws of the corporation; he formerly raised by contributions a sum of money for the expenses of the corporation as such, and for the support of his own dignity as its head; he suggested improvements for the benefit of the association, and marshalled the members to aid him in maintaining the public peace; he dispensed and still dispenses civil justice as a patriarch to those who choose to submit to his decision as referee or arbitrator; or he presides over the proceedings of others whom either he himself or the parties might nominate as arbitrators of their disputes."

The next most important feature of society under the Mahratta rule was the cultivation of the land by peasant proprietors, called Mirasdars or hereditary owners of their fields. Elphinstone tells us that "a large portion of the Ryots are the proprietors of their estates, subject to the payment of a fixed land tax to Government; that their property is hereditary and saleable; and they are never dispossessed while they pay their tax." "He is in no way inferior," writes Captain Robertson, "in point of tenure on its original basis, as described in the quotation, to the holder of the most undisputed freehold estate in England." The Mirasi tenure, says Chaplin, "is very general through-out the whole of that part of the conquered territory which extends from the Krishna to the range of Ghats." And Mr. Chaplin adds that "the Collector [of Poona] is very properly an advocate for preserving the rights of Mirasdars, a line of policy which he strenuously recommends in several places; but as nobody, I trust, has ever thought of invading their rights, the discussion of the question at any length would be superfluous."

It is a lamentable fact that both these ancient institutions, the Village Community and the Mirasi tenure, virtually ceased to exist before the first generation of British administrators had closed their labours in the conquered territories. A fixed resolve to make direct arrangements with every separate cultivator, and to impose upon him a tax to be revised at each recurring settlement, necessarily weakened Village Communities and extinguished Mirasi rights. No impartial historian compares the Mahratta rule with its interminable wars, with the British rule which has given peace and security to the people. At the same time no impartial historian notes without regret the decay of the old self-governing institutions, the extinction of the old tenant-rights, and the consequent increase of the burdens on the soil, which have been the results of British administration in India. It is an unwise policy to efface the indigenous self-governing institutions of any country; and the policy is specially unwise under an alien rule which can never be in touch with the people, except through the natural leaders and representatives of the people. Eighty-five years have elapsed since the British conquest of the Deccan, but the system of rural self-government, which the Village Commu-nities represented, has never been replaced.

Land Settlements were made temporarily in different districts immedi-ately after the Conquest of the Deccan; and regular Survey Settlements were commenced by Pringle of the Bombay Civil Service in 1824–28, but ended in failure. His assessment was based on a measurement of fields and an estimate of the yield of various soils, and the Government demand was fixed at 55 per cent. of the produce. The measurement, however, was faulty; the estimates of produce were erroneous; the revenue demand was excessive; and the Settle-ment operations ended in oppression. "Every effort, lawful and unlawful, was made to get the utmost out of the wretched peasantry, who were subjected to torture, in some instances cruel and revolting beyond all description if they would not or could not yield what was demanded. Numbers abandoned their homes and fled into the neighbouring Native States. Large tracts of land were thrown out of cultivation, and in some districts no more than a third of the cultivable area remained in occupation."

A re-survey was commenced by Goldsmid and Lieutenant Wingate in 1835, and they founded the system on which land revenue administration in Bombay is based up to the present time. This date marks, therefore, the commencement of the current land system of Bombay, as 1833 marks the commencement of the current land system of Northern India. And both in Bombay and in Northern India, Settlements have been made for long periods of thirty years from these dates.

The plan adopted by Goldsmid and Wingate was very simple. They classed all soils into nine different classes according to their quality; they fixed the assessment of a district after inquiries into its circumstances and previous history; and they distributed the district demand among the villages and fields contained in the district. The owner of each field was then called upon to cultivate his holding on payment of the Land Tax fixed for his field. "The assessment was fixed by the Superintendent of Survey without any reference to the cultivator; and when those rates were introduced, the holder of each field was summoned to the Collector and informed of the rate at which his land would be assessed in future; and if he chose to retain it on those terms, he did; if he did not choose, he threw it up."

It will be seen that this simple scheme entirely ignored the Village Communities of the Deccan, and extinguished the rights of Mirasi tenants to hold their hereditary lands at fixed rates. British administrators judged it wise to make a settlement directly with every individual tenant; and they imposed on each field a Land Tax according to their own judgment. The new assessment, too, was more or less guess-work, and was therefore subject to the same uncertainty which vitiated the system of Northern India. It was liable to vary as the Settlement Officer was moderate or severe. And moderation shown at one Settlement, during a time of distress, was liable to be followed by severity at the succeeding Settlement, at the first signs of prosperity. The accumulation of agricultural wealth was impossible so long as Settlement Officers retained the power of varying the Land Tax at each recurring settlement according to their own judgment. And any permanent improvement in the condition of the peasantry possessed no security against arbitrary enhancements of the State-demand.

QUESTIONS TO CONSIDER

1. What are Dutt's chief criticisms of British rule? How do they differ from those of Harriet Martineau (chapter 33)?
2. What kind of evidence does Dutt present to support his interpretation of history?
3. Why does Dutt contend that economic history is important? What does it tell us about the Indian-British encounter that we would not learn about from another type of history?

FOR FURTHER READING

Dutt, R. C. *The Economic History of India Under Early British Rule*. London: Routledge and Kegan Paul, 1950; orig. 1902.
———. *The Economic History of India in the Victorian Age*. London: Routledge and Kegan Paul, 1950; orig. 1904.

_____ . *A History of Civilisation in Ancient India.* London: Kegan Paul, Trench, Trubner, 1893.

_____ . *The Peasantry of Bengal.* Calcutta: Thacker and Spink, 1874.

Sen, S. P. *Historians and Historiography in Modern India.* Calcutta: Institute of Historical Studies, 1973.

NOTES

1. Romesh Dutt, *The Economic History of India Under Early British Rule* (London: Routledge and Kegan Paul; 1950, orig. 1904), v–ix.
2. Dutt, *The Economic History of India in the Victorian Age* (London: Routledge and Kegal Paul, 1950; orig. 1904), 50–54. Footnotes omitted.

CHAPTER 35

Samuel Johnson

History and the Nigerian Tradition

Dr. Obadiah Johnson, editor of *The History of the Yorubas*,
by Samuel Johnson
From The History of the Yorubas *by The Rev. Samuel
Johnson, C.M.S. (Nigeria) Bookshops, Lagos*

Hegel reflected a common European view when he remarked, in a Berlin lecture in 1830, that "Africa was not a historical part of the world" (Ranger, 74). People who subscribed to this view did not necessarily mean that nothing had happened there. But the Western definition of history as written accounts of the past overlooked the historians of nonliterate societies. Africa had little writing; outsiders assumed that it had no history as well.

We have already encountered the Sundiata epic—an oral history of an eleventh-century Mande king. Though distorted, the epic is based in fact; we find independent confirmation of it in Arab texts. West African *griots* (bards) were the keepers of the African tradition, and they kept it more or less well until the modern age.

Yet an African historiography emerged at the end of the nineteenth century, influenced by, yet independent of, both the *griots* and the West. Like political institutions, technology, and other aspects of contemporary life on that continent, it was a blend of imported and indigenous elements. Respect for oral sources plus Western critical analysis have produced a new approach that uses evidence of many types to uncover the past. Like a good navigator or geographer, it triangulates: it takes many bearings to get a clearer picture of what happened.

Samuel Johnson's *The History of the Yorubas,* a selection from which follows, is an early example of this trend. Like others who had been educated by missionaries, Johnson originally knew more about England, Greece, and Rome than he did about his own continent. Yet it became clear to him and to some of his contemporaries that Europeans did not fully understand the African past. Europeans overemphasized their own role and played down indigenous developments. Like James Africanus Horton of Sierra Leone, Apolo Kagwa of Uganda, and Otomba Payne of his own adopted land, Johnson uncovered and wrote Yoruba history in order to portray its people as proud actors in a proud land.

Johnson was born in 1846 in Sierra Leone. He moved to Nigeria as a boy, was educated, and became a teacher and Protestant catechist in Yorubaland— that country's southwestern corner. He became pastor at Oyo in 1887, where he also served as a messenger between the local rulers and the British at Lagos. Little else is known of his personal life, other than that he married twice and was survived by five daughters. He saw—and favored—the expansion of British rule; he believed that it would give his people the possibility of peace and civilization. On the other hand, he did not want the Yorubas to lose their sense of themselves. He sought to preserve their heritage, which was dying with the *griots* of his day. He believed that with British help and a knowledge of their own past greatness, the Yorubas could be great again.

Although Johnson's work has been surpassed by modern Africanists, it provides a good illustration of their tradition's beginnings. Unable to compare oral history with archaeological, linguistic, and other evidence, he relied on the *griots* for the ancient and mythological period. He admitted that he could not test the truth of all their tales. He strung those he found most plausible into a history of the wars and doings of former kings. Where two stories seemed to conflict, he presented both and suggested an interpretation that might reconcile them. He avoided or explained away the truly fanciful elements, fitting the rest into a reconstructed past that emphasized the dual suzerainty of Oyo and Ife over Yoruba life. In his reconstruction, the former took political precedence, the latter spiritual. Recent historians question this analysis, as they do the naivete with which he assumed the historical accuracy of some of the stories. Yet his overall account is still consulted today.

Of course, Johnson did better with more recent events: he consulted those who had seen them. Some he named; others he did not. Such eyewitnesses and participants inform his account for most of the nineteenth century. Indeed, he saw some events himself as a go-between in various political negotiations. Here and there he appears in his own text; in those instances, we can be sure of the source of his information. As is apparent, he wrote the history of this period much as a European might have written it, focused on war and politics, yet incorporating an indigenous point of view.

The History of the Yorubas has itself an interesting history. As his brother Dr. Obadiah Johnson writes in its preface, Samuel Johnson finished the manuscript in 1897, then mailed it to England to be published. Four years later, he died at the relatively young age of 55. Obadiah Johnson reported that he then inquired, only to discover that the publisher had lost Johnson's original, and so the manuscript had to be recreated from his brother's papers and notes. That was again sent to England, but it did not appear in print until 1921, 24 years after the original composition. Surely such perseverance deserves remembrance in modern days!

The following selection consists of passages from two parts of Johnson's work. In the first, Johnson presented a compilation of bardic stories about Atiba, a prince and warrior. In the larger section from which this passage is taken, we see the story of his birth, something about his life and character, and the political consequences of his acts. Johnson did not hide his opinions about these, but the opinions do not get in the way of the story.

The second passage (in two subsections) is more contemporary. It comes from Johnson's account of the war between Ibadan and its neighbors. Ibadan was locked out of the coastal trade, but picked this fight for political, not just economic ends. Again, Johnson saw the war as a tragedy, a symptom of the social dislocation that he hoped would end with British rule. Unlike later Africanist historians such as K. O. Dike and Walter Rodney, Johnson did not consider that perhaps the British caused the dislocation that they then stepped in to end.

History of the Yorubas[1]

Prince Atiba: His Early Life and History

Prince Atiba was the son of King Abiodun by an Akeitan woman. According to one account, he was born in the city of Oyo, his father died when he was but a child, and when Abiodun's children were being ill-treated by King Aole his mother fled with him to her own town in the country.

But another account was of a more romantic interest and is more probable, as being characteristic of that age. According to this account, his mother, a slave at Gudugbu, was given as a hostage to the Alafin of Oyo. She had an intimate friend who was much distressed by this separation. After 8 or 10 weary months, she was resolved at all costs to go up to the city to visit her friend with whom she had been associated from childhood.

The Gudugbu hostage was too insignificant to be noticed among the crowd of women in the King's harem until this strange visit of her friend drew the King's attention to her. The visitor from the country loitering within the precincts of the palace was asking all whom she saw coming from the women's quarters to call her Eni-Olufan one of the King's wives, but no one knew who that was. At length King Abiodun was told that a woman from the country was asking for one of his wives, and this unusual incident aroused the King's curiosity. The Gudugbu woman was called to his presence to state the object of her visit. She replied—"May your majesty live long. The young woman from Gudugbu given as a hostage was my bosom friend, and for the past 8 months or more I have had no one to talk to, and hence I was resolved to visit her."

The King then said to her, "Are you not afraid to come here to enquire for my wife? Suppose I add yourself to the harem or kill you or sell you?" She replied, "For my friend's sake I am prepared to undergo any treatment, and if your majesty make a wife of me I shall be happy as my friend and I will see each other every day."

The King greatly admired their friendship; he gave permission for her to be lodged with her friend, and was by this led to pay some attention to the Gudugbu hostage.

For three months these two friends enjoyed each other's company and as the King's wife was now in the way of becoming a mother, he was graciously pleased to send them home. He sent for both of them one morning, and after a few approbatory remarks on their friendship, he loaded them with presents, and said to his wife's friend, "I am sending your friend home with you in order that you may not fail to have some one to unbosom your mind to as hitherto. I make you both my deputy for that part of the country. All matters to be referred to Oyo will henceforth be brought to you for decision, all the tribute monies will be paid to you also, and as my wife will be unable to undertake a journey, I expect your visit here as often as you can come." With this instruction he dismissed them and sent several Eunuchs and Ilaris with them as escort and to commend them formally to the care and protection of the Bale of Gudugbu. Both these women returned to Gudugbu in quite a different capacity from that in which they left it. The little town was all astir on their arrival, and many were the private murmurs against Eni-Olufan's friend for the heavy responsibilities she had brought upon them. Great deference, however, was paid to them both, and they became practically the supreme rulers and judges of that district. The King's wife in course of time gave birth to a son who was named Atiba; her friend also (who was a married woman) gave birth to a son named Onipede. The intimacy existing between the two mothers re-appeared also in the boys from childhood up to manhood.

(This account is reconcilable with the first as it is possible that as an infant, Atiba may have been taken to Oyo to see his father, and may have been there till Aole's reign when the mother had to flee with him back to the country as stated above.)

Atiba grew up a wild and reckless lad. When he was of age, his father ordered that the mother should apportion to him the tribute money of that district, this continued until the succeeding reign when the country was thrown into confusion and anarchy.

This circumstance probably led his mother to remove with him from Gudugbu to Akeitan her own home. Here Atiba was under the care of his maternal uncle who was now head of the house and the family estate.

Atiba was brought up as a tailor, but he preferred a wild and predatory life, for which the circumstances of the times afforded great opportunities. A story was told of him that once being very hungry, he asked his uncle for a yam, and the uncle not only refused it him, but took the opportunity of reprimanding him sharply for living the idle life of a kidnapper. "If I had lived on man-stealing like you," said he "I could not have got any yam." But Yesufu the younger uncle felt sorry for his nephew and said to Atiba that whilst he (the uncle) was living, he (Atiba) would never suffer the pinch of hunger. This incident had its reward hereafter as will be noticed in its place.

From Akeitan Prince Atiba made several incursions into the Gudugbu farms, and was generally a pest to the country round about.

In order not to bring trouble on the Akeitan people, Atiba was urged to remove his residence to the town of Ago where he would find in Oja the chief of that place a man of a like spirit to his own, of a warlike disposition, and he did so.

But when Atiba arrived at Ago, Oja was strongly advised not to let him settle down there, because a man like him would eventually become master of the town. Elebu, Oja's brother was the chief opponent. But Oja did not follow this advice. "How can I," said he "an officer on the staff of the Kakanfo, and a titlebearer in the kingdom, turn away my prince? Oja continued friendly to him until his fall in the Kanla expedition.

Their kidnapping expeditions were at that time chiefly directed against the Egbas in the Oke Ogun districts near Sagaun. They found them so simple and unsophisticated in those days that when a kidnapper had captured several of them and was in quest for more he had only to leave his cap or his spear or any other personal property by the side of them, and bid them wait for him there, and should another kidnapper fall in with them he was to be shown the sign of prepossession, and thus they would be left untouched until their captor returned. These captives never made any effort to escape.

Atiba rose to importance by committing acts of violence and extortion with impunity, from the great deference paid to his high birth. In that age of anarchy and confusion he collected around himself all lawless men, insolvent debtors, slaves who had deserted their masters. His wealth was continually augmented by fresh marauding expeditions, his men behaving like the Jamas, himself at the head of them.

* * *

The Bokofi Expedition

Since the Ijaye war (1860–62) the Ijebus and the Egbas had strictly forbidden ammunition to be sold to any of the interior tribes, notably Ibadan. On the restoration of peace in 1865 the trade between them consisted of foreign clothes, salt, rum and gin from the coast in exchange for produce, chiefly palm oil, kernels, cotton, etc., from the interior. In order to obtain ammunition, the late Basorum Ogunmola opened the Oke Igbo road via Ife to Benin solely for that purpose.

The late King Adelu, however, had purchased a large quantity of gunpowder at Porto Novo which was sent half way to Bokofi but no further for fear of the Egbas kidnapping the whole. On hearing this, the Are was resolved to send the youngest Mogajis for it, secretly wishing they might encounter the Egbas or the Dahomians who might probably help him to get rid of one or other of them. Ilori the Osi, and Iyapo the Seriki were sent on this expedition under the elderly chief Olupoyi as Baba Isale.

The name of Iyapo drew the whole of young men of Ibadan to this expedition leaving only the Are, the Balogun and the Otun at home. Their simple instructions were:—"Molest no one, steer clear of Egba territory, go straight by Oke'ho, Igana to Meko; but if any one molest or interfere with you, follow the party home, and we shall come and meet you outside their gates." The Are hurried the Seriki out of home the same day he gave him the order, the less prepared the better the chances of his fall in the Are's opinion.

The expedition left Ibadan on the 26th April, 1877, and returned safely on the 21st June, without encountering either Egbas or Dahomians. They brought with them about 800 kegs of gunpowder, a few Dane guns, and casks of rum, etc. On the next day the whole of the powder was forwarded to the Alafin who took a few kegs and made a present of the rest to the Ibadan chiefs. During this expedition there was a great stir among the Egbas. They charged the Ibadans with seeking an occasion of quarrel with them by sending an army into their "backyard" as they styled it, but as the Ibadan government had sent formally to apprise the Egba chiefs of their movement and object before the expedition left, the responsible chiefs of Abeokuta like Ogundipe, and others paid no heed to the hue and cry that was being made. But the great majority of them at a meeting at Sodeke street decided to close the roads against Ibadan and forbid especially the exportation of salt and foreign goods.

Ajagunjeun the Balogun of Itoko took the lead and went to the caravan town gate to turn the Ibadan traders back home and to see that those already in the town leave empty handed.

This was really the first hostile act that led up eventually to the 16 years' war, which involved practically the whole Yoruba country, and caused so much loss of lives, and much distress and misery, and destruction of towns, subjugation of the Ijebus by the British government, reduction of the military power of Ibadan, the placing of a British Resident in that town, and of District Commissioners in the principal towns of the Yoruba country.

The First Act of War

The Are's avarice and ambition at this time were unbounded.

His ambition was to eclipse the fame of the two greatest chiefs of undying memory at Ibadan, viz, Ibikunle and Ogunmola (his late master) who both left a name behind them, and sons who upheld the fame and greatness of their father. To this end he sought occasion first against Ilori Ogunmola's son, and then against Seriki Iyapo, Ibikunle's son. If he could reduce these men who eclipsed himself in all that made for feudal greatness and glory, his own star would then shine undimmed.

Further, he now undertook to organize a military band for his own house, raising some of the principal slaves to power and greatness, some of them commanding from 400 to 1,000 soldiers each, horse and foot; and accumulated also a vast store of ammunition in his own house. Also he put up his eldest son as a rival to the other Mogajis in the town, and organized a military band for him, and a guard consisting of the sons of the well-to-do men in the town.

These doings of the Are did not escape the observation of the chiefs. It seemed to them that the Are wanted to perpetuate the administration of Ibadan in his own family, and they were determined to resist this with all their might. The Are on the other hand was much elated with his military organization, and he made it clear that he was bent on an enterprise which he was determined to prosecute to a successful issue with or without the help of his chiefs.

On the 25th of June, 1877, the Are declared at the meeting of the Town Council that as the Egbas first shut their gates against Ibadan since the 3rd of June they must now shut theirs against the Egbas, and 17 days hence commence hostilities.

The chiefs one and all remonstrated with him against this enterprise, but he was obdurate. Messengers were despatched to their neighbours the Ijebus, Ilorins, the Ijesas, Ekitis and Ifes telling them of the impending struggle and requesting their cooperation. The *casus belli* were stated as follows:—

1. That they only performed an act of loyalty towards the King by sending to Porto Novo to bring home ammunition he had bought there, when the Egbas refused to sell to them.
2. They never trespassed on Egba territory, nor gave any cause of offence to any, and yet the Egbas resented their action by closing their roads against Oyos forbidding all trade and intercourse with them.

3. Hundreds of their people who went to Abeokuta for trade had been stolen and sold into slavery which alone gave them the right to demand redress.

But before the return of the messengers the Egba chiefs sent their ambassadors headed by one Leasu to negotiate peace and on the 12th of July, 1877, a full meeting was convened to hear them. But Leasu proved himself most unfit to play the part entrusted to him; he spoke disrespectfully and in an impertinent manner, addressing the Are by name, but his own head chief by his title Alatise. The chiefs were indignant at this and the Seriki Iyapo at once confronted him with "You ought rather be gone as you are most unfit to discharge the duties of a messenger. Why did you not call your own chief Ogudipe by name but by his title Alatise, but our own chief you keep calling by name Latosisa? That is his name true, but he has a title and he is the ruler of this town. If you cannot do him respect we will show you the gate."

Leasu had to leave the town the next day without a reply to his message.

Whilst the chiefs were for negotiation, the Are was bent on hostilities. He found in this affair a plausible pretext for a thing he had long premeditated to carry out, viz., the subjugation of Abeokuta as the first step towards bringing the whole country again under one head.

Seeing the storm brewing the native missionaries in a body interviewed him and endeavoured to dissuade him from prosecuting his mad project. They pointed out to him that the thing could not be done, as the Egbas were well supplied with breach-loading guns which are terrible weapons of precision, whilst he had none. He laughingly replied "And with muzzle-loading ones will I break them." They further remonstrated with him saying "Ote aladugbo ko dara" (warfare between neighbours is a great evil). He received them hitherto with his usual smiles and affability, extenuating his actions, etc., but now, all of a sudden (probably thinking they were moved thereto by the chiefs) he grew stern and resolute, not to say fierce (his Kakanfo blood seemingly flying into his head) and he said "I am going to perform a task which God has allotted to me to do, and those who say they shall see that I do not accomplish it will not live to see it done, as done it shall be, and when I have finished there shall be no more wars for ever in the Yoruba country." How truly prophetic his words turned out to be, but how differently from what he intended them to be.

Kidnapping Expedition to the Egba farms.—The Are was as determined to commence hostilities as the chiefs were against it. Hence at the meeting of the Town Council on the 31st of July, he said to the chiefs, "There is no subject for discussion to-day but you should all go home and prepare for a kidnapping expedition to the Egba farms to-marrow morning." The Balogun and the other chiefs were against the proposal, they said they were not prepared for such a big undertaking. But the Are coolly returned this ironical answer, "Very well, as you are not prepared you can have as much time at home as you wish, meantime I go, and perhaps by the time I return you may then be ready." This sarcastic reply was felt, and each one went home for a hasty preparation for the marrow.

The Are led out the Ibadan host to the Egba farms on the 1st August and captured Atadi, and Alagbara, and pushed on as far as Arakanga behind the gates of Abeokuta, and captured a young bride there. The Egbas were not prepared for this. At the instance of Chief Ogundipe they were about to send another ambassador to undo the mischief done by Leasu, but this attack on their farms and villages put an end to their pacific intentions.

As it was now evident that war was inevitable, the Ijebus to show on which side their sympathy lay, recalled their Agurin at Ibadan, a sign of declaration of war.

The Are with reference to Abeokuta said "Too large for a close siege but for that reason the more vulnerable to famine." Hence in his expeditions, the main object was to destroy foodstuffs, fire the barns, cut down standing corn, chop in pieces yam and other tuberous foodstuffs.

The second expedition was known as "Igbe Igbin" (the Igbin expedition), because some of the Ibadan soldiers encountered Igbin an Egba war chief. But the Ibadan war-chiefs had made a compact among themselves not to fight, but leave the brunt of everything to the Are alone; therefore when they reached the farms they located themselves at short distances from one another, leaving Aturu the Balogun's head slave to lead the men in search of prey. There was no chief with them when Igbin attacked them vigorously and pursued them a great distance until they reached the vicinity of the Seriki's location when he sent a body of men to drive back the pursuers. Aturu also rallied those within his reach, and led them back safe.

This second expedition was less beneficial to them than the first.

* * *

Closure of Roads and the Results

The greatest needs of the Ibadan now were ammunitions and salt, and the only route by which they could obtain them even in small quantities was the roundabout way *via* Oke Igbo to Ondo and thus to the coast. Hence they endeavoured to keep on friendly terms with Derin Ologbenla, the Bale of Oke Igbo, and humoured him every now and then by sending him presents of slaves.

Derin was an Ife prince, and as to the Ifes themselves, although their army was in the Ibadan camp, yet their sympathies were all on the other side.

But it happened in March, 1881, that the Ibadans suspecting treachery in a town named Osu, situated between Ile Ife and Ilesa, sent a small force secretly by Awo, son of the late Labosinde, against the place, to capture it by surprise in order to keep their rear clear of any trouble. But all the towns in the neighbourhood were in the secret of the expedition and in sympathy with the Ekitis as men striking for freedom, therefore it leaked out. Osu was prepared and reinforced against a surprise, and hence the expedition failed.

The town of Osu not being far from the city of Ife, to suspect Osu is to suspect Ife itself, and Derin of Oke Igbo, taking this as a cause of offence, openly declared for the Ekitis and endeavoured to close even this road to all

Oyos by allowing the Ijesas to kidnap caravans on the road. But the Ogunsua or Bale of Modakeke, knowing that the safety of his town is linked with that of Ibadan, by protecting caravans and attacking kidnappers did not allow the road to be altogether closed. In vain the Ifes tried to win the Ogunsua over: the position of Modakeke to Ife is analogous to that of Belfast to the south of Ireland; the Modakekes are Oyos and of the same tribal affinity with Ibadan with which their own safety is linked.

The price of salt rose so high that a pound of salt could not be had for less than ten shillings when it could be obtained at all. Poor people therefore could not even think of preparing their meals with salt; those who could obtain a few grains of it, ate their meals insipid, and then qualified the tastelessness in their mouths with the few grains of salt afterwards!

But the distress in the country was not all on one side. The Egbas also were indirectly affected by this closure of the roads against the interior tribes. They were free to trade with Lagos indeed, but they wanted produce from the interior and slaves to work their farms. They therefore managed to open a circuitous route to Ketu and Ejio, where they and the Porto Novians established a market to trade with all Oyos from different parts of the country, but they still rigidly excluded all sale of ammunition, only cloth and salt were the articles of merchandise, and even this was considered a godsend by the interior folks, for their distress from want of salt was by this greatly alleviated.

An anecdote from an actual occurrence will forcibly illustrate the point of desperation to which these people were driven at this time:

A man with his wife and daughter—a marriageable young woman—went to Ejio to trade. At the close of the fair, the woman was being taken away by an Egba man; a hue and cry was immediately raised, and the Egba was arrested as a manstealer. He denied the charge and told his tale. The woman had been bartered to him for salt and cloth, he only claimed what was his by right. Upon investigation it was found that he was quite right, the seller was the woman's own daughter! She had bartered away her own mother for salt! But the man could not allow his wife to be taken away, a compromise must be made. So after he and the woman had consulted together they agreed that this undutiful daughter was to be given to the Egba in exchange: they showed him that the mother was old and would be a little service to him, whereas the young woman might be taken by him for a wife and that they, the parents, would regard the cloths and salt as an adequate dowry given by him. The Egba man was highly pleased with the offer and went home delighted with having had the best of the bargain, and the parents on the other hand were satisfied that to all intents and purposes their daughter had been comfortably settled. This was by no means a solitary instance of desperate acts such as this.

The distress at the seat of war at this time was indescribable: the Oke Igbo road being closed there was a great dearth of ammunition. The Ekitis knowing this from escaped slaves often came as near as possible to the gate of the camp and assaulted them. The Ibadan army would be drawn up but they could not return the fire of the enemy. They could hardly muster 100 kegs of powder throughout the whole army, and this they reserved for an extreme case of emergency. The writer was present in the camp on one such occasion, when Chief Babalola sent a slave wife of his round to all the traders present in the camp for even a handful of powder if possible. From private soldiers who had not exhausted their allowance, and others who did not use theirs in previous fights she collected a small quantity in exchange for food! The writer being a friend of the Seriki's brother, asked him confidentially on that occasion, "Supposing the Ijesas and Ekitis were to come upon you suddenly one day to rush the camp, what will you do?" He replied, " 'Tis true we have no ammunition, but there are not wanting among us about 5,000 accomplished swordsmen who will be more than a match for the Ekitis with their guns at close quarters, and they know it or they would have attempted to do so."

Further, the Ekitis often taunted them by appearing on top of a rock where they could well be seen by the Ibadans, and tantalized them by emptying kegs of gunpowder on the rock, throwing a lighted torch on the pile, and blazing all away.

The muster for battle at this time took place almost every day. The Ekitis came as near as possible to the camp, firing into it. The method adopted by the Ibadans to meet the present crisis was to assemble near the gate of the camp, and thence make a sudden and vigorous dash on the Ekitis driving them back to the battlefield: then the swordsmen would spread themselves in the valley and trenches awaiting those who would venture near; the Ekitis being on higher ground could be seen by them much sooner. Now and then as opportunity offered they would pounce upon them sword in hand, and often come back with captives. Thus they would hold out till about five or six in the evening before the main Ibadan army marched out, when they could not all fire more than one round before nightfall.

For months and months affairs dragged on in this way, each party being afraid of the other. The sentries at the camp gate were doubled for fear of the night attack.

On one occasion a few kegs of powder were obtained at Ejio at a very high price; when these reached the camp such a shout of joy was raised as if they had won a victory; a *Feu de joie* was fired that evening. The shout was heard at the Ekiti camp. But this joy was short lived, for a grave danger threatened the Yoruba country from another direction.

QUESTIONS TO CONSIDER

1. How does Johnson shape oral traditions into an account that looks like the histories that Westerners write?
2. How does Johnson portray the leaders of the Yoruba, Egba, and other African groups in each of these two passages?
3. Compare these passages to Dutt's account of British rule in India. Why does Johnson welcome British rule, whereas Dutt criticizes it?

FOR FURTHER READING

Ajayi, J. F. Ade. "Samuel Johnson: Historian of the Yoruba." *Nigeria Magazine* 81 (1964), 141–46.

Johnson, Samuel. *The History of the Yorubas, from the Earliest Times to the Beginning of the British Protectorate.* Ed. O. Johnson. London: Lowe and Brydone, 1921.

Law, Robin. "How Truly Traditional is our Traditional History? The Case of Samuel Johnson and his Recording of Yoruba Oral Tradition." *History in Africa* 11 (1984), 195–221.

Mwase, George S. *Strike a Blow and Die: A Narrative of Race Relations in Colonial Africa.* Cambridge, MA: Harvard University Press, 1967.

Oyemakinde, J. O. "Samuel Johnson and his History of the Yorubas." *The Historian* (Ibadan) 5 (1968), 166–222.

Ranger, T. O., ed. *Emerging Themes of African History.* Nairobi: East African Publishing House, 1968.

NOTES

1. Samuel Johnson, *The History of the Yorubas, from the Earliest Times to the Beginning of the British Protectorate,* ed. O. Johnson (London: Lowe and Brydone, 1921), 274–76, 413–17, 452–54.

CHAPTER 36

Fukuzawa Yukichi

Apostle of the West

Fukuzawa Yukichi
From The Autobiography of Fukuzawa Yukichi,
The Hokuseido Press, Tokyo.

One of the ways that people outside Europe could choose to respond to the spread of European power and culture across the globe was imitation. Fukuzawa Yukichi (1835–1901)—scholar, educator, journalist, public policy advocate—had tremendous impact on Japan's modern response to the West. He advocated frank cultural and intellectual emulation of Europe and North America as necessary to preserving Japan's political independence and to creating a powerful modern nation.

Fukuzawa was born in Osaka to a poor, low-ranking samurai family in the last decades of Tokugawa rule and raised in Kyushu. He studied Confucianism and the Chinese classics, but also the Dutch and English languages and Western sciences as they began to leak through the cracks in the Tokugawa seal. He started a school of Western studies in Edo (now Tokyo) in 1858; it later became Keio University. When Western gunboats and merchants came to Japan in the 1850s, Fukuzawa determined to see the West for himself and discover what made it strong, traveling to the U.S. and Europe three times in the 1860s.

Thereafter, Fukuzawa spent his life teaching and writing about the strong nation Japan could become—culturally and spiritually as well as economically and militarily. His books *Seiyo Jijo* (*Conditions of the West*, 1866) and *Gakumon no Susume* (*Encouragement of Learning*, 1872–76) were bestsellers in a Japan eager to avoid the colonial traps that had caught China and India and would soon ensnare the peoples of Africa. In America, a translation of the *Autobiography of Yukichi Fukuzawa* has been almost continuously in print, testimony to Fukuzawa's attractiveness to Westerners as their disciple in Asia, as well as to his keen powers of observation regarding life in the era of cataclysmic change that was Meiji Japan.

Bunmeiron no Gairyaku (*An Outline of a Theory of Civilization*, 1875), partly reproduced here, is Fukuzawa's most scholarly and historical work. It argues that history proceeds in stages (he seems to have acquired this idea from Henry Thomas Buckle and François Guizot). All the world's peoples can be characterized as primitive, semideveloped, or civilized. The European countries he saw as civilized; Japan, he said, was only semideveloped. Yet he believed that, by learning about Western nations and emulating them, Japan, too, could quickly become civilized.

Others of Fukuzawa's day argued for only adopting Western technology, strictly retaining Japan's traditional Confucian and Shinto value systems. Fukuzawa took a more radical position, arguing for a remaking of Japanese values, to democratize society and free it from what he saw as the dead hand of feudal hierarchy. He saw this as primarily an intellectual and moral, not a political or economic task—a remolding of the spirit of the Japanese people, building on such Western ideas as equality and individualism.

Fukuzawa's *Outline* is not exactly a history. In some ways it resembles the policy-advocacy-with-historical-examples of Machiavelli. Yet Fukuzawa's ideas about history had tremendous impact on generations of Japanese historians and other scholars, even though the Japanese government adopted a more conservative approach. The work of Fukuzawa Yukichi shows vividly one prominent response of Third World peoples to the growth of Western power.

An Outline of a Theory of Civilization[1]
Western Civilization As Our Goal

When we are talking about civilization in the world today, the nations of
Europe and the United States of America are the most highly civilized, while
the Asian countries, such as Turkey, China, and Japan, may be called
semi-developed countries, and Africa and Australia are to be counted as still
primitive lands. These designations are common currency all over the world.
While the citizens of the nations of the West are the only ones to boast of
civilization, the citizens of the semi-developed and primitive lands submit to
being designated as such. They rest content with being branded semi-
developed or primitive, and there is not one who would take pride in his own
country or consider it on a par with nations of the West. They groan, they
grieve; some are for learning from the West and imitating it, others are for
going it alone and opposing the West. The overriding anxiety of Asian
intellectuals today is this one problem to the exclusion of all others. At any
rate, the designations 'civilized,' 'semi-developed,' and 'primitive' had been
universally accepted by people all over the globe. Why does everybody accept
them? Clearly, because the facts are demonstrable and irrefutable. I shall
explain this point further below. For these are stages through which mankind
must pass. These may be termed the stages of civilization.

First, there is the stage in which neither dwellings nor supplies of food are
stable. Men form communal groups as temporary convenience demands;
when that convenience ceases, they pull up stakes and scatter to the four
winds. Or even if they settle in a certain region and engage in farming and
fishing, they may have enough food and clothing, but they do no yet know
how to make tools. And though they are not without writing, they produce no
literature. At this stage man is still unable to be master of his own situation; he
cowers before the forces of nature and is dependent upon arbitrary human
favor or accidental blessings. This is called the stage of primitive man. It is still
far from civilization.

Secondly, there is the stage of civilization wherein daily necessities are not
lacking, since agriculture has been started on a large scale. Men build houses,
form communities, and create the outward semblance of a state. But within
this facade there remain very many defects. Though literature flourishes, there
are few who devote themselves to practical studies. Though in human
relations sentiments of suspicion and jealousy run deep, when it comes to
discussing the nature of things men lack the courage to raise doubts and ask
questions. Men are adept at imitative craftsmanship, but there is a dearth of
original production. They know how to cultivate the old, but not how to
improve it. There are accepted rules governing human intercourse, and slaves
of custom that they are, they never alter those rules. This is called the
semi-developed stage. It is not yet civilization in the full sense.

Thirdly, there is the stage in which men subsume the things of the
universe within a general structure, but the structure does not bind them.

Their spirits enjoy free play and do not adhere to old customs blindly. They act autonomously and do not have to depend upon the arbitrary favors of others. They cultivate their own virtue and refine their own knowledge. They neither yearn for the old nor become complacent about the new. Not resting with small gains, they plan great accomplishments for the future and commit themselves wholeheartedly to their realization. Their path of learning is not vacuous; it has, indeed, invented the principle of invention itself. Their business ventures prosper day by day to increase the sources of human welfare. Today's wisdom overflows to create the plans of tomorrow. This is what is meant by modern civilization. It has been a leap far beyond the primitive or semi-developed stages.

Now, if we make the above threefold distinction, the differences between civilization, semi-development, and the primitive stage should be clear. However, since these designations are essentially relative, there is nothing to prevent someone who has not seen civilization from thinking that semi-development is the summit of man's development. And, while civilization is civilization relative to the semi-developed stage, the latter, in its turn, can be called civilization relative to the primitive stage. Thus, for example, present-day China has to be called semi-developed in comparison with Western countries. But if we compare China with countries of South Africa, or, to take an example more at hand, if we compare the Japanese people with the Ezo, then both China and Japan can be called civilized. Moreover, although we call the nations of the West civilized, they can correctly be honored with this designation only in modern history. And many of them, if we were to be more precise, would fall well short of this designation.

For example, there is no greater calamity in the world than war, and yet the nations of the West are always at war. Robbery and murder are the worst of human crimes; but in the West there are robbers and murderers. There are those who form cliques to vie for the reins of power and who, when deprived of that power, decry the injustice of it all. Even worse, international diplomacy is really based on the art of deception. Surveying the situation as a whole, all we can say is that there is a general prevalence of good over bad, but we can hardly call the situation perfect. When, several thousand years hence, the levels of knowledge and virtue of the peoples of the world will have made great progress (to the point of becoming utopian), the present condition of the nations of the West will surely seem a pitifully primitive stage. Seen in this light, civilization is an open-ended process. We cannot be satisfied with the present level of attainment of the West.

Yes, we cannot be satisfied with the level of civilization attained by the West. But shall we therefore conclude that Japan should reject it? If we did what other criterion would we have? We cannot rest content with the stage of semi-development; even less can the primitive stage suffice. Since these latter alternatives are to be rejected, we must look elsewhere. But to look to some far-off utopian world thousands of years hence is mere daydreaming. Besides, civilization is not a dead thing; it is something vital and moving. As such, it must pass through sequences and stages; primitive people advance to semi-developed forms, the semi-developed advance to civilization, and civilization itself is even now in the process of advancing forward. Europe also had to pass through these phases in its evolution to its present level. Hence present-day Europe can only be called the highest level that human intelligence has been able to attain at this juncture in history. Since this is true, in all countries of the world, be they primitive or semi-developed, those who are to give thought to their country's progress in civilization must necessarily take European civilization as the basis of discussion, and must weigh the pros and cons of the problem in the light of it. My own criterion throughout this book will be that of Western civilization, and it will be in terms of it that I describe some-thing as good or bad, in terms of it that I find things beneficial or harmful. Therefore let scholars make no mistake about my orientation.

Some people say that, just as the world is divided into separate lands, so also men's sentiments and social customs, as well as their national polities and governments, are different. Therefore, they argue, is it not unwise to take European civilization as the model of modernization for every country? Shall we not attain the proper balance only if Western civilization is adapted to each country's own sentiments and social customs, and only if, while preserving each national polity and government, we select what is suitable, adopting or rejecting as circumstances dictate? My reply to this is that of course we should be selective in applying foreign civilization to a semi-developed country. We can distinguish in civilization between its visible exterior and its inner spirit. It is easy enough to adopt the former, but difficult to pursue the latter. Now, when one aims at bringing civilization to a country, the difficult part must be done first and the easier left for later; then, as the difficult part is acquired, stock should be taken of how much it has taken hold, and at a suitable junctures the easier part can be added to it in the same measure, in this way assuring a constant balance. But if the wrong order is followed and the easier part is adopted before the difficult, *the easier part often will prove not only useless but harmful as well.*

In the first place, the externals of civilization are all empirical details, from food, clothing, shelter, implements, and so forth, to government decrees and laws. If only these external things were regarded as civilization, we would naturally have to be selective in adapting them to the distinctive ways of each country. Even the nations of the West, though they border on one another, are not uniform in manners and customs. Much less can the countries of Asia, so different from the West, imitate Western ways in their entirety. And even if they did imitate the West, that could not be called civilization.

For example, can we say that the current Western styles seen more and more in daily Japanese life are a proof of civilization? Can we call those men with Western haircuts whom we meet on the street civilized persons? Shall we call a person enlightened just because he eats meat? Hardly. I am always a bit upset at the way the Japanese government is building stone buildings and iron bridges, or at the way Chinese, in order to reform their military system all at once, are building warships, buying cannons, and so on, without regard for their national resources and at unreasonable expense. These things all can be built through manpower or purchased with money. They are the most tangible of material things and the easiest of easy things to obtain. Should we then, when adopting such things, proceed without due consideration of consequences and priorities? Due regard must always be had for the sentiments and customs of one's own nation; the resources of one's own country must always be consulted. This is what ought to be meant by those who speak of adapting to 'sentiments and social customs.' I have no argument with them on this score, but some of them seem to be talking about only the external forms of civilization while neglecting its spirit.

But what, then, is the spirit of civilization? It is a people's spiritual makeup. This spirit can be neither bought nor sold. Nor again can it be readily created through use of manpower. It permeates the entire lifestream of a people and is manifest on a wide scale in the life of the nation. But since it has no one visible form, it is difficult to ascertain its existence. Let me try to describe it as best as I can.

If scholars read widely into the histories of the world and compare Asia and Europe, and if they inquire into the points in which the two areas of the world differ—without going into such things as their geographies and products, their ordinances and laws, their technical skills or technical backwardness, their religious differences or similarities, and so forth—they will definitely discover a certain spiritual entity behind these respective differences. This spiritual entity is difficult to describe. But when it is nourished it grows to embrace the myriad things of the earth; if repressed or restrained, its external manifestations will also vanish. It is in constant motion, advancing or retreating, waxing or waning. It may seem a will-o'-the-wisp or an apparition, but if we look at its real manifestations within present-day Asia and Europe, we can clearly see it is not illusory.

Let us now call this the 'spirit of a people.' In respect to time, it may be called the 'trend of the time.' In reference to persons, it may be called 'human sentiments.' With regard to a nation as a whole, it may be called 'a nation's ways' or 'national opinion.' These things are what is meant by the spirit of civilization. And it is this spirit of civilization that differentiates the manners and customs of Asia and Europe. Hence the spirit of civilization can also be described as the sentiments and customs of a people.

Considered in these terms, the statement of those who say that even if we intend to adopt Western civilization we must first consider the sentiments and customs of our own nation, however inadequately expressed and vague their view may be, when understood correctly means that we must not import only the outward forms of civilization, but must first make the spirit of civilization ours and only then adopt its external forms. What I mean when I say that we should take European civilization as our goal is that we should turn to Europe in order to make the spirit of civilization ours, and thus I am in complete accord with their opinion. However, there are those who, in the pursuit of civilization, would give priority to external forms. As a result, when they suddenly encounter obstacles they do not know how to handle them. I differ from them only in wanting to give priority to the spirit of civilization in order to eliminate the obstacles in advance, and thus to facilitate the assimilation of external civilization. Still others, finally, are not opposed to civilization, but they have not committed themselves to its pursuit as wholeheartedly as I have. They have simply not fully thought through their own positions.

QUESTIONS TO CONSIDER

1. What, according to Fukuzawa, are the stages of civilization? At what stage did he believe Japan was at the time of his writing?
2. Which aspects of this presentation likely stem from Japanese culture and history, and which probably represent Western intrusions?
3. This selection is extremely philosophical. In what ways is it also a style of writing history?

FOR FURTHER READING

Craig, Albert. "Fukuzawa Yukichi: The Philosophical Foundations of Meiji Nationalism." In *Political Development in Modern Japan,* edited by Robert Ward. Princeton, NJ: Princeton University Press, 1968.
_____ . *An Encouragement of Learning.* Trans. David A. Dilworth and Umeyo Hirano. Tokyo: Sophia University Press, 1969.
Pyle, Kenneth. *The New Generation in Meiji Japan: Problems of Cultural Identity, 1885–1895.* Stanford, CA: Stanford University Press, 1969.
Sansom, G. B. *The Western World and Japan.* New York: Knopf, 1950.
Yukichi, Fukuzawa. *The Autobiography of Yukichi Fukuzawa.* Trans. Eiichi Kiyooka. New York: Schocken, 1972.

NOTES

1. Fukuzawa Yukichi, *An Outline of a Theory of Civilization,* trans. David A. Dilworth and G. Cameron Hurst (Tokyo: Sophia University, 1973), 13–17, 138–45.

CHAPTER 37

Liang Qichao and Hu Shi

Western Ideas to Strengthen China

Hu Shi
The Bettmann Archive

T hroughout the nineteenth century China, which had only recently been
the world's greatest empire, gradually crumbled under the pressure of
European gunboats, traders, and missionaries. By the last decades of that
century China could no longer control its own borders, the government was
near collapse, and foreign powers were poised to carve up the country.

In 1898 a group of bright, young intellectuals—all aspiring to become
Confucian scholars as Sima Guang had been—gained the attention of the
young emperor. With his backing they initiated a flurry of reforms to save
China from dismemberment before the colonialist onslaught. They proposed
to rebuild China, using Western-style science and technology, but founding
the operation on a Confucian philosophical base. Their leader, Kang Youwei
(1858–1927) epitomized the group's blending of old and new, China and the
West, in a book called *K'ung-tzu kai-chih k'ao (Confucius As a Reformer)*. The
1898 reform movement was crushed by conservatives, the emperor was
imprisoned by his aunt, the reformers either were killed or fled to Japan, and
China's last dynasty kept its date with destruction.

One of those who fled was Kang's disciple Liang Qichao (1873–1929). In
Japan he learned more about the West and about Japan's greater success at
resisting colonialism. First a journalist for 20 years and then a scholar toward
the end of his life, Liang gradually gave up Kang's Confucian devotion to
ancient Chinese philosophical commitments (however revised for the modern
era) and adopted a more forward-looking political allegiance to China as an
emerging modern nation-state. He loved Chinese culture, especially Buddhism, deeply, but he strove to find a basis for that love which was not
backward-looking but pointed toward hope for the future. He found that basis
in nationalism.

Liang gave up many of the remodelled Confucian ideas of Kang and
adopted instead a Social Darwinist view of history as a survival-of-the-fittest
contest among nations—a contest he insisted China must win. In a series of
books on Chinese history and historiography, Liang derided traditional
Confucian historians as backward-looking elitists who merely taught emperors how to govern and doted on the past, without reference to the needs of the
future. Liang called instead for widespread popular education and a history
written on scientific principles that would instill nationalistic pride and hope
for the future in the Chinese people. Liang wanted to introduce foreign
learning to China, including the evolving Western scientific standards of
historical scholarship, in order to make China strong. The selection reproduced here is from Liang's *Intellectual Trends in the Qing Period (Ch'ing-tai
hsüeh-shu kai-lun)*. In it, Liang contrasts the still backward-looking approach of
Kang Youwei with the more radical thinking of another of the late-Qing
reformers, Tan Situng (1866–1898).

Just as Liang's reformism outpaced that of his mentor Kang, so in turn
Liang was quickly overtaken himself. The Qing dynasty fell of its own weight
in 1911. There followed a generation of chaos, warlordism, and groping toward
the future. One of Liang's ideas—history for the people—broadened rapidly
into the New Culture Movement of the 1910s and '20s. This wide-ranging

movement of young intellectuals produced an outpouring of literature in the vernacular rather than in the language of Confucian scholars. The New Culture devotees espoused mass education and the introduction of Western philosophy and ideas, not just science and technology. They published and demonstrated against weak government and tried on many new ideas from the West.

A leading light of the New Culture Movement was Hu Shi (1891–1962). Hu took his higher education in America at Cornell and Columbia Universities, where he became a disciple of John Dewey. Back in Beijing as a philosophy professor in 1917, Hu combined Dewey's pragmatism with his own passionate devotion to a literature that would open up the lives of common people. The selection by Hu, which follows Liang's passage, is from *The Development of the Logical Method in Ancient China*, a revision of Hu's Columbia dissertation and a work of both history and philosophy. By recourse to ancient poetry, this selection brings to life the suffering of common people in a bygone age. Hu also casts ancient Chinese history in terms similar to early modern European history. He writes not the history of a unitary empire, of the sort one would find in the work of the Ban family or of Sima Guang, but the history of a number of small, emerging nations. In this, Hu echoes Liang's nationalism and at the same time marks himself as an imitator of Europe.

Like Kang and Liang, Hu too was passed by the whirl of intellectual trends. Soon his contemporaries Li Dazhao, Chen Duxiu, and Mao Zedong were trying on another import from the West: Marxism. As Hu moved to the right politically in the 1920s, the center of Chinese historical thinking came to be dominated by Marxists. Since that time, and especially in recent decades in the People's Republic of China, there have been many fine Chinese historians. But they have not gone far beyond Karl Marx himself (see Chapter 39) in their fundamental thinking.

Intellectual Trends in the Qing Period[1]

K'ang [Youwei]'s second work was the *K'ung-tzu kai-chih k'ao* (*A Study of Confucius on Institutional Reform*) and his third, the *Ta-t'ung shu* (*Book of the Universal Commonwealth*). If his Study of the Classics Forged during the Hsin Period is comparable to a cyclone, these two works were a mighty volcanic eruption and huge earthquake. He studies the *Kung-yang Commentary* without bothering with the minutiae of the rules of writing composition; he was only looking for the great principles hidden in esoteric language which Ho Hsiu (129–192 AD) labelled "the extraordinary and the marvelous." He decided that the *Spring and Autumn Annals* had been Confucius' creation for the purpose of institutional reforms, and that written words were nothing but symbols, like a secret telegraphic code and the notes of musical scores, which cannot be understood without oral instructions. Moreover, he said that not only the *Spring and Autumn Annals,* but all of the Six Classics had been written by Confucius; men in the past were wrong when they said that Confucius had merely edited them. He believed that Confucius wanted to establish an independent criterion by which to promote or demote the men of old and to select or discard the ancient texts. He always tried to justify his institutional reforms on the basis of antiquity, relying on Yao (2357?–2256? BC) and Shun (2255?–2206? BC), although we do not know whether there actually were such men, and even if there were, they must in all probability have been very ordinary men; their salient virtues and great accomplishments, depicted in the classical canon, were all figments of Confucius' imagination. Not only was this the case with Confucius, but all the philosophers of the Chou (1122?–256 BC) and Ch'in (255–207 BC) too advocated institutional reforms on the basis of antiquity. For instance, Lao-tzu relied on the Yellow Emperor; Mo-tzu, on the Great Yü; and Hsü Hsing, on the Divine Husbandman.

More recently, men who have looked to Ho Hsiu (129–182 AD) for guidance in the study of the *Kung-yang Commentary* like Liu Feng-lu (1776–1829), Kung Tzu-chen (1792–1841), and Ch'en Li (1809–1869) have all talked of changing institutions, but K'ang's doctrine was quite different from theirs. What he called institutional change involved a kind of political revolution and reform of society; for this reason he liked to talk about "going through the three periods of unity." "Three periods" implied that the three dynasties of Hsia (2205?–1766? BC), Shang (1766?–1123? BC), and Chou (1122?–256 BC) were different from each other; hence, reforms should be made as time went on. He was also fond of speaking of "the unfolding of the three epochs," the "three epochs" being "the epoch of disorder," "the epoch of rising peace," and "the epoch of universal peace." The more one made changes, the more one would progress. K'ang's advocacy of political "reform and restoration" was indeed based on these ideas. He said that Confucius' institutional reforms had covered a hundred generations before him and a hundred generations after him, and therefore K'ang honored him as the founder of a religion. But since K'ang mistakenly considered Christian worship in Europe as the basis of good government and state power, he frequently attempted to equate Confucius with Christ by quoting a variety of apocryphal prognostications to support his thesis, and consequently, Confucius, as K'ang saw him, was imbued with a "quality of mystery." These, in brief, are the contents of his *Study of Confucius on Institutional Reform*. The influence of this work on the intellectual world may be said to have been the following:

1. It taught men not to study the ancient works with the intention of seeking out the trivialities of commentary on isolated phrases, or philology, or the terms for artifacts, or minute details concerning institutions, but to study them for their general meaning. On the other hand, their general meaning was not to be found in the discussion of Mind and Human Nature, but rather in the basic ideas with which ancient men initiated laws and established institutions. As a result, both Han and Sung learning were rejected, and this opened up new frontiers to the academic world.
2. In asserting that Confucius' greatness lay in his establishing a new school of learning (i.e., initiating a religion), it encouraged men's creative spirit.
3. Since the *Wei-ching k'ao* had already condemned the majority of the classics as Liu Hsin's forgeries, and the *Kai-chih k'ao* had gone further to say that the entire corpus of the true classics had been created by Confucius under the pretense of their antiquity, the classical canon, which had commonly been considered sacrosanct and inviolable for the past several thousand years, was now laid open to question to its very foundations. This prompted scholars to a more critical and skeptical attitude.
4. Although K'ang praised Confucius highly, he nevertheless said that Confucius had established a school of learning with the same motives, the same means, and the same objectives as had the other philosophers in establishing theirs. In this way he relegated Confucius to the rank of other philosophers, dissolving the so-called notion of "a black-white demarcation and a fixed orthodoxy" and so leading men into comparative studies.

*   *   *

T'an Ssu-t'ung's . . . work of the "New Studies" was the *Jen-hsüeh* (The Book on Benevolence), also known as "The Writing of a Formosan," containing many sharp satires on the Ch'ing court, in which he assumed the guise of a Formosan giving vent to his anger. Having completed the manuscript, he kept it to himself and sent a duplicate to his friend Liang Ch'i-ch'ao, who published it for distribution in Japan, and the book thus came into general circulation. The author's preface to the *Jen-hsüeh* states:

> I shall shed tears of agony and make strong outcries in order to hasten the breaking out of the entangling nets in which we are enmeshed; to break out of the entangling net created by the pursuit of selfish interests and of official emoluments; to break out of the net of such vulgar teachings as those of the school of textual criticism and of stylistic formalism; to break out of the net of all confining theories and teachings throughout the globe; to break through the trammels imposed by rulers; to break out of the net of the "basic human relationships"; and to break out of the net of "heaven." . . . Since these nets can be broken through, they really do not exist, and it is only when there are no nets in reality that it is possible to speak of breaking through.

This, in brief, is the spirit of *Jen-hsüeh*. The Englishman Newton inaugurated modern science when he advocated "iconoclasm"; T'an's "breaking out of the notes" was in this same vein.

The *Jen-hsüeh* was written with the intent of fusing science, philosophy, and religion in a single furnace to make them more useful to human life. This can indeed be called an extremely bold and far-reaching project. However, while I dare not say that such a project may not be carried out someday, yet when viewed in the light of the general state of the intellectual progress of the modern world, it still seems somewhat premature. How much more so in the China of T'an's day!

As a boy, T'an had studied mathematics with considerable success, and had also read exhaustively various translations in the field of what was called "physics" and made full use of all the scientific knowledge then available to him. He had also studied the "Vijnanamatra" and "Avatamsaka" schools of Buddhism, using them as the basis of his thinking and correlating them with science. Furthermore, he adopted the ideas of "The Universal Peace" and "The Universal Commonwealth" of the Modern Text scholars as the ultimate goal for a "World Order," also correlating these ideas with Buddhism. His book derived its material from these three fields (i.e., science, philosophy, and religion), which he organized as a basis for his own ideas, and while it is undeniable that it contains many inconsistent, disorderly, and childish arguments, still it broke so entirely free and independent of the fetters of the traditional thinking that it had no equal throughout the Ch'ing period.

At bottom, T'an opposed the idea of prefering antiquity. He once asked, "If antiquity is so admirable, what is the point of being a modern man?" His general criticism of Chinese history runs as follows:

> The governments of the past two thousand years have all been modeled on that of the Ch'in, hence all of them have been great predators. The dominant doctrine of the past two thousand years has been Hsün-tzu's, which has produced good prudent villagers (i.e., sycophants). It is the great predators who have utilized the good prudent villagers, and it is the good prudent villagers who have known how to flatter the great predators.

At that time, the pronouncements of T'an Ssu-t'ung, Liang Ch'i-ch'ao, Hsia Tseng-yu, and their circle were mostly based on this thesis, and T'an was the bravest of them all.

The Development of the Logical Method in Ancient China[2]

The great Chow Empire, founded in 1122 B.C., fell in 771 B.B., when the imperial domains were invaded by the Dog Barbarians, and the Emperor, Yu-Wang, was slain by the invaders. The next Emperor, Ping-Wang, fled to the Eastern capital in 770, thus beginning the Eastern Chow dynasty which lasted until

256 BC In the glorious days of the Chow Empire, the Emperor reigned supreme over the several hundred vassal states or principalities into which China was then divided. The Emperor, or "Son of Heaven," was not only the temporal but also the spiritual head of the empire, ruling in the name of Heaven to which he alone was privileged to sacrifice, the vassal lords and their subordinates sacrificing only to the lesser deities. The feudal hierarchy, which comprised the Emperor as liege lord, the five ranks of vassal lords, the Grand Officers, the knights (sze), and the common people, was governed by rules prescribing inter-class and intra-class relations and duties with the minutest detail. This system seems to have worked remarkably well for several centuries. Then it began to decay. The Imperial government, under weak and wicked emperors, gradually declined in prestige and power until it finally succumbed to the barbarian invasion in 771. In the meantime, some of the vassal states had gradually increased both in territory and in prestige by conquering surrounding states and barbarian tribes which were then quite numerous. The Imperial government never recovered the lost authority and potency. In the early years of the Eastern dynasty, as, for instance, in 707, the Emperor was still able to send a punitive expedition against a disobedient vassal state. Such attempts, however, were futile. Several powerful states had arisen to assume the leadership of the states. One of them, the State of Chu, had, in 704, proclaimed itself a "kingdom."

There were alliances of states formed for defensive and aggressive purposes. Most of the important wars of the sixth and fifth centuries were fought between groups or alliances, each under the "presidency" of one leading power. Such wars occurred very frequently. Attempts at international conciliation and disarmament by agreement were made, e.g., in BC 546, by the pacifists of the time, but they were without success. It has been estimated that at the beginning of the Chow Empire, there were at least eight hundred vassal states. Many of these states were conquered and their territory annexed by the few great powers. About the end of the fifth century BC, the numerous states had been reduced to seven powers with a few buffer states subsisting betwixt them. Six of these seven were finally conquered by the State of Chin towards the last quarter of the third century BC, the period of "contending states" thus passing into the Empire of Chin.

The numerous wars and frequent transfers of political allegiance had of course tremendous effects on the social and intellectual conditions of the time. They had brought about a gradual breakdown of the feudal hierarchy. The lords of the vanquished states were naturally degraded, while the needs of the time—the wars, the demand for diplomatic talents as well as for domestic statesmanship—elevated many a great talent from lowliness and obscurity. Peasants' sons, and even slaves not infrequently rose to Ministership of State, and a few ministers became so powerful as to overshadow their princes and afterwards actually to replace the ruling houses. Merchants—a class which had long been considered the lowest of all the classes of freemen—too began to play an important role in the politics of nations. In short, the rigid class demarcations characteristic of every feudal system were swept away by the rapid political and social upheavals and transformations.

Nowhere can we find more vivid descriptions of the social conditions of the age than in the popular songs and poems that have been edited and preserved to us by Confucius in the *Book of Poetry*. I shall now resort to this remarkable collection for contemporary testimonies of the conditions of social and intellectual life of the time.

The reduction of many a ruling house to conditions of dependence and misery is seen in the following utterances of an officer who had followed his prince into exile after the downfall of his principality:

"Reduced! Reduced!
Why not return?
If it were not for your person, O Prince
How should we be here in the mire?"
    (Pt. I, Bk. III, XI.)

The rise of the lowly and unprivileged class to wealth and positions of power is seen in the following complaint:

"The sons of boatmen
Are wrapped in furs of the bear and the grisly bear!
And sons of servitude
Form the officers in public employment!"
    (Pt. II, Bk. V, IX.)

If the misery and suffering attendant upon the frequent wars and expeditions and devastations, the *Book of Poetry* furnishes a wealth of vivid pictures. Here is a song of a soldier:

"How freely are the wild geese on their wings,
And the rest they find on the bushy yu trees!
But we, ceaseless toilers in the king's service,
Cannot even plant our millet and rice.
What will our parents have to rely on?
O thou distant and azure Heaven!
When shall all this end?"
    (Pt., Bk. X, VIII.)

*   *   *

And the inequality and the injustice of it all!

"Under the wide heaven,
All is the king's land;
Within the sea-boundaries,
All are his servants.
How unjust are those in power
Who made me toil so, as if I alone were worthy! . . .
"Some enjoy their ease and rest,
And some are worn out in serving the State!
Some lie and loll upon their couches,
And some never cease marching about!'
    (Pt. II, Bk. VI, I.)

Glimpses of the economic life of the time may be gathered from the following songs:

"Shoes thinly woven of the dolichos fibre
May be used to walk on the hoarfrost!
And the delicate fingers of women
May be used to make clothes!
Sew the waistband and sew the collar!
And the good man wears them!"
  (Pt. I, Bk. IX, I.)

*   *   *

"The mother-wort of the valley
Is scorched everywhere.
There is a woman left homeless.
Ever flow her tears!
Ever flow her tears!
But of what avail is her lament?"
  (Pt. I, Bk. VI, VI.)

*   *   *

"You awe-inspiring Ministers of State,
Why are you so unjust?
Heaven is multiplying its afflictions;
The people are grumbling,
And yet you do not correct nor bemoan yourselves!"
  (Pt. II, Bk. IV, VII.)

*   *   *

"Men had their land and farms,
But you have them now.
Men had their people and their retainers,
But these you have taken from them.
Here is an innocent man,
But you have imprisoned him.
There is a guilty man,
But you have let him go free."

*   *   *

"When the people are going away,
The country is sure to go to ruin."
  (Pt. III, Bk. III, X.)

QUESTIONS TO CONSIDER

1. What differences does Liang see between Kang Youwei and Tan Situng?
2. What is the effect on the reader of Hu's recourse to poetry in the selection presented here?

3. In what respects do these passages bear continuity with the earlier Chinese histories of Sima Qian (Chapter 10), Ban Zhao (11), and Sima Guang (22)? In what respects (and for what probable reasons) do they diverge?

4. How do Liang's and Hu's perspectives on response to the West differ from other Third World historians such as Dutt, Johnson, and Fukuzawa?

FOR FURTHER READING

Beasley, W. G., and E. G. Pulleyblank, eds. *Historians of China and Japan.* Oxford: Oxford University Press, 1961.

Chow Tse-tung. *The May Fourth Movement: Intellectual Revolution in Modern China.* Stanford, CA: Stanford University Press, 1960.

Compilation Group for the "History of Modern China" series. *The Reform Movement of 1898.* Beijing: Foreign Languages Press, 1976.

Grieder, Jerome. *Hu Shih and the Chinese Renaissance.* Cambridge, MA: Harvard University Press, 1970.

Levenson, Joseph R. *Liang Ch'i-ch'ao and the Mind of Modern China.* Cambridge, MA: Harvard University Press, 1953.

Li Chien-nung. *The Political History of China, 1840–1928.* Trans. and ed. Ssu-yu Teng and Jeremy Ingalls. Princeton, NJ: Van Nostrand, 1956.

Meisner, Maurice. *Li Ta-chao and the Origins of Chinese Marxism.* Cambridge, MA: Harvard University Press, 1967.

Schneider, Laurence A. *Ku Chieh-kang and China's New History.* Berkeley, CA: University of California Press, 1971.

Schwarcz, Vera. *The Chinese Enlightenment: Intellectuals and the Legacy of the May Fourth Movement of 1919.* Berkeley, CA: University of California Press, 1986.

Teng, Ssu-yu, and John K. Fairbank. *China's Response to the West.* New York: Atheneum, 1970.

NOTES

1. Liang Ch'i-ch'ao, *Intellectual Trends in the Ch'ing Period*, trans. Immanuel C. Y. Hsu (Cambridge, MA: Harvard University Press, 1959), 94–95, 107–108.

2. Hu Shih, *The Development of the Logical Method in Ancient China* (New York: Paragon, 1963; orig. Shanghai, 1922), 1–9.

PART FIVE

Science and Critique

*A*ll the historians of Part 5 conceived themselves, on one level or another, to be engaged in science. They worked in the nineteenth and early twentieth centuries, either in the West or in other parts of the world that had been deeply affected by Euroamerican colonialism, hence by Western modes of thought. As surely as Marie Curie sought the underlying laws of physics, and Herbert Spencer sought the underlying principles shaping human behavior, these historians were seeking the underlying laws that guided history.

Marx told stories about Louis Bonaparte or the Paris Commune, yet he saw those stories not as unconnected events, but as part of a large pattern of historical forces. It was the pattern, the universal laws of history that captivated him. So, too, it was the big social forces, not the intimate details of daily living that animated Marc Bloch's study of feudal Europe. Da Cunha told the story of some rebels in Bahia, Brazil, but first he spent half his book placing them in the context of geology, race mixing, climate, and other forces. Weber, too, looked for the deep underlying cultural changes that lay behind events; he found

them in the social ethics of the Protestant reformers and in the writings of Benjamin Franklin.

Note that this scientific approach does not allow much room for the supernatural. Heirs of the eighteenth-century Enlightenment, our scientific historians sought naturalistic explanations for events even where eyewitnesses saw God or the gods at work. Da Cunha, for example, explained Antonio Conselheiro's religious rebellion as a combination of insanity and credulity--and in the process maintained a post-Enlightenment naturalism, even as his explanation belittled the people he described.

If there was an element of epistemological arrogance to this approach, there was also an element of faith. The historians we treat here were all devoted to what the Germans call *wissenschaft*—the muse of objective knowledge. Thus Ranke could seek objective truth by carefully collecting and analyzing documents, yet could also believe that the spirit of God animated human history. Thus, too, Marx could possess a faith in the inevitable progression of historical stages that lay near the heart of his analysis of capitalism. Charles and Mary Beard believed

403

deeply that American democracy would ultimately correct its mistakes. And Frederick Jackson Turner exhibited a similar faith in the transformative power of the American frontier. Each of these, nonetheless, perceived his or her own particular faith to be grounded in scientific objectivity.

What unites all these historians is a dedication to method. Weber's method was broadly philosophical, based on reasoning and on observation of civic affairs in the world around him. Ranke's method was textual, and included exhaustive research in primary sources as well as absolute interpretive fidelity to the documents. Dike advocated a multidisciplinary team approach: a historian, an anthropologist, an art historian, a linguist, and an archaeologist collectively analyzing a historical period and pooling their knowledge. Yanagita Kunio drew his methodology from the folklorist wing of anthropology. Panikkar called for a scientific attention to Indian historical sources as a corrective to an overreliance on European ones. These were all hard-headed, no-nonsense analysts, dedicated to the idea that they could discover objective truth through a careful application of scientific principles.

Each of these authors also offered a critique. Marx's life work was a critique of capitalism. Panikkar opposed British colonialism. Mary Ritter Beard criticized capitalist exploitation but also the male domination of women and women who allowed themselves to be dominated. Da Cunha criticized those leaders of the Brazilian republic who failed to incorporate the people of rural Bahia in their plans for the nation.

Science and critique: these are the two themes unifying the historians in Part 5. Their critiques were different, as were their sciences, but their commitments to both were remarkably uniform.

FOR FURTHER READING

Collingwood, R. G. *The Idea of History.* New York: Oxford University Press, 1956.

Fustel de Coulanges, N. O. *The Ancient City.* Baltimore: Johns Hopkins University Press, 1980; orig. 1864.

Hughes, H. Stuart. *History as Art and as Science.* New York: Harper and Row, 1964.

Landes, Davis S., and Charles Tilly, eds. *History as Social Science.* Englewood Cliffs, NJ: Prentice Hall, 1971.

Lewis, William Todd. *History as Applied Science.* Detroit, MI: Wayne State University Press, 1972.

Novick, Peter. *That Noble Dream: The "Objectivity Question" and the American Historical Profession.* Cambridge, UK: Cambridge University Press, 1988.

Sarkar, Benoy Kumar. *The Science of History and the Hope of Mankind.* London: Longmans, Green, 1912.

CHAPTER 38

Leopold von Ranke

Realist, Idealist

Leopold von Ranke
Courtesy of the German Information Center

No man or woman has more profoundly affected what modern historians have conceived their work to be about than Leopold von Ranke. He was the most prolific and honored member of a nineteenth-century German school of writers whose work was labelled *historismus* ("historicism" in English; quite different from the "new historicism" that has arisen in Europe and America in recent years). These historians reacted against the interpretive self-absorption and rhetorical flights of Enlightenment historians like Voltaire (see Chapter 30). Ranke's goal was set forth in the preface to his first book, *Histories of the Latin and Germanic Nations from 1494 to 1514* (1824): "History has been assigned the office of judging the past, of instructing our time for the benefit of future years. This essay does not aspire to such high offices; it wants only to show how it had really been—*wie es eigentlich gewesen.*"

Wie es eigentlich gewesen ("as it actually was") was repeated as a mantra by European and American historians for a century and a half. Ranke saw the world as made up of many different peoples with different ways of seeing what went on around them. The historian's task, he said, was to see the world from the point of view of the people under study, using documents as windows into their mental universe. To that end, he prescribed a careful method of exhaustive research in primary sources, documentation using footnotes, and scrupulous objectivity in interpretation, much like Arai Hakuseki in Japan (see Chapter 26).

Yet Ranke was also a product of the Romantic era, a Protestant, and a German. Born in a small town in Thuringia in 1795, Ranke came of age during the Romantic period, and identified especially with the nationalist and religious expressions of that movement. He was deeply religious, and convinced that spirit and intuition ought to drive historical interpretation. In a lecture in 1845 he said the following:

> No one could be more convinced than I that historical research requires the strictest method: criticism of the authors, the banning of all fables, the extraction of the pure facts. But I am also convinced that this fact has a spiritual content. For any action is not the outermost limit. The external appearance is not the final thing which we have to discover; there is still something which occurs within. The event occurs only as the result of a spiritually combined series of actions. It is our task to recognize what really happened in the series of facts which German history comprises: their sum. After the labor or criticism, intuition is required. (*The Secret of World History*, 21)

Still, despite this reliance on spirit and intuition, Ranke disagreed with the willingness of Romantics like Walter Scott to reshape the past to fit their own visions. In the end, he stood for objectivity as the queen of virtues.

Some recent interpreters such as Peter Novick have tried to undermine Ranke's commitment to objectivity, arguing that *eigentlich* in the nineteenth-century German meant something more like "essentially" than "actually"; one suspects they stretch Ranke to fit their own, late-twentieth-century, relativist preoccupations. Whatever Ranke actually thought, the way he was used for over a century by historians was as an icon of scientific objectivity.

Ranke spread his ideas as a professor at the University of Berlin from 1825 to 1865 (he lived on to 1886). Students came to him from all over Europe and from North America. His seminar method of teaching revolutionized postgraduate education. Ranke was midwife at the birth of a professional class of historians, trained in graduate schools and employed by universities as teachers and scholars. Since his time there have been relatively few gentlemen and -women historians, a marked departure from the previous centuries; professional historians have become the norm.

Ranke wrote some 60 volumes in a career that spanned six decades. He built a body of work dedicated both to universal history (by which he meant the entire history of the peoples of western Europe, not the world) and to immersion in individual events and personalities. Among Ranke's many books, none is more significant than his *History of the Popes,* a portion of which is reproduced here. The book resulted from years spent reading thousands of documents in the Vatican archives. In this study, Ranke's purpose was to illuminate the development of Europe's most important institution from earliest times to his own day, with detailed emphasis on the sixteenth and seventeenth centuries. Although Ranke was a dedicated Lutheran, and the modern reader can see evidence of his Lutheran convictions, the *History of the Popes* embodied a degree of impartiality that brought him criticism from many of his fellow Protestants. The selection chosen here is not the story of a Pope, but a portion of Ranke's memorable treatment of Ignatius Loyola, founder of the Society of Jesus.

The History of the Popes[1]

Ignatius Loyola

The chivalry of Spain was the only one that had preserved a certain remnant of its religious character, down to the period before us. The war with the Moors, but just arriving at its conclusion in the Peninsula, and still proceeding in Africa; the vicinity of the subjugated Moriscoes still remaining, and with whom the intercourse held by the victors was marked by the rancor characteristic of religious hatred; with the adventurous expeditions yet undertaken against infidels beyond the seas; all combined to perpetuate this spirit. In such books as the "Amadis de Gaul," full of a simple, enthusiastic loyalty and bravery, that spirit was idealized.

Don Iñigo Lopez de Recalde,[2] the youngest son of the house of Loyola, was born in a castle of that name, between Azpeitia and Azcoitia, in Guipuscoa. He was of a race that belonged to the nobles in the land—"de parientes mayores"—and its head claimed the right of being summoned to do homage by special writ. Educated at the court of Ferdinand the Catholic, and in the train of the Duke of Najara, Iñigo was deeply imbued with the spirit of his nation and class. He aspired to knightly renown, and for none of his compatriots had the glitter of arms, the fame of valor, the adventures of single combat and of love, more attractive charms than for him; but he also displayed an extraordinary fervor of religious enthusiasm, and had already celebrated the first of the apostles, in a romance of chivalry, at this early period of his life.[3]

It is, nevertheless, probable, that his name would have become known to us, only as one of those many brave and noble Spanish leaders, to whom the wars of Charles V gave opportunities so numerous for distinguishing themselves, had he not been wounded in both legs, at the defence of Pampeluna, against the French, in 1521. Of these wounds he was never completely cured; twice were they reopened, and such was his fortitude, that, in these severe operations, the only sign of pain he permitted to escape him was the firm clenching of his hands. His sufferings were, unhappily, unavailing; the cure remained deplorably incomplete.

He was much versed in, and equally attached to, the romances of chivalry, more especially to the Amadis. During his long confinement, he also read the life of Christ, and of some of the saints.

Visionary by nature, and excluded from a career that seemed to promise him the most brilliant fortunes, condemned to inaction, and at the same time rendered sensitive and excitable by his sufferings, he fell into the most extraordinary state of mind that can well be conceived. The deeds of St. Francis and St. Dominic, set forth by his favorite books in all the lustre of their saintly renown, not only seemed to him worthy of imitation, but, as he read, he believed himself possessed of the courage and strength required to follow in their footsteps, and to vie with them in austerity and self-denial.[4] It is true that these exalted purposes were sometimes chased by projects of a much more worldly character. Then would he picture himself repairing to the city where dwelt the lady to whose service he had devoted himself. "She was no countess," he said, "and no duchess, but of yet higher degree." The gay and graceful discourses with which he would address her, how he would prove his devotion, the knightly exploits he would perform in her honor; such were the fantasies between which his mind alternated.

The more his recovery was protracted, and his hope of ultimate cure was deferred, the more also did the spiritual revery gain ascendancy over the worldly vision. Shall we do him wrong, if we impute this result to the increased conviction that his former vigor could not be restored, that he could not hope again to shine in military service or the knightly career?

Not that the transition was so abrupt, or to so opposite an extreme, as it might, on the first view, appear to be. In his spiritual exercises, the origin of which was coincident with the first ecstatic meditations of his awakened spirit, he imagines two camps, one at Jerusalem, the other at Babylon; the one belonging to Christ, the other to Satan; in the one is every thing good—in the other, whatever is most depraved and vicious. These are prepared for combat. Christ is a king who has signified his resolve to subjugate all unbelievers; whoever would fight beneath his banners must be fed with the same food, and clad in like garments with him; he must endure the same hardships and vigils; according to the measure of his deeds, shall he be admitted to share in the victory and rewards. Before Christ, the Virgin, and the whole court of heaven, shall each man then declare that he will truly follow his lord, will share with him in all adversities, and abide by him in true poverty of body and of spirit.[5]

By these fanciful imaginations, it probably was that his transition from the chivalry of arms to that of religion was facilitated; for it was indeed to a sort of spiritual knighthood that his aspirations now tended, the ideal perfection of which was to consist in emulation of the achievements performed, and privations endured, by the saints. Tearing himself from home and kindred, he now sought the heights of Montserrat, not driven to this by remorse for his sins, nor impelled by any reality of religious feeling, but, as he has himself declared, merely by the desire of achieveing deeds equally great with those to which the saints are indebted for their renown. His weapons and armor he hung up before an image of the Virgin; kneeling or standing in prayer, with his pilgrim's staff in his hand, he here passed the night, holding a vigil somewhat different from that of knighthood, but expressly suggested by the Amadis,[6] where all the rites proper to it are minutely described. The knightly dress in which he had arrived at Montserrat he gave away, assuming the coarse garb of the hermits, whose lonely dwellings are scooped among those naked rocks. After having made a general confession, he set off toward Jerusalem, not going direct to Barcelona, lest he should be recognized on the highways, but making a round by Manresa, whence, after new penances, he meant to gain his port of embarkation for the holy city.

But in Manresa he was met by other trials; the fantasies to which he had shielded himself, not so much from conviction as caprice, began here to assume the positive mastery. He devoted himself to the severest penances in the cell of a convent of Dominicans; he scourged himself thrice a day, he rose to prayer at midnight, and passed seven hours of each day on his knees.

He found these severities so difficult of practice that he greatly doubted his own ability to persevere in them for his whole life, but, what was still more serious, he felt that they did not bring him peace. He had spent three days on Montserrat in confessing the sins of all his past life; but, not satisfied with this he repeated it in Manresa, recalling many faults before forgotten, nor permitting the most trifling errors to escape him; but the more laborious his exploration, so much the more painful became the doubts that assailed him. He did not believe that he should be either accepted by or justified before God. Having read in the works of the fathers that a total abstinence from food had once moved the compassion and obtained the mercy of the Almighty, he kept rigid fast from one Sunday to another, but his confessor forbad him to continue this attempt, and Iñigo, who placed the virtue of obedience above all others, desisted immediately; occasionally it appeared to him that his melancholy had been removed, falling away as does a heavy garment from the shoulders, but his former sufferings soon returned. His whole life seemed to him but one continuous series of sin, and he not unfrequently felt tempted to throw himself from the window.[7]

This relation cannot fail to remind us of the nearly similar sufferings endured by Luther some twenty years before, when he was assailed by similar doubts. The great demand of religion, a perfect reconciliation with God, and its full assurance, could never be obtained in the ordinary manner prescribed by the Church, with such certainty as to satisfy the unfathomable longings of a soul at enmity with itself. But out of this labyrinth Ignatius and Luther escaped by very different paths, the latter attained to the doctrine of reconciliation through Christ without works; this it was that laid open to him the meaning of the Scriptures which then became his strong support; but of Loyola we do not find that he examined the Scriptures or became impressed by any particular dogma. Living in a world of internal emotion, and amid thoughts arising for ever within him, he believed himself subjected to the influence now of the good, and now of the evil spirit. He arrived finally at the power of distinguishing the inspirations of the one from that of the other, perceiving that the soul was cheered and comforted by the first, but harassed and exhausted by the latter.[8] One day he seemed to have awakened from a dream, and thought he had tangible evidence that all his torments were assaults of Satan. He resolved to resign all examination of his past life from that hour, to open those wounds no more, never again to touch them. This was not so much the restoration of his peace as a resolution, it was an engagement entered into by the will rather than a conviction to which the submission of the will is inevitable. It required no aid from Scripture, it was based on the belief he entertained of an immediate connection between himself and the world of spirits. This would never have satisfied Luther. No inspirations—no visions would Luther admit; all were in his opinion alike injurious. He would have the simple, written, indubitable word of God alone.

Loyola, on the contrary, lived wholly in fantasies and inward apparitions; the person best acquainted with Christianity was, as he thought, an old woman, who had told him, in the worst of his mental anguish, that Christ would yet appear to him in person. For some time this was not clear to him; but at length he believed not only to have the Saviour in person before his eyes, but the Virgin Mother also. One day he stood weeping aloud on the step of the church of St. Dominick, at Manresa, because he believed himself to see the mystery of the Trinity at that moment standing before his sight.[9] He spoke of nothing else through the whole day, and was inexhaustible in similes and comparisons respecting it. Suddenly also the mystery of the creation was made visible to him in mystic symbols. In the host he beheld the God and the Man. Proceeding once along the banks of the Llobregat to a distant church, he sat down and bent his eyes earnestly on the deep stream before him, when he was suddenly raised into an ecstasy wherein the mysteries of the faith were visibly revealed to him. He believed himself to rise up a new man. Thenceforth neither testimony nor Scripture was needful to him; had none such existed he would have gone without hesitation to death for the faith which he had before believed, but which he now saw with his eyes.[10] If we have clearly comprehended the origin and development of this most peculiar state of mind, of this chivalry of abstinence, this pertinacity of enthusiasm, and fantastic asceticism, we shall not need to follow Iñigo Loyola through every step of his progress. He did, in fact, proceed to Jerusalem, in the hope of confirming the faith of the believer as well as that of converting the infidel. But how was this last purpose to be accomplished, uninstructed as he was, without associates, without authority? Even his intention of remaining in the Holy Land was frustrated by an express prohibition from the heads of the Church at Jerusalem, who had received from the Pope the privilege of granting or refusing permissions of residence there. Returning to Spain he had further trials to encounter, being accused of heresy on attempting to teach and inviting others to participate in those spiritual exercises on which he had now entered. It would have been an extraordinary sport of destiny, if Loyola, whose Society, centuries later, ended in Illuminati, had himself been associated with a sect of that name;[11] and it is not to be denied that the Spanish Illuminati of that day—the Alumbrados— did hold opinions bearing some analogy to his fantasies. They had rejected the doctrine then taught in Christendom, of salvation by works, like him they gave themselves up to ecstasies, and believed, as he did, that they beheld religious mysteries, above all that of the Trinity, in immediate and visible revelation. They made general confession a condition to absolution, and insisted earnestly on the necessity for inward prayer, as did Loyola and his followers of later times. I would not venture to affirm that Loyola was entirely untouched by these opinions, but neither would I assert that he belonged to the sect of Alumbrados. The most striking distinction betwen them and him is, that whereas they believed themselves to be exalted by the claims of the spirit above all the common duties of life, he, on the contrary, still impressed by his early habits, placed the soldier's virtue, obedience, before all others; his every conviction and whole enthusiasm of feeling he compelled himself to place in subjection to the Church and to all who were invested with her authority.

*   *   *

He proceeded then to Paris, which at that time was the most celebrated university of the world.

*   *   *

Of the two companions who shared the rooms of Loyola in the college of St. Barbara, one, Pater Faber, a Savoyard, proved an easy conquest; growing up among his father's flocks, he had one night devoted himself solemnly, beneath the canopy of heaven, to study and to God. He went through the course of philosophy with Ignatius (the name that Loyola received among foreigners), and the latter communicated to him his own ascetic principles. Ignatius taught his young friend to combat his faults, prudently taking them not altogether, but one by one, since there was always some virtue to the possession of which he should more especially aspire. He kept him strictly to confession and to frequent participation of the Lord's Supper. They lived in the closest intimacy. Ignatius received alms in tolerable abundance from Spain and Flanders, these he constantly divided with Faber. His second companion, Francis Xavier of Pampeluna, in Navarre, was by no means so easily won; his most earnest ambition was to ennoble still further the long series of his ancestors, renowned in war during five hundred years, by adding to their names his own, rendered illustrious by learning. He was handsome and rich, possessed high talent, and had already gained a footing at court. Ignatius was careful to show him all the respect to which he laid claim, and to see that others paid it also, he procured him a large audience for his first lectures, and, having begun by these personal services, his influence was soon established by the natural effect of his pure example and imposing austerity of life. He at length prevailed on Xavier, as he had done on Faber, to join him in the spiritual exercises. He was by no means indulgent; three days and three nights did he compel them to fast. During the severest winters, when carriages might be seen to traverse the frozen Seine, he would not permit Faber the slightest relaxation of discipline. He finished by making these two young men entirely his own, and shared with them his most intimate thoughts and feelings.[12]

How full of mighty import was that little cell of St. Barbara, uniting as it did these three men, who there formed plans and devised enterprises, inspired by their visionary and enthusiastic ideas of religion, and that were to lead, they themselves could have conception whither.

*   *   *

In the year 1540, he [the pope] gave his sanction to their institute, at first with certain restrictions, but afterward, in 1543, the Society of Jesus was absolutely and unconditionally established.

*   *   *

. . . [T]hey devoted all their energies and every hour of their lives to the essential duties of their office; not to one only, as did the Barnabites, although they attended sedulously to the sick as one measure toward acquiring a good name; nor with the restrictions that fettered the Theatines, but to all the greater duties equally, and with whatever force they could command. First to preaching; before separating in Vicenza, they had mutually agreed to preach chiefly for the common people, to think more of themselves by display of eloquence, and to this system they adhered. Secondly to confession: for by this they were to hold the immediate guidance and government of consciences. The spiritual exercises by which they had themselves become united with Ignatius afforded them important aid. Finally, they devoted themselves to the education of youth: they had intended to bind themselves to this last by a special clause in their vows, and although they had not done so, yet the practice of this duty was made imperative by the most stringent rules; to gain the rising generation was among the purposes most earnestly pursued. They laid aside, in short, all secondary matters, devoting themselves wholly to such labors as were essential, of immediate result, and calculated for the extension of their influence.

Thus was a system pre-eminently practical evolved from the visionary aspirations of Ignatius; and from the ascetic conversions he had made, there resulted an institution, framed with all that skillful adaptation of means to their end which the most consummate worldly prudence could suggest.

His most sanguine hopes were now more than fulfilled—he held the uncontrolled direction of a society, among whose members his own peculiar views found cordial acceptance, and wherein the religious convictions at which he had arrived by accident or the force of his genius, were made the object of profound study, and the venerated basis and guide of belief. His plan relating to Jerusalem was not, indeed, to be carried out, for nothing useful could now be obtained by it; but in other directions the company he ruled went forth on the most remote, and above all, most successful missions. The care of souls, which he had so earnestly enforced, was entered on with a zeal that he could not have hoped for, and to an extent surpassing his highest anticipations. And lastly, he was himself the object of an implicit obedience, combining that of the soldier to his captain with that of the priest to his spiritual chief.

NOTES

1. Leopold von Ranke, *History of the Popes*, vol. 1, trans. E. Fowler (New York: Frederick Ungar, 1966; orig. 1901), 123–29, 130–31, 133, 134–35. Footnotes renumbered to fit abridgment.
2. He is so called in judicial acts. How he became possessed of the name "Recalde" is not known, but this does not impugn its authenticity. "Acta Sanctorum, 31 Julii, Commentarius praevius," p. 410.
3. Maffei, "Vita Ignatii."
4. The "Acta antiquissima, a Ludovico Consalvo ex ore Sancti excepta, AA. SS. LL." p. 634, gives very authentic information on the subject. The

thought occurred to him once: "Quid, si ego hoc agerem, quod fecit b. Franciscus, quid si hoc, quod b. Dominicus?" Again: "Of many vain things that offered themselves to his mind, one he retained." The honor that he meant to pay his lady ["non era condesa ni duquesa mas era su estado mas alto que ninguno destas"], a singularly frank and simple acknowledgment.

5. "Exercitia spirtuali: Secunda Hebdomada." "Contemplatio regni Jesu Christi ex similitudine regis terreni subditos suos evocantis ad bellum"; and in other places.

6. "Acta antiquissima." A strange mistake of the compiler, for certainly Amagis is not an author. "When his mind was filled with things from Amadis of Gaul, and other writers of that sort, many of which he met with."

7. Maffei, Ribadeneira, Orlandino, and all his other biographers describe these struggles; but more authentic than all are the writings of lgnatius himself on this subject; the following passage, for example, clearly depicts his condition: "When agitated by these thoughts he was often sorely tempted to throw himself from a large window in his cell, near the place where he prayed; but when he saw that it was a sin to destroy himself, he cried out again, 'Lord, I will not do aught that may offend thee.'"

8. One of his most peculiar and most original perceptions, the beginning of which is referred by himself to the fancies of his illness. In Manresa it became a certainty, and it is described with great expansion in the "Spiritual Exercises," wherein are found especial rules: "For discovering whether the movements of the soul proceed from good spirits or evil, so that the first be admitted and the last repelled."

9. Figured by three keys of a musical instrument.

10. "Acta antiguissima:" "his visis haud mediocriter tun confirmatus est" (the original has "y le dieron tanta confirmacione siempre de la fe") "ut saepe etiam id cogitarit, quod etsi nulla scriptura mysteria illa fidei doceret, tamen ipse ob ea ipsa quae viderat, statueret sibi pro is esse moriendum." (See the text.)

11. This charge was made against Lainez and Borgia also—Llorente, "Hist. de l'Inquisition," iii. 83. Melchior Cano calls them plainly illuminati, the gnostics of the age.

12. Orlandinus, who likewise wrote a life of Faber, which I have not seen, is more circumstantial on this point also (in his great work, "Historiae Societatis Jesu," past i. p. 17) that is Ribadeneira.

QUESTIONS TO CONSIDER

1. To what extent did Ranke succeed in his attempt to portray history *"wie es eigentlich gewesen"* ("as it actually was")?

2. How might Ranke's employment by a university, rather than reliance on a personal fortune or patronage, have affected his work?

3. What do Ranke's footnotes add to his account and to the reader's reaction to it?

4. To what extent does this passage show signs of idealistic as well as rational values?

FOR FURTHER READING

Iggers, Georg G., and James M. Powell, eds. *Leopold von Ranke and the Shaping of the Historical Discipline.* Syracuse, NY: Syracuse University Press, 1990.

Krieger, Leonard. *Ranke: The Meaning of History.* Chicago: University of Chicago Press, 1977.

Ranke, Leopold von. *The History of Servia.* Trans. Mrs. Alexander Kerr. London: Henry G. Bohn, 1853.

_____ . *History of the Popes.* 3 vols. Trans. E. Fowler. New York: Frederick Ungar, 1966; orig. 1901.

_____ . *History of the Reformation in Germany.* Trans. Sarah Austin. New York: Frederick Ungar, 1966; orig. 1905.

_____ . *Memoirs of the House of Brandenburg, and History of Prussia.* 3 vols. Trans. Alexander and Duff Gordon. New York: Greenwood, 1968; orig. 1849.

_____ . *The Secret of World History.* Ed. and trans. Roger Wines. New York: Fordham University Press, 1981.

_____ . *The Theory and Practice of History.* Ed. and trans. Georg G. Iggers, Wilma A. Iggers, and Konrad von Moltke. Indianapolis, IN: Bobbs-Merrill, 1973.

CHAPTER 39

Karl Marx

Historical Materialist

Karl Marx
Courtesy of the German Information Center

The average person does not think of Karl Marx as a historian. Agitator, communist, radical economist (if an academic discipline must be assigned)—yes. But historian? Yet Marx's tremendous knowledge of history shows in all his writings. He developed his economic theories out of a desire to understand how history works. What universal principles govern the rise and fall of peoples and nations? Why was the Europe of his day so different from the Europe of centuries past? Revolutions, coups d'etat, the elimination of one class of people and the emancipation of another—for Marx, these were but the signs of the underlying socio-economic forces that are the topic of his major works.

Marx wrote histories, too. He analyzed the rise of capitalism in France and England. He wrote about workers' rebellions like the Paris Commune of 1871. And he wrote at length about the revolution of 1848: why it happened, and above all, why it failed. His books have inspired later historians to look behind "the facts" to the socio-economic processes that guide events in particular ways.

Karl Marx was born in 1818 in Trier, on the western edge of what is now Germany (Germany was not, of course, unified until 1871). His father was a well-to-do lawyer, who encouraged young Karl's intellectual inquisitiveness. Though expected to follow his father's profession, Marx gravitated to philosophy in school. He was especially influenced by the work of G. W. F. Hegel. Then he became involved in student politics at the Universities of Bonn and Berlin. We would not consider his student politics to be radical today. But his support for popular democracy and his exposés of the plight of impoverished workers won him no friends in the Prussian government, nor even in the more liberal Rhineland. Unable to find work, he emigrated to Paris in 1843 to edit a journal with other "left Hegelians." This journal lasted only one issue. While working there, he met Friedrich Engels, with whom he established a lifelong intellectual partnership. Marx was expelled from France, then Belgium, and— after the revolution of 1848—from Germany. He settled in London, where he lived in poverty until his death in 1883.

Marx's work can be divided into three periods. His writings before 1848 most clearly show his Hegelianism. Though centered on social problems, they are abstract and philosophical, concerned with how to develop freedom in an oppressive world. Some of the most significant were not published until after his death—left, as Marx put it, to "the gnawing criticism of the mice." Despite their difficulty—and they are hard reading—they show the germ of his view of history.

Marx presented that view more clearly in a series of pamphlets he wrote between 1848 and 1855, selections from which follow. These portray history as the result of a series of class struggles: master against slave, townspeople against country folk, rich against poor. In this vision, individuals do not matter much; underlying economic developments do. As Marx put it: "Men make their history, but they do not make it exactly as they please." Their efforts are constrained by the amount and kinds of goods a society can produce and by the way that production is organized. By knowing the roles different classes play in economic life and the ways in which classes oppose one another, the historian can show why events occur as they do. Marx's own analyses of mid-nineteenth century political events, for instance, in *The Eighteenth Brumaire of Louis Bonaparte* and *The Class Struggles in France*, are models of the genre.

After 1855, Marx devoted himself to tracing the economic underpinnings of capitalist society. In *Das Kapital*, his most significant book, Marx works out the "laws of motion" of economic life in an attempt to prove that capitalism will ultimately fail. Though the working class did not overthrow it in the French and German revolutions of 1848, he argued that a free society will in the end emerge from capitalism's wreckage. People will be neither rich nor poor. Instead, all will share in the wealth that they collectively produce. And all will determine their own economic fate—as only the rich do today. Though he had not worked out these details at the time he wrote the passages excerpted here, one can see their outline clearly.

Our first selection, from *The Communist Manifesto*, presents Marx's view of history at the most general level. Co-authored with Engels, this passage looks at the history of economic relations. These clearly determine political events, in the view of the authors. The second passage, from *The Class Struggles in France*, traces the history of the French revolution of 1848. Here, individuals are eclipsed by classes, and political events are mere manifestations of deeper class conflicts. Yet the result is still history, rather than economics or sociology. Marx, like all historians, is trying to explain why things happened the way they did.

The Communist Manifesto[1]

The History of All Hitherto Existing Society is the History of Class Struggles

Freeman and slave, patrician and plebeian, lord and serf, guild-master and journeyman, in a word, oppressor and oppressed, stood in constant opposition to one another, carried on an uninterrupted, now hidden, now open fight, a fight that each time ended, either in a revolutionary reconstitution of society at large, or in the common ruin of the contending classes.

In the earlier epochs of history, we find almost everywhere a complicated arrangement of society into various orders, a manifold gradation of social rank. In ancient Rome we have patricians, knights, plebeians, slaves; in the Middle Ages, feudal lords, vassals, guild-masters, journeymen, apprentices, serfs; in almost all of these classes, again, subordinate gradations. The modern bourgeois society that has sprouted from the ruins of feudal society has not done away with class antagonisms. It has but established new classes, new conditions of oppression, new forms of struggle in place of the old ones.

Our epoch, the epoch of the bourgeoisie, possesses, however, this distinctive feature: it has simplified the class antagonisms. Society as a whole is more and more splitting up into two great hostile camps, into two great classes directly facing each other: Bourgeoisie and Proletariat.

From the serfs of the Middle Ages sprang the chartered burghers of the earliest towns. From these burgesses the first elements of the bourgeoisie were developed.

The discovery of America, the rounding of the Cape, opened up fresh ground for the rising bourgeoisie. The East Indian and Chinese markets, the colonization of America, trade with the colonies, the increase in the means of exchange and in commodities generally, gave to commerce, to navigation, to industry, an impulse never before known, and thereby, to the revolutionary element in the tottering feudal society, a rapid development.

The feudal system of industry, under which industrial production was monopolized by closed guilds, now no longer sufficed for the growing wants of the new markets. The manufacturing system took its place. The guild-masters were pushed on one side by the manufacturing middle class; division of labor between the different corporate guilds vanished in the face of division of labor in each single workshop.

Meantime the markets kept ever growing, the demand ever rising. Even manufacture no longer sufficed. Thereupon, steam and machinery revolutionized industrial production. The place of manufacture was taken by the giant, Modern Industry, the place of the industrial middle class, by industrial missionaires, the leaders of whole industrial armies, the modern bourgeois.

Modern industry has established the world market, for which the discovery of America paved the way. This market has given an immense development to commerce, to navigation, to communication by land. This development has, in its turn, reacted on the extension of industry; and in proportion as industry, commerce, navigation, railways extended, in the same proportion the bourgeoisie developed, increased its capital, and pushed into the background every class handed down from the Middle Ages.

We see, therefore, how the modern bourgeoisie is itself the product of a long course of development, of a series of revolutions in the modes of production and of exchange.

Each step in the development of the bourgeoisie was accompanied by a corresponding political advance of that class. An oppressed class under the sway of the feudal nobility, an armed and self-governing association in the medieval commune; here independent urban republic (as in Italy and Germany), there taxable "third estate" of the monarchy (as in France), afterward, in the period of manufacture proper, serving either the semifeudal or the absolute monarchy as a counterpoise against the nobility, and, in fact, cornerstone of the great monarchies in general, the bourgeoisie has at last, since the establishment of Modern Industry and of the world market, conquered for itself, in the modern representative State, exclusive political sway. The executive of the modern State is but a committee for managing the common affairs of the whole bourgeoisie.

The Bourgeoisie, Historically, has Played a Most Revolutionary Part

The bourgeoisie, wherever it has got the upper hand, has put an end to all feudal, patriarchal, idyllic relations. It has pitilessly torn asunder the motley feudal ties that bound man to his "natural superiors," and has left remaining no other nexus between man and man than naked self-interest, than callous "cash payment." It has drowned the most heavenly ecstasies of religious fervor, of chivalrous enthusiasm, of philistine sentimentalism, in the icy water of egotistical calculation. It has resolved personal worth into exchange value, and in the place of the numberless indefeasible chartered freedoms, has set up that single, unconscionable freedom—Free Trade. In one word, for exploitation, veiled by religious and political illusions, it has substituted naked, shameless, direct, brutal exploitation.

* * *

The bourgeoisie cannot exist without constantly revolutionizing the instruments of production, and thereby the relations of production, and with them the whole relations of society. Conservation of the old modes of production in unaltered form was, on the contrary, the first condition of existence for all earlier industrial classes. Constant revolutionizing of production, uninterrupted disturbance of all social conditions, everlasting uncertainty and agitation distinguish the bourgeois epoch from all earlier ones. All fixed, fast-frozen relations, with their train of ancient and venerable prejudices and opinions are swept away, all new-formed ones become antiquated before they can ossify. All that is solid melts into air, all that is holy is profaned, and man is at last compelled to face with sober senses his real conditions of life, and his relations with his kind.

The need of a constantly expanding market for its products chases the bourgeoisie over the whole surface of the globe. It must nestle everywhere, settle everywhere, establish connections everywhere.

*   *   *

The bourgeoisie, by the rapid improvement of all instruments of production, by the immensely facilitated means of communication, draws all, even the most barbarian, nations into civilization. The cheap prices of its commodities are the heavy artillery with which it batters down all Chinese walls, with which it forces the barbarians' intensely obstinate hatred of foreigners to capitulate. It compels all nations, on pain of extinction, to adopt the bourgeois mode of production; it compels them to introduce what it calls civilization into their midst, i.e., to become bourgeois themselves. In one word, it creates a world after its own image.

The bourgeoisie has subjected the country to the rule of the towns. It has created enormous cities, has greatly increased the urban population as compared with the rural, and has thus rescued a considerable part of the population from the idiocy of rural life. Just as it has made the country dependent on the towns, so it has made the barbarian and semibarbarian countries dependent on the civilized ones, nations of peasants on nations of bourgeois, the East on the West.

The bourgeoisie keeps more and more doing away with the scattered state of the population, of the means of production, and of property. It has agglomerated population, centralized means of production, and has concentrated property in a few hands. The necessary consequence of this was political centralization. Independent, or but loosely connected, provinces with separate interests, laws, governments and systems of taxation, became lumped together into one nation, with one government, one code of laws, one national class-interest, one frontier and one customs tariff.

*   *   *

The weapons with which the bourgeoisie felled feudalism to the ground are now turned against the bourgeoisie itself.

But not only has the bourgeoisie forged the weapons that bring death to itself; it has also called into existence the men who are to wield those weapons—the modern working class—the proletarians.

In proportion as the bourgeoisie, i.e., capital, is developed, in the same proportion is the proletariat, the modern working class, developed—a class of laborers, who live only so long as they find work, and who find work only so long as their labor increases capital. These laborers, who must sell themselves piecemeal, are a commodity, like every other article of commerce, and are consequently exposed to all the vicissitudes of competition, to all the fluctuations of the market.

Owing to the extensive use of machinery and to division of labor, the work of the proletarians has lost all individual character, and, consequently, all charm for the workman. He becomes an appendage of the machine. . . . In proportion, therefore, as the repulsiveness of the work increases, the wage decreases.

*   *   *

Modern industry has converted the little workshop of the patriarchal master into the great factory of the industrial capitalist. Masses of laborers, crowded into the factory, are organized like soldiers. As privates of the industrial army they are placed under the command of a perfect hierarchy of officers and sergeants. Not only are they slaves of the bourgeois class, and of the bourgeois State; they are daily and hourly enslaved by the machine, by the overlooker, and, above all, by the individual bourgeois manufacturer himself.

* * *

Hitherto, every form of society has been based, as we have already seen, on the antagonism of oppressing and oppressed classes. But in order to oppress a class, certain conditions must be assured to it under which it can, at least, continue its slavish existence. The serf, in the period of serfdom, raised himself to membership in the common, just as the petty bourgeois, under the yoke of feudal absolutism, managed to develop into a bourgeois. The modern laborer, on the contrary, instead of rising with the progress of industry, sinks deeper and deeper below the conditions of existence of his own class. He becomes a pauper, and pauperism develops more rapidly than population and wealth. And here it becomes evident that the bourgeoisie is unfit any longer to be the ruling class in society, and to impose its conditions of existence upon society as an overriding law. It is unfit to rule because it is incompetent to assure an existence to its slave within his slavery, because it cannot help letting him sink into such a state, that it has to feed him, instead of being fed by him. Society can no longer live under this bourgeoisie, in other words, its existence is no longer compatible with society.

The essential condition for the existence, and for the sway of the bourgeois class, is the formation and augmentation of capital; the condition of capital is wage labor. Wage labor rests exclusively on competition between the laborers. The advance of industry, whose involuntary promoter is the bourgeoisie, replaces the isolation of the laborers, due to competition, by their revolutionary combination, due to association. The development of Modern Industry, therefore, cuts from under its feet the the very foundation on which the bourgeoisie produces and appropriates products. What the bourgeoisie, therefore, produces, after all, is its own gravediggers. Its fall and the victory of the proletariat are equally inevitable.

The Class Struggles in France²

After the July Revolution, when the liberal banker Laffitte led his *compère*, the Duke of Orleans, in triumph to the Hôtel de Ville, he let fall the words: "From now on the bankers will rule." Laffitte had betrayed the secret of the revolution.

It was not the French bourgeoisie that ruled under Louis Philippe, but one faction of it: bankers, stock-exchange kings, railway kings, owners of coal and iron mines and forests, a part of the landed proprietors associated with them—the so-called finance aristocracy. It sat on the throne, it dictated laws in the Chambers, it distributed public offices, from cabinet portfolios to tobacco bureau posts.

The industrial bourgeoisie proper formed part of the official opposition, that is, it was represented only as a minority in the Chambers. Its opposition was expressed all the more resolutely, the more unalloyed the autocracy of the finance aristocracy became, and the more it itself imagined that its domination over the working class was ensured after the mutinies of 1832, 1834 and 1839, which had been drowned in blood. Grandin, Rouen manufacturer and the most fanatical instrument of bourgeois reaction in the Constitutent as well as in the Legislative National Assembly, was the most violent opponent of Guizot in the Chamber of Deputies. Léon Faucher, later known for his impotent efforts to climb into prominence as the Guizot of the French counter-revolution, in the last days of Louis Philippe waged a war of the pen for industry against speculation and its train-bearer, the government. Bastiat agitated in the name of Bourdeaux and the whole of wine-producing France against the ruling system.

The petty bourgeoisie of all gradations, and the peasantry also, were completely excluded from political power. Finally, in the official opposition or entirely outside the *pays légal,* there were the ideological representatives and spokesmen of the above classes, their savants, lawyers, doctors, etc., in a word: their so-called men of talent.

Owing to its financial straits, the July monarchy was dependent from the beginning on the big bourgeoisie, and its dependence on the big bourgeoisie was the inexhaustible source of increasing financial straits. It was impossible to subordinate the administration of the state to the interests of national production without balancing the budget, without establishing a balance between state expenditures and state revenues. And how was this balance to be established without limiting state expenditures, that is, without encroaching on interests which were so many props of the ruling system, and without redistributing taxes, that is, without shifting a considerable share of the burden of taxation onto the shoulders of the big bourgeoisie itself?

On the contrary, the faction of the bourgeoisie that ruled and legislated through the Chambers had a direct interest in the indebtedness of the state. The state deficit was really the main object of this speculation and the chief source of its enrichment. At the end of each year a new deficit. After the lapse of four or five years a new loan. And every new loan offered new opportunities to the finance aristocracy for defrauding the state, which was kept artificially on the verge of bankruptcy—it had to negotiate with the bankers under the most unfavourable conditions. Each new loan gave a further opportunity, that of plundering the public which had invested its capital in state bonds by means of stock-exchange manipulations, into the secrets of which the government and the majority in the Chambers were initiated. In general, the instability of state credit and the possession of state secrets gave the bankers and their associates in the Chambers and on the throne the possibility of evoking sudden, extraordinary fluctuations in the quotations of government securities, the result of which was always bound to be the ruin of a mass of smaller capitalists and the fabulously rapid enrichment of the big gamblers. As the state deficit was in the direct interest of the ruling faction of the bourgeoisie, it is clear why the extraordinary state expenditure in the last years of Louis Philippe's reign was far more than double the extraordinary expenditure under Napoleon, indeed reached a yearly sum of nearly 400,000,000 francs, whereas the whole average annual export of France seldom attained a volume amounting to 750,000,000 francs. The enormous sums which, in this way, flowed through the hands of the state facilitated, moreover, swindling contracts for deliveries, bribery, defalcations and all kinds of roguery. The defrauding of the state, practised wholesale in connection with loans, was repeated retail in public works. What occurred in the relations between Chamber and Government became multiplied in the relations between individual departments and individual entrepreneurs.

The ruling class exploited the building of railways in the same way as it exploited state expenditures in general and state loans. The Chambers piled the main burdens on the state, and secured the golden fruits to the speculating finance aristocracy. One recalls the scandals in the Chamber of Deputies, when by chance it leaked out that all the members of the majority, including a number of ministers, had been interested as shareholders in the very railway constructions which as legislators they caused to be carried out afterwards at the cost of the state.

On the other hand, the smallest financial reform was wrecked due to the influence of the bankers. For example, the postal reform. Rothschild protested. Was it permissible for the state to curtail sources of revenue out of which interest was to be paid on its ever-increasing debt?

The July monarchy was nothing but a joint-stock company for the exploitation of France's national wealth, the dividends of which were divided among ministers, Chambers, 240,000 voters and their adherents. Louis Philippe was the director of this company—Robert Macaire on the throne. Trade, industry, agriculture, shipping, the interests of the industrial bourgeoisie, were bound to be continually endangered and prejudiced under this system. Cheap government, *gouvernment à bon marché*, was what it had inscribed in the July days on its banner.

*   *   *

The eruption of the general discontent was finally accelerated and the mood for revolt ripened by two economic world events.

The potato blight and the crop failures of 1845 and 1846 increased the general ferment among the people. The dearth of 1847 called forth bloody conflicts in France as well as on the rest of the Continent. As against the shameless orgies of the finance aristocracy, the struggle of the people for the prime necessities of life! At Buzançais, hunger rioters executed; in Paris, oversatiated *escrocs* snatched from the courts by the royal family!

The second great economic event which hastened the outbreak of the revolution was a general commercial and industrial crisis in England. Already heralded in the autumn of 1845 by the wholesale reverses of the speculators in railway shares, stayed off during 1846 by a number of incidents such as the impending abolition of the corn duties, the crisis finally burst in the autumn of

1847 with the bankruptcy of the London wholesale grocers, on the heels of which followed the insolvencies of the land breaks and the closing of the factories in the English industrial districts. The after-effect of this crisis on the Continent had not yet spent itself when the February Revolution broke out.

The devastation of trade and industry caused by the economic epidemic made the autocracy of the finance aristocracy still more unbearable. Throughout the whole of France the bourgeois opposition agitated at banquets for an electoral reform which should win for it the majority in the Chambers and overthrow the Ministry of the Bourse. In Paris the industrial crisis had, moreover, the particular result of throwing a multitude of manufacturers and big traders, who under the existing circumstances could no longer do any business in the foreign market, onto the home market. They set up large establishments, the competition of which ruined the small *épeciers and boutiquiers en masse*, hence the innumerable bankruptcies among this section of the Paris bourgeoisie, and hence their revolutionary action in February. It is well known how Guizot and the Chambers answered the reform proposals with an unambiguous challenge, how Louis Philippe too late resolved on a ministry led by Barrot, how things went as far as hand-to-hand fighting between the people and the army, how the army was disarmed as a result of the passive conduct of the National Guard, how the July monarchy had to give way to a Provisional Government.

*   *   *

Up to noon of February 25 the republic had not yet been proclaimed; on the other hand, all the ministries had already been shared out among the bourgeois elements of the Provisional Government and among the generals, bankers and lawyers of the National. But the workers were determined this time not to put up with any fraud like that of July 1830. They were ready to take up the fight anew and to get a republic by force of arms. With this message, Raspail betook himself to the Hôtel de Ville. In the name of the Paris proletariat he commanded the Provisional Government to proclaim a republic; if this order of the people were not fulfilled within two hours, he would return at the head of 200,000 men. The bodies of the fallen were scarcely cold, the barricades were not yet cleared away, the workers not yet disarmed, and the only force which could be opposed to them was the National Guard. Under these circumstances the doubts born of considerations of state policy and the juristic scruples of conscience entertained by the Provisional Government suddenly vanished. The time limit of two hours had not yet expired when all the walls of Paris were resplendent with the historic, momentous words:

République française! Liberté, Egalité, Fraternité!

QUESTIONS TO CONSIDER

1. What does Marx say are the forces that move history? How do they compare with the forces that Eusebius (Chapter 15), Sima Guang (22), and Ibn Khaldûn (23) thought moved history?

2. How does Marx portray individuals? Does he think that they have any real importance?
3. In Marx's view, what role do revolutionaries and revolutionary intellectuals (such as Marx himself) play in social transformation?

FOR FURTHER READING

Elster, Jon. *An Introduction to Marx.* Cambridge, UK: Cambridge University Press, 1985.

Gandy, D. Ross. *Marx and History.* Austin, TX: University of Texas Press, 1979.

Marx, Karl. *The Civil War in France.* New York: International Publishers, 1968.

———. *The Eighteenth Brumaire of Louis Bonaparte.* New York: International Publishers, 1963.

McClellan, David, ed. *Karl Marx: Selected Writings.* Oxford: Oxford University Press, 1977.

Rader, Melvin. *Marx's Interpretation of History.* New York: Oxford University Press, 1979.

Rius. *Marx for Beginners.* Trans. Richard Appignanesi. New York: Pantheon, 1976.

NOTES

1. Frederick L. Bender, ed., *Karl Marx: The Essential Writings,* 2nd ed. (Boulder, CO: Westview, 1986), 241–53.
2. Jon Elster, ed., *Karl Marx: A Reader* (Cambridge, MA: Cambridge University Press, 1986), 244–50.

CHAPTER 40

Max Weber

The Spiritual Origins of Capitalism

Max Weber
Courtesy of the German Information Center

M ax Weber was a complex scholar. Modern sociology claims him as a founding father, yet he was trained in jurisprudence and saw himself as an economic historian. An intellectual prodigy, he was a full professor by age 30. Yet four years later he had a nervous breakdown and never returned to full-time teaching. He wrote massively, yet published few books, none of them during the 30 years before his death at age 57. His most famous works were long journal articles or compiled notes that he never put into final form. Many of these have been translated into English. Yet translators uniformly agree that the English versions fail to do justice to Weber's German. And the imprecision of Weber's German is legendary: one translator writes that it is sometimes hard to tell just what Weber is talking about. Yet both his ideas and his scholarship are held in high regard.

Max Weber was born in 1864 in Erfurt, Germany, the son of a wealthy and politically connected family. His father was a legislator from the National Liberal party. Learning and policy debates were both valued in his natal household. Weber showed his intellectual skills early, applying them at first to law and history. He wrote his PhD thesis on the legal history of medieval trading firms; his "habilitation" (the "second doctorate" required of German scholars) was on the agrarian history of Rome. A few years after taking his first professorship, he threw his autocratic father out of the house. When the old man died a few weeks later, Weber suffered what H. Stuart Hughes describes as a classic Oedipal breakdown. He could not work intellectually for five years.

Although Weber endured periodic relapses for the rest of his life, he began writing again in 1903. His most famous work, *The Protestant Ethic and the Spirit of Capitalism,* appeared as two long journal articles in 1904–5. In it, he traced the ethical origins of Western capitalism to Calvinist theology. His thesis is complex. In brief, he said that ascetic Calvinism got people used to working hard in a worldly profession. It taught them to order their lives rationally in the service of God. This ethic has an "elective affinity" for capitalism, which requires people to work hard and order their businesses rationally in the service of profit. Calvinists' ethics gave them a competitive economic advantage that others had to match to survive. The result, said Weber, was an "iron cage" of hard work and self-denial that traps all who are heirs to Calvinist values.

Until his premature death in 1920, Weber wrote on many other topics: world religions, politics, types of rulership, Western rationalism, and so on. His historical work probed the economies of ancient Rome, medieval Europe, and nineteenth-century Germany. In all these eras, and places, he tried to trace the connection between economic changes (especially in land tenure and the organization of labor), social changes, and changes in politics. He also charted the results of these structural changes for everyday life among different social groups.

Seen as a whole, two projects ran through all Weber's work. On the one hand, he looked at the role of status groups, social classes, and political forces in various eras. On the other, he traced the impact of religious ethics, norms and values, and ideas of lawful authority. Karl Marx had argued that both sprang from the economy. Weber tried to show that economic, political, and ideological factors were each important. He sought to explain which social forces make things happen in various eras, how and in what degrees, and in what combinations. Yet he refused to reduce the historical facts to one underlying structure. Thus Weber is the intellectual progenitor of much of the social-scientific history that dominated American historical writing in the mid-twentieth century.

The passages that follow come from Weber's comparative study of the economic ethics of the major world religions—a project of which *The Protestant Ethic* was the first part. He was, in effect, seeking the origins of Western culture, which he saw to be ruled by rationality. Weber argued that though Western rationalism in general—and rational capitalism in particular—had many causes, most of those causes were also found in other times and places. Only in the West had religion added to the needed material resources an ethic that encouraged self-denying work in a career. This ethic was not capitalist by intent. Yet it became capitalist in practice, as it lost its religious roots and grew into a secular world view.

The passages that follow show Weber working with this theme in excerpts from *The Protestant Ethic*. In it, Weber tries to identify the cultural "spirit of capitalism": that ethical demand to organize one's life rationally of which he finds Ben Franklin such a good example. Historians of European religion would quarrel with Weber's designation of Franklin as a Calvinist and his rough equation of Calvinism and Lutheranism, but they would not dispute his analysis of Franklin's values and their efficacy for capitalism. The second passage deals with Martin Luther's concept of the "calling," another key ingredient, according to Weber's understanding, in the relationship between Protestant values and the rise of capitalism. In these selections, Weber works as a historian of culture. His approach is comparative yet specific. Though sociologists have been the main consumers of his work so far, that work is ripe for reappropriation by historians, among whom he would be most comfortable.

The Protestant Ethic and the Spirit of Capitalism[1]

The Spirit of Capitalism

In the title of this study is used the somewhat pretentious phrase, the *spirit of capitalism*. What is to be understood by it? The attempt to give anything like a definition of it brings out certain difficulties which are in the very nature of this type of investigation.

If any object can be found to which this term can be applied with any understandable meaning, it can only be an historical individual, i.e. a complex of elements associated in historical reality which we unite into a conceptual whole from the standpoint of their cultural significance.

Such an historical concept, however, since it refers in its content to a phenomenon significant for its unique individuality, cannot be defined according to the formula *genus proximum, differentia specifica*, but it must be gradually put together out of the individual parts which are taken from historical reality to make it up. Thus the final and definitive concept cannot stand at the beginning of the investigation, but must come at the end. We must, in other words, work out in the course of the discussion, as its most important result, the best conceptual formulation of what we here understand by the spirit of capitalism, that is the best from the point of view which interests us here. This point of view (the one of which we shall speak later) is, further, by no means the only possible one from which the historical phenomena we are investigating can be analysed. Other standpoints would, for this as for every historical phenomenon, yield other characteristics as the essential ones. The result is that it is by no means necessary to understand by the spirit of capitalism only what it will come to mean to us for the purposes of our analysis. This is a necessary result of the nature of historical concepts which attempt for their methodological purposes not to grasp historical reality in abstract general formula, but in concrete genetic sets of relations which are inevitably of a specifically unique and individual character.

Thus, if we try to determine the object, the analysis and historical explanation of which we are attempting, it cannot be in the form of a conceptual definition, but at least in the beginning only a provisional description of what is here meant by the spirit of capitalism. Such a description is, however, indispensable in order clearly to understand the object of the investigation. For this purpose we turn to a document of that spirit which contains what we are looking for in almost classical purity, and at the same time has the advantage of being free from all direct relationship to religion, being thus, for our purposes, free of preconceptions.

> "Remember, that *time* is money. He that can earn ten shillings a day by his labour, and goes abroad, or sits idle, one half of that day, though he spends but sixpence during his diversion or idleness, ought not to reckon *that* the only expense; he has really spent, or rather thrown away, five shillings besides.

"Remember, that *credit* is money. If a man lets his money lie in my hands after it is due, he gives me the interest, or so much as I can make of it during that time. This amounts to a considerable sum where a man has good and large credit, and makes good use of it.

"Remember, that money is of the prolific, generating nature. Money can beget money, and its offspring can beget more, and so on. Five shillings turned is six, turned again it is seven and threepence, and so on, till it becomes a hundred pounds. The more there is of it, the more it produces every turning, so that the profits rise quicker and quicker. He that kills a breeding-sow, destroys all her offspring to the thousandth generation. He that murders a crown, destroys all that it might have produced, even scores of pounds."

*   *   *

"For six pounds a year you may have the use of one hundred pounds, provided you are a man of known prudence and honesty.

"He that spends a groat a day idly, spends idly above six pounds a year, which is the price for the use of one hundred pounds.

"He that wastes idly a groat's worth of his time per day, one day with another, wastes the privilege of using one hundred pound each day.

"He that idly loses five shillings' worth of time, loses five shillings, and might as prudently throw five shillings into the sea.

"He that loses five shillings, not only that sum, but all the advantage that might be made by turning it in dealing, which by the time that a young man becomes old, will amount to a considerable sum of money."

It is Benjamin Franklin who preaches to us in these sentences, the same which Franklin Kurnberger satirizes in his clever and malicious *Picture of American Culture* as the supposed confession of faith of the Yankee. That it is the spirit of capitalism which here speaks in characteristic fashion, no one will doubt, however little we may wish to claim that everything which could be understood as pertaining to that spirit is contained in it. Let us pause a moment to consider this passage, the philosophy of which Kurnberger sums up in the words, "They make tallow out of cattle and money out of men." The peculiarity of this philosophy of avarice appears to be the ideal of the honest man of recognized credit, and above all the idea of a duty of the individual toward the increase of his capital, which is assumed as an end in itself. Truly what is here preached is not simply a means of making one's way in the world, but a peculiar ethic. The infraction of its rules is treated not as foolishness but as forgetfulness of duty. That is not mere business astuteness, that sort of thing is common enough, it is an ethos. This is the quality which interests us.

When Jacob Fugger, in speaking to a business associate who had retired and who wanted to persuade him to do the same, since he had made enough money and should let others have a chance, rejected that as pusillanimity and answered that "he [Fugger] thought otherwise, he wanted to make money as long as he could," the spirit of his statement is evidently quite different from that of Franklin. What in the former case was an expression of commercial daring and a personal inclination morally neutral, in the latter takes on the character of an ethically coloured maxim for the conduct of life. The concept spirit of capitalism is here used in this specific sense, it is the spirit of modern capitalism. For that we are here dealing only with Western European and

American capitalism is obvious from the way in which the problem was stated. Capitalism existed in China, India, Babylon, in the classic world, and in the Middle Ages. But in all these cases, as we shall see, this particular ethos was lacking.

Now, all Franklin's moral attitudes are coloured with utilitarianism. Honesty is useful, because it assures credit; so are punctuality, industry, frugality, and that is the reason they are virtues. A logical deduction from this would be that where, for instance, the appearance of honesty serves the same purpose, that would suffice, and an unnecessary surplus of this virtue would evidently appear to Franklin's eyes as unproductive waste. As a matter of fact, the story in his autobiography of his conversion to those virtues, or the discussion of the value of a strict maintenance of the appearance of modesty, the assiduous belittlement of one's own deserts in order to gain general recognition later, confirms this impression. According to Franklin, those virtues, like all others, are only in so far virtues as they are actually useful to the individual, and the surrogate of mere appearance is always sufficient when it accomplishes the end in view. It is a conclusion which is inevitable for strict utilitarianism. The impression of many Germans that the virtues professed by Americanism are pure hypocrisy seems to have been confirmed by this striking case. But in fact the matter is not so simple. Benjamin Franklin's own character, as it appears in the really unusual candidness of his autobiography, belies that suspicion. The circumstance that he ascribes his recognition of the utility of virtue to a divine revelation which was intended to lead him in the path of righteousness, shows that something more than mere garnishing for purely egocentric motives is involved.

In fact, the *summum bonum* of this ethic, the earning of more and more money, combined with the strict avoidance of all spontaneous enjoyment of life, is above all completely devoid of any eudamonistic, not to say hedonistic, admixture. It is thought of so purely as an end in itself, that from the point of view of the happiness of, or utility to, the single individual, it appears entirely transcendental and absolutely irrational. Man is dominated by the making of money, by acquisition as the ultimate purpose of his life. Economic acquisition is no longer subordinated to man as the means for the satisfaction of his material needs. This reversal of what we should call the natural relationship, so irrational from a naive point of view, is evidently as definitely a leading principle of capitalistic influence. At the same time it expresses a type of feeling which is closely connected with certain religious ideas. If we thus ask, why should "money be made out of men," Benjamin Franklin himself, although he was a colourless deist, answers in his autobiography with a quotation from the Bible, which his strict Calvinistic father drummed into him again and again in his youth: "Seest thou a man diligent in his business? He shall stand before kings" (Prov. xxii. 29). The earning of money within the modern economic order is, so long as it is done legally, the result and the expression of virtue and proficiency in a calling; and this virtue and proficiency are, as it is now not difficult to see, the real Alpha and Omega of Franklin's ethic, as expressed in the passages we have quoted, as well as in all his works without exception.

And in truth this peculiar idea, so familiar to us to-day, but in reality so little a matter of course, of one's duty in a calling, is what is most characteristic of the social ethic of capitalistic culture, and is in a sense the fundamental basis of it. It is an obligation which the individual is supposed to feel and does feel towards the content of his professional activity, no matter in what it consists, in particular no matter whether it appears on the surface as a utilization of his personal powers, or only of his material possessions (as capital).

Of course, this conception has not appeared only under capitalistic conditions. On the contrary, we shall later trace its origins back to a time previous to the advent of capitalism. Still less, naturally, do we maintain that a conscious acceptance of these ethical maxims on the part of individuals, entrepreneurs or labourers, in modern capitalistic enterprises, is a condition of the further existence of present-day capitalism. The capitalistic economy of the present day is an immense cosmos into which the individual is born, and which presents itself to him, at least as an individual, as an unalterable order of things in which he must live. It forces the individual, in so far as he is involved in the system of market relationships, to conform to capitalistic rules of action. The manufacturer who in the long run acts counter to these norms, will just as inevitably be eliminated from the economic scene as the worker who cannot or will not adapt himself to them will be thrown into the streets without a job.

Thus the capitalism of to-day, which has come to dominate economic life, educates and selects the economic subjects which it needs through a process of economic survival of the fittest. But here one can easily see the limits of the concept of selection as a means of historical explanation. In order that a manner of life so well adapted to the peculiarities of capitalism could be selected at all, i.e., should come to dominate others, it had to originate somewhere, and not in isolated individuals alone, but as a way of life common to whole groups of men. This origin is what really needs explanation. Concerning the doctrine of the more naïve historical materialism, that such ideas originate as a reflection or superstructure of economic situations, we shall speak more in detail below. At this point it will suffice for our purpose to call attention to the fact that without doubt, in the country of Benjamin Franklin's birth (Massachusetts), the spirit of capitalism (in the sense we have attached to it) was present before the capitalistic order. There were complaints of a peculiarly calculating sort of profit-seeking in New England, as distinguished from other parts of America, as early as 1632. It is further undoubted that capitalism remained far less developed in some of the neighboring colonies, the later Southern States of the United States of America, in spite of the fact that these latter were founded by large capitalists for business motives, while the New England colonies were founded by preachers and seminary graduates with the help of small bourgeois, craftsmen and yeomen, for religious reasons. In this case the causal relation is certainly the reverse of that suggested by the materialist standpoint.

*   *   *

Luther's Conception of the Calling

Now it is unmistakable that even in the German word *Beruf,* and perhaps still more clearly in the English *calling,* a religious conception, that of a task set by God, is at least suggested. The more emphasis is put upon the word in a concrete case, the more evident is the connotation. And if we trace the history of the word through the civilized languages, it appears that neither the predominantly Catholic peoples nor those of classical antiquity have possessed any expression of similar connotation for what we know as a calling (in the sense of a life-task, a definite field in which to work), while one has existed for all predominantly Protestant peoples. It may be further shown that this is not due to any ethical peculiarity of the languages concerned. It is not, for instance, the product of a Germanic spirit, but in its modern meaning the word comes from the Bible translations, through the spirit of the translator, not that of the original. In Luther's translation of the Bible it appears to have first been used at a point in Jesus Sirach (xi. 20 and 21) precisely in our modern sense. After that it speedily took on its present meaning in the everyday speech of all Protestant peoples, while earlier not even a suggestion of such a meaning could be found in the secular literature of any of them, and even, in religious writings, so far as I can ascertain, it is only found in one of the German mystics whose influence on Luther is well known.

Like the meaning of the word, the idea is new, a product of the Reformation. This may be assumed as generally known. It is true that certain suggestions of the positive valuation of routine activity in the world, which is contained in this conception of the calling, had already existed in the Middle Ages, and even in late Hellenistic antiquity. We shall speak of that later. But at least one thing was unquestionably new: the valuation of the fulfillment of duty in worldly affairs as the highest form which the moral activity of the individual could assume. This it was which inevitably gave every-day worldly activity a religious significance, and which first created the conception of a calling in this sense. The conception of the calling thus brings out that central dogma of all Protestant denominations which the Catholic division of ethical precepts into *precepta* and *consilia* discards. The only way of living acceptably to God was not to surpass worldly morality in monastic asceticism, but solely through the fulfillment of the obligations imposed upon the individual by his position in the world. That was his calling.

Luther developed the conception in the course of the first decade of his activity as a reformer. At first, quite in harmony with the prevailing tradition of the Middle Ages, as represented, for example, by Thomas Aquinas, he thought of activity in the world as a thing of the flesh, even though willed by God. It is the indispensable natural condition of a life of faith, but in itself, like eating and drinking, morally neutral. But with the development of the conception of *sola fide* in all its consequences, and its logical result, the increasingly sharp emphasis against the Catholic *consilia evangelica* of the monks as dictates of the devil, the calling grew in importance. The monastic life is not only quite devoid of value as a means of justification before God, but he also looks upon its renunciation of the duties of this world as the product of selfishness, withdrawing from temporal obligations. In contrast, labour in a calling appears to him as the outward expression of brotherly love. This he proves by the observation that the division of labour forces every individual to work for others, but his view-point is highly naive, forming an almost grotesque contrast to Adam Smith's well-known statements on the same subject. However, this justification, which is evidently essentially scholastic, soon disappears again, and there remains, more and more strongly emphasized, the statement that the fulfillment of the worldly duties is under all circumstances the only way to live acceptably to God. It and it alone is the will of God, and hence every legitimate calling has exactly the same worth in the sight of God.

That this moral justification of worldly activity was one of the most important results of the Reformation, especially of Luther's part in it, is beyond doubt, and may even be considered a platitude. This attitude is worlds removed from the deep hatred of Pascal, in his contemplative moods, for all worldly activity, which he was deeply convinced could only be understood in terms of vanity of low cunning. And it differs even more from the liberal utilitarian compromise with the world at which the Jesuits arrived. But just what the practical significance of this achievement of Protestantism was in detail is dimly felt rather than clearly perceived.

In the first place it is hardly necessary to point out that Luther cannot be claimed for the spirit of capitalism in the sense in which we have used that term above, or for that matter in any sense whatever. The religious circles which to-day most enthusiastically celebrate that great achievement of the Reformation are by no means friendly to capitalism in any sense. And Luther himself would, without doubt, have sharply repudiated any connection with a point of view like that of Franklin. Of course, one cannot consider his complaints against the great merchants of his time, such as the Fuggers, as evidence in this case. For the struggle against the privileged position, legal or actual, of single great trading companies in the sixteenth and seventeenth centuries may best be compared with the modern campaign against the trusts, and can no more justly be considered in itself an expression of a traditionalistic point of view. Against these people, against the Lombards, the monopolists, speculators, and bankers patronized by the Anglican Church and the kings and parliaments of England and France, both the Puritans and the Huguenots carried on a bitter struggle. Cromwell, after the battle of Dunbar (September 1650), wrote to the Long Parliament: "Be pleased to reform the abuses of all professions: and if there be any one that makes many poor to make a few rich, that suits not a Commonwealth." But, nevertheless, we will find Cromwell following a quite specifically capitalist line of thought. On the other hand, Luther's numerous statements against usury or interest in any form reveal a conception of the nature of capitalistic acquisition which, compared with that of late Scholasticism, is from a capitalistic view-point, definitely backward. Especially, of course, the doctrine of the sterility of money which Anthony of Florence had already refuted.

But it is unnecessary to go into detail. For, above all, the consequences of the conception of the calling in the religious sense for worldly conduct were susceptible to quite different interpretations. The effect of the Reformation as such was only that, as compared with the Catholic attitude, the moral emphasis on and the religious sanction of, organized worldly labour in a calling was mightily increased. The way in which the concept of the calling, which expressed this change, should develop further depended upon the religious evolution which now took place in the different Protestant Churches.

QUESTIONS TO CONSIDER

1. According to Weber, what role do ideas play in history? How do they do so?
2. Today we describe capitalism as the pursuit of profit. Is this what Weber meant by "the spirit of capitalism"? If not, what did he mean by the term?
3. Weber wrote that "Luther cannot be claimed for the spirit of capitalism." How, then, does he trace that spirit to Luther's idea of a "calling"?

FOR FURTHER READING

Bendix, Reinhard. *Max Weber, An Intellectual Portrait.* 2nd ed. Berkeley, CA: University of California Press, 1979.

Hughes, H. Stuart. *Consciousness and Society: The Reorientation of European Social Thought, 1890–1930.* New York: Knopf, 1958.

Macrae, Donald G. *Weber.* London: Fontana/Collins, 1974.

Schaff, Lawrence A. *Fleeing the Iron Cage: Culture, Politics, and Modernity in the Thought of Max Weber.* Berkeley, CA: University of California Press, 1989.

Weber, Max. *The Agrarian Sociology of Ancient Civilizations.* Trans. R. I. Frank. London: NLB, 1976.

_____ . *Capitalism, Bureaucracy, and Religion: A Selection of Texts.* Ed. Stanislav Andreski. London: George Allen & Unwin, 1983.

_____ . *From Max Weber: Essays in Sociology.* Ed. Hans Gerth and C. Wright Mills. New York: Oxford University Press, 1946.

NOTES

1. Max Weber, *The Protestant Ethic and the Spirit of Capitalism,* trans. Talcott Parsons (New York: Scribner's, 1958), 47–56, 79–83. Footnotes have been omitted.

CHAPTER 41

Frederick Jackson Turner

The American West

Frederick Jackson Turner
State Historical Society of Wisconsin WHi(x3)48588

N o anthology of great historians written for American students would be complete without Frederick Jackson Turner. No similar anthology for non-American students would include him. Despite this lack of international recognition at the highest level, for several generations of American history students, Turner was held up as *the* historian. This was not because he pioneered a new approach to historical writing. Nor was it because he wrote a large number of influential books; he wrote only a few books and never went far beyond the ideas expressed in the essay reproduced here. Turner was viewed as important because he had one simple, powerful idea that affirmed the temper of his people and his time.

Turner was in his own mind a product of the American West, born at Portage, Wisconsin, in 1861 when the upper Midwest still remembered frontier days. He was educated at the fledgling University of Wisconsin and at Johns Hopkins and then went back to Wisconsin in 1889 to teach. Four years later he presented his essay "The Significance of the Frontier in American History" to the American Historical Association. Turner stayed at Wisconsin until 1910, when he moved to Harvard to teach frontier history. On his retirement in 1924 he moved to the Huntington Library in California, where he remained until his death in 1932.

Turner's idea was that the frontier explains American history. Like most other European Americans, Turner conceived of North America as an empty continent before Europeans arrived. There was a perceptible area of "settlement" moving ever westward, a line where civilization met savagery. Out of the rough and tumble of life on the frontier, thought Turner, came most of America's distinctive traits—most notably democratic political habits. America was unlike any other nation on earth, and the reason was the frontier.

Turner was not the first major American historian to write rhapsodically about the West. Francis Parkman, a nineteenth-century Bostonian, wrote many books about westward movements in American history, and especially about the contest between France and England for what is now the U.S. Midwest. Dime novelists in the nineteenth century, movie producers in the twentieth, and pulp novelists like Louis L'Amour have made a steady living off romantic tales of pioneers, gunslingers, Indian fighters, and outlaws. By comparison with these, Turner's was a gentler, less violent, more pastoral frontier. He wrote of farmers and ranchers, not cowboys and Indians. Yet he wrote affirmingly of America's uniqueness and its essential goodness, of Europeans bringing civilization to Eden and in the process finding themselves. That was the heart of his message: that America was an exception among nations, more marvelous than any other, made so by the frontier.

Turner spawned generations of disciples who elaborated his fundamental ideas, and who wrote some of the liveliest historical prose in the English language; they included Herbert Eugene Bolton, Walter Prescott Webb, Bernard DeVoto, and Ray Allen Billington. Billington described the appeal of Turner's ideas to Americans at the turn of the twentieth century:

> Turner's thesis appealed to a people suddenly aware that their efforts to build
> a powerful nation had not been in vain; it was equally alluring to all who

believed that their revered democratic institutions had wrought this miracle. Turner's America was a land in which all, humble and proud alike, had contributed to the national grandeur, where the individual had proven his worth by the conquest of nature, and where continuing progress was ordained by the excellence of time-proven institutions no less than by the perfection of the American character. (Foreword to Turner, *Frontier in American History*, x)

After midcentury, other historians of the West, such as Henry Nash Smith, Richard Slotkin, and Francis Paul Prucha, began to take off in new directions. Smith and Slotkin analyzed the West as a system of symbols that gave clues to the evolving American character. Prucha and others noticed as Turner had not that the American continent was occupied before Europeans went there, and they began to take seriously the relationships between European Americans and Native Americans. Many others, less concerned with the West, simply thought Turner ignored most of the really important things that were happening in American history—industry, immigration, the rise of cities, and so forth.

These historians were followed in the century's last two decades by historians who proclaimed a "New Western History." One of them, Patricia Limerick, wrote as follows:

[T]he New Western History offers a more balanced view of the western past. It includes failure as well as success; defeat as well as victory; sympathy, grace, villainy, and despair as well as danger, courage, and heroism; women as well as men; varied ethnic groups and their differing perspectives as well as white Anglo-Saxon Protestants; an environment that is limiting, interactive, and sometimes ruined as well as mastered and made to bloom; a parochial economy alternately fueled and abandoned by an interlocking national and world order; and, finally, a regional identity as well as a frontier ethic. Frederick Jackson Turner, father of the frontier thesis, comes in for hard criticism for having bequeathed what many historians regard as an interpretive straightjacket. (*Trails*, xi)

Yet, even as these New West historians proclaimed their independence from Turner and their embrace of the historical passions of their generation (those passions are detailed in the last section of this book), they found themselves Turner's captives at every turn: they mentioned Turner on 81 out of the 214 pages in the book just quoted. And at this writing, there are far more historians writing about the American West in the romantic mode of Turner, Parkman, and L'Amour than in the more analytical mode of the New West historians.

The Significance of the Frontier in American History[1]

In a recent bulletin of the Superintendent of the Census for 1890 appear these significant words: "Up to and including 1880 the country had a frontier of settlement, but at present the unsettled area has been so broken into by isolated bodies of settlement that there can hardly be said to be a frontier line. In the discussion of its extent, its westward movement, etc., it can not, therefore, any longer have a place in the census reports." This brief official statement marks the closing of a great historical movement. Up to our own day American history has been in large degree the history of the colonization of the Great West. The existence of an area of free land, its continuous recession, and the advance of American settlement westward, explain American development.

Behind institutions, behind constitutional forms and modifications, lie the vital forces that call these organs into life and shape them to meet changing conditions. The peculiarity of American institutions is, the fact that they have been compelled to adapt themselves to the changes of an expanding people—to the changes involved in crossing a continent, in winning a wilderness, and in developing at each area of this progress out of the primitive economic and political conditions of the frontier into the complexity of city life. Said Calhoun in 1817, "We are great, and rapidly—I was about to say fearfully—growing!" So saying, he touched the distinguishing feature of American life. All peoples show development; the germ theory of politics has been sufficiently emphasized. In the case of most nations, however, the development has occurred in a limited area; and if the nation has expanded, it has met other growing peoples whom it has conquered. But in the case of the United States we have a different phenomenon. Limiting our attention to the Atlantic coast, we have the familiar phenomenon of the evolution of institutions in a limited area, such as the rise of representative government; the differentiation of simple colonial governments into complex organs; the progress from primitive industrial society, without division of labor, up to manufacturing civilization. But we have in addition to this a recurrence of the process of evolution in each western area reached in the process of expansion. Thus American development has exhibited not merely advance along a single line, but a return to primitive conditions on a continually advancing frontier line, and a new development for that area. American social development has been continually beginning over again on the frontier. This perennial rebirth, this fluidity of American life, this expansion westward with its new opportunities, its continuous touch with the simplicity of primitive society, furnish the forces dominating American character. The true point of view in the history of this nation is not the Atlantic coast, it is the great West. Even the slavery struggle, which is made so exclusive an object of attention by writers like Prof. von Holst, occupies its important place in American history because of its relation to westward expansion.

In this advance, the frontier is the outer edge of the wave—the meeting point between savagery and civilization. Much has been written about the frontier from the point of view of border warfare and the chase, but as a field for the serious study of the economist and the historian it has been neglected.

The American frontier is sharply distinguished from the European frontier—a fortified boundary line running through dense populations. The most significant thing about the American frontier is, that it lies at the hither edge of free land. In the census reports it is treated as the margin of that settlement which has a density of two or more to the square mile. The term is an elastic one, and for our purposes does not need sharp definition. We shall consider the whole frontier belt, including the Indian country and the outer margin of the "settled area" of the census reports. This paper will make no attempt to treat the subject exhaustively; its aim is simply to call attention to the frontier as a fertile field for investigation, and to suggest some of the problems which arise in connection with it.

In the settlement of America we have to observe how European life entered the continent, and how America modified and developed that life and reacted on Europe. Our early history is the study of European germs developing in an American environment. Too exclusive attention has been paid by institutional students to the Germanic origins, too little to the American factors. The frontier is the line of most rapid and effective Americanization. The wilderness masters the colonist. It finds him a European in dress, industries, tools, modes of travel, and thought. It takes him from the railroad car and puts him in the birch canoe. It strips off the garments of civilization and arrays him in the hunting shirt and the moccasin. It puts him in the log cabin of the Cherokee and Iroquois and runs an Indian palisade around him. Before long he has gone to planting Indian corn and plowing with a sharp stick; he shouts the war cry and takes the scalp in orthodox Indian fashion. In short, at the frontier the environment is at first too strong for the man. He must accept the conditions which it furnishes, or perish, and so he fits himself into the Indian clearings and follows the Indian trails. Little by little he transforms the wilderness, but the outcome is not the old Europe, not simply the development of Germanic germs, any more than the first phenomenon was a case of reversion to the Germanic mark. The fact is, that here is a new product that is American. At first, the frontier was the Atlantic coast. It was the frontier of Europe in a very real sense. Moving westward, the frontier became more and more American. As successive terminal moraines result from successive glaciations, so each frontier leaves its traces behind it, and when it becomes a settled area the region still partakes of the frontier characteristics. Thus the advance of the frontier has meant a steady movement away from the influence of Europe, a steady growth of independence on American lines. And to study this advance, the men who grew up under these conditions, and the political, economic, and social results of it, is to study the really American part of our history.

Stages of Frontier Advance

In the course of the seventeenth century the frontier was advanced up the Atlantic river courses, just beyond the "fall line," and the tidewater region became the settled area. In the first half of the eighteenth century another advance occurred. Traders followed the Delaware and Shawnese Indians to the Ohio as early as the end of the first quarter of the century. Gov. Spotswood, of Virginia, made an expedition in 1714 across the Blue Ridge. The end of the first quarter of the century saw the advance of the Scotch-Irish and the Palatine Germans up the Shanandoah Valley into the western part of Virginia, and along the Piedmont region of the Carolinas. The Germans in New York pushed the frontier of settlement up the Mohawk to German Flats. In Pennsylvania the town of Bedford indicates the line of settlement. Settlements had begun on New River, a branch of the Kanawha, and on the sources of the Yadkin and French Broad. The King attempted to arrest the advance by his proclamation of 1763, forbidding settlements beyond the sources of the rivers flowing into the Atlantic; but in vain. In the period of the Revolution the frontier crossed the Alleghenies into Kentucky and Tennessee, and the upper waters of the Ohio were settled. When the first census was taken in 1790, the continuous settled area was bounded by a line which ran near the coast of Maine, and included New England except a portion of Vermont and New Hampshire, New York along the Hudson and up the Mohawk about Schenectady, eastern and southern Pennsylvania, Virginia well across the Shenandoah Valley, and the Carolinas and eastern Georgia. Beyond this region of continuous settlement were the small settled areas of Kentucky and Tennessee, and the Ohio, with the mountains intervening between them and the Atlantic area, thus giving a new and important character to the frontier. The isolation of the region increased its peculiarly American tendencies, and the need of transportation facilities to connect it with the East called out important schemes of internal improvement, which will be noted farther on. The "West," as a self-conscious section, began to evolve.

From decade to decade distinct advances of the frontier occurred. By the census of 1820 the settled area included Ohio, southern Indiana and Illinois, southeastern Missouri, and about one-half of Louisiana. This settled area had surrounded Indian areas, and the management of these tribes became an object of political concern. The frontier region of the time lay along the Great Lakes, where Astor's American Fur Company operated in the Indian trade, and beyond the Mississippi, where Indian traders extended their activity even to the Rocky Mountains; Florida also furnished frontier conditions. The Mississippi River region was the scene of typical frontier settlements.

The rising steam navigation on western waters, the opening of the Erie Canal, and the westward extension of cotton culture added five frontier states to the Union in this period. Grund, writing in 1836, declares: "It appears then that the universal disposition of Americans to emigrate to the western wilderness, in order to enlarge their dominion over inanimate nature, is the actual result of an expansive power which is inherent in them, and which by continually agitating all classes of society is constantly throwing a large portion of the whole population on the extreme confines of the State, in order to gain space for its development. Hardly is a new State or Territory formed before the same principle manifests itself again and gives rise to a further emigration; and so is it destined to go on until a physical barrier must finally obstruct its progress."

In the middle of this century the line indicated by the present eastern boundary of Indian Territory, Nebraska, and Kansas marked the frontier of the Indian country. Minnesota and Wisconsin still exhibited frontier conditions, but the distinctive frontier of the period is found in California, where the gold discoveries had sent a sudden tide of adventurous miners, and in Oregon, and the settlements in Utah. As the frontier has leaped over the Alleghenies, so now it skipped the Great Plains and the Rocky Mountains; and in the same way that the advance of the frontiersmen beyond the Alleghenies had caused the rise of important questions of transportation and internal improvement, so now the settlers beyond the Rocky Mountains needed means of communication with the East, and in the furnishing of these arose the settlement of the Great Plains and the development of still another kind of frontier life. Railroads, fostered by land grants, sent an increasing tide of immigrants into the far West. The United States Army fought a series of Indian wars in Minnesota, Dakota, and the Indian Territory.

By 1880 the settled area had been pushed into northern Michigan, Wisconsin, and Minnesota, along Dakota rivers, and in the Black Hills region, and was ascending the rivers of Kansas and Nebraska. The development of mines in Colorado had drawn isolated frontier settlements into that region, and Montana and Idaho were receiving settlers. The frontier was found in these mining camps and the ranches of the Great Plains. The superintendent of the census for 1890 reports, as previously stated, that the settlements of the West lie so scattered over the region that there can no longer be said to be a frontier line.

In these successive frontiers we find natural boundary lines which have served to mark and to affect the characteristics of the frontiers' names: The "fall line"; the Allegheny Mountains; the Mississippi; the Missouri, where its direction approximates north and south; the line of the arid lands, approximately the ninety-ninth meridian; and the Rocky Mountains. The fall line marked the frontier of the seventeenth century; the Alleghenies that of the eighteenth; the Mississippi that of the first quarter of the nineteenth; and the Missouri that of the middle of this century (omitting the California Movement); and the belt of the Rocky Mountains and the arid tract, the present frontier. Each was won by a series of Indian wars.

The Frontier Furnishes a Field for Comparative Study of Social Development

At the Atlantic frontier one can study the germs of processes repeated at each successive frontier. We have the complex European life sharply precipitated by the wilderness into the simplicity of primitive conditions. The first frontier had to meet its Indian question, its question of the disposition of the public domain, of the means of intercourse with other settlements, of the extension of political organization, of religious and educational activity. And the settlement of these and similar questions for one frontier served as a guide for the next. The American student needs not to go to the "prim little townships of Sleswick" for illustrations of the law of continuity and development. For example, he may study the origin of our land policies in the colonial land policy; he may see how the system grew by adapting the statutes to the customs of the successive frontiers. He may see how the mining experience in the lead regions of Wisconsin, Illinois, and Iowa was applied to the mining laws of the Rockies, and how our Indian policy has been a series of experimentations on successive frontiers. Each tier of new States has found in the older ones material for its constitutions. Each frontier has made similar contributions to American character, as will be discussed farther on.

But with all these similarities there are essential differences, due to the place element and the time element. It is evident that the farming frontier of the Mississippi Valley presents different conditions from the mining frontier of the Rocky Mountains. The frontier reached by the Pacific Railroad, surveyed into rectangles, guarded by the United States Army, and recruited by the daily immigrant ship, moves forward at a swifter pace and in a different way than the frontier reached by the birch canoe or the pack horse. The geologist traces patiently the shores of ancient seas, maps their areas, and compares the older and the newer. It would be a work worth the historian's labors to mark these various frontiers and in detail compare one with another. Not only would there result a more adequate conception of American development and characteristics, but invaluable additions would be made to the history of society.

Loria, the Italian economist, has urged the study of colonial life as an aid in understanding the stages of European development, affirming that colonial settlement is for economic science what the mountain is for geology, bringing to light primitive stratifications. "America," he says, "Has the key to the historical enigma which Europe has sought for centuries in vain, and the land which has no history reveals luminously the course of universal history." There is much truth in this. The United States lies like a huge page in the history of society. Line by line as we read this continental page from west to east we find the record of social evolution. It begins with the Indian and the hunter; it goes on to tell of the disintegration of savagery by the entrance of the trader, the pathfinder of civilization; we read the annals of the pastoral stage in ranch life; the exploitation of the soil by the raising of unrotated crops of corn and wheat in sparsely settled farming communities; the intensive culture of the denser farm settlement; and finally the manufacturing organization with city and factory system. This page is familiar to the student of census statistics, but how little of it has been used by our historians. Particularly in eastern States this page is a palimpsest. What is now a manufacturing State was in an earlier decade an area of intensive farming. Earlier yet it had been a wheat area, and still earlier the "range" had attracted the cattle-herder. Thus Wisconsin, now developing manufacture, is a State with varied agricultural interests. But earlier it was given over to almost exclusive grain-raising, like North Dakota at the present time.

Each of these areas has had an influence in our economic and political history; the evolution of each into a higher stage has worked political trans-formations. But what constitutional historian has made any adequate attempt to interpret political facts by the light of these social areas and changes?

The Atlantic frontier was compounded of fisherman, fur-trader, miner, cattle-raiser, and farmer. Excepting the fisherman, each type of industry was on the march toward the West, impelled by an irresistible attraction. Each passed in successive waves across the continent. Stand at Cumberland Gap and watch the procession of civilization, marching single file—the buffalo following the trail to the salt springs, the Indian, the fur-trader and hunter, the cattle-raiser, the pioneer farmer—and the frontier has passed by. Stand at South Pass in the Rockies a century later and see the same procession with wider intervals between. The unequal rate of advance compels us to distin-guish the frontier into the trader's frontier, the rancher's frontier, or the miner's frontier, and the farmer's frontier. When the mines and the cow pens were still near the fall line the traders' pack trains were tinkling across the Alleghenies, and the French on the Great Lakes were fortifying their posts, alarmed by the British trader's birch canoe. When the trappers scaled the Rockies, the farmer was still near the mouth of the Missouri.

* * *

Having now roughly outlined the various kinds of frontiers, and their modes of advance, chiefly from the point of view of the frontier itself, we may next inquire what were the influences on the East and on the Old World. A rapid enumeration of some of the more noteworthy effects is all that I have time for.

Composite Nationality

First, we note that the frontier promoted the formation of a composite nationality for the American people. The coast was preponderantly English, but the later tides of continental immigration flowed across to the free lands. This was the case from the early colonial days. The Scotch Irish and the Palatine Germans, or "Pennsylvania Dutch," furnished the dominant element in the stock of the colonial frontier. With these peoples were also the freed indentured servants, or redemptioners, who at the expiration of their time of service passed to the frontier. Governor Spottswood of Virginia writes in 1717, "The inhabitants of our frontiers are composed generally of such as have been transported hither as servants, and, being out of their time, settle themselves where land is to be taken up and that will produce the necessarys of life with little labour." Very generally these redemptioners were of non-English stock. In the crucible of the frontier the immigrants were Americanized, liberated, and fused into a mixed race, English in neither nationality or characteristics. The process has gone on from the early days to our own. Burke and other writers in the middle of the eighteenth century believed that Pennsylvania was "threatened with the danger of being wholly foreign in language, manners, and perhaps even inclinations." The German and Scotch-Irish elements in the frontier of the South were only less great. In the middle of the present century the German element in Wisconsin was already so considerable that leading publicists looked to the creation of a German state out of the commonwealth by concentrating their colonization. Such examples teach us to beware of misinterpreting the fact that there is a common English speech in America into a belief that the stock is also English.

Industrial Independence

In another way the advance of the frontier decreased our dependence on England. The Coast, particularly of the South, lacked diversified industries, and was dependent on England for the bulk of its supplies. In the South there was even a dependence on the Northern colonies for articles of food. Governor Glenn, of South Carolina, writes in the middle of the eighteenth century: "Our trade with New York and Philadelphia was of this sort, draining us of all the little money and bills we could gather from other places for their bread, flour, beer, hams, bacon, and other things of their produce, all which, except beer, our new townships begin to supply us with, which are settled with very industrious and thriving Germans. This no doubt diminishes the number of shipping and the appearance of our trade, but it is far from being a detriment to us." Before long the frontier created a demand for merchants. As it retreated from the coast it became less and less possible for England to bring her supplies directly to the consumers' wharfs, and carry away staple crops, and staple crops began to give way to diversified agriculture for a time. The effect of this phase of the frontier action upon the northern section is perceived when we realize how the advance of the frontier aroused seaboard cities like Boston, New York, and Baltimore, to engage in rivalry for what Washington called "the extensive and valuable trade of a rising empire."

*   *   *

Growth of Democracy

But the most important effect of the frontier has been in the promotion of democracy here and in Europe. As has been indicated, the frontier is productive of individualism. Complex society is precipitated by the wilderness into a kind of primitive organization based on the family. The tendency is anti-social. It produces antipathy to control, and particularly to any direct control. The tax-gatherer is viewed as a representative of oppression. Prof. Osgood, in an able article, has pointed out that the frontier conditions prevalent in the colonies are important factors in the explanation of the American Revolution, where individual liberty was sometimes confused with absence of all effective government. The same conditions aid in explaining the difficulty of instituting a strong government in the period of the confederacy. The frontier individualism has from the beginning promoted democracy.

The frontier States that came into the Union in the first quarter of a century of its existence came in with democratic suffrage provisions, and had reactive effects of the highest importance upon the older States whose peoples were being attracted there. An extension of the franchise became essential. It was *western* New York that forced an extension of suffrage in the constitutional convention of that State in 1821; and it was *western* Virginia that compelled the tide-water region to put a more liberal suffrage provision in the constitution framed in 1830, and to give to the frontier region a more nearly proportionate representation with the tide-water aristocracy. The rise of democracy as an effective force in the nation came in with western preponderance under Jackson and William Henry Harrison, and it meant the triumph of the frontier—with all of its good and with all of its evil elements.

*   *   *

So long as free land exists, the opportunity for a competency exists, and economic power secures political power. But the democracy born of free land, strong in selfishness and individualism, intolerant of administrative experience and education, and pressing individual liberty beyond its proper bounds, has its dangers as well as its benefits. Individualism in America has allowed a laxity in regard to governmental affairs which has rendered possible the spoils system and all the manifest evils that follow from the lack of a highly developed civic spirit. In this connection may be noted also the influence of frontier conditions in permitting lax business honor, inflated paper currency and wild-cat banking. The colonial and revolutionary frontier was the region whence emanated many of the worst forms of an evil currency. The West in the War of 1812 repeated the phenomenon on the frontier of that day, while the speculation and wild-cat banking of the period of the crisis of 1837 occurred on the new frontier belt of the next tier of States. Thus each one of the periods of lax financial integrity concides with periods when a new set of frontier communities had arisen, and concides in an area with these successive frontiers, for the most part. The recent Populist agitation is a case in point. Many a State that now declines any connection with the tenets of the Populists, itself adhered to such ideas in an earlier stage of the development of the State. A primitive society can hardly be expected to show the intelligent appreciation of the complexity of business interests in a developed society. The continual recurrence of these areas of paper-money agitation is another evidence that the frontier can be isolated and studied as a factor in American history of the highest importance.

*   *   *

Intellectual Traits

From the conditions of frontier life came intellectual traits of profound importance. The works of travelers along each frontier from colonial days onward describe certain common traits, and these traits have, while softening down, still persisted as survivals in the place of their origin, even when a higher social organization succeeded. The result is that to the frontier the American intellect owes its striking characteristics. That coarseness and strength combined with acuteness and inquisitiveness; that practical, inventive turn of mind, quick to find expedients; that masterful grasp of material things, lacking in the artistic but powerful to effect great ends; that restless, nervous energy; that dominant individualism, working for good and for evil, and withal that buoyancy and exuberance which comes with freedom—these are traits of the frontier, or traits called out elsewhere because of the existence of the frontier. Since the days when the fleet of Columbus sailed into the waters of the New World, America has been another name for opportunity, and the people of the United States have taken their tone from the incessant expansion which has not only been open but has even been forced upon them. He could be a rash prophet who should assert that the expansive character of American life has now entirely ceased. Movement has been its dominant fact, and, unless this training has no effect upon a people, the American energy will continually demand a wider field for its exercise. But never again will such gifts of free land offer themselves. For a moment, at the frontier, the bonds of custom are broken and unrestraint is triumphant. There is not *tabula rasa*. The stubborn American environment is there with its imperious summons to accept its conditions; the inherited ways of doing things are also there; and yet, in spite of environment, and in spite of custom, each frontier did indeed furnish a new field of opportunity, a gate of escape from the bondage of the past; and freshness, and confidence, and scorn of older society, impatience of its restraints and its ideas, and indifference to its lessons, have accompanied the frontier. What the Mediterranean Sea was to the Greeks, breaking the bond of custom, offering new experiences, calling out new institutions and activities, that, and more, the ever retreating frontier has been to the United States directly, and to the nations of Europe more remotely. And now, four centuries from the discovery of America, at the end of a hundred years of life under the Constitution, the frontier has gone, and with its going has closed the first period of American history.

QUESTIONS TO CONSIDER

1. What does Turner believe are the unique features of American civilization that were created by the frontier?
2. What are the similarities between Turner's vision of America expanding westward, Bradford's (Chapter 28) portrait of Pilgrims journeying to America, and Martineau's (33) portrayal of British civilization expanding into India?
3. Turner describes the frontier as the leading edge of American expansion. How would this picture be different if one viewed it as a meeting ground of several cultures—for example, Native, Spanish, and British American?

FOR FURTHER READING

Billington, Ray Allen. *Frederick Jackson Turner.* New York: Oxford University Press, 1973.

_____, and Martin Ridge. *Westward Expansion: A History of the American Frontier.* 5th ed. New York: Macmillan, 1982.

Bolton, Herbert Eugene. *The Spanish Borderlands.* New Haven, CT: Yale University Press, 1921.

DeVoto, Bernard. *The Year of Decision: 1846.* Boston: Houghton Mifflin, 1942.

Limerick, Patricia Nelson. *Legacy of Conquest: The Unbroken Past of the American West.* New York: Norton, 1987.

_____, et al., eds. *Trails: Toward a New Western History.* Lawrence, KS: University Press of Kansas, 1991.

Malone, Michael P., ed. *Historians and the American West.* Lincoln, NE: University of Nebraska Press, 1983.

Parkman, Francis. *The Discovery of the Great West.* Boston: Little, Brown, 1869.

_____. *The Jesuits in North America in the Seventeenth Century.* Boston: Little, Brown, 1886.

_____. *The Oregon Trail.* New York: Heritage Press, 1943.

Prucha, Francis Paul. *The Great Father: The United States Government and the American Indians.* Lincoln, NE: University of Nebraska Press, 1984.

Slotkin, Richard. *Regeneration through Violence: The Mythology of the American Frontier, 1600-1860.* Middletown, CT: Wesleyan University Press, 1973.

Smith, Henry Nash. *Virgin Land: The American West as Symbol and Myth.* Cambridge, MA: Harvard University Press, 1950.

Stegner, Wallace. *Wolf Willow.* New York: Viking, 1962.

Taylor, George Rogers, ed. *The Turner Thesis.* 3rd ed. Lexington, MA: Heath, 1972.

Turner, Frederick Jackson. *The Frontier in American History.* New York: Holt, Rinehart & Winston, 1962; orig. 1920.

_____. *Rise of the New West.* New York: Harper, 1906.

_____. *The United States, 1830–1850: The Nation and Its Sections.* New York: Henry Holt, 1935.

Utley, Robert. *Billy the Kidd.* Lincoln, NE: University of Nebraska Press, 1989.

Webb, Walter Prescott. *The Great Frontier.* Boston: Houghton Mifflin, 1952.

_____. *The Great Plains.* Boston: Ginn, 1931.

NOTES

1. Frederick J. Turner, *The Significance of the Frontier in American History* (Ann Arbor, MI: University Microfilms, 1966; orig. Washington, DC: American Historical Association 1894), 199–208, 215–17, 221–23, 226–27. Footnotes have been omitted.

CHAPTER 42

Euclides da Cunha

A Vision of a New Nation

Euclides da Cunha
© Gary Olsen

B razil also had its frontier, and its frontier historian, but both were different from the North American counterparts just described. Between 1893 and 1897, thousands of frontier Brazilians flocked to the small town of Canudos in the state of Bahia. Drawn by the sermons of a rustic prophet, Antônio Conselheiro, they formed a rebellious, if mystical, community, at odds with the ways of the coastal elite. That elite saw them as a threat and sent troops to quell them. The backlanders fought fiercely; they held off the army for a year before their last fighters fell dead into graves they had dug with their own hands.

The Canudos rebellion unnerved the Brazilian upper class. They had just overthrown the monarchy, and so saw the revolt as the Brazilian equivalent of the French Vendée: an anti-Republican rural uprising. As progressive and urban "Europeans," they feared the unlettered rural folk, most of whom were of mixed African, Indian, and European ancestry. They saw their own good-hearted efforts to revamp Brazilian society slipping into a racially degenerate abyss.

To these progressives, Canudos symbolized all that was wrong with their nation. More than the naval revolt of a few years earlier, or the just-ended civil war in the south, Canudos combined a perceived threat to the Republic with a slap at the elite sense of Brazil's identity. The rebels' initial defeat of the army made the progressives fear that all they had gained would vanish under a semicivilized deluge.

Euclides da Cunha was a young engineer and journalist at the time of the rebellion. Born in 1866, he was raised in the style of the second-tier elite. His most influential teacher, Benjamin Constant, was one of the founders of the Republic, an abolitionist, and a staunch admirer of August Comte, the creator of the French variety of the intellectual movement, positivism. He trained da Cunha to believe in progress, science, and a duty to bring European civilization to his country. Da Cunha learned this lesson well. He joined the army and tried to make it a center of Republican feeling. When he found himself unsuited to military life, he took up civil engineering, then went as a journalist to report on the Canudos campaign for *O Estado de Sao Paulo*.

At first, da Cunha supported the army. Frontier life was something of a scandal for him, as it was for many upper class Brazilians. His nation was split: its cities were as modern as any, but the countryside was poor, backward, and morally intemperate. How could their nation enter the modern world with such a burden? His early field dispatches cast the *conselheiristas* as rude fanatics and the army as Romans fighting the barbarians: cruel, yet needed to guard civilization.

Yet as da Cunha looked at frontier Bahia with a scientist's eye, his views began to change. He saw the great extremes of climate and imagined their effect on the inhabitants. He looked at the area's topography and saw how hard it made their living. And he began to see their race mixing in a new way: not as a degenerate form of humanity but as the foundation of a new stock: a true Brazilian people. Though raw, these rustics had a strength of character that could not be denied. Five years after the war, when he wrote *Os Sertoes*

(Rebellion in the Backlands), da Cunha found them courageous and worth praise. He described his history as a "cry of protest" against the Republican government's massacre of them. If Brazil was to make progress, such people must be brought into the mainstream, not be killed by it.

In fact, da Cunha was wholly with neither the rebels nor the government. The near instant acclaim that met *Os Sertoes* came partly from da Cunha's ambivalence. He portrayed both army and insurgents as flawed. Although both fought for a cause, and the former had right on their side, yet only the latter were fully committed. Their faithful struggle was blind, yet worth emulating for its ardor. Would that the Republic had such defenders!

At first da Cunha could not find a publisher for his manuscript, and so he printed it privately. That printing sold out in two months, so more followed, as did three revised editions. Da Cunha gained instant celebrity, with which he was not entirely comfortable. He worked as an engineer and surveyor until 1909, when he was killed by his estranged wife's lover. His death left unfinished his second book about Brazil, titled *Paradise Lost*.

Os Sertoes has been called the "Bible of Brazilian nationality." It shaped educated Brazilians' sense of themselves and their society for at least the first 60 years of this century. Though recent historians now doubt some of its stories—da Cunha only came to the front as the fighting ended, and spent most of that time a half-day's march from Canudos itself —its influence is indisputable. By situating the revolt in its climatic, geological, and demographic context, da Cunha drew a new picture of Brazil's past and of its future possibilities.

This, of course, is da Cunha's lasting achievement. Though few modern historians embrace his environmental and racial determinism, all agree that he used them to make a masterpiece. The book is worth reading today for its style and for its historical vision as much as for the events it relates. Unfortunately, no excerpt can give more than a taste of that style. The following passage, taken from "Chapter 2: Man," touches on several of da Cunha's themes.

Rebellion in the Backlands[1]

Origin Of The Jagunços

There can be no doubt that there is a notable trace of originality in the formation of our backlands population, we shall not say of the North, but of subtropical Brazil. Let us try to sketch it in; and, in order not to stray too far from the subject, let us keep close to that theater in which the historic drama of Canudos was unfolded, by traversing rapidly the reaches of the Sao Francisco, that "great highway of Brazilian civilization," as one historian has put it.

From the bird's-eye view given in the foregoing pages, we have seen that this river flows through regions that differ greatly in character. At its headwaters it spreads out, its expanded basin with its network of numerous tributaries taking in the half of Minas, in the zone of mountains and forests. Later, along its middle portion, it narrows, in the extremely beautiful region of the Campos Gerais. Along its lower course, downstream from Joazeiro, where it is confined between slopes which render its bed uneven and which twist it about in the direction of the sea, it becomes poor in tributaries, almost all of them intermittent, and flows away hemmed in a single corredeira of several hundred miles in length, extending to Paulo Affonso—and here it is that it cuts through the semidesert tract of caatingas.

In the threefold aspects of this river we have a diagram of the course of our history, one that reflects in parallel fashion its varying manifestations. It balances the influence of the Tieté. Whereas this latter river, with a course incomparably better suited to purposes of colonization, became the chosen pathway of pioneers seeking, above all, the enslavement and corruption of the savage, the Sao Francisco at its headwaters was essentially the center of the movement to the mines; in its lower course it was the scene of missionary activity; and, in its middle region, it became the classic land of the herdsman, representing the only mode of life compatible with existing social and economic conditions in the colony. Its banks were trod alike by the bandeirante, the Jesuit, and the vaqueiro.

When, at some future date, a more copious supply of documents shall enable us to reconstruct the life of the colony from the seventeenth century to the end of the eighteenth, it is possible that the vaqueiro, wholly forgotten today, will stand out with that prominence which he deserves, by reason of his formative influence on the life of our people. Brave and fearless as the bandeirante, as resigned and tenacious as the Jesuit, he had the advantage of a supplementary attribute which both the others lacked—he had his roots fixed in the soil.

* * *

He is a retrograde, not a degenerate, type. The vicissitudes of history, by freeing him, in the most delicate period of his formation, from the disproportionate exigencies of a borrowed culture, have fitted him for the conquest of that culture some day. His psychic evolution, however backward it may be, has therefore the guaranty of a strong, well-constituted physique. This crossed race, then, makes its appearance as an autonomous and, in a way, an original one, transfiguring within itself all the inherited attributes; so that, unfettered at last of a savage existence, it may attain to civilized life as a result of the very causes which prevent it from doing so at once. Such is the logical conclusion.

The situation here is the reverse of that to be observed in the cities of the seaboard, where an extravagant inversion prevails, highly complex functions being there imposed on feeble organisms, with the effect of compressing and atrophying them before they have attained their full development. In the backlands, on the other hand, the robust organic integrity of the mestizo remains unimpaired, inasmuch as, being immune to foreign admixtures, he is capable of evolving and differentiating himself in accommodation to new and loftier destinies; for the solid physical basis is there for the moral development that is to come.

*   *   *

The Sertanejo

The sertanejo, or man of the backlands, is above all else a strong individual. He does not exhibit the debilitating rachitic tendencies of the neurasthenic mestizos of the seaboard.

His appearance, it is true, at first glance, would lead one to think that this was not the case. He does not have the flawless features, the graceful bearing, the correct build of the athlete. He is ugly, awkward, stooped. Hercules-Quasimodo reflects in his bearing the typical unprepossessing attributes of the weak. His unsteady, slightly swaying, sinuous gait conveys the impression of loose-jointedness. His normally downtrodden mien is aggravated by a dour look which gives him an air of depressing humility. On foot, when not walking, he is invariably to be found leaning against the first doorpost or wall that he encounters; while on horseback, if he reins in his mount to exchange a couple of words with an acquaintance, he braces himself on one stirrup and rests his weight against the saddle. When walking, even at a rapid pace, he does not go forward steadily in a straight line but reels swiftly, as if he were following the geometric outlines of the meandering backland trails. And if in the course of his walk he pauses for the most commonplace of reasons, to roll a cigarro, strike a light, or chat with a friend, he falls—"falls" is the word—into a squatting position and will remain for a long time in this unstable state of equilibrium, with the entire weight of his body suspended on his great-toes, as he sits there on his heels with a simplicity that is at once ridiculous and delightful.

He is the man who is always tired. He displays this invincible sluggishness, this muscular atony, in everything that he does: in his slowness of speech, his forced gestures, his unsteady gait, the languorous cadence of his ditties—in brief, in his constant tendency to immobility and rest.

Yet all this apparent weariness is an illusion. Nothing is more surprising than to see the sertanejo's listlessness disappear all of a sudden. In this weakened organism complete transformations are effected in a few seconds. All that is needed is some incident that demands the release of slumbering energies. The fellow is transfigured. He straightens up, becomes a new man, with new lines in his posture and bearing; his head held high now, above his massive shoulders; his gaze straightforward and unflinching. Through an instantaneous discharge of nervous energy, he at once corrects all the faults that come from the habitual relaxation of his organs; and the awkward rustic unexpectedly assumes the dominating aspect of a powerful, copper-hued Titan, an amazingly different being, capable of extraordinary feats of strength and agility.

This contrast becomes evident upon the most superficial examination. It is one that is revealed at every moment, in all the smallest details of back-country life—marked always by an impressive alternation between the extremes of impulse and prolonged periods of apathy.

It is impossible to imagine a more inelegant, ungainly horseman: no carriage, legs glued to the belly of his mount, hunched forward and swaying to the gait of the unshod, mistreated backland ponies, which are sturdy animals and remarkably swift. In this gloomy, indolent posture the lazy cowboy will ride along, over the plains, behind his slow-paced herd, almost transforming his "nag" into the lulling hammock in which he spends two-thirds of his existence. But let some giddy steer up ahead stray into the tangled scrub of the caatinga, or let one of the herd at a distance become entrammeled in the foliage, and he is at once a different being and, digging his broad-roweled spurs into the flanks of his mount, he is off like a dart and plunges at top speed into the labyrinth of jurema thickets.

Let us watch him at this barbarous steeple chase.

Nothing can stop him in his onward rush. Gullies, stone heaps, brush piles, thorny thickets, or riverbanks—nothing can halt his pursuit of the straying steer, for wherever the cow goes, there the cowboy and his horse go too. Glued to his horse's back, with his knees dug into its flanks until horse and rider appear to be one, he gives the bizarre impression of a crude sort of centaur: emerging unexpectedly into a clearing, plunging into the tall weeds, leaping ditches and swamps, taking the small hills in his stride, crashing swiftly through the prickly briar patches, and galloping at full speed over the expanse of tablelands.

His robust constitution shows itself at such a moment to best advantage. It is as if the sturdy rider were lending vigor to the frail pony, sustaining it by his improvised reins of caroá fiber, suspending it by his spurs, hurling it onward—springing quickly into the stirrups, legs drawn up, knees well forward and close to the horse's side—"hot on the trail" of the wayward steer; now bending agilely to avoid a bough that threatens to brush him from the saddle; now leaping off quickly like an acrobat, clinging to his horse's mane, to avert collision with a stump sighted at the last moment; then back in the saddle again at a bound—and all the time galloping, galloping, through all obstacles, balancing in his right hand, without ever losing it once, never once dropping it in the liana thickets, the long, iron-pointed, leather-headed goad which in itself, in any other hands, would constitute a serious obstacle to progress.

But once the fracas is over and the unruly steer restored to the herd, the cowboy once more lolls back in the saddle, once more an inert and unprepossessing individual, swaying to his pony's slow gait, with all the disheartening appearance of a languishing invalid.

*   *   *

Mestizo Religion

Isolated in this manner in a country that knows nothing of him, and engaged in an open warfare with an environment which would appear to have stamped upon his physical organism and his temperament its own extraordinary ruggedness, the sertanejo, either a nomad or with few roots in the soil, does not, to tell the truth, possess the organic capacity for attaining a loftier place in life. The restricted circle of his activities retards his psychic development. His religion is a monotheism which he does not understand, marred by an extravagant mysticism, with an incongruous admixture of the fetishism of the Indian and the African. He is the primitive individual, bold and strong, but at the same time credulous, readily permitting himself to be led astray by the most absurd superstitions. An analysis of these will reveal a fusion of distinct emotional states.

His religion is, like himself, mestizo in character. A resume of the physical and physiological characteristics of the races from which he springs would likewise serve to summarize their moral qualities. It is an index to the life of the three peoples. And the sertanejo's religious beliefs reflect this violent juxtaposition of distinct tendencies. It is not necessary to describe them. The hair-raising legends of the waggish and wanton *caapora*, mounted on a peevish caitetú and crossing the plains on mysterious moonlit nights; the diabolic *sacy*, a vermilion-colored bonnet on its head, assaulting the belated traveler on unlucky Good Friday eves; along with the werewolves and the night-wandering headless she-mules; all the temptations of the evil one, or Devil, that tragic bearer of celestial grievances, commissioned to the earth; the prayers addressed to Sao Campeiro, canonized *in partibus,* to whom candles are lighted on the plains to obtain his help in recovering lost objects; the cabalistic conjurings for the curing of animals, for "bruising" and "selling" fevers; all the visions, all the fantastic apparitions, all the fanciful prophecies of the insane messiahs; and the pious pilgrimages and the missions and the penances—all these complex manifestations of an ill-defined religiosity are wholly explicable.

It would not be too far amiss to describe them as a miscegenation of beliefs. Here they are, plain to be seen: the anthropomorphism of the savage, the animism of the African, and, what is more worthy of note, the emotional attitude of the superior race itself in the period of discovery and colonization. This last is a notable instance of historical atavism.

*   *   *

Indeed, as we view the backland disorders of today and the insane messiahs who provoke them, we are forcibly struck by their resemblance to the prophetic figures in the [Iberian] peninsula of former days—the King of "Penamacor," the King of "Ericeira," consecrated to martyrdom and wandering over the mountain slopes, infecting credulous multitudes with the same mad ideals, the same harassing dream.

This historical analogy is one that goes back for three centuries; but it is an exact one, complete and flawless. In the rustic society of the backlands time has stood still; this society has not been affected by the general evolutionary movement of the human race; it still breathes the moral atmosphere of those mad visionaries who pursued a Miguelhino or a Bandarra. Nor is there lacking, by way of rounding out the comparison, the political mysticism of *Sebastianism*. Extinct in Portugal, it persists unimpaired today, under a singularly impressive form, in our northern backcountry. But let us not run ahead of our story.

*   *   *

Antônio Conselheiro, Striking Example of Atavism

It was natural that the deep-lying layers of our ethnic stratification should have cast up so extraordinary an anticlinal as Antonio Conselheiro.

The metaphor is quite correct. Just as the geologist, by estimating the inclination and orientation of the truncated strata of very old formations, is enabled to reconstruct the outlines of a vanished mountain, so the historian in taking the stature of this man, who in himself is of no worth, will find it of value solely in considering the psychology of the society which produced him. As an isolated case, this is one lost amid a multitude of commonplace neurotics; it could be included under the general category of progressive psychoses. Taken in connection with the social background, on the other hand, it is sufficiently alarming. It is at once a diathesis and a synthesis. The various phases of this man's career do not, it may be, represent the successive stages of a serious ailment, but they most certainly afford us a condensed summary of a very grave social malady. As the upshot of it all, this unfortunate individual, a fit subject for medical attention, was impelled by a power stronger than himself to enter into conflict with a civilization and to go down in history when he should have gone to a hospital. For to the historian he is not an unbalanced character but rather appears as the integration of various social traits—vague, indecisive, not readily perceived when lost in the multitude, but well defined and forceful when thus summed up in a human personality.

All the naive beliefs from a barbarous fetishism to the aberrations of Catholicism, all the impulsive tendencies of lower races given free outlet in the undisciplined life of the backlands, were condensed in his fierce and extravagant mysticism. He was at once an active and a passive element of that agitation which sprang up about him. A highly impressionable temperament led him merely to absorb the beliefs and superstitions of his environment, in which process his mind, tormented by adversity, was at first little more than the morbidly passive recipient; and, reflected by a consciousness that was in a state of delirium, these influences, greatly strengthened, in turn reacted upon the surroundings which had produced them.

In this particular case it is difficult to draw a dividing line between individual and collective tendencies. The life of this man at once becomes a synoptic chapter in the life of a society. In tracing the individual tendencies, we at the same time draw a rapid parallel for the social forces, and, in following out these two lines, we have a perfect example of the reciprocality of influences.

* * *

Early Reverses

It is at this point that the drama of his life begins. A wife was for him merely an additional deadweight to the tremendous burden of his tarnished heredity, and marriage led to the unbalancing of a life which had begun promisingly enough. From 1858 on, everything that he does shows him to be a changed man. For one thing, he has lost his old sedentary habits. It may have been the incompatibility of genius or, what is more likely, his wife's bad disposition; but, whatever the cause, his existence was now an exceedingly unsettled one. Within the course of a few years, we find him living in various towns and cities and following various occupations.

Amid all this restlessness, nevertheless, there is to be perceived a character engaged in struggle, one that does not mean to let itself be defeated. Being left without any worldly fortune, Antonio Maciel, in this preparatory phase of his career, in spite of his unhappy home life, no sooner arrives at a new place of residence than he at once starts looking for employment, any means whatsoever of earning an honest livelihood. In 1859, removing to Sobral, he obtains a position as cashier, but does not remain there long. Going on to Campo Grande, he there finds work as scrivener to a justice of the peace; but again his stay is a brief one, and he is off for Ipú, where he becomes a court attaché.

In all this there is to be noted an evergrowing predilection for those occupations which are least laborious, requiring less and less of an expenditure of energy. Antonio Maciel is getting away from the discipline of his youth and displays a marked tendency toward those forms of activity which are more exciting and less productive; he is on the downward path which leads to open vagabondage. At the same time his troubles at home are robbing him of his old serenity.

This period of his life, nevertheless, shows him to be endowed still with worthy sentiments. Round about him permanent party strifes were going on, offering an adventurous career upon which, like so many others, he might have embarked, by allying himself with the first victor at the polls who came along; and he would have been welcome by reason of his family's traditional prestige. He always avoided this, however; and throughout the whole of his downward course there is to be glimpsed a man who is giving ground, it may be, but who does so slowly, struggling painfully to keep his footing, but with all the exhaustion of a weakened constitution.

Downfall

Then of a sudden he meets with a violent mishap, and the inclined plane of his life at once comes to an end with a terrifying crash. At Ipú his wife left him, ran away with a police officer. This proved his complete undoing. Overcome with shame, the poor fellow sought to bury himself in the depths of the backlands, seeking out the most remote regions, where no one would even know his name and where he might find the shelter of complete obscurity. His course was to the south of Ceará. Upon passing through Páos Brancos, on the Crato Highway, he made an attack one night, with all the fury of a madman, upon a relative who had put him up. There was a brief investigation by the police, which was halted when the victim declared that his assailant had not been to blame. In this manner the latter was saved from going to prison. He then went on south, as fast as his legs could carry him, in the direction of Crato, and dropped out of sight.

Ten years passed by, and the unfortunate youth of Quixeramobim appeared to have been completely forgotten. Only once in a long while would someone recall his name and the scandal which had marked the close of his life in those parts—a scandal in which a certain local bigwig, a police sergeant, was *magna pars,* the Lovelace of the episode. Thanks to this somewhat ludicrous incident, the name of Antonio Maciel was barely kept alive on his native heath; but he might, to all intents and purposes, have been dead.

And so there appeared in Baía the somber anchorite with hair down to his shoulders, a long tangled beard, an emaciated face, and a piercing eye, a monstrous being clad in a blue canvas garment and leaning on the classic staff which is used to stay the pilgrim's tottering steps.

* * *

It is not surprising, then, if to these simple folk he became a fantastic apparition, with something unprepossessing about him; nor is it strange if, when this singular old man of a little more than thirty years drew near the farmhouses of the *tropeiros,* the festive guitars at once stopped strumming and the improvisations ceased. This was only natural. Filthy and battered in appearance, clad in his threadbare garment and silent as a ghost, he would spring up suddenly out of the plains, peopled by hobgoblins. Then he would pass on, bound for other places, leaving the superstitious backwoodsmen in a daze. And so it was, in the end, he came to dominate them without seeking to do so.

* * *

More Legends

Still without interference, the "Counselor" continued on his mission of arousing and perverting the popular imagination. It was at this time that the first legends about him became current. We shall not endeavor to exhume them all from the archives, but here are a few of them.

He it was who founded the settlement of Bom Jesus; and the astounded folk tell of him that on a certain occasion, as the lovely church that stands there was being built, and as a dozen workmen were doing their utmost to hoist a heavy beam, the Predestined stepped upon the plank and then ordered two of the men to lift the beam and himself, and those two succeeded in doing what all the others had not been able to do, quickly and without the slightest exertion.

Another time—and I had this from persons who had not been taken in by his fanaticism —he came to Monte Santo and announced that there would be a procession to the summit of the mountain, up to the last of the chapels, on the top. The ceremony began in the afternoon, the multitude spreading out slowly up the steep incline, intoning benedicites and pausing contritely at the stations. He preceded them—a grave and sinister figure—head bared, his long hair floating on the wind, and leaning on his inseparable staff. Night fell, the tapers of the penitents were lighted, and the procession along the line of peaks was like a luminous highway up the mountain.

Upon reaching the Holy Cross, on the top, Antonio Conselheiro, panting for breath, seated himself upon the first step of the stairway of rough-hewn stone, and sat there ecstatically contemplating the heavens, his gaze fixed on the stars.

The first wave of the faithful then began overflowing into the small chapel, while others remained without, kneeling on the hard rock. The contemplative mystic then arose, for weariness was something that he frowned upon. Making his way through the ranks of his respectful followers drawn up on either side, he in turn now entered the chapel, with lowered head, humble and downcast, gasping still. As he approached the great altar, however, his pallid face framed by his disorderly locks was upraised, and it was then that the multitude beheld a terrifying sight. Two bloody tears were slowly trickling down the immaculate face of the Blessed Virgin.

These and other legends are still current in the backlands. And this is quite natural. A species of great man gone wrong, Antonio Conselheiro in his sorrowing mysticism brought together all those errors and superstitions which go to form the coefficient of reduction of our nationality. He drew the people of the backlands after him, not because he dominated them, but because their aberrations dominated him. He was favored by his milieu, and at times, as we have seen, he had a realization of the utility of the absurd. He acted in obedience to the irresistible finality of old ancestral impulses and, in the grip of those impulses, displayed in everything he did the placidity of an incomparable evangelist. It was, indeed, this inexplicable placidity of his which deadened his neurasthenia.

QUESTIONS TO CONSIDER

1. According to da Cunha, what roles do climate and geography play in shaping Brazilian character and history?
2. Da Cunha speaks much of physical and ethnic types and related moral characteristics among the people of the backlands. Is this mere prejudice, or is it clear-headed analysis? How does it shape da Cunha's interpretation?

3. How does da Cunha explain Antônio Conselheiro's path to becoming a prophet? How is this different than the way he might have been described by one of his followers or by a religious believer?
4. How does da Cunha's perspective on the role of the frontier in constructing a Brazilian national identity differ from Turner's perspective on the role of the frontier in constructing an American national identity?

FOR FURTHER READING

Azevedo, Aluísio. *Mulatto*. Trans. Murray Graeme MacNicoll. Ed. Daphne Patai. Austin, TX: University of Texas Press, 1990.
Bello, José Maria. *A History of Modern Brazil, 1889–1964*. Trans. James L. Taylor. Stanford, CA: Stanford University Press, 1966.
Levine, Robert M. *Vale of Tears: Revisiting the Canudos Massacre in Northeast Brazil, 1893–1897*. Berkeley, CA: University of California Press, 1992.

NOTES

1. Euclides da Cunha, *Rebellion in the Backlands*, trans. Samuel Putnam (Chicago: University of Chicago Press, 1944), 71–73, 88–91, 110–12, 117–18, 126–28, 139–40. Footnotes have been omitted.

CHAPTER 43

K. M. Panikkar

Indian Diplomat and Historian

Vasco Da Gama
© *North Wind Pictures*

Kavalam Madhava Panikkar (1895–1963) made Indian history as much as he studied it. A diplomat and journalist as well as a historian, he pioneered a critical reinterpretation of Western colonialism that stressed Indian resistance to Western rule. He also focused attention on the complex interplay between indigenous and European institutions over the four-and-a-half centuries of modern contact between these civilizations. He sought to place that interplay in a world context: as an interplay, rather than a glorious Western advance. In doing so, he offended some Westerners. Yet he gave voice to a postcolonial Asia that needed to see itself in a new light. And he did so through careful scholarship, not mere propaganda.

Panikkar was born in Kerala State, on India's southwest coast. He took his college degrees at Madras and at Oxford, where he won a First in History. After obtaining a law degree, he returned to India to teach at the Aligarh Muslim University. He soon left that post to edit the *Hindustan Times.* He did not find journalism rewarding, and shifted to a career of public service in various of the Indian states. From 1936 to 1939, for example, he was the Foreign Minister of Patiala State. From 1939 to 1944, he held the same post for Bikaner State; he then became its Prime Minister until Indian independence. It was here that he earned the Rajput honorific "Sardar," by which he is sometimes known. After independence, Nehru chose Panikkar for various diplomatic missions; he was, for example, the ambassador to the People's Republic of China and the chief architect of the early friendship between India and that land. On retiring from public service, he spent the last two years of his life as the vice-chancellor of two Indian universities.

Through it all, Panikkar wrote histories. Two early volumes on Kerala's encounter with colonialism (*Malabar and the Portuguese* and *Malabar and the Dutch,* both 1931) were followed by several historical biographies. He wrote histories of some of the other Indian states, focusing on their relations with the nation as a whole. He wrote an overall *Survey of Indian History,* which some critics argue gives too much weight to Hinduism at the expense of Islam. He wrote an essay on sea power in Indian history before composing his most influential book, *Asia and Western Dominance,* which appeared in 1953.

This book presented a history of colonialism seen through Indian eyes. Unlike most European histories of the topic, it used both native and European sources, and examined both the subregional encounters (e.g., Portugal vs. Malabar) and the overall pattern of encounter (Europe vs. India as a whole). It emphasized the role of gunnery, sea power, and military organization in the West's early triumphs, but also pointed to the various Indian states' abilities to fend off the European advance. In Panikkar's view, European political dominance came quite late. It should thus not be too hard for India to make its way in the postcolonial era.

Panikkar is remembered most of all for the novelty of his ideas. Here are some of the more important ones. He focused his histories of the Princely States on their relationships with the British Raj, to which his diplomatic experience most surely added insight. He looked at India in geopolitical terms, a new approach at the time, but one with great relevance to understanding the broad sweep of the colonial encounter. He saw India in the context of Asia, not merely as one separate subcontinent, and treated Europe as a whole civilization rather than a collection of separate countries. He thus framed the "Vasco da Gama Epoch" as a meeting of civilizations, rather than just of states. And he believed that the impact of the East on the West was as important as that of the West on the East; though he did not trace this in detail in his histories, he pointed it out as a direction other historians should explore.

Despite his prolific pen, Panikkar has been criticized in all these areas for failing to delve deeply enough. He is said to have presented overviews rather than the details that would have proved his points. Surely this is unjust with respect to his work on Kerala; his two books on the Malabar coast and the early sections of *Asia and Western Dominance* show a fine regard for details. But many of his other works are indeed broad—a perhaps inevitable failing of a life spent in diplomacy rather than professional scholarship. Be that as it may, Panikkar did enunciate a new historical vision, one that has been highly influential in India and in the postcolonial world.

The following passage is taken from an early chapter of *Asia and Western Dominance*. In it, Panikkar traces the interplay between European and Indian power before the former triumphed. The Portuguese bested the Indians and Arabs at sea, but the Indians won on land. It was not until later that this early stalemate was to dissolve.

Asia and Western Dominance[1]

India and the Indian Ocean

The Indian Ocean had from time immemorial been the scene of intense commercial trade. Indian ships had from the beginning of history sailed across the Arabian Sea up to the Red Sea ports and maintained intimate cultural and commercial connections with Egypt, Israel and other countries of the Near East. Long before Hippalus disclosed the secret of the monsoon to the Romans, Indian navigators had made use of these winds and sailed to Bab-el-Mandeb. To the east, Indian mariners had gone as far as Borneo and flourishing Indian colonies had existed for over 1,200 years in Malaya, the islands of Indonesia, in Cambodia, Champa and other areas of the coast. Indian shops from Quilon made regular journeys to the South China coast. A long tradition of maritime life was part of the history of Peninsula India. In fact the spice trade which fed Europe and which was so potent an attraction to the Westerners did not all come from India, though it was carried from Indian ports along the Red Sea route. India was primarily the country of pepper and cardamom, while cloves, nutmegs and other equally valuable spices came from the islands of Indonesia. This was so from the early times of the Christian era, for we have an allusion in Kalidasa's epic *Raghuvamsa* of ships loaded with fragrant spices from the islands across the seas.

The supremacy of India in the waters that washed her coast was unchallenged till the rise of Arab shipping under the early khalifs. But the Arabs and Hindus competed openly, and the idea of 'sovereignty over the sea' except in narrow straits was unknown to Asian conception. It is true that the Sri Vijaya Empire dominating the Straits of Malacca exercising control of shipping through that sea lane for two centuries, but there was no question at any time of any Asian power exercising or claiming the right to control traffic in open seas. It follows from this conception of the freedom of the seas that Indian rulers who maintained powerful navies like the Chola Emperors, or the Zamorins, used it only for the protection of the coast, for putting down piracy and, in case of war, for carrying and escorting troops across the seas. Thus during the hundred years' war between the Sailendra Kings of Sri Vijaya and the Chola Emperors, the reported battles are all on land, the Chola king carrying whole armies across to the Malayan Peninsula and fighting successive campaigns in the territories of the Malayan ruler. Naval fights on any large scale, in the manner of the wars between Carthage and Rome, seem to have been unknown in India before the arrival of the Portuguese. The Indian ships therefore were not equipped for fighting in distant seas.

Arab mercantile activity had never been political. The Arabs traded freely in all the Indian ports, sailed out to the Pacific and reached even the China coast. After the ninth century they seem to have entered into effective competition with Gujerati merchants for the spice trade of the Indonesian islands, for when Affonso Albuquerque arrived on the Malayan coast he noticed Arab, Hindu and Chinese merchants competing openly in the markets of that area.

From quite early times Chinese junks had also appeared in the Malayan waters and occasionally also in Indian ports. But systematic Chinese maritime expansion to the south began only in the Ming period. In the time of the Ming Emperor Yung Lo successive naval expeditions had been fitted out under a great captain, Cheng Ho, a full description of whose voyages in the southern seas has been left by the eunuch Ma Huan who accompanied the party as an interpreter. One of Cheng Ho's armadas consisted of no less than sixty-five ships, some of which were of very considerable size. In the Indian Ocean area he visited Ceylon and Calicut a number of times and even sailed up to Aden. This outburst of maritime activity was only temporary and after Cheng Ho's death we do not hear of any further organized Chinese activity on the sea. The Ming Admiral's repeated visits to Malaya were, however, not without political consequences. For the first time the Malayan rulers became aware of the might of the Celestial Empire, and without presuming to challenge it they willingly became tributaries and accepted the suzerainty of the Emperor in Peking. This vassalage continued for a hundred years, in fact till the Portuguese warships arrived off the coast and, as we shall see at the proper time, the conduct of the Portuguese authorities towards these Muslim potentates was destined to have far-reaching consequences for the relations of the Western Powers with the Chinese Empire.

* * *

As the first voyage was only exploratory da Gama confined himself to a request for permission to trade, which the Zamorin freely granted. But the Portuguese captain's refusal to pay the customs duty was an indication of the troubles that lay ahead. Also da Gama had noted with surprise and alarm the presence of the 'Moors' in the city and the influence which they enjoyed at court. For this he had not been prepared. It would be remembered that the Bull of Nicholas V had proceeded on the assumption that the people of India were Christians. Da Gama even mistook a Hindu temple at Calicut for a Christian church. The presence of the Muslims, their practical monopoly of trade and their influence with the Zamorin were, therefore, matters of unpleasant surprise, which went against the presuppositions of the Portu-guese authorities.

After a formal exchange of compliments and the sale of the goods he had brought in exchange for spices, da Gama sailed back to Portugal to report the success of his expedition to his master. Dom Manoel and his advisers realized that in the Indian Ocean also they had come up against their mortal enemies, 'the Moors,' and that without a prolonged and major effort the advantages of the discovery of an all-sea route to India would not accrue to them. The second expedition which the King ordered to be fitted out was on a much larger scale. It consisted of 33 ships and 1,500 men, with ample military equipment. It was a great naval expedition meant to assert the authority of the King of Portugal over the Indian seas. This powerful armada was commanded by Pedro Alvarez Cabral, a nobleman of distinction, and the officers of other ships were recruited from the flower of Portuguese nobility. The orders to Cabral were to sail directly to Calicut and to demand from the Zamorin, on threat of war, the right to establish a trading post and permission for five Franciscan fathers to preach the gospel. Of this armada, only six reached the Indian coast. The Zamorin was in no way displeased by the return of the Portuguese and sent a message welcoming Cabral to Calicut. But the Admiral was in no mood for friendship. He asked for an audience with the Zamorin, insisting at the same time that hostages should be delivered to him before he landed. The Zamorin agreed to this unusual proposal and the Portuguese envoy was received cordially and was allotted a place for trade. But the high-handed actions of one of Cabral's assistants, Correa, led to a popular outbreak, which cost the Portuguese many lives. Correa himself, who started the fight, was killed with fifty of his men. On this Cabral withdrew his ships and bombarded the city. The Zamorin fitted out a fleet of eighty ships carrying fifteen hundred men to avenge this act of barbarism. Cabral, however, sailed away on sighting the Calicut ships.

Though Cabral had sailed away, the Portuguese had not abandoned the Indian Ocean. On the contrary, Dom Manoel assumed for himself the title of 'The Lord of the Navigation, Conquest and Commerce of Ethiopia, Arabia, Persia and India' and fitted out an even stronger expedition with orders to enforce his claim to the supremacy of the Indian seas. It was Vasco da Gama himself who was appointed captain-major of this fleet. The fleet consisted of fifteen ships of which six were larger and more powerfully equipped than those which had previously arrived in the Indian sea. *San Jeronymo* was the flagship. The other five were lateen rigged caravels fitted with heavy artillery and the expedition carried 800 trained soldiers. Since it was realized that there might be serious opposition a reinforcement of five vessels under Estavo da Gama was sent five months later.

The most impressive fact about this first and most decisive period of Portuguese endeavour is the remarkable manner in which the fleets in the East were kept reinforced by the Portuguese home government. Armada followed armada in unending succession under trained captains, and the Portuguese chiefs in the Indian waters knew that men and ships were on the way bringing succour to them. Even in the most difficult circumstances they could therefore hold out with the firm conviction that help was not far away. In this work, the Portuguese Government had the financial backing of the great merchant princes of Antwerp who, realizing the revolutionary change in trade that the Portuguese discoveries involved, had hastened to annex the benefits. The Weslers, for example, had invested in the Portuguese voyages of 1503 to open a depot for spices in Antwerp. To this system of continuous reinforcements, worked out by Dom Manoel with the assistance of Antwerp capital, must be attributed the success that attended the navies of Portugal on the Eastern seas.

Da Gama and his associates, even before they reached the coast of India, began to enforce the claim of his sovereign to be 'the Lord of Navigation.' Without any kind of warning he intercepted and destroyed any vessel he came across on his voyage. The following incident quoted in *Lendas da India* is typical of the policy of terrorism and piracy that he introduced into Indian waters. The Portuguese armada ran across some unarmed vessels returning from Mecca. Vasco da Gama captured them and in the words of Lendas, 'after making the ships empty of goods, prohibited anyone from taking out of it any Moor and then ordered them to set fire to it.' The explanation for capturing the vessel is perhaps to be found in Barroes' remark: 'It is true that there does exist a common right to all to navigate the seas and in Europe we recognize the rights which others hold against us; but the right does not extend beyond Europe and therefore the Portuguese as Lords of the Sea are justified in confiscating the goods of all those who navigate the seas without their permission.'

Strange and comprehensive claim, yet basically one which every European nation, in its turn, held firmly almost to the end of Western supremacy in Asia. It is true that no other nation put it forward so crudely or tried to enforce it so barbarously as the Portuguese in the first quarter of the sixteenth century, but the principle that the doctrines of international law did not apply outside Europe, that what would be barbarism in London or Paris is civilized conduct in Peking (e.g. the burning of the Summer Palace) and that European nations had no moral obligations in dealing with Asian peoples (as for example when Britain insisted on the opium trade against the laws of China, though opium smoking was prohibited by law in England itself) was part of the accepted creed of Europe's relations with Asia. So late as 1870 the President of the Hong Kong Chamber of Commerce declared: 'China can in no sense be considered a country entitled to all the same rights and privileges as civilized nations which are bound by international law.' Till the end of European domination the fact that rights existed for Asians against Europeans was conceded only with considerable mental reservation. In countries under direct British occupation, like India, Burma and Ceylon, there were equal rights established by law, but that as against Europeans the law was not enforced very rigorously was known and recognized. In China, under extra-territorial jurisdiction, Europeans were protected against the operation of Chinese laws. In fact, except in Japan this doctrine of *different rights* persisted to the very end and was a prime cause of Europe's ultimate failure in Asia.

Da Gama's barbarous acts of piracy reached the ears of the Zamorin even before his ships were sighted off the coast, and the Lord of Mountains and the Seas was ready to meet the challenge. After Cabral's bombardment, the Zamorin had strengthened his naval forces, and these were reinforced by a fleet of heavier vessels belonging to Khoja Ambar, one of Calicut's leading merchants engaged in Red Sea trade. Though the Calicut fleet had the advantage of speed, it did not possess the fire power of the Portuguese ships fitted with heavy artillery. In the engagement that followed off Cochin, Khoja Ambar's ships suffered as a result of Portuguese fire, but the Zamorin's Admiral Kassim was able to manoeuvre his small ships like wasps, and the result was that da Gama broke off the engagement and sailed away with his ships to Europe.

Though the honours of the battle off Cochin lay with the Calicut Navy, the Kassim's inability to chase da Gama nullified the fruits of his victory. The

Calicut Navy was not a high sea fleet, and was at best able to fight only in coastal waters. Near the coast it could meet the Portuguese fleet on more than equal terms, but the Calicut vessels were wholly unsuited for operations at any distance from their base. At the battle off Cochin the Portuguese discovered this secret and exploited it later to the fullest advantage.

* * *

With the departure of Mir Hussain and the Egyptian fleet from Indian waters in 1509, the Portuguese may be said to have established their claim to be 'Lord of Navigation' in the Eastern seas. Though it is true that the Zamorin's naval power was unbroken and Calicut was able for another ninety years (till 1599) to challenge Portuguese authority in the coastal waters of Malabar and fought numerous successful actions against them, in the high seas the Portuguese established an unchallenged mastery which placed the seaborne commerce of India at their mercy for over a century-and-a-half. The man who organized this maritime empire and carried it virtually to the Pacific was Affonso Albuquerque, undoubtedly one of the greatest names in the history of Europe's relations with Asia and the architect of Western domination in the East.

Albuquerque came out to the East, first in 1506, when he accompanied Tristan da Cunha on an expedition which had been sent out to attack the Red Sea traders and to blockade the entrance to that sea. This first cruise around Aden, Socotra and Ormuz gave Albuquerque the basic strategic conceptions of his oceanic policy. Socotra he seized and converted into a naval base, recognizing its importance for the control of the Red Sea trade. Acting on his own and without authority from anyone he demanded and obtained tribute from the King of Ormuz. It is also important to note that an Embassy from the King of Portugal to the legendary 'Prester John,' King of Ethiopia, consisting of Joao Gomez and Joao Sanches with Sidi Mahmmed, a Tunisian Moor, as their guide, had accompanied the expedition and had been landed at Melinde to make their way to the Ethiopian capital. The party, however, reappeared after a year and presented themselves to Albuquerque who gave them letters in Arabic and Portuguese to the Christian Emperor. It will be seen from these preliminary activities that Albuquerque's vision had already embraced the entire Arabian and Red Seas when he actually assumed the Governorship of Portuguese possessions.

His first object was to establish an impregnable base in India from where he could enforce complete and undisturbed mastery of the Indian seas. The only Portuguese possession at the time was the fortress of Cochin situated on a small island, barely half a square mile in extent. Albuquerque decided that Cochin was unsuitable and it was to Calicut, still the great centre of the spice trade, that he turned. Previous failures in their encounters with the Zamorin rankled in the minds of the Portuguese, and Dom Manoel had sent out no less a person than the Grand Marshal of Portugal, Dom Fernando Coutinho, with express orders to reduce Calicut and destroy the power of the Zamorin. A surprise attack was decided upon. Two fleets, known respectively as the fleet of Portugal and the fleet of India under the separate commands of the Marshal and the Governor, appeared before Calicut carrying a large expeditionary force. A landing was effected without much difficulty. The Zamorin was away from the capital at the time, but the palace guard who engaged the Portuguese invaders found no difficulty in defeating them. In a sharp engagement the Portuguese forces were cut to pieces, the Grand Marshal along with seventy hidalgos losing their lives. Albuquerque himself received two wounds, one on the left arm and the other on the neck. A cannon shot felled him to the ground and he was carried unconscious to the ship. Thus ended in disaster the first attempt to challenge the power of an Indian ruler on land.

The defeat of the Portuguese under their greatest leader at Calicut had far-reaching consequences. For two hundred and thirty years after this, no European nation attempted any military conquest or tried to bring any ruler under his control. Goa was no doubt occupied and converted into a great base, but this was with the help of Tulaji, the Hindu chief of the area, who joined with the Portuguese in order to weaken the Adil Shahi Sultan's authority in the neighbourhood. Also, it should be remembered that Goa was at an extremity of Adil Shai's extensive dominions and its conquest and fortification by the Portuguese were matters of great importance to the Hindu Empire of Vijayanagar in its campaigns against Islam. The Vijayanagar Emperors were quick to realize that Goa provided them an outlet to the sea, through which they could get not only arms and equipment, but the horses which they needed so much for their cavalry. Actually, therefore, the conquest of Goa was not the establishment of the Portuguese as a land power in India, but the creation of a suitable place for naval operations in the Indian Ocean.

Albuquerque reported to his master that he had put every Moor in Goa to the sword, adding 'wherever he could find them no Moor was spared and they filled mosques with them and set them on fire.' This bitter hatred of Islam brought the Portuguese into friendly relations with the Hindu monarchs of Vijayanagar, who had been carrying on relentless war against Islam for 170 years. In 1509 Krishna Deva Raya, the greatest ruler of the dynasty, and the inveterate enemy of the Muslim Rulers of the Deccan, ascended the throne of Vijayanagar. Not only did he welcome the occupation of Goa by the Portuguese, which enabled him to receive military supplies from abroad, but maintained cordial relations with them. In 1510, Albuquerque sent a mission to him soliciting permission for an establishment at Bhatkal and this was freely granted. The friendly relations between the Hindu Empire and the Portuguese authorities, united in their enmity to Islam, is a fact which is generally overlooked in considering how Portugal was able to maintain herself in Goa with little or no military power after the first fifty years of her appearance in Indian waters.

*   *   *

We may at this stage consider why the aggrandisement of the Portuguese in the Indian Ocean and their activities in their coastal establishments did not create any widespread reaction in India, for the one thing that stands out most clearly in the relations of the Portuguese with the Indian Powers at this time is the general attitude of friendliness and tolerance towards the newcomers in the Hindu courts of the South with the exception of Calicut. As we have noticed, the great Hindu Empire of Vijayanagar maintained cordial relations with the Portuguese at Goa and permitted them to trade in its extensive dominions. With the rulers of Cochin, where the Portuguese had their first establishments, the Portuguese authorities maintained very cordial relations. With the smaller chiefs along the coast they traded freely and without political complications. In fact, it would not be incorrect to say that the Portuguese met with no hostility at the courts of Hindu rulers, except at Calicut.

The case of the Zamorin was very special. His State was the one considerable naval power on the coast and the Portuguese claims of supremacy on the sea conflicted with his own authority. For a hundred years the naval fight between the Zamorin's fleets and the Portuguese from Goa and Cochin continued without intermission, and it was only in 1599 that a treaty was signed between them. Also, it should be remembered that the prosperity of Calicut State, for over 400 years, had been bound up with the activities of Arab spice merchants. The Portuguese attempt to displace them affected the basic policy of the Zamorins on which the strength of Calicut had been built up. The hostility of the Zamorin was therefore understandable and it was based on considerations which were particular to his own State.

For the rest, the activities of the Portuguese affected only the Muslim traders, and this was a part their settled policy. We have noticed how at the conquest of Malacca, Hindu, Chinese and Burmese traders were left unmolested by Albuquerque. The carrier trade in the Indian Ocean had become a monopoly of the Arabs and the determined Portuguese attempt to dispossess them of it did not affect Indian rulers or their merchants. It made no difference to the Indian rulers whether their merchants sold their goods to the Portuguese or to the Arabs. In fact the Portuguese had an advantage in that they were able to sell to Indian rulers arms and equipment which they required. So far as the Indian merchants were concerned, very soon they worked out a system of permits by which they were able to carry on their trade without the competition of Arab merchants, and in that sense the Portuguese monopoly may be said to have helped them. The achievement of the Portuguese during the first period of their supremacy was to have swept the sea of Arabian traders and to have effectively extinguished the monopoly which they had enjoyed for so long. This was not unwelcome to the Hindus and does not seem to have been actively opposed by the non-Arab Muslim merchants of Cambay and Gujerat.

Also, after the disaster that their arms suffered at Calicut, the Portuguese seem to have divested themselves of any territorial ambitions which they might have originally entertained in regard to the mainland of India. The islands of Diu and Bombay and trading posts at different places on the coast, apart from the territory of Goa and the fort of Cochin, were all that they possessed and with these they seem to have been wisely content. Though the viceroys kept great pomp and style at Goa, and pretended almost to imperial dignities, they were realistic enough in their relations with Indian rulers. They exchanged embassies and missions, received and returned presents, and on the whole maintained the decencies of inter-State intercourse. They had in effect become a minor 'country power'—except, of course, on the sea where their claims were truly universal and their authority undisputed.

QUESTIONS TO CONSIDER

1. How does Panikkar portray early European contact with India? How does this differ from European portrayals?
2. To what does Panikkar attribute the eventual European domination of the Indian Ocean?
3. What kinds of events does Panikkar include in his history? What does he leave out?

FOR FURTHER READING

Banerjee, Tarasankar. *Sardar K. M. Panikkar: The Profile of a Historian.* Calcutta: Ratna Prakashan, 1977.

Panikkar, K. M. *An Autobiography.* Trans. K. Krishnamurthy. Madras: Oxford University Press, 1977.

———. *India and the Indian Ocean.* London: G. Allen and Unwin, 1945.

———. *Malabar and the Dutch, Being the History of the Fall of the Nayar Power in Malabar.* Bombay: D. B. Taraporevala, 1931.

———. *Malabar and the Portuguese, Being a History of the Relations of the Portuguese with Malabar from 1500 to 1663.* Bombay: D. B. Taraporevala, 1929.

———. *Survey of Indian History.* London: Meridian Books, 1947.

Sen, S. P. *Historians and Historiography in Modern India.* Calcutta: Institute of Historical Studies, 1973.

NOTES

1. K. M. Panikkar, *Asia and Western Dominance: A Survey of the Vasco Da Gama Epoch of Asian History, 1498–1945* (New York: John Day, 1953), 34–36, 40–48, 52–54. Footnotes have been omitted.

CHAPTER 44

Kenneth Onwuka Dike

Father of Modern African Historiography

Kenneth Onwuka Dike
Harvard University Archives

W e have previously seen the work of African historians develop from the oral epics of the Mande to the blending of oral, written, and eyewitness accounts introduced by Samuel Johnson. African historiography has continued this trajectory in the twentieth century. Its most important shaper, Dr. Kenneth Onwuka Dike (1917–1983), argued that Africa needs to come to terms with the European powers, not by abandoning its traditions, but by combining them with Western ones. From his early articles describing the native sources available to the African historian, through his solo work on the history of the Niger River delta, to the multidisciplinary Benin project, Dike advocated seeing African history through new eyes.

Dike was born in Awka, in southeastern Nigeria. He was the first Nigerian to be professionally trained as a historian in the Western tradition, receiving his PhD from the University of London in 1950. He supervised Nigerian public records in the British colonial government for several years, then became a professor and vice-chancellor at the University of Ibadan. His career suffered a hiatus during the 1966-1970 Nigerian civil war, a fate suffered by many southwesterners. He then took a professorship at Harvard, where he stayed for ten years. He returned to Nigeria in 1979, and headed the Anambra State University of Technology in Enugu until his death.

Dike set forth his historiographic views most clearly in an early article "African History and Self-Government," which was a response to the charge that Africa lacked history because it lacked written records. He argued for the integrity of African oral histories, saying that these were no less trustworthy than the records of European explorers; both had to be read with a critical eye. He later filled out this approach in an encyclopedia entry, "African Historiography," written with his colleague Ade Ajayi. Here he argued that the oral accounts of the African past depend for their accuracy on specialized institutions, which are in the modern era slipping away. By combining such accounts with anthropological and linguistic evidence, and also with European written records, one can approach the African past much more closely than historians once believed.

Dike embodied these views most fully in his revised doctoral dissertation, *Trade and Politics in the Niger Delta 1830-1885,* a selection from which follows. It is this work on which his reputation as a historian is based. The passage we have chosen comes from an early chapter. In it, Dike argues that population movements in the Niger Delta were responses to the new trade opportunities that the Europeans offered. Africans came into the Delta, which had previously been sparsely populated. They built kingdoms and took and traded slaves there because the Europeans provided a ready market for them. But the structures of those kingdoms and slaving houses were not dictated from abroad. European documents of the early period show the independence of native institutions; African oral histories show that these institutions responded both to outside pressures and to opportunities. We can only understand African history, said Dike, by seeing events with both native and European eyes; the former give us the context by which the records of the latter may be understood.

Trade and Politics is not the sole source of Dike's historiographic influence. In the 1950s and 1960s, he sponsored the multidisciplinary Benin project, a team effort that combined the talents of a historian, an archaeologist, an anthropologist, an art historian, and a linguist to unravel the history of Benin, the most significant of the Delta kingdoms. The African past, Dike believed, is found in art and music, religion, language, and physical remains as well as in stories and writing. One can only determine the past through a multifaceted investigation that combines the talents of several scholars. Dike devoted much of his later professional effort to organizing these investigations, to the detriment of his own writing.

Above all, Dike believed in balance. In rejecting a European historiography that limited itself to written records, Dike was not arguing that one had to limit oneself to African sources. He did not think that Africans had any monopoly on historical truth. Indeed, he applied the critical techniques of the best Western scholarship to sources of all kinds. Just as African oral histories need written supplements for rigor, European writings about Africa are meaningless unless they are illuminated by the myriad sources of native knowledge at the historian's disposal. To reject these sources is to condemn oneself to failure.

Finally, Dike drew political consequences from his historiographic views. As a Nigerian nationalist, he saw African history as relevant to the present. Only after Africans could come to reject a historiography that placed Europeans and their writing at the center of history, could they assume the active role in the modern world that Dike believed they deserved.

Trade and Politics in the Niger River Delta[1]

The Delta and Its People

From Lagos to the Cameroons lies the low country of the Nigerian coastal plain. The Niger Delta occupies the greater part of this lowland belt and may be described as the region bounded by the Benin river on the west and the Cross river in the east, including the coastal area where the Cameroon mountains dip into the sea. It covers an area of some 270 miles along the Atlantic coast and is 120 miles in depth. The two mouths of the Niger are the Forcados and the Nun, but the rivers Benin, Brass, Bonny, Kwa-Ibo, the Cross, and other separate streams are linked to these by a labyrinth of creeks and lagoons. "I believe," wrote Mary Kingsley, "the great swamp region of the Bight of Biafra [Niger Delta] is the greatest in the world, and that in its immensity and gloom, it has a grandeur equal to that of the Himalayas."[2] There remains, however, the intriguing paradox that this area, notorious among nineteenth-century travellers for its unhealthiness, with a soil too poor "to produce a ton of oil" as Macgregor Laird put it in 1832, and practically uninhabited by the tribes of the Nigerian interior before the Portuguese adventure to the Guinea coasts began, had become by 1830 the greatest single trading area in West Africa.

It was as navigable waterways that the rivers of the Niger Delta became so important in the economic history of modern Nigeria. A canoe could be taken from Badagry on the west coast of Nigeria to Rio del Rey in the east without going into the open sea. This "Venice of West Africa," as Winwood Reade described it in 1867, linked together not only places in the Delta but towns and villages along the 2,600 miles of the Niger valley. "The Oil Rivers are chiefly remarkable among our West African Possessions," wrote Sir Harry Johnston in 1888, "for the exceptional facilities which they offer for penetrating the interior by means of large and navigable streams and by a wonderful system of natural canalization which connects all the branches of the lower Niger by means of deep creeks. There are hardly any roads existing in the Delta; the most trivial distance that a native requires to go, he generally achieves in a canoe." This water system links the Delta with "the markets and sources of production far inland."[3]

Geographically the Delta divides easily into two sections. The northern section is comparatively drier and higher than the area of swampland to the south. Even in the lowland belt the dank and humid surroundings are interspersed with vast stretches of dry land, a maze of islands intersected by creeks and rivers, and on these settlements have been built. Some of these southern colonies, being placed on points of control for internal and external commerce, quickly grew in importance and became the trading centres on the Atlantic seaboard. Just as the growing volume of Atlantic commerce drew Europe irresistibly to the lands of Guinea, so the natives of tribal areas, impelled by the urge "to traffic and exchange," flocked to the coast to do trade. From now on the coastland became the frontier of opportunity. As in medieval West Africa trade with the Arabs by way of the Sahara caravans led to an outcrop of commercial cities on the Niger bend such as Jenne, Timbuktu, Gao, and others, so the rise of Lagos, Accra, Dahomey, and the Delta states must be attributed to the development of maritime commerce. The seaboard trading communities which emerged with this commerce transcended tribal boundaries; their history belongs both to Atlantic and to tribal history.

Every item of the export trades in the ports of Biafra was a product of the tribal interior, and the carrying-trade on which the prosperity and greatness of the Delta states rested linked their fortunes decisively with those of producers in the tribal locations. The coastal communities united in their blood and institutions elements of the Atlantic and tribal societies which fashioned them. Each of the adventurous groups that pioneered these settlements was different in language and culture and in political and social organization. The Jekris of Warri (on the Benin river) could not understand the Ijaws on the Brass River. These migrants represented many Nigerian tribes in movement—Ibos, Binis, semi-Bantus from the Cameroons Highlands, Ijaws, Efiks, Ibibios, to name only a few of the most important. This fact must be noted. It helps to explain the haphazard way in which the Delta communities grew. Down to the nineteenth century this movement of population continued. Opobo, the main center of trade and politics in the eighties, was founded in 1870.

Perhaps the Niger Delta was peopled by three distinct waves of migration from the tribal hinterland. The earliest, that of the Ijaws, appears to have preceded the Portuguese advent. A detailed analysis of their tradition of origin indicates that they believe Benin to have been their ancestral habitat. This claim, which may be true of some places, must be received with reservations in the case of others until more supporting evidence is forthcoming, especially as the temptation to claim Benin origins is very strong.[4]

Throughout medieval West Africa the kingdom of Benin was the dominant power in southern Nigeria and extended its conquests from Lagos in the west, to Bonny river in the east, and northward to Idah. It was the one state with which the Portuguese, during their early visit to the Delta, maintained diplomatic relations.[5] The persistence and the universality of the claims to Benin origin in Delta traditions is evidence, at least, of the powerful influence which this kingdom exerted over the imagination of her neighbours, particularly in southern Nigeria, where her military power was felt by Ibos and Ibo-speaking peoples east of the Niger.

* * *

The most important movement of populations occurred between 1450 and 1800, and gradually converted the little Ijaw fishing villages into city-states. This second wave of migration followed the development of the slave trade and involved all the tribes to the Delta hinterland; it was a movement in which the Ibos, being numberically superior, were predominant. Points on the Delta coast, suitable as harbours for the European sailing ships, were quickly occupied. Such was the case with Bonny. According to tradition, a famous chief and hunter, Alagbariye, on his regular hunting expeditions to the coast, came upon the site on which Bonny now stands, and aware of its potentialities for directing the new trade, brought his people there to found the town. Variations of this account have been recorded by European travellers from Barbot to Bailie and Leonard.[6] The site so admirably chosen by the newcomers proved to be the best port of the Niger Delta and remained so till the nineteenth century. "By its safe and extensive anchorage," wrote Hope Waddell in 1846, "its proximity to the sea, and connection with the great rivers of Central Africa, Bonny is now the principal seat of palm oil trade as it was formerly of the slave trade" in West Africa. That it was practically uninhabited before this migration is indicated by its original name. According to tradition the first settlers on arrival found the island full of birds, mostly curlews, and called it "Okoloama" (*Okolo*, curlew; *Ama*, town; the town of curlews).[7] Similarly the occupation of the site now known as Old Calabar by the Efik tribe, who were formerly domiciled in Ibibio territory, shows that everywhere vantage points for the Atlantic trade were quickly seized upon. The port they occupied is, as a natural harbour, second only to Bonny in importance. Various accounts of the Calabar migration have been given by European travellers and traders since the seventeenth century, and in the nineteenth century a number of writers have dealt with Efik tribal history.[8] By the end of the sixteenth century the process of forming the city-states may be said to have been complete. From the seventeenth century onwards the Delta became the most important slave mart in West Africa.

Once the states were founded and the settlers' position as middlemen consolidated, fresh voluntary migrations from the hinterland to the coast were practically impossible. Yet large accessions of people continued to flow into and swell the Delta population, mainly by way of the slave trade. It was during the era of traffic in human beings that the Delta gained the bulk of her population. A study of contemporary literature will reveal that in the nineteenth century by far the greater number of the Delta population were "in a state of serfdom" and not a few great chiefs were of slave descent. Particularly was this the case with Bonny. The influx of slaves seemed to have reduced the number of freemen to an absolute minimum. In 1848 Koehler noted that "only a small proportion" of Bonny population is "free-born."[9] In 1863 Richard Burton recorded that apart from the Bonny royal family and one or two others, the rest were of slave origins and of the latter "some few are 'Bonny free' [born in Bonny] but none 'proper free.'"[10] Hugh Goldie, whose knowledge of Old Calabar was unrivalled, stated in 1890 that the "slaves greatly outnumber the freemen."[11] It would appear that marriage between slave women and freemen led inevitably to the greater absorbing the less. Few men were free from the stigma of slavery, and consequently the surviving free classes wielded power out of all proportion to their numbers.

With further migrations to the coast barred by the rise of the city-states, the lure of the great commercial highway of the Niger valley itself stimulated another migration within the hinterland, and the hardy and adventurous people from the Benin area once again established themselves at places on the riverbank favourable to the trade. The Ibo-speaking people living to the west of the Niger call themselves Ika, and the people of Arbo, Assay, and Onitsha on the west bank have a tradition that their ancestors came from Benin. This third migratory wave is generally accepted to have taken place about the middle of the seventeenth century, at a time when the Delta middlemen having fortified their privileged position on the Atlantic coast brooked no rivals. According to an Onitsha writer the date of their arrival at the present site was about 1630.[12] The tradition of these seventeenth-century migrants, which is closely related to that of Benin, shows that although they are Ibo-speaking, they were not originally Ibos. Moreover, whereas the Ibos east of the Niger have no kings—an Ibo proverb has it, "Ndi Igbo Echi Eze," i.e. "the Ibos make no kings"—yet these Ibo-speaking riverine towns to the west of the Niger have a society patterned after the semi-divine kingship of Benin. Even in the nineteenth century their Benin origin was perceptible to European observers. In 1832 Macgregor Laird said of Obi Ossai, king of Abo, "From his fondness for coal ornaments, I should imagine him to be of Benin extraction."[13]

* * *

The eastward movement into Iboland from the Benin area, stimulated by trade in the Niger valley, was paralleled by a comparable movement from the north. The northern branch was a direct result of the slave trade. The indigenous home of the Ibos, which lies mainly to the east of the Niger valley, is within the forest belt where the cavalry used by the Fulani in their annual slave-raids could not operate. These raids were conducted mainly in the plains north of the forest region, and were organized from Kano, Sokoto, Bida, and Ilorin. They inevitably led to the movement of tribes, south of the Benue, to inaccessible areas and places of safety such as the Ibo forest area provided.

> Here and there are still to be found people who have a vague tradition of their fathers having been driven from the Ilorin-region, and settled among a people of a strange tongue which they adopted. At Ukwu-Nzu are to be seen ancient ivory tusks in a shrine which it is said were deposited by an Oba or King of Benin, whose mother came from that town, which is one of the small group speaking both Ibo and a corrupt Yoruba called "Onukwumi," who say they were driven by slave-raiders in the neighbourhood of Ilorin.[14]

The effects of these migrations on Iboland and its history may now be assessed.

The density of population which was and still is a main feature of the Ibo country was due in part at least to this accession of new blood from the west and north. The Ibos might be, as has often been asserted, a prolific race, but there can be little doubt that the new migrants from the seventeenth century onward added not a little to the existing population and occupied lands the original tribe could ill afford to lose. Professor W. M. Macmillan has in various writings consistently maintained that Africa is underpopulated, and he attributes much of her backwardness to her lack of human resources necessary for taming what, according to him, is an inhospitable and poor continent.[15] This view cannot apply to Iboland.

Perhaps the most important factor conditioning Ibo history in the nineteenth century and in our own time is land hunger. Yorubaland, occupying a
greater area of land, has a smaller population. Hence the Ibos pressing against
limited land resources had, of necessity, to seek other avenues of livelihood
outside the tribal boundaries. In the nineteenth century and earlier the growth
of a large non-agricultural population in areas where the land was too small or
too poor to sustain the people gave rise to some measure of specialization
among sections of the tribe: the Aros became the middlemen of the hinterland
trade; the Ada and the Abam constituted mercenaries; Awka men were the
smiths and the doctors, while the Nkwerre people, in addition to their work in
iron, played the role of professional spies and diplomatists. If we may judge
from nineteenth-century records, in spite of this specialization, over-
population was the rule in all sections of the tribe. This reservoir of manpower
accounts for the fact that Iboland supplied the greater part of the slaves
shipped to the New World from the bights of Benin and Biafra. Professor M. J.
Herskovits has shown that there were four principal slaving areas in West
Africa: "The Senegal and the Guinea Coast" are two of the areas mentioned in
contemporary writings. "The regions about the mouth of the Niger, named
Bonny and Calabar in the documents, and the Congo are the other two." He
went on to show that "large numbers of slaves were shipped from the Niger
Delta region, as indicated by the manifests of ships loaded at Calabar and
Bonny, the principal ports. These were mainly Ibo slaves representing a people
which today inhabits a large portion of this region."[16] Contemporary sources
clearly indicate that the Delta formed the most important slave mart in West
Africa, equalling the trade of all West Africa put together. Delta ascendancy in
this traffic dated from the closing years of the seventeenth century. Between
1786 and 1800 Captain John Adams carried out scientific research into the
West African trade and people. In 1822 he wrote:

> This place [Bonny] is the wholesale market for slaves, as not fewer than 20,000
> are annually sold here; 16,000 of whom are members of one nation, called
> Heebo [the Ibos], so that this single nation . . . during the last 20 years
> [exported no less] than 320,000; and those of the same nation sold at New
> Calabar [a Delta port], probably amounted, in the same period of time, to
> 50,000 more, making an aggregate amount of 370,000 Heebos. The remaining
> part of the above 20,000 is composed of the native of the Brass coun-
> try . . . and also of Ibbibbys [Ibibios] or Quaws.[17]

These figures have been borne out by other witnesses. Macgregor Laird
put the Delta export slave trade between 1827–34 "at the lowest calculation"
as 200,000 slaves.[18]

This over-population explains the great preponderance of the same tribe
in the Delta itself, even in areas like Old Calabar and the Cameroons not
dominated by the Ibo interior. In 1853, when Creek Town was the leading
trading community of Old Calabar, Ibos formed more than half the population.[19] "The King of New Calabar . . . and Pepple King of Bonny, were both
of Ibo descent, of which also are the mass of the natives."[20] This was

confirmed by Dr. W. B. Baikie after an interview with King William Dappa Pepple at Fernando Po in 1854.[21]

Impressed by this Ibo ubiquity, Dr. J. A. B. Horton, a West African writing in 1868, declared that Iboland "is separated from the sea only by petty tribes [the Delta communities], all of which trace their origin from the great race."[22] The mistake of ascribing Ibo origins to all the Delta peoples was common among nineteenth-century writers. It can only be accounted for by the great influx of Ibo migrants which blurred the lines of the earlier migrations. The statement fails to take note of the fact that in the peopling of the Delta no one Nigerian tribe had a monopoly. Benis, Ijaws, Sobos, Jekris, Ekoi, Ibibios, Efik, and even northern Nigerian tribes were represented. The following contemporary statement on the composition of Old Calabar's population was true of almost any Delta state: "We have amongst us [in Old Calabar] captives of the slave-raids of the Tibari, as the Fulatos or Fellani [Fulani] are called here. Thus about 13 different tribes are represented in our population."[23]

To sum up, it is broadly true to say that owing to their numerical superiority[24] and consequent land hunger the Ibo migrants (enforced or voluntary) formed the bulk of the Delta population during the nineteenth century. They bequeathed their language to most of the city-states—to Bonny, Okrika, Opobo, and to a certain extent influenced the language and institutions of Old and New Calabar. But the population which evolved out of this mingling of peoples was neither Benin nor Efik, Ibo nor Ibibio. They were people apart, the product of the clashing cultures of the tribal hinterland and of the Atlantic community to both of which they belonged. The tribal Ibos called them Ndi Mili Nnu (People of the Salt Water), and so long as the frontier of trade was confined to the Atlantic seaboard so long did they remain the economic masters of these territories.[25]

NOTES

1. K. Onwuka Dike, *Trade and Politics in the Niger River Delta, 1830–1885: An Introduction to the Economic and Political History of Nigeria* (Oxford: Clarendon Press, 1956), 19–21, 24–26, 27–30. Footnotes renumbered to fit abridgement.
2. *Travels in West Africa* (1897). Cf. A. C. C. Hastings, *The Voyage of the Day Spring* (London, 1857), pp. 73–74.
3. F. O. 84/1882, Memorandum by Consul H. H. Johnston on the British Protectorate of the Oil Rivers, Part II.
4. Conclusions reached in this chapter, particularly on the question of migrations, are tentative. Until authoritative local histories of the Delta states are written, and the conflicting theories now in circulation carefully sifted and checked, one can only write in very board terms. See Jacob Egharevba, *A Short History of Benin* and his *Famous Iyases of Benin*, published locally. Chief Egharevba's dating of epic events in Benin history is arbitrary, but his knowledge of local history is wide. Cf. J. W. Blake, *Europeans in West Africa* (London, 1942), i. 78–79.

5. P. A. Talbot, *Peoples of Southern Nigeria* (London, 1926), i. 155–56. Cf. J. W. Blake, *European Beginnings in West Africa* (London, 1937), pp. 11–12, and E. Prestage, *The Portuquese Pioneers* (London, 1933), pp. 212–16.

6. Talbot, *Peoples of Southern Nigeria*, i. 238. Cf. A. Leonard, *The Lower Niger and Its Tribes* (London, 1906), pp. 22–23.

7. It is important to note that "Bonny" is the corruption of the word "Ibani" (name of the Patriarch of the founders of Okoloama) by Europeans; Ubani by the Ibos; Umani by the Ibibios; and Ebi-nya by the Andonis.

8. H. M. Waddell, *Twenty-nine Years in the West Indies and Central Africa* (London, 1863, pp. 343–61, H. Goldie, *Old Calabar and Its Mission* (Edinburgh, 1890), p. 12, and M. D. W. Jeffreys, *Old Calabar* (Calabar, 1935), pp. 1–22. The Efiks disagree with Jeffreys that they are Ibibio and with Goldie that they occupied their present site in the seventeenth century. They believe they arrived at the present site during the fifteenth century. Their traditions of origin indicate that they came from the region of the Cameroons.

9. Talbot, *Peoples of Southern Nigeria*, i. 256.

10. Ibid., p. 269.

11. Goldie, op. cit., p. 18.

12. M. O. Ibesiako, *Some Aspects of Ancient Civilization* (1937), p. 13; also Talbot, op. cit., pp. 167–9 and 234–5.

13. Laird and Oldfield, *Narrative of an Expedition into the Interior of Africa* (London, 1837), i. 101.

14. S. R. Smith, "The Ibo People" (unpublished manuscript, 1929), pp. 1–7.

15. W. M. Macmillan, *Africa Emergent* (London, 1938).

16. M. J. Herskovits, *The Myth of the Negro Past* (New York, 1941), p. 36.

17. J. Adams, *Sketches Taken During Ten Years Voyage to Africa between the Years 1786–1800* (London, n.d.), p. 38.

18. Parl. Pap. 1842, XI, Pt. I, Appendix and Index, No. 7.

19. *Church Missionary Intelligencer* (London, 1853), xiv. 255; cf. H. Goldie, *Efik Dictionary* (Edinburgh, 1874), p. 355.

20. H. Crow, *Memoirs* (London, 1830), p. 197.

21. W. B. Baikie, *An Exploring Voyage into the Rivers Quorra and Tchadda* (London, 1854), p. 355.

22. J. A.B. Horton, *West African Countries and Peoples* (London, 1868), p. 171.

23. H. Goldie, *Calabar and Its Mission* (Edinburgh, 1890), p. 18.

24. Horton, ibid., pp. 174–5, estimates Ibo population in the middle of the nineteenth century "at from 10,000,000 to 12,000,000" people. This seems an exaggeration, but confirms the common nineteenth-century belief that population density was high.

25. The term "Ijaw," still used to describe the Delta inhabitants, although convenient for purposes of classification, takes no account of the co-mingling of peoples we have just discussed. For Ibo influence on Old Calabar language, &c., see Jeffreys, op. cit., pp. 44–45. For European influence, e.g. in language, ibid., pp. 55–59:

amik	hammock	*ankisi*	handkerchief	*bhibe*	bible
abranken	blanket	*bensin*	pencil	*etombit*	tumbler
tase	thousand	*nwaba*	guava	*suap*	soap

QUESTIONS TO CONSIDER

1. According to Dike, what was the impact of slave trading on the Niger Delta region?
2. What kind of evidence does Dike use to demonstrate the population shifts in the Niger Delta prior to European rule? How does this evidence determine the kinds of things Dike is able to investigate?
3. What is Dike's view of the role of oral versus written sources in reconstructing West African history?

FOR FURTHER READING

Ajayi, J. F. A. "The Place of African History and Culture in the Process of Nation-building in Africa South of the Sahara." *Journal of Negro Education* 30 (1961): 206–13.

Dike, Kenneth O. "African History and Self-Government." *West Africa* 37 (1953): 177–78, 225–26, 251.

———. *Trade and Politics in the Niger Delta 1830-1885: An Introduction to the Political and Economic History of Nigeria.* Oxford: Clarendon, 1956.

———, and J. F. A. Ajayi. "African Historiography." In *International Encyclopedia of the Social Sciences,* edited by David L. Sills, Vol. 6, 394–400. New York: Macmillan, 1968.

Omer-Cooper, J. D. "The Contribution of the University of Ibadan to the Spread of the Study and Teaching of African History within Africa." *Journal of the Historical Society of Nigeria* 10:3 (1980): 23–31.

Smith, H. F. C. "The Benin Study." *Journal of the Historical Society of Nigeria* 1:1 (1956): 60–61.

CHAPTER 45

Charles and Mary Beard

Activists as Historians

Charles Beard
The Bettmann Archive

Mary Beard
Courtesy of DePauw University

Charles and Mary Beard, among the most influential historians in twentieth-century America, translated Marx's class analysis into an everyday feature of historical study and brought to their work a lifelong commitment to improving public policy in the service of the common good. They were at heart progressive political activists who shaped their scholarship to support their political agenda. At the time they wrote (roughly the first half of the twentieth century) scholars paid far more attention to Charles than to Mary. His ideas were the subject of fierce debate for decades. In time, however, those ideas were corrected and qualified into practical inconsequence, though he remained a major figure in the history of the discipline. By contrast, Mary Ritter Beard was initially treated as a mere appendage to her husband, but later came to be seen as one of the founders of a new woman's perspective on history.

Charles A. Beard (1874–1948) could never quite choose between the study and the soapbox. Educated at DePauw University, Oxford, and Columbia, he worked at Hull House and considered a career as a labor organizer in England before settling on the writing of history. He taught at Columbia University, but resigned over infringements of academic freedom in 1917. Thereafter he pursued a varied career as a writer of monographs, essays, and textbooks in history and political science; as a lecturer in this country and abroad; and as an adviser to municipal governments and labor groups. His historical writing combined an objective, scientific tone and method—he often used words like "science" and "data"—with a passionate conviction that history existed for the good of humankind and must be bent to the tasks of the age. For Charles Beard as for his wife, the historian's calling was to an engagement with social responsibility. Mary Ritter Beard (1876–1958) was a student with Charles Beard at DePauw. The couple was married in 1900. Like her husband, Mary Beard spent most of her life writing, speaking, and working for a number of progressive causes. Unlike Charles Beard, she never held an academic post. Her prose was florid and rich with anecdotes, in striking counterpoint to her husband's pose of objectivity.

The Beards together wrote some of the best known books of American history ever published. Their four-volume work, *The Rise of American Civilization* (1927–42), offered a sweeping analysis of all of American history. The basis of their analysis was a broad theory of economic determinism. Titles of chapters indicate their preoccupation with the material concerns of large classes of people: "The Sweep of Economic Forces," "The Triumph of Business Enterprise," and the "Rise of the National Labor Movement." The Beards' *Basic History of the United States* (1944) was a paperback best seller, the most widely read history of their half-century.

Some readers have assumed, perhaps because Charles Beard had a PhD and a professor's position and perhaps because he was male, that the couple's common writings were in fact his work, not Mary's. There is no record of the method by which the Beards produced their books, but there is every reason to believe that, since both also wrote books individually, the volumes that appeared under both their names were in fact joint products. Charles Beard was proudest of the work he and Mary did together, and frequently identified himself as the "Co-Author of *The Rise of American Civilization*." Certainly, the prose style seems a blend of their distinctness: enriched by her taste for grand phrases, disciplined by his careful structure.

The following selections are from individually written volumes, because it is these two individual studies that have had the most lasting impact on historiography, and because one can judge more clearly the contributions and preoccupations of each author by examining the products of their individual labors. Charles Beard, in *An Economic Interpretation of the Constitution of the United States* (1939), set the terms of debate about American politics for the next several decades. He argued that class factors, not high-minded public spirit, predominated in the writing and ratification of the U.S. Constitution. He argued that the framers and ratifiers of the Constitution stood to gain monetarily from that document's insistence on providing a solid base to the economy, and on repaying the government's debts. Beard's position was desperately contested, reasserted, and revised by others, on grounds of increasingly sophisticated quantitative methodology. Later scholars judged him either half right or half wrong. But Beard had enduring influence, in that almost no one is willing any longer to assert that material factors are unimportant in shaping political alignments.

Mary Beard's *Woman as Force in History* did not spark such an immediate debate when it was published in 1946. The rise of a new feminist generation after World War II, however, brought Mary Beard's ideas about women's history to the fore. There they remain today. Mary Ritter Beard was hotly at odds with feminists of the nineteenth and early twentieth centuries. She adamantly supported their goals but thought their belief in a traditional and universal subjugation of women, against which they had to do battle, was ahistorical nonsense. Despite laws and customs that circumscribed women in times past, Beard argued, up until the Industrial Revolution women found ways to act effectively in the world. Only with the rise of industry were women forced as a class into subjection. Her contention is still part of the debate over women's history today.

An Economic Interpretation of the Constitution of the United States[1]

In fact, the inquiry which follows is based upon the political science of James Madison, the father of the Constitution and later President of the Union he had done so much to create. This political science runs through all of his really serious writings and is formulated in its most precise fashion in *The Federalist* as follows: "The diversity in the faculties of men, from which the rights of property originate, is not less an insuperable obstacle to a uniformity of interests. The protection of these faculties is the first object of government. From the protection of different and unequal faculties of acquiring property, the possession of different degrees and kinds of property immediately results; and from the influence of these on the sentiments and views of the respective proprietors, ensues a division of society into different interests and parties. . . . The most common and durable source of factions has been the various and unequal distribution of property. Those who hold and those who are without property have ever formed distinct interests in society. Those who are creditors, and those who are debtors, fall under a like discrimination. A landed interest, a manufacturing interest, a mercantile interest, a moneyed interest, with many lesser interests, grow up of necessity in civilized nations and divide them into different classes, actuated by different sentiments and views. The regulation of these various and interfering interests forms the principal task of modern legislation, and involves the spirit of party and faction in the necessary and ordinary operations of the government."

Here we have a masterly statement of the theory of economic determinism in politics. Different degrees and kinds of property inevitably exist in modern society; party doctrines and "principles" originate in the sentiments and views which the possession of various kinds of property creates in the minds of the possessors; class and group divisions based on property lie at the basis of modern government; and politics and constitutional law are inevitably a reflex of those contending interests. Those who are inclined to repudiate the hypothesis of economic determinism as a European importation must, therefore, revise their views, on learning that one of the earliest, and certainly one of the clearest, statements of it came from a profound student of politics who sat in the Convention that framed our fundamental law.

The requirements for an economic interpretation of the formation and adoption of the Constitution may be stated in a hypothetical proposition which, although it cannot be verified absolutely from ascertainable data, will at once illustrate the problem and furnish a guide to research and generalization.

It will be admitted without controversy that the Constitution was the creation of a certain number of men, and it was opposed by a certain number of men. Now, if it were possible to have an economic biography of all those connected with its framing and adoption,—perhaps about 160,000 men altogether,—the materials for scientific analysis and classification would be available. Such an economic biography would include a list of the real and personal property owned by all of these men and their families: lands and houses, with incumbrances, money at interest, slaves, capital invested in shipping and manufacturing, and in state and continental securities.

Suppose it could be shown from the classification of the men who supported and opposed the Constitution that there was no line of property division at all; that is, that men owning substantially the same amounts of the same kinds of property were equally divided on the matter of adoption or rejection—it would then become apparent that the Constitution had no ascertainable relation to economic groups or classes, but was the product of some abstract causes remote from the chief business of life—gaining a livelihood.

Suppose, on the other hand, that substantially all of the merchants, money lenders, security holders, manufacturers, shippers, capitalists, and financiers and their professional associates are to be found on one side in support of the Constitution and that substantially all or the major portion of the opposition came from the non-slaveholding farmers and the debtors—would it not be pretty conclusively demonstrated that our fundamental law was not the product of an abstraction known as "the whole people," but of a group of economic interests which must have expected beneficial results from its adoption? Obviously all the facts here desired cannot be discovered, but the data presented in the following chapters bear out the latter hypothesis, and thus a reasonable presumption in favor of the theory is created.

* * *

The Economic Interests

A survey of the economic interests of the members of the Convention presents certain conclusions:

A majority of the members were lawyers by profession.

Most of the members came from towns, on or near the coast, that is, from the regions in which personalty [personal property] was largely concentrated.

Not one member represented in his immediate personal economic interests the small farming or mechanic classes.

The overwhelming majority of members, at least five-sixths, were immediately, directly, and personally interested in the outcome of their labors at Philadelphia, and were to a greater or less extent economic beneficiaries from the adoption of the Constitution.

[There follows a long list of names of participants in the Constitutional Convention, grouped according to their investments in government securities, lands for speculation, trade, manufacturing, shipping, and slaves.]

* * *

It cannot be said, therefore, that the members of the Convention were "disinterested." On the contrary, we are forced to accept the profoundly significant conclusion that they knew through their personal experiences in economic affairs the precise results which the new government that they were setting up was designed to attain.

* * *

The Economics of the Vote on the Constitution

[Following upon an exhausive catalogue (with maps) of the pattern of popular voting with regard to ratification of the Constitution, Beard writes:] Three conclusions seem warranted by the data presented in this chapter:

Inasmuch as the movement for the ratification of the Constitution centred particularly in the regions in which mercantile, manufacturing, security, and personalty interests generally had their greatest strength, it is impossible to escape the conclusion that holders of personalty saw in the new government a strength and defence to their advantage.

Inasmuch as so many leaders in the movement for ratification were large security holders, and inasmuch as securities constituted such a large proportion of personalty, this economic interest must have formed a very considerable dynamic element, if not the preponderating element, in bringing about the adoption of the new system.

The state conventions do not seem to have been more "disinterested" than the Philadelphia convention; but in fact the leading champions of the new government appear to have been, for the most part, men of the same practical type, with actual economic advantages at stake.

The opposition to the Constitution almost uniformly came from the agricultural regions, and from the areas in which debtors had been formulating paper money and other depreciatory schemes.

* * *

Conclusions

At the close of this long and arid survey—partaking of the nature of catalogue—it seems worth while to bring together the important conclusions for political science which the data presented appear to warrant.

The movement for the Constitution of the United States was originated and carried through principally by four groups of personalty interests which had been adversely affected under the Articles of Confederation: money, public securities, manufactures, and trade and shipping.

The first firm steps toward the formation of the Constitution were taken by a small and active group of men immediately interested through their personal possessions in the outcome of their labors.

No popular vote was taken directly or indirectly on the proposition to call the Convention which drafted the Constitution.

A large propertyless mass was, under the prevailing suffrage qualifications, excluded at the outset from participation (through representatives) in the work of framing the Constitution.

The members of the Philadelphia Convention which drafted the Constitution were, with a few exceptions, immediately, directly, and personally interested in, and derived economic advantages from, the establishment of the new system.

The Constitution was essentially an economic document based upon the concept that the fundamental private rights of property are anterior to government and morally beyond the reach of popular majorities.

The major portion of the members of the Convention are on record as recognizing the claim of property to a special and defensive position in the Constitution.

In the ratification of the Constitution, about three-fourths of the adult males failed to vote on the question, having abstained from the elections at which delegates to the state conventions were chosen, either on account of their indifference or their disfranchisement by property qualifications.

The Constitution was ratified by a vote of probably not more than one-sixth of the adult males.

It is questionable whether a majority of the voters participating in the elections for the state conventions in New York, Massachusetts, New Hampshire, Virginia, and South Carolina, actually approved the ratification of the Constitution.

The leaders who supported the Constitution in the ratifying conventions represented the same economic groups as the members of the Philadelphia Convention; and in a large number of instances they were also directly and personally interested in the outcome of their efforts.

In the ratification, it became manifest that the line of cleavage for and against the Constitution was between substantial personalty interests on the one hand and the small farming and debtor interests on the other.

The Constitution was not created by "the whole people" as the jurists have said; neither was it created by "the states" as Southern nullifiers long contended; but it was the work of a consolidated group whose interests knew no state boundaries and were truly national in their scope.

Woman as Force in History[2]

Everybody's Interest: Man and Woman

Fatefully interlocked with all the visible, vocal, and revolutionary upheavals which, in our own time, have been ripping open and transforming great societies inherited from the nineteenth century and its long past are the relations between men and women. Even underground movements for counter-revolutions, revolutions against revolutions, take vitality from these relations. Thrust into the global violence which marks our age is the dynamism of women who, with men, have set the world on fire and helped to frame plans for its reconstruction. . . .

The competition among the revolutionists for mastery in the human world has been emphatically marked by a competition in conceptions of sex relations. Three views of perfection in these relations have been struggling for victory in this rivalry.

One is the view that the "woman's problem," a definition respecting woman's place in society satisfactory to herself, can only be solved by complete equality with men, and that the equality can only be established under Communism. A second view is that woman must find her greatest happiness and contribute most to the State by limiting her ambitions to domesticity and still more narrowly to child-bearing, in order that the population rate may be high enough to keep a given nation secure against crowded societies on its borders, and strong enough within for aggressive action when desired against neighbors or more distant communities; this is the ideology of Fascism. The third view is that woman must have the right to choose her way of life even to the point of self-centered interests; this is one among the ideologies of Democracy.

*   *   *

The Haunting Idea: Its Nature and Origin

It is difficult, admittedly, to trace all the mental processes which converged into the idea that women were a subject sex or nothing at all—in any past or in the total past—until they began to win "emancipation" in our age of enlightenment. But, if one works backward in history hunting for the origin of this idea, one encounters, near the middle of the nineteenth century, two illuminating facts: (1) the idea was first given its most complete and categorical form by American women who were in rebellion against what they regarded as restraints on their liberty; (2) the authority whom they most commonly cited in support of systematic presentations of the idea was Sir William Blackstone of *Commentaries on the Laws of England*—the laws of the mother country adopted in part by her offspring in the new world. The first volume of this work appeared in 1765 and the passage from that volume which was used with unfailing reiteration by insurgent women in America was taken from Blackstone's chapter entitled "Of Husband and Wife."

That passage (7th edition, 1775) ran as follows: "By marriage, the husband and wife are one person in law; that is, the very being or legal existence of the woman is suspended during the marriage, or at least is incorporated and consolidated into that of the husband; under whose wing, protection, and *cover*, she performs every thing."

*   *   *

Such was the nature of Blackstone's dictum to the effect that woman was civilly dead after she married, that her personality was merged into that of her husband and lord. To what extent and with what meaning was it true, if true at all?

*   *   *

For the moment it may be said that there are some truths in it, that it contains a great deal of misleading verbalism, and that in upshot it is false. We must remember, moreover, very distinctly, that he was, at this point in his *Commentaries*, dealing solely with the rights or rightlessness of the married woman only, with her position, as he said, "in law." Now the words "in law" actually meant in common law. Blackstone so understood it and understood it as a qualification on all the passage. So did his readers who were trained in the law.

The common law was, however, only one branch of English law, one of the laws of England, or bodies of law. Other bodies of law were acts of

Parliament often drastically modifying the common law and old customs left undisturbed by the common and statutory laws; and, as Blackstone remarked casually, "over and above" these laws was Equity, "frequently called in to assist, to moderate, and to explain the other laws."

It was Equity administered by a special court, having no jury, that provided, in the name of justice, remedies for wrongs for which the Common Law afforded no remedies. Equity enforced trusts and other understandings that assured to married women rights of property denied to them by the Common Law. . . .

Besides, there were the private practices and agreements of men and women in the ordinary affairs of daily living, which as a rule prevailed undisturbed unless perchance became involved in actions before the courts and were declared illegal, contrary to law or good morals.

*   *   *

Did Blackstone willfully intend to mislead his readers into believing that the legal status of married women in England in 1765 was correctly and fully described in his statement on husband and wife?

Whatever his intentions Blackstone could have avoided the charge of distortion by including in his chapter on husband and wife another statement correctly presenting the rules of equity jurisprudence under which the wife could be fully protected in the enjoyment of her separate property rights.

*   *   *

Equality as the Escape from Subjection

The dogma of woman's complete historic subjection to man must be rated as one of the most fantastic myths ever created by the human mind.

Leaders of the woman movement at some times and in some places stood fast by the contention in the Seneca Falls Declaration of Sentiments that the overweening object of man had been to hold woman in servitude to him and that the "history of mankind" is a history of "man's repeated injuries and usurpations," at least as far as women are concerned. At such times and places they represented women as rightless in long history and passive in that condition. Yet at other times and places, confronted with the question as to how a creature who had been nothing or nearly nothing in all history could suddenly, if ever, become something—something like man, his equal—a few leaders in the woman movement used history to show what force women had displayed in history.

This contradiction is manifest in the volumes of the huge *History of Woman Suffrage* put together from the archives of the campaign for woman's enfranchisement from 1848 to the 1880's by Susan B. Anthony, Elizabeth Cady Stanton, Ida Husted Harper, and other workers in that movement. In the first volume the dilemma is disclosed. The first chapters of that volume deal almost entirely with the great "achievements" of women in times past, from the Abbess of Whitby in the ninth century to George Sand, Florence Nightengale, and Clara Barton in the nineteenth century. The second chapter is devoted entirely to women in journalism and it presents historical facts about important women editors, publishers, and writers from colonial times in America to the very moment when the very doctrine of subjection was being stoutly asserted in the best Blackstonian style. In Chapter IV, so closely following the accounts of women, single and married, who were not mere victims of men's "tyranny," occurs the Seneca Falls Declaration against man the tyrant and the attendant Resolutions of resistance to his mastery. Yet throughout the mammoth volumes of this *History of Woman Suffrage,* a record setting forth women's labors in this cause, are scattered extensive references to women as writers, speakers, agitators, business enterprisers, doctors, teachers, and other types of non-domestic activists, most of whom were wives and mothers living on good terms with their husbands and sons.

*   *   *

Theory of Subjection Tested by Long Legal History

In summary, what does modern critical scholarship find in the long review of English legal history prior to 1765? It finds men and women, in many fundamental respects, on a similar footing with regard to their property holdings under the requirements of a strong feudal State. It finds men and women making powerful efforts, individually and together, to protect their families against the encroachments of that State. It finds an early and persistent recognition, especially with the development of Equity, of justice as the ideal for adjusting and determining the relations of men and women as members of families and communities, and as individuals.

This is not to deny that there were discriminations between men and women in the feudal law—civil and criminal—which were in various cases carried forward through the centuries. There were many discriminations against women in both branches of the law; but many responsibilities, which may in some instances be called "unfair" discriminations, were imposed on men, independently and in connection with discriminations against women. To the enlightened conscience of modern times, several of the discriminations against women, such as the right of the husband to inflict punishment on his wife, are barbaric; but even as to that it must be remembered that the husband was at law responsible for his wife's behavior and women were by no means all peaceable by nature. Other discriminations associated with the feudal state and manners—now deemed forms of tyranny—should more properly be regarded as anachronisms. Yet all of the discriminations combined do not add up to the utter subjection of women, single and married, under the sovereign power of men at law, to say nothing of practice, in feudal economy or as it was revolutionized and feudal impulses were checked by changes in economy and improvements in morals.

QUESTIONS TO CONSIDER

1. In each case, how might Charles and Mary Beard's respective political commitments have affected the questions they chose to investigate and their interpretations?

2. The Beards have been accused of being interpretation-rich and data-poor, even by scholars who share their conclusions. Can you see evidence for or against this charge?
3. How might Charles Beard, as an economic determinist, have written about women as a force in history? How might Mary Ritter Beard, as a feminist historian, have interpreted the U.S. Constitution?

FOR FURTHER READING

Beale, Howard K., ed. *Charles A. Beard: An Appraisal.* Lexington, KY: University of Kentucky Press, 1954.

Beard, Charles A. *American Foreign Policy in the Making, 1932–1940.* New Haven, CT: Yale University Press, 1946.

_____ . *The Economic Basis of Politics.* New York: Knopf, 1922.

_____ . *An Economic Interpretation of the Constitution of the United States.* New York: Free Press, 1913.

_____ . *Economic Origins of Jeffersonian Democracy.* New York: Macmillan, 1915.

_____ . *The Enduring Federalist.* Garden City, NY: Doubleday, 1948.

_____ . *The Nature of the Social Sciences.* New York: Scribner's, 1934.

Beard, Charles A., and Mary R. Beard. *A Basic History of the United States.* New York: Doran, 1944.

_____ . *History of the United States.* New York: Macmillan, 1921.

_____ . *The Making of American Civilization.* New York: Macmillan, 1937.

_____ . *The Rise of American Civilization.* 4 vols. New York: Macmillan, 1927–42.

Beard, Mary Ritter. *The Force of Women in Japanese History.* Washington, DC: Public Affairs Press, 1953.

_____ . *On Understanding Women.* New York: Longmans, Greene, 1931.

_____ . *A Short History of the American Labor Movement.* New York: Worker's Education Bureau of America, 1920.

_____ . *Woman as Force in History.* New York: Macmillan, 1946.

_____ . *Woman's Work in Municipalities.* New York: National Municipal League, 1915.

Cott, Nancy F. *A Woman Making History: Mary Ritter Beard Through Her Letters.* New Haven, CT: Yale University Press, 1991.

Hofstadter, Richard. *The Progressive Historians: Turner, Beard, Parrington.* New York: Knopf, 1968.

Lane, Ann J., ed. *Mary Ritter Beard: A Sourcebook.* New York: Schocken, 1977.

Turoff, Barbara K. *Mary Beard as Force in History.* Dayton, OH: Wright State University, 1979.

NOTES

1. Charles A. Beard, *An Economic Interpretation of the Constitution of the United States* (New York: Free Press, 1913), 14–17, 149–51, 290–91, 324–35. Footnotes have been omitted.
2. Mary R. Beard, *Woman as Force in History: A Study in Traditions and Realities* (New York: Macmillan, 1946), 1–2, 78–84, 155–56, 203–4. Footnotes have been omitted.

CHAPTER 46

Marc Bloch

Annaliste

Marc Bloch
© *Gary Olsen*

Marc Bloch (1886–1944) was the most visible of a coterie of historians who changed the emphasis in historical research in Europe and America in the twentieth century. The *Annales* school, so-called after the journal Bloch cofounded with Lucien Febvre in 1929, relied heavily on the other social sciences—economics, psychology, anthropology, sociology, and especially geography—for method and technique. It refocused historical studies from an emphasis on politics and diplomacy to a concern for the nameless, faceless masses and the everyday quality of past lives. Gradually, this social history came to dominate academic research and even to show up in books written for a popular audience.

Bloch came from an academic family. Both his father and grandfather were teachers and scholars, while his great grandfather had been an important rabbi. The family was originally from Strasbourg, but when Alsace became German after the Franco-Prussian War in 1870, they moved to Paris. Bloch was an intense lover of France and, like his ancestors for five generations, patriotically went to war when called up. He entered World War I as a sergeant and ended up a captain. Wounded once, almost killed by typhoid fever, and decorated four times, Bloch emerged from the war with a profound respect for the common enlisted men but with near contempt for the arrogance and incompetence of most officers. Bloch joyfully participated in the French reoccupation of Strasbourg and was drafted even before he demobilized to help in the re-Frenchification of the University there. From 1919 to 1936 he remained teaching medieval history at Strasbourg. He then taught at Paris, volunteered for the army in 1939–40, was evacuated from Dunkirk and later repatriated to France. After the French capitulation to the Germans in June 1940, Bloch taught at provincial universities at Clermont and Montpelier. Increasing anti-Semitic restrictions by the Vichy regime found Bloch striving to feed and protect his large family—at one point he sought to secure passage to the United States unsuccessfully. Perhaps naively, Bloch thought that his family's five generations of service in the French military or his own status as a war hero would protect him from the worst of his neighbors' anti-Semitism, but as the Germans increasingly dominated even the southern part of France, he joined the Resistance. Assigned a significant coordinator's role in Lyons, he was betrayed and captured in March 1944, tortured, and shot shortly after the D-Day invasion.

The *Annales* school has a complex series of interrelated components. One aspect is an appreciation for highly detailed studies of small geographic regions. A famous example is the study of one small village in the Pyrenees during the Albigensian heresy of the Middle Ages. Another emphasis is on interdisciplinary studies, perhaps stimulated at Strasbourg where faculty offices were in a single building and so facilitated interdisciplinary exchange. The history of commoners and the use of a variety of means to ferret out the structures of their lives is deemed significant. Especially important was the archeological reconstruction of the tools used in daily toil and an understanding of climates and weather.

Although Bloch was not a cultural materialist (he recognized, for example, that the disappearance of slavery in medieval Europe was due primarily to theological ideas), he thought that an understanding of the material condition of life was vital to reconstruct the life of the non-nobles and the politically insignificant. Thus his famous discussion of feudal society rested less than other scholars' on legal and institutional descriptions and more on how the system actually functioned on the ground. Likewise anyone attempting to do agrarian history should not only be a good historian who can work with texts but also be familiar with farming practices and realities to interpret those texts, a "dirty hands" approach.

The *Annalistes* also like comparative history—sometimes comparing developments across regions in the same time period, sometimes comparing the same region in several time periods. Bloch's posthumously published *Seigneurie francaise et manor anglais* (Paris, 1960) compared manorialism in its English and French varieties. In contrast to narrative history, historians in the *Annales* tradition favor a variety of analytic approaches. Whereas a narrative historian might supply battlefield maps, the Annaliste would show maps of medieval drainage schemes in Picardy and include a statistical table of estimated yearly rainfall reconstructed from records of the wine harvest or tree ring analysis.

Bloch was revered by European and American historians for two generations after World War II, for his heroism, for the journal he helped found, and for his vision of history. He enunciated that vision clearly in an uncompleted set of essays, *The Historian's Craft*. The fullest expression of his mode of historical writing is his magisterial *Feudal Society*. The table of contents reads like a sociological survey of the whole of Europe over several hundred years. It moves from the invasions of Muslims and Northmen, to material conditions and economic characteristics, to modes of feeling and thought, to kinship ties, to vassalage, to the nature of the fief, to the ties that bind society's lower orders, to social classes, to political organization. In the selection that follows, Bloch describes one of the central institutions of feudalism: the vassal tie. Here he exhibits the broad generalizations, the comparisons between regions and time periods, and the humane personal interest that are the hallmarks of his work.

Feudal Society[1]
The Vassal Tie

1. The Man of Another Man

To be the "man of another man": in the vocabulary of feudalism, no combination of words was more widely used or more comprehensive in meaning. In both the Romance and the Germanic tongues it was used to express personal dependence *per se* and applied to persons of all social classes regardless of the precise legal nature of the bond. The count was the "man" of the king, as the serf was the "man" of his manorial lord. Sometimes even in the same text, within the space of a few lines, radically different social stations were thus evoked. An instance of this, dating from the end of the eleventh century, is a petition of Norman nuns, complaining that their "men"—that is to say their peasants—were forced by a great baron to work at the castles of his "men," meaning the knights who were his vassals. The ambiguity disturbed no one, because, in spite of the gulf between the orders of society, the emphasis was on the fundamental element in common: the subordination of one individual to another.

If, however, the principle of this human nexus permeated the whole life or society, the forms which it assumed were none the less very diverse—with sometimes almost imperceptible transitions, from the highest to the humblest. Moreover there were many variations from country to country. It will be useful if we take as a guiding thread one of the most significant of these relationships of dependence, the tie of vassalage; studying it first in the most highly "feudalized" zone of Europe, namely, the heart of the former Carolingian Empire, northern France, the German Rhineland and Swabia; and endeavoring, before we embark on any inquiries into its origins, to describe the most striking features of the institution at the period of its greatest expansion, that is to say, from the tenth to the twelfth century.

2. Homage in the Feudal Era

Imagine two men face to face; one wishing to serve, the other willing or anxious to be served. The former puts his hands together and places them, thus joined, between the hands of the other man—a plain symbol of submission, the significance of which was sometimes further emphasized by a kneeling posture. At the same time, the person proffering his hands utters a few words—a very short declaration—by which he acknowledges himself to be the "man" of the person facing him. Then chief and subordinate kiss each other on the mouth, symbolizing accord and friendship. Such were the gestures—very simple ones, eminently fitted to make an impression on minds so sensitive to visible things—which served to cement one of the strongest social bonds known in the feudal era. Described or mentioned in the texts a hundred times, reproduced on seals, miniatures, bas-reliefs, the ceremony was called "homage" (in German, *Mannschaft*). The superior party, whose position was created by this act, was described by no other term than the very general one of "lord." Similarly, the subordinate was often simply called the "man" of this lord; or sometimes, more precisely, his "man of mouth and hands" (*homme de bouche et de mains*). But more specialized words were also employed, such as "vassal" or, till the beginning of the twelfth century at least, "commended man" (*commendé*).

In this form the rite bore no Christian impact. Such an omission, probably explained by the remote Germanic origins of the symbolism, in due course ceased to be acceptable to a society which had come to regard a promise as scarcely valid unless God were guarantor. Homage itself, so far as its form was concerned, was never modified. But, apparently from the Carolingian period, a second rite—an essentially religious one—was superimposed on it; laying his hand on the Gospels or on relics, the new vassal swore to be faithful to his master. This was called fealty, *foi* in French (in German *Treue*, and, formerly, *Hulde*).

The ceremony therefore had two stages, but they were by no means of equal importance. For in the act of fealty there was nothing specific. In a disturbed society, where mistrust was the rule and the appeal to divine sanctions appeared to be one of the few restraints with any efficacy at all, there were a great many reasons why the oath of fealty should be exacted frequently. Royal or seignorial officials of every rank took it on assuming their duties; prelates often demanded it from their clergy; and manorial lords, occasionally, from their peasants. Unlike homage, which bound the whole man at a single stroke and was generally held to be incapable of renewal, this promise—almost a commonplace affair—could be repeated several times to the same person. There were therefore many acts of fealty without homage: we do not know of any acts of homage without fealty—at least in the feudal period. Furthermore, when the two rights were combined, the pre-eminence of homage was shown by the fact that it was always given first place in the ceremony. It was this alone that brought the two men together in close union; the fealty of the vassal was a unilateral undertaking to which there was seldom a corresponding oath on the part of the lord. In a word, it was the act of homage that really established the relation of vassalage under its dual aspect of dependence and protection.

The tie thus formed lasted, in theory, as long as the two lives which it bound together, but as soon as one or other of these was terminated by death it was automatically dissolved. We shall see that in practice vassalage very soon became, in most cases, hereditary; but this *de facto* situation allowed the legal rule to remain intact to the end. It mattered little that the son of the deceased vassal usually performed his homage to the lord who had accepted his father's or that the heir of the previous lord almost invariably received the homage of his father's vassals: the ceremony had none the less to be repeated with every change of the individual persons concerned. Similarly, homage could not be offered or accepted by proxy; the examples to the contrary all date from a very late period, when the significance of the old forms was already almost lost. In France, so far as it applied to the king, this privilege was legalized only under Charles VII and even then not without many misgivings. The social bond seemed to be truly inseparable from the almost physical contact which the formal act created between the two men.

The general duty of aid and obedience incumbent on the vassal was an obligation that was undertaken by anyone who became the "man" of another man. But it shaded off at this point into special obligations, which we shall discuss in detail later on. The nature of these corresponded to conditions of rank and manner of life that were rather narrowly defined, for despite great differences of wealth and prestige, vassals were not recruited indiscriminately from all levels of society. Vassalage was the form of dependence peculiar to the upper classes who were characterized above all by the profession of arms and the exercise of command. At least, that is what it had become. In order to obtain a clear idea of the nature of vassalage, it will be well at this point to inquire how it had progressively disentangled itself from a whole complex of personal relationships.

3. The Origins of Ties of Personal Dependence

To seek a protector, or to find satisfaction in being one—these things are common to all ages. But we seldom find them giving rise to new legal institutions save in civilizations where the rest of the social framework is giving way. Such was the case in Gaul after the collapse of the Roman Empire.

Consider, for example, the society of the Merovingian period. Neither the State nor the family any longer provided adequate protection. The village community was barely strong enough to maintain order within its own boundaries; the urban community scarcely existed. Everywhere, the weak man felt the need to be sheltered by someone more powerful. The powerful man, in his turn, could not maintain his prestige or his fortune or even ensure his own safety except by securing for himself, by persuasion or coercion, the support of subordinates bound to his service. On the one hand, there was the urgent quest for a protector; on the other, there were usurpations of authority, often by violent means. And as notions of weakness and strength are always relative, in many cases the same man occupied a dual role—as a dependent of a more powerful man and a protector of humbler ones. Thus there began to be built up a vast system of personal relationships whose intersecting threads ran from one level of the social structure to another.

In yielding thus to the necessities of the moment, these generations of men had no conscious desire to create new social forms, nor were they aware of doing so. Instinctively each strove to turn to account the resources provided by the existing social structure and if, unconsciously, something new was eventually created, it was in the process of trying to adapt the old. Moreover, the society that emerged from the invasions had inherited a strange medley of institutions and practices in which the traditions of the Germans were intermingled with the legacy of Rome, and with that of the peoples whom Rome had conquered without ever completely effacing their native customs. Let us not at this point fall into the error of seeking either in vassalage or, more generally, in feudal institutions a particular ethnological origin; let us not imprison ourselves once more in the famous dilemma: Rome or "the forests of Germany." Such phantasies must be left to those ages which—knowing less than we do of the creative power of evolution—could believe, with Boulain-villiers, that the nobility of the seventeenth century was descended almost entirely from Frankish warriors, or which, like the young Guizot, could interpret the French Revolution as a *revanche* of the Gallo-Romans. In the same way the old physiologists imagined in the sperm a fully formed *homunculus*. The lesson of the feudal vocabulary is nevertheless clear. This vocabulary is, as we shall see, full of elements of diverse origin subsisting side by side, some borrowed from the speech of the conquered people or that of the conquerors, or newly coined, like "homage" itself. Such a vocabularly is surely a faithful reflection of a social régime which, though itself deeply moulded by a composite past, was above all the product of contemporary conditions. "Men," says the Arab proverb, "resemble their own times more than they do their father."

Among the lowly people who sought a protector, the most unfortunate became simply slaves, thereby binding their descendants as well as them-selves. Many others, however, even among the most humble, were anxious to maintain their status as free men; and the persons who received their allegiance had as a rule little reason to oppose such a wish. For in this age when personal ties had not yet strangled the institutions of government, to enjoy what was called "freedom" meant essentially to belong by undisputed right to the people ruled by the Merovingian kings—to the *populus Francorum*, as contemporaries called it, lumping together under the same name the conquerors and the conquered. As a result, the two terms "free" and "frank" came to be regarded as synonymous and continued to be so regarded through the ages. To be surrounded with dependents who enjoyed the judicial and military privileges characteristic of free men was, for a chief, in many respects more advantageous than to command only a horde of slaves.

These dependent relationships "befitting a freeman" (*ingenuili ordine*)—as they are called in a formula from Tours—were described by terms derived for the most part from classical Latin. For through all the vicissitudes of an eventful history the ancient practices of the patron-client relationship had never disappeared from the Roman or Romanised world. In Gaul especially they took root all the more easily since they were in keeping with the customs of these subject populations. Before the coming of the legions there was no Gaulish chieftan who was not surrounded by a group of retainers, either peasants or warriors. We are very ill informed as to how far these ancient native practices survived the Roman conquest and lived on under the veneer of an ecumenical civilization. Nevertheless, everything leads to the conclusion that, though profoundly modified by the pressure of a very different political régime, they continued to exist in one form or another. In any case, the troubles of later centuries in every part of the Empire made it more than ever necessary to look for aid to powers closer at hand and more effective than the institutions of public law. In the fourth or the fifth century, at all levels of society, if one wished to protect oneself from the harsh exactions of the tax-collector, to influence in one's own favour the decisions of the judges or merely to ensure for oneself an honourable career, one could do no better— even though free and perhaps a man of position—than attach oneself to someone more highly placed. Ignored or even prohibited by public law, these ties had no legal force. They constituted none the less one of the strongest of social bonds. In making increasing use of pacts of protection and obedience, the inhabitants of what had now become Frankish Gaul were therefore not aware that they were doing anything for which there was no ready term in the language of their ancestors.

The old word *clientela*, except as a literary anachronism, fell into disuse in the later centuries of the Empire. But in Merovingian Gaul, as at Rome, one continued to say of the chief that he "took charge" (*suscipere*) of the subordi- nate whose "patron" he thereby became; and of the subordinate that he "commended" himself—that is to say "entrusted" himself—to his protector. The obligations thus accepted were generally called "service" (*servitium*). Not so long before, the word would have horrified a free man. In classical Latin it was used only in the sense of slavery; the only duties compatible with freedom were *officia*. But by the end of the fourth century *servitium* had lost this original taint.

Germania also made its contribution. The protection which the powerful man extended to his weaker neighbour was often termed *mundium*, *mundeburdum*—which became *maimbour* in medieval French—or again *mitium*, this latter term expressing more particularly the right and the duty of representing the dependent in judicial matters. All these were Germanic words ill-disguised by the Latin dress in which they appear in the charters.

These various expressions were almost interchangeable and were used regardless of whether the contracting parties were of Roman or of barbarian origin. The relationships of private dependence were not subject to the principle of the "personality of laws," since they were still on the fringe of all legal systems. The fact that they were not officially controlled rendered them all the more capable of being adapted to an infinite variety of circumstances. The king himself, in his capacity as leader of his people, owed his support to all his subjects without discrimination and was entitled in turn to their allegiance as confirmed by the universal oath of free men; nevertheless he granted to a certain number of them his personal *maimbour*. A wrong done to persons thus placed "within his word" was regarded as an offence against the king himself and was in consequence treated with exceptional severity. Within this rather ill-assorted group there arose a more restricted and more distin- guished body of royal retainers who were called the *leudes* of the prince, that is to say his "men"; in the anarchy of later Merovingian times, they more than once controlled both king and state. As in Rome, a little earlier, the young man of good family who wished to get on in the world "entrusted" himself to a powerful man—if his future had not already in his childhood been assured in this way by a far-sighted father. In spite of the prohibitions of councils, many ecclesiastics of every rank did not scruple to seek the protection of laymen. But it was apparently in the lower strata of society that the relationships of subordination were most widely diffused as well as most exacting. The only formula of "commendation" that we possess shows us a poor devil who only accepts a master because "he lacks the wherewithal to feed and clothe himself." There was no distinction of words, however, and no difference—at least no very clear one—in conception between these diverse aspects of dependence, despite all differences of social status.

Whatever the status of the person who commended himself, he seems almost invariably to have taken an oath to his master. Was it also customary for him to make a formal act of submission? We do not know with any certainty. The official legal systems, which are concerned only with the old institutions regulating the affairs of the people and the family, are silent on this point. As to the agreements themselves, they were hardly ever put in writing, which alone provides definite evidence. From the second half of the eighth century, however, the documents begin to mention the ceremony of the joined hands. The very first example shown us is a case where the persons involved are of the highest rank, the protégé being a foreign prince, the protector the king of the Franks; but we must not be deceived by this one-sidedness on the part of those who compiled the records. The ceremony did not seem worth describing unless, being associated with matters of high policy, it was one of the features of an interview between rulers; in the normal course of life it was regarded as a commonplace event and so was passed over in silence. Undoubtedly the ceremony had been in use for a considerable time before it thus suddenly appeared in the texts. The similarity of the custom among the Franks, the Anglo-Saxons and the Scandinavians attests its Germanic origin. But the symbolism was too obvious for it not to be readily adopted by the whole population. In England and among the Scandinavians we find it being used indiscriminately to express very different forms of subordination—that of the slave to the master, that of the free companion to the warrior chieftain. Everything points to the conclusions that this was also the case for a long time in Frankish Gaul. The gesture served to conclude protective contracts of various kinds; sometimes performed, sometimes omitted, it did not seem indispensable to any of them. An institution requires a terminology without too much ambiguity and a relatively stable ritual, but in the Merovingian world personal relationships remained on the level of customary procedure.

QUESTIONS TO CONSIDER

1. How does Bloch typify the relationship between lord and vassal? Do similar relationships exist in the modern world?
2. How is Bloch's portrayal of social forces similar to and different from those by Ibn Khaldûn (Chapter 23), Karl Marx (39), and Charles Beard (45)?
3. Bloch gives full weight to historical forces and almost no weight to the actions of individuals. What are the strengths and weaknesses of this approach?

FOR FURTHER READING

Annales: Economies, Sociétés, Civilisations (formerly *Annales d'histoire économique et sociale*).

Bloch, Marc. *French Rural History.* Trans. J. Sondheimer. Berkeley, CA: University of California Press, 1966.

_____ . *The Historian's Craft.* Trans. Peter Putnam. New York: Knopf, 1953.

_____ . *Land and Work in Medieval Europe: Selected Papers by Marc Bloch.* Trans. J. E. Anderson. Berkeley, CA: University of California Press, 1967.

Burke, Peter. *The French Historical Revolution: The Annales School, 1929–89.* Stanford, CA: Stanford University Press, 1990.

Febvre, Lucien. *The Coming of the Book: The Impact of Printing, 1450–1800.* Trans. David Gerard. London: NLB, 1976.

_____ . *Life in Renaissance France.* Trans. Marian Rothstein. Cambridge, MA: Harvard University Press, 1977.

_____ . *The Problem of Unbelief in the Sixteenth Century.* Trans. Bernice Gottlieb. Cambridge, MA: Harvard University Press, 1982.

Fink, Carole. *Marc Bloch: A Life in History.* Cambridge, UK: Cambridge University Press, 1989.

Ladurie, Emmanuel LeRoy. *Montaillou: The Promised Land of Error.* Trans. Barbara Bray. New York: George Braziller, 1978.

Lefebvre, Georges. *The Coming of the French Revolution.* Trans. R. R. Palmer. Princeton, NJ: Princeton University Press, 1989; orig. 1947.

_____ . *The French Revolution.* 2 vols. Trans. John Hall Stewart and James Fruglietti. New York: Columbia University Press, 1962–64.

Stoianovich, Traian. *French Historical Method: The Annales Paradigm.* Ithaca, NY: Cornell University Press, 1976.

NOTES

1. Marc Bloch, *Feudal Society*, 2 vols., trans. L. A. Manyon (Chicago: University of Chicago Press, 1961), I:145–51. Footnotes have been omitted.

CHAPTER 47

Yanagita Kunio

Historian of the People

Japanese Woman Farm Worker
Hulton-Deutsch Collection/Corbis

While Marc Bloch was in France constructing his *magnum opus* on the role of broad historical forces, half a world away Yanagita Kunio (1875–1962) was revolutionizing Japanese historical writing. A generation before Europeans or Americans caught a similar vision, Yanagita Kunio ended the single-minded preoccupation of Japanese scholars with the history of politics and the military, and wrote powerfully the history of everyday people.

Yanagita was a child of some privilege, the son of a medical doctor and a graduate of Japan's finest schools. Upon graduation from Tokyo Imperial University in 1900, he married into the wealthy Yanagita family, took his wife's name (a common practice in Japan), and embarked on a career as a government bureaucrat. Two decades later he switched to journalism, and then after 1930 devoted himself almost entirely to scholarship. Yanagita's main contribution was to bring British folklore studies to Japan. Indeed, his folklore writings have become the subject of a distinct subfield in Japanese universities and have their own journal. The best known of these is *Tono Monogatari* (1910), translated as *The Legends of Tono*. Yanagita's collections of folk stories comprise dozens of volumes.

Yanagita Kunio also turned his attention to Japanese history. Unlike Arai Hakuseki, Motoori Norinaga, or other great Japanese historians, Yanagita cared not a whit for politics, warfare, or tales of heroism. His interest was in the lives of everyday people, whom he regarded as the primary actors in history. Yanagita used anthropological methods to illuminate historical questions a generation and more before Americans like Lawrence Levine won acclaim for the same achievement.

Yanagita set forth his historical method in *Kyodo Seikatsu no Kenkyu Ho* (*Research Methods for the Study of Community Daily Life*, 1935). After choosing a subject, he would gather hundreds of stories and oral histories through interviews with ordinary people; collect the stories to publish as a separate literary volume; then write a volume of historical analysis describing the themes he found in the interviews and comparing them with the interpretations of historians who worked with literary sources. In the historical volumes, he eschewed personal narrative and described broad sociological trends. This was his method in many books of history, including *Kaijo no Michi* (*A Road on the Sea*, 1961), which revolutionized thinking about the peopling of the Japanese islands by noting cultural similarities with Pacific peoples and positing migration routes from the Pacific Islands; *Nihon Nomin Shi* (*The History of Japanese Common People*); and *Meiji Taisho Shi: Shiso Hen* (*The History of Common Life in the Meiji and Taisho Periods*, 1931).

The selection that follows is taken from *Japanese Manners and Customs in the Meiji Era*. The volume describes the rapid changes experienced by ordinary Japanese in the social upheavals that attended the end of feudalism and isolation and the rise of a modern state in touch with the outside world. The book describes such mundane issues as changes in language, food, clothing, housing, family structure, the roles of children and adults, funerals and other ceremonies, travel, and religion. The section reproduced here shows Yanagita's sympathy for the lot of women in a rapidly industrializing society.

Several other twentieth-century Japanese historians are worthy of note. Two in particular are Naito Konan (1866–1934) and Ienaga Saburo (1913–   ). Naito was the dean of Chinese historical studies, a field in which Japan is a world leader. He insisted in the 1910s and '20s that the historian must go beyond simple dynastic labels and seek the underlying changes in Chinese society and economics, and so construct a more meaningful periodization. This idea anticipated by 50 years a similar development in Euroamerican studies of China. Ienaga is best known in the West for his criticism of Japan's imperial aggression in the 1930s and '40s and his unflinching description of World War II in Japan and its colonies.

Japanese Manners and Customs in the Meiji Era[1]

The Bride's Lot

The old system of village marriage had been based on a spirit of mutual cooperation among the members of community, and since women as a group had performed important tasks, their position had been relatively strong. During the late Tokugawa and early Meiji periods, however, there was pronounced tendency for each family to become a separate unit, dependent solely on its own efforts for survival. As this occurred, the position of the head of the house became much more important, and his authority virtually absolute. Herein lies the basic cause of the miserable existence led by so many young brides in this epoch. After going to live at the house of a father-in-law, a young woman had to be moulded to fit his idea of what a wife should be. Her conduct had to convince him that she would be a credit to his house. She was directly under the control of her mother-in-law, and the latter was usually blamed for her sufferings, but in a broader sense, the bride's basic difficulty was that her marriage was subordinated to what her elders conceived of as the benefit of the tribe. The relationship between herself and her husband became a thing of secondary importance. Often a young bride would be sent back to her home before there had been time to tell whether she and her husband would be compatible or not. The divorce rate in the middle years of the Meiji period was scandalous, and while there were numerous other reasons, one of the main ones was certainly that marriage arrangements were transferred from the hands of young people to those of their parents.

Ironically, wedding celebrations became more festive than ever, and the bride was increasingly beautiful and doll-like. There were no doubt many young women who realized that their married life would not be as joyful and splendid as their weddings, but there were few who did not prefer to submit to the accepted conditions rather than to remain spinsters. The fear of not being married at all or of being discarded after marriage was a great weight on young women's minds.

The Restoration was supposed to have brought equality and enlightenment to all, but the unfortunate fact is that many of the common people squandered their new freedom in an attempt to ape the prestigious military class. The Confucian ideas of marriage held by the latter were widely accepted, and the heads of houses assumed all control over matrimonial matters. Sons or daughters who did not conform to their will could do little other than leave home or commit suicide, and brides who did not produce a child for two or three years after marriage were often returned to their parents. Not infrequently wives were divorced on the vague grounds that they did not fit perfectly with family life in their new homes. Of course, many girls did manage somehow to suit their parents-in-law, but the sacrifice was often very great.

The Work of Housewives

If a bride survived the ordeal of living under the watchful eyes of her husband's parents for a sufficient number of years, she became mistress of the family in her own right, and her condition improved immeasurably. She now had the responsibility of feeding the family, keeping them in clothing, and in general caring for the household finances, and she was likely to have her hands busy at sewing, cooking, and cleaning much of the time, but the work was rewarded with appreciation and respect.

The following description of a housewife was written by Ema Mieko in a book entitled *Hida No Onnatachi (The Women of Hida):*

> I went to a very small mountain village in the upper region of the Akao River (Ono County, Toyama Prefecture) and visited a farm house where three families lived together. The mistress of the house not only looked after her eighty-year-old parents-in-law, but also directed her son and daughter-in-law in their work and helped train their children. This woman was about fifty. Her forehead was rather broad, and her hair had a slight wave. There was an air of great tenderness about her, but one also received the impression that she was alert and diligent. I had dinner with her family and watched her as she sat by the hearth and ladled out the food to them. As I looked at the scene, I became aware that this woman, and her simple, brisk, and efficient manner had a sort of majestic dignity, but the traditional dignity of a matriarch presiding over her clan at table. Sitting there quietly and unperturbed, she was truly beautiful.

During the Meiji period the mistress of the house usually had such dignity and authority. In later times people often said that in comparison with the past housewives lived as queens, but as the work that women contributed decreased, the authority that they had possessed also tended to disappear.

Women at Work

The women in Meiji literature generally seem modest and reserved, if not actually servile and ineffectual. In this respect they accord with the prevailing conception of Oriental womanhood, but the literary picture of wives totally dependent on their husbands was hardly valid. The average woman did her share of the family work, and her contribution insured her the respect of society. However, a number of people under the influence of Confucian ideas considered it proper for women to be entirely subordinate to men and were shocked to see women of the modern era taking up new work and attempting to advance their social position. This attitude unfortunately became common, though there was little basis for it in fact.

Even in city shops women performed much of the daily work, and in the rural districts they were much more actively connected with the production and circulation of goods. All over the country the annual transplantation of rice shoots was considered a woman's task, and in many areas women were held responsible for the original seeding. The harvest was usually brought in by men and women together, but in many places the women threshed the grain, and in almost all instances they hulled and milled it. Tasks like this were more and more carried out with the help of simple machines, but the division of labor between men and women was maintained.

In mountain communities of the past, forestry and hunting were the exclusive province of men while the same was true of the various work involving boats and nets in fishing communities. In such places, however, women took complete charge of gardening and farming, and at times they maintained fields up in the mountains at a considerable distance from their homes. Sericulture was carried on entirely by them, and since most fishing villages became more and more reliant on farming, the part played by women became increasingly important. Most fishermen took little interest in household affairs and simply left the management of finances to their wives. During the Meiji period agriculture grew so vital to the economic life of the islands in the Seto Inland Sea that women gained much authority with regard not only to household economy but to village economy as well. In some cases the money that a man retained for his personal needs was called by the name now ordinarily used for the small change that wives of salary earners pilfer from the household money.

In fishing communities where women worked all day as divers, men were little more than accessories. The reputation of a woman rested on the question of whether she could provide her husband's keep or not, and as a consequence the social standing of women was very high. In most fishing villages it was left up to the women to sell the fish, and often they traveled as merchants to nearby farming villages.

The Public Activities of Women

Despite the large part played by women in production, they were surprisingly inactive in public life, simply because they were largely confined to their houses and had little chance to associate with outsiders. Even the most domineering shopkeepers' wives in Asakusa district of Tokyo—on the whole a rather terrifying class—were forced to take a back seat to their husbands in public. Still the women of many communities maintained organizations, usually a religious nature, which gave them a chance to express their views on a number of public questions.

In the Meiji period a few women began against almost over-whelming obstacles to perform welfare work for the benefit of the many people who had become destitute as a result of the prevailing social confusion. As a rule the efforts of these ladies were directed primarily at providing protection and education for unfortunate children. Such work was exceedingly rare before the Restoration, and it appears to have owed much to the influence of Western women, but the inspiration was not entirely from without. A woman named Uriu Iwako established a school and welfare agency for children in the earliest years of the Meiji period, before foreign ideas of charity work had been imported to any appreciable degree, and we might note that a statue was later erected to this lady in Asakusa Park in Tokyo by her admirers and helpers.

A number of women educators appeared on the scene, but instead of advocating a common education for men and women, they usually were interested only in the domestic training of girls, and aside from a few who promoted Western-style learning, most of them retained the traditional strong emphasis on ethics and house-hold virtues.

There were some who advocated increased political rights for women, but as a rule they eventually settled down in conservative movements for promoting women's education. During the third decade of the Meiji period, a number of feminine writers became prominent. Also, around the same time newspapers began to include columns on domestic matters, and the first women's magazine appeared. Around 1900 people were discussing such questions as whether women ought to be allowed to climb Mount Fuji, hitherto reserved for men, or to ride bicycles in the public streets. In 1910 a society called the Seito-sha or Association of Bluestockings began promoting equal rights for women, and there was much talk of "awakened womanhood."

Women and Religion

a. The Woman's Part in Family Worship
Women were usually left out of the public rituals during festivals, but often they played the principal role in family worship, and in general, they were considered to be in relatively close spiritual contact with the gods. Japan has always had a good number of mediums and sorceresses, and there appears to have been a general belief in the past that women possessed great religious powers.

It is clear from examples found around Okinawa, for example, that the gods were considered far more likely to speak through women than through men, and it is possible that the men of the past in general relied on the spiritual strength of their wives or sisters to protect them from harm. Many of the customs that ostensibly indicate scorn for the feminine sex may be seen upon further study to be based on an ancient fear of women's supernatural powers.

During the Meiji period household worship underwent many changes, but the *bon* festival remained one of its most important aspects. It was considered that the spirits of ancestors, particularly ancestors not long dead, returned to earth in this season, and despite the exegetical reasons offered by Buddhists for the *bon,* it was largely a non-Buddhist form of ancestor worship by individual households. As spiritual mentors of the family the mistress of the house and her mother-in-law waited on the dead almost as though they were still alive.

b. Clairvoyants
Prior to the Meiji period, female clairvoyants occupied a fairly important place in Shinto shrines, but when the Meiji government reorganized the shrine system, they were either turned out or given purely formal positions. The government also tried on occasion to suppress independent sorceresses, who

commanded a considerable following, but no sooner than old ones disappeared, new ones took their place. These women took a large part in local religious festivals and exerted much influence on household religion. The average housewife, if told by one of them that she was not paying sufficient attention to the spirits of her family's ancestors, trembled to the depths of her soul. Local religious societies of women often sought the teaching and guidance of such people, and two religious groups, Tenri-kjyo and Omoto-kyo, both of which believed in them, spread throughout the country during Meiji because of the adherence of country women to them.

Around 1910 a number of women who claimed to be clairvoyant caught the public eye. As they competed among themselves for supremacy, scholars pronounced some genuine and others fraudulent, while the general public listened avidly, if not always credulously, to the various predictions. The flame soon died, but the phenomenon as a whole illustrates the deep-seated Japanese belief in the spiritual powers of women.

The Conception of Women's Work

a. From Old to New Work

As we have seen, women of pre-modern times played an important part in production. Both in the country and in the cities, however, most of them did little work outside the home, and most of those who did were actresses, music teachers, hairdressers, or midwives. In addition a number of young girls served as maids, and a few of them continued to do so throughout their lives.

During the middle years of the Meiji period new forms of employment became available to women. They began, for instance, to be hired by large textile mills, and before long they held between seventy and eighty per cent of the jobs in this industry. They were employed largely because they were content to work hard for a small salary, and their working conditions were often miserable. Many of them lived in extreme poverty and contacted serious diseases, in particular tuberculosis. Almost invariably they quit working when they married, at the latest, and there were very few who were interested enough in a career to attempt to improve their position as workers.

As time went on, however, a number of women gained a place for themselves as public servants, most notably as telephone operators. Women were first hired for this work in 1899, and they performed so creditably that in the next year they were also employed in other phases of communications work. They were made to work in different rooms from the male employees, however, and were not put in charge of tasks that involved direct contact with the public. Obviously, the practice of hiring them was still regarded with considerable caution.

As time went on they were accepted by more and more businesses. In 1903 they began to work in the Bureau of Railway Operation, the Tokyo Electric Light Company, and Shimbashi Station (as ticket sellers). The Mitsui Clothing Store went so far as to set them to work selling goods to the public. In 1907 the

Ministry of Communication attracted some attention by making female employees eligible for promotions hitherto reserved for men. The consensus at the time was that the ministry cognizant of their ability, diligence, and tractability, as well as of the fact that they would work for less money than men, took this measure in order to keep them from transferring to private companies and banks. People who held high hopes for the emancipation of the feminine sex read the ministry's action as a sign of the times and predicted that one day women would even be able to serve the public as lawyers and judges.

Women also took up intellectual occupations, the number of them engaged as school teachers being particularly large. Twenty-five hundred were employed in primary schools only ten years after the establishment of the school system in 1872. To be sure, this number represented only three per cent of the total number of teachers, but considering that the only women hitherto engaged as educators had been a handful of Buddhist nuns working in temple schools, the figure is quite remarkable. Many young women began to go to normal school, and various prefectures established new institutions of this type especially for them. High schools for girls also increased notably in number.

Music schools attracted quite a few young ladies, and in 1899 a women's school of medicine was established. In the same year, we might note, laws governing midwifery were enacted, and modern practices introduced into this ancient profession.

The current conceptions of women's work remained old-fashioned. Though young women were being employed in increasing numbers, few people devoted much thought to the special new provisions needed for their health, education, and discipline. The employers, the employed, and even the latters' parents usually considered women's working careers as only temporary. Young women with no more than high school education were not equipped to consider the larger economic implications of their position, but they usually were dimly aware of inconsistencies between home life and the office, and they preferred the former. As a consequence, they did not often seriously consider trying to advance in their working careers.

QUESTIONS TO CONSIDER

1. How were the life experiences of Japanese women changing in the late nineteenth and early twentieth centuries?
2. In what ways is Yanagita's background in anthropology and folklore apparent in this passage?
3. For what kinds of investigations is Yanagita's method likely to be most effective?

FOR FURTHER READING

Fogel, Joshua A. *Politics and Sinology: The Case of Naito Konan.* Cambridge, MA: Harvard University Press, 1984.

Gluck, Carol. *Japan's Modern Myths: Ideology in the Late Meiji Period.* Princeton, NJ: Princeton University Press, 1985.

Ienaga Saburo. *The Pacific War, 1931–1945.* New York: Pantheon, 1978.

Yanagita Kunio. *About Our Ancestors: The Japanese Family System.* Trans. Fanny Hagin Mayer and Ishiwara Yasuyo. Tokyo: Japan Society for the Promotion of Science, 1970.

————. *Japanese Folk Tales.* Trans. Fanny Hagin Mayer. Taipei: Orient Cultural Service, 1966.

————. *The Legends of Tono.* Trans. Ronald A. Morse. Tokyo: Japan Foundation, 1975.

NOTES

1. Yanagita Kunio, *Japanese Manners and Customs in the Meiji Era,* trans. Charles S. Terry (Tokyo: Obunsha, 1957), 242–51.

PART SIX

Passions of the Present

A historian is in danger when he or she ventures out of the past and into the present. As a class of scholars, historians are used to making judgments about the lives and work of the long dead. They are much less comfortable when rendering similar judgments about people who can talk back. Thus it is with some trepidation that the editors of this volume turn in Part 6 to a contemplation of the themes that have dominated historical writing in the last third of the twentieth century. Yet we must do so, for the student of history should be apprised of the state of the discipline as it is being practiced today, just as he or she ought to learn of the development of the discipline from earliest times.

Our choices in this section are not arbitrary, but we are well aware that many a historian working today would put together a somewhat different list of themes to characterize the concerns of the present generation than have we. He or she might also estimate differently the best authors to choose as examples of each theme. A historian may be so wrapped up in the theme of his or her own work as to be unable to see that there are people working on

many different themes today. One historian may believe that the only important history being written today is quantitative social scientific history; another may believe that the social scientific paradigm has proven bankrupt, and that postmodernist cultural history is the only legitimate history being done these days. The editors of this book each concentrate their own historical writing on a couple of themes, but they recognize that there are fine historians working in many areas.

We have surveyed the historical writing of the generations of historians currently at work, and we believe we see nine themes that characterize them most prominently. We have chosen Fernand Braudel to stand for the school of French historians gathered around the journal *Annales* who have elaborated and taken in quite new directions the work begun by Marc Bloch. Robert Fogel is our choice to represent the quantitative social scientific historians who so dominated the 1950s and 1960s, and who continue to work to good effect near the end of the century. John Blassingame is our choice to represent the work being done on race, E. P. Thompson for class, and

Caroline Walker Bynum on gender, three issues that currently dominate historical writing in the United States. Natalie Zemon Davis stands as an exemplar of the work being done in cultural history, as Walter Rodney does for that group of historians who study the entire world as a single system. Gertrude Himmelfarb is a fine example of the reaction by neoconservatives against all the other trends represented in this part of the book. Edward Said is a similarly excellent example of the rising group of Third World scholars who actively question the judgments, even the categories of analysis, of European and North American historians. All of these authors have influenced the current generations of writers of history, and all except Braudel, Thompson, and Rodney are still alive and active at the time of this writing.

There are, of course, many other themes on which historians have spent effort in recent years—as there are other fine historians who could represent the themes we have chosen. People continue to use intellectual history, religious history, agricultural history, military history, and many other labels to describe their work. There are disciples in our era of Frederick Jackson Turner, Karl Marx, and Naito Konan, if not of Gibbon or Thucydides. Among the other types of history currently being written, four stand out as particularly important in our era: studies of environmental history, histories of the family, psychological histories, and microstudies of particular communities. These are rela-

tively new themes in historical writing, and they are important. But they have not affected the whole discipline as thoroughly as have the nine themes represented by the selections included in Part 6. Perhaps they will emerge in future years as dominant themes in historical writing, but at this point they do not seem so important as the others we have chosen. We have listed some works illustrating those themes below, in the hope that interested readers will pursue them on their own.

The historians in Part 6 are selected rather differently from those in the previous parts. In the cases of the authors whose work appears in the earlier five sections, centuries of readers have decreed that these are among the finest historians of all time. In this last section, however, we can make no such claim. As we turn to the most recent generations of historians, judgments as to greatness and lasting importance can be less sure. We cannot be certain that, two centuries from now, people will be reading the work of Natalie Davis, John Blassingame, and Walter Rodney; they might just as likely be reading Robert Darnton, Winthrop Jordan, and William McNeill as exemplars of the finest historical writing that the late twentieth century has to offer. What we can be sure of is that culture, race, and world systems are three of the themes that dominate late-twentieth-century historical writing, and that these six historians—and the other writers mentioned in the bibliographies in Part 6—are among the finest practitioners working in our era.

FOR FURTHER READING

Novick, Peter. *That Noble Dream: The "Objectivity Question" and the American Historical Profession.* New York: Cambridge University Press, 1988.

The Environment

Cronon, William. *Changes in the Land: Indians, Colonists, and the Ecology of New England.* New York: Hill and Wang, 1983.

Crosby, Alfred W. *The Columbian Exchange: Biological and Cultural Consequences of 1492.* Westport, CT: Greenwood, 1972.

————— . *Ecological Imperialism: The Biological Expansion of Europe, 900–1900.* New York: Cambridge University Press, 1986.

Nash, Roderick. *Wilderness and the American Mind,* 3rd ed. New Haven, CT: Yale University Press, 1982.

Worster, Donald. *Dust Bowl: The Southern Plains in the 1930s.* New York: Oxford, 1979.

————— , ed. *Ends of the Earth: Perspectives on Modern Environmental History.* New York: Cambridge University Press, 1991.

Family

Ariés, Philippe. *Centuries of Childhood: A Social History of Family Life.* New York: Knopf, 1962.

Gutman, Herbert. *The Black Family in Slavery and Freedom.* New York: Random House, 1976.

Hareven, Tamara. *Family Time and Industrial Time.* New York: Cambridge University Press, 1982.

Ryan, Mary P. *The Cradle of the Middle Class: The Family in Oneida County, New York, 1790–1865.* New York: Cambridge University Press, 1981.

Stone, Lawrence. *The Family, Sex and Marriage In England 1500–1800.* New York: Harper and Row, 1977.

Psychohistory

Brodie, Fawn. *No Man Knows My History: The Life of Joseph Smith, the Mormon Prophet.* New York: Knopf, 1945.

————— . *Thomas Jefferson: An Intimate Portrait.* New York: Norton, 1974.

Erikson, Erik. *Gandhi's Truth: On the Origins of Militant Nonviolence.* New York: Norton, 1969.

————— . *Young Man Luther: A Study in Psychoanalysis and History.* New York: Norton, 1962.

Gay, Peter. *Freud for Historians.* New York: Oxford University Press, 1985.

Greven, Philip. *The Protestant Temperament: Patterns of Child-Rearing, Religious Experience, and the Self in Early America.* New York: Knopf, 1977.

Communities

Dawley, Alan. *Class and Community: The Industrial Revolution in Lynn.* Cambridge, MA: Harvard University Press, 1976.

Greven, Philip J., Jr. *Four Generations: Population, Land, and Family in Colonial Andover, Massachusetts.* Ithaca, NY: Cornell University Press, 1970.

Gross, Robert A. *The Minutemen and Their World.* New York: Hill and Wang, 1976.

Ladurie, Emmanuel Le Roy. *Montaillou: The Promised Land of Error.* New York: George Braziller, 1978.

Matsumoto, Valerie J. *Farming the Home Place: A Japanese American Community in California, 1919–1982.* Ithaca, NY: Cornell University Press, 1993.

Wallace, Anthony F. C. *Rockdale: The Growth of an American Village in the Early Industrial Revolution.* New York: Norton, 1978.

CHAPTER 48

Annales

Fernand Braudel

Fernand Braudel
Fernand Braudel Center/Binghamton University

If Marc Bloch was the most influential European historian of the first half of the twentieth century, Fernand Braudel (1902–1985) occupied the same place of honor in the second. Braudel was the towering figure of the second generation of the *Annales* school (see Chapter 46). Historian Samuel Kinser said of him, "If the Nobel Prize were given to historians, it would almost certainly have been awarded to Fernand Braudel."[1]

Braudel was the son of a schoolmaster in a town in Lorraine in northeastern France. He studied in Paris as a youth and then at the Sorbonne, where his professors bored him with narrative accounts of political and diplomatic history. After university Braudel spent a decade teaching history in Algeria and traveling around the Mediterranean collecting photographic copies of old documents. Then he taught at secondary schools in Paris and at a university in Brazil. All the while he was poring over the documents, trying to shape them into a usable historical account. In 1937 Braudel returned to Paris to take up a position at Ecole des Hautes Etudes and join Lucien Febvre and Marc Bloch on the board of *Annales*. World War II provided the occasion for Braudel's breakthrough as a scholar. Joining the army, he was captured in 1940 and spent the rest of the war in a German prisoner-of-war camp. While there, he wrote, based on his memory of the documents he had kept for so many years, the first draft of an interdisciplinary study of the entire Mediterranean basin, which he managed to smuggle out to Febvre. After the war Braudel presented the manuscript as his dissertation and was granted a doctorate from the Sorbonne. Braudel taught for many years at the Collège de France and the Sixth Section, and he served as editorial director of the *Annales*, retiring from teaching and administration to continue writing in 1972.

The hallmark of Braudel's approach to history was an attempt to understand society as a total, interrelated system. It was based on a three-tiered notion of historical time that gave rise to three modes of analysis. The base was *structure* or the *long durée*[2]—time periods of hundreds of years. On this tier, the actors were climate and geography and long-term economic forces. The second tier was *conjoncture*, periods lasting from a decade to a generation or so. Here the main issues were sociological and economic, and the actors were classes and other large groupings of people. On the third tier, *événement*, one found events, institutions, and people. These were derivative of the first two tiers. Braudel and the *Annalistes* gave French intellectuals the first systematic theory for understanding history since Marx, and as such provided a counterbalance to other scholars who continued to pursue Marxist analysis.

Braudel's masterwork—the doctoral dissertation that took more than two decades to write—was not about a person or an event, but about an ocean and the region that surrounded it. *The Mediterranean and the Mediterranean World in the Age of Philip II* (1949) embodies the three-tiered approach. In "The Role of the Environment," it treats the physical world as causal, starting with detailed descriptions of mountains and plains, ocean and desert, coastline and islands, climate and seasons, and proceeding to note the shape of human habitation. The second level of analysis, "Collective Destinies and General Trends," has to do with the structures of human relationships, starting with 300 pages on the economic systems of the Mediterranean world. Thus ends the first volume. The second level is completed in volume two, with descriptions of empires and states, the clash of classes, varieties of culture, and modes of warfare. Only in the last third of a work nearly 1,400 pages long does Braudel even begin to mention "Events, Politics and People"—the wars and politics that would have occupied the entire attention of a historian like Voltaire or Macaulay.

Fernand Braudel's research went wide and deep. As much academic entrepreneur in his latter years as practicing scholar, he organized a legion of graduate students to ferret out materials in archives all over Europe, then wove the treasures they uncovered into a single, complex yet compelling tapestry. The selection reproduced here is from Braudel's second great work, completed late in life, *Civilization and Capitalism: 15th–18th Century* (1979). Again, the emphasis is on Europe, but in this book the scale is even larger: 2,000 pages, surveying four centuries of time, with forays around the globe to Japan, the Americas, Turkey, India, Africa, and China. It is an attempt, after Braudel's own kind, at universal history. Unlike *The Mediterranean*, in *Civilization and Capitalism* Braudel never gets down to politics and events. His attention is relentlessly tuned to the market economy and its interactions with the material world and the human world writ large.

Nonetheless, though hardly a human passes through its pages, *Civilization and Capitalism* is a profoundly humane book. Braudel's compelling vision and his sparkling prose work magic on the reader. One may find oneself, much to one's surprise, wanting to know more and more about the lengths of cart axles, the grades of wine, the changes in coinage, the different yokes used in harnessing animals. In lesser hands these might seem pedestrian matters, even antiquarian and obscure. In Braudel's, they illumine the lives of people who have passed.

The third generation of *Annales* scholars, working after 1960, had less interest in work on the scope of Bloch or Braudel. Maintaining fidelity to the three tiers of analysis, they nonetheless chose to work increasingly on the third tier and to study *mentalités*. By this they did not mean the consciousness of individuals, but the "collective mentality that regulates, without their knowing it, the representations and judgments of social subjects."[3] As time passed, the younger *Annales* scholars like Emmanuel Le Roy Ladurie got further and further from the grand structures, wide geographical scope, and long time frame of Braudel's work. In books like *Montaillou* and *Carnival in Romans*, Le Roy Ladurie concerned himself with the very local, personal, short-term, and particular—and formed a bridge to the generation of cultural historians who were to come. Other scholars, such as Philippe Ariès and Michel Foucault in France and Natalie Davis and Robert Darnton in the United States (see Chapter 53), also studied *mentalités*, without necessarily maintaining adherence to the analytical structure imposed by the *Annales* school.

Thus the *Annalistes* have provided the foundation for much of the work that has been done in the present generations, particularly in social scientific and cultural history (see Chapters 49 and 53), and also in the history of the environment, although those subdisciplines have non-*Annaliste* roots as well.

The Structures of Everyday Life[4]
Daily Bread

Men's diet between the fifteenth and the eighteenth centuries essentially consisted of vegetable foods. This was clearly the case in pre-Columbia America and Black Africa, and strikingly so in the Asiatic rice-growing civilizations, not only in earlier times but today. The early settlement and then the spectacular increase in population in the Far East were only possible because of the small amount of meat eaten. The reasons for this are very simple. If the choices of an economy are determined solely by adding up calories, agriculture on a given surface area feeds ten to twenty times as many people. Montesquieu made the point with reference to the rice-growing countries: "Land which elsewhere is used to feed animals there directly serves as sustenance for men."[5]

But everywhere in the world, and not only from the fifteenth to the eighteenth centuries, any population-increase beyond a certain level means greater recourse to vegetable foods. The choice between cereals and meat depends on the number of people. This is one of the great tests of material life: "Tell me what you eat, and I will tell you who you are." A German proverb using a play on words, says the same thing, *Der Mensch ist was er isst* (man is what he eats).[6] His food bears witness to his social status and his civilization or culture.

A journey from a culture to a civilization, or from a low density of population to a relatively high one (or vice versa), can mean significant changes in diet for a traveller. Jenkinson, the leading merchant of the Muscovy Company, arrived in Moscow in 1558 from distant Archangel and proceeded down the Volga. Before reaching Astrakhan, he saw on the river bank "a great herd of Nagay Tartars." These were nomadic shepherds ("towne or house they had none") who robbed and murdered and knew none but the skills of war, who neither ploughed nor sowed, and who had nothing but scorn for the Russians they fought. How could such Christians, they said, be men, since they not only ate wheat, "the top of a weede," but drank it too (since beer and vodka were made from grain). The Nagays drank milk and ate meat, which was quite different. Jenkinson continued his journey across the deserts of Turkestan, risking death from thirst or hunger. When he reached the valley of the Amu Dar'ya, he found fresh water, mares' milk and meat from wild horses, but no bread.[7] The same differences and the same exchange of insults between herdsmen and husbandmen were just as likely to be found in the West, between the graziers of Bray and the cereal-growers of the Beauvaisis, for instance,[8] or between the Castilians and the cattle-farmers of the Béarn, "cowherds" as the southerners called them—but they gave as good as they got. More spectacular, and particularly visible in Peking, was the contrast between the eating habits of the Mongols—and later Manchus—who ate meat in large slices, in the European style, and the attitude towards food of the Chinese. For the Chinese, cooking was an almost ritual art, in which basic cereals—*fan*—were always served with an accompaniment known as the *ts'ai*, in which vegetables, sauces and spices were skillfully combined with a little meat or fish, which had to be cut up into small pieces.[9]

Europe was on the whole a region of meat-eaters: "butchers had catered for the belly of Europe for over a thousand years."[10] For centuries during the middle ages, its tables had been loaded with meat and drink worthy of Argentina in the nineteenth century. This was because the European country-side, beyond the Mediterranean shores, had long remained half empty with vast lands for pasturing animals, and even in later times its agriculture left plenty of room for livestock. But Europe's advantage declined after the seventeenth century. The general rule of vegetable supremacy seemed to be re-asserting itself with the increase in population in Europe up to at least the middle of the nineteenth century.[11] Then and only then, scientific stock-raising and massive arrivals of meat from America, salted and then frozen, enabled it to break its fast.

Furthermore the European, true to his long-established tastes, regularly and promptly demanded they be catered for when he was overseas. Abroad, the lords and masters ate meat. They stuffed themselves with it unrestrainedly in the New World, recently populated by herds from the Old. Their appetite for meat roused opprobrium and astonishment in the Far East: "One has to be a very great lord in Sumatra," said one seventeenth-century traveller, "to have a boiled or roast chicken, which moreover has to last for the whole day. Therefore they say that two thousand Christians [meaning Westerners] on their island would soon exhaust the supply of cattle and poultry."[12]

These dietary choices and the conflicts they implied were the result of very long-term processes. Maurizio goes so far as to write: "A thousand years bring scarcely any changes in the history of diet."[13] In fact the broad outlines of man's dietary history were laid down and directed by two ancient revolutions. At the end of the Paleolithic Age the "omnivores" moved on to hunting large animals. "Great carnivorism" was born and the taste for it has never disappeared: "a craving for flesh and blood, a 'hunger for nitrogen,' in other words for animal protein."[14]

The second revolution, in the seventh or sixth millenium before the Christian era, was neolithic agriculture with the arrival of cultivated cereals. Now fields were cultivated, at the expense of hunting-ground and extensive grazing. As the centuries passed, the expanding population was reduced to eating vegetable foods, raw or cooked, often insipid and always monotonous whether they were fermented or not: gruels, sops and bread. From now on, history records two opposing species of humanity: the few who ate meat and the many who fed on bread, gruel, roots and cooked tubers. In China in the second millenium, "the administrators of the great provinces were designated . . . meat-eaters."[15] In ancient Greece it was said that "the eaters of barley gruel have no desire to make war."[16] An Englishman centuries later (1776) stated: "Vigour and Fortitude of Heart are much more generally found in Persons that live on Flesh, than in such as live on lighter Meat."[17]

Having said this, we will concentrate first on the food of the majority between the fifteenth and the eighteenth centuries and therefore on those foods supplied by agriculture, the oldest industry of all. Wherever it began, agriculture had from the start been obliged to opt for one of the major food-plants, and had been built up around this initial choice of priority on which everything or almost everything would thereafter depend. Three of these plants were brilliantly successful: wheat, rice and maize. They continue to share world arable land between them today. The "plants of civilization,"[18] they have profoundly organized man's material and sometimes his spiritual life, to the point where they have become almost ineradicable structures. Their history and the "determinism of civilization"[19] they have exercised over the world's peasantry and human life in general are the subject of the present chapter. Our journey from one to the other of these cereals will take us round the world.

Wheat

Wheat is primarily—but not only—found in the West. Well before the fifteenth century, it was growing on the plains of northern China side by side with millet and sorghum. It was "planted in holes" there and not reaped but "uprooted with its whole stem," with a hoe. It was exported by the Un Leang Ho—"the grain-bearing river"—up to Peking. It was even found from time to time in Japan and southern China where, according to Father de Las Cortes (1626), the peasant sometimes succeeded in obtaining a wheat harvest between two harvests of rice.[20] This was simply an extra, because the Chinese "did not know how to knead bread any more than they knew how to roast meat" and because, as a minor product, "wheat [in China] is always cheap." Sometimes they made a sort of bread from it, cooked in steam over a cauldron and mixed "with finely chopped onions." The result, according to one Western traveller, was "a very heavy dough that lay like a stone on the stomach."[21] Biscuit was made at Canton in the sixteenth century, but it was for Macao and the Philippines. Wheat also provided the Chinese with vermicelli, gruels and lard cakes, but not bread.[22]

An excellent type of wheat was also grown in the dry plains of the Indus and in the upper Ganges, and immense caravans of oxen effected exchanges of rice and wheat across all India. In Persia a rudimentary type of bread, a plain biscuit made without leaven, was generally on sale at a low price. It was often the result of enormous peasant labour. In the neighbourhood of Ispahan for example, "the wheat lands are heavy and need four or even six oxen to till them. And a child is placed on the yoke of the first pair to drive them on with a stick."[23] And of course wheat grew all round the Mediterranean, even in the oases of the Sahara, and especially in Egypt. As the Nile floods in summer, the crops there are always produced in winter, when the water has receded from the land. The climate at this time of year is scarcely favourable to tropical plants but it suits wheat, which is also found in Ethiopia.

From Europe, wheat travelled far and made many conquests. Russian colonization carried it eastward to Siberia, beyond Tomsk and Irkutsk; as early as the sixteenth century, the Russian peasant established its success in the black earth country of the Ukraine (where Catherine II eventually completed her conquests in 1793). Wheat had triumphed there well before that date, even somewhat inopportunely: "At present," states a report of 1771, "piles of grain the size of houses, enough to feed all Europe, are again rotting in Podolia and Volhynia."[24] The same catastrophic superabundance happened in 1784. Wheat was "at such a low price in the Ukraine that many landowners have abandoned its cultivation," noted a French agent.[25] "However, stocks of this grain are already so plentiful that they not only feed a large part of Turkey but even supply exports for Spain and Portugal." And for France as well, via Marseilles. Boats from Marseilles took on grain from the Black Sea either in the Aegean islands or in the Crimea, for example at Gozlev, the future Eupatoria, the crossing of the Turkish straits being effected, one surmises, by administrative collusion.

In fact, the great period of "Russian" wheat was still to come. The arrival in Italy of boats loaded with Ukrainian wheat in 1803 seemed like a disaster to the landowners. The same threat was denounced in the French Chamber of Deputies a little later in 1818.[26]

Wheat had crossed the Atlantic from Europe well before these events. In Latin America it had to contend with excessively hot climates, destructive insects and rival crops (maize and manioc). Its success in America came later on, in Chile; on the banks of the St. Lawrence; in Mexico; and later still in the English colonies in America, in the seventeenth and particularly the eighteenth centuries. At that time Boston sailing ships were carrying flour and grain to the sugar islands of the Caribbean, then to Europe and the Mediterranean. From 1739, American ships were unloading grain and flour in Marseilles.[27] In the nineteenth century, wheat triumphed in Argentina, southern Africa, Australia, the Canadian prairies and the Middle West, everywhere asserting by its presence the expansion of European civilization.

Wheat and Other Grains

To return to Europe: as soon as one looks at the question of grain, one realizes what a complicated phenomenon it is. It would be better to put it in the plural—*los panes*, as so many Spanish texts say. In the first place there were different qualities of grain: in France the best was often called "the head of the corn": sold side by side with it were medium-quality wheat, "small corn" or maslin, a mixture of wheat with another cereal, often rye. Moreover, wheat was never grown by itself. Despite its great age, even older cereals grew alongside it. Spelt, a cereal with a "dressed grain," was still grown in the fourteenth century in Italy; in 1700 in Alsace, the Palatinate, Swabia and the Swiss uplands, where it was regarded as suitable for making bread; and in the late eighteenth century in Gelders and the county of Namur (where it was chiefly used, like barley, for pig-feed and to make beer); and until the early nineteenth century in the Rhône valley.[28] Millet was even more widely grown.[29] When Venice was besieged by the Genoese in 1372, it was saved by its stocks of millet. In the sixteenth century, the Venetian government deliberately kept stocks of this long-lasting cereal (it could sometimes be kept for twenty or so years) in the fortified towns of the Terra Firma. And millet rather than wheat was sent to the *presidios* in Dalmatia or the islands of the Levant when they were short of food.[30] Millet was still grown in Gascony, Italy and central Europe in the eighteenth century. But it produced a very coarse foodstuff to judge by the comments of a Jesuit at the end of the century. He admired the use the Chinese made of their various millets and exclaimed: "With all our progress in the sciences of curiosity, vanity and uselessness, our peasants in Gascony and the Bordelais *Landes* are as little advanced as they were three centuries ago in methods of making their millet into a less uncivilized and less unhealthy food."[31]

Wheat had other and more important associates; for example barley, which was used to feed horses in the south. "No barley harvest, no war," could have been said in the sixteenth century and later, of the long Hungarian frontier where battles between Turks and Christians were inconceivable without cavalry.[32] Towards the north, hard grains gave way to soft grains, barley to oats and more especially rye, which came late to the north— probably not before the great invasions of the fifth century; after this it seems to have become established and spread there at the same time as triennial rotation.[33] Boats from the Baltic, very soon attracted farther and farther from home by hungry Europe, carried as much rye as wheat. First they came as far as the North Sea and the Channel, then to the Iberian ports on the Atlantic and finally, on a massive scale at the time of the great crisis of 1590, as far as the Mediterranean.[34] All these cereals were used to make bread, even in the eighteenth century, whenever wheat was in short supply. "Rye bread," wrote a doctor, Louis Lemery, in 1702, "is not as nourishing as wheat and loosens the bowels a little." Barley bread, he added, "is refreshing but less nourishing than wheat or rye bread"; only the northern peoples make bread from oats "which suits them very well."[35] But it is a harsh fact that throughout the eighteenth century, in France, arable land was almost equally divided between *"bled"* (that is bread cereals, wheat and rye) and *"menus grains"* (or lesser cereals: barley, oats, buckwheat, millet); and that rye, which was about equal to wheat in 1715, was grown in a ratio of two to one in 1792.[36]

NOTES

1. Samuel Kinser, *"Annaliste* Paradigm? The Geohistorical structuralism of Fernand Braudel," *American Historical Review* 86 (1981): 63–105.
2. It is worth noting in passing that, while Braudel's approach was original, it was not unique. Asakawa Kanichi (1873–1948), a Japanese historian working at Yale a generation before Braudel, did local history over the *long durée.*
3. Roger Chartier, "Intellectual History or Sociocultural History? The French Trajetories," in *Modern European Intellectual History,* ed. Dominick La Capra and Steven L. Kaplan (Ithaca, NY: Cornell University Press, 1982), 23.
4. Fernand Braudel, *The Structures of Everyday Life,* trans. Siân Reynolds (New York: Harper and Row, 1981), 104–14. Footnotes edited to fit abridgement.

5. Montesquieu, *De l'Esprit des lois,* book XXII chap. 14, in *Oevres complètes,* 1964 edn., p. 690.

6. This proverb seems to have been invented by L. A. Feuerbach.

7. *Haklyut's Voyages,* 1927 edn., vol. I, pp. 441, 448–9.

8. P. Goubert, *op. cit.,* pp. 108, 111.

9. K. C. Chang, *Food in Chinese Culture,* 1977.

10. Claude Manceron, *Les Vingt Ans du Roi,* 1972, p. 614.

11. Wilhelm Abel, "Wandlungen des Flesichverbrauchs und der Bleischversorgung in Deutschland seit dem ausgehenden Mittelalter," in *Berichte über Landswirtschaft,* XXII, 3, 1937, pp. 411–52.

12. Abbé Prévost, *op. cit.,* IX, p. 342 (Beaulieu's voyage).

13. A. Maurizio, *op. cit.,* p. 168.

14. Dr. Jean Claudian, Preliminary report of the International Conference of F.I.P.A.L., Paris, 1964, typescript, pp. 7–8, 19.

15. Marcel Granet, *Danses et légendes de la Chine ancienne,* 1926, pp. 8 and 19, note.

16. J. Claudian, *art. cit.,* p. 27.

17. *An Account of the Character and Manners of the French* [by J. Andrews], 1770, p. 58.

18. M. Sorre, *op. cit.,* vol. I, pp. 162–3.

19. Pierre Gourou, "La civilisation du végétsal," in *Indonesie,* no. 5, pp. 385–96, reviewed by Lucien Febvre, in *Annales E.S.C.,* 1949, p. 73.

20. P. de Las Cortes, *doc. cit.* fo. 75.

21. Abbé Prevost, *op. cit.,* vol. V, p. 486.

22. G. F. Gemelli Careri, *op. cit.,* vol. IV, p. 79.

23. *Ibid.,* vol. II, p. 59.

24. Memorandum on the port of Oczaskov and the trade for which it might act as an entrepot, Affaires Etrangères, Paris (henceforth, A. E.), M and D, Russia, 7, fo. 229.

25. A. E., M and D, Russia, 17, fos. 78 and 194–96.

26. V. Dandolo, *Sulle Cause dell'avvilimanto delle nostre granaglie e sulle industrie agrarie . . .,* 1820, XL, p. 1.

27. *Histoire du commerce de Marseille,* ed. G. Rambert, 1954, IV, pp. 625ff.

28. Étienne Juillard, *La Vie rurale dans la plaine de Basse-Alsace,* 1953, p. 29; J. Ruwet, E. Hélin, F. Ladrier, L. vanBuyten, *Marché des céréals à Ruremonde, Luxembourg, Namur et Diest, XVIIe et XVIIIx siècles,* 1966, pp. 44, 57ff., 283–4, 299ff; Daniel Faucher, *Plaines et bassins du Rhône moyen,* 1926, p. 317.

29. M. Sorre, *op. cit.,* vol. I, map, p. 241: an area covering the whole Mediterranean and central and southern Europe.

30. *Medit.,* vol. I, pp. 595, 596.

31. Bibliothèque Nationale, Paris, Estampes, Oe 73.

32. *Medit.,* vol. I, p. 244.

33. Hans Haussherr, *Wirtschaftsgeschichte der Neuzeit, vom des 14. bis zur Höhe des 19. J.,* 3rd edn., 1954, p. 1.

34. *Medit.,* vol. I, p. 600 and note 370.

35. Louis Lemery, *Traité des aliments, où, l'on trouve la différence et le choix qu'on doit faire de chacun d'eux en particulier . . .,* 1702, p. 113.

36. Cf. J. C. Toutain's table, "Le produit de l'agriculture française de 1700 à 1958", in *Histoire quantitative de l'économie française,* ed. J. Marczewski, 1961, p. 57.

QUESTIONS TO CONSIDER

1. What does Braudel mean by "the structures of everyday life"?
2. How does a description of diet help us understand history?
3. Braudel presents this as a world history, but focuses largely on European artifacts and practices. How might this same subject be viewed in a world perspective?

FOR FURTHER READING

Asakawa Kanichi. *The Documents of Iriki.* New Haven, CT: Yale University Press, 1929.

Braudel, Fernand. *Civilization and Capitalism, 15th–18th Century.* Berkeley, CA: Trans. Siân Reynolds. University of California Press, 1992; orig. New York: Harper and Row, 1981.
Volume I. *The Structures of Everyday Life.*
Volume II. *The Wheels of Commerce.*
Volume III. *The Perspective of the World.*
_____ . *The Mediterranean and the Mediterranean World in the Age of Philip II.* 2 vols. Trans. Siân Reynolds. New York: Harper and Row, 1972–73.
_____ . *On History.* Trans. Sarah Matthews. Chicago: University of Chicago Press, 1980.

Hexter, J. H. "Fernand Braudel and the *Monde Braudellian.*" *Journal of Modern History* 44 (1972).

Hunt, Lynn. "French History in the Last Twenty Years: The Rise and Fall of the *Annales* Paradigm." *Journal of Contemporary History* 21 (1986): 209–24.

Ladurie, Emmanuel Le Roy. *Carnival in Romans.* New York: Braziller, 1980.
_____ . *The Mind and Method of the Historian.* Trans. Siân Reynolds and Ben Reynolds. Chicago: University of Chicago Press, 1981.
_____ . *Montaillou: The Promised Land of Error.* Trans. Barbara Bray. New York: George Braziller, 1978.
_____ . *The Territory of the Historian.* Trans. Ben and Siân Reynolds. Chicago: University of Chicago Press, 1979.

Trevor-Roper, H. R. "Fernand Braudel, the *Annales,* and the Mediterranean." *Journal of Modern History* 44 (1972).

See also the readings suggested for Chapter 46.

CHAPTER 49

Numbers

Robert William Fogel

Robert William Fogel
Courtesy of the University of Chicago

T he middle third of the twentieth century was the era of the social scientist in America at large and of the social scientific historian in the groves of academe. In the wake of the startling success of physics as an instrument of national policy at the end of World War II, scientists of all sorts achieved an unprecedented height of prestige in the United States. To be a "rocket scientist" was to be smart, capable, and worthy of holding the reins of public decision making. Some of that same prestige attached to those who applied the scientific techniques of massive data collecting, quantitative analysis, hypothesis testing, and experimental replication to matters social and political: the social scientists. One early example was Gunnar Myrdal, the Swedish economist whose massive *An American Dilemma* (1944) set the agenda for two generations of American race relations. A parade of young social scientists— "the best and the brightest" in David Halberstam's phrase—went to Washington with John F. Kennedy in 1960 to study and to fix America, and did a lot that was intelligent and useful (and some that was not).

So it was in the academy as well. Social scientific methods were one of the great themes of the second half of the twentieth century in intellectual life in Europe and America. Marshalling the quantitative tools and intellectual prestige of physicists and mathematicians (everything but the white lab coats), quantitative social scientific historians promised to give us answers we could depend on because they were scientifically derived. This positivist search for objective, scientific truth—even universal laws of human behavior—was a continuation of the movement begun by such as Ranke and Henry Buckle in the mid-nineteenth century.

The advocates of quantitative social scientific history managed two great achievements. First, they succeeded in getting many historians to think about the structures of society rather than mere events, about political forces rather than single elections, about economic forces rather than the successes or failures of individuals or companies. Second, they tried to get them to think systematically about how they know the things they think they know. In the latter regard, quantitative historians tried to get beyond the ad hoc judgments of what they regarded as less rigorous historians and debunk commonsense conclusions. They would take a widely accepted generalization, such as the idea that there was a rise of the middle classes in Europe at the beginning of the modern age, and test it: establish criteria for judging if, when, where, and to what extent such a rise may have occurred; gather data scientifically; and make the judgment. (In the case of the middle class in Europe, quantitative historians found far less rise than literary historians had imagined.)

These were signal virtues, but there were also some problems that came with quantitative approaches to history. First, there was a tendency to claim too much. Quantitative history—cliometrics, as some called it—consumed larger amounts of time, energy, and money to establish a single fact than did archival research of a literary sort. There was a tendency to expand one's conclusions to fit the size of the project rather than the number of new facts actually produced. Second, quantitative historians, like other social scientists, sometimes treated their mathematical tools as if they were magic wands, as substitutes for thinking, rather than as precise tools with clearly limited explanatory powers. Third, quantitative history was history with the people left out. This imposed the dryness of aggregate statistics on many otherwise interesting subjects. Despite such limitations, however, quantitative social scientific history has contributed enormously to our understanding of complex issues.

No historian has practiced quantitative social scientific history to greater applause than Robert William Fogel. The son of Russian immigrants, Fogel was a Communist organizer, then studied statistics at Columbia University. He was a longtime professor at several universities, including the University of Chicago and Rochester University.

A passage from Fogel's first major work, *Railroads and American Economic Growth* (1964), follows. In that book Fogel overturned the conventional wisdom that railroads had been one of the key factors in the explosive growth of the United States economy in the nineteenth century. His main technique of analysis here is testing the "counterfactual hypothesis": measuring as precisely as he can just how different things would have been if the railroads had not been built. *Railroads and American Economic Growth* did what quantitative social scientific history was supposed to do: it took an important assertion; examined it carefully, objectively, and quantitatively; and settled the question.

Ten years later, *Time on the Cross*, his book with Stanley Engerman, caused a firestorm of controversy for its conclusions. One of these was that the lives of slaves were not so bad, at least when one compared the clothing they were issued with that worn by free workers in the northern cities, or the number of calories ingested by the two sets of people. *Time on the Cross* came in two volumes: one, in big print with lots of bar graphs, laid out the main ideas of the authors but contained none of the proof; the second, in small print with lots of tables and equations, contained the data and the mathematical apparatus used to analyze it. Most people read the first volume and were appalled; most did not read the second or did not understand it. *Time on the Cross* sparked a cottage industry of historians and economists who spent several years refuting the majority of its conclusions one by one.

Fogel won a Bancroft Prize with Stanley Engerman for *Time on the Cross*, and a Nobel Prize for economics (together with Douglass C. North) for his life's work: creating the subdiscipline of cliometrics. His most mature expression was *Without Consent or Contract: The Rise and Fall of American Slavery* (1989), in which he argued that slavery came to an end because of politics, not economics. In that book Fogel belatedly proved himself an adept narrative historian as well as a cliometrician, in an extended discussion of the people and personalities who opposed slavery.

As the twentieth century drew to a close, there were lots of working social scientific historians, but their movement seemed on the wane. They were beginning to bow, not before before what J. Morgan Kousser called "the neo-Luddite posture" ("Quantitative Social-Scientific History," 434) of such older-fashioned historians as Arthur Schlesinger, Jr. ("Almost all important questions are important precisely because they are not susceptible to quantitative answers"), but before the antipositivist mood of postmodernist cultural history (see Chapter 53).

Railroads and American
Economic Growth[1]

To establish the proposition that railroads substantially altered the course of economic growth one must do more than provide information on the services of railroads. It must also be shown that substitutes for railroads could not (or would not) have performed essentially the same role. Writers who have held either that railroads were crucial to American economic growth or enormously accelerated this growth implicitly asserted that the economy of the nineteenth century lacked an effective alternative to the railroad and was incapable of producing one. This assertion is without empirical foundation; the range and potentiality of the supply of alternative opportunities is largely unexplored.

In the investigation of the incremental contribution of the railroad to economic growth it is useful to distinguish between the primary and the derived consequences of this innovation. The primary consequence of the railroad was its impact on the cost of transportation. If the cost of rail service had exceeded the cost of equivalent service by alternative forms of transportation over all routes and for all items, railroads would not have been built and all of the derived consequences would have been absent. The dervied consequences or aspects of the innovation included changes in the spatial distribution of economic activity and in the mix of final products. They also included the demand for inputs, especially manufactured goods and human skills, required for railroad construction and operation as well as the effects of that construction and operation on human psychology, political power, and social organization. Those who have held that railroads were indispensable to American economic growth could have based their position either on the ground that the reduction in transportation costs attributable to railroads was large or on the ground that the derived consequences of railroads were crucial (even if the reduction in transportation costs were small) or on some combination of the two types of effects.

The Primary Effect of Railroads

Summary of the Findings

In this study the investigation of the primary effect of railroads is limited to transportation costs connected with the distribution of agricultural products. Chapters II and III discuss the increase in the production potential of the economy made possible by the availability of railroads for the transportation of such goods. The main conceptual device used in the analysis of this problem is the "social saving." The social saving in any given year is defined as the difference between the actual cost of shipping agricultural goods in that year and the alternative cost of shipping exactly the same collection of goods between exactly the same set of points without railroads.

This cost differential is in fact larger than the "true" social saving. Forcing the pattern of shipments in a non-rail situation to conform to the pattern that actually existed is equivalent to the imposition of a restraint on society's freedom to adjust to an alternative technological situation. If society had had to ship by water and wagon without the railroad it could have altered the geographical locus of agricultural production or shifted some productive factor out of agriculture altogether. Further, the sets of primary and secondary markets through which agricultural surpluses were distributed were surely influenced by conditions peculiar to rail transportation; in the absence of railroads some different cities would have entered these sets, and the relative importance of those remaining would have changed. Adjustments of this sort would have reduced the loss of national income occasioned by the absence of the railroad.

For analytical convenience the computation of the social saving is divided into two parts. Chapter II deals with the social saving in interregional distribution.

* * *

While the interregional social saving is large compared to the actual transportation cost, it is quite small compared to annual output of the economy— just six-tenths of one per cent of gross national product. Hence the computed social saving indicates that the availability of railroads for the interregional distribution of agricultural products represented only a relatively small addition to the production potential of the economy.

The Social Saving in the Interregional
Distribution of Agricultural Commodities

First approximation	$38,000,000
Neglected cargo losses	6,000,000
Transshipping costs	16,000,000
Supplementary wagon haulage	23,000,000
Neglected capital costs	18,000,000
Additional inventory costs	48,000,000
Total	$73,000,000

The estimation of the social saving is more complex in intraregional trade (movements from farms to primary markets) than in long-haul trade. Interregional transportation represented a movement between a relatively small number of points—eleven great collection centers in the Midwest and ninety secondary markets in the East and South. But intraregional transportation required the connection of an enormous number of locations. Considering each farm as a shipping point, there were not 11 but 4,565,000 interior shipping locations in 1890; the number of primary markets receiving farm commodities was well over a hundred. These points were not all connected by the railroad network, let alone by navigable waterways. The movement of commodities from farms to primary markets was never accomplished exclusively by water or by rail. Rather it involved a mixture of wagon and water or wagon and train services.

This is the crux of the intraregional problem. If the evaluation of the impact of interior railroads merely involved an analysis of the substitution of water for rail transportation, there would be no reason to expect a large social saving. Considered in isolation, boats were a relatively efficient substitute for the iron horse. However the absence of the railroad would have required greater utilization not only of water service but also of wagon service. It is the additional amount of very costly wagon transportation that would have been needed for the shipment of each ton of agricultural produce leaving the farm which suggests that the social saving attributable to interior railroads probably exceeded the social saving of the more celebrated trunk lines.

The intraregional social saving—which covers twenty-seven commodities—is estimated in two ways. The first computation (estimate α) is a direct extension of the method used for long-distance shipments. It is the difference between the actual cost of shipping goods from farms to primary markets in 1890 and the cost of shipping in exactly the same pattern without the railroad. However, in the intraregional case the assumption that pattern of shipments would have remained unchanged despite the absence of railroads implies that wagons would have carried certain agricultural commodities over distances in which wagon haulage costs greatly exceeded the market value of the produce. As a result estimate α introduces an upward bias that is too large to ignore.

It is possible to estimate the intraregional social saving by a method that reduces this upward bias. Without railroads the high cost of wagon transportation would have limited commercial agricultural production to areas of land lying within some unknown distance of navigable waterways. If the boundaries of this region of feasible commercial agriculture were known, the social saving could be broken into two parts: (1) the difference between the cost of shipping agricultural commodities from farms lying within the feasible region to primary markets with the railroad and the cost of shipping from the same region without the railroad (i.e., an α estimate for the feasible region), and (2) the loss in national product due to the decrease in the supply of agricultural land. The social saving estimated in this manner (estimate β) would be less than the previous measure since it allows for a partial adjustment to a non-rail situation. Moreover, by disaggregating the social saving, estimate β provides additional information on the gestalt of the railroad's influence on the development of agriculture.

A first approximation of the α estimate can be computed on the basis of the relationship shown in equation 3.2.

$$(3.2) \qquad \alpha = x\,[w(D_{fb} - D_{fr}) + (BD_{bp} - RD_{rp})]$$

where

x = the tonnage of agricultural produce shipped out of counties by rail

w = the average wagon rate per ton-mile

B = the average water rate per ton-mile

R = the average rail rate per ton-mile

D_{fb} = the average distance from a farm to a water shipping point

D_{fr} = the average distance from a farm to rail shipping point

D_{bp} = the average distance from a water shipping point to a primary market

D_{rp} = the average distance from a rail shipping point to a primary market.

*   *   *

It thus appears that while railroads were more important in short-haul movements of agricultural products than in long-haul movements, the differences are not as great as is usually supposed. It is very likely that even in the absence of railroads the prairies would have been settled and exploited. Cheap transportation rather than railroads was the necessary condition for the emergence of the North Central states as the granary of the nation. The railroad was undoubtedly the most efficient form of transportation available to the farmers of the nation. But the combination of wagon and water transportation could have provided a relatively good substitute for the fabled iron horse.

*   *   *

The Derived Effects

*   *   *

The "Take-Off" Thesis

Perhaps the most persuasive theory of embodied consequences is the one which holds that the inputs required for railroad construction induced the rise of industries, techniques and skills essential to economic growth. Chapters IV and V examine the widely discussed version of this theory authored by W. W. Rostow. According to Rostow the growth of America's modern basic industrial sectors can be traced directly to the requirements for building and, especially, maintaining the railway system. Through their demand for coal, iron, machinery, and other manufactured goods railroads are supposed to have ushered the United States into a unique period of structural transformation that built modern growth into the economy. Rostow calls this period of radical transformation, the "take-off into self-sustained growth." He holds that it occurred between 1843 and 1860.

At first sight it might appear that available data support Rostow's contention that the eighteen years from 1843 through 1860 witnessed a unique structural transformation in the economy. According to data compiled by Robert Gallman the manufacturing share of commodity output increased from 21.1 per cent to 32.0 per cent over a period closely approximating the one singled out by Rostow—1844 through 1859. While this shift towards manufacturing is impressive, averaging 3.6 percentage points per quinquennium, it is by no means unique. Gallman's series extends from 1839 to 1899. Of the 12 quinquennia included in the study, the manufacturing share increased by 3.0 points or more in half. However, only one of these high-rate-of-change periods falls during Rostow's "take-off" years. Four belong to the epoch following the Civil War. Indeed, the increase in the manufacturing share during the fifteen years from 1879 to 1894 exceeded that of 1844-59 by 50 per cent.

Unfortunately there is no aggregate measure equivalent to Gallman's for the period prior to 1839. Available information indicates, however, that the decade of the 1820's may have witnessed a shift toward manufacturing comparable to that observed for the "take-off" years. This possibility is supported by the sharp decline in the home manufacture of consumer's goods and by the fact that urban population increased at twice the rate of the population as a whole. It is also buttressed by the rapid rise of the cotton textile and iron industries. The production of cotton cloth increased by over 500 per cent between 1820 and 1831. In the latter year the output of textiles was 40 per cent greater in America than it had been in Great Britain at the close of its "take-off." The growth of iron production outstripped that of cotton. The output of pig iron increased from 20,000 tons in 1820 to 192,000 tons in 1830, a rise of nearly 900 per cent. By 1830 iron, like textiles, was a substantial industry. In this branch of manufacture too, American production in 1830 exceeded British production at the close of the era that Rostow designated as the British "take-off."

The development of cotton textiles and iron during the 1820's was so rapid that even if all other commodity producing sectors grew no faster than the population, the manufacturing share of commodity output would have increased 1.5 percentage points. And if manufacturing industries other than iron and cotton grew at three times the rate of population, the manufacturing share in commodity output would have risen by nearly 6 percentage points. Since the production of woolen textiles, carpets, paper, primary refined lead, sugar, and meat packing expanded from three to twenty-five times as rapidly as the population, the last alternative seems quite reasonable.

Available evidence thus tends to controvert the view that the period from 1843 to 1860 or any other eighteen-year period was one of unique structural change. Instead, the data suggest a process of more or less continuous increase in the absolute and relative size of manufacturing extending from 1820—a good argument can be made for viewing 1807 as the starting date—through the end of the century.

The doubt attached to Rostow's dictum on the existence of very short periods of decisive structural transformation does not imply that historians must abandon the concept of "industrial revolution." One should not, however, require a revolution to have the swiftness of a coup d'etat. That manufacturing accounted for about 10 per cent of commodity production in 1820 and 48 per cent in 1889 is certainly evidence of a dramatic change in what was, by historical standards, hardly more than a moment of time. One need not arbitrarily abstract eighteen years out of a continuum to uphold the use of a venerable term.

If the growth of manufacturing during the two decades prior to the Civil War was not the crossing of the Rubicon pictured by Rostow, it was nonetheless large and impressive. The question of the relationship between this growth and the materials required for the construction and maintenance of railroads still remains.

The Iron Industry

Iron is the most frequently cited example of an industry whose rise was dominated by railroads. Hofstadter, Miller, and Aaron, for example, report that the railroad was "by far the biggest user of iron in the 1850's" and that by 1860 "more than half the iron produced annually in the United States went into rails" and associated items. Such reports, however, are not based on systematic measurements but on questionable inferences derived from isolated scraps of data. Casual procedures have led to the use of an index that grossly exaggerates the rail share, to the neglect of the rerolling process, and to a failure to consider the significance of the scrapping process.

The systematic reconstruction of the position of rails in the market for iron requires the development of a model of rail consumption that incorporates the largest number of available data fragments in an internally consistent manner. A model which meets this specification involves the following variables:

R_t = tons of rails consumed in year t

R_{dt} = tons of rails produced domestically in year t

R_{ft} = tons of rails imported in year t

R_{jt} = tons of worn rails scrapped in year t

M_t = track-miles of rails laid in year t; a track-mile of rails is defined as one-half of the miles of rails in a mile of single track

w_t = the average weight of rails in year t per track-mile of rails laid in year t; i.e., $w_t = \dfrac{R_t}{M_t}$

Mst = track-miles of rails used in the construction of new single track in year t

Met = track-miles of rails used in the construction of new extra track in year t; extra track refers to second and third tracks on a given line, sidings, etc.

Mrt = track-miles of rails used in the replacement of worn out rails in year t

t = time measured in years.

The model can be set forth as follows:

(5.1) R_t = $M_t W_t$

(5.2) R_{dt} = $R_t - R_{ft}$

(5.3) M_t $=$ $Mst + Met + Mrt$

t

ΣMet

(5.4) $\dfrac{0}{t}$ $=$ αt

ΣMst

0

(5.5) Mrt $=$ $\beta 1 M_t - 1 + \beta 2 M_t - 2 + \ldots + \beta n M_t - n; \Sigma\beta = 1$

* * *

The strongest statement that can be made in support of Rostow's thesis is that the demand for railroad iron played an increasingly important role during the fifties in maintaining the *previous* level of production when the demand for other items sagged. Otherwise one could just as well argue that nails rather than rails triggered the 1845–49 leap in iron production. Indeed in 1849 the domestic production of nails probably exceeded that of rails by over 100 per cent.

QUESTIONS TO CONSIDER

1. What is the core of Fogel's argument?
2. Fogel has been accused of reducing history to numbers. What are the strengths and weaknesses of this quantitative approach to the past?
3. How does Fogel's treatment of economic history differ from Dutt's?

FOR FURTHER READING

Aydelotte, William O., Allan G. Bogue, and Robert William Fogel, eds. *The Dimensions of Quantitative Research in History.* Princeton, NJ: Princeton University Press, 1972.

Benson, Lee. *The Concept of Jacksonian Democracy.* Princeton, NJ: Princeton University Press, 1961.

_____ . *Toward the Scientific Study of History.* Philadelphia: Lippincott, 1972.

Bruchey, Stuart. *The Roots of American Economic Growth, 1607–1861: An Essay in Social Causation.* New York: Harper and Row, 1965.

David, Paul A., et al. *Reckoning with Slavery: A Critical Study in the Quantitative History of American Negro Slavery.* New York: Oxford University Press, 1976.

Dawley, Alan. *Class and Community: The Industrial Revolution in Lynn.* Cambridge, MA: Harvard University Press, 1976.

Engerman, Stanley L., and Robert E. Gallman, eds. *Longterm Factors in American Economic Growth.* Chicago: University of Chicago Press, 1986.

Fogel, Robert William. *Without Consent or Contract.* New York: Norton, 1989.

_____ , and G. R. Elton. *Which Road to the Past? Two Views of History.* New Haven, CT: Yale University Press, 1983.

_____ , and Stanley L. Engerman. *Time on the Cross: The Economics of American Negro Slavery.* 2 vols. Boston: Little, Brown, 1974.

Gutman, Herbert. *Slavery and the Numbers Game: A Critique of Time on the Cross.* Urbana, IL: Univerity of Illinois Press, 1975.

Hareven, Tamara K. *Family Time and Industrial Time.* Cambridge, UK: Cambridge University Press, 1982.

Kousser, J. Morgan. "Quantitative Social-Scientific History." In *The Past Before Us,* edited by Michael Kammen, 433–56. Ithaca, NY: Cornell University Press, 1980.

Landes, David S., and Charles Tilly. *History as Social Science.* Englewood Cliffs, NJ: Prentice Hall, 1971.

Lee, Susan Previant, and Peter Passell. *A New Economic View of American History.* New York: Norton, 1979.

Modell, John. *Into One's Own: From Youth To Adulthood In The United States, 1920–1975.* Berkeley, CA: University of California Press, 1989.

Myrdal, Gunnar. *An American Dilemma.* New York: Harper, 1944.

North, Douglass C. *Growth and Welfare in the American Past.* 2nd ed. Englewood Cliffs, NJ: Prentice Hall, 1974.

———. *Structure and Change in Economic History.* New York: Norton, 1981.

Ransom, Roger L., Richard Sutch, and Gary M. Walton, eds. *Explorations in the New Economic History.* New York: Academic Press, 1982.

Ryan, Mary P. *The Cradle of the Middle Class: The Family in Odeida County, New York, 1790–1865.* Cambridge, UK: Cambridge University Press, 1981.

Thernstrom, Stephan. *The Other Bostonians: Poverty and Progress in the American Metropolis, 1880–1970.* Cambridge, MA.: Harvard University Press, 1973.

Tilly, Charles. *The Vendee.* Cambridge, MA: Harvard University Press, 1964.

NOTES

1. Robert William Fogel, *Railroads and American Economic Growth* (Baltimore: Johns Hopkins Press, 1964), 207–9, 211–13, 219, 228–31, 233.

CHAPTER 50

Race

John W. Blassingame

THE BROOMSTICK WEDDING.
"Look squar' at de broomstick! All ready now! one-two-three-jump!"

A slave wedding
© North Wind Pictures

I n 1900, W. E. B. DuBois wrote that the problem of the twentieth century would be the problem of the color line. That is no less true as the century draws to a close than it was when DuBois wrote it more than nine decades earlier. Much of the best historical writing has been on race, and much of the best work on race has been on America's biggest racial problem: slavery. From the nuanced perceptions and lyrical prose of Winthrop Jordan to the method-ological innovations of Lawrence Levine, slavery has occupied the pens of many of America's finest historians. John Blassingame is one.

Blassingame was born in Georgia in 1940 and educated there, at Howard University, and at Yale. Since 1970 he has taught African American studies and history at Yale. He is coauthor of an interpretive history of African Americans, author of a study of the Black people of New Orleans during and after the Civil War, and editor of several collections of documents, including the papers of Frederick Douglass, the giant of nineteenth-century African American history.

The selection here is taken from Blassingame's masterwork, *The Slave Community.* Here Blassingame engaged in a debate with two writers of earlier generations, Ulrich B. Phillips and Stanley Elkins. Writing in the first half of the twentieth century, Phillips was one of the main propounders of the mint julep school of American historical writing. He argued that slavery, while it seemed awfully unfair, was really a pretty good thing for the slaves—in part because African Americans in Phillips's view were best characterized by the stereotype of Sambo, an infantile, fawning creature incapable of taking care of himself. Elkins, writing after World War II, thought that slavery was terrible, and that Sambo was proof: slavery had reduced competent human beings to miserable, dependent creatures. Together with Sterling Stuckey, Eugene Gen-ovese, Lawrence Levine, and several other writers of the 1960s and '70s, Blassingame took exception to both viewpoints. The image of Sambo, said Blassingame and the others, told much more about White slave masters than it did about Black slaves. Slaves had many more resources than Elkins gave them credit for—among them religion, songs, stories, family, community, and covert resistance. In framing his argument and supporting his points, Blassin-game draws on the techniques and concerns of other passions of the present in historical writing: culture, family, and psychological interpretations.

Blassingame's writing is in line with the main thrust of writing on race in the latter twentieth century: a concentration on African Americans and other people of color as actors, rather than simply the objects of actions by Whites. He tells the history of African Americans from the points of view of African Americans. One sees a similar emphasis in the writing of Ronald Takaki on Asian Americans, Mario García on Chicanos, Albert Hurtado on Native Americans, and Karen Leonard on people of mixed racial ancestry. One theme of very recent work on race, including that of Leonard and of George Sanchez, and a theme that is not evident in Blassingame, is the idea of race as a plastic category, a social construction that changes its content and meaning over time.

The Slave Community[1]

Culture

Antebellum black slaves created several unique cultural forms which lightened their burden of oppression, promoted group solidarity, provided ways for verbalizing aggression, sustaining hope, building self-esteem, and often represented areas of life largely free from the control of whites. However oppressive or dehumanizing the plantation was, the struggle for survival was not severe enough to crush all of the slave's creative instincts. Among the elements of slave culture were: an emotional religion, folk songs and tales, dances, and superstitions. Much of the slave's culture—language, customs, beliefs, and ceremonies—set him apart from his master. His thoughts, values, ideals, and behavior were all greatly influenced by these processes. The more his cultural forms differed from those of his master and the more they were immune from the control of whites, the more the slave gained in personal autonomy and positive self-concepts.

The social organization of the quarters was the slave's primary environment which gave him his ethical rules and fostered cooperation, mutual assistance, and black solidarity. The work experiences which most often brought the slave in contact with whites represented his secondary environment and was far less important in determining his personality than his primary environment. The slave's culture or social heritage and way of life determined the norms of conduct, defined roles and behavioral patterns, and provided a network of individual and group relationships and values which molded personality in the quarters. The socialization process, shared expectations, ideals, and enclosed status system of the slave's culture promoted group identification and a positive self-concept. His culture was reflected in socialization, family patterns, religion, and recreation. Recreational activities led to cooperation, social cohesion, tighter communal bonds, and brought all classes of slaves together in common pursuits.[2]

The few periods of recreation the slave enjoyed and his religious beliefs gave him some hours of joy and a degree of hope amid his sufferings. Since his recreation was less supervised than his labor, these hours were especially important to him. Leisure time and religious activities broke the monotony of daily toil and permitted the slave to play roles other than that of the helpless dependent driven to this tasks. During his leisure hours the slave could take out his anger towards whites in physical contests with other slaves or seek relief in religious devotion by turning to One more powerful than his earthly master. Religious and recreational activities and the differences between the slave's and the master's customs prevented his total identification with the slaveholder's interests and gave him some respite from constant toil.[3]

* * *

Slaves spent their Sundays fishing, hunting, wrestling, running races, strumming the banjo, singing, dancing, playing marbles, recounting tales, fiddling, drinking whiskey, gambling, or simply visiting and conversing with friends. With or without their master's permission, they often organized dances and parties to which all of the slaves in the neighborhood were invited.

The social leaders at many of these affairs were the house slaves to whom the field slaves looked "as a pattern of politeness and gentility."[4] At one of the balls, Austin Steward recalled that the domestic servants came dressed in their masters' cast-off clothing and brought some of their owners' silverware, table cloths, wine, and food for the guests who were dancing to the tunes played by a slave fiddler. Anderson reported that his overseer once even permitted the slaves to use his master's house for a dance when the master and his family went visiting.

Apparently the European reels, minuets, and schottishes were too sedate and formalized for the slave. In the quarters the dance was more often a test of physical endurance, a means of winning praise and expressing the slave's inner feelings. Often openly lascivious, the dances involved wild gyrations to a furious rhythm.[5] According to a former slave,

> These dances were individual dances, consisting of shuffling of the feet, swinging of the arms and shoulders in a peculiar rhythm of time developed into what is known today as the Double Shuffle, Heel and Toe, Buck and Wing, Juba, etc. The slaves became proficient in such dances, and could play a tune with their feet, dancing largely to an inward music, a music that was felt, but not heard.[6]

The unrestrained exhibitions gave the slave some escape, some temporary relaxation from toil and refreshed his spirit.

In addition to these activities, several other customs prevented the slaves from identifying with the ideals of their masters. Because of their superstitions and belief in fortune tellers, witches, magic, and conjurers, many of the slaves constructed a psychological defense against total dependence on and submission to their masters. Whatever his power, the master was a puny man compared to the supernatural. Often the most powerful and significant individual on the plantation was the conjurer.

The conjurers gained their control over the slaves in various ways. Shrewd men, they generally were industrious enough to avoid punishment. They then told the slaves they were not punished because they had cast a spell on their masters. Claiming the ability to make masters kind, prevent floggings and separations, cause and prevent pain and suffering, insure love and happiness, the conjurers were often very successful in gaining adherents. Frequently they were able to do this because they used their knowledge of the medicinal value of roots and herbs to cure certain illnesses.

William Webb, who became a conjurer after observing a skillful practitioner at work, explained how he obtained complete sway over the slaves on one plantation in Kentucky. Observing that the slaves were disgruntled over their master's cruel treatment, Webb visited the quarters secretly, prayed for better treatment for the slaves, and then had the slaves collect various roots, put them in bags, march around the cabins several times, and point the bags toward the master's house every morning. When the master started treating his slaves better (because he had a dream in which they wreaked vengeance on him), the slaves were completely in Webb's power: they regaled him with sumptuous meals nightly, and the women were especially attentive.[7]

Faith in the conjurer was so strong that slaves often appealed to him to prevent floggings. M. F. Jamison declared that the conjurer on his plantation claimed that he "could prevent the white folks from mistreating you, hence those of us who could believe in such would visit him and have him 'fix' us." In many instances, the conjurer had more control over the slaves than the master had. Henry Clay Bruce felt that conjurers were so successful that the slaves had a mortal fear of them and "believed and feared them almost beyond their masters."[8]

Sometimes the charms the slaves obtained from the conjurers bolstered their courage and caused them to defy their masters. For example, after the powders and roots a conjurer gave to Henry Bibb appeared to prevent him from receiving a flogging, Bibb then had, he wrote,

> great faith in conjuration and witch-craft. I was led to believe that I could do almost as I pleased without being flogged. . . . [after going off the plantation without permission] my master declared that he would punish me for going off; but I did not believe that he could do it, while I had this root and dust; and as he approached me, I commenced talking saucy to him.[9]

* * *

Among the most important distinctive cultural forms in the quarters were folk songs and tales. It must be acknowledged at the outset that there are innumerable problems involved in using folk tales and songs to delineate the slave's world view. The major problem in attempting to analyze these elements of the culture is that all too many of the eyewitness accounts were recorded long after slavery ended. While undoubtedly many of the tales and songs recorded in the nineteenth century reflected the slave experience, they had, in effect, been corrupted by freedom. Even when authentic antebellum sources are used, they are limited because they generally represented only what blacks wanted white folks to hear. When this fact is added to the unfamiliarity of many of the whites with the slaves' language patterns and their general ignorance of music and folklore, the complexities of the problem are manifest. Then, too, many of the profane tales and secular songs were ignored by most witnesses. While some of these problems are insurmountable, others can be eliminated by a strict application of the rules of evidence. This is especially true in regard to slave music. Only evidence from witnesses who actually heard this music before and during the Civil War has been relied upon in this analysis.[10]

The secular songs told of the slave's loves, work, floggings, and expressed his moods and the reality of his oppression. On a number of occasions he sang of the proud defiance of the runaway, the courage of the black rebels, the stupidity of the patrollers, the heartlessness of the slave traders, and the kindness and cruelty of masters.[11]

* * *

Most slaves, repelled by the brand of religion their masters taught, formulated new ideas and practices in the quarters. The slave's religious principles were colored by his own longings for freedom and based on half-understood sermons in white churches or passages from the Old Testament, struggles of the Jews, beautiful pictures of a future life, enchantment and fear, and condemnation of sin. Frequently the praise meetings started on Saturday or Sunday evenings and lasted far into the night.[12]

A syncretism of African and conventional religious beliefs, the praise meeting in the quarters was unique in the United States. While whites might be carried away by religious frenzy at occasional "Awakenings," slaves had an even more intense emotional involvement with their God every week. In contrast to most white churches, a meeting in the quarters was the scene of perpetual motion and constant singing. Robert Anderson recalled that in meetings on his plantation there was much singing and "While singing these songs, the singers and the entire congregation kept time to the music by the swaying of their bodies, or by the patting of the foot or hand. Practically all of their songs were accompanied by a motion of some kind."[13] A black plantation preacher testified to the uniqueness of the religion in the quarters when he asserted:

> The way in which we worshipped is almost indescribable. The singing was accompanied by a certain ecstasy of motion, clapping of hands, tossing of heads, which would continue without cessation about half an hour; one would lead off in a kind of recitative style, others joining in the chorus. The old house partook of the ecstasy; it rang with their jubilant shouts, and shook in all its joints.[14]

* * *

The Slave Family

The family, while it had no legal existence in slavery, was in actuality one of the most important survival mechanisms for the slave. In his family he found companionship, love, sexual gratification, sympathetic understanding of his sufferings; he learned how to avoid punishment, to cooperate with other blacks, and to maintain his self-esteem. However frequently the family was broken, it was primarily responsible for the slave's ability to survive on the plantation without becoming totally dependent on and submissive to his master. The important thing was not that the family was not recognized legally or that masters frequently encouraged monogamous mating arrangements in the quarters only when it was convenient to do so, but rather that some form of family life did exist among slaves.

While the form of family life in the quarters differed radically from that among free Negroes and whites, this does not mean that the institution was unable to perform many of the traditional functions of the family. The rearing of children was one of the most important of these functions. Since slave parents were primarily responsible for training their children, they could cushion the shock of bondage for them, help them to understand their situation, teach them values different from those their masters tried to instill in them, and give them a referent for self-esteem other than their masters.

* * *

The degree to which slaves were able to give their children hope in the midst of adversity is reflected in the attitudes the black autobiographers held toward their parents. Fathers were loved and respected because of their physical strength, courage, and compassion. Austin Steward described his father as "a kind, affectionate husband and a fond, indulgent parent." James Watkins admired his father because he was "a clever, shrewd man." James Mars stood in awe of his father who "was a man of considerable muscular strength, and was not easily frightened into obedience." Although they were not always perfect male models, most slave fathers had the respect of their children. Viewing the little things that they did to make life more pleasant for their children, Charles Ball asserted: "Poor as the slave is, and dependent at all times upon the arbitrary will of his master, or yet more fickle caprice of the overseer, his children look up to him in his little cabin, as their protector and supporter."[15]

Slave mothers were, of course, held in even greater esteem by their children. Frequently small children fought overseers who were flogging their mothers. Even when they had an opportunity to escape from bondage, many slaves refused to leave their mothers. As a young slave, William Wells Brown did not run away because he "could not bear the idea" of leaving his mother. He felt that he, "after she had undergone and suffered so much for me would be proving recreant to the duty which I owed to her."[16]

* * *

Plantation Stereotypes and Institutional Roles

Personal relations on the plantation were, as in most institutions, determined by spatial arrangements, the frequency of interaction between high- and low-powered individuals, and how the high-powered individual defined the behavioral norms. In practice, of course, many of the institutionally defined roles were imperfectly played. Before one can examine the *actual* behavior on the plantation, however, the societal images and the planter's expectations of the slave must be compared. In the final analysis, the planter's expectations were more closely related to the slave's actual behavior than publicly held stereotypes. Even so, neither the planter's expectations nor the stereotypes were proscriptive. In other words, the slave did not necessarily act the way white people expected him to behave or the way they perceived him as behaving. . . .

The portrait of the slave which emerges from antebellum Southern literature is complex and contradictory.[17] The major slave characters were Sambo, Jack, and Nat. The one rarely seen in literature, Jack, worked faithfully as long as he was well treated. Sometimes sullen and uncooperative, he generally refused to be driven beyond the pace he had set for himself. Conscious of his identity with other slaves, he cooperated with them to resist the white man's oppression. Rationally analyzing the white man's overwhelming physical power, Jack either avoided contact with him or was deferential in his presence. Since he did not identify with his master and could not always keep up the facade of deference, he was occasionally flogged for insubordination. Although often proud, stubborn, and conscious of the wrongs he suffered, Jack tried to repress his anger. His patience was, however, not unlimited. He raided his master's larder when he was hungry, ran away when he was tired of working or had been punished, and was sometimes ungovernable. Shrewd and calculating, he used his wits to escape from work or to manipulate his overseer and master.

Nat was the rebel who rivaled Sambo in the universality and continuity of his literary image. Revengeful, bloodthirsty, cunning, treacherous, and savage, Nat was the incorrigible runaway, the poisoner of white men, the ravager of white women who defied all the rules of plantation society. Subdued and punished only when overcome by superior numbers or firepower, Nat retaliated when attacked by whites, led guerilla activities of maroons against isolated plantations, killed overseers and planters, or burned plantation buildings when he was abused. Like Jack, Nat's customary obedience often hid his true feelings, self-concept, unquenchable thirst for freedom, hatred of whites, discontent, and manhood, until he violently demonstrated these traits.[18]

Sambo, combining in his person Uncle Remus, Jim Crow, and Uncle Tom, was the most pervasive and long lasting of the three literary stereotypes. Indolent, faithful, humorous, loyal, dishonest, superstitious, improvident, and musical, Sambo was inevitably a clown and congenitally docile. Characteristically a house servant, Sambo had so much love and affection for his master that he was almost filio-pietistic; his loyalty was all-consuming and self-immolating. The epitome of devotion, Sambo often fought and died heroically while trying to save his master's life. Yet, Sambo had no thought of freedom; that was an empty boon compared to serving his master.[19]

The Sambo stereotype was so pervasive in antebellum Southern literature that many historians, without further research, argue that it was an accurate description of the dominant slave personality. According to historians of this stripe, the near unanimity of so many white observers of the slave cannot be dismissed.[20] While this is obviously true, it does not follow that the Sambo stereotype must be treated uncritically. Instead, it must be viewed in the context of the other slave stereotypes, and from the perspective of psychology and comparative studies in literature.

* * *

Another factor which compelled Southern writers to portray the slave as Sambo was their need to disprove the allegations of anti-slavery novelists. Facing the withering attack of the abolitionists, they had to prove that slavery was not an unmitigated evil. The loyal contented slave was a *sine qua non* in Southern literary propaganda. Whether he existed in fact was irrelevant to the writer. Without Sambo, it was impossible to prove the essential goodness of Southern society.[21]

Another of the important reasons for the pervasiveness of the Sambo stereotype was the desire of whites to relieve themselves of the anxiety of thinking about slaves as men. In this regard, Nat, the actual and potential rebel, stands at the core of white perceptions of the slave. With Nat perennially in the wings, the creation of Sambo was almost mandatory for the Southerner's emotional security. Like a man whistling in the dark to bolster his courage, the white man *had* to portray the slave as Sambo. This public stereotype only partially hid a multitude of private fears, which reached the proportion of mass hysteria at the mere mention of the word "rebellion." Generally, historians have been so intent upon proving that these fears were groundless that they have ignored the relationship between the countless rumors of rebellions and the white man's stereotype of the slave and the slave's actual behavior. If whites really believed that a majority of slaves were Sambos, how could they also believe that these pathetically loyal and docile blacks would rise up and cut their throats?

Judging from the ease with which whites conjured up Nat, they apparently felt that the relationship between the planter and the slave was one of continual war requiring eternal vigilance in order for the master to maintain the upper hand. In a sense, this is indicated by the constant changes in the slave codes. If the slave had accepted the Sambo role, there would have been little need to continue changing the codes after the first generation of American-born slaves had grown to adulthood. Slaveholders apparently believed in Sambos, for they were constantly searching for new ways to guarantee the subordination of slaves. Was this search simply a result of the formulation of new management techniques, or did it reflect slave behavior which contradicted the Sambo stereotype?

From an analysis of the constantly recurring rumors of insurrections, it is obvious that many whites considered black slaves dangerous, insubordinate, bold, evil, restless, turbulent, vengeful, barbarous, and malicious. The white man's fear and his anxiety about the slave was so deep and pervasive that it was sometimes pathological. An epidemic of runaways, a group of whispering slaves, mysterious fires, or almost any suspicious event caused alarm, apprehension, and a deepening state of paranoia among whites.[22]

* * *

It is almost impossible to square the white's fear of Nat with the predominance of the Sambo stereotype in plantation literature. Apparently both slave characters were real. The more fear whites had of Nat, the more firmly they tried to believe in Sambo in order to escape paranoia. This psychological repression was augmented by public acts to relieve anxiety. Every effort was made to keep the slaves in awe of the power of whiteness and ignorant of their own potential power. The congregation of crowds of slaves, their independent movement, possession of arms, and degree of literacy, were all strictly regulated. The rebellious slave was punished swiftly and cruelly to discourage others. The oppressive acts consisted of cropping ears, castrating, hanging, burning, and mutilating. The army, the militia, and the entire white community stood ready to aid any embattled region. In all of these actions, the whites demonstrated that, even if slaves did not revolt, they were considered rebellious. Consequently, Southern whites restricted their own freedom of speech, censored their newspapers, interfered with the U. S. mails, and lynched abolitionists to make sure that no one incited the rebellious slaves.[23]

NOTES

1. John W. Blassingame, *The Slave Community: Plantation Life in the Antebellum South* (New York: Oxford University Press, 1972), 41–42, 44–45, 48, 49–50, 64, 78–79, 102–103, 132–35, 138–40, 141. Footnotes have been renumbered to fit abridgement.
2. Milton M. Gordon, *Assimilation in American Life* (New York, 1964), 19–39; Leslie A. White, *The Science of Culture* (New York, 1949), 121–89.
3. Practically all secondary accounts of slavery discuss what could be generally described as slave "culture," but give little solid information on life in the quarters. See: Charles Sydnor, *Slavery in Mississippi* (New York, 1933), 55–66; Joe G. Taylor, *Negro Slavery in Louisiana* (Baton Rouge, 1963), 125–52; J. Winston Coleman, *Slavery Times in Kentucky* (Chapel Hill, 1940), 67–80.
4. Austin Steward, *Twenty-Two Years A Slave, and Forty Years A Freeman* (Rochester, New York, 1861), 32.
5. Philip V. Fithian, *Journal and Letters of Philip Vickers Fithian, 1773–1774* (Williamsburg, Va., 1943), 83; Nicholas Cresswell, *The Journal of Nicholas Cresswell, 1774–1777* (New York, 1924), 18–19, 30; James K. Paulding, *Letters From the South . . .* (New York, 1817), 119; Charles Lanman, *Haw-He-Noo: Or the Records of a Tourist* (Philadelphia, 1850), 144–45; Francis and Theresa Pulzsky, *White, Red, and Black* (3 vols., London, 1853), III, 13; John Finch, *Travels in the United States of America and Canada* (London, 1833), 237.
6. Robert Anderson, *From Slavery to Affluence* (Hemingford, Nebraska, 1927), 30–31.
7. Henry Bibb, *Narrative of the Life and Adventures of Henry Bibb, An American Slave* (New York, 1849), 24–32; William Wells Brown, *Narrative of William W. Brown, A Fugitive Slave* (Boston, 1847), 90–96; A. M. Bacon, "Conjuring and Conjure Doctors," *Southern Workman* XXIV (Nov. 1895), 193–94, (Dec. 1895), 209–11; Thaddeus Norris, "Negro Superstitions," *Lippincott's Magazine* VI (July 1870), 90–95.
8. Monroe F. Jamison, *Autobiography And Work of Bishop M. F. Jamison, D. D.* (Nashville, 1912), 34; Henry Clay Bruce, *The New Man, Twenty-Nine Years A Slave, Twenty-Nine Years A Free Man* (York, Pa., 1895), 54.
9. Bibb, *Adventures*, 26–27.
10. Many recent essays on the subject, while often informative, are marred by their heavy reliance on songs written and recorded after the Civil War or those popularized and commercialized by such groups as the Fisk Jubilee Singers and the New Orleans University Singers. See Sterling Stuckey, "The Black Ethos in Slavery," *Massachusetts Review* IX (Summer 1968),

417–37; David McD. Simms, "The Negro Spiritual: Origin and Themes," *Journal of Negro Education* XXXV (Winter, 1966), 35–41; John Lovell, "The Social Implications of the Negro Spiritual," *Journal of Negro Education* XVIII (Oct. 1939), 634–43.

11. George W. Cable, "Creole Slave Songs," *Century Magazine* XXXI (April 1886), 807–28; William C. Bryant, *Letters of a Traveller* (London, 1850), 85–86; Paulding, *Letters*, 126–27; Henry B. Whipple, *Bishop Whipple's Southern Diary* (Minneapolis, 1937), 33–34; Benjamin W. Griffith, "Longer Version of 'Guinea Negro Song' From A Georgia Frontier Songster," *Southern Folklore Quarterly* XXVIII (June 1964), 117.

12. Louis Hughes, *Thirty Years a Slave* (Milwaukee, 1897), 39–58; William Webb, *The History of William Webb* (Detroit, 1873), 8–12; Bruce, *New Man*, 72–77; Peter Randolph, *Sketches of Slave Life* (Boston, 1855), 67–69, 77.

13. Anderson, *From Slavery*, 24–25.

14. James L. Smith, *Autobiography of James L. Smith* (Norwich, Conn., 1881), 27.

15. Steward, *Twenty-Two Years*, 126; James Watkins, *Narrative of the Life of James Watkins* (Bolton, England, 1852), 7; James Mars, *Life of James Mars, A Slave Born and Sold in Connecticut* (Hartford, 1864), 3; Charles Ball, *Slavery in the United States: A Narrative of the Life and Adventures of Charles Ball* (Lewistown, Penn., 1836), 211.

16. W. W. Brown, *Narrative*, 31–32.

17. Francis P. Gaines, *The Southern Plantation: A Study in the Development and Accuracy and Tradition* (New York, 1925); Tremaine McDowell, "The Negro in the Southern Novel Prior to 1850," *Journal of English and Germanic Philology* XXV (Oct. 1926), 455–73; Charles E. Burch, "Negro Characters in the Novels of William Gilmore Simms," *Southern Workman* LII (April 1923), 192–95; Jack B. Moore, "Images of the Negro in Early American Short Fiction," *Mississippi Quarterly* XXXII (Winter 1968–69), 47–57; Sterling A. Brown, *The Negro in American Fiction* (Washington, D.C., 1937), 1–47; John H. Nelson, *The Negro Character in American Literature* (Lawrence, Kansas, 1926), 23–48, 86–92; Catherine J. Starge, *Black Portraiture in American Fiction* (New York, 1971), 30–45.

18. Howard Braverman, "An unusual Characterization by a Southern Ante-Bellum Writer," *Phylon* XIX (Summer 1958), 171–79; Calvin H. Wiley, *Life in the South: A Companion to Uncle Tom's Cabin* (1852); Bayard R. Hall, *Frank Freeman's Barbershop* (1852).

19. For portraits of Sambo risking his life to save his master see: Hector, Cato, Scipio, Braugh, and Tom in William Gilmore Simms, *The Yemasee* (1832), *The Foragers* (1855), *Mellichampe* (1836), *Southward Ho!* (1854), and *The Partisan* (1835).

20. Stanley Elkins, *Slavery: A Problem in American Institutional and Intellectual Life* (New York, 1963), 86–89.

21. Jeanette Tandy, "Pro-Slavery Propaganda in American Fiction of the Fifties," *South Atlantic Quarterly* XXI (Jan. 1922), 41–50, (April 1922), 170–78; Jay B. Hubbell, *Southern Life in Fiction* (Athens, Ga., 1960).

22. Herbert Aptheker, *American Negro Slave Revolts* (New York, 1943); Thomas
    W. Higginson, "Nat Turner's Insurrection," *Atlantic Monthly* VIII (Aug.
    1861), 173–87; Robert N. Elliott, "The Nat Turner Insurrection As Reported
    in the North Carolina Press," *North Carolina Historical Review* XXXVIII (Jan.
    1861), 1–18; Donald B. Kelley, "Harper's Ferry: Prelude to Crisis in
    Mississippi," *Journal of Mississippi History* XXVII (Nov. 1865), 351–72.
23. Clement Eaton, *Freedom of Thought in the Old South* (New York, 1951),
    89–117; Herbert Aptheker, *One Continual Cry: David Walker's Appeal to the
    Colored Citizens of the World* (New York, 1965), 45–53.

QUESTIONS TO CONSIDER

1. What materials does Blassingame use to open up the psychic world of
   African American slaves?
2. How might these same slaves have looked different to their White masters?
   How might they have looked different to historians in the Southern White
   tradition?
3. What is the relationship between Blassingame's assertion of Black agency
   and the anticolonial narratives of the Aztec and Mayan chroniclers (29),
   Panikkar (43), and Said (56)?

FOR FURTHER READING

Axtell, James. *The Invasion Within: The Contest of Cultures in Colonial North America.*
    New York: Oxford University Press, 1985.
Berry, Mary Frances, and John W. Blassingame. *Long Memory: The Black Experience in
    America.* New York: Oxford, 1982.
Blassingame, John W. *Black New Orleans, 1860–1880.* Chicago: University of Chicago
    Press, 1973.
———, ed. *Slave Testimony: Two Centuries of Letters, Speeches, Interviews, and
    Autobiographies.* Baton Rouge, LA: Louisiana State University Press, 1977.
———, et al., eds. *The Frederick Douglass Papers.* Multiple volumes. New Haven, CT:
    Yale University Press, 1979–present.
Deloria, Vine. *Custer Died for Your Sins.* New York: Macmillan, 1969.
DuBois, Ellen, and Vicki Ruiz, eds. *Unequal Sisters: A Multicultural Reader in U.S.
    Women's History.* New York: Routledge, 1990.
DuBois, W. E. B. *Black Reconstruction in America.* Cleveland, OH: World, 1962.
———. *The Suppression of the African Slave-Trade to the United States of America,
    1638–1870.* New York: Russell and Russell, 1965; orig. Longmans, Green, 1896.
Elkins, Stanley. *Slavery: A Problem in American Institutional and Intellectual Life.*
    Chicago: University of Chicago Press, 1959.
Franklin, John Hope. *The Free Negro in North Carolina, 1790–1860.* Chapel Hill, NC:
    University of North Carolina Press, 1943.
Genovese, Eugene. *Roll, Jordan, Roll: The World the Slaves Made.* New York: Random
    House, 1974.

Gilmore, Al-Tony. *Revisiting Blassingame's The Slave Community: The Scholars Respond.* Westport, CT: Greenwood, 1978.

Gutiérrez, Ramón A. *When Jesus Came, the Corn Mothers Went Away: Marriage, Sexuality, and Power in New Mexico, 1500–1846.* Stanford, CA: Stanford University Press, 1991.

Hurtado, Albert L. *Indian Survival on the California Frontier.* New Haven, CT: Yale University Press, 1988.

Jennings, Francis. *The Invasion of America: Indians, Colonialism, and the Cant of Conquest.* New York: Norton, 1975.

Jordan, Winthrop D. *White Over Black: The Origins of American Race Relations.* Chapel Hill, NC: University of North Carolina Press, 1968.

Leonard, Karen Isaksen. *Making Ethnic Choices: California's Punjabi Mexican Americans.* Philadelphia: Temple University Press, 1992.

Levine, Lawrence W. *Black Culture and Black Consciousness.* New York: Oxford University Press, 1977.

Monroy, Douglas. *Thrown Among Strangers: The Making of Mexican Culture in Frontier California.* Berkeley, CA: University of California Press, 1990.

Phillips, Ulrich B. *Life and Labor in the Old South.* Boston: Little, Brown, 1929.

Raboteau, Albert J. *Slave Religion.* New York: Oxford University Press, 1978.

Sanchez, George J. *Becoming Mexican American: Ethnicity, Culture, and Identity in Chicano Los Angeles, 1900–1945.* New York: Oxford University Press, 1993.

Stampp, Kenneth. *The Peculiar Institution.* New York: Random House, 1956.

Stuckey, Sterling. *Slave Culture: Nationalist Theory and the Foundations of Black America.* New York: Oxford University Press, 1987.

Takaki, Ronald. *Strangers from a Different Shore: A History of Asian Americans.* Boston: Little, Brown, 1989.

CHAPTER 51

Class

E. P. Thompson

Edward Palmer Thompson
© Gary Olsen

E dward Palmer Thompson (1924–1994) was born into a British intellectual family noted for its liberalism and for its opposition to British rule in India. The family home was host to Tagore, Gandhi, Nehru, and other luminaries of the independence movement, each of whom left a mark on the young man. His father was a historian, and Edward gravitated to that field just as he gravitated to his father's politics. He even went beyond the politics, joining the British Communist Party while at university, before commanding a tank troop in World War II. Thompson stayed with the Party until 1956, when he left over its residual Stalinism.

A founder and editor of *The New Left Review,* Thompson taught in the adult education program at Leeds University and at the Centre for the Study of Social History at Warwick. At both these posts and through his continued political activism, he helped bring a humanized Marxism to the emerging New Left of the sixties and seventies. In the 1980s, Thompson was a major figure in the European Campaign for Nuclear Disarmament. One opinion poll in that decade found him the second most trusted politican in Britain after the Queen.

Thompson's historical works reflect his political commitments. This is not unusual; most historians' work does so, but few have commitments so far outside the mainstream. Rather than focusing on history from above— politicians and captains of industry—Thompson wrote history from below. He wanted to recount the past as experienced by, reacted to, and formed in the lives of ordinary people. He had a particular concern for the perspectives of the industrial working class.

Thompson's first major work was a biography of William Morris, a nineteenth-century British Romantic whose work contained a radical critique of the capitalist order. Thompson, still a Party member when it appeared in 1955, portrayed Morris as possessing a Communist vision, even though he lacked the Marxist conceptual resources that Thompson then believed were necessary to make an accurate analysis of capitalism.

By the time he came to write *The Making of the English Working Class* (1963), Thompson had modified both his historical and his political views. In that work, which has had as great an effect on late-twentieth-century historical writing as any other single book, Thompson tried to trace the emergence of a self-conscious nineteenth-century working class out of the mass of the poor with which that century began. Rather than following Marx in seeing this as an automatic result of capitalism, Thompson found a varied series of struggles in different locales. Some were leaderless responses to a new economic order. More, however, were conscious attempts to defend previously guaranteed rights that the British ruling class was trying to sweep away. And most were led by revolutionary intellectuals who convinced others of the need to struggle, even when the odds against them seemed overwhelming. Thompson showed how the development of a working class did not proceed in a straight line; it occurred only gradually and with many setbacks. That it occurred at all, he believed, was a tribute to the independence of the human spirit.

Thompson's third major historical study, *Whigs and Hunters* (1975), continued his revisionism. Where he had previously seen the law as mainly an upper-class tool, as it had been at the time of Pitt's repression during the

Napoleonic War, he now emphasized the ways that the poor and their rulers contested over it. Both could use the law, and it was not always the upper class that won. Sometimes British magistrates even had to rule against the law to maintain upper-class privilege—violating, for example, the still-standing Elizabethan apprenticeship codes so as to give manufacturers fuller control over their workers. At other times the poor were actually able to use the law to defend their rights. Thompson had thus moved from the Marxist assumption that the law invariably reflects the interests of the governing classes to a more inductively analytical posture.

Although Thompson maintained his progressive political commitments, during the last two decades of his life he made as many enemies on the left as he had previously made on the right. His *Poverty of Theory* (1978) contained a blistering critique of Louis Althusser's structural Marxism; accusing Althusser of turning people into robots by denying them even the smallest ability to control their lives. Instead, Thompson set forth a vision of social change arising out of individual (and sometimes heroic) human action. People could and did act for themselves, not impelled inexorably by historical forces. But their actions seldom worked out as they intended. Thompson cited William Morris, who argued that "men fight and lost the battle, and the thing they fought for comes about in spite of their defeat, and when it comes [it] turns out not to be what they meant, and other men have to fight for what they meant under another name." For Thompson, this "involuntary volunteerism" typified human history.

All of Thompson's historical works are rich in detail, reflecting his ever increasing distrust of theories and generalizations purporting to summarize events. A huge book, *The Making of the English Working Class* is filled with such humanizing details, as the following passage shows. Thompson used government figures, industrial records, reminiscences, letters to newspapers— anything that could shed light on the lives of people he wrote about. In writing the history of the poor, however, Thompson would not accept these sources at face value, always analyzing the perspective of the writers. Most writers documenting the poor of the Industrial Revolution saw them as rabble; the historian had to read through their descriptions to see the lives of the poor people behind. The historian's job was not to parrot any particular observer but to recreate the context so that the evidence would illumine real lives.

Yet for all its particularity, Thompson's work also has theoretical significance. He rescued the concept of class from deterministic Marxism and reestablished it to indicate a social stratum combining economic situation with self-consciousness. The modern working class was thus not something that simply sprang into existence; it had to be made. The first part of the following passage describes the making of one segment of that class. It traces the transformation of weavers from independent artisans to oppressed workers. The last part of the selection gives some of Thompson's conclusions about that process; these conclusions parallel those of the eighteenth-century writer Thompson respected most, the poet William Blake.

The Making of the
English Working Class[1]
The Weavers

The history of the weavers in the 19th century is haunted by the legend of better days. The memories are strongest in Lancashire and Yorkshire. But they obtained in most parts of Britain and in most branches of textiles. Of the Midlands stocking-weavers in the 1780s:

> When the wake came, the stocking-maker had peas and beans in his snug garden, and a good barrel of humming ale.

He had "a week-day suit of clothes and one for Sundays and plenty of leisure."[2] Of the Gloucestershire weavers:

> Their little cottages seemed happy and contented . . . it was seldom that a weaver appealed to the parish for a relief. . . . Peace and content sat upon the weaver's brow.[3]

Of the linen-weaving quarter of Belfast:

> . . . a quarter once remarkable for its neatness and order; he remembered their whitewashed houses, and their little flower gardens, and the decent appearance they made with their families at markets, or at public worship. These houses were now a mass of filth and misery. . . .[4]

Dr. Dorothy George, in her lucid and persuasive *England in Transition*, has argued that the "golden age" was in general a myth. And her arguments have carried the day.

They have, perhaps, done so too easily. After all, if we set up the ninepin of a "golden age" it is not difficult to knock it down. Certainly, the condition of the Spitalfields silk-weavers in the 18th century was not enviable. And it is true that capitalist organisation of the woollen and worsted industries of the south-west and of Norwich early gave rise to many forms of antagonism which anticipate later developments in Lancashire and Yorkshire. Certainly, also, the conditions of the 18th century weaving communities were idealised by Gaskell in his influential *Manufacturing Population of England* (1833); and by Engels when (following Gaskell) he conjured up a picture of the grandparents of the factory operatives of 1844 "leading a righteous and peaceful life in all piety and probity."

But the fact of 18th-century hardship and conflict on the one hand, and of 19th-century idealisation on the other, does not end the matter. The memories remain. And so does plentiful evidence which does not admit of easy interpretation. The existence of supplementary earnings from small farming or merely slips of garden, spinning, harvest work, etc., is attested from most parts of the country. There is architectural evidence to this day testifying to the solidity of many late 18th-century weaving hamlets in the Pennines. The commonest error today is not of Gaskell and Engels but that of the optimist

who muddles over the difficult and painful nature of the change in status from
artisan to depressed outworker in some such comforting phrases as these:

> The view that the period before the Industrial Revolution was a sort of golden
> age is a myth. Many of the evils of the early factory age were no worse than
> those of an earlier period. Domestic spinners and weavers in the eighteenth
> century had been "exploited" by the clothiers as ruthlessly as the factory
> operatives were "exploited" by the manufacturers in the 1840s.[5]

We may distinguish between four kinds of weaver-employer relationship
to be found in the 18th century. (1) The customer-weaver—the Silas Marner,
who lived in independent status in a village or small town, much like a
master-tailor, making up orders for customers. His numbers were declining,
and he need not concern us here. (2) The weaver, with the status of a superior
artisan, self-employed, and working by the piece for a choice of masters.
(3) The journeyman weaver, working either in the shop of his master clothier,
or, more commonly, in his own home and at his own loom for a single master.
(4) The farmer or smallholder weaver, working only part-time in the loom.

The last three groups all run into each other, but it is helpful if the
distinctions are made. For example in the mid 18th century, the Manchester
small-ware and check trades were largely conducted by weaver-artisans
(group 2), with a high degree of organisation. As the cotton industry
expanded in the latter half of the century, more and more small farmers
(group 4) were attracted by the high wages to becoming part-time weavers. At
the same time the West Riding woollen industry remained largely organised
on the basis of small working-clothiers employing only a handful of journeymen and apprentices (group 3) in their own domestic unit. We may simplify
the experiences of the years 1780–1830 if we say that they saw the merging of
all three groups into a group, whose status was greatly debased—that of the
proletarian outworker, who worked in his own home, sometimes owned and
sometimes rented his loom, and who wove up the yarn to the specifications of
the factor or agent of a mill or of some middleman. He lost the status and
security which groups 2 and 3 might expect, and the side-earnings of group 4:
he was exposed to conditions which were, in the sense of a London artisan,
wholly "dishonourable."

Among the weavers of the north memories of lost status were grounded
in authentic experiences and lingered longest. In the West Country by the end
of the 18th century the weavers were already outworkers, employed by the
great gentlemen clothier who "buys the wool, pays for the spinning, weaving,
Milling, Dying, Shearing, Dressing, etc.," and who might employ as many as
1,000 workers in these processes. A Yorkshire witness in 1806 contrasted the
two systems. In the West Country,

> there is no such thing as what we in Yorkshire call the domestic system; what
> I mean by the domestic system is the little clothiers living in villages, or in
> detached places, with all their comforts, carrying on business with their own
> capital. . . . I understand that in the west of England it is quite the reverse of

that, the manufacturer there is the same as our common workman in a factory in Yorkshire, except living in a detached house; in the west the wool is delivered out to them to weave, in Yorkshire it is the man's own property.[6]

But in the Yorkshire domestic industry of the 18th century, the wool was the property, not of the weaver, but of the little master-clothier. Most weavers were journeymen, working for a single clothier, and (however much this was later idealised) in a dependent status.

*   *   *

It was the loom, and not the cotton-mill, which attracted immigrants in their thousands. From the 1770s onwards the great settlement of the uplands— Middleton, Oldham, Mottram, Rochdale—commenced. Bolton leapt from 5,339 inhabitants in 1773 to 11,739 in 1789: at the commencement of the Wars—

> notwithstanding the great numbers who have enlisted, houses for the work-ing class are not procured without difficulty; and last summer many houses were built in the skirts of town, which are now occupied.[7]

Small farmers turned weaver, and agricultural labourers and immigrant artisans entered the trade. It was the fifteen years between 1788 and 1803 which Radcliffe described as "the golden age of this great trade" for the weaving communities:

> Their dwellings and small gardens clean and neat,—all the family well clad,—the men with each a watch in his pocket, and the women dressed to their own fancy,—the church crowded to excess every Sunday,—every house well furnished with a clock in elegant mahogany or fancy case,—handsome tea services in Staffordshire ware . . . Birmingham, Potteries, and Sheffield wares for necessary use and ornament . . . many cottage families had their cow. . . .[8]

Experience and myth are intermingled, as they are in Gaskell's account of weaving families earning 4 pounds per week at the turn of the century, and in Bamford's description of his own *Early Days* in Middleton. We know from an Oldham diarist that the prosperity did not extend to fustians, the coarsest branch of the trade.[9] In fact, probably only a minority of weavers attained Radcliffe's standard; but many aspired towards it. In these fifteen or twenty years of moderate prosperity a distinct cultural pattern emerges in the weaving communities: a rhythm of work and leisure: a Wesleyanism in some villages softer and more humanised than it was to be in the first decades of the 19th century (Bamford's Sunday school taught him to write as well as to read), with class leaders and local preachers among the weavers: a stirring of political Radicalism, and a deep attachment to the values of independence.

But the prosperity induced by the soaring output of machine yarn disguised a more essential loss of status. It is in the "golden age" that the artisan, or journeyman weaver, becomes merged in the generic "hand-loom weaver." Except in a few specialised branches, the older artisans (their apprenticeship walls being totally breached) were placed on a par with the new immigrants; while many of the farming-weavers abandoned their small-holdings to concentrate upon the loom. Reduced to complete dependence upon the spinning-mill or the "putters-out" who took yarn into the uplands, the weavers were now exposed to round after round of wage reductions.

Wage cutting had long been sanctioned not only by the employer's greed but by the widely-diffused theory that poverty was an essential goad to industry. The author of the *Memoirs of Wool* had probably the industry of the west of England in mind when he wrote:

> It is a fact well known . . . that scarcity, to a certain degree, promotes industry, and that the manufacturer who can subsist on three days work will be idle and drunken the remainder of the week. . . . The poor in the manufacturing counties will never work any more time in general than is necessary just to live and support their weekly debauches. . . . We can fairly aver that a reduction of wages in the woollen manufacture would be a national blessing and advantage, and no real injury to the poor. By this means we might keep our trade, uphold our rents, and reform the people into the bargain.[10]

But the theory is found, almost universally, among employers, as well as among many magistrates and clergy, in the cotton district as well.[11] The prosperity of the weavers aroused feelings of active alarm in the minds of some masters and magistrates. "Some years ago," wrote one magistrate in 1818, the weavers were "so extravagantly paid that by working three or four days in the week they could maintain themselves in a comparative state of luxury." They "spent a great portion of their time and money in alehouses, and at home had their tea-tables twice a day provided with a rum bottle and the finest wheaten bread and butter."[12]

Reductions, during the Napoleonic Wars, were sometimes forced by large employers, sometimes by the least scrupulous employers, sometimes by little masters or self-employed weavers working for "commission houses." When markets were sluggish, manufactures took advantage of the situation by putting out work to weavers desperate for employment at any price, thereby compelling them "to manufacture great quantities of goods at a time, when they are absolutely not wanted."[13] With the return of demand, the goods were then released on the market at cut price; so that each minor recession was succeeded by a period in which the market was glutted with cheap goods thereby holding wages down to their recession level. The practices of some employers were unscrupulous to a degree, both in the exaction of fines for faulty work and in giving false weight in yarn. Yet at the same time as wages were screwed lower and lower, the number of weavers continued to increase over the first three decades of the 19th century; for weaving, next to general labouring, was the grand resource of the northern unemployed. Fustian weaving was heavy, monotonous, but easily learned. Agricultural workers, demobilised soldiers, Irish immigrants—all continued to swell the labour force.

* * *

iv. Myriads of Eternity

If we can now see more clearly many of the elements which made up the working-class communities of the early 19th century, a definitive answer to the "standard-of-living" controversy must still evade us. For beneath the word "standard" we must always find judgements of value as well as questions of fact. Values, we hope to have shown, are not "imponderables" which the historian may safely dismiss with the reflection that, since they are not amenable to measurement, anyone's opinion is as good as anyone else's. They are, on the contrary, those questions of human satisfaction, and of the direction of social change, which the historian ought to ponder if history is to claim a position among the significant humanities.

The historian, or the historical sociologist, must in fact be concerned with the judgements of value in two forms. In the first instance, he is concerned with the values *actually held* by those who lived through the Industrial Revolution. The old and newer modes of production each supported distinct kinds of community with characteristic ways of life. Alternative conventions and notions of human satisfaction were in conflict with each other, and there is no shortage of evidence if we wish to study the ensuing tensions.

In the second instance, he is concerned with making some judgement of value upon the whole process entailed in the Industrial Revolution, of which we ourselves are an end-product. It is our own involvement which makes judgement difficult. And yet we are helped towards a certain detachment, both by the "romantic" critique of industrialism which stems from one part of the experience, and by the record of tenacious resistance by which the hand-loom weaver, artisan or village craftsman confronted this experience and held fast to an alternative culture. As we see them change, so we see how we became what we are. We understand more clearly what was lost, what was driven "underground," what is still unresolved.

Any evaluation of the quality of life must entail an assessment of the total life-experience, the manifold satisfactions or deprivations, cultural as well as materiel, of the people concerned. From such a standpoint, the older "cata-clysmic" view of the Industrial Revolution must still be accepted. During the years between 1780 and 1840 the people of Britain suffered an experience of immiseration, even if it is possible to show a small statistical improvement in material conditions. When Sir Charles Snow tells us that "with singular unanimity . . . the poor have walked off the land into the factories as fast as the factories could take them," we must reply, with Dr. Leavis, that the "actual history" of the "full human problem [was] incomparably and poignantly more complex than that".[14] Some were lured from the countryside by the glitter and promise of wages of the industrial town; but the old village economy was crumbling at their backs. They moved less at their own will than at the dictate of external compulsions which they could not question; the enclosures, the Wars, the Poor Laws, the decline of rural industries, the counter-revolutionary stance of their rulers.

The process of industrialization is necessarily painful. It must involve the erosion of traditional patterns of life. But it was carried through with exceptional violence in Britain. It was unrelieved by any sense of national participation in communal effort, such as is found in countries undergoing a national evolution. Its ideology was that of the masters alone. Its messianic prophet was Dr. Andrew Ure, who saw the factory system as "the great minister of civilization to the terraqueous globe," diffusing "the life-blood of science and religion to myriads . . . still lying 'in the region and shadow of death.' "[15] But those who served it did not *feel* this to be so, and any more than those "myriads" who were served. The experience of immiseration came upon them in a hundred different forms; for the field labourer, the loss of his common rights and the vestiges of village democracy; for the artisan, the loss of his craftsman's status; for the weaver, the loss of livelihood and of independence; for the child, the loss of work and play in the home; for many groups of workers whose real earnings improved, the loss of security, leisure and the deterioration of the urban environment. R. M. Martin, who gave evidence before the Hand-Loom Weaver's committee of 1834, and who returned to England after an absence from Europe of ten years, was struck by the evidence of physical and spiritual deterioration:

> I have observed it not only in the manufacturing but also in agricultural communities in this country; they seem to have lost their animation, their vivacity, their field games and their village sports; they have become a sordid, discontented, miserable, anxious, struggling people, without health, gaiety, or happiness.

It is misleading to search for explanations in what professor Ashton has rightly described as "tedious" phrases,—man's "divorce" from "nature" or "the soil." After the "Last Labourers' Revolt," the Wiltshire field labourers— who were close enough to "nature"—were far worse degraded than the Lancashire mill girls. This violence was done to *human* nature. From one standpoint, it may be seen as the outcome of the means of production was freed from old sanctions and had not yet been subjected to new means of social control. In this sense we may still read it, as Marx did, as the violence of the capitalist class. From another standpoint, it may be seen as a violent technological differentiation between work and life.

It is neither poverty nor disease but work itself that casts the blackest shadow over the years of the Industrial Revolution. It is Blake, himself a craftsman by training, who gives us the experience:

> Then left the sons of Urizen the plow & Harrow, the loom,
> The hammer & the chisel & the rule & compasses . . .
> And all the arts of life they chang'd into the arts of death.
> The hour glass contemn'd because its simple workmanship,
> Was the workmanship of the plowman & the water wheel
> That raises water into Cisterns, broken & burn'd in fire
> Because its workmanship was like the workmanship of the shepherds
> And in their stead intricate wheels invented, Wheel without wheel,
> To perplex youth in their outgoings & to bind to labours
> Of day & night the myriads of Eternity, that they might file

And polish brass & iron hour after hour, laborious workmanship,
Kept ignorant of the use that they might spend the days of wisdom
In sorrowful drudgery to obtain a scanty pittance of bread,
In ignorance to view a small portion & think that All,
And call it a demonstration, blind to all the simple rules of life.

These "myriads of eternity" seem at times to have been sealed in their work
like a tomb. Their best efforts, over a lifetime, and supported by their own
friendly societies, could scarcely ensure them that to which so high a popular
value was attached—a "Decent Funeral." New skills were arising, old satisfactions persisted, but over all we feel the general pressure of long hours of
unsatisfying labour under severe discipline for alien purposes. This was at the
source of that "ugliness" which, D. H. Lawrence wrote, "betrayed the spirit of
man in the nineteenth century."[16] After all other impressions fade, this one
remains; together with that of the loss of any felt cohesion in the community,
save that which the working people, in an antagonism to their labour and to
their masters, built for themselves.

NOTES

1. E. P. Thompson, *The Making of the English Working Class* (New York:
   Vintage, 1963), 269–72, 275–78, 444–47. Notes have been renumbered to
   fit abridgement.
2. W. Gardiner, *Music and Friends* (1838), I, p. 43. See also M. D. George,
   England in Transition (Penguin edn. 1953), p. 63.
3. T. Exell, *Brief History of the Weavers of Gloucestershire*, cited in E. A. L. Moir,
   "The Gentlemen Clothiers," in (ed.) H. P. R. Finberg, *Gloucestershire Studies*
   (Leicester, 1957), p. 247.
4. Emmerson Tennant, M.P. for Belfast, in House of Commons, 28 July 1835.
   See also (for the Spitalfields silk-weavers) Thelwall's account, above,
   p. 143.
5. Introduction by W. O. Henderson and W. H. Chaloner to F. Engels,
   Condition of the Working Class in England in 1844 (1958), p. xiv.
6. Cited by E. A. L. Moir, op. cit. p. 226. For the West of England industry, see
   also D. M. Hunter, *The West of England Woolen Industry* (1910) and J. de L.
   Mann, "Clothiers and Weavers in Wiltshire during the Eighteenth Century," in (ed.) L. S. Presnell, *Studies in the Industrial Revolution* (1960).
7. J. Aikin, *A Description of the Country . . . round Manchester* (1795), p. 262.
   Note the early use of "working class."
8. W. Radcliffe, *Origin of Power Loom Weaving* (Stockport, 1828), p. 167.
9. See S. J. Chapman, *The Lancashire Cotton Industry* (Manchester, 1904), p. 40.
   There are indications of widespread reductions commencing in about
   1797. An Association of Cotton Weavers, based on Bolton, claimed that
   wages had fallen by 1/3rd between 1797 and 1799; Rev. R. Bancroft, 29
   April, 1709, P.C. A.155; A. Weaver, *Address to the Inhabitants of Bolton*

(Bolton, 1799); Radcliffe, op. cit. pp. 72–7. But wages seem to have reached a peak of 45s. to 50s. a week in Blackburn in 1802: *Blackburn Mail*, 26 May 1802.

10. J. Smith, *Memoirs of Wool* (1747), II, p. 308.
11. See A. P. Wadsworth and J. de L. Mann, *The Cotton Trade and Industrial Lancashire* (Manchester, 1931), pp. 387 ff.
12. Aspinall, op. cit., p. 271.
13. Weavers' petition in favour of a minimum wage bill, 1807, signed—it is claimed—by 130,000 cotton weavers: see J. L. and B. Hammond, *The Skilled Laborer*, p. 74.
14. C. P. Snow, *The Two Cultures* (1959); F. R. Leavis, "The Significance of C. P. Snow," *Spectator*, 9 March 1962.
15. *Philosophy of Manufactures*, pp. 18–19.
16. "Nottingham and the Mining Country," *Selected Essays* (Penguin edn.), pp. 119, 122.

QUESTIONS TO CONSIDER

1. Out of what historical materials does Thompson fashion his picture of life during the Industrial Revolution?
2. What does Thompson say is the difficulty in determining a people's "standard-of-living"? What factors does he say are essential in evaluating how well people lived?
3. Imagine that Thompson were to write a history of the Information Revolution of the late twentieth century. What might he say about our changing quality of life? What kind of evidence might he present to support his views?

FOR FURTHER READING

Brody, David. *Steelworkers in America*. New York: Harper and Row, 1969.
Cohen, Lizabeth. *Making a New Deal: Industrial Workers in Chicago, 1919–1939*. New York: Cambridge University Press, 1990.
Dawley, Alan. *Class and Community: The Industrial Revolution in Lynn*. Cambridge, MA: Harvard University Press, 1976.
Dubofsky, Melvin. *We Shall Be All: A History of the Industrial Workers of the World*. New York: Quadrangle, 1969.
Gutman, Herbert. *Work, Culture, and Society in Industrializing America*. New York: Knopf, 1976.
Hane, Mikiso. *Peasants, Rebels, and Outcastes: The Underside of Modern Japan*. New York: Pantheon, 1982.
Hareven, Tamara. *Family Time and Industrial Time*. Cambridge, U.K.: Cambridge University Press, 1982.
Kazin, Michael. *Barons of Labor*. Urbana, IL: University of Illinois Press, 1987.

Patterson, Orlando. *Freedom in the Making of Western Culture.* New York: Basic Books, 1991.

Thompson, E. P. *Customs in Common.* New York: New Press, 1993.

———. *Making History: Writings on History and Culture.* New York: New Press, 1994.

———. *The Poverty of Theory and Other Essays.* New York: Monthly Review, 1978.

———. *Whigs and Hunters.* London: Allen Lane, 1975.

———. *William Morris: Romantic to Revolutionary.* London: Lawrence and Wishart, 1955.

———. *Witness Against the Beast: William Blake and the Moral Law.* New York: New Press, 1993.

CHAPTER 52

Gender

Caroline Walker Bynum

Caroline Walker Bynum
Courtesy of Columbia University/Joe Pineiro photo

G ender: perhaps no other recent trend has more thoroughly changed the shape of historical writing. Wherever one looks, whatever topic one chooses, someone is investigating the gender aspects of that subject. Much gender history is women's history, and almost every department of history in the United States has at least one specialist. Women's history tells the stories of women as actors in the historical drama from the dawn of time to yesterday. The selections by Mary Ritter Beard and Ban Zhao above (Chapters 45 and 11) are women's history. In its post–World War II incarnation, women's history began as the study of women's movements for political and social equality. It then moved to a more general consideration of women as actors in society and culture.

One major theme has been the history of patriarchy, of the oppression of women by men. This has resulted, for example, in works such as Gerda Lerner's on the creation and sustenance of patriarchy, and then on the creation of feminist consciousness. A second theme has been to tell the stories of those people—in this case, women—whom male historians have systematically left out; such is the work of Laurel Thatcher Ulrich. A third theme is the phenomenon of gender itself. In this category falls recent work on the construction of femaleness, and of maleness, and on the history of gays and lesbians, including the writing of John Boswell.

Some excellent historians writing on gender are interested, like Ban Zhao, in the particular perspectives of women as historical actors. They use women's lives and concerns to illuminate subjects that male-oriented historians either ignore or do not find ways to understand. The work of Caroline Walker Bynum is such an instance. She is not concerned merely to tell us the history of males dominating females in medieval Europe, although surely they did and that is part of her argument. Instead, Bynum looks where men historians have not looked—at the particularities of medieval European women's sphere—and paints a picture of daily life and spirituality that we could not learn about from one with purely male interests. Male-oriented historians have sought to understand medieval Christianity and have written about theology, church leaders, and church institutional developments. Bynum is just as interested in medieval Christianity, but she looks instead at the rituals of women's lives, and she uncovers daily spirituality and deep psychological issues. She goes on to a contemplation of the place of women and the meaning of femaleness in medieval European society.

Caroline Walker Bynum has taught at Harvard, the University of Washington, and Columbia University. Her work focuses on women and spirituality in the Middle Ages, and is collected in three books: *Jesus as Mother: Studies in the Spirituality of the High Middle Ages* (1982), *Holy Feast and Holy Fast: The Religious Significance of Food to Medieval Women* (1987), and *Fragmentation and Redemption: Essays on Gender and the Human Body in Medieval Religion* (1991). She brings together a feminist concern for understanding her subject from women's points of view; a willingness to take seriously the religious experiences of medieval people without trying to reduce them to superstition or psychological dysfunction; and a cultural anthropologist's interest in the meaning of ritual and symbol for the interior life of individuals.

Holy Feast and Holy Fast[1]
The Religious Significance of Food to Medieval Women

A number of recent works on sanctity provide quantitative evidence that food is a more important motif in women's piety than in men's. Donald Weinstein and Rudolph Bell, in their study of 864 saints from 1000 to 1700, demonstrate conclusively that all types of penitential asceticism, including fasting, are significantly more common in female religiosity. Although only 17.5 percent of those canonized or venerated as saints from 1000 to 1700 were women, women accounted for almost 29 percent of those saints who indulged in extreme austerities, such as fasting, flagellation, or sleep deprivation; 23.3 percent of those who died from such practices; and 53.2 percent of those in whose lives illness was the central factor in reputation for sanctity.[2] Richard Kieckhefer, in his examination of fasting by fourteenth-century saints, cites almost as many examples of women as of men, despite the fact that fewer than 30 percent of those revered as saints were women. Kieckhefer also finds that in the period he has studied, Henry Suso is almost the only male to receive eucharistic visions.[3] André Vauchez, in his study of late medieval canonizations, suggests that fasting was important for only one type of male saint—the hermit (who was often a layman)—whereas it was a crucial component of the reputation of holy women.[4] The older work of Herbert Thurston, which attempts a "scientific" approach no longer fashionable, nonetheless assembles a wide range of cases. It is, therefore, worth noting that Thurston's discussion of "authentic" food multiplication miracles lists almost as many performed by women as by men.[5]

Peter Browe's work on the eucharist indicates, moreover, that the eucharistic miracle is almost entirely a female genre.[6] If one accepts Browe's categories (of twenty types of eucharistic miracle), only two types occur primarily to males, and both of these are associated with the act of consecration, which could be performed only by men. The two male types are the miracle of the spider in the chalice, traditionally told of priests, and the miracle of transformation at the moment of consecration, which was by definition limited to priests. At least eight types of eucharistic miracle, however, are predominantly or exclusively female. Four types occur almost exclusively to women: miracles in which the recipient becomes a crystal filled with light, miracles in which the recipient distinguishes consecrated and unconsecrated hosts, miracles in which worthy and unworthy recipients and celebrants are distinguished, and miracles in which the eucharist has a special effect on the senses (smelling sweet, ringing with music, filling the mouth with honey, announcing its presence when hidden away or hoarded, etc.). Predominantly but not exclusively female are miracles in which the host or chalice changes into a beautiful baby—miracles that sometimes (but not always) have highly erotic overtones for both men and women. Most striking of all, there is only one male example (after the patristic period) of the common story of the saint who lives largely or entirely on the eucharist. There are very few male cases of the various distribution miracles in which the eucharist is brought by doves or angels or flies by itself through the air, and these are mostly told of low-status males—lay brothers or altar boys. And there appears to be only one male case of the miracle in which Christ becomes the priest and offers himself as food—an act sometimes accomplished with frightening literalism, as when he tears off the flesh from the palm of his hand for Adelheid of Katharinental.[7] Not only are these patterns striking in themselves, it is also clear that the male miracles underline the power of the priests, whereas in at least half of the women's miracles it is the quality of the eucharist as food that is stressed.[8] The eucharist is offered as flesh or honeycomb; it affects the tastes; it sustains life; it is vomited out if unconsecrated.

A cursory glance at the history of eucharistic piety indicates that women were prominent in the creation and spread of special devotions such as the feast of Corpus Christi (revealed to Juliana of Cornillon)[9] or the devotion to the Sacred Heart (found especially in the Flemish saint Lutgard of Aywiéres and the many visions of the nuns of the Saxon monastery of Helfa).[10] So important was the eucharist that some thirteenth-century women (e.g., Ida of Nivelles and the Viennese beguine Agnes Blannbekin) made vocational decisions or changed orders out of desire to receive it more frequently.[11] Stories of people levitating, experiencing ecstasy during the mass, or racing from church to church to attend as many eucharistic services as possible are usually told of women—for example, of Hedwig of Silesia (d. 1241), Douceline of Marseilles (d. 1274), and several of the Flemish holy women described by James of Vitry (see the epigraph to chapter I above).[12] The work of Imbert-Gourbeyre, despite its scanty documentation and notoriously uncritical stance, nonetheless provides a revealing idea of what the pious expected of religious heroes and heroines. Imbert-Gourbeyre culled from saints' lives nine cases of miraculous abstinence, all of them female, and fifty-two cases of miraculous communion (between the thirteenth and sixteenth centuries), of which forty-five are female.[13]

Even in accounts written by medieval males for male audiences, we find the eucharist and the attendant theme of the humanity of Christ associated especially with women. For example, Caesarius of Heisterbach, writing in the early thirteenth century for male novices and drawing on his own male world, in general told overwhelmingly male stories. In his treatment of dying, in the *Dialogue on Miracles*, he gives fifty-four stories about men and eight about women; on punishment of the dead, he gives forty-seven male stories and eight female; on such topics as lust and despair, he preserves a similar ratio. But we find as many cases of nuns as of monks receiving the infant Jesus in visions, and there are more than half as many appearances of the crucifix to women as to men. In the section on the eucharist, where he turns from celebrant (all male stories, of course) to recipient, we find almost as many miracles occurring to women as to men.[14] Although several early collections of exempla addressed to men (for example, Conrad of Eberbach's, Peter the Venerable's, and Gerald of Wales's) contain stories only about males,[15] both James of Vitry and Thomas of Cantimpré, writing in the thirteenth century, give female as well as male examples of eucharistic miracles and devotion.[16] Tubach's index of exempla lists thirty-two miracles concerning the host that occurred to men, twenty to women. Of the male miracles, twelve occurred to priests.[17]

* * *

Not only did preachers tell a disproportionate number of stories about women and food practices; they also tended to advise women about both fast and feast. Even in the patristic period, writers who addressed women tended to associate food and lust and to devote an inordinate amount of the relatively little writing they directed toward women to these topics. Two of Jerome's most extensive discussions of food as incentive to licentiousness were addressed to women,[18] and Fulgentius of Ruspe (d. 533), a disciple of Augustine, wrote several letters on fasting to women, urging a fine balance between abstinence and moderation:

> We must practice such moderation in fasting that our body is not excited by the full satisfaction of the appetite or enfeebled by too much privation. It is necessary then that the fast of virgins be followed by eating such that the body is not drawn by the pleasures of eating nor excited by its fulfillment.[19]

Medieval preachers such as Peter the Chanter repeated Jerome's advice to women and cited patristic examples of female ascetics and fasters.[20]

* * *

Male theologians wrote much on the eucharist, and certain formal theological considerations of the sacrament were (like all scholastic theology) exclusively male genres. But it is striking how many important treatises on the eucharist or on the closely connected theme of the humanity of Christ were addressed by men to women. One thinks, for example, of the works of Jan van Ruysbroeck (d. 1381), Richard Rolle (d. 1349), Henry Suso, and Dionysius the Carthusian (d. 1471).[21] It is also noteworthy that many of the preachers who were central in elaborating eucharistic piety preached most often to women (for example, Guiard of Laon [d. 1248] and John Tauler).[22] Moreover, many of the earliest texts recommending frequent communion were directed to women, although, in general, little theological injunction was written for them. In the eleventh century, John of Fécamp, Peter Damian, and Pope Gregory VII all recommended to women eucharistic devotion and frequent reception.[23]

Iconographic evidence also suggests that medieval people of both sexes associated food and fasting with women. In particular, the eucharist was associated with female saints. The communion of the Virgin, of Mary Magdalen, and of Mary the Egyptian was a fairly common theme in painting.[24] The saints most frequently depicted on eucharistic tabernacles were the Virgin, the Magdalen, Christopher, and little Saint Barbara, as she was known from the *Golden Legend*.[25] Dumoutet comments that Barbara was probably the saint most frequently associated with the eucharist in iconography. (See plate 7 for a retable with saints Barbara and Catherine.) Popular wisdom held that Barbara's devotees would not die without a chance to receive the sacrament at the end. Mary Magdalen was the saint most closely linked with fasting, owing to the version of her legend that circulated in the Middle Ages and attributed to her a fast of many years in the desert near Marseilles. As the cult of the host grew in the later Middle Ages, tabernacles came to associate the consecration with the Incarnation, and therefore with the Virgin Mary. The Cistercians generally stressed the association of Mary with the sacrament, and at Citeaux the pyx was held by an image of the Virgin. The angel's words of salutation to Mary were sometimes reproduced on tabernacles. In his explanation of the mass (1285–1291), William Durandus said that the pyx or tabernacle or reliquary in which the host is kept signifies Mary's body. There is even an extant tabernacle that explicitly identifies the container with Mary. (It is surrounded by Anne, Mary's mother, and thus suggests that it is Mary herself.) As retables developed, they also tended to link the moment of consecration (sometimes depicted as the Mystical Mill or the baby Christ in the chalice) with the Annunciation or some other scene suggesting the Incarnation or the reception of Christ—for example, the Virgin capturing the unicorn, meeting with her cousin Elizabeth, or nursing the Christ child (see frontispiece and plates 1, 6, and 7). Depictions of the iconographic motifs of the Eucharistic Man of Sorrows or Christ in the winepress (see plates 1, 5, 25, 26, and 30) often include nuns or other female figures (Mary or Caritas), not only as recipients of food but also as providers or celebrants. Quantitative evidence is, however, the least reliable type of evidence on this matter. This is so not only because the total number of recorded eucharistic miracles, exempla, saints' lives, causes for canonization, retables and pyxes, and treatises on asceticism is sometimes too small for percentages to be trustworthy idices. It is also because the stories themselves are misleading. To say this is not to raise the question of whether the miracles reported in these writings "really happened." My point here is merely that the numerous passing references to eucharistic devotion and food asceticism in saints' *Vitae* and other sources must be viewed with skepticism, because, if they are only passing references, there is a distinct possibility that the authors themselves may not have meant them literally. There is reason to suspect that fasting and visions were sometimes described or attributed where neither was experienced and conversely, that they were sometimes discouraged in individuals who were driven obsessively toward them. Both these points deserve elaboration.

Among early Christian writers, both Jerome and Cassian had taught that meat and wine excited sexual lust and that gluttony was the basic source from which flowed others sins. A number of the Desert Fathers (for example, Anthony, Hilarion Simeon Stylites, and Gerasimus) were said to have practiced extreme food asceticism, combined with intense eucharistic piety. Many hagiographers and saints from the eleventh to the fifteenth century bore this model in mind. Peter Damian told of Italian hermits who mimicked Paul and Anthony. In the *vita* of Mary of Oignies, James of Vitry underlined the ways in which Mary imitated the Desert Fathers, and Raymond of Capua made the same point about Catherine of Siena. Peter of Vaux claimed that Colette of Corbie surpassed the Fathers in her food asceticism. Henry Suso posted the sayings of the Fathers on the walls of his cell, and a number of the aphorisms he chose dealt with fasting.

By high Middle Ages, fasting and eucharistic devotion were expected of saints, especially hermit saints and women. Those, such as Richard Rolle, who were not able to maintain fasts were criticized for their failure; and a writer like Tauler who did not have the gift of food asceticism felt it necessary to apologize for the lack. Witnesses in canonization proceedings regularly testified to the fasting of candidates for sanctity, although additional evidence sometimes suggests that the testimony was not true. Vanchez cites, for example, witnesses who deposed that Philip of Bourges (d. 1261) and Thomas of Cantilupe (d. 1282) practiced abstinence, although a cleric of Philip's diocese refused to believe in his sanctity because he "drank and ate normally," and several other witnesses testified that Thomas did not try to be better than other men. At various points in Raymond of Capua's account of Catherine of Siena he tells us that "after this" she "ate nothing"; but later in the narrative there is clear evidence of eating—perhaps even of binge eating. For example, two witnesses recount that she once broke a fast of fifty-nine days by eating large amounts of food on the feast of the Ascension. Alpaïs of Cudot's hagiographer reports simultaneously that she lived without corporeal food and that she sucked morsels of food three times a week to quell gossip. "Eating nothing" in hagiographical accounts often means "not eating normally."

* * *

To holy people themselves, fasting, meditation, and eucharistic devotion were often merely steps toward God, part of the preparation for contemplation. To their adherents, however, abstinence or trances were signs and sources of supernatural power. Thus we sometimes find that the further an account of a saint is from the saint herself, the more her food asceticism or paramystical phenomena are emphasized. For example, the biographer of the peasant saint Alpaïs, who supposedly lived for forty years on the eucharist alone, devotes much attention to the saint's visions and spiritual teacher, whereas the contemporary chroniclers and collectors of exempla who picked up her story focused almost exclusively on the miraculous non-eating, including clinical details about her failure to excrete and the emptiness of her intestines. In the second book of the *Herald of Divine Love*, Gertrude the Great strained to express an ultimately inexpressible union, more or less ignoring the paramystical phenomena that dominate the other four books, which she did not write. Simone Roisin has found that in general, thirteenth-century saints' *vitae* written for the laity contain more miraculous elements, whereas those composed for the cloistered stress inner spiritual development and mystical union. Culling references to fasts and eucharist from biographies of holy people thus tells us more about the stereotypes of holiness held by different audiences than about the exact distribution of ascetic or pious practices.

If adherents encouraged feats and miracles of abstinence, church authorities on the other hand were often suspicious, especially of the abstinence and piety of women. As I explained in chapter 2, the twelfth and thirteenth centuries saw the curious conjunction of a new wave of extreme ascetic practices with repeated exhortations to moderation. Spiritual writers such as Bernard of Clairvaux stressed inner rather than outward response, while theologians such as Peter the Chanter and Aquinas urged common sense and "rationality." These calls for reasonableness and interiority were clearly in part a response to such alarming austerities as wearing iron plates, mutilating one's flesh and rubbing lice into the wounds or even jumping into ovens or hanging oneself. But the austerities were in part a response to the injunctions to moderation. In such an environment, women's asceticism often came in for particular criticism.

* * *

Women sometimes internalized such suspicion of their piety or evidenced a deep ambivalence about their own yearnings toward supernatural power or extraordinary penitential practices. Clare of Assisi, herself a practitioner of extreme food deprivation, encouraged Agnes of Prague to mildness and prudence in fasting. Angela of Foligno called the idea that she give up eating a "temptation." Beatrice of Nazareth and Columba of Rieta feared that their eucharistic devotion and asceticism were inspired by the devil. Lutgard of Aywiéres was required by her own abbess to omit frequent communion, and Catherine of Siena's fellow tertiaries at one point urged that she be deprived of reception and ejected from the church because of her exuberant ecstasies. Margaret of Cortona, though repeatedly urged by Christ himself to daily communion, went through agonies of uncertainty that led her repeatedly to abstain. Gertrude the Great worried about the dangers of private revelation; if she introduced new prayers on the authority of visions alone, she reasoned, then the community would have no protection against false sisters who claimed similar inspiration.

* * *

There is no evidence that mothers were generally more supportive of future saints than were fathers, and it can be demonstrated that daughters' vocations met with more parental opposition than sons'. Nonetheless, a number of saints' *vitae* suggest that mothers or surrogate mothers taught their children fasting and eucharistic devotion. Aelred of Rievaulx (d.1167) reports that King David of Scotland (d. 1153) learned fasting and eucharistic devotion from his mother, herself a saint. Peter of Luxembourg, one of the few males who broke his health with fasting, had models of asceticism in both mother and father. But Peter's biographer tells us that his mother was more active in charity, providing meals for the needy three times a week and sending delicacies from her own table to women in childbirth. Peter later followed the example of both parents, giving money and food to the poor. The author of the *vitae* of Colette of Corbie implies a similar contrast between male and female practice when he notes that Colette's father gave money to the poor, especially reformed prostitutes, whereas her mother lived parsimoniously, undertook many penances, meditated every day on the life of Christ, and went to weekly confession and communion. It appears to have been a cliché of hagiography that pious fathers gave alms while pious mothers gave (and gave up) food. Moreover, in praising the patience displayed by saintly girls toward unsympathetic mothers, hagiographers often reveal that girls were carrying to extremes devout practices learned from other women. When little Dorothy of Montau wished to practice the severe fasting she saw her mother perform, conflict flared between mother and daughter. Juliana of Cornillion, taught fasting by the religious woman who was caring for her, was punished while a child for taking the teaching too much to heart. Elizabeth of Hungary may have found a model for her extreme fasting and compulsive food distribution in the behavior of her future mother-in-law Sophia, who raised her (although subsequent commentators suggest only there was tension between Elizabeth and her surrogate mother).

Other vignettes from chronicles and saints' *vitae* suggest that food absti-nence frequently characterized women who were not considered saints. Catherine of Siena's fasting developed in the course of conflict with her parents about her religious vocation, but her biographer tells of another girl in the family whose self-starvation began in response to the dissolute behavior of her young husband. The early fifteenth-century English laywoman Margery Kempe, upon Christ's advice, manipulated her husband into accepting conti-nence by offering to give up the public fasts with which she was embarrassing him before the neighbors.

Because medieval people loved marvels, chroniclers often preserved stories of strange eating behavior. Most of the surviving tales are about women. Ninth-century chronicles report, without much detail, two cases of twelve-year-old girls who refused to eat for three years. In one of these stories, told by Einhard and picked up by a number of other chroniclers, the girl began her fast "first from bread and then from all food and drink" after receiving Easter communion from the priest. Readers are then told simply that, after three years, she "began to eat again."

Far more interesting are two healing miracles recounted in the earliest *vita* of Walburga (d. 779), written by Wolfhard, priest of Eichstätt, about a hundred years after her death. Many food-related themes cluster about Walburga's life. That she herself fasted and sometimes remained in the church after Vespers while the other nuns took supper in the refectory is one of the relatively few details we know about her own piety. She was also one of the most famous myroblytes, or oil-producing saints, curing the afflicted for more than a thousand years after her death with an aromatic fluid that flowed from the stone on which her relics rested—some said from her breastbone. The symbol of ears of corn with which she is associated iconographically seems to have been borrowed, along with other details, from an earlier fertility cult, that of Walborg or Walpurg, the earth goddess. Not surprisingly, then, two of Walburga's early posthumous miracles were cures of what can quite accu-rately be called "eating disorders." Wolfhard recounts that a man named Irchinbald was in danger of becoming a glutton until he was suddenly seized with loathing for food. He then went for twenty-seven weeks without bread or meat, taking only a few vegetables or a little egg yolk. When he had become emaciated and extremely ill, he heard a voice telling him to go to Monheim (to which some of Walburga's relics had been translated), to pray to Walburga and drink from the consecrated chalice that would be offered to him by three nuns standing near the altar. As soon as he drank, he felt hungry for bread. A similar story is told of a servant girl named Friderade. But, in her case, the self-starvation was not cured. Rather, it was elaborated into a miracle.

Friderade, so the story goes, suffered from a voracious appetite; she ate until she grew enormous with gout or dropsy. When she visited Walburga's shrine her swollen feet were cured, but not her appetite. She then confessed to a sister Deithilda and received consecrated bread from the priest. After this she felt a loathing for all food except the eucharist. Deithilda, who worried about her, persuaded her to drink a little beer, but it merely gushed out again from her mouth and nose. Friderade subsequently passed three years without eating. A priest who observed her for the local bishop testified that she indeed survived without food. Thus, in these two ninth-century miracles, a man's loathing for food was cured by a sacred drink administered by nuns, whereas a woman's greed was cured by sacred bread administered by a priest. As the hagiographer tells the story, Irchinbald's transition from gluttony to starvation is natural; it is his return to eating that is the miraculous cure. In contrast, Friderade's loss of appetite is the miracle. The implication is that her subsequent return to eating needs no explanation.

*   *   *

An impressive array of examples can thus be collected to show that fasting and eucharistic miracles were more prominent in women's religiosity than in men's. But my purpose in this book is not simply to count cases of male and female behavior. It is, rather, to demonstrate that food was an obsessive and overpowering concern in the lives and writings of religious women between the twelfth and fifteenth century. It was women, not men, who were reputed to live for years on the eucharist alone or whose abstinence went so far that normal bodily functions such as excretion ceased. It was women who in story after story drank pus or filth from the sick they cared for, while abstaining from ordinary food. Moreover, it was women who developed eucharistic piety, including the cult of the Sacred Heart and the feast of Corpus Christi: women who in vision after vision saw Christ in the host or chalice; women who gave food from their tables to the sick or the poor, frequently in defiance of husband or family; women whose miracles in life multiplied food for others and whose bodies after death exuded healing liquid. Finally, it was women who in their writings repeatedly used bread, blood, hunger, and eating as their dominant images for union with God and neighbor—language which appears in male writers but is never central to their piety.

Quantitative patterns are thus no more than the beginning of my inquiry. Indeed, such patterns obscure even while they elucidate. For, in order to be counted, phenomena must be cut apart from each other and put into countable categories. What is really important to an understanding of women's piety, however, is not the number of food miracles or fasts or the frequency of eucharistic ecstasies, but the way in which food as a polysemous symbol of suffering and fertility lies at the center of how women thought and how they survived. In the rest of this book, therefore, I shall be concerned with particular lives and particular texts, in all their complexity of lived and literary metaphor. I shall try to demonstrate, by exploring women's stories, that food was an overwhelming concern, that denial and devotion—fast and feast—were connected in basic and complex ways, and that the causes of women's piety lie deep within the structures of medieval assumptions and medieval society.

NOTES

1. Caroline Walker Bynum, *Holy Feast and Holy Fast: The Religious Significance of Food to Medieval Women* (Berkeley, CA: University of California Press, 1987). Notes have been renumbered to fit abridgement.
2. Weinstein and Bell, SS, table 18, p. 234.
3. Kieckhefer, UnS, p. 172. Ruysbroeck also received ecstasies (if not actual visions) while celebrating; see below, nn. 24 and 240. All sorts of visions were more common with women than with men in this period; see Dinzelbacher, *Vision and visionsliteratur*, pp. 151–55, 226–28.
4. Vauchez, *La Saintetee*, pp. 224–26, 347–48, 405–6, 450–51.
5. Thurston, PP, pp, 385–91. Thurston, who includes modern saints as well, lists twenty-three men and twenty women. On the common hagiographical motif of women's distribution of bread that turns into roses, see below, chap. 7 n. 13.
6. The following paragraph is based on Browe, *Die Wunder*. For other miracles, see Corblet, *Histoire dogmatique*, vol. I, pp. 447–515.
7. Browe, *Die Wunder*, p. 23.
8. For an early example of the kind of eucharistic miracle that supports priestly authority, see the early-ninth-century Life of Evurtius in *Catalogus codicum hagiogtaphicorum latinorum Bibliotheca nationali Parisiensi*, Subsidia hagiographica 2, vol. 2 (Brussels: The Bollandists, 1890), pp. 317–18: and the later version in the *Libersancti Jacobi*, ed. Jeanne Vielliard, in *Le Guide du pélerin de Saint-Jacques de Compostelle* (Macon: Protat, 1938), pp. 58–60. In this miracle the hand of God appeared over the head of the celebrating priest, imitating his actions (and thereby demonstrating that Christ offers the sacrifice in every mass). For a fourteenth-century example, see the Life of Jan van Ruysbroeck by Henry Uten Boghaerde (Henry Pomer), which is bk. 2 of "De origine monasterii Viridisvallis una cum vitis B. Joannis Rusbrochii primi prioris hujus monasterii et aliquot coaetaneorum ejus" (AB 4 [1885], chap. 28, pp. 302–3). In this account we are told that Ruysbroeck, old and blind, was forbidden by his superior to celebrate because of his feebleness. Ruysbroek defended himself, claiming that the feebleness was ecstasy and that Jesus had come to him to say, "Tu es meus et ego tuus."
9. See McDonnell, *Beguines*, pp. 305–15; Hontoir, "Sainte Julienne"; Baix and Lambot, *La Dévotion*, pp. 75–80; and the Life of Juliana of Cornillon, AASS April, vol. I, pp. 442–75.

10. Cyprien Vagaggini, "La Dévotion au Sacré-Coeur chez sainte Mechtilde et sainte Gertrude," *Cor Jesu: Commentationes in litteras encyclicas Pii PP. XII 'Haurietis aquas,'* 2 vols. (Rome: Herder, 1959), vol. 2, pp. 31–48; Ursmer Berliére, *La Dévotion au Sacré-Coeur dans l'ordre de saint Benoit,* Collection Pax 10 (Paris: Lethiellux, 1923); Gougaud, DAP, pp. 75–130.

11. McDonnell, *Beguines,* p, 313. On Agnes Blannbekin and the scandal caused by the publication of her revelations in 1731, see G. Allmang, "Agnés Blannbekin," DHGE, vol. 1 (1912), col. 977; and Peter Dinzelbacher, "Die 'Vita et Revelationes' der Wiener Begine Agnes Blannbekin (†1315) im Rahmen der Viten- und Offenbarungsliteratur ihrer Zeit," in Dinzelbacher and Bauer, *Frauenmystik,* pp. 152–77.

12. Jungmann, *Mass of the Roman Rite,* vol. 2, pp. 20–21; Vauchez, *La Sainteté,* pp. 431–32; Duhr, "Communion fréquente," cols. 1256–68.

13. Imbert-Gourbeyre, *Stigmatisation,* Vol. 2, pp. 183, 408–9. For criticisms of Imbert Gourbeyre, see Pierre Debongnie, "Essai critique sur l'histoire des stigmatisations au moyen age," *Etudes carmélitaines,* 21.2 (October 1936): 22–59; and E. Amann, "Stigmatisation," DTC, vol. 14, pt. 1 (1939), cols. 2617–19.

14. Caesarius, *Dialogus.* Bk. 11 concerns dying; bk. 12 concerns the punishment of the dead. In bk. 8 (visions), there are three appearances of the Christ child to women (chaps. 3, 7, 8) and two to men (chaps. 2, 5); eight appearances of the crucifix to men (chaps. 11, 13, 14, 17, 18, 20, 21, 23) and four to women (chaps 10, 15, 16, 22; one might also count chap. 9). The opening and closing chapters of bk. 9 (on the eucharist) deal with celebrants and the proof of transubstantiation and are about males; chaps. 33–51 (which deal with the laity) have nine visions to women (chaps, 33, 34, 35, 36, 39, 40, 46, 47, 50) and ten to men (chaps. 37, 38, 41, 42, 43, 44, 45, 48, 49, 51); of the scattered remaining chapters on recipients, three are about males (chaps. 24, 63, 64)) and one about a female (chap. 25).

15. Conrad of Eberbach, *Exordium magnum cisterciense,* ed. Bruno Griesser, Series scriptorum s. ordinis cisterciensis 2 (Rome: Editiones Cistercienses, 1961); Peter the Venerable, *Liber de miraculis,* PL 189, cols. 851–954; Gerald of Wales, *Gemma ecclesiastica* in Gerald of Wales, *Opera,* ed. J. S. Brewer, vol. 2 (London: Longman, 1862).

16. See James of Vitry, *The Historia occidentalis of Jacques de Vitry: A Critical Edition,* ed. John F. Hinnebusch, Spicilegium Friburgense 17 (Fribourg, Switzerland: University Press, 1972); and Thomas of Cantimpré, *Liber qui dicitur bonum universale de proprietatibus apum* (Cologne: Johan Koelhoff, ca. 1479). The eucharist is, however, unimportant in James's *sermones vulgares;* see James of Vitry, *The Exempla of Illustrative Stories from the Sermones Vulgares of Jacques de Vitry,* ed. Thomas F. Crane, Publications of the Folk-lore Society 26 (London: Nutt, 1890).

17. Tubach, *Index,* pp. 207–12.

18. Jerome, Letter 54, *Ad Furia de viduitate servanda,* in *Sancti Eusebii Hieronymi epistulae,* pt. 1, ed. Hilberg, pp. 466–85; and idem, Letter 22, *Ad Eustochium,* chaps. 17–18, PL 22, cols. 404–5. Jerome's other major discussion of

fasting, food, and lust is in *Contra Jovinianum*, bk. 2, chaps. 5–17, PL 23, cols. 290–312. Jerome also urged women to avoid excessive abstinence; see Arbesmann, "fasting and Prophecy," pp. 38–39.

19. Fulgentius of Ruspe, Letter 3, chap. 13, PL 65, col. 332. See also PL 65, col. 132.
20. Peter the Chanter, chapter on fasting from *Verbum abbreviatum*, PL 205, cols. 327–28.
21. Richard Rolle's *Form of Living*, like his two other English epistles, was written for a woman. Henry Suso's *Little Book of Eternal Wisdom*, the heart of which is meditations on Christ's death, is addressed chiefly to nuns, as is his *Book of Letters*. The second part of Ruysbroeck's *Mirror of Eternal Salvation* is a treatise on the eucharist that was probably written for Margaret of Meerbeke. He also addressed his *Book of the Seven Cloisters* to her. Dioysius the Carthusian wrote six sermons on the eucharist for Mechtild of Nimégue and other ecstatics.
22. On Guiard see P. C. Boeren, *La Vie et les oeuvres de Guiard de Laon, 1170 env.–1248* (The Hague: Nijhoff, 1956), pp. 157–58. Tauler preached most of his sermons, which stress mysticism and frequent communion, in German to nuns; see Karl Boeckl, *Eucharistie-Lehre der deutschen Mystiker des Mittelalters* (Freiburg: Herder, 1924, pp. 74–122).
23. Baix and Lambot, *La Dévotion*, pp. 48–52.
24. Corblet, *Histoire dogmatique*, vol. 2, passim, esp. pp. 513–51.
25. Dumouter, CD, p. 80; and Corblet, *Histoire dogmatique*, Vol. 2, p. 550.

QUESTIONS TO CONSIDER

1. According to Bynum, how did women's spiritual practices in medieval Europe differ from those of their male contemporaries?
2. What, in Bynum's view, was the relationship between the body and spirituality?
3. How does Bynum's focus on medieval women's lives illuminate parts of history that other approaches fail to grasp?
4. How is Bynum's presentation of medieval Christianity as a whole different from Bede's?

FOR FURTHER READING

Bernstein, Gail Lee. *Recreating Japanese Women, 1600–1945*. Berkeley, CA: University of California Press, 1991.
Boswell, John. *Same-Sex Unions in Premodern Europe*. New York: Villard, 1994.
Bynum, Caroline Walker. *Fragmentation and Redemption: Essays on Gender and the Human Body in Medieval Religion*. New York: Zone Books, 1990.
——— . *Jesus as Mother: Studies in the Spirituality of the High Middle Ages*. Berkeley, CA: University of California Press, 1982.

Cott, Nancy F. *The Bonds of Womanhood: "Woman's Sphere" in New England, 1780–1835.* New Haven, CT: Yale University Press, 1977.

DuBois, Ellen Carol, and Vicki Ruiz, eds. *Unequal Sisters: A Multicultural Reader in U.S. Women's History.* New York: Routledge, 1990.

Flexner, Eleanor. *Century of Struggle: The Woman's Rights Movement in the United States.* Rev. ed. Cambridge, MA: Harvard University Press, 1975.

Jones, Jacqueline. *Labor of Love, Labor of Sorrow: Black Women, Work, and the Family from Slavery to the Present.* New York: Basic Books, 1985.

Karlsen, Carol F. *The Devil in the Shape of a Woman: Witchcraft in Colonial New England.* New York: Norton, 1987.

Lerner, Gerda. *The Creation of Feminist Consciousness.* New York: Oxford University Press, 1993.

———. *The Creation of Patriarchy.* New York: Oxford University Press, 1986.

Pantel, Pauline Schmitt, et al., eds. *A History of Women in the West.* 5 vols. Cambridge, MA: Harvard University Press, 1992.

Perrot, Michelle, ed. *Writing Women's History.* Trans. Felicia Pheasant. Oxford: Blackwell, 1984.

Pomeroy, Sarah B. *Goddesses, Whores, Wives, and Slaves: Women in Classical Antiquity.* New York: Schocken, 1975.

Scott, Ann Firor. *The Southern Lady: From Pedestal to Politics, 1830–1930.* Chicago: University of Chicago Press, 1970.

Sklar, Kathryn Kish. *Catherine Beecher: A Study in American Domesticity.* New Haven, CT: Yale University Press, 1973.

Ulrich, Laurel Thatcher. *A Midwife's Tale.* New York: Vintage, 1991.

Warner, Marina. *Alone of All Her Sex: The Myth and the Cult of the Virgin Mary.* New York: Vintage, 1993.

CHAPTER 53

Culture

Natalie Zemon Davis

Natalie Zemon Davis
Courtesy of Princeton University/Denise Applewhite

Cultural history is not new. There have always been historians who have written about culture. Frequently, they have written about what some call high culture—music, painting, theater, dance, and other art forms that have been formally presented. Usually, cultural historians have operated as a subgroup of intellectual historians. They have used literary modes of analysis, asking questions like the following: Is this not a wonderful artifact or performance? What are the major features that went into its construction? What are the ideas that the author/painter/ sculptor/choreographer is trying to impart to us? Where does this item stand in the stream of development of artistic technique?

The new cultural historians of the 1970s, '80s, and '90s are a very different lot. Some deal with formal cultural presentations, but more deal with aspects of popular culture: advertising, jokes, popular music, crowd behavior at sporting events, food, clothing, parades, riots. Their focus is not primarily on the authors or creators of culture but on its consumers. They try to unpack the meaning of everyday items and behavior in order to catch glimpses of the minds of ordinary people. They employ the ethnographic perspectives of cultural anthropologists, notably Clifford Geertz and Mary Douglas, and the interpretive methods of a generation of literary critics led by Jacques Derrida and Paul De Man, to try to understand people's experiences by illuminating what may be unseen in the texts, written or symbolic, that they have left us.

Two of the foremost practitioners of this type of history are Lawrence Levine and Robert Darnton. Darnton is particularly concerned with the history of mentalities and by the uses to which historians can put the ethnographic methods of anthropologists. Darnton's method is frequently ethnographic: pulling at the loose thread, the seeming anomaly, to try to find one's way into the minds of one's subjects. "Straying from the beaten path," he wrote in *The Great Cat Massacre* (pp. 6, 75–78),

> may not be much of a methodology, but it creates the possibility of enjoying some unusual views, and they can be the most revealing. [For exam-ple] . . . The funniest thing that ever happened in the printing shop of Jacques Vincent, according to a worker who witnessed it, was a riotous massacre of cats. [There follows a gruesome description of the event.] . . . Yet it strikes the modern reader as unfunny, if not downright repulsive. Where is the humor in a group of grown men bleating like goats and banging with their tools while an adolescent reenacts the ritual slaughter of a defenseless animal? Our own inability to get the joke is an indication of the distance that separates us from the workers of preindustrial Europe. . . . [T]he best points of entry in an attempt to penetrate an alien culture can be those where it seems to be most opaque. When you realize that you are not getting something—a joke, a proverb, a ceremony—that is particularly meaningful to the natives, you can see where to grasp a foreign system of meaning in order to unravel it.

Levine has spent a career looking in odd places—slave songs, jokes, old photographs, blues lyrics—and unpacking their symbolic and experiential significance. He is a master of asking the untutored question—the one that no sensible person would ask because everyone knows that it is not important—to throw new light on what people did not even know were unsettled issues. For instance, he used slave songs and stories to uncover a world of psychic resistance to slavery that previous scholars had simply not noticed because they presumed slaves to be voiceless. On another occasion he noticed what seemingly no one had noticed before: that William Shakespeare's plays were seen and known by all classes of Americans in the nineteenth century (they were then popular culture like the Flintstones) but that they had somehow become the exclusive property of the upper classes by the twentieth. In *Highbrow/Lowbrow*, Levine expanded that insight into an interpretation of the ways in which culture was used to reinforce increasing class divisions as America became an industrial society. Levine and the other new cultural historians insist that intellectual history is not the history of ideas, but the history of men and women thinking. Just so, the history of mentalities is not the history of popular beliefs and attitudes, but of people believing and acting.

Natalie Zemon Davis operates in an intellectual world closely related to those of Darnton and Levine. Through a series of germinal essays, including "Printing and the People," reproduced in part here, and her teaching at the University of California and then at Princeton, Davis has done much to shape the vision of a generation of cultural historians. *The Return of Martin Guerre*, a book which was later made into movies in France and the United States, tells the story of a man in sixteenth-century France who returns to his wife and village after years away at war. He is welcomed and resumes his former life, but then the question crops up: Is he really Martin Guerre, or is he the imposter Pansette? The story has several twists, but ultimately the villagers and legal authorities decide. Davis agrees with their decision, concluding her book with these words: "I think I have uncovered the true face of the past—or has Pansette done it once again?" (p. 125). Such an embrace of the plasticity of truth is one of the hallmarks of the new cultural historians.

Some cultural historians take an additional postmodernist step. Dominick La Capra, Hayden White, and Michel Foucault are examples, although there is great variety among such writers and they would not all accept the label. Such historians try to deconstruct—to take apart and leave the parts lying around unconnected—most aspects of received wisdom: the idea of truth, linear time, even geography. Unlike Ranke and the positivists, they do not seek primarily to find out how the past really was. To the contrary, the more extreme of such writers contend that it is not possible to know the past—that an actual past may not in fact even have existed, since all we have of the past is the interpretations, the constructions, the shards that have been preserved. The author, they say, is as much a text to be interpreted as is his or her writing or the documents on which his or her writing is based.

Many such historians would characterize the turn to culture and the postmodernist enterprise as a reaction against the extreme positivism of quantitative social science. They would say that it signals the end of the empirical age. There is in this movement a rejection of the arrogant certainties of those who think counting uncovers meaning. The turn has taken place, not only in historical studies, but in literary criticism, anthropology, legal scholarship, sociology, art history, linguistics, and other fields. It has resulted in unprecedented discussions across former disciplinary boundaries. Those boundaries, so carefully constructed by the positivists, are being deconstructed by the postmodernists, and new hybrid fields like cultural studies and critical theory are being formed.

At this moment, it is not possible to determine whether postmodernism is simply an intellectual movement of temporary influence, or whether it signals a sea change in the ways people think in Europe, North America, and perhaps the world, on a par with the Reformation or the Enlightenment. There are vociferous advocates of both positions. What one can say for sure is that the historical writing of Natalie Zemon Davis is vivid, intelligent, and thought provoking. In the essay reprinted here, "Printing and the People," Davis shows us, not just what the text said, but how it was used and what it meant to the lives of the people who read or heard it. We have all heard that printing revolutionized the lives of Europeans in the sixteenth century; now we can begin to understand what that meant.

Printing and the People[1]

Here are some voices from the sixteenth century. "The time has come. . . . for women to apply themselves to the sciences and disciplines." Thus the ropemaker's daughter Louise Labé addresses her sex when her collected poems are printed in Lyon in 1556. "And if one of us gets to the point where she can put her ideas in writing, then take pains with it and don't be reluctant to accept the glory." Ten years later in Cambrai, a Protestant linen-weaver explains to his judges about the book in his life: "I was led to knowledge of the Gospel by . . . my neighbor, who had a Bible printed at Lyon and who taught me the psalms by heart. . . . The two of us used to go walking in the fields Sundays and feast days, conversing about the Scriptures and the abuse of priests." And listen to the printers' journeymen of Paris and Lyon in 1572, in a brief they printed to convince Parlement and public that they needed better treatment from their employers: "Printing [is] an invention so admirable, . . . so honorable in its dignity, and profitable above all others to the French. Paris and Lyon furnish the whole of Christendom with books in every language." And yet "the Publishers and master Printers . . . use every stratagem to oppress . . . the Journeymen, who do the biggest and best part of the work of Printing." And finally, Pierre Tolet, doctor of medicine, justifying in 1540 his translation of some Greek texts into French, printed for the use of surgeons' journeymen: "If you want a servant to follow your orders, you can't give them in an unknown tongue."[2]

These quotations suggest the several and complex ways in which printing entered into popular life in the sixteenth century, setting up new networks of communication, facilitating new options for the people, and also providing new means of controlling the people. Can this be true? Could printing have mattered that much to *the people* in a period when literacy was still so low?

We can best understand the connections between printing and the people if we do two things: first, if we supplement thematic analysis of texts with evidence about audiences that can provide context for the meaning and uses of books; second, if we consider a printed book not merely as a source for ideas and images, but as a carrier of relationships. The data to support such an approach are scattered in the pages of the original editions themselves; in studies of literacy and dialects, book ownership and book prices, authorship and publication policy; and in sources on the customs and associational life of peasants and artisans. The theory to assist such an approach can be found in part in the work of Jack Goody and his collaborators on the implications of literacy for traditional societies—especially in their discussion of the relations between those who live on the margins of literacy and those who live at its center. Additional theoretical support exists in the fertile essays of Elizabeth L. Eisenstein on the impact of printing on literate elites and on urban populations in early modern Europe—especially when she talks of "cross-cultural interchange" between previously "compartmentalized systems." Both Goody and Eisenstein have insisted to critics that they do not intend technological determinism, and I am even more ready than they to emphasize the way that social structure and values channel the uses of literacy and printing.[3]

This essay, then will consider the context for using printed books in defined popular milieus in sixteenth-century France and the new relations that printing helped to establish among people and among hitherto isolated cultural traditions. Were there new groups who joined the ranks of known authors? What was the composition of "audiences"—those who actually read the books—and of "publics"—those to whom authors and publishers addressed their works?[4]

* * *

[I]

Let us look first to the peasants. The penetration of printing into their lives was a function not just of their literacy but of several things: the cost and availability of books in a language that they knew; the existence of social occasions when books could be read aloud; the need or desire for information that they thought could be found in printed books more easily than elsewhere; and in some cases the desire to use the press to say something to someone else.

Rural literacy remained low throughout the sixteenth century. Of the women, virtually none knew their ABC's, not even the midwives. As for the men, a systematic study of Emmanuel Le Roy Ladurie of certain parts of the Languedoc from the 1570's through the 1590's found that three percent of the agricultural workers and only ten percent of the better-off peasants— the *laboureurs* and *fermiers*—could sign their full names.[5] In the regions north and southwest of Paris, where the speech was French, the rates may have been slightly higher, and rural schools have been noted in several places. But the pupils who spent a couple of years at such places learning to read and write and sing were drawn from special families (such as that of a barber-surgeon in the Forez, who sent his boys to a school and rewarded its rector with a chapel in 1557) or were intended for nonagricultural occupations (such as the serf's son in the Sologne who went to school "to learn science" because he was "weak of body and could not work the soil").[6]

Surely a lad ambitious to be a *fermier* in the mid-sixteenth century would need to keep accounts, yet not all economic pressures pushed the prosperous peasant to literacy. Charles Estienne's agricultural manual advised the landed proprietor that his tenant farmer need not have reading and writing (one can lie on paper, too) so long as he was experienced and wise in agricultural ways. A peasant in the Haut-Poitou in 1601, designated tax assessor of his village, tried to get out of it by pleading illiteracy. As for sales of land, marriage contracts, and wills, there were itinerant scribes and notaries aplenty who were happy to add to their income by performing these services for the peasants.[7]

The country boys who really learned their letters, then, were most likely those who left for the city to apprentice to crafts or to become priests, or the few lucky sons of *laboureurs*, who, at a time when fellowships for the poor were being taken over by the rich, still made it to the University of Paris. One such, the son of a village smith from Brie, became a proofreader in Lyon after his university years, and at his death in 1560 was in possession of a precious manuscript of the theodosian code.[8]

But when they came back to visit, such men did not leave books in their villages. "Our little Thomas talks so profoundly, almost no one can under-stand him" was the observation of Thomas Platter's relatives when he passed through his Swiss mountain home during his student years in the early sixteenth century. One can imagine similar remarks exchanged by peasants in France about a son who had studied books in a strange language or learned his craft in a different dialect. As the peasants' inventories after death were virtually without manuscripts in the fifteenth century, so they were almost without printed books in the sixteenth.[9] Why should this be so? Surely a *laboureur* who could afford many livres worth of linens and coffers in the 1520's could afford three sous for a *Calendrier des bergers*, two sous for the medical manual *Le Tresor des povres*, or even two and a half livres for a bound and illustrated Book of Hours, which might be credit to his family for generations.[10]

Yet just because one can afford books does not mean that one can have ready access to them or need them or want them. A literate laboureur in some parts of France during the sixteenth century might never meet a bookseller: his nearest market town might have no presses if it were a small place, and peddlers' itineraries still reached relatively few parts of the countryside.[11] If he did come upon a bookseller, his wares might be in a language the peasant had difficulty reading, since so little printing was done in vernaculars other than French. Only five books printed in Breton during the sixteenth century could be found by an eighteenth-century student of that language, and the first work in Basque came out in 1545 and had very few imitators.[12] Provencal was favored by several editions, mostly of poetry, but the various regional dialects, from Picard to Poitevin, rarely appeared in print at all.[13]

* * *

And yet there were a few ways that printing did enter rural life in the sixteenth century to offer some new options to the peasants. The important social institution for this was the *veillée*, an evening gathering within the village community held especially during the winter months from All Saints' Day to Ash Wednesday.[14] Here tools were mended by candlelight, thread was spun, the unmarried flirted, people sang, and some man or woman told stories—of Mélusine, that wondrous woman-serpent with her violent husband and sons; of the girl who escaped from incest to the king's palace in a she-donkey's hide; of Renard and other adventuresome animals.[15] Then, if one of the men were literate and owned books, he might read aloud.

In principle, printing increased significantly the range of books available for the *veillée*. In fact, given the limited channels of distribution in the sixteenth century and the virtuosity of the traditional storyteller, even a rural schoolteacher might have very few books. According to Noel du Fail, a young lawyer from a seigneurial family in upper Brittany who wrote in 1547 a story of a peasant village, the village books were "old": *Aesop's Fables* and *Le Roman de la Rose*. Now both of these had printed editions and urban readers in the late fifteenth and early sixteenth centuries. By the 1540's, however, the learned were enjoying Aesop in fresh Latin and Greek editions or in new French rhyme; and, though still appreciative of the thirteenth-century *Roman*, they were feeling ever more distant from its sense and style, even in the updated version given them by Clément Marot. In contrast, peasants would have had no reason to supplant the early editions that Marot and his publisher disdained as full of printing errors and *"trop ancien langaige."*[16]

Did such reading aloud change things much in the village? *Reading* aloud? We might better say "translating," since the reader was inevitably turning the French of his printed text into a dialect his listeners could understand. And we might well add "editing"—if not for *Aesop's Fables,* whose form and plots were already familiar to peasants, then for the 22,000 lines and philosophical discourses of the *Roman.* In a community hearing parts of the *Roman* for the first time, new relationships were perhaps set up with old chivalric and scholastic ways of ordering experience; some new metaphors were acquired and varied images of women and love added to the listeners' existing stock.[17] Who do you yearn to be, or to love? Mélusine of the Rose? A good question, but it hardly constitutes a connection with the disctinctive features of "print culture."[18]

As early as the 1530's, however, some *veillées* were being treated to a book that was in the vanguard and more disruptive of traditional rural patterns than Aesop, the *Roman de la Rose,* of the *Calendrier*: the vernacular Bible. In Picardy a cobbler reads it to the villagers at the veillées until he is discovered by a nearby abbey. Here the literalness of the text was important. The Bible could not be "edited" or reduced to some formulaic magic. It had to be understood, and there were probably no pictures to help. In the Saintonge and elsewhere during the 1550's, Philibert Hamelin, his pack filled with Bibles and prayer books that he had printed at Geneva, comes to sit with peasants in the fields during their noonday break and talks of the Gospel and of a new kind of prayer. Some are delighted and learn; others are outraged and curse and beat him. He is sure that one day they will know better.[19]

In the Orléanais a forest ranger buys a vernacular New Testament, a French Psalter, and the Geneva catechism from a bookseller at a fair and goes alone into the forest of Marchenoir to read them. Over in the mountains of the Dauphiné a peasant somehow teaches himself to read and write French and divides his time between plowing and the New Testament. The story goes that when reproached by the priests because he did not know the Scripture in Latin, he laboriously spelled it out until he could contradict them with Latin citations.[20]

Finally, evangelical peddlers begin to work the countryside systematically. A carter, a native of Poitiers, loads up in Geneva with Bibles, Psalters, and Calvinist literature published by Laurent de Normandie and looks for buyers in the Piedmont and the rural Dauphiné. Five craftsmen from scattered parts of France are arrested in 1559 in a village in the Lyonnais with literature from Geneva in their baskets. Even the Inquisitor wonders why they should want to sell such books to *"gens rustiques."*[21]

Still, even if the Bible did not become a permanent fixture in most rural households, merely to think of selling to them on a large scale was something new. Who first opened up the rural markets for the peddlers' books of the seventeenth century? Not a simple printer of rural background; he would remember the illiteracy of his village. Not an ordinary publisher of popular literature; he would worry about meager profits. But zealous Protestants could overlook all that, could face the possibilities of destroyed merchandise and even death for the sake of "consoling poor Christians and instructing them in the law of God."[22]

If printing and Protestantism opened new routes for selling books in the countryside, the press also facilitated the *writing* of a few new books for a peasant public. What happened, I think, was that the printing of "peasant lore," as in the *Shepherds' Calendar* and in the books of common proverbs, brought it to the attention of learned men in a new way. These men were discovering the thoughts not of their local tenants or of the men and women from whom they bought grain at market, but of The Peasants. And, dedicated to the "illustration" of the national tongue and to the humanist ideal of practical service, they decided that they must correct rural lore and instruct The Peasants. Thus, Antoine Mizaud, doctor of medicine, mathematician, and professor at Paris, writes an *Astrologie des Rustiques* to tell countryfolk without the time to acquire perfect knowledge of the heavens how to predict the weather by sure terrestrial signs. (Mariners, military commanders, and physicians should find it useful, too.)[23] Thus, somewhat later, the royal surgeon Jacques Guillemeau writes a book on pregnancy and childbirth "not for the learned . . . but for young Surgeons, little versed in the art, dispersed here and there, far way from the cities."[24]

Some new almanacs appear on an annual basis now, authored by doctors of medicine and "mathematicians," containing bits of possible novel *agricultural* information, such as when to plant fruits and market vegetables. ("Tested by M. Peron and Jean Lirondes, old gardeners at Nimes," says one edition, which then tells about the *choux cabus*, artichokes, melons, and other plants that distinguished the seventeenth-century Languedoc garden from its mode's fifteenth-century forebear.)[25] Though these almanacs were conceived for a diverse public, they probably were expected to reach some peasant readers— certainly more than were the justly celebrated agricultural manuals of Charles Estienne, Jean Liebault, and others. These latter treatises were intended for landowners, gentlemen farmers, and seigneurs, who would then teach their lessees, tenants, and hired servants what to do.

What can we conclude, then, about the consequences of printing for the sixteenth-century peasant community? Certainly they were limited. A few lines of communication were opened between professor and peasant—or rather between bodies of cultural materials, as in the case of some traditional lore that was standardized and disseminated by the press, perhaps with a little correction from above. Expectations were higher by 1600 that a printed book might come into the village and be read aloud at the *veillée*, even where the little spark of Protestantism had burned out in the countryside. But oral culture was still so dominant that it transformed everything it touched; and it still changed according to the rules of forgetting and remembering, watching and discussing. Some printed medieval romances may have come to the peasants from the cities, but they cannot have played the escapist role that Mandrou has claimed for them in the seventeenth century. Peasants in the Lyonnais, in the Ile-de-France, and in the Languedoc put on tithe strikes just the same; villages in Burgundy forced their lords to enfranchise about half of their servile population; peasants in Brittany, the Guyenne, Burgundy, and the Dauphiné organized themselves into emergency communes, communicated with each other, and rebelled under traditional slogans, ensigns, and captives with festive titles—all neither deflected nor aided by what was being said in print.[26] Indeed, those who wished to control the countryside and bring it to order by means other than sheer force—whether bishop, seigneur, or king— would have to send not books but messengers, whose seals would not be mocked and who would disclose verbally the power behind the papers that they read.

[II]

In the cities, the changes wrought or facilitated by printing in the life of the *menu peuple* had greater moment. . . .

NOTES

1. Natalie Zemon Davis, "Printing and the People," *Society and Culture in Early Modern France* (Stanford, CA: Stanford University Press, 1975), 189–226. Footnotes renumbered to fit abridgement.
2. *Euvres de Louize Labé Lionnoize. Revues et Corrigees par ladite Dame* (Lyon: Jean I de Tournes, 1556), Dedication. Trial of *meulquinier* Antoine Setppen, native of Cambrai, in C. L. Frossard, "La réforme dans le Cambrésis au XVle siècle," *Bulletin de la société de l'histoire du protestantisme français* 3 (1854): 530. *Remonstrances, et Memoires, pour les Compangnons Imprimeurs, de Paris et Lyon: Opposans. Contre les Libraires, maistres Imprimeurs desdits lieux: Et adiointz* (n.p., n.d. [Lyon, 1572]), f. A ir (hereafter cited as *Remonstrances*). *Le Chirurgie de Paulus Aegineta Maistre Pierre Tolet Medecin de l'Hospital de Lyon* (Lyon: Etienne Dolet, 1540), p. 6.
3. J. R. Goody, ed., *Literacy in Traditional Societies* (Cambridge, 1968). Elizabeth L. Eisenstein, "Some Conjectures About the Impact of Printing on Western Society and Thought: A Preliminary Report," *Journal of Modern History* 40 (1968): 1–56; *idem*, "The Advent of Printing and the Problem of the Renaissance," *Past and Present* 45 (Nov. 1969): 19–89; *idem* (with T. K. Rabb), "Debate. The Advent of Printing and the Problem of the Renais- sance," *Past and Present* 52 (Aug. 1971): 134–44; *idem*, "L'avènement de l'imprimerie et la Réforme," Annales ESC 26 (1971): 1355–82. For a study of popular culture that uses a "relational" approach, see M. Agulhon, "Le problème de la culture populaire en France autour de 1848," Davis Center Seminar, Princeton University (May 1974).

4. This distinction is a necessary one, but is not made in everyday speech. I follow the terminology of T. J. Clark, *Image of the People. Gustave Courbet and the Second French Republic, 1848–1851* (New York, 1973), p. 12.

5. Estimates of ability to read based on studies of ability to sign one's name are, of course, approximate. One can learn to read without learning to write and vice versa. Nevertheless, the two skills were most often taught together in the sixteen century. Statistics on ability to sign, then, give us the order of magnitude of the number of readers. For a discussion of techniques of measuring literacy in the early modern period, see R. S. Schofield, "The Measurement of Literacy in Pre-Industrial England," in J. R. Goody, ed., *Literacy in Traditional Societies* (Cambridge, Eng., 1968), pp. 311–25, and F. Furet and W. Sachs, "La corissance de l'alphabétisation en France, XVIIIe–XIX siècle," *Annals. Economies, Sociétés, Civilisations* 29 (1974): 714–37.

6. Bernard Guenee, *Tribunaux et gens de justice dans le bailliage de Senlis à la fin du moyen âge (vers 1380–vers 1550)* (Paris, 1963).

7. Charles Estienne, *L'agriculture et maison rustique* (Paris: Jacques du Puys, 1564), chap. 7, f. 9r. Paul Raveau, *l'agriculture et les classes paysannes. La transformation de la propriété dans le haut Poitou au 16e siècle* (Paris, 1926), p. 259. René Choppin, *Traité de Privileges des Personnes Vivans aux Champs* [1st ed. in Latin, 1575] in *Oeuvres* (Paris, 1662–63), 3:16. René Fédou, *Les hommes de loi lyonnais à la fin du moyen age* (Paris, 1964), pp. 158–60.

8. E. Campardon and A. Tuetey, eds., *Inventaire des registres des insinuations du Châtelet de Paris pendant les règnes de François 1er et de Henti II* (Paris, 1906), no. 735. Archives Départementales du Rhône, B, Insinuations, Testaments, 1560–61, ff. 9r–10v; Henri and Julien Baudrier, *Bibliographie lyonnaise* (Lyon, 1895–1912), 9:306.

9. Thomas Platter (1499–1582), *Autobiographie*, trans. M. Helmer (*Cahiers des Annales* 22 [Paris, 1964]) p. 42. Thomas taught one of his young cousins his ABC's in one day and that lad left the village soon after for a scholarly career (p. 50). When Platter returned much later to found a school for a short period, it was with a special evangelical mission.

    No books are mentioned in the reviews of household possessions and wills made by Bézard, *Vie rurale;* Guérin, *Vie rurale;* Gonon, *Vie quotidienne;* and Raveau, *Agriculture.* Note the remarkably infrequent mention of books in notarial acts in the rural Mâconnais even in the seventeenth through the nineteenth centuries (Suzanne Tardieu, *La vie domestique dans le mâconnais rural préindustriel* [Paris, 1964], p. 358 and p. 358, n. 2).

10. Albert Labarre, *Le livre dans la vie amie noise du seizième siècle. L'enseignement des inventions après decès* (Paris, 1971).

11. Martin, *Livre, pouvoirs et société*, pp. 319–20. When the Sire de Gouberville acquired books for his little library at the manor of Mesnil-au-Val in Normandy, they were purchased in Paris and Bayeux (A. Tollemer, *Un Sire de Gouberville, gentilhomme campagnard au cotentin de 1553 à 1562* [Paris, 1972], pp. 204–9). In the 1570's and early 1580's, the bibliophile François de La Croix du Maine found it much harder to acquire books in Le Mans

and vicinity than in Paris (*Premier volume de la Bibliotheque du Sieur de la Croix-du-Maine* [Paris 1584], Preface, f. a viir). A 1635 Paris edition of a book on surgery and health by H. Fierabras was purchased in July 1669 "a la foire de beaucaire" (written in the copy at the medical library of the University of California at San Francisco). It seems unlikely that books were sold at the Beaucaire fairs a century earlier.

12. On the variety of speech and dialect in sixteenth-century France and the growing separation between written and spoken language, see F. Brunot et al., *Histoire de la langue française des origines à 1900* (Paris, 1905–53), 1:xiii–xiv, 304ff; 2:174–75.

    Grégoire de Rostrenin, *Dictionnaire françois-celtique ou françois-Breton* (Rennes, 1732), preface; a Breton-French-Latin dictionary (Tréquier: Jean Calvet, 1499); a book of the Passion and Resurrection, the Death of the Virgin, and the Life of Man in Breton verse (Paris: Yves Quillevere, 1530); the Four Ends of Man in Breton verse (Morlaix, 1570); and two saints' lives in Breton.

    G. Brunet, *Poésies basques de Bernard Dechepara . . . d'après l'édition de Bordeaux, 1545* (Bordeaux, 1847). Julien Vinson, *Essai d'une bibliographie de la langue basque* (Paris, 1891–98), 1, nos. 1–5 (only two of these entries were published in France; the others were printed in Pamplona or Bilbao).

13. *Chansons nouvelles en lengaige provensal* (black-letter; n.p., n.d.). Augier Gaillard, *Las Obras* (Bordeaux, 1574); L. Bellaud de la Bellaudière, *Obros et rimos provenssalos* (Marseille: P. Mascaron, 1595). La Croix du Maine lists four persons with manuscripts in Provençal (Jean de Nostredame, Guillaume Boyer, Olivier de Lorgues, and Pierre de Bonifaccis), but I cannot find any evidence of their being printed in that language.

14. Roger Vaultier, *Le folklore pendant la guerre de Cent Ans d'après les lettres de rémission du trésor des chartes* (Paris, 1965); Robert Mandrou, De la culture populaire aux 17e et 18e siècles, La bibliothèque bleue de Troyes (Paris, 1964).

15. Marc Soriano, Les contes de Perrault. Culture savante et traditions populaires (Paris, 1968).

16. Du Fail, *Propos*, pp. 15, 51. French editions of Aesop: Lyon, 1490 and 1499, prepared by the Augustinian Julien de Macho; new rhymed edition by Guillaume Corrozet, Paris 1542 and after. Greek and Latin editions: Elizabeth Armstrong, *Robert Estienne, Royal Printer* (Cambridge, 1954), p. 97; Germaine Warkentin, "Some Renaissance School books in the Osborne Collection," *Renaissance and Reformation* 5, 3 (May 1969): 37. Urban ownership of Aesop: Labarre, *Livre*, p. 208; Schutz, *Vernacular Books*, p. 72–73.

    Editions of the *Roman de la Rose* in its "ancient language": fourteen between 1481 and 1528; four editions between 1526 and 1538 in the translation attributed to Marot. No further editions until 1735! (Clearly the *Roman* did not become part of the peddlers' literature.) On these editions, on interest in the *Roman* among poets and on Marot as probable translator, see Antonio Viscardi, "Introduction," in *Le Roman de la Rose, dans la version attribuée à Clément Marot,* ed. S. F. Bariton (Milan, 1954), pp. 11–90. Urban ownership of the *Roman:* Labarre, *Livre,* p. 210; Schutz, *Vernacular Books,* p. 67; Doucet, *Bibliothèques,* p. 87, n. 39.

17. I am grateful to E. Howard Bloch, Joseph Duggan, and John Benton for suggestions on this subject. Though many medieval manuscripts remain of the *Roman de la Rose*—some 300—they are unlikely to have circulated among the peasants in this form. There is a short version of the *Roman* in manuscript, with much of the philosophical material omitted (E. Langlois, *Les manscrits du Roman de la Rose. Description et classement* [Lille, 1910], pp. 385–86). Here again there is no evidence that these excisions were made to prepare it for reading to peasants.

18. Noel du Fail was quite particular about the books that he placed in the village. When a pirated edition of his *Propos* came out in Paris in 1548 with other books added to his list, he suppressed them in his new edition at Lyon in 1549. In 1573, however, the Parisian publisher Jean II Ruelle added five titles that may have had some hearing in the countryside: a late-fifteenth-century poetic history of the reign of Charles VII; two medieval romances (including *Valentine et Orson,* which has thematic material relating to the old rural custom of the chase of the wildman or of the bear); an account by Symphorien Champier of the chivalric deeds of the good knight Bayard; and the Miracles of Our Lady. Some of these were part of the *Bibliothèque bleue* of the seventeenth century (du Fail, *Propos,* pp. iv-xii, 138, 187).

   On a rainy evening in February 1554, the Norman gentleman Gilles de Gouberville read to his household, including the male and female servants, from *Amadis de Gaule* (A. Tollemer, *Un Sire de Gouberville, gentihomme campagnard au contentin de 1553 à 1562,* with introduction by E. Le Roy Ladurie [reprint of the 1873 ed., Paris, 1972], p. 285). This chivalric tale had only recently been translated from the Spanish and printed in France.

   I think these books would have been received by peasants in the same way as the *Roman de la Rose* and *Aesop's Fables.*

19. Jean Crespin, *Histoire des Martyrs persecutez et mis a mort pour la verite d'Evangelie, depuis le temps des Apostres jusques a present (1619),* ed. D. Benoit (Toulouse, 1885–89) 2: 423–25; 1: 335.

20. On the carter Barthélemy Hector: *Livres des habitants de Genève,* ed. P.-F. Geisendorg (Geneva, 1957); H. L. Schlaepfer, "Laurent de Normandie," in *Aspects de la propagande religieuse* (Geneva, 1957), p. 198; Crespin, *Martyrs,* 2: 437–38. On the peddlers in the Lyonnais, ADR, B, Sénéchaussée, Sentences, 1556–1559, Sentence of July 1559. Two of them, the dressmaker Girard Bernard, native of Champagne, and the shoemaker Antoine Tallencon or Tannenton, native of Gascony, purchased books from Laurent de Normandie a few months before their arrest (Schlaepfer, "Laurent de Normandie," p. 200).

21. See, for instance, Marcel Cauvin, "Le protestantisme cans le Contentin," BSHPF 112 (1966): 367–68; 115 (1960): 80–81. Le Roy Ladurie, *Paysans,* 348–51. For a picture of Protestant congregations in the seventeenth

century in which individual *laboureurs* play their part, see P. H. Chaix, "Les protestants en Bresse en 1621," *Cahiers d'histoire* 14 (1969): 252–54.

22. Crespin, *Martyrs,* 2:438. The publisher of Protestant propaganda some-times shared part of the risk with the peddler, contracting, for instance, that if the books were seized within a two-month period by the "enemies of the Gospel," the *libraire* would bear all the loss (Schlaepfer, "Laurent de Normandie," p. 199, n. 10; P. H. Chaix, "Les protestants en Bresse en 1621," *Cahiers d'histoire* 14 (1969), p. 59.

23. [Antoine Mizaud], *Les Ephemerides perpetuelles de l'air: autrement l'Astrologie des Rustiques* (Paris: Jacques Kerver, 1554), dedication. Signatures in the Houghton Library copy: "Claude Lorot, nimdunois[?], Claude Rinart son nepveu. Arte collude." On Mizaud's other works, see La Croix de Maine, *Bibliothèque,* pp. 17–18.

24. Jacques Guillemeau, *De la grossesse et accouchement des femmes . . . Par feu Jacques Guillemeau, Chirigien ordinaire du Roy* (Paris, 1620; 1st ed. Paris, 1609), f. a iiir–v.

25. Le Sieur L'Estoile, *Ephemerides ou Almanach iournalier pour l'an 1625* (Lyon, n.d. [1625]), pp. 75–78. On gardens in the Languedoc, see Le Roy Ladurie, *Paysans,* pp. 60–68.

26. N. Weiss, "Vidimus des lettres patentes de François ler, 1529" BSHPF 59 (1910), 501–4; Le Roy Ladurie, *Paysans,* 380–404; Bézard, *Vie rurale,* 289–90; V. Carrière, *Introduction aux études d'histoire ecclésiastique locale* (Paris, 1936), 3: 319–52. S. Gigon, *La révolte de la gabelle en Guyenne* (Paris, 1906); G. Procacci, *Classi socioli e monarchia assoluta nella Francia della prima metà del secolo XVI* (Turin, 1955), pp. 161–73, 213–30; Choppin, *Oeuvres* (162–63), 3:22 ("*la multitude des Rustiques de la Guyenne, qui alloient tumuiltueusement armée de villages en villages en l'an 1594"*). Jean Moreau, *Mémoires . . . sur les Guerres de la Ligue en Bretagne,* ed. H. Waquet (Archives historiques de Bretagne, 1; Quimper, 1906), pp. 11–14, 75–76. A. Le M. de La Borderie and B. Pocquet, *Histoire de Bretagne* (Rennes, 1906), 5:173–81. Henri Drouot, *Mayenne et la Bourgogne, Etude sur la Ligue (1587–1596)* (Paris, 1937, 1:39–55; 2:291–92. Claude de Rubys, *Histoire veritable de la ville de Lyon* (Lyon, 1604), pp. 430–31; Daniel Hlchek, "The Socio-Economic Context of the French Wars of Religion. A Case Study: Valentinois-Diois" (unpublished Ph.D. dissertation, Dept. of History, McGill University, 1973), chap. 4; L. S. Van Doren, "Revolt and Reaction in the City of the Romans, Dauphiné, 1579–80," *Sixteenth Century Journal* 5 (1974): 72–77. See also Madeleine Foisil, *La révolte des Nu-Pieds et les révoltes normandes de 1639* (Paris, 1970), 178–83, on nicknames and organization of the Nu-Pieds.

QUESTIONS TO CONSIDER

1. How did printing change the lives of ordinary people in sixteenth-century France?

2. What does Davis mean when she asks her reader to "consider a printed book not merely as a source for ideas and images, but as a carrier of relationships"?
3. In what ways is Davis's cultural history similar to and different from the cultural histories of Weber (Chapter 40), Yanagita (47), Blassingame (50), Thompson (51), and Bynum (52)?

FOR FURTHER READING

Chartier, Roger. *Cultural History: Between Practices and Representations.* Trans. Lydia G. Cochrane. Ithaca, NY: Cornell University Press, 1988.

Darnton, Robert. *The Great Cat Massacre and Other Episodes in French Cultural History.* New York: Basic Books, 1984.

_____ . *The Kiss of Lamourette: Reflections in Cultural History.* New York: Norton, 1990.

Davis, Natalie Zemon. *The Return of Martin Guerre.* Cambridge, MA: Harvard University Press, 1983.

Foucault, Michel. *The Archaeology of Knowledge.* Trans. A. M. Sheridan Smith. New York: Pantheon, 1972.

_____ . *Discipline and Punish: The Birth of the Prison.* Trans. Alan Sheridan. New York: Random House, 1978.

_____ . *Madness and Civilization.* Trans. Richard Howard. New York: Random House, 1965.

Geertz, Clifford. *The Interpretation of Cultures.* New York: Basic Books, 1973.

_____ . *Local Knowledge: Further Essays in Interpretive Anthropology.* New York: Harper and Row, 1983.

Hunt, Lynn, ed. *The New Cultural History.* Berkeley, CA: University of California Press, 1989.

LaCapra, Dominick. *Rethinking Intellectual History: Texts, Contexts, Language.* Ithaca, NY: Cornell University Press, 1983.

Levine, Lawrence W. *Black Culture and Black Consciousness.* New York: Oxford University Press, 1977.

_____ . *Highbrow/Lowbrow: The Emergence of Cultural Hierarchy in America.* Cambridge, MA: Harvard University Press, 1988.

_____ . *The Uncertain Past: Essays in American Cultural History.* New York: Oxford University Press, 1993.

Miller, Jim. *The Passion of Michel Foucault.* New York: Simon and Schuster, 1993.

Palmer, Bryan D. *Descent into Discourse: The Reification of Language and the Writing of Social History.* Philadelphia: Temple University Press, 1990.

Susman, Warren. *Culture as History: The Transformation of American Society in the Twentieth Century.* New York: Pantheon, 1984.

White, Hayden. *The Content of the Form: Narrative Discourse and Historical Representation.* Baltimore: Johns Hopkins University Press, 1987.

_____ . *Metahistory: The Historical Imagination in Nineteenth-Century Europe.* Baltimore: Johns Hopkins University Press, 1973.

CHAPTER 54

World Systems

Walter Rodney

Walter Rodney
Courtesy of Boston University

The attempt to write universal history—the history of the whole world through all time—goes very far back in the Western historiographical tradition. The Bible is, after all, a kind of universal history, a writing about God's dealings with humankind. Although its narrative has a parochial focus on the Hebrews, in its implications it extends beyond them to the rest of the world. Augustine's *City of God* is a later attempt to bring under one compass all of humankind's history (and its future) and to find meaning there.

Such attempts at universal history have been a minor key, not the norm in the Western tradition. They have long alternated with the more common national histories of writers like Tacitus, Bede, Guicciardini, and Ranke. Non-Western traditions have been even less interested in writing about the whole world; in China, India, and Persia, histories have almost always concentrated on the people from the writers' own countries.

It has been argued that, especially in the twentieth century, global or universal history has taken on special urgency as a substitute for God in humankind's search for meaning. In *World Historians and Their Goals*, Paul Costello writes:

> In the study of world history one confronts civilizations or unified cultural systems made up of habitual patterns of symbols and material life—as wholes—that live and progress, or die and disintegrate, in rhythm with a hidden underlying reality. To grasp this reality is essential to the resolution of the crisis of the twentieth century, where old symbols have broken down, old faiths have been lost or betrayed, where God is dead and progress becomes a fearful passage of Faustian striving toward ends that lose their attraction with our approach, where the old utopias become prisons and asylums. To most of the major world historians of the twentieth century, modern man has lost his connection with a unity beyond his own self-interest; through progress he has broken his connection to a meaningful cosmos. The modern individual's vision of the world is distracted by his concern for detail; the mechanical increment is taken for reality as a whole and consequently he cannot come to grips with the ultimate issues of his time or the eternal ones of his nature. To the world historians there is a crisis in modern man's epistemology; as the frame of reference is constricted so is the possibility of any meaning in the world beyond a narrowly circumscribed sensate experience. As reality is broken down to its constituent data nothing can be known except the quantitative, and the person becomes a fragment. . . . [W]orld history . . . has come to provide psychological grounding for life in an age without a common faith. (pp. 3–5)

The list of world historians in the modern West includes some distinguished and many very popular historians, including H. G. Wells, Oswald Spengler, and Arnold Toynbee, among others. Professional historians have liked world historians rather less than has the general public. Formally trained historians generally have considered world history as painted with much too broad a brush, as too far removed from its sources to be concretely verifiable, and therefore as unreliable. In a secular age, they have also been uncomfortable with the religious overtones of some world histories.

In recent years there has arisen a particular kind of world historian, one who portrays the history of the world, not just as a collection of national histories, but as a single, interlocking world system. William McNeill is one of these. In a dozen books beginning with *The Rise of the West* in 1963, McNeill has tried to paint a detailed portrait of the "history of the human community." He has chosen broad themes, such as warfare, technology, disease, nationalism, and freedom. In each case, he has drawn his theme across the entire globe, people from each continent, and a long period of time. In *Plagues and Peoples,* for example, he has gone beyond the conventional account of the bubonic plague's devastation of Europe, to show the disease migrating across the Eurasian land mass more than once. He assays its impact on China and India as well as on France and England. He contemplates the meaning of disease in various cultures, and shows how diseases acted decisively at certain critical moments to change the courses of nations' histories.

A sharp economic undertone marks the work of Immanuel Wallerstein in *The Modern World-System* and L. S. Stavrianos in *Global Rift.* These writers see the creation of a world system of capitalist economic institutions as the decisive development of modern history. They describe all of the history of modern nations as an outworking of the development of that world system. Their influence has spread primarily in sociological and political scientific circles to scholars like Daniel Chirot, Lucy Cheng, and Edna Bonacich who build arguments about modern history, class relationships, and international relations.

Walter Rodney's book *How Europe Underdeveloped Africa,* reproduced in part here, strikes a similar chord. He argues that, at the time Europeans first came to sub-Saharan Africa in the fifteenth century, Western Europe and West Africa stood at approximately the same level of economic, social, and technological development, with the Europeans having certain advantages such as guns and large, ocean-going ships that proved decisive in the encounter. Four centuries later, Europe had forged ahead dramatically and Africa had declined.

Rodney regards these transformations as mutually produced. His argument is subtle and complex, but it boils down to this: Europe developed economically by stealing from Africa. The stealing began with the slave trade and continued through colonial and quasi-colonial extractive economic arrangments in later centuries. African labor and resources, Rodney argues, provided the key factor that spurred the economic development of European industrial capitalism. Meanwhile, Africa's losses to European theft kept it from developing economically at an equal pace. In the end, Rodney calls for Africa to throw off not only the yoke of formal colonialism but also the residual harness of international capitalism.

Many Third World scholars and sympathizers have found Rodney's arguments persuasive. Other scholars, mainly people from Europe and North America, have questioned Rodney's figures. Few doubt the negative impact of slavery on Africa, but some question how much resource rape and slave production actually contributed to the rise of industrial capitalism in Europe, as compared with domestic European sources of capital formation. And some see continuing economic relationships between Europe and Africa as more beneficial to Africa than Rodney (or Wallerstein or Stavrianos) will admit. An analysis of Indonesia's relationship to the Netherlands, however, undertaken by noted anthropologist Clifford Geertz, finds an economic dynamic similar to the one Rodney describes for Africa.

Walter Rodney was a Guyanese scholar and political activist. Educated in history at the University of the West Indies in Jamaica and at the University of London, he was the author of several books of West African history. He was killed in political violence in Guyana in 1980.

How Europe Underdeveloped Africa[1]
The European Slave Trade as a Basic Factor in African Underdevelopment

To discuss trade between Africans and Europeans in the four centuries before colonial rule is virtually to discuss slave trade. Strictly speaking, the African only became a slave when he reached a society where he worked as a slave. Before that, he was first a free man and then a captive. Nevertheless, it is acceptable to speak of the trade in slaves when referring to the shipment of captives from Africa to various other parts of the world where they were to live and work as the property of Europeans. The title of this section is deliberately chosen to call attention to the fact that the shipments were all by Europeans to markets controlled by Europeans, and this was in the interest of European capitalism and nothing else. In East Africa and the Sudan, many Africans were taken by Arabs and were sold to Arab buyers. This is known (in European books) as the "Arab Slave Trade." Therefore, let it be clear that when Europeans shipped Africans to European buyers it was the "European Slave Trade" from Africa.

Undoubtedly, with few exceptions such as Hawkins, European buyers purchased African captives on the coasts of Africa and the transaction between themselves and Africans was a form of trade. It is also true that very often a captive was sold and resold as he made his way from the interior to the port of embarkation—and that too was a form of trade. However, on the whole, the process by which captives were obtained on African soil was not trade at all. It was through warfare, trickery, banditry, and kidnaping. When one tries to measure the effect of European slave trading on the African continent, it is essential to realize that one is measuring the effect of social violence rather than trade in any normal sense of the word.

Many things remain uncertain about the slave trade and its consequences for Africa, but the general picture of descructiveness is clear, and that destructiveness can be shown to be the logical consequence of the manner of recruitment of captives in Africa. One of the uncertainties concerns the basic question of how many Africans were imported. This has long been an object of speculation, with estimates ranging from a few million to over one hundred million. A recent study has suggested a figure of about ten million Africans landed alive in the Americas, the Atlantic islands, and Europe. Because it is a low figure, it is already being used by European scholars who are apologists for the capitalist system and its long record of brutality in Europe and abroad. In order to whitewash the European slave trade, they find it convenient to start by minimizing the numbers concerned. The truth is that any figure of Africans imported into the Americas which is narrowly based on the surviving records is bound to be low, because there were so many people at the time who had a vested interest in smuggling slaves (and withholding data). Nevertheless, if the low figure of ten million was accepted as a basis for evaluating the impact of slaving on Africa as a whole, the conclusions that could legitimately be drawn would confound those who attempt to make light of the experience of the rape of Africans from 1445 to 1870.

On any basic figure of Africans landed alive in the Americas, one would have to make several extensions—starting with a calculation to cover mortality in transshipment. The Atlantic crossing, or "Middle Passage," as it was called by European slavers, was notorious for the number of deaths incurred, averaging in the vicinity of 15 or 20 per cent. There were also numerous deaths in Africa between time of capture and time of embarkation, especially in cases where captives had to travel hundreds of miles to the coast. Most important of all (given that warfare was the principal means of obtaining captives) it is necessary to make some estimate as to the number of people killed and injured so as to extract the millions who were taken alive and sound. The resultant figure would be many times the millions landed alive outside of Africa, and it is that figure which represents the number of Africans directly removed from the population and labor force of Africa because of the establishment of slave production by Europeans.

The massive loss to the African labor force was made more critical because it was composed of able-bodied young men and young women. Slave buyers preferred their victims between the ages of fifteen and thirty-five, and preferably in the early twenties; the sex ratio being about two men to one woman. Europeans often accepted younger African children, but rarely any older person. They shipped the most healthy wherever possible, taking the trouble to get those who had already survived an attack of smallpox, and who were therefore immune from further attacks of that disease, which was then one of the world's great killer diseases.

Absence of data about the size of Africa's population in the fifteenth century makes it difficult to carry out any scientific assessment of the results of the population outflow. But, nothing suggests that there was any increase in the continent's population over the centuries of slaving, although that was the trend in other parts of the world. Obviously, fewer babies were born than would otherwise have been the case if millions of child-bearing ages were not eliminated. Besides, it is essential to recognize that the slave trade across the Atlantic Ocean was not the only connection which Europeans had with slaving in Africa. The slave trade on the Indian Ocean has been called the "East African Slave Trade," and the "Arab Slave Trade" for so long that it hides the extent to which it was also a European slave trade. When the slave trade from East Africa was at its height in the eighteenth century and in the early nineteenth century, the destination of most captives was the European-owned plantation economies of Mauritius, Réunion, and Seychelles—as well as the Americas, via the Cape of Good Hope. Besides, Africans laboring as slaves in certain Arab countries in the eighteenth and nineteenth centuries were all ultimately serving the European capitalist system which set up a demand for slave-grown products, such as the cloves grown in Zanzibar under the supervision of Arab masters.

No one has been able to come up with a figure representing total losses to the African population sustained through the extraction of slave labor from all

areas to all destinations over the many centuries that slave trade existed. However, on every other continent from the fifteenth century onwards, the population showed constant and sometimes spectacular natural increase; while it is
striking that the same did not apply to Africa. One European scholar gave the
following estimates of world population (in millions) according to continents:

	1650	1750	1850	1950
Africa	100	100	100	120
Europe	103	144	274	423
Asia	257	437	656	857

None of the above figures is really precise, but they do indicate a consensus
among researchers on population that the huge African continent has an
abnormal record of stagnation in this respect, and there is no causative factor
other than the trade in slaves to which attention can be drawn.

An emphasis on population loss as is highly relevant to socio-economic
development. Population growth played a major role in European development in providing labor, markets, and the pressures which led to further
advance. Japanese population growth had similar positive effects; and in other
parts of Asia which remained pre-capitalist, the size of the population led to a
much more intensive exploitation of the land than has ever been the case in
which is still a sparsely peopled African continent.

So long as the population density was low, then human beings viewed as
units of labor were far more important than other factors of production such
as land. From one end of the continent to the other, it is easy to find examples
showing that African people were conscious that population was in their
circumstances the most important factor of production. Among the Bemba, for
instance, numbers of subjects were held to be more important than land.
Among the Shambala of Tanzania, the same feeling was expressed in the
saying, "A king is people." Among the Balanta of Guinea-Bissau, the family's
strength is represented by the number of hands there are to cultivate the land.
Certainly, many African rulers acquiesced in the European slave trade for
what they considered to be reasons of self-interest, but on no scale of
rationality could the outflow of population be measured as being anything but
disastrous for African societies.

African economic activity was affected both directly and indirectly by
population loss. For instance, when the inhabitants of a given area were
reduced below a certain number in an environment where the tsetse fly was
present, the remaining few had to abandon the area. In effect, enslavement
was causing these people to lose their battle to tame and harness nature—a
battle which is at the basis of development. Violence almost meant insecurity.
The opportunity presented by European slave dealers became the major
(though not the only) stimulus for a great deal of social violence between
different African communities and within any given community. It took the
form more of raiding and kidnaping than of regular warfare, and that fact
increased the element of fear and uncertainty.

Both openly and by implication, all the European powers in the nineteenth century indicated their awareness of the fact that the activities connected with producing captives were inconsistent with other economic pursuits. That was the time when Britain in particular wanted Africans to collect palm produce and rubber and to grow agricultural crops for export in place of slaves; and it was clear that slave raiding was violently conflicting with that objective in Western, Eastern, and Central Africa. Long before that date, Europeans accepted that fact when their self-interest was involved. For example, in the seventeenth century, the Portuguese and Dutch actually discouraged slave trade on the Gold Coast, for they recognized that it would be incompatible with gold trade. However, by the end of that century, gold had been discovered in Brazil, and the importance of gold supplies from Africa was lessened. Within the total Atlantic pattern, African slaves became more important than gold, and Brazilian gold was offered for African captives at Whyday (Dahomey) and Accra. At that point, slaving began undermining the Gold Coast economy and destroying the gold trade. Slave raiding and kidnaping made it unsafe to mine and to travel with gold; and raiding for captives proved more profitable than gold mining. One European on the scene noted that "as one fortunate marauding makes a native rich in a day, they therefore exert themselves rather in war, robbery and plunder than in their old business of digging and collecting gold."

The above changeover from gold mining to slave raiding took place within a period of a few years between 1700 and 1710, when the Gold Coast came to supply about five thousand to six thousand captives per year. By the end of the eighteenth century, a much smaller number of captives were exported from the Gold Coast, but the damage had already been done. It is worth noting that Europeans sought out different parts of West and Central Africa at different times to play the role of major suppliers of slaves to the Americas. This meant that virtually every section of the long western coastline between the Senegal and Cunene rivers had at least a few years' experience of intensive trade in slaves—with all its consequences. Besides, in the history of eastern Nigeria, the Congo, northern Angola, and Dahomey, there were periods extending over decades when exports remained at an average of many thousands per year. Most of those areas were also relatively highly developed within the African context. They were leading forces inside Africa, whose energies would otherwise have gone towards their own self-improvement and the betterment of the continent as a whole.

The changeover to warlike activities and kidnaping must have affected all branches of economic activity, and agriculture in particular. Occasionally, in certain localities food production was increased to provide supplies for slave ships, but the overall consequences of slaving on agricultural activities in Western, Eastern, and Central Africa were negative. Labor was drawn off from agriculture and conditions became unsettled. Dahomey, which in the sixteenth century was known for exporting food to parts of what is now Togo, was suffering from famines in the nineteenth century. The present generation of Africans will readily recall that in the colonial period when able-bodied men left their homes as migrant laborers, that upset the farming routine in the home districts and often caused famines. Slave trading after all meant migration of labor in a manner one hundred times more brutal and disruptive.

To achieve economic development, one essential condition is to make the maximum use of the country's labor and natural resources. Usually, that demands peaceful conditions, but there have been times in history when social groups have grown stronger by raiding their neighbors for women, cattle, and goods, because they then used the "booty" from the raids for the benefit of their own community. Slaving in Africa did not even have that redeeming value. Captives were shipped outside instead of being utilized within any given African community for creating wealth from nature. It was only as an accidental by-product that in some areas Africans who recruited captives for Europeans realized that they were better off keeping some captives for themselves. In any case, slaving prevented the remaining population from effectively engaging in agriculture and industry, and it employed professional slave-hunters and warriors to destroy rather than build. Quite apart from the moral aspect and the immense suffering that it caused, the European slave trade was economically totally irrational from the viewpoint of African development.

*   *   *

One tactic that is now being employed by certain European (including American) scholars is to say that the European slave trade was undoubtedly *a moral evil*, but it was *economically good* for Africa. Here attention will be drawn only very briefly to a few of those arguments to indicate how ridiculous they can be. One that receives much emphasis is that African rulers and other persons obtained European commodities in exchange for their captives, and this was how Africans gained "wealth." This suggestion fails to take into the account the fact that several European imports were competing with and strangling African products; it fails to take into account the fact that none of the long list of European articles were of the type which entered into the productive process, but were rather items to be rapidly consumed or stowed away uselessly; and it incredibly overlooks the fact that the majority of the imports were of the worst quality even as consumer goods—cheap gin, cheap gunpowder, pots and kettles full of holes, beads, and other assorted rubbish.

Following from the above, it is suggested that certain African kingdoms grew strong economically and politically as a consequence of the trade with Europeans. The greatest of the West African kingdoms, such as Oyo, Benin, Dahomey, and Asante are cited as examples. Oyo and Benin were great long before making contact with Europeans, and while both Dahomey and Asante grew stronger during the period of the European slave trade, the roots of their achievements went back to much earlier years. Furthermore—and this is the major fallacy in the argument of the slave-trade apologists—the fact that a given African state grew politically more powerful at the same time as it engaged in selling captives to Europeans is not automatically to be attributed to the credit of the trade in slaves. A cholera epidemic may kill thousands in a country and yet the population increases. The increase obviously came about *in spite of* and not because of the cholera. This simple logic escapes those who speak about the European slave trade benefiting Africa. The destructive tendency of slave trading can be clearly established; and, wherever a state seemingly profressed in the epoch of slave trading, the conclusion is simply that it did so in spite of the adverse effects of a process that was more damaging than cholera. This is the picture that emerges from a detailed study of Dahomey, for instance, and in the final analysis although Dahomey did its best to expand politically and militarily while still tied to slave trade, that form of economic activity seriously undermined its economic base and left it much worse off.

A few of the arguments about the economic benefits of the European slave trade for Africa amount to nothing more than saying that exporting millions of captives was a way of avoiding starvation in Africa! To attempt to reply to that would be painful and time-wasting. But, perhaps a slightly more subtle version of the same argument requires a reply: namely, the argument that Africa gained because in the process of slave trading new food crops were acquired from the American continent and these became staples in Africa. The crops in question are maize and cassava, which became staples in Africa late in the nineteenth century and in the present century. But the spread of food crops is one of the most common phenomena in human history. Most crops originated in only one of the continents, and then social contact caused their transfer to other parts of the world. Trading in slaves has no special bearing on whether crops spread— the simplest forms of trade would have achieved the same result. Today, the Italians have (hard) wheat foods like spaghetti and macaroni as their staple, while most Europeans use the potato. The Italians took the idea of the spaghetti-type foods from the Chinese noodle after Marco Polo returned from travels there, while Europe adopted the potato from American Indians. In neither case were Europeans enslaved before they could receive a benefit that was the logical heritage of all mankind, but Africans are to be told that the European slave trade developed us by bringing us maize and cassava.

All of the above points are taken from books and articles published recently, as the fruit of research in major British and American universities. They are probably not the commonest views even among European bourgeois scholars, but they are representative of a growing trend that seems likely to become the new accepted orthodoxy in metropolitan capitalist countries; and this significantly coincides with Europe's struggle against the further decolonization of Africa economically and mentally. In one sense, it is preferable to ignore such rubbish and isolate our youth from its insults; but unfortunately one of the aspects of current African underdevelopment is that the capitalist publishers and bourgeois scholars dominate the scene and help mold opinions the world over. It is for that reason that writing of the type which justifies the trade in slaves has to be exposed as racist bourgeois propaganda, having no connection with reality or logic. It is a question not merely of history but of present-day liberation struggle in Africa.

QUESTIONS TO CONSIDER

1. What evidence does Rodney use to argue that "Europe underdeveloped Africa"?
2. How is Rodney's sense of Africans as a single people related to the racial definitions employed by DaCunha (Chapter 42), Dike (44), and Blassingame (50)?
3. How successful are histories that try to work on such a grand, comparative scale? Are they more or less convincing than detailed analyses of more narrowly conceived topics?

FOR FURTHER READING

Cheng, Lucie, and Edna Bonacich, eds. *Labor Migration Under Capitalism.* Berkeley, CA: University of California Press, 1984.

Costello, Paul. *World Historians and Their Goals.* DeKalb, IL: Northern Illinois University Press, 1993.

Curtin, Philip. *The African Slave Trade.* Madison, WI: University of Wisconsin Press, 1969.

Bentley, Jerry H. *Old World Encounters: Cross-Cultural Contacts and Exchanges in Pre-Modern Times.* New York: Oxford, 1993.

Durant, Will and Ariel. *The Story of Civilization.* 11 vols. New York: Simon and Schuster, 1935–75.

Fanon, Frantz. *The Wretched of the Earth.* New York: Grove, 1963.

Geertz, Clifford. *Agricultural Involution: The Processes of Ecological Change in Indonesia.* Berkeley, CA: University of California Press, 1963.

Kennedy, Paul. *The Rise and Fall of Great Powers: Economic Change and Military Conflict from 1500 to 2000.* New York: Random House, 1988.

McNeill, William H. *The Human Condition: An Ecological and Historical View.* Princeton, NJ: Princeton University Press, 1980.

_____. *Mythistory and Other Essays.* Chicago: University of Chicago Press, 1986.

_____. *Plagues and Peoples.* Garden City, NY: Doubleday, 1976.

_____. *The Pursuit of Power: Technology, Armed Force, and Society since A.D. 1000.* Chicago: University of Chicago Press, 1982.

_____. *The Rise of the West: A History of the Human Community.* Chicago: University of Chicago Press, 1963.

Mumford, Lewis. *The City in History.* New York: Harcourt, Brace and World, 1961.

_____. *Technics and Civilization.* New York: Harcourt, Brace, 1934.

Ortega y Gasset, José. *An Interpretation of Universal History.* New York: Norton, 1973.

Rodney, Walter. *A History of the Upper Guinea Coast, 1545 to 1800.* Oxford: Clarendon Press, 1970.

_____. *West Africa and the Atlantic Slave Trade.* Nairobi: East African Publishing House, 1969.

Spengler, Oswald. *The Decline of the West.* 2 vols. Trans. Charles Francis Atkinson. New York: Knopf, 1926–28.

Stavrianos, L. S. *Global Rift: The Third World Comes of Age.* New York: Morrow, 1981.

Toynbee, Arnold J. *A Study of History.* 12 vols. London: Oxford University Press, 1933–1961. Rev. and abr. ed. with Jane Caplan, Oxford: Oxford University Press, 1972.

Wallerstein, Immanuel. *The Modern World-System.* 3 vols. New York: Academic Press, 1974–89.

Wolf, Eric R. *Europe and the People Without History.* Berkeley, CA: University of California Press, 1982.

NOTES

1. Walter Rodney, *How Europe Underdeveloped Africa* (Washington, DC: Howard University Press, 1974), 95–103.

CHAPTER 55

Neoconservative Reaction

Gertrude Himmelfarb

Gertrude Himmelfarb
Courtesy of CUNY Graduate Office

Not everyone likes the trends of the current generations of historical thinking. There are more than a few historians, some of them quite distinguished, who cringe at quantifying, criticize class, joust at gender, condemn culture, scorn systems, and reject race as unfit subjects for the historian. All these, they say, are perversions of the true calling of historians to record, analyze, and criticize the deeds of the central actors of Western civilization: the men who ran the governments of Europe and North America and others of their class who were the leading lights in economic and intellectual life.

Many of these critics of the other varieties of history set forth in this section are members of the Cold War generation and were once called liberals. Now, in a different age, they are called neoconservatives. They are repulsed by the trends of the last third of the twentieth century, not only in historical writing but in American intellectual life in general. Among them are not only historians but intellectuals from other disciplines, such as the late philosopher Allan Bloom, whose influential book *The Closing of the American Mind* is a clarion call against the multicultural trends of our era; Nathan Glazer, a sociologist of ethnicity and prominent critic of affirmative action; and Norman Podhoretz, a once-liberal journalist.

The list of kindred spirits includes Thomas Sowell, an African American economist-turned-historian, who argues in several books that the relatively lower position occupied by Black people in American society can be attributed to their inferior culture and moral qualities, compared with people such as Whites and Asian Americans whom he regards as better disciplined and possessors of superior cultural attributes. A conservative of a younger generation is Francis Fukuyama, whose *End of History and the Last Man* argues that all of history has been pointing to the present moment, when, according to his view, liberal democracy of the American sort is permanently triumphant everywhere in the world. Human existence, in Fukuyama's interpretation, can get no better than this. Sowell and Fukuyama are intellectual heirs of Voltaire in their shining faith in progress, and of Macaulay and Martineau in their belief in the superiority of European civilization (along with, in the modern case, certain Asian cognates) over the darker peoples of the earth.

One of the foremost current practitioners of the old history and perhaps the most articulate critic of all the varieties of the new is Gertrude Himmelfarb (1922–). No one could be farther than she from the ideas summarized in the Culture section (Chapter 53). Educated at Brooklyn College, Jewish Theological Seminary, and the University of Chicago, Himmelfarb chose as her first book an intellectual biography of Lord Acton, a famous parliamentarian and historian of Victorian England. In 1942 Himmelfarb married Irving Kristol, who is now an urban studies professor and a neoconservative activist. She devoted her thirties to writing and to raising children, among them later conservative political strategist William Kristol. Gertrude Himmelfarb resumed a formal academic career in the mid-1960s and became Distinguished Professor of History at the City University of New York by the 1980s.

The moral dimensions of politics are always close to the core of Himmelfarb's work. She is far more, however, than simply a throwback to history as
past politics. In a string of books on Victorian England she has written subtle
and persuasive intellectual history as well. Her essay reproduced here first
appeared in *Harper's* magazine in 1984, and later in a book called *The New
History and the Old*. In crackling prose it argues, perhaps convincingly, that the
new varieties of history that excite the passions of many of her colleagues are
not really all that important or interesting, and that the old history has more
life in it than they suppose—in fact, that history ought to be about past politics
and the intellectual life of elites. Himmelfarb, like other neoconservatives,
holds up individual liberty as the highest human value; and like them, she
tends to label as Marxist or perverse the things that she does not like. Indeed,
there is a great deal of name calling in her essay. Yet beneath it there is a
serious argument for caution about embracing current fads.

The New History and the Old[1]

The "Old New Social History" and the "New Old Social History": thus one eminent social historian (Charles Tilly) distinguishes his mode of history from that of another eminent social historian (Lawrence Stone).[2] Recalling the history of this genre, one might be tempted to add some additional "old's" and "new's" to accommodate the several varieties that have emerged since James Harvey Robinson proclaimed the advent of the "New History."

Even in 1912, when Robinson issued that manifesto, the "new history" was not all that new. In 1898 the *American Historical Review,* bastion of the old history, published an essay, "Features of the New History," commending the "new" *Kulturgeschichte* as practiced by Karl Lamprecht—which itself was not so new, Jakob Burckhardt's classic work on the Renaissance having appeared almost half a century earlier. Lamprecht's new history was not quite Burckhardt's; nor was Robinson's Lamprecht's. But they had much in common with one another and with later versions of the new history, for they all rejected the basic premises of the old history: that the proper subject of history is essentially political and that the natural mode of historical writing is essentially narrative. Lamprecht's "genetic" method, emphasizing causation rather than narration, presaged the "analytic" method favored today. And Robinson's plea for a history of the "common man," which would dispense with the "trifling details" of dynasties and wars and utilize the findings of "anthropologists, economists, psychologists, and sociologists," is still the agenda of the new history.[3]

England had its own. . . . In 1900 [H. G. Wells] offered a "prospectus" for a history of mankind that would take into account all the forces of social change: biologic, demographic, geographic, economic. Later, in his autobiography, Wells remarked that if he were a multimillionaire, he would establish "Professorships of Analytic History" to endow a new breed of historians— "human ecologists."[4]

As it happened, the French had already started to produce that new breed. The *Annales d'histoire économique et sociale* was founded in 1929 in opposition to the political and diplomatic historians who dominated the academic establishment—the Sorbonnistes, as they were contemptuously called. That epithet lost some of its sting when the *Annales* moved from Strasbourg to Paris, where one of its editors (Marc Bloch) joined the faculty of the Sorbonne and the other (Lucien Febvre) the Collège de France. With the establishment after the war of the Sixième Section of the Ecole Pratique des Hautes Etudes, the Annalistes acquired a powerful institutional base, and under the editorship of Fernand Braudel their journal became the most influential historical organ in France, possibly in the world.[5] It has also proved to be remarkably innovative. Going well beyond the more traditional forms of economic and social history, it now derives both its subjects and its methods from anthropology, sociology, demography, geography, psychology, even semiotics and linguistics.

While Americans have been developing their own modes of new history—econometric and cliometric, black and ethnic, feminist and sexual, psychoanalytic and populist—they have also been much influenced by their colleagues abroad. A large contingent of historians may be found making annual or sabbatical pilgrimages to Paris to take instruction from the masters. Others look to Britain for inspiration, especially to the Marxists, whose work has been used to fortify the indigenous tradition of radical history (typified by Robinson's student and collaborator, Charles A. Beard). Thus E. P. Thompson's *Making of the English Working Class* has become the model for the making of the American working class; Eric Hobsbawm's concept of "primitive rebels" is taken as the prototype of inner-city gangs; and Perry Anderson's version of "Althusserian" Marxism is the point of departure for discussions of the theory and methodology of Marxism.

If the new history, as we know it today, is not as novel as some of its younger enthusiasts might think, neither is the old history as archaic as its critics assume. The old history, traditional history, has had a long time to assimilate and accommodate itself to the new. Indeed, even before the advent of the new, it was never as homogeneous or simplistic as the stereotype has it. German history managed to make room for a Burckhardt as well as a Ranke, for cultural history as well as political and "scientific" history. The English Whig historians, descending from Burke and Macaulay, came in many sizes and shapes, including some notably un-Whiggish types. And their contemporaries in France had a breadth and liberality of spirit that even the Annalistes admire; one of the complaints of the new historians is that the Sorbonnistes abandoned the grand tradition of Guizot, Thierry, and Michelet. Nor are the great American classics merely political chronicles. Bancroft's history was not only a paean to Jacksonian democracy; it also reflected his predilection for German idealism and romanticism. And Parkman's "history of the American forest," as he called his work on the Great West,[6] was as rooted in anthropology, geography, and ecology as the work of any new historian; the wilderness was as surely his hero as the Mediterranean was Braudel's.

The new history, then, is older than one might think, and the old not quite so antiquated. But what is undeniably new is the triumph of the new. In the historical profession as a whole the new history is now the new orthodoxy. This is not to say that the old history is no longer being written. Political, constitutional, diplomatic, military, and intellectual histories continue to be written by some eminent senior historians and even some enterprising young ones. (Although more often the old history is rewritten in the light of the new. Thus political history is quantified and sociologized, and intellectual history—the study of ideas—is converted to *mentalité* history—the study of popular beliefs and attitudes). Yet the old history, if not entirely superseded, has been largely displaced. What was once at the center of the profession is now at the periphery. What once defined history is now a footnote to history.

. . . By now there are historians—serious, reputable, senior historians—who know no other kind of history and can do no other kind. For them the new history has lost its distinctive character. They recognize no legitimate criticism of the genre as such, any more than of history as such. To the arguments that quantitative history, for example, has a tendency to elevate method over substance, permitting statistics to define the subject, they reply that this is not different from constitutional history, which takes its themes from whatever documents are available. To the charge that social history tends to be unduly concerned with the minutiae of everyday life, they respond by pointing to the no less tedious machinations that make up a good deal of political history. The issue, we are told, is not the new history or the old, but good history or bad.

* * *

"New history" has become the accepted shorthand term for modes of history that may not be consistent with one another but that do represent, singly and collectively, a challenge to traditional history. . . . social history, . . . "History with the politics left out" is the way G. M. Trevelyan described social history almost half a century ago. . . . a mode of history that either ignores politics, or relegates it to the realm of "epiphenomena," or recognizes it as a subject deserving of study only when it has been transmuted into social or political science. . . . quantohistory and psychohistory. . . . Marxist history [having] its origins in the Communist Party.

* * *

In 1980, in a review of *The Past before Us* (a volume of historiographic essays commissioned by the American Historical Association), I wrote of "intimations" in this book and elsewhere that some new historians were becoming sensitive to the concerns of traditional historians. I predicted that "the 'humanization' of social history will eventually lead, not to a restoration of the old history, but to an accommodation in which old and new can live together."[7] I came to this conclusion despite other intimations in the same work that so far from seeking an accommodation with the old history, some new historians were embarking on a still more radical mission. In his contribution to that volume Carl Degler observed that while a great deal of attention was being directed to the history of women and the family, these subjects had still not been properly integrated into the "mainstream" of history, and that this could be achieved only by altering our conception of history and our sense of the past: "In sum, what is meant by history or the past will have to be changed before these two subdisciplines become an integral part of it."[8]

Since the publication of *The Past before Us* the demand for "mainstreaming" has been echoed by other subdisciplines dealing with workers, blacks, ethnic groups, and social and sexual "deviants." One might well wonder whether anything would remain of the discipline of history if these subdisciplines were brought into the mainstream, and whether such an effort of integration would not result in the disintegration of the whole. The "total" history that some new historians pride themselves on might turn out to be a total dissolution of history—history in any form recognizable to either the new or the old historian. . . .

Even some of the Annalistes are beginning to suspect that they have unleashed a force they cannot control. The very disciplines they have used to subvert the conventions of the old history threaten to subvert history itself. It is curious to find the editors of a collection of essays by prominent annalistes complaining of the "aggression of social sciences," and still more curious to hear of the effect of that aggression on history: "The field which it [history] used to occupy alone as the systematic explanation of society in its time dimension has been invaded by other sciences with ill-defined boundaries which threaten to absorb and dissolve it."[9] The same volume contains an essay by one of the editors with the provocative title "The Return of the Event." But the "return" heralded there is not of the kind of "event" familiar in traditional history. On the contrary, Pierre Nora confirms "the effacement of the event, the negation of its importance and its dissolution," as the great triumph of the new history. It is quite another event that he sees as returning: one that has been produced by the mass media of modern industrial society and that is often indistinguishable from a "nonevent" or "illusion," a "sign" or a "function."[10]

A similar retreat, more semantic than substantive, may be noted in the United States, where one of the founders of the new history has called for a "new old history" to correct the excesses of the new and restore some of the virtues of the old. But the "*mentalité* history" that Lawrence Stone invokes as the distinctive mode of this "new old history" is nothing like traditional intellectual or even cultural history. And the "revival of narrative" he points to—the "narration of a single event" exemplified by Emmanuel Le Roy Ladurie's *Montaillou*, Carlo Cipolla's *Faith, Reason and the Plague in Seventeenth Century Tuscany*, Eric Hobsbawm's *Primitive Rebels*, E. P. Thompson's *Whigs and Hunters*—is far from the old narrative history, where the narration was not of a single event but precisely of a series of events chronologically connected so as to tell a story over a significant span of time.

One is not surprised to find other signs of misgiving and dissidence. Orthodoxies breed heresies; dominance generates discontent. As the new history loses the glamour of novelty, the old acquires a new allure. More and more often one hears confessions of nostalgia for an old-fashioned history that has dramatic movement and literary grace; for a political history that regards constitutions and laws as something more than ploys in the manipulation of power; for an intellectual history that takes serious ideas seriously, as ideas, rather than as instruments of production and consumption; even for a social history that does not presume to be dominant or superior, let alone "total." It may be that we are witnessing the beginning of yet another wave of historical revisionism—not the restoration of an old regime (historians are skeptical of such restorations) but the inauguration of a new regime.

It is tempting to say (as I once did) that we can now look forward to a real accommodation of new and old, a merging of the best of both. It is a pleasing prospect but not a very hopeful one. . . . There is a good deal at stake, not only in terms of professional interests (careers dependent upon particular subjects, methods, and institutional affiliations), but of philosophical convictions—ideas about history, politics, society, even human nature. The new historian cannot concede the preeminence of politics in the Aristotelian sense, which supposes man to be a "political animal"; and the old historian cannot admit the superiority, let alone totality, of a mode of history that takes man to be a "social animal." Nor can the new historian conceal his contempt for a history that persists in studying "important people, significant events, and successful historical movements";[11] nor the old historian find it anything but bizarre that such subjects should be derided and that *l'histoire historisante* should be used as an invidious term.[12] So long as new historians announce that "Mickey Mouse may in fact be more important to an understanding of the 1930s than Franklin Roosevelt,"[13] or that "the history of menarche" should be recognized as "equal in importance to the history of monarchy,"[14] traditional historians will feel confirmed in their sense of the enormous gap separating the two modes of history.

One would like to think that reality will inevitably assert itself to produce a more sensitive and realistic history. But here too one cannot be sanguine. It was, after all, during the most catastrophic event in modern times that two of the greatest Annalistes affirmed their faith in a doctrine that belittled events and located reality in the "impersonal forces" of history. In his moving account of the fall of France in 1940, Marc Bloch alluded to the theory of history that contributed to the prevailing mood of "intellectual lethargy."

> We were all of us either specialists in the social sciences or workers in scientific laboratories, and maybe the very disciplines of those employments kept us, by a sort of fatalism, from embarking on individual action. We had grown used to seeing great impersonal forces at work in society as in nature. In the vast drag of these submarine swells, so cosmic as to seem irresistible, of what avail were the petty struggles of a few shipwrecked sailors? To think otherwise would have been to falsify history.[15]

Even then Bloch did not consider that this "cosmic" theory may have falsified history itself, that it was not only politically enervating but historically stultifying. One wonders whether that possibility occurred to him when he later joined the Resistance movement—and gave his life to it.

It was the same tragic event, the fall of France, that ironically provided another historian with the opportunity to launch an attack on *l'histoire événementielle*.[16] Historians have paid homage to Fernand Braudel, who managed to write the first draft of his monumental work, *The Mediterranean and the Mediterranean World in the Age of Philip II*, while confined in a prisoner-of-war camp in Germany during World War II. That work extolled *la longue durée*: the "inanimate" forces of geography, demography, and economy that were the "deeper realities" of history, compared with which the passions of Philip II and the ideas of the Renaissance were "cockleshells" tossed on the waters of history.[17] The book was indeed an impressive achievement, but also a profoundly ironic, even perverse one. For it was written at a time when Europe was being convulsed by the passions of a single man and by ideas that very nearly destroyed a people and a religion of considerable *durée*. Braudel himself has said that he wrote it in prison, partly as a "direct existential response to the tragic times I was passing through."

> All those occurrences which poured in upon us from the radio and the newspapers of our enemies, or even the news from London which our clandestine receivers gave us—I had to outdistance, reject, deny them. Down with occurrences, especially vexing ones! I had to believe that history, destiny, was written at a much more profound level.[18]

It is curious that historians, admiring the intrepid spirit that could bring forth so bold a theory in the midst of such tragic "occurrences," have failed to note the gross disparity between that theory and those occurrences—the extent to which the theory did indeed "outdistance, reject, deny them." It is still more curious that in the years following the war, as historians tried to assimilate the enormity of the individuals and ideas responsible for those "short-term events" (known as World War II and the Holocaust), the theory of history that belittled individuals, ideas, and above all events became increasingly influential. The irony is compounded by the fact that what Braudel took to be an "existential response" to reality—distancing himself from it and seeking a "much more profound level" of meaning—was exactly the opposite from the response of the Existentialists, who found meaning precisely in the actuality of events, however contingent and ephemeral. Because the Existentialists respected the meaning of events, they also respected the integrity of the individuals involved in them—the conscious, responsible, autonomous individuals whose actions were freely willed, even "gratuitous." Braudel, by denying the "underlying reality" of events, denied both the efficacy of individuals and the possibility of freedom. *The Mediterranean* concludes by asserting the triumph of the long term over the individuals doomed to live in the short term.

> So when I think of the individual, I am always inclined to see him imprisoned within a destiny in which he himself has little hand, fixed in a landscape in which the infinite perspectives of the long term stretch into the distance both behind him and before. In historical analysis, as I see it, rightly or wrongly, the long term always wins in the end. Annihilating innumerable events—all those which cannot be accommodated in the main ongoing current and which are therefore ruthlessly swept to one side—it indubitably limits both the freedom of the individual and even the role of chance.[19]

. . . Bertrand Russell [wrote]: "If life is to be saved from boredom, relieved only by disaster, means must be found of restoring individual initiative not only in things that are trivial but in the things that really matter."[20] Some new historians have confessed that their initial disaffection with traditional history came from boredom with the old subjects: dynasties and governments, wars and laws, treaties and documents. So it may be that a new generation of historians, bored with the "everyday life of common people" and the "long-term structures" of geography and demography, may find a renewed excitement in the drama of events, the power of ideas, and the dignity of individuals—"not only in things that are trivial but in the things that really matter."

NOTES

1. Gertrude Himmelfarb, "Introduction" to *The New History and the Old* (Cambridge, MA: Harvard University Press, 1987), 1–12. Footnotes have been renumbered and slightly revised to fit the abridgement.

2. Charles Tilly, "The Old New Social History and the New Old Social History," *Review* [journal of the Fernand Braudel Center, Binghamtom, NY], Winter 1984.

3. James Harvey Robinson, *The New History: Essays Illustrating the Modern Historical Outlook* (New York, 1965 [1st ed., 1912]), pp. 132, 8, 24.

4. H. G. Wells, *Experiment in Autobiography: Discoveries and Conclusions of a Very Ordinary Brain* (New York, 1934), pp. 551–552.

5. The title of the journal has changed several times; it is currently *Annales. Economies. Sociétés. Civilisations.* For the French literature on this school, see the bibliographies in Hervé Coutau-Bégarie, *Le phénomène "Nouvelle Histoire": stratégie et idéologie des nouveaux historiens* (Paris, 1983); and Traian Stoianovich, *French Historical Method: The Annales Paradigm* (Ithaca, 1976). One of the earliest serious critiques in America was by Bernard Bailyn, "Braudel's Geohistory—A Reconsideration," *Journal of Economic History,* Summer 1951. Among the notable English critiques are Richard Cobb, "Nous des *Annales*" (1966), reprinted in Cobb, *A Second Identity: Essays on France and French History* (London, 1969); J. H. Hexter, "Fernand Braudel and the *Monde Braudellien*," *Journal of Modern History,* December 1972; Samuel Kinser, "*Annaliste* Paradigm" The Geohistorical Structuralism of Fernand Braudel," *American Historical Review,* February 1981; David Gress, "The Pride and Prejudice of Fernand Braudel," *New Criterion,* April 1983. Some of these authors (Kinser, for example) offset their criticism with effusive praise, and others deal with Braudel rather than the Annalistes in general.

6. *The Journal of Francis Parkman,* ed. Mason Wade (New York, 1947), p. xi. A more recent "classic" in the same vein is Walter Prescott Webb, *The Great Plains* (Boston, 1931), where the chief protagonists are the soil and the climate.

7. Gertrude Himmelfarb, review of *The Past before Us, New York Times Book Review,* August 17, 1980, p. 3.

8. Carl Degler, "Women and the Family," in *The Past before Us: Contemporary Historical Writing in the United States,* ed. Michael Kammen (Ithaca, 1980), p. 326.

9. Colin Lucas, "Introduction," *Constructing the Past: Essays in Historical Methodology,* ed. Jacques Le Goff and Pierre Nore (Cambridge, 1985), p. 10. Lucas is quoting the introduction by Le Goff and Nora to the original four-volume collection of essays, *Faire de l'histoire* (Paris, 1974), from which *Constructing the Past* is a selection.

10. Pierre Nora, "Le retour de l'événement," in *Faire de l'histoire,* I, 227. The "return of the event" in this special sense of "event"—was a subject much

discussed among the Annalistes at this time. Stoianovich, *French Historical Method*, pp. 228–231.

11. *Perspectives* [newsletter of the American Historical Association], February 1986. Report of comments by E. J. Hobsbawn during a conference at the New School for Social Research, October 30, 1985.
12. The phrase is generally attributed to Henri Berr. See Fernand Braudel, "Personal Testimony," *Journal of Modern History*, December 1972, p. 467; idem, *On History*, trans. Sarah Matthews (Chicago, 1980), p. 64.
13. Warren I. Susman, *Culture as History: The Transformation of American Society in the Twentieth Century* (New York, 1985), pp. 103, 197.
14. Peter N. Stearns, "Coming of Age," *Journal of Social History*, Winter 1976, p. 250.
15. Marc Bloch, *Strange Defeat: A Statement of Evidence Written in 1940*, trans. Gerard Hopkins (New York, 1968), pp. 172–73.
16. Braudel assigns this term to Paul Lacombe and Fracois Simiand. See his "Personal Testimony," p. 467, and *On History*, p. 27.
17. Braudel, *The Mediterranean and the Mediterranean World in the Age of Philip II*, trans. Sian Reynolds (New York, 1972), I, 21 preface to 1st French ed., 1946).
18. Braudel, "Personal Testimony," p. 454.
19. Braudel, *Mediterranean*, II, 1244.
20. Robert Nisbet. *Prejudices: A Philosophical Dictionary* (Cambridge, Mass., 1982), pp. 22, 28.

QUESTIONS TO CONSIDER

1. What are the things that Gertrude Himmelfarb does not like about the "New History"?
2. What does Himmelfarb mean when she asserts that individuals and individual choices make the essential difference in history?
3. Looking back at the table of contents, which of the historians in this anthology would Himmelfarb like, which not, and why?

FOR FURTHER READING

Bailyn, Bernard. "The Challenge of Modern Historiography." *American Historical Review* 87 (1982).
_____ . *The Ordeal of Thomas Hutchinson*. Cambridge, MA: Harvard University Press, 1974.
Bennett, William J. *The Book of Virtues*. New York: Simon and Schuster, 1993.
Bloom, Allan. *The Closing of the American Mind*. New York: Simon and Schuster, 1987.
D'Souza, Dinesh. *Illiberal Education*. New York: Free Press, 1991.
Fukuyama, Francis. *The End of History and the Last Man*. New York: Free Press, 1992.

Gay, Peter. *Art and Act: On Causes in History.* New York, 1976.

_____ . *Style in History.* New York: Basic Books, 1974.

Glazer, Nathan. *Ethnic Dilemmas.* Cambridge, MA: Harvard University Press, 1983.

Himmelfarb, Gertrude. *The Idea of Poverty: England in the Early Industrial Age.* New York: Knopf, 1983.

_____ . *Lord Acton: A Study in Conscience and Politics.* San Francisco, CA: ICS Press, 1994; orig. Chicago: University of Chicago Press, 1952.

_____ . *Marriage and Morals among the Victorians.* New York: Knopf, 1986.

_____ . *On Liberty and Liberalism: The Case of John Stuart Mill.* San Francisco, CA: ICS Press, 1990.

_____ . *On Looking Into the Abyss: Untimely Thoughts on Culture and Society.* New York: Knopf, 1994.

_____ . *Poverty and Compassion: The Moral Imagination of the Late Victorians.* New York: Knopf, 1991.

_____ . *Victorian Minds.* New York: Knopf, 1968.

Kristol, Irving. *Reflections of a Neoconservative.* New York: Basic Books, 1983.

Pells, Richard H. *The Liberal Mind in a Conservative Age.* New York: Harper and Row, 1985.

Pipes, Richard. *Russia Observed.* Boulder, CO: Westview, 1989.

_____ . *The Russian Revolution.* New York: Knopf, 1990.

Podhoretz, Norman. *Breaking Ranks: A Political Memoir.* New York: Harper and Row, 1979.

Sowell, Thomas. *Ethnic America: A History.* New York: Basic Books, 1981.

CHAPTER 56

The Third World Talks Back

Edward W. Said

Edward W. Said
Courtesy of Columbia University/Joe Pineiro photo

This entire anthology proceeds from the understanding that late-twentieth-century civilization is worldwide, not regional. Although East Asia, Africa, Europe, India, and the Americas were at one time separate, they are no longer so. Their past is now our past—no matter which "their" and which "our" we mean.

Edward Said's work highlights this new reality, but in a peculiar way. Said is concerned with the relationship between East and West, particularly their colonial history. Specifically, he focuses on the conceptual systems that justified nineteenth-century colonialism—that made the quest for empire possible for the admittedly freedom-loving West. As he points out in *Orientalism*, his major historical work, the West created the idea of "the Orient" and endowed its inhabitants with certain features that made them seem to need outside rulers. By the same act, Westerners endowed themselves with the ability to carry this "White man's burden." This dual accomplishment created a world view that the West has yet to shake entirely. It also generated an anticolonial opposition and much world conflict.

As is obvious in the passage that follows, Said's method borrows much from literary criticism. He analyzes exemplary texts to reveal the cultural attitudes they embody. These attitudes, he believes, create the events that lie on history's surface. Balfour's speech before the British parliament, for example, did not itself effect much. Yet it expressed the attitude that shaped British colonialism as a whole. Exposing the logic of such attitudes helps us understand the past better than would any mere record of events as they occurred.

This textual criticism comes naturally to Said, most of whose career has been devoted to literature. Born in 1935 in Palestine, he fled to Egypt with his family at the time of the first Arab-Israeli war (1947–48). He was educated in Cairo and the United States, including a stint at Princeton where he studied English and history. He received a PhD in comparative literature from Harvard, writing a dissertation on Joseph Conrad—an exile like himself who was also interested in the effect of colonialism on East and West alike. A professor at Columbia University, Said is one of a growing number of scholars from what has sometimes been called the Third World who spend at least part of their working lives in Europe or the United States, yet who maintain ties to the perspectives of nationalist movements in their countries of origin. As such, they are part of the whirl of peoples migrating around the globe with increasing velocity and with multicontinental impact.

Before the 1970s, Said stuck to the field in which he had been trained. After the 1967 Arab-Israeli war, his writings grew in political and historical directions as he became a speaker for the Palestine Liberation Organization. He has since become something of a public intellectual, regularly called upon by the British and American news media for commentary "from a Palestinian point of view." But he recognizes the contradictoriness of this attention. The Western media, he has argued, do not understand Palestine; they try to reduce it to simple stereotypes that fail to grasp the multisided meaning behind events. Said himself embodies much of this multivocality. Raised Christian in a supposedly Muslim Middle East, a stateless Arab in a world of nations, a foreign devotee of Western literature, a literary critic who also writes history, he brings a unique perspective to his analysis.

That analysis is admittedly controversial. Both the method and the substance of his work are unusual for a historian—one of the reasons we have included him in this anthology. By writing about colonialism as a form of thought, and using literary analysis to uncover it, he implies a relationship between history and culture that seems strange to positivist and materialist historians. It would, however, be familiar to a cultural historian like Max Weber or Natalie Davis. Note, however, that where they ranged widely in search of evidence, Said dives deeply into a few key texts; each method, in its own way, discloses a culture's assumptions.

Orientalism is Said's most straightforward historical work. *The Question of Palestine* is also historical, with a large admixture of contemporary politics. Said's most recent book, *Culture and Imperialism,* is more literary in form. Yet it, too, provides deep historical insights that standard historical methodologies miss. In *Culture and Imperialism* Said analyzes works by Conrad, Kipling, Yeats, C. L. R. James, Ranajit Guha, and Jane Austen, among others, looking for artifacts of the colonial encounter. Not only does his delving enrich our feeling for the texts; it also gives us a more nuanced sense of the colonial period. It matters, for example, that the British public debated the end of the slave trade prior to 1807, and that Austen reflected this debate in her novels. The ironies that Said catches keep us from painting either the victims or the beneficiaries of colonialism monochromatically, even while they remind us of the cultural assumptions on which those people built their worlds. In *Culture and Imperialism,* as in the passage from *Orientalism* that follows, Said uses literature and literary techniques to make a historical point about the attitudes that shaped events. To this historian, culture shapes the world.

Orientalism[1]
Knowing the Oriental

On June 13, 1910, Arthur James Balfour lectured the House of Commons on "the problems with which we have to deal with in Egypt." These, he said, "belong to a wholly different category" than those "affecting the Isle of Wight or the West Riding of Yorkshire." He spoke with the authority of a long-time member of Parliament, former private secretary to Lord Salisbury, former chief secretary for Ireland, former secretary for Scotland, former prime minister, veteran of numerous overseas crises, achievements, and changes. During his involvement in imperial affairs Balfour served a monarch who in 1876 had been declared Empress of India; he had been especially well placed in positions of uncommon influence to follow the Afghan and Zulu wars, the British occupation of Egypt in 1882, the death of General Gordon in the Sudan, the Fashoda Incident, the battle of Omdurman, the Boer War, the Russo-Japanese War. In addition his remarkable social eminence, the breadth of his learning and wit—he could write on such varied subjects as Bergson, Handel, theism, and golf—his education at Eton and Trinity College, Cambridge, and his apparent command over imperial affairs all gave considerable authority to what he told the Commons in June 1910. But there was still more to Balfour's speech, or at least to his need for giving it so didactically and moralistically. Some members were questioning the necessity for "England in Egypt," the subject of Alfred Milner's enthusiastic book of 1892, but here designating a once-profitable occupation that had become a source of trouble now that Egyptian nationalism was on the rise and the continuing British presence in Egypt no longer so easy to defend. Balfour, then, to inform and explain.

Recalling the challenge of J. M. Robertson, the member of Tyneside, Balfour himself put Robertson's question again: "What right have you to take up these airs of superiority with regard to people whom you choose to call Oriental?" The choice of "Oriental" was canonical; it had been employed by Chaucer and Mandeville, by Shakespeare, Dryden, Pope, and Byron. It designated Asia or the East, geographically, morally, culturally. One could speak in Europe of an Oriental personality, an Oriental atmosphere, an Oriental tale, Oriental despotism, or an Oriental mode of production, and be understood. Marx had used the word, and now Balfour was using it; his choice was understandable and called for no comment whatever.

> I take up no attitude of superiority. But I ask [Robertson and anyone else] . . . who has even the most superficial knowledge of history, if they will look in the face the facts with which a British statesman has to deal when he is put in a position of supremacy over great races like the inhabitants of Egypt and countries in the East. We know civilization of Egypt better than we know the civilization of any other country. We know it further back; we know it more intimately; we know more about it. It goes far beyond the petty span of the history of our race, which is lost in the prehistoric period at a time when the Egyptian civilisation had already passed its prime. Look at all the Oriental countries. Do not talk about superiority or inferiority.

Two great themes dominate his remarks here and in what will follow: knowledge and power, the Baconian themes. As Balfour justifies the necessity for British occupation of Egypt, supremacy in his mind is associated with "our" knowledge of Egypt and not principally with military or economic power. Knowledge to Balfour means surveying a civilization from its origins to its prime to its decline—and of course, it means being able to do that. Knowledge means rising above immediacy, beyond self, into the foreign and distant. The object of such knowledge is inherently vulnerable to scrutiny; this object is a "fact" which, if it develops, changes, or otherwise transforms itself in the way that civilizations frequently do, nevertheless is fundamentally, even ontologically stable. To have such knowledge of such a thing is to dominate it, to have authority over it. And authority here means for "us" to deny autonomy to "it"—the Oriental country—since we know it and it exists, in a sense, as we know it. British knowledge of Egypt is Egypt for Balfour, and the burdens of knowledge make such questions as inferiority and superiority seem petty ones. Balfour nowhere denies British superiority and Egyptian inferiority; he takes them for granted as he describes the consequences of his knowledge.

> First of all, look at the facts of the case. Western nations as soon as they emerge into history show the beginnings of those capacities for self-government . . . having merits of their own. . . . You may look through the whole history of Orientals in what is called, broadly speaking, the East, and you never find traces of self-government. All their great centuries—and they have been very great—have been passed under despotisms, under absolute government. All their great contributions to civilisation—and they have been great—have been made under that form of government. Conqueror has succeeded conqueror; one domination has followed another; but never in all the revolutions of fate and fortune have you seen one of those nations of its own motion establish what we, from a Western point of view, call self-government. That is the fact. It is not a question of superiority and inferiority. I suppose a true Eastern sage would say that the working government which we have taken upon ourselves in Egypt and elsewhere is not a work worthy of a philosopher—that it is the dirty work, the inferior work, of carrying on the necessary labour.

Since these facts are facts, Balfour must then go on to the next part of his argument.

> Is it a good thing for these great nations—I admit their greatness—that this absolute government should be exercised by us? I think it is a good thing. I think that experience shows that they have got under it far better government than in the whole history of the world they ever had before, and which not only is a benefit to them, but is undoubtedly a benefit to the whole of the civilised West. . . . We are in Egypt not merely for the sake of the Egyptians, though we are there for their sake; we are there also for the sake of Europe at large.

Balfour produces no evidence that Egyptians and "the races with whom we deal" appreciate or even understand the good that is being done them by colonial occupation. It does not occur to Balfour, however, to let the Egyptian speak for himself, since presumably any Egyptian who would speak out is more likely to be "the agitator [who] wishes to raise difficulties" than the good native who overlooks the "difficulties" of foreign domination. And so, having settled the ethical problems, Balfour turns at last to the practical ones. "If it is our business to govern, with or without gratitude, with or without the real and genuine memory of all the loss of which we have relieved the population [Balfour by no means implies, as part of that loss, the loss or at least the indefinite postponement of Egyptian independence] and no vivid imagination of all the benefits which we have given to them; if that is our duty, how is it to be performed?" England exports "our very best to these countries." These selfless administrators do their work "amidst tens of thousands of persons belonging to a different creed, a different race, a different discipline, different conditions of life." What makes their work of governing possible is their sense of being supported at home by a government that endorses what they do. Yet

> directly the native populations have that instinctive feeling that those with whom they have got to deal have not behind them the might, the authority, the sympathy, the full and ungrudging support of the country which sent them there, those populations lose all that sense of order which is the very basis of their civilization, just as our officers lose all that sense of power and authority, which is the very basis of everything they can do for the benefit of those among whom they have been sent.

Balfour's logic here is interesting, not least for being completely consistent with the premises of his entire speech. England knows Egypt; Egypt is what England knows; England knows that Egypt cannot have self-government; England confirms that by occupying Egypt; for the Egyptians, Egypt is what England has occupied and now governs; foreign occupation therefore becomes "the very basis" of contemporary Egyptian civilization; Egypt requires, indeed insists upon, British occupation. But if the special intimacy between governor and governed in Egypt is disturbed by Parliament's doubts at home, then "the authority of what . . . is the dominant race—and as I think ought to remain the dominant race—has been undermined." Not only does English prestige suffer; "it is vain for a handful of British officials—endow them how you like, give them all the qualities of character and genius you can imagine—it is impossible for them to carry out the great task which in Egypt, not we only, but the civilised world would have imposed upon them."

As a rhetorical performance Balfour's speech is significant for the way in which he plays the part of, and represents, a variety of characters. There are of course "the English," for whom the pronoun "we" is used with the full weight of a distinguished, powerful man who feels himself to be representative of all that is best in his nation's history. Balfour can also speak for the civilized world, the West, and the relatively small corps of colonial officials in Egypt. If he does not speak directly for the Orientals, it is because they after all speak another language; yet he knows how they feel since he knows their history, their reliance upon such as he, and their expectations. Still, he does speak for them in the sense that what they might have to say, were they to be asked and might they be able to answer, would somewhat uselessly confirm what is already evident: that they are a subject race, dominated by a race that knows them and what is good for them better than they could possibly know for themselves. Their great moments were in the past; they are useful in the modern world only because the powerful and up-to-date empires have effectively brought them out of the wretchedness of their decline and turned them into rehabilitated residents of productive colonies.

Egypt in particular was an excellent case in this point, and Balfour was perfectly aware of how much right he had to speak as a member of his country's parliament on behalf of England, the West, Western civilization, about modern Egypt. For Egypt was not just another colony: it was to become the triumph of English knowledge and power. Between 1882, the year in which England occupied Egypt and put an end to the nationalist rebellion of Colonel Arabi, and 1907, England's representative in Egypt, Egypt's master, was Evelyn Baring (also known as "Over-baring"), Lord Cromer. On July 30, 1907, it was Balfour in the Commons who had supported the project to give Cromer a retirement prize of fifty thousand pounds as a reward for what he had done in Egypt. Cromer *made* Egypt, said Balfour:

> Everything he has touched he has succeeded in. . . . Lord Cromer's services during the past quarter of a century have raised Egypt from the lowest pitch of social and economic degradation until it now stands among Oriental nations, I believe, absolutely alone in its prosperity, financial and moral.

* * *

Unlike Balfour, whose theses on Orientals pretended to objective universality, Cromer spoke about Orientals specifically as what he had ruled or had to deal with, first in India, then for the twenty-five years in Egypt during which he emerged as the paramount consul-general in England's empire. Balfour's "Orientals" are Cromer's "subject races," which he made the topic of a long essay published in the *Edinburgh Review* in January 1908. Once again, knowledge of subject races or Orientals is what makes their management easy and profitable; knowledge gives power, more power requires more knowledge, and so on in increasingly profitable dialectic of information and control. Cromer's notion is that England's empire will not dissolve if such things as militarism and commercial egotism at home and "free institutions" in the colony (as opposed to British government "according to the code of Christian morality") are kept in check. For if, according to Cromer, logic is something "the existence of which the Oriental is disposed to ignore," the proper method of ruling is not to impose ultrascientific measures upon him or to force him bodily to accept logic. It is rather to understand his limitations and "endeavor to find, in the contentment of the subject race, a more worthy and, it may be hoped, a stronger bond of union between the rulers and the ruled." Lurking everywhere behind the pacification of the subject race is imperial might, more effective for its refined understanding and infrequent use than for its soldiers, brutal tax gatherers, and incontinent force. In a word, the Empire must be wise; it must temper its cupidity with selflessness, and impatience with flexible discipline.

*   *   *

Now at last we approach the long-developing core of essential knowledge, knowledge both academic and practical, which Cromer and Balfour inherited from a century of modern Western Orientalism: knowledge about and knowledge of Orientals, their race, character, culture, history, traditions, society, and possibilities. This knowledge was effective: Cromer believed he had put it to use in governing Egypt. Moreover, it was tested and unchanging knowledge, since "Orientals" for all practical purposes were a Platonic essence, which any Orientalist (or ruler of Orientals) might examine, understand, and expose. Thus in the thirty-fourth chapter of his two-volume work *Modern Egypt,* the magisterial record of his experience and achievement, Cromer puts down a sort of personal canon of Orientalist wisdom:

> Sir Alfred Lyall once said to me: "Accuracy is abhorrent to the Oriental mind. Every Anglo-Indian should always remember that maxim." Want of accuracy, which easily degenerates into untruthfulness, is in fact the main characteristic of the Oriental mind.
>
> The European is a close reasoner; his statements of fact are devoid of any ambiguity; he is a natural logician, albeit he may not have studied logic; he is by nature skeptical and requires proof before he can accept the truth of any proposition; his trained intelligence works like a piece of mechanism. The mind of the Oriental, on the other hand, like his picturesque streets is eminently wanting in symmetry. His reasoning is of the most slipshod description. Although the ancient Arabs acquired in a somewhat higher degree the science of dialectics, their descendants are singularly deficient in the logical faculty. They are often incapable of drawing the most obvious conclusions from any simple premises of which they may admit the truth. Endeavor to elicit a plain statement of facts from any ordinary Egyptian. His explanation will generally be lengthy, and wanting in lucidity. He will probably contradict himself half-a-dozen times before he has finished his story. He will often break down under the mildest process of cross-examination.

Orientals or Arabs are thereafter shown to be gullible, "devoid of energy and initiative," much given to "fulsome flattery," intrigue, cunning, and unkindness to animals; Orientals cannot walk on either road or a pavement (their disordered minds fail to understand what the clever European grasps immediately, that roads and pavements are made for walking); Orientals are inveterate liars, they are "lethargic and suspicious," and in everything oppose the clarity, directness, and nobility of the Anglo-Saxon race.

Cromer makes no effort to conceal that Orientals for him were always and only the human material he governed in British colonies. "As I am only a diplomatist and an administrator, whose proper study is also man, but from a point of view of governing him," Cromer says, "I content myself with noting the fact that somehow or other the Oriental generally acts, speaks, and thinks in a manner exactly opposite to the European." Cromer's descriptions are of course based partly on direct observation, yet here and there he refers to orthodox Orientalist authorities (in particular Ernest Renan and Constantin de Volney) to support his views. To these authorities he also defers when it comes to explaining why Orientals are the way they are. He has no doubt that *any* knowledge of the Oriental will confirm his views, which to judge from his description of the Egyptian breaking under cross-examination, find the Oriental to be guilty. The crime was that the Oriental was an Oriental, and it was an accurate sign of how commonly acceptable such a tautology was that it could be written without even an appeal to European logic or symmetry of mind. Thus any deviation from what were considered the norms of Oriental behavior was believed to be unnatural; Cromer's last annual report from Egypt consequently proclaimed Egyptian nationalism to be an "entirely novel idea" and "a plant of exotic rather than of indigenous growth."

We would be wrong, I think, to underestimate the reservoir of accredited knowledge, the codes of Orientalist orthodoxy, to which Cromer and Balfour refer everywhere in their writing and in their public policy. To say simply that Orientalism was a rationalization of colonial rule is to ignore the extent to which colonial rule was justified in advance by Orientalism, rather than after the fact. Men have always divided up the world into regions having real or imagined distinction from each other. The absolute demarcation between East and West, which Balfour and Cromer accept with such complacency, had been years, even centuries, in the making. There were of course innumerable voyages of discovery; there were contacts through trade and war. But more than this, since the middle of the eighteenth century there had been two principle elements in the relation between East and West. One was a growing systematic knowledge in Europe about the Orient, knowledge reinforced by the colonial encounter as well as by the widespread interest in the alien and unusual, exploited by the developing sciences of ethnology, comparative anatomy, philology, and history; furthermore, to this systematic knowledge was added a sizable body of literature produced by novelists, poets, translators, and gifted travelers. The other feature of Oriental-European relations was that Europe was always in a position of strength, not to say domination. There is no way of putting this euphemistically. True, the relationship of strong to weak could be disguised or mitigated, as when Balfour acknowledged the "greatness" of Oriental civilizations. But the essential relationship, on political, cultural, and even religious grounds, was seen—in the West, which is what concerns us here—to be one between a strong and weak partner.

Many terms were used to describe the relation: Balfour and Cromer, typically, used several. The Oriental is irrational, depraved (fallen), childlike, "different"; thus the European is rational, virtuous, mature, "normal." But the way of enlivening the relationship was everywhere to stress the fact that the Oriental lived in a different but thoroughly organized world of his own, a world with its own national, cultural, and epistemological boundaries and principles of internal coherence. Yet what gave the Oriental's world its intelligibility and identity was not the result of its own efforts but rather the whole complex series of knowledgeable manipulations by which the Orient was defined by the West. Thus the two features of cultural relationship I have been discussing come together. Knowledge of the Orient, because generated out of strength, in a sense *creates* the Orient, the Oriental, and his world. In Cromer's and Balfour's language the Oriental is depicted as something one judges (as in a court of law), something one studies and depicts (as in curriculum), something one disciplines (as in a school or prison), something one illustrates (as in a zoological manual). The point is that in each of these cases the Oriental is *contained* and *represented* by dominating frameworks. Where do these come from?

*   *   *

During the early years of the twentieth century, men like Balfour and Cromer could say what they said, in the way they did, because a still earlier tradition of Orientalism than the nineteenth-century one provided them with a vocabulary, imagery, rhetoric, and figures with which to say it. Yet Orientalism reinforced, and was reinforced by, the certain knowledge that Europe or the West literally commanded the vastly greater part of the earth's surface. The period of immense advance in the institutions and content of Orientalism coincides exactly with the period of unparalleled European expansion; from 1815 to 1914 European direct colonial dominion expanded from about 35 percent of the earth's surface to about 85 percent of it. Every continent was affected, none more so than Africa and Asia. The two greatest empires were the British and French; allies and partners in some things, in others they were hostile rivals. In the Orient, from the eastern shores of the Mediterranean to Indochina and Malaya, their colonial possessions and imperial spheres of influence were adjacent, frequently overlapped, often were fought over. But it was in the Near Orient, the lands of the Arab Near East, where Islam was supposed to define cultural and racial characteristics, that the British and the French encountered each other and "the Orient" with the greatest intensity, familiarity, and complexity. For much of the nineteenth century, as Lord Salisbury put it in 1881, their common view of the Orient was intricately problematic: "When you have got a . . . faithful ally who is bent on meddling in a country in which you are deeply interested—you have three courses open to you. You may renounce—or monopolize—or share. Renouncing would have been to place the French across our road to India. Monopolizing would have been very near the risk of war. So we resolved to share."

And share they did, in ways that we shall investigate presently. What they shared, however, was not only land or profit or rule; it was the kind of intellectual power I have been calling Orientalism. In a sense Orientalism was a library or archive of information commonly and, in some of its aspects, unanimously held. What bound the archive together was a family of ideas and a unifying set of values proven in various ways to be effective. These ideas explained the behavior of Orientals; they supplied Orientals with a mentality, a genealogy, an atmosphere; most important, they allowed Europeans to deal with and even to see Orientals as a phenomenon possessing regular characteristics. But like any set of durable ideas, Orientalist notions influenced the people who were called Orientals as well as those called Occidental, European, or Western; in short, Orientalism is better grasped as a set of constraints upon and limitations of thought than it is simply as a positive doctrine. If the

essence of Orientalism is the ineradicable distinction between Western superiority and Oriental inferiority, then we must be prepared to note how in its
development and subsequent history Orientalism deepened and even hard-
ened the distinction. When it became common practice during the nineteenth
century for Britain to retire its administrators from India and elsewhere once
they had reached the age of fifty-five, then a further refinement in Orientalism
had been achieved; no Oriental was ever allowed to see a Westerner as he aged
and degenerated, just as no Westerner needed ever to see himself, mirrored in
the eyes of the subject race, as anything but a vigorous, rational, ever alert
young Raj.

QUESTIONS TO CONSIDER

1. What does Said mean by "Orientalism"? Why does he say that this
   ideology is historically important?
2. Said opens with an analysis of Balfour's reply to Robertson, who had
   challenged Britain's imperial rule over "Oriental" peoples. Why does he
   choose this particular speech to make his point?
3. How might Said interpret the passages by Martineau (Chapter 33), Dutt
   (34), Fukuzawa (36), Liang and Hu (37), all of whom write about the
   Western-colonial encounter?
4. What are the strengths and weaknesses of a literary or textual approach to
   history such as the one employed by Said?

FOR FURTHER READING

Barakat, Halim. *The Arab World: Society, Culture, and State.* Berkeley, CA: University
    of California Press, 1993.
Deloria, Vine, Jr. *Custer Died for Your Sins.* New York: Macmillan, 1969.
Diop, Cheikh Anta. *Precolonial Black Africa.* Trans. Harold J. Salemson. Brooklyn, NY:
    Lawrence Hill Books, 1987.
Maalouf, Amin. *The Crusades Through Arab Eyes.* Trans. Jon Rothschild. New York:
    Schocken, 1984.
Mazrui, Ali A. *Towards a Pax Africana: A Study of Ideology and Ambition.* Chicago:
    University of Chicago Press, 1967.
Said, Edward W. *Culture and Imperialism.* New York: Knopf, 1994.
_____ . *The Question of Palestine.* New York: Times Books, 1979.
Sprinkler, Michael, ed. *Edward Said: A Critical Reader.* Oxford: Blackwell, 1992.
Trask, Haunani-Kay. *From a Native Daughter: Colonialism and Sovereignty in Hawai'i.*
    Monroe, ME: Common Courage Press, 1993.
Turner, Brian S. *Orientalism, Postmodernism and Globalism.* New York: Routledge, 1994.
Wood, Michael. "Lost Paradises." *New York Review of Books* (March 3, 1994): 44–47.

NOTES

1. Edward W. Said, *Orientalism* (New York: Patheon, 1978), 31–42.

Credits

Chapter 1

From *Big Falling Snow: A Tewa-Hopi Indian's Life and Times and the History and Traditions of His People* by Albert Yava, edited and annotated by Harold Courlander. (1978) New York: Crown Publishing Group.

Chapter 2

Thomas O. Beidelman, "Myth, Legend, and Oral History: A Kaguru Traditional Text," *Anthropos* 65 (1970): 78–87. Reprinted by permission of the publisher.

Chapter 3

The Kumulipo: A Hawaiian Creation Chant, trans. and ed. Martha Warren Beckwith. (1972, orig. 1951) Honolulu, HI: University of Hawaii Press. Reprinted by permission of the publisher.

Chapter 4

Djibril Tamsir Niane, *Sundiata: An Epic of Old Mali*, trans. G. D. Pickett. (1965) White Plains, NY: Addison Wesley Longman Ltd. Reprinted by permission of Addison Wesley Longman Ltd.

Chapter 5

All scripture quotations are taken from the *Holy Bible, New International Version*. Copyright © 1973, 1978, 1984 by International Bible Society. Used by permission of Zondervan Publishing House. All rights reserved.

Chapter 6

Homer, *The Iliad of Homer*, trans. Richmond Lattimore. (1951) Chicago, IL: University of Chicago Press. Used by permission of the publisher.

Chapter 7

Clae Waltham, *Shu Ching: Book of History: A Modernized Edition of the Translation of James Legge.* (1971) Chicago, IL: Regnery. Reprinted by permission of the publisher.

Chapter 8

Herodotus, *The Persian Wars,* trans. Aubrey de Selincourt. (1954) London: Penguin Books, Ltd. Reprinted by permission of the publisher.

Chapter 9

Thucydides, *History of the Peloponnesian War,* trans. Rex Warner. (1954) London: Penguin Books, Ltd. Reprinted by permission of the publisher.

Chapter 10

Ssu-ma Ch'ien [and Ssu-ma T'an], *Records of the Historian: Chapters from the Shih Chi of Ssu-ma Ch'ien,* trans. Burton Watson. (1969) New York: Columbia University Press. Reprinted by permission of the publisher.

Chapter 11

Pan Ku [and Pan Chao], *Courtier and Commoner in Ancient China,* trans. Burton Watson. (1974) New York: Columbia University Press. Reprinted by permission of the publisher.

Chapter 12

Gaalya Cornfeld, et al., eds., *Josephus: The Jewish War.* (1982) Grand Rapids, MI: Zondervan.

Chapter 13

From *The Complete Works of Tacitus* by A. J. Church and W. J. Brodribb, translators. Copyright © 1940 and renewed 1970 by Random House, Inc. Reprinted by permission of Random House, Inc.
Tacitus, *The Annals of Imperial Rome,* trans. Michael Grant. (1973) Harmondsworth, UK: Penguin. Reprinted by permission of the publisher.

Chapter 14

All scripture quotations are taken from the *Holy Bible, New International Version.* Copyright © 1973, 1978, 1984 by International Bible Society. Used by permission of Zondervan Publishing House. All rights reserved.

Chapter 15

Eusebius, *The Ecclesiastical History,* trans. Kirsopp Lake and J. E. L. Oulton. (1926–42) London: Heinemann Publishers. Reprinted by permission of the publisher.

Chapter 16

Abu Ja'far Muhammad al-Tabari, *The History of al-Tabari,* trans. W. Montgomery Watt and M. V. McDonald. (1988) Albany, NY: State University of New York Press. Reprinted by permission of the publisher.

Chapter 17

Kalhana, *Rajatarangini: The Saga of the Kings of Kasmir,* trans. Ranjit Sitaram Pandit. (1935) New Delhi: Sahitya Akademi.

Chapter 18

History and Mythology of the Aztecs: The Codex Chimalpopoca, trans. John Bierhorst. (1992) Tucson, AZ: University of Arizona Press. Reprinted by permission of the publisher.

Chapter 19

From *History of the Franks,* translated by Ernest Brehaut. Copyright © 1974 by Columbia University Press. Reprinted with permission of the publisher.

Chapter 20

Bede, *A History of the English Church and People,* trans. Leo Sherley-Price. (1955) London: Penguin. Reprinted by permission of the publisher.

Chapter 21

E. R. A. Sewter, trans., *The Alexiad of Anna Comnena.* (1969) London: Penguin. Reprinted by permission of the publisher.

Chapter 22

Reprinted with the permission of Scribner, a Division of Simon & Schuster from *The Civilization of China,* translated and edited by Dun J. Li. Copyright © 1975 by Dun J. Li.

Chapter 23

Ibn Khaldûn, *The Muqaddimah,* trans. Franz Rosenthal. (1958) Princeton, NJ: Princeton University Press. Reprinted by permission of the publisher.

Chapter 24

Abu'l Fazl, *Akbar-Nama.* (1975) Lahore, India: Hafiz Press.

Chapter 25

Gul-Badan Begam, *The History of Humayun (Humayun-nama)*, trans. Annette S. Beveridge. (1901, reprinted 1972) Delhi, India: Idarah-i Adabiyat-i Delli.

Chapter 26

Arai Hakuseki, *Lessons from History: The Tokushi Yoron*, trans. Joyce Ackroyd. (1982) St. Lucia, Australia: University of Queensland Press. Reprinted by permission of the publisher.

Chapter 27

Niccolò Machiavelli, *Florentine Histories*, trans. Laura F. Banfield and Harvey C. Mansfield, Jr. (1968) Princeton, NJ: Princeton University Press. Reprinted by permission of the publisher.

Francesco Guicciardini, *The History of Italy*, trans. Sidney Alexander. (1969) New York: Macmillan Publishers. Reprinted by permission of the publisher.

Chapter 28

William Bradford, *Of Plymouth Plantation*, trans. Harold Paget. (1948) Toronto: Van Nostrand.

Chapter 29

Fray Bernardino do Sahagún, *General History of the Things of New Spain (The Florentine Codex: Book 12 — The Conquest of Mexico)*, trans. from the Aztec by Arthur J. O. Anderson and Charles E. Dribble. (1955) Santa Fe, NM: School of American Research Press, University of Utah Press. Reprinted by permission of the publisher.

The Annals of the Cakchiquels, trans. Adrián Recinos and Delia Goetz. (1953) Norman, OK: University of Oklahoma Press. Reprinted by the permission of the publisher.

Chapter 30

Voltaire, *The Age of Louis XIV*, trans. Martyn P. Pollack. (1961) New York: Dutton Publishers.

Chapter 31

Reprinted from *Great Books of the Western World*. Copyright © 1952, 1990 Encyclopaedia Britannica, Inc.

Chapter 32

Thomas Babington Macaulay, *The History of England*, vol. 1. (1887) New York: Allison.

Chapter 33

Harriet Martineau, *British Rule in India: A Historical Sketch.* (1857) London: Smith, Elder.

Chapter 34

Romesh Dutt, *The Economic History of India Under Early British Rule.* (1950, orig. 1904) London: Routledge and Kegan Paul.
Romesh Dutt, *The Economic History of India in the Victorian Age.* (1950, orig. 1904) London: Routledge and Kegan Paul.

Chapter 35

Samuel Johnson, *The History of the Yorubas, from the Earliest Times to the Beginning of the British Protectorate,* ed. O. Johnson. (1921) London: Lowe and Brydone.

Chapter 36

Fukuzawa Yukichi, *An Outline of a Theory of Civilization,* trans. David A. Dilworth and G. Cameron Hurst. (1973) Tokyo: Sophia University. Reprinted by permission of the publisher.

Chapter 37

From *Intellectual Trends in the Ch'ing Period* by Liang Ch'i-Ch'ao. Copyright © 1959 by the President and Fellows of Harvard College. Reprinted by permission of Harvard University Press.
Hu Shih, *The Development of the Logical Method in Ancient China.* (1963, orig. Shanghai, 1922) New York: Paragon.

Chapter 38

Leopold von Ranke, *History of the Popes,* vol. 1, trans. E. Fowler. (1996, orig. 1901) New York: Frederick Ungar Books. Reprinted by permission of the publisher.

Chapter 39

Reprinted from Frederic L. Bender (ed.), *Karl Marx: The Communist Manifesto, A Norton Critical Edition.* New York: W. W. Norton & Co., 1988.
Jon Elster, ed., *Karl Marx: A Reader.* (1986) Cambridge, MA: Cambridge University Press. Reprinted with the permission of Cambridge University Press.

Chapter 40

Max Weber, *The Protestant Ethic and the Spirit of Capitalism,* trans. Talcot Parsons. (1958) New York: Scribner's.

Chapter 41

Frederick J. Turner, *The Significance of the Frontier in American History.* (1966, orig. Washington, DC: American Historical Association, 1894) Ann Arbor, MI: University Microfilms.

Chapter 42

Euclides da Cunha, *Rebellion in the Backlands,* trans. Samuel Putnam. (1944) Chicago: University of Chicago Press. Reprinted by permission of the publisher.

Chapter 43

K. M. Panikkar, *Asia and Western Dominances: A Survey of the Vasco da Gama Epoch of Asian History, 1498–1945.* (1953) New York: John Day. Reprinted with permission of HarperCollins Publishers, Inc.

Chapter 44

Reprinted from *Trade and Politics in the Niger Delta 1830–1885* by Kenneth Onwuka Dike (1956) by permission of Oxford University Press.

Chapter 45

Reprinted with the permission of Simon & Schuster from *An Economic Interpretation of the Constitution of the United States* by Charles A. Beard. Copyright © 1935 by Macmillan Publishing Company; copyright renewed 1963 by William Beard and Miriam B. Vagts.

Reprinted with the permission of Simon & Schuster from *Woman as a Force in History* by Mary R. Beard. Copyright © 1946 by Mary R. Beard; copyright renewed 1974 by William Beard and Miriam B. Vagts.

Chapter 46

Marc Bloch, *Feudal Society,* 2 vols., trans. L. A. Manyon. (1961) Chicago: University of Chicago Press. Reprinted by permission of the publisher.

Chapter 47

Yanagita Kunio, *Japanese Manners and Customs in the Meiji Era,* trans. Charles S. Terry. (1957) Tokyo: Obunsha.

Chapter 48

Copyright 1979 by Librairie Armand Colin. English translation copyright © 1981 by William Collins Ltd. and Harper & Row, Publishers, Inc. Reprinted by permission of HarperCollins Publishers, Inc.

Chapter 49

Robert William Fogel, *Railroads and American Economic Growth*. (1964) Baltimore, MD: Johns Hopkins Press. Reprinted by permission of the publisher.

Chapter 50

From *The Slave Community: Plantation Life in the Antebellum South* by John Blassingame. © 1972 by Oxford University Press, Inc. Used by permission of Oxford University Press, Inc.

Chapter 51

From *The Making of the English Working Class* by E. P. Thompson. Copyright © 1963 by E. P. Thompson. Reprinted by permission of Pantheon Books, a division of Random House, Inc.

Chapter 52

Caroline Walker Bynum, *Holy Feast and Holy Fast: The Religious Significance of Food to Medieval Women*. (1987) Berkeley, CA: University of California Press. Reprinted by permission of the publisher.

Chapter 53

Excerpted from *Society and Culture in Early Modern France* by Natalie Zemon Davis with permission of the publishers, Stanford University Press. Copyright © 1975 by the Board of Trustees of the Leland Stanford Junior University.

Chapter 54

Walter Rodney, *How Europe Underdeveloped Africa*. (1974) Washington, DC: Howard University Press. Reprinted by permission of Howard University Press.

Chapter 55

Reprinted by permission of the publisher from *The New History and the Old* by Gertrude Himmelfarb, Cambridge, Mass.: Harvard University Press, Copyright © 1987 by the President and Fellows of Harvard College.

Chapter 56

From *Orientalism* by Edward W. Said. Copyright © 1978 by Edward W. Said. Reprinted by permission of Pantheon Books, a division of Random House, Inc.